Anita Sawyer Hollander

Anita Hollander is the Chapman Professor in the College of Business at ... been selected as a 1999–2000 Carnegie Foundation Pew Scholar, and is one of only three business professors selected nationwide to receive this honor.

Professor Hollander is currently serving as director of the School of Accounting and chair of the MIS Department. Anita came to TU in 1996 after serving on the faculty at Florida State University from 1987 through 1996. She received her Ph.D. from the University of Tennessee—Knoxville. Anita's teaching interest is information systems. She has received several teaching awards including a University of Tulsa Innovation in Teaching Award, two Florida State University Beta Alpha Psi Professor of the Year Awards, a Florida State University Teaching Award, and a State of Florida Legislature Teaching Incentive Program Award. She was also honored with the TU Mortar Board Professor of the Year.

Anita is a past recipient of a Price Waterhouse Foundation grant and an Institute of Internal Auditors research grant. In addition to *Accounting, Information Technology, and Business Solutions,* she coauthored the professional book *Event-Driven Business Solutions: Today's Revolution in Information Technology.* Anita serves on the editorial board of the *Journal of Information Systems* and reviews papers for numerous information systems journals.

In addition to her service assignments at the University of Tulsa and Florida State, Anita has been active in the American Accounting Association (AAA) and the American Institute of Certified Public Accountants (AICPA). She has served as Chairperson of the Information Systems Section of the AAA. Anita has twice served as the Information Systems group leader at the Arthur Andersen New Faculty Consortium and has served as a faculty facilitator at the Deloitte and Touche Youth Leadership Conference.

Eric L. Denna

Eric Denna is currently serving as Vice President—Technology and Chief Information Officer at Brigham Young University. He began his professional career as an EDP auditor and consultant to Ernst & Whinney after completing his bachelor degree in accounting and a master degree in information systems at Brigham Young University's (BYU) School of Accountancy.

In 1988 Eric joined the faculty of BYU's School of Accountancy. In 1989 he was instrumental in combining the accounting and IS faculties to create The School of Accountancy and Information Systems (SOAIS). The SOAIS was subsequently awarded the first Innovations in Accounting Education Award by the American Accounting Association in 1993. In 1991 he was also awarded the university's William C. Brown Teaching Excellence Award for his innovation in the classroom.

Eric has worked as a consultant to several organizations helping them develop and implement innovative business, information, and decision processes. Some of Eric's consulting clients include IBM, Price Waterhouse, Sears, Geneva Steel, Scott Paper, The State of Washington, Times Mirror, Utah Technology Finance Corporation, Novell, The State of Michigan, and Farm Management Corporation. He is also a member of Patty Seybold's Pioneer Group, a technology think tank in Boston.

Eric has written several books and articles on a variety of topics. In addition to *Accounting, Information Technology, and Business Solutions,* Eric is the lead author of the professional book *Event-Driven Business Solutions: Today's Revolution in Business and Information Technology.* He has also written several articles describing innovations in business, information, and decision processes. Eric is known as one who challenges traditional thinking about how organizations work and their use of information technology.

J. Owen Cherrington

J. Owen Cherrington earned MBA and Ph.D. degrees at the University of Minnesota. He is a CPA, a member of the AICPA and the UACPA, and licensed to practice public accounting in Utah. After working as a principal in the management consulting division of Arthur Young & Co., Owen came to Brigham Young University where he currently serves as the director of the information systems faculty and programs in the Marriott School of Management. Previously, he was on the faculty of Utah State University and Pennsylvania State University.

Owen has an extensive list of publications including four major college textbooks in introductory accounting, cost and managerial accounting, information systems, and CPA review. He has over 50 articles and monographs in professional books and journals. In addition, he has written training materials, or conducted training programs for IBM, AICPA, Utah Association of CPAs, Arthur Young, Ernst & Young, Alexander Grant & Co., Price Waterhouse, and BYU Conferences and Workshops. Owen is the Mary & Ellis Distinguished Professor of Accounting at BYU and was recently recognized as the 1997 Marriott School Outstanding Professor.

A high priority for Owen is his teaching. Areas of instruction include business ethics, analysis and design of information systems, and management consulting. He has been recognized by the Marriott School of Management for his outstanding teaching and awarded the NAC Outstanding Faculty Award, Exxon Outstanding Teaching Award, William C. Brown Teaching Excellence Award, and the Outstanding Educator Award given by the Utah Association of CPAs.

Second Edition

ACCOUNTING, INFORMATION TECHNOLOGY, AND BUSINESS SOLUTIONS

ANITA S. HOLLANDER
Chapman Professor of Accounting
University of Tulsa
Department of Accounting

ERIC L. DENNA
Warnick/Deloitte & Touche Faculty Fellow
Brigham Young University
School of Accountancy
and
Information Systems

J. OWEN CHERRINGTON
Director, Information Systems Group
Brigham Young University
School of Accountancy
and
Information Systems

Boston Burr Ridge, IL Dubuque, IA Madison, WI New York San Francisco St. Louis
Bangkok Bogotá Caracas Lisbon London Madrid
Mexico City Milan New Delhi Seoul Singapore Sydney Taipei Toronto

To
our families
Thank you for your love and support.

McGraw-Hill Higher Education

*A Division of The **McGraw-Hill** Companies*

ACCOUNTING, INFORMATION TECHNOLOGY, AND BUSINESS SOLUTIONS

This book is printed on acid-free paper.

2 3 4 5 6 7 8 9 0 DOC/DOC 9 0 9 8 7 6 5 4 3 2 1 0 9

ISBN 0-256-21789-0

Publisher: *Jeffrey J. Shelstad*
Vice president/editor-in-chief: *Michael W. Junior*
Developmental editor: *Kelly Lee*
Senior marketing manager: *Michelle Hudson*
Project manager: *Alisa Watson*
Production associate: *Debra R. Benson*
Designer: *Kiera Cunningham*
Supplement coordinator: *Marc Mattson*
Compositor: *ElectraGraphics, Inc.*
Typeface: *10/12 Times Roman*
Printer: *R. R. Donnelley & Sons Company*

Library of Congress Cataloging-in-Publication Data

Hollander, Anita Sawyer
    Accounting, information technology, and business solutions/Anita
Sawyer Hollander, Eric L. Denna, J. Owen Cherrington. — 2nd ed.
      p. cm.
    Includes bibliographical references and index.
    ISBN 0-256-21789-0
    1. Managerial accounting. 2. Information technology.
3. Information storage and retrieval systems—Accounting.
I. Denna, Eric L. II. Cherrington, J. Owen. III. Title.
HF5657.4.H65 1999
658.15'11—dc21   98-55219

http://www.mhhe.com

PREFACE

THE APPROACH: A FOUNDATION FOR LIFELONG LEARNING

In this text, you are presented with nine main chapters that "tell our story" and seven supplemental chapters that complement this material. This text is not intended to be all encompassing, but lays a foundation for a philosophy of lifelong learning

Our intent is to lay a foundation for students as future business professionals to begin thinking about innovative methods for providing accounting user support, information technology, and problem solving. This text is not intended to serve as an exhaustive, all inclusive reference. In an ever-changing world, professionals must continue to learn and gather new information throughout their professional lives.

OBJECTIVES AND CONTENT

In this book, you will see an integration of both "traditional" knowledge and "state of the art" knowledge. We have combined knowledge about business, the profession, information customers, information technology, information systems, and accounting to create a framework for the Accounting Information Systems course. The objective of this text is to instill a philosophy in the information age accounting professionals of today and tomorrow. The philosophy is based on teaching students how to learn, and how to adapt to or hopefully lead change. Understanding organizations (their activities, processes, and the information needs of organization stakeholders) is the focus of this book. Information technology is presented as an enabler of organization activities and objectives, rather than as the focus of study.

The book is comprised of a series of modules intended to make teaching these objectives easier.

Module 1 (Chapter 1) An Introduction.

Goal: This module introduces accounting; the objectives, calls for change, challenges and opportunities. It includes a discussion of information systems and explains the role and purpose of accounting information systems. The module also reviews the accounting and information system profession relationship (stressing the need to merge knowledge from the two professions to effectively use, design, and evaluation accounting information systems).

The accounting profession is presented as an organization support function. Accountants strive to support the planning, execution, and evaluation activities of organizations and organization stakeholders (both internal and external), thus they must truly understand the business world. Students are taught that accounting professionals should strive to add value to organizations, and this will require our profession to be associated with less clerical, bookkeeping tasks, and to be associated with more real-time business and information support. Specifically, we suggest

> The need for accounting support, and thus AIS design, to be user driven;
> The need for a proactive, business support philosophy;
> The ability of accountants to impact (rather than simply report) the bottom line;
> The ability of accountants to facilitate reengineering efforts;
> The opportunity to move from a historical perspective, "bean counter" identity to a valuable, real time organization support function.

Students are taught that a change in the way accountants use technology can enable change in the profession and in the role accountants play within organizations.

Enhancement: Chapter 1 has been revised to describe the relationship between business, management, and information processes. This chapter includes additional coverage of why change and the changes occurring in information technology. It also contains a summary of CPA Vision Project. Discussion of history of information technology and explanation of traditional information technology system eliminated from this chapter.

Module 2 (Chapter 2, Supplements A and B) Modeling Business Processes

Goal: Chapter 2 helps students develop an understanding of business processes, which includes the ability to identify and model both business events and processes. These models serve as the basis for planning an IT architecture. Chapter 4 teaches students how to use their model (developed in Chapter 3) to plan an event-driven architecture and develop a prototype to test their process model. The objective is to build an IT application that supports business processes in Real-Time. The events-driven design is an integrated, data-oriented/business process design based on a semantic REAL model. This model was chosen because it is not relational data base specific; it is equally applicable to object oriented implementations.

We offer semantic modeling as a tool to communicate organization understanding. We highlight the need to learn important elements of organization understanding that will enable professionals to better design, use, and evaluate information systems designs, including:

> organization processes and the activities that comprise those processes,
> the sequence of activities in an organization process,
> relationships between organization activities and processes,
> complete documentation of organization activities and stakeholder,
> the activity that triggers business activities,
> business rules relating to activities and participants, and
> the roles of organization participants (authorization, custody, control/info support)

We feel this approach of developing a semantic mental model of an organization helps students establish a system standard which can be used to critique and analyze a variety of system designs. When the concepts are used to determine the requirements of an IT application, the result is an architecture where IT supports those managing the organization, rather than IT imposing a structure and an agenda on the organization.

Enhancement: The new Chapter 2 has been reorganized to contain revised material from the former Chapter 3 on Modeling Business Processes. In this chapter, students are asked to identify events that comprise a business model. Business Processes are covered earlier in the chapter. The discussion of different processes and business activities for different organizations based on an organizations' is also covered in this chapter. Students are shown a business process example. The discussion on Linking Processes has been moved closer toward the end of the chapter and the discussions of prioritizing business events, decomposing business processes, and essential characteristics of relevant business events have been eliminated. The following discussions have been moved to an Appendix for Chapter 2: further practice using real modeling, selling a service, providing public assistance, and making steel.

Enhancement: Supplement A has been completely revised and updated for this edition. Supplement B contains new coverage on General Ledger Software Packages. A list of ERP Software vendors available via the Internet is offered.

Module 3 (Chapters 3 and 4, Supplement C) The Traditional AIS Architecture

This module reviews the accounting information systems architecture (the traditional, file oriented, manual design; the traditional, file oriented, automated design; and the event-driven design), focusing on the general ledger and the accounting cycle. Understanding the general ledger design provides insights to some of the limitations accounting professionals have in producing the outputs desired by information customers. We objectively review the criticisms of traditional designs, and stress that these criticisms are feedback from an increasingly demanding, sophisticated user group whose expectations are grounded in the real-time information age. These users are concerned with organization efficiency, reengineering, restructuring, downsizing, streamlining, complex financial transactions and international markets. Their demands are broadening the transaction documentation and boundaries of the accounting system. This module presents a challenge to accounting information professionals. The challenge is to effectively use IT to build information system architectures that improve the ability of accounting to support organizations. To meet this challenge, accounting professionals need to develop a strategic, conceptual understanding of IT resources, and the ability to understand and model business activities and processes.

Chapter 4 helps students develop an understanding of business processes, which includes the ability to identify and model both business events and processes. These models serve as the basis for planning an IT architecture. Chapter 4 teaches students how to use their model (developed in Chapter 3) to plan an event-driven architecture and develop a prototype to test their process model. The objective is to build an IT application that supports business processes in Real-Time. The events-driven design is an integrated, data-oriented/business process design based on a semantic REAL model. This model was chosen because it is not relational data base specific; it is equally applicable to object oriented implementations.

We offer semantic modeling as a tool to communicate organization understanding. We highlight the need to learn important elements of organization understanding that will enable professionals to better design, use, and evaluate information Systems designs, including:

> organization processes and the activities that comprise those processes,
> the sequence of activities in an organization process,
> relationships between organization activities and processes,
> complete documentation of organization activities and stakeholder,
> the activity that triggers business activities,
> business rules relating to activities and participants, and
> the roles of organization participants (authorization, custody, control/info support)

We feel this approach of developing a semantic mental model of an organization helps students establish a system standard which can be used to critique and analyze a variety of system designs. When the concepts are used to determine the requirements of an IT application, the result is an architecture where IT supports those managing the organization, rather than IT imposing a structure and an agenda on the organization.

Enhancements: Revised former Chapter 2 now makes up Chapter 3 on The Traditional Accounting Information System Architecture. Students will learn about the nature of the traditional accounting cycle and its' relationship to business events. They will also understand the impact of IT on the traditional accounting system and be able to describe the limitations of the traditional accounting system architecture. This chapter also discusses how the traditional architecture can limit accounting's ability to enhance its value and an alternative accounting system architecture.

The discussion of traditional accounting cycle and information systems is pretty consistent with previous edition. The discussion of an alternative information systems architecture has been added to this chapter.

Enhancements: Chapter 4 is entirely new to this edition. This chapter is designed to help students understand the key steps in analyzing and designing information technology applications. It also explains how to use the REAL business process model to analyze and design IT applications that support those responsible for defining and managing organization activities. This chapter is best learned by applying it. Therefore, you are encouraged to implement the concepts by using the software package of your choice.

Enhancements: Supplement C contains new coverage on File Versus Data Base Environments and Data Warehouses. The coverage of Flat Files has been eliminated.

Module 4 (Chapter 5 and Supplement D) Business and Information Process Rules, Risks, and Controls

This module includes a discussion of traditional efforts to identify and control business and information process risk and ways to improve control strategies. We emphasize the control component of organization understanding. Our approach includes training students to first identify both business and information risk exposures, then develop control strategies. Control strategies lead to implementing specific control procedures. Due to the changing nature of organizations and systems, students learn that to implement control strategies, they may need to review existing control procedures and update or revise them. This helps students understand recent calls for reengineering traditional accounting controls, and the risks of applying traditional control procedures to transformed environments.

Increasingly, organizations are embedding information processes into business processes. This provides accountants with a strategic opportunity to help management use IT as a resource to effectively control the execution of business activities, while capturing accurate and complete data about business activities - in Real-Time. We emphasize the need (and ability using technology) to control organizations at each point in a business process, the ability to implement more proactive control, the ability to use technology as a control resource, and the opportunity to create more complete, per transaction audit trails, rather than separate process, batch audit trails

Enhancement: This chapter has been heavily revised. Students will understand the re-lationship between risks, opportunities, and controls and will be able to explain each of the components of an internal control system. In this chapter the weaknesses in the traditional control philosophy are discussed and an outline of control philosophy applicable to an in-formational technology environment is provided. This chapter also discusses the types of business and information process risks.

The discussions regarding timing the design and implementation of controls, size of business, and the process of developing a system of internal controls has been retained from the First Edition.

Enhancement: Supplement D includes new coverage of the control environment, risk assessment, information and communication and monitoring. The Coverage of Templates for Event Processes moved to Appendix D. 1.

Module 5 (Chapters 6-8 and Supplement E): Business processes and AIS designs for supporting these processes.

The most significant module (in terms of suggested class and project time) is the business process module. It incorporates systems analysis and design knowledge, and it builds on and applies the knowledge learned in Chapters 1 through 5. Using the framework estab-lished in the previous module, we discuss the processes from a business perspective. We try to refrain from focusing student attention on memorizing a series of process sequences, tasks, or a series of control procedures. We want to train students to be adaptable to a changing world by basing their evaluation of systems design or organization controls on a (system or control) objective, rather than whether a system uses a familiar design or fa-miliar set of control procedures.

We first examine each process in business, rather than information terms. We discuss the objectives of each process, the relationships between processes, the roles of process participants, and the decision and business information needs relating to each process activity. We examine the variations of processes (e.g., retailing, manufacturing, credit versus cash sales, etc.) and the effects of EDI and trading partner alliances on the processes. The input, processing, output, and risk exposure of each activity is examined from a business perspective (e.g., an order request from a customer leads to a need to review the order to see if the customer and business can complete a sales transaction - the customer is credit worthy and the business can provide the goods or services; if so, this results in an authorization from sales to continue the process). Finally, we discuss the management and information activities, including the recording, maintenance, and reporting (including queries, reports, and documents) activities relating to each process and process activity.

Next, each process is analyzed in the context of various AIS designs. We feel it is important to teach both traditional and nontraditional designs (the traditional, file oriented manual design; the traditional, file oriented, automated design; and the events-driven design). Each design is evaluated for its ability to meet user information needs and support organization objectives. We examine how controls are implemented in each design (and when controls are triggered); the audit trails of each design; the physical and logical data structures of each design; and the specific input, process, and output steps required for each design. We also compare the timing and flexibility of the reporting and document generation capabilities of each.

Surprisingly, we have found that the event-driven design perspective is a great tool for ensuring that accounting students understand and can explain concepts normally associated with only traditional designs (e.g., understanding and applying GAAP and explaining the meaning of financial statement outputs.) This alternative model also helps students understand duality and other economic concepts represented in the traditional accounting model.

Enhancements: Chapters 6, 7, 8, and Supplement E have been completely revised and updated from the First Edition.

Module 6 (Chapter 9)) Developing and Implementing Business Solutions: The Need for Lifelong Learning.

The final module includes discussion of application planning and development (the need for solutions - not just more software), reengineering efforts, managing change, and the opportunity for accounting and IT professionals to play a significant role in the development of business solutions. It reminds students that our text is not all inclusive, and encourages them to integrate concepts in this text with other business classes and topics. Our study concludes by discussing the types of skills needed to be a valuable member of a solution development team, and the need to continue learning and experimenting throughout ones professional life. We finish on the same note that we started. This is a time of great opportunity for the profession. All we need to do is *Seize the Day!*

Enhancement: Chapter 9 includes new coverage regarding the types of organizational change, deciding when to change, and managing change. In this chapter, students will also learn to create a common vision. The following discussions have been eliminated: from Chapter 9: information technology applications planning and development, planned and unplanned application development project, existing system details and limitations, clarifying information technology application requirements, and event-driven solutions and reengineering.

Module 7 (Supplements F and G) Information Technology - Resources Available to Build AIS

This module examines the effects of technology. It includes an introduction to various types of IT components and their development as well as assessing their business value. The resource module examines hardware/software concepts and trends. The objective is a strategic, conceptual understanding of information technology as a resource to enable organization objectives. As these technologies change and become more user friendly and advanced, the opportunity to more effectively and efficiently support organizations is enhanced. Due to continual change, students are taught that it is their responsibility to improve their understanding of technology, and to remain informed over time. We do suggest references, sources, and techniques for obtaining additional information. Students are taught that an ill-prepared professional will quickly learn that improperly managed technology is a risk or problem, rather than a useful resource. The professional should control the technology, rather than vice-versa.

Students are challenged to consider how we, as accounting information support professionals, can effectively use today's more complete, timely documentation of business activities to support the decision making of organization stakeholders. However, technology is not presented as a panacea. Students are reminded that technology is only useful and effective if properly implemented and used. Before designing or implementing a system, a professional must understand the system domain and system objectives.

Enhancements: Supplement F has been completely revised and updated for this edition. Supplement G, newly titled *Information Technology: Software Applications,* includes new coverage regarding enterprise resource planning software and software used to enhance organization productivity

APPLIED LEARNING

To help students apply their knowledge, the end of chapter material includes review and discussion questions and problems; sample cases and vignettes; and suggestions for individual and group projects, presentations, written papers and other active learning exercises.

Like the business world and the field of systems, we are sure this approach requires maintenance, periodic review and upgrade to keep it applicable for preparing accounting information professionals. We hope that you enjoy reading this AIS text. We look forward to hearing your comments. With your suggestions we will be able to make improvements in this on-going project.

Anita S. Hollander
Eric L. Denna
J. Owen Cherrington

SUPPLEMENTS

New to this Edition! Solutions Manual with Instructor Supplement CD-ROM (0-07-561948-2)

This supplement packages the Solutions Manual with a CD containing an electronic version of the Solutions Manual, Test Bank questions, Ready Shows (or PowerPoint®), additional PowerPoint in the form of exhibits taken from the text, and data files needed to answer selected end-of-chapter material.

The Solutions Manual provides solutions to all the end-of-chapter material in the text. The Test bank, authored by Cheryl Dunn of Florida State University, is also available on this CD to allow you to customize testing material according to your needs. The Ready Shows (PowerPoint), authored by Bruce MacLean of Dalhousie University, offers in-depth coverage of each chapter in the text and additional PowerPoint taken from the exhibits in the text provide a variety of material for your class lecture.

New to this Edition! Test Bank (0-256-23595-3)

The printed Test Bank offers a variety of true/false, multiple choice, discussion questions, and mini cases. The complete test bank is also available in electronic form on the Instructor Supplement CD-ROM.

New to this Edition! On the Web

Be sure to visit the Hollander web site at *www.mhhe.com/hollander* to find links to related web sites of interest, online instructor supplements, sample syllabi, and additional projects and cases.

ACKNOWLEDGEMENTS

This edition is based on the careful comments and suggestions of the following people. We extend our sincere thanks for their insightful comments and their efforts to guide us in this revision.

Darrell Brown
Portland State University

Doug Stein
Northern Illinois University

Dan O'Leary
University of Southern California

Dena Johnson
Texas Tech. University

Robert Kneckel
University of Florida

Janet Gillespie
University of Texas, Austin

Cheryl Dunn
Florida State University

Carol E. Brown
Oregon State University

Faye Borthick
Georgia State University

Melvin Jolly
University of Idaho

Ceil Pillsbury
University of Wisconsin–Milwaukee

Bernadette M. Ruf
Florida International University

Dan Stone
University of Illinois

Doug Stein
Northern Illinois University

Ralph Viator
University of Kentucky

Judith K. Welch
Central Florida University

Tarek S. Amer
Northern Arizona University

Carolyn Hartwell
University of Dayton

Alan Sangster
The Queen's University, Belfast

Doris Duncan
California State University, Hayward

Eric Johnson
University of Texas at Arlington

BRIEF CONTENTS

CONTENTS

An Introduction to Accounting, Information Technology, and Business Solutions

CHAPTER OBJECTIVE

The objective of this chapter is to enhance your understanding of the dynamic profession you have chosen. After studying this chapter, you should be able to:

- Describe how organizations create value for their customers.
- Describe the relationship between business, management, and information processes.
- Describe three ways accounting professionals can increase their value.
- Identify reasons for changing the nature of accounting and how the use of information technology (IT) can enable such change.

INTRODUCTION

Close your eyes and create a mental picture of an accountant. What did you see? Did you visualize a person with a green eye shade and a pocket protector, who loves numbers and likes to sit in a back room away from other people in the organization? Or did you see an articulate, personable, innovative, and critical member of a business team? Ask a friend to complete the exercise. Why is this exercise useful?

Many forward-looking members of the accounting profession are all too aware that the world in which we live is rapidly changing in profound ways. As a result, the accounting profession is in a mode of serious introspection, evaluating all facets of what it does and creating a vision of what it can and should be in the future. They realize the need to proactively prepare for the future and convince other businesspersons of their preparation and ability to provide valuable services. American Institute of Certified Public Accountants (AICPA)

President Barry Melancon has stated that "the changes the profession needs to make are probably the most fundamental ever faced by the CPA . . . [we] want to reposition the CPA as a strategic business advisor . . . lift the CPA from routine or compliance services and low end number crunching to the heart of business decision making." This requires that accounting professionals objectively examine criticisms about the profession and challenge themselves to find new ways to improve the quality of their information products and services.

Today's students need to understand the history of traditional accounting as performed in the industrial age, and acquire the skills and knowledge necessary to excel as professionals in the information age. This text educates future professionals to face the challenges of the information revolution. Our objective is to prepare you to become an active participant in the evolution of business information systems. Probably the most important contribution this book makes is to propose a different philosophy underlying the design, use, and evaluation of accounting information systems.

Obviously, no one textbook can incorporate all there is to know about this complex topic. We will often refer you to other sources to learn more about specific concepts or issues. However, we think this book provides you with a good foundation for this period of monumental change in the business world and in the accounting profession.

A CHANGING WORLD

Many people have discussed the profound effect information technology (IT) will have on the accounting profession since the early days of modern IT. Bob Elliott, national partner with the accounting firm of KPMG/Peat Marwick, is one of the more outspoken accounting futurists. In his 1992 *Accounting Horizons* article, Elliott begins with, "Information technology (IT) is changing everything."[1] Drawing on the work of Alvin Toffler,[2] Elliott uses the imagery of the "third wave" to predict impending and significant changes in accounting practice, education, and research. Elliott concludes his article with the following:

> IT is creating a wave of change that is crashing over accounting's shoreline. It crashed across industry in the 1970s. Then it crashed across the services in the 1980s. And it will crash across accounting in the 1990s. It is changing the way business is done and the problems faced by managers. Managers now need new types of information in order to make decisions, so internal and external accounting must be changed. Higher education can simply react to these changes, or it can take a more active role, embracing the future, adapting rapidly, and facilitating the adaptations of others. The challenge to academic accountants is to invent the third-wave accounting paradigm and produce the graduates who can function effectively in the third-wave organizations they will be joining. The challenge to non-academic accountants is to make the organizational and political changes to implement the new accounting paradigm.

Elliott's predictions have stimulated discussion about the likelihood and degree of impending changes in accounting practice and education. Many people are currently exploring the role IT will play in enabling such changes.

---

1 B. Elliott, "The Third Wave Breaks on the Shores of Accounting," *Accounting Horizons,* June 1992, p. 61.
2 A. Toffler, *The Third Wave* (New York: Bantam Books, 1990), p. 2.

Elliott is not the first, nor will he be the last, to suggest the need for and likelihood of change in the accounting profession. Nor is he the only person predicting a change in accounting. Al Pipkin, controller[3] for Coors Brewing Company, observes that IT is:

> bringing about a total transformation of the controller's [accounting] staff, and a re-definition of the overall financial system. Technology is changing the culture of the controller's organization just as it is impacting the entire business. In the 21st century, there will be fewer accountants on the controller's staff, but they will perform in totally new and exciting ways.

You can pick up dozens of newspapers and magazines today that proclaim "the age of no paper is no longer a pipe dream." The drudgery of shuffling paper and doing routine manipulations of data soon will be gone. From now on, the controller's staff will add value to the business or it won't exist.[4]

Although we agree with Elliott's and Pipkin's predictions, change to this point has focused on the need to improve the relevance and usefulness of accounting information. We do not believe the profession has used IT resources to significantly affect the nature of accounting practice, education, or research. IT will not fundamentally change the nature of accounting until we rethink the traditional accounting process and effectively utilize IT to enhance the process. Innovative uses of IT can enable significant changes in accounting. The question of how to effectively use IT to bring about desired changes is still an unanswered, yet critical, question.

This book encourages and enables your exploration of IT's potential effect on accounting and business (both private and public, for-profit and not-for-profit entities). Our objective is ambitious. Typically, texts present material as though the nature of the accounting profession is rather stable. This text differs in that we want to spark your imagination and creativity. By having you focus your attention on what *can* happen, we believe you can play a significant role in defining what *will* happen. As Pipkin points out, professionals who can create and add value will have a profound impact on shaping the future.

THE NATURE AND PURPOSE OF AN ORGANIZATION—CREATING VALUE

Everything an organization does should create value for its customers according to Michael Porter in his book titled *Competitive Advantage*.[5] Creating value has a cost. For example, assembling an automobile creates value but it also requires the organization to pay for various inputs (e.g., materials, supplies, and time of employees). Porter computes an organization's "margin" as the difference between value and cost. This definition is much broader than the typical accounting definition of *margin* because Porter's calculation includes all value and all cost, much of which is difficult to measure financially.

---

3 The controller is the individual or function responsible for using, designing, and evaluating an organization's financial information system. The controller is typically an accounting executive responsible for developing and maintaining an organization's financial records.

4 A. Pipkin, "The 21st Century Controller," *Management Accounting,* February 1989, p. 24.

5 M. Porter, *Competitive Advantage: Creating and Sustaining Superior Performance* (New York: The Free Press, 1985), p. 12.

The concept of creating value applies to both for-profit and not-for-profit organizations. For-profit organizations try to maximize their margins. Not-for-profit organizations, such as charitable or governmental entities, seek to maximize the goods and services they provide with the resources (funds) they receive. Over the long run, charitable and governmental organizations seek to optimize their services while matching outflows to inflows. Whether for-profit or not-for-profit, viable organizations provide goods and services that customers value in a cost-effective way.

Every organization seeks to create value by providing goods and services customers want. For example:

- A grocery store creates value by providing food in a clean and convenient location for customers to purchase.
- An airline company creates value by safely transporting passengers and cargo in a timely manner.
- An automobile manufacturer creates value by manufacturing safe, reliable vehicles to transport people and cargo.
- A municipality creates value by providing essential community services (e.g., police protection, fire protection, emergency services, and utilities) to its citizens.

Organizations and individuals that provide goods and services their customers value will survive and grow while those who do not will shrink and die. Due to competition for scarce resources, each organization or individual must provide value in a cost-effective manner. Although some organizations manage to defer their demise through deceit, disguise, or political influences, ultimately every organization has to answer to the final arbiter of value—the customer.

CASE IN POINT

In the late 1970s and early 1980s with gas prices rising rapidly and our oil supplies in doubt, most new car buyers favored smaller, more gas efficient automobiles. America's automobile manufacturers had several lean years as they modified their automobile designs to smaller, fuel-efficient vehicles. Over the next decade as the percentage of small cars increased, most parking lots adjusted the size of the parking stalls from 8 or 9 feet wide to 7 feet wide. But since 1987 the size of America's cars is getting bigger. In sprawling western and southwestern cities, the popularity of sport-utility vehicles and pickup trucks can make parking a hassle. Parking lots with larger parking stalls are now able to charge a premium price. Parking problems will likely increase as the popularity of the Hummer increases. The Hummer is the civilian adaptation of a military vehicle that is 8 feet wide, including the mirrors.[6]

Organizations create value by developing and providing the goods and services customers desire. Goods and services are provided through a series of business processes. A *business process* is a series of activities that accomplishes a business objective. Regardless

---

6 Neal Templin, "Big Cars and Little Spaces Cause Mayhem," *The Wall Street Journal,* March 11, 1998, pp. B1, 8.

of the type of goods or services provided, each organization has at least three business processes (see Exhibit 1–1):

1. *Acquisition/payment process.* The objective of the acquisition/payment process is to acquire, maintain, and pay for the resources needed by the organization. Many resources are required including human resources, property, plant, equipment, financial resources, raw materials, and supplies. Resources are acquired from external entities like suppliers or vendors. These are the inputs required by the organization to provide goods and services to its customers.

2. *Conversion process.* The objective of the conversion process is to convert the acquired resources into goods and services for customers. The raw inputs are transformed into finished goods and services by this process.

3. *Sales/collection process.* The objective of the sales/collection process is to sell and deliver goods and service to customers and collect payment. The finished goods and services from the conversion process are sold to customers (external entities) in exchange for their payment, usually in the form of cash.

Leaders of an organization are responsible for managing the business processes. Management activities can be broadly categorized into planning, executing, controlling, and evaluating (see Exhibit 1–2). Planning requires leaders to define the business

EXHIBIT 1–1

Business Processes

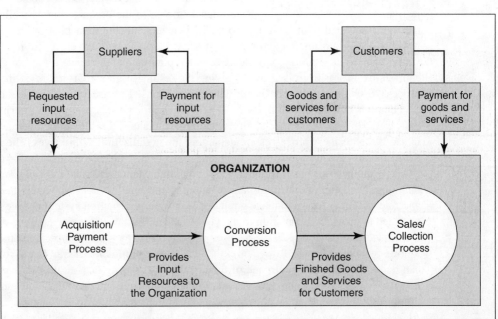

E X H I B I T 1–2

Management Activities

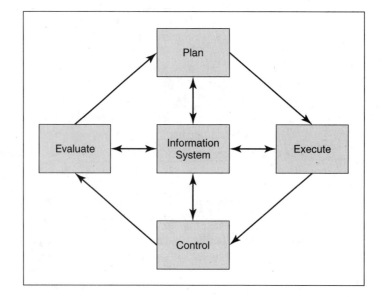

objectives, to prioritize business processes, and to provide a blueprint for achieving the objectives. They must identify opportunities available to the organization as well as assess the risk associated with each opportunity. Managers execute their plan by dividing business processes into smaller activities, assigning people to perform each activity, and motivating them to do a good job. A clearly defined plan increases the likelihood of proper execution. Control is exercised by reviewing the results of an activity or an entire business process to see if they are consistent with expectations. The review may cause a change in expectations or a change in the way an activity or a process is performed to bring the actual results in line with expectations. Periodically, managers evaluate the operating results to see if the business processes are achieving the organization's objectives. The results of the evaluation are used to modify the plans, objectives, or expectations.

At the heart of *managing* is decision making. Managers make multiple decisions in planning, executing, controlling, and evaluating the organization. Managers need timely and relevant information to make good decisions. An information system is developed and operated to provide information to managers. The information system captures data about the organization and its activities, stores and maintains the data, and prepares meaningful reports for management. These activities, called *information processes* (see Exhibit 1–3), can be broadly classified into one of three groups: *recording* data about business activity, *maintaining* or keeping the data about an organization relevant and up to date, and *reporting* useful information to those who execute, control, and evaluate the business processes.

EXHIBIT 1–3

The Information System and Information Processes

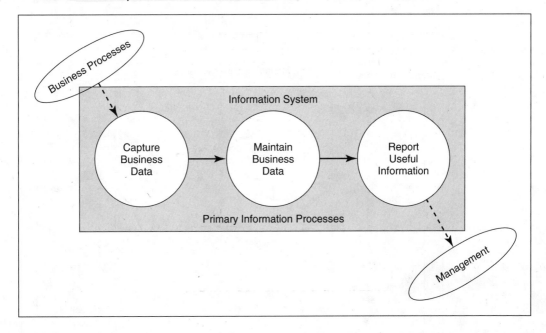

Notice the difference between *data* and *information* in the above discussion. *Data* are the inputs into the information system; they are facts and figures about business activities and business processes. In and of itself, data are generally not useful for decision making. The information system captures, stores, combines, summarizes, and organizes data into *information* that is meaningful to management for decision making. Information is defined as data that have meaning to the receiver—the information customer. If a report truly contains information, it should enable the information customer to use the information to make a management decision.

In summary, business processes are directly associated with providing goods and services to customers. The three main business processes are acquiring and paying for input resources, converting inputs into finished goods and services, and selling and collecting payment from customers for the goods and services provided (see Exhibit 1–4). Managers obtain information from an information system to help them manage the business processes. They must make decisions about planning, executing, controlling, and evaluating each business process. An information system provides this information through three main information processes: recording business activity data, maintaining the stores of data, and reporting information to management. Information processes capture, store, and maintain data and report useful information about the business processes.

EXHIBIT 1–4

Relationship between Business Processes, Information Processes, and Management Activities

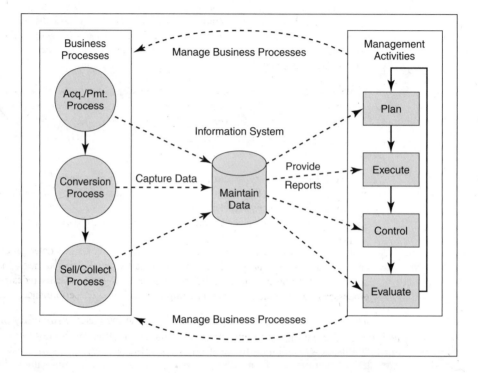

As an organization's business processes and management processes change, so must its information processes. When business processes, management processes, and information processes are integrated, they greatly enhance the likelihood of the organization achieving its overall objective (providing value to its customers). When they are not well integrated or well aligned, the organization sputters and limps along just like an automobile that is out of tune, a frustrating condition.

An important theme of this book is the integration of business, management, and information processes. Subsequent chapters will discuss the nature of business processes in more detail and promote the use of business process understanding as a basis for designing information systems.

THE CALL FOR CHANGE

Creating value for customers in today's world is particularly challenging. The steady, somewhat predictable world of the past has been replaced with constant change. Organizations have more opportunities, but they also face more threats from changes in competition, regulations, customer demands, operating risks, and employee demands. Futurist Alvin Toffler suggests that this new world:

> challenges all our old assumptions. Old ways of thinking, old formulas, dogmas, and ideologies, no matter how cherished or how useful in the past, no longer fit the facts. The world that is fast emerging from the clash of new values and technologies, new geopolitical relationships, new lifestyles and modes of communication, demands wholly new ideas and analogies, classifications and concepts.[7]

Many organizations are reconsidering how they operate to create value. One approach to change is to reengineer business processes. *Reengineering* is often an overused (and sometimes misused) term. Reengineering requires an organization to rethink how it operates to provide greater value to its customers. Michael Hammer initially popularized the concept.

> Despite a decade or more of restructuring and downsizing, many U.S. companies are still unprepared to operate in the 1990s . . . heavy investments in information technology have delivered disappointing results—largely because companies tend to use technology to mechanize old ways of doing business. They leave the existing processes intact and use computers simply to speed them up.
>
> It is time to stop paving the cow paths. Instead of embedding outdated processes in silicon and software, we should obliterate them and start over. We should "reengineer" our businesses: use the power of modern information technology to radically redesign our business processes in order to achieve dramatic improvements in their performance.[8]

These radical changes in organizations and the increased availability of information technology are beginning to put pressure on the accounting profession to do things differently. Some of the more significant challenges facing the accounting profession include the following:

- Much of what accountants do was developed by "precomputer thinking." For example, the accounting process used today was documented by Pacioli several hundred years ago and it has not changed substantially. If the accounting profession doesn't reinvent itself in light of information technology it risks being pushed aside and perhaps replaced by a profession with a more innovative vision of how information, analysis, and attest services should be provided.[9]
- Most revenues for public accounting firms in the United States (approximately 70%) have come from auditing public financial statements and compliance tax services. The need for an audit was created by the Securities Act of 1933 and the Securities and Exchange Act of 1934. The first income tax laws passed in 1913 created the need for

---

7 Toffler, *The Third Wave*, p. 2.
8 Michael Hammer, "Reengineering Work: Don't Automate, Obliterate," *Harvard Business Review*, July–August 1990, pp. 104–12.
9 See Robert Mednick, "Our Profession in the Year 2000: A Blueprint of the Future," *Journal of Accountancy*, August 1988.

compliance tax services. These two services have dominated the public accounting profession for the last 60 to 80 years, but both of them are in the latter stages of their product life cycle. Firms are extremely competitive in pricing services in these areas and profit margins are very narrow. Projections over the next 20 years indicate there will not be adequate revenue in these areas to support the public accounting profession as we know it today.[10]

- Many managers are dissatisfied with the quality and timeliness of information provided by the accounting systems. As the gap widens between manager's information needs and traditional management reports, many managers are creating their own information system. Many companies now support two, often irreconcilable, sets of books: (1) an official accounting system consisting of traditional ledgers and controls, and (2) a separate information network developed by managers who aren't receiving the information they need from the formal system. Information in the latter system is considered by management to be essential in determining the business's financial condition, in executing business transactions, and in making business decisions. As operating managers collect and maintain more and more financial data, accountants risk being excluded from the management team that runs the business and being responsible only for documenting its history.[11]

- Traditional financial statements are extremely compressed and not released for several weeks after the end of the year. All the business activity for an entire accounting period is summarized in financial statements that cover approximately three pages and footnotes that are not more than five to seven pages long. Figuratively, an analyst using financial statements as an information source is forced to look at a company through a keyhole that permits only a small part of available information to be seen. Some people predict that once capital suppliers have real-time access to an enterprise's databases, they will have little interest in annual financial statements and, by extension, auditor's opinions on them. What they might be far more interested in is real-time assurance from the auditor that either the information in the enterprise's database is reliable or the system itself is likely to produce reliable data.[12]

As we begin to change accounting it is important to realize that accounting is one of the oldest professions on record and that it has changed many times previously. Book-keeping has been practiced from very early times. For example, the Romans had an elaborate system of keeping accounts and used a double-entry system. A review of accounting over the ages indicates accountants have not always done the same work, but they have performed similar functions. The primary functions of accounting that have been practiced for thousands of years include:

---

10 See Richard Greene and Katherine Barrett, "Auditing the Accounting Firms: Under Heavy Fire, the Big Six Firms Are Finally Changing How They Do Business," *Financial World*, September 27, 1994, pp. 30–34.

11 See John S. Fisher, "What's Ahead in Accounting: The New Finance," *Journal of Accountancy*, August 1994.

12 See Robert K. Elliott, "What's Ahead in the Assurance Function: The Future of Audits," *Journal of Accountancy*, September 1994.

- *Recording data about business transactions.* There has always been a group of people responsible to record data about business events. In the Egyptian era they used a quill pen to record the data and stored it on papyrus scrolls. Today we might use a bar code and scan data into a computer system and store it on a magnetic disk.

- *Summarizing results of business activity into useful reports.* Kings, government leaders, and business managers have always relied on accounting people to summarize the results of business activity into meaningful reports. The balance sheet and income statement have been standard reports for many years. More recently we added a statement of cash flows. However, managers in today's environment demand more detailed reports such as sales by district or sales by product type. Accountants have always played a key role in helping a variety of people understand and use the reports for a variety of purposes.

- *Providing assurances that the business is operating as intended and that the assets of the organization are protected.* All parties to a business event have looked to accountants to provide assurance that the transaction is properly handled, accurately recorded, and accurately reported. Hundreds of years ago an accountant had to be physically present to observe the business activity. Based on physical observation the accountant vouched for the accuracy of the results. Throughout most of this century the assurance has been based on a system of internal controls and an audit of the published financial statements.

These functions are necessary for any business or government entity to operate and will always be needed. However, we don't have to do them the same way today as they have been performed for hundreds of years. For example, the accounting system may not need double-entry postings using debits and credits. Financial information need not be provided in the same financial statements as we know them today, or based on the same generally accepted accounting principles. Assurances need not be provided by audits of public financial statements. Nevertheless, business activity must be recorded and reported and controls must be in place to protect various people's interests. A variety of people need help understanding business information and using it properly in a variety of decisions.

The infrastructure that supports the production and delivery of accounting's information products is the *accounting information system.* Simply defined, a *system* is a set of resources brought together to achieve some common goal. For example, a fire is a system. It has a set of resources (match and wood) to accomplish a goal (generate heat). The resources available to build accounting information systems include people and technologies. The objective of the accounting information system is to collect and store data about business processes that can be used to generate meaningful reports for decision makers to help them plan, execute, control, and evaluate organization activities.

The accounting information system has traditionally captured and stored data about a selected subset of business events, namely activities that meet the definition of an accounting transaction. Only those events that change the composition of the company's assets, liabilities, or owners' equity have data about them captured and stored in the accounting information system. Could we modify the set of business events and capture data about a broader set of business events than "accounting transactions"? Sure! Do we want to broaden the set of business events? Maybe, depending on the type of information our information customers need to make good decisions. Remember, the customer is king or queen and the system must provide what the customer wants to continue to be successful and add value. It is exciting that people are rethinking important decisions such as What is the role of accounting and accountants? What constitutes accounting data and accounting information?, and How (and when) should accounting information be processed and distributed?

Technologies have evolved and advanced over the years from manual resources (e.g., paper, quill, and ink) to advanced information systems (e.g., scanners, disks, and printers). As new technologies are developed we must seek creative ways to utilize their capacity to improve the accounting system. New technologies may enable us to do things we could not economically perform with prior technologies. We must constantly be looking for ways to use new technology to reengineer the accounting system and improve the information it provides.

Traditionally, accounting professionals have added value by providing information to information customers who are responsible for managing an organization. However, because of the diversity of the information customer's needs, various accounting specialties have evolved, such as financial accounting and reporting, managerial and cost accounting, auditing, assurance services, and tax compliance and planning. Often, each accounting specialty is viewed as a separate and distinct profession with its own systems of capturing and processing data and its own body of knowledge that is somewhat related to, but largely separate from, the others. Developing and maintaining these separate systems is costly and is often unnecessary given today's information technology. The challenge facing accounting today is the growing diversity of information requirements that go well beyond traditional definitions of accounting and the capabilities of traditional accounting systems.

CHANGES IN PROCESS

The accounting profession is seriously evaluating its competitive strengths, the services it provides, and the competencies required to perform those services. The American Institute of Certified Public Accountants (AICPA) is currently sponsoring the CPA Vision Project.[13] Meetings are being held throughout the country to obtain grassroots input on what the accounting profession might be like 10 to 15 years from now. The objective is to create a comprehensive and integrated vision of the profession's future that will:

- Build awareness of future opportunities and challenges for all segments of the profession.
- Lead the profession as it navigates the changing demands of the marketplace.

---

13 Articles about the results of the Vision Project are being regularly published in the *Journal of Accountancy*. Information is also being published on the Internet—see http://www.cpavision.org.

* Draw together the profession to create a vibrant and viable future.
* Leverage the CPA's core competencies and values.
* Guide current and future initiatives in support of the profession and the protection of public interest.

Fundamental in creating a vision of the future is identifying the values and competencies of accountants. The top five values and competencies identified in the Vision Project are shown in Table 1–1. The top values and competencies possessed by accountants are those that provide them with a competitive advantage in delivering selected services to customers. But there are issues that must be addressed in successfully delivering those services. Table 1–2 contains the top five services accountants are expected to provide and the top five issues in providing those services.

As noted in Table 1–1, people value accounting services because they see accountants as competent, broad-based businesspeople with integrity and objectivity, who constantly learn new things and keep up to date with their profession. One of the distinguishing competencies of accountants will be their technological ability (i.e., ability to utilize and leverage technology as an enabler and strategic tool).

The services identified in Table 1–2 are much broader than the traditional tax and audit services. Assurance services will continue to be a dominant activity, but they are expected to be more than audited financial statements. Assurance services are expected to

TABLE 1–1

CPA Vision Project Values and Competencies

Top Five Values	Top Five Competencies
Continuing education and lifelong learning. CPAs highly value continuing education beyond certification and believe it is important to continuously acquire new skills and knowledge.	*Communication skills.* Ability to give and exchange information with meaningful relationships.
Competence. CPAs are able to perform work in a capable, efficient, and appropriate manner.	*Strategic and critical thinking skills.* Ability to link data, knowledge, and wisdom together to provide quality advice.
Integrity. CPAs conduct themselves with honesty and professional ethics.	*Focus on client and market.* Ability to meet the changing needs of clients better than competitors can.
Attunement with broad business issues. CPAs are in tune with overall realities of business enterprises.	*Interpretation of converging information.* Ability to provide interpretation of financial and nonfinancial information as they interface with each other.
Objectivity. CPAs are able to be nonbiased and nonjudgmental.	*Technologically adept.* Ability to utilize and leverage technology.

TABLE 1–2

CPA Vision Project Services and Issues

Top Five Services	Top Five Issues
Assurance. Attesting to the reliability of information and systems.	The future success of the profession relies a great deal upon *public perceptions* of the CPAs' abilities and roles.
Technology. Providing services in system analysis, information management, and system security.	CPAs must become *market driven* and not dependent upon regulations to keep them in business.
Management consulting. Providing advice to organizations on management and performance improvements.	The market demands *less auditing and accounting* and *more value-added consulting* services.
Financial planning. Providing advice in the broad areas of financial planning.	*Specialization* is critical for the future survival of the CPA profession.
International services. Providing services in the international arena such as cross-border tax planning, multinational company mergers, multinational company joint ventures, and so on.	The marketplace demands that CPAs be *conversant in global business* practices and strategies.

cover everything from home pages on the Internet to the financial systems themselves. Analysis, design, implementation, and security of information systems will continue to grow. Also, general management consulting on managing and improving the performance of organizations is expected to increase.

Critical to the success of future accountants is their ability to change the public's perception of the CPA's abilities and roles. CPAs themselves must become more market driven, more specialized, less dependent on auditing and accounting, and more driven by value-adding consulting services in a globalized business environment.

Other professional organizations like the Financial Executives Institute and the Institute of Management Accountants have each organized committees to consider needed changes in the services provided by the accounting profession. Many ideas have been advanced but none of them have received as much publicity as the CPA Vision Project of the AICPA.

Calls for change are impacting university classrooms. To promote changes in accounting education, the accounting profession funded the Accounting Education Change Commission (AECC) in the late 80s and early 90s. The AECC has released a series of reports that explain the need for change in accounting education and provide some guidance for promoting such change. The American Accounting Association, a professional association of accounting academicians and practicing professionals, continues to promote change and innovation in accounting education. As the AECC explained in their report *The First Course in Accounting:* "[Students should] gain an appreciation that accounting as a discipline is the focus of constructive debate and intensive rethinking caused by economic and technological change, and one that will continue to evolve in the future."[14]

The criticisms and changes may irritate some people. However, demands for change do not mean that accounting has not provided a valuable service and can't continue to do so in the future. Instead, change represents a significant opportunity to provide even greater value to organizations, industries, and society. The question, therefore, is how can the accounting profession increase its value?

HOW CAN ACCOUNTING PROFESSIONALS ENHANCE THEIR VALUE?

Accounting has a natural, strategic opportunity to enhance its value by helping to solve *business* problems, not just traditional *accounting* problems. Individuals that perform the role of a business solution professional merge business, accounting, and IT skills and knowledge. By doing this they can ensure for themselves a key role in shaping the future of an organization. Solving business problems requires an integration of the organization's strategy, structure, business processes, information technology, and business measurements as illustrated in Exhibit 1–5. Although there is some value in focusing attention on each component individually, an integrated solution that addresses all of them is necessary. We suggest the following guidelines as a framework for solving business problems:

1. Remember that all solution components—strategy, structure, business processes, measurements, and IT—are important. Meaningful solutions are rarely found by focusing only on strategy, measurement, or some other subset of the components. Focusing on one solution component without considering its impact on the other components is unproductive.

2. Align each business solution to the organization's business processes. A business solution is any plan to solve a business problem. Part of most business solutions includes the effective use of IT; however, it may also include changes in organization structure, measurements, and strategy. Focusing on business processes allows us to consider all solution components together because they provide a common thread across what was previously considered diverse disciplines and specialties.

3. Encourage continuous organizational learning and real-time adaptation to a complex and ever-changing world. As the popular philosopher Eric Hoffer observes: "In times of change, learners inherit the earth, while the learned find themselves beautifully equipped to deal with a world that no longer exists." People are learning that there is no such thing as a permanent, integrative business solution.

Exhibit 1–5 illustrates the nature of a business solution framework that follows these three guidelines: all factors are important, they are aligned to business processes, and they

---

14 Accounting Education Change Commission, *The First Course in Accounting,* 1992, p. 3.

EXHIBIT 1–5

Business Solution Framework

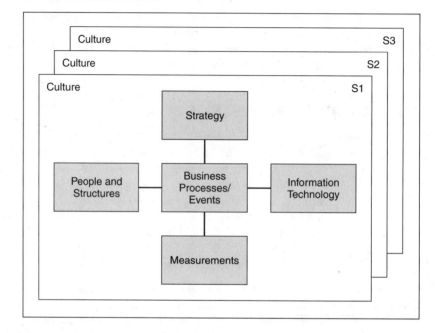

change (learn) over time. Although strategy, structures, business processes, measurements, and IT are all important, this book will focus primarily on three of the areas—business processes, IT, and measurements. We will provide glimpses into strategy and structures at times, but will not provide the same background and depth as with business processes, IT, and measurements.

Accountants have the opportunity to use these solution guidelines and to help organizations provide value by integrating their business, information, and management processes. Simply put, accounting can enhance its value to an organization by constantly improving its ability to:

1. Provide useful information for the decision makers that plan, execute, control, or evaluate the organization's activities.

2. Help embed information processes into business processes. Increasingly, organizations are embedding technology into business processes. Accountants can help ensure that the information processes embedded into the business processes execute rules to control the business process while also capturing and storing detailed data about the business processes in real time.

3. Help management define business policies to shape and control its business processes.

This book illustrates how working on all three of these opportunities provides accountants with a tremendous opportunity to enhance their value. When accounting professionals overlook any of these opportunities, they limit their potential value to the organization. Furthermore, being involved in all three areas makes the accounting professional a key player in developing innovative business solutions.

The three opportunities outline potential deliverables for future accounting professionals. While some may feel these deliverables lie outside the current or traditional domain of the accounting profession, we believe they are key to increasing the value of accounting in the future. Our objective is to explore how accounting can provide greater value. This may require the nature and scope of accounting to change. However, we should not be surprised that a focus on adding greater value might require us to start doing some things we have not done before, and stop doing other things we have done for years.

Business professionals should view IT and its capabilities as an integral part of a tool set to provide business solutions. However, do not allow an interest in IT to take you off course. Focus on how technology can be used as a resource to build business solutions rather than on the study of IT as a discipline of its own. IT use must be driven by the nature of the desired business process, the data to be captured, and the information to be provided, rather than IT shaping the nature of business processes, data, and information. Without this perspective the proverbial tail can begin to wag the dog.

CONCLUDING COMMENTS

We hope we have persuaded you to at least consider the possibility that:

1. The accounting profession may need to change.
2. Any changes in the accounting profession should focus on helping organizations provide greater value to customers.
3. Accounting and IT must be integrated to develop business solutions.
4. IT has a role to play in the future of the accounting profession.

This book is written to help you understand the direction of, and reasons for, changes in both accounting and IT professions. Some of you may wonder why accounting professionals should worry about IT. Should they simply relinquish the IT domain to others? Several years ago Howard Armitage observed:

> Despite the fact that information systems design is among the most vital components of successful corporate management, accountants have found themselves increasingly playing a peripheral role in what was once regarded as their exclusive domain. Among the reasons for this role reversal have been the general absence of adequate systems training and background on the part of the accountant and the technical complexities of earlier computer systems which effectively reduced accounting input. . . . It is of interest to note that while the definitions of Management Accounting and Management Information Systems have striking parallels, it is the latter group which has been marshaling responsibility for such accounting functions as determining user requirements, data classification, results communication, and decision support.

. . . accountants should be taking a more active role in such vital concerns. Since accountants have expertise in accounting concepts, they clearly must be more heavily involved in accounting information system design. To date, accounting emphasis has focused on the control of information systems. This is a crucial area of inquiry. . . . Of equal importance, however, is the expertise that management accountants can offer to the design and development of other corporate information systems which rely on the accounting function for data. Recent methodological advances in system analysis and design permit this re-entry to take place.[15]

Today, more than at any other time in history, accountants have a strategic opportunity to add value in this dynamic, international economy. Again, this can prove as exhilarating as it is terrifying. As Tom Peters points out:

The way we organize and get things done in the public and private sectors, and in general, is undergoing the most profound shift since (at least) the Industrial Revolution. It's no wonder that we all, clerk, middle manager, government minister, and chairman of the board alike, feel a disquiet, bordering on despair. . . . The story that unfolds from CNN to The Body Shop (and even the Union Pacific Railroad) is in equal parts terrifying and liberating. Terrifying because all old bets are off, from the boardroom (which *may* disappear) to the factory (which, in the form we've lived with for the last 150 years, *will* disappear). Liberating because there's never been a time so laden with opportunity for anyone, receptionist or bank president, with a mind to shuck tradition and take the plunge.[16]

AICPA Chair Robert Mednick has stated that he hopes to see accountants become the "premier information professional in a world of electronic commerce and virtual global trade." Achieving such a lofty status will require much hard work from accountants. They must strive to acquire the necessary financial, information technology, information systems, and business skills and competencies, as well as convincing other business professionals that the goal has been met. If you are interested, we encourage you to strive toward accomplishing this goal. We hope this book can convince you to take the plunge and work toward changing the perception and reality so that everyone who closes their eyes and visualizes an accounting information professional sees an articulate, personable, innovative, and critical member of a business team. We hope this book makes the difference between your plunge resulting in a swan dive rather than a belly flop.

Those who accept such possibilities can expect to greatly increase their value to organizations. Others will find themselves at a significant disadvantage. As Machiavelli explained to the ruling family of Florence:

It must be considered that there is nothing more difficult to carry out, nor more doubtful of success, nor more dangerous to handle than to initiate a new order of things. For the reformer has enemies in all those who profit by the old order, and only lukewarm defenders by all those who could profit by the new order. This lukewarmness arises partly from fear of their adver-

---

15 H. Armitage, *Linking Management Accounting Systems with Computer Technology* (Ontario, Canada: The Society of Management Accountants of Canada, 1984).

16 T. Peters, *Liberation Management: Necessary Disorganization for the Nanosecond Nineties* (New York: Alfred A. Knopf, 1992), p. 345.

saries who have the laws in their favor, and partly from the incredulity of mankind who do not truly believe in anything new until they have had actual experience with it.[17]

Let's begin the task of exploring the future of accounting, IT, and business solutions. To help you gain the knowledge and skills necessary to perform the role of a business information professional, this text will cover the following:

Topic 1. Understanding and modeling business processes and business events. As noted earlier, business processes provide the basis for understanding how a business works and linking the functional areas of an organization like production, accounting, finance, and human resources. Business processes can be broken into a series of separate activities we call business events. We introduce a means of identifying and modeling business processes and their events (Chapter 2).

Topic 2. The evolution of the accounting information system architecture. The architecture of the accounting process has not changed substantially for several hundred years. Nevertheless, many companies continue to use the traditional architecture. We analyze this architecture and how it has been computerized. We identify criticisms of the architecture and explore an alternative to improve it (Chapter 3).

Topic 3. Planning and building an IT architecture. The conceptual models of business processes/events serve as the basis for planning and building an IT architecture to support business processes and management activities (Chapter 4).

Topic 4. Business and information process risk analysis. We consider the impact of the changing nature of the accounting system on identifying and controlling business and information process risk and control design (Chapter 5).

Topic 5. Business solutions. With our foundation in place, we compare the business processes, measurements, and IT application architecture of traditional business processes with each of the components of event-driven solutions (Chapters 6–8).

Topic 6. Continuous improvement. Nothing is so constant as change in today's world of information technology. We discuss the challenge of managing change and the opportunity to play a significant role in the development of business solutions. We conclude by discussing the skills that are needed to be a valuable member of a solution development team, and the need to continue learning and experimenting throughout one's professional life (Chapter 9).

Supplemental Topics. While the first nine chapters of the book have a definite agenda, there are a few other topics your instructor may wish to cover. These topics complement the material in the main chapters by including information about tools and techniques for building IT applications. They include: documentation skills, the general ledger architecture, database concepts, data processing controls, the changing nature of journals and ledgers, and the

---

17 Niccolo Machiavelli, The Prince, trans. Luigi Rice and Rev. E. R. P. Vincent (New York: New American Library, 1952), p. 10.

information technology resource. Documentation skills (Supplement A) and the general ledger architecture (Supplement B) fit nicely with your study of Chapters 2 and 3. You will use the documentation skills in almost every chapter in this text. Supplement C discusses database concepts and technology in nontechnical terms. This material complements Chapter 4. Supplement D provides an overview of sample information system controls, and complements the material presented in Chapters 5 through 8. The best time to read Supplement E (about the changing nature of journals and ledgers) is after reading Chapter 6. Finally, the IT resource material (Supplements F and G) includes an introduction to various types of IT components and their development, as well as assessing the business value of IT. Your instructor will advise you on when to study this material.

Again, our intent is to give you a foundation to begin thinking innovatively about accounting, IT, and solving business problems. Enjoy!

CHECKLIST OF KEY TERMS AND CONCEPTS

Accounting	Industrial age
Accounting Education Change Commission	Information
Accounting information system	Information age
Accounting "specialties" (financial accounting and reporting, managerial and cost accounting, and tax compliance and planning)	Information customers
	Information processes
	Information system
	Information technology
Acquisition/payment business process	Managing business and information processes
American Accounting Association	Margin
American Institute of Certified Public Accountants	Not-for-profit organizations
	Real-time access
Auditing	Reengineering
Business cycle	Relationship between accounting and IT professionals
Business processes	
Business solution professional	Sales/collection business process
Business solutions	System
Conversion business process	Value
For-profit organizations	

REVIEW QUESTIONS

1. What does it mean to create value? How do organizations create value?
2. What is an organization's margin?
3. Differentiate between the objectives of a for-profit and a not-for-profit organization.
4. Explain each of the following elements of managing: planning, executing, controlling, and evaluating.

5. What is a business process? Describe each of the major business processes found in most organizations.

6. Give three examples of each type of business process.

7. Define and give three examples of *information processes.*

8. How are management, business, and information processes related?

9. Define *reengineering.*

10. What is an accounting information system? How does it differ from other information systems within an organization?

11. Briefly describe each of the competencies of future accountants as identified by the CPA Vision Project.

12. Describe what is meant by a business solution professional.

13. Discuss each of the proposed guidelines for solving business problems.

14. What is a business solution framework?

15. How can accountants increase the value they add to an organization?

DISCUSSION QUESTIONS

1. How is accounting reacting to calls for change? Will the way accounting uses IT affect its ability to react to calls for change? Explain.

2. You and a friend are debating whether IT advancements have had an impact on the accounting profession. Prepare an argument that IT advancements have not significantly impacted accounting. Prepare an alternative argument that IT advancements have significantly impacted the accounting profession. Why are you seemingly able to argue both sides?

3. Why does accounting need to rethink its processes to derive the most benefit from IT advancements?

4. Should a business's needs mandate the uses of IT, or should IT mandate the nature of business processes? Explain.

5. Read Hammer's article on reengineering. Is reengineering the same as automating or computerizing traditional methods of conducting business? Explain.

6. Why must accounting and information systems personnel work together to provide useful information? What happens if they do not work together?

7. What are the drawbacks or roadblocks that make it difficult for accountants to help create greater value for an organization? What will be your role in solving these roadblocks?

8. What are the major challenges facing the accounting profession?

9. If only businesses that truly create value survive, how do tobacco companies stay in business? How do illegal drug markets survive?

10. Who are accounting's information customers?

11. If accountants begin to take a larger role in solving business problems, why will some people object and argue that this is not within the realm or the responsibility of accounting?

12. The CPA Vision Project identified five issues facing the accounting profession. Identify the issue you think is the most important. Summarize the issue and describe why you think it is the most important.

MINICASES AND OTHER APPLIED LEARNING

1. **Owen's Farm.** Owen's Farm owns approximately 50 acres of peach trees. Migrant farm workers perform almost all of the work. In the late winter and early spring they prune the trees. During the mid-spring they thin the fruit from the trees, and in late summer and early fall they pick the fruit.

   The farm manager does most of the other work, such as spraying the trees, irrigating, and selling the fruit. Spray concentrate, fruit boxes, and other supplies are purchased on account from the local co-op stores. Fruit is sold on account to major food chains such as Krogers and Albertsons.

   Required:

   Identify and classify the major activities of Owen's Farm into *(a)* the acquisition/payment process, *(b)* the conversion process, and *(c)* the sales/collection process.

2. Research published literature regarding proposed changes in accounting education. Should the emphasis of accounting education change? Explain.

3. Research the changes that have occurred in the structure and services provided by professional accounting firms during the past five years. Prepare a summary of your findings. Why are the firms changing?

4. **An Analysis of the Financial Accounting Specialty.** Consider the following background overview of financial accounting history:

   Due to the composition of courses in an accounting major, students are most familiar with financial accounting. Financial accounting's main function is to report information about an organization's activities to external information customers (investors, creditors, and regulators). As an organization's dependence on external financing sources increases, an organization assumes increased reporting responsibilities to investors and creditors. External investors, creditors, and regulators want information to help them decide whether to invest their resources in the organization.

   Historical events help explain the current state of financial accounting. Organizations grew rapidly during the early 1900s and most organizations became dependent on investors and creditors for external sources of capital to fund industrial growth. As organizations became more and more dependent upon external sources of funding, they had to provide investors and creditors (information customers) with useful information to aid their evaluation of the organization's performance.

   For several years everything seemed to be just fine. Organizations sold ownership interests (shares of stock) to investors and borrowed money from creditors (notes, mortgages, and bonds). The organizations provided the investors and creditors with information regarding their performance, often suggesting a very healthy return on their investment. There were no strict guidelines regarding financial reporting, but no one really seemed to care. Millions of dollars were being exchanged each day and everyone seemed very content with the situation.

The stock market crash of 1929 drastically changed the way organizations reported their financial information. Thousands of individuals and organizations were ruined financially. Hundreds of banks failed, and the United States was thrust into the Great Depression. In response to the collapse of the financial markets, the U.S. Congress passed the Securities Act of 1933 and the Securities Exchange Act of 1934, which established the Securities Exchange Commission (SEC). The SEC became the federal agency overseeing all organizations with publicly traded securities (e.g., stocks and bonds).

The SEC established reporting requirements for publicly held organizations. Creditors quickly adopted the SEC's requirements for their own purposes. Since the formation of the SEC, various standard-setting bodies have been given responsibility to identify generally accepted accounting principles (GAAP). Today the SEC has delegated the primary responsibility for establishing GAAP for publicly held companies to the Financial Accounting Standards Board (FASB). To date the FASB has issued well over 100 Statements of Financial Accounting Standards (SFASs) to govern the reporting of an organization's financial information. In addition to the FASB, the Governmental Accounting Standards Board (GASB) has been formed to set standards for financial reporting by federal, state, and local governments.

The primary objective of financial accounting is to provide external information customers with financial information regarding an organization's financial status, operating results, and financing methods. This is typically accomplished for publicly held companies through the release of three financial reports:

Income statement. A report of the operating results of an organization for a certain period of time.

Balance sheet. A report of the financial status of an organization at a given point in time.

Statement of cash flows. A report of the sources and uses of cash for a period of time.

Although the format and guidelines for preparing these statements vary by industry and by country, the financial reports of diverse organizations are surprisingly similar. The underlying theory is that financial accountants can produce general purpose financial statements that provide a uniform view for information customers. Keeping abreast of the many standards governing financial reporting is very challenging. Nonetheless, unless an organization adheres to established reporting standards, it could be subject to stiff fines or even lose its opportunity to seek investment capital. For most organizations, losing external funding sources could seriously jeopardize their ability to continue operations. Therefore, they spend large sums of money to adhere to the rules and regulations of those governing the external reporting process.

Financial accounting has an explicit set of concepts to guide the development of published financial reports. The accounting profession expended a great deal of effort in establishing a theory to support financial accounting. This effort culminated with the release of the *conceptual framework* consisting of six Financial Accounting Concept Statements beginning in November 1978 and ending in December 1985. These six statements (one of which was superseded) provide financial accounting with a foundation to guide the development of specific reporting standards.

One of the more significant contributions of the conceptual framework was the FASB's definition of useful information. Although these standards were intended to provide universal definitions of useful information, many people argue that financial accounting is no closer to adhering to these definitions than the day the Conceptual Statements were issued.

Financial reporting requirements are particularly important because of their impact on the allocation of financial resources in our economy. Inadequate reporting to the financial markets can result in tremendous waste of scarce capital resources. When the financial market fails, such as in the crash of 1929, it can result in disaster.

Required:

Perform the following for private or public financial reporting.

   a. Research the most recent year of business and accounting publications (e.g., *The Wall Street Journal, Business Week, Fortune, Journal of Accountancy,* AICPA releases, and FASB and GASB releases) for articles about financial reporting. Summarize your findings in a written report.

   b. Research the recent history of financial reporting (the last three to five years). Explain the most significant changes in financial accounting during that time.

   c. What are the major challenges facing the financial reporting specialty?

5. **An Analysis of the Auditing Specialty.** Consider the following background overview of auditing history:

> The auditor's information customer is anyone who wants some assurance that information about the organization is reliable and meets prescribed reporting rules, regulations, and procedures. The auditing profession started in response to the needs of 15th century shipping merchants who wanted to ensure that their cargo investments were accounted for properly. The need arose because merchants could not always personally oversee the shipping and selling of their goods. Over the years, auditing has evolved into a critical service to many information customers who are not able to personally attest to the reliability of business information.
>
> Today, there are three basic types of audits and auditors:
>
> > *Operational audits* focus on evaluating the effectiveness and efficiency of an organization's activities and are typically performed by *internal auditors.* Internal auditors represent, and report to, the organization's management (the information customer).
> >
> > *Compliance audits* focus on determining whether prescribed rules and regulations have been followed by the organization in managing and reporting its activities. Internal auditors can perform compliance audits when the organization's management has established the applicable rules, but the information customer performs most compliance audits. For example, government or regulatory agencies such as the IRS, SEC, or other federal, state, and local authorities each have their own audit staffs who audit information provided by organizations and individuals.
> >
> > *Financial statement audits* focus on determining whether an organization's financial statements adhere to generally accepted accounting principles (GAAP). The Securities and Exchange Commission (SEC), by law, has authority to establish GAAP, but they have generally given a professional organization the responsibility to set the rules. Financial statement audits are performed by certified public accountants (CPAs)—

external auditors who offer an independent evaluation of the financial statements for information customers.

Regardless of the type of audit, the auditor attempts to provide an objective evaluation of the operating activities, the compliance procedures, or the financial statements of the organization. Independence is a critical feature of the auditor. As Arens and Loebbecke explain:

> Auditing is the process by which a competent, independent person accumulates and evaluates evidence about quantifiable information related to a specific economic entity for the purpose of determining and reporting on the degree of correspondence between the quantifiable information and established criteria.[18]

Because auditors are somewhat unique in their purpose within the field of accounting, Arens and Loebbecke go on to contrast auditing and traditional accounting:

> *Accounting* is the process of recording, classifying, and summarizing economic events in a logical manner for the purpose of providing financial information for decision making. The function of accounting, to an entity [organization] and to society as a whole, is to provide certain types of quantitative information that management and others can use to make decisions. To provide relevant information, accountants must have a thorough understanding of the principles and rules that provide the basis for preparing the accounting information. In addition, accountants must develop a system to make sure the entity's economic events are properly recorded on a timely basis and at a reasonable cost.
>
> In *auditing* accounting data, the auditor is concerned with determining whether the recorded information properly reflects the economic events that occurred during the accounting period. Since the accounting rules are the criteria for evaluating whether the accounting information is properly recorded, any auditor involved with these data must also thoroughly understand the rules. In the context of the audit of financial statements, the rules are the generally accepted accounting principles.[19]

Over the past 50 years, the duties and responsibilities of auditors have evolved under the influence of regulatory agencies, the courts, and professional associations. The auditing profession consists of tens of thousands of individuals working for public accounting firms, profit-oriented organizations, and public agencies and institutions. With today's challenging operating environment, the need for useful information is greater than ever. Auditing simply attempts to provide some assurance as to the accuracy of the information.

Required:

a. Research the most recent year of business and accounting publications (e.g., *The Wall Street Journal, Business Week, Fortune, Journal of Accountancy,* AICPA releases, FASB and GASB releases, and auditing journals) for articles about the auditing specialty. Summarize your findings in a written report.

b. Research the recent history of the auditing specialty (the last three to five years). Explain the most significant changes in the auditing specialty during that time.

c. What are the major challenges facing the audit specialty?

---

18 A. A. Arens and J. K. Loebbecke, *Auditing: An Integrated Approach,* 5th ed. (Englewood Cliffs, NJ: Prentice Hall, 1991), p. 1.
19 Ibid.

6. **An Analysis of the Management Accounting Specialty.** Consider the following background overview of management accounting history:

> Until the late 1800s managers, who were also the owners, maintained and analyzed their own information. As organizations grew management needed more and more information to effectively plan, control, and evaluate the organization's activities. The increase in size and complexity made it impossible for managers to keep abreast of everything that was happening in their organizations and still perform all their planning, controlling, and evaluating activities. This spawned the management accounting specialty.

As the Institute of Management Accountants explains:

> Management accounting is the process of identification, measurement, accumulation, analysis, preparation, interpretation, and communication of financial information used by management to plan, evaluate, and control within an organization and to assure appropriate use of and accountability for its resources. Management accounting also comprises the preparation of financial reports for non-management groups such as shareholders, creditors, regulatory agencies, and tax authorities.[20]

Managerial accounting deals primarily with supporting the needs of information customers inside the organization (most notably management). Internal information customers are responsible for planning, controlling, and evaluating the organization's operations. To do this requires useful information. Information is, in this sense, the fuel that makes management go. Without it, management efforts are often futile, if not impossible, because the decision-making process is left to a "gut feeling" rather than an intelligent choice among alternatives.

Although managerial accountants tend to specialize in providing financial information, this information must be integrated with nonfinancial information about market share, customer satisfaction, and employee attitudes. In comparing managerial and financial accounting, Garrison and Noreen identify eight major differences. In contrast to financial accounting, managerial accounting:

1. Focuses on providing data for internal uses by the manager.
2. Places more emphasis on the future.
3. Emphasizes the relevance and flexibility of data.
4. Places less emphasis on precision and more emphasis on nonmonetary data.
5. Emphasizes the segments of an organization, rather than just looking at the organization as a whole.
6. Draws heavily from other disciplines.
7. Is not governed by generally accepted accounting principles.
8. Is not mandatory.[21]

The role of managerial accounting is critical to the success of the organization in today's complex operating environment. Unions, watch groups, and government lobbyists all demand

---

20 Management Accounting Practices Statement Promulgation Subcommittee, *Statement on Management Accounting* (New York, National Association of Accountants, 1981), p. 4.
21 Ray Garrison and E. Noreen, *Managerial Accounting,* 7th ed. (Burr Ridge, IL: Richard D. Irwin, 1994), p. 14.

information from management. The demands of these additional groups greatly increase the responsibility and burden of reporting organizational information and this responsibility is increasingly assigned to the managerial accountant.

Required:

  a. Research the most recent year of business and accounting publications (e.g., *The Wall Street Journal, Business Week, Fortune, Management Accounting, Journal of Accountancy,* AICPA releases, and FASB and GASB releases) for articles about the management accounting specialty. Summarize your findings in a written report.

  b. Research the recent history of the management accounting specialty (the last three to five years). Explain the most significant changes in the management accounting specialty during that time.

  c. What are the major challenges facing the management accounting specialty?

7. **An Analysis of the Tax Accounting Specialty.** Consider the following background overview of tax accounting history:

> Governmental units have taxed their citizenry from the earliest days of recorded history. Although tax collectors have existed as long as there have been tax laws, as tax laws have become more complex the need for tax planning and reporting specialists has grown. In the United States, the need for tax expertise has grown almost exponentially since 1913 when Congress passed the Revenue Act. This act authorized the federal government to begin taxing U.S. citizens and residents. Since then, both U.S. and foreign governments have developed very complex tax laws for individuals and all forms of business organizations.
>
> Numerous tax laws instituted by federal, state, and municipal authorities underlie the rules and regulations governing tax reporting. These laws provide the basis for requiring organizations and individuals to report information about their operations and pay taxes. Much of a tax accountant's work has traditionally focused on preparing tax documents. Recently, computer technology has automated many aspects of this reporting process. At the same time, the complexity of tax law and its impact on future business events have made tax specialists a critical consultant to those planning an organization's activities. People look to tax experts to provide useful information regarding the tax effect of alternative decision choices. Thus, a tax accounting specialty has become a significant part of the accounting profession.
>
> Notwithstanding the efforts of the U.S. Congress and others to simplify tax reporting processes (e.g., the 1986 Tax Simplification Act), tax accounting continues to become more and more complex. The challenge for the tax specialist is to keep abreast of the changes in the various tax laws to which individuals and organizations are accountable. As a result, the demand for knowledgeable tax accounting specialists continues to grow.

Required:

  a. Research the most recent year of business and accounting publications (e.g., *The Wall Street Journal, Business Week, Fortune, Journal of Accountancy,* AICPA releases, FASB releases, and tax journals) for articles about the tax specialty. Write a report that summarizes your findings.

  b. Research the recent past of the tax specialty (three to five years). Explain the most significant changes in the tax accounting specialty during that time.

c. What are the major challenges facing the tax accounting specialty?

d. Is it better to specialize in tax compliance or tax planning/strategy? Justify your response.

8. **Accounting Specialties and Accounting Information Systems Design.** Although there is an increasingly diverse set of skills required to support each accounting specialty (e.g., financial accounting, management accounting, and tax reporting), the specialties are surprisingly similar in that each has a basic goal of providing useful information about the organization's performance to information customers. Unfortunately, the diverse needs of these information customers have translated over the years into the need for separate information systems for each type of information customer.

Developing separate systems for each accounting specialty suggests differences in the reference point of each area or specialty. Yet, tax specialists strive to plan tax strategies and report tax liabilities based on the activities of the organization. Managerial accountants strive to support decision makers who are responsible for planning, executing, controlling, and evaluating the activities of the organization. Financial accountants report on the financial results of an organization's activities, and auditors attest to the usefulness of financial statements that summarize the organization's activities. Notice how all the specialties draw from the same point of reference—a common data pool describing the activities of an organization.

The reason for the diverse accounting disciplines lies in the diversity of reporting needs across information customers, rather than diversity in what they are actually looking at—the underlying organization activities. As analysts and designers of accounting information systems, we need to consider and support all accounting specialties. Accounting information systems should collect and store data that reflect the activities and performance of an organization. Accounting specialties will define the form and content of the output needed by their information users, but they should not dictate how business data are processed and stored. As we discuss specific system design concepts throughout this text, you will learn that supporting the various accounting specialties does not mandate developing a variety of diverse, independent (yet very redundant) systems.

Required:

Develop a list of potential problems associated with having separate accounting information subsystems for financial accounting and reporting, management accounting, and tax accounting.

9. **Management Misinformation Systems.** Five assumptions people typically make about information systems are summarized below. The author, Russell L. Ackoff,[22] contends these are erroneous assumptions and identifies reasons why he feels

---

22 Russell L. Ackoff, "Management Misinformation Systems," *Management Science* 14, no. 4 (December 1967), pp. B-147 to B-156.

they are in error. The objective of this assignment is to help you to begin to identify factors that distinguish good information systems from bad information systems.

Assumption 1—Give Them More

Most MISs [management information systems] are designed on the assumption that the critical deficiency under which most managers operate is the *lack of relevant information*. I do not deny that most managers lack a good deal of information that they should have, but I do deny that this is the most important informational deficiency from which they suffer. It seems to me that they suffer more from an *overabundance of irrelevant information*.

This is not a play on words. The consequences of changing the emphasis of an MIS from supplying relevant information to eliminating irrelevant information is considerable. If one is preoccupied with supplying relevant information, attention is almost exclusively given to the generation, storage, and retrieval of information: hence emphasis is placed on constructing data banks, coding, indexing, updating files, access languages, and so on. The ideal which has emerged from this orientation is an infinite pool of data into which a manager can reach to pull out any information he wants. If, on the other hand, one sees the manager's information problem primarily, but not exclusively, as one that arises out of an overabundance of irrelevant information, most of which was not asked for, then the two most important functions of an information system become *filtration* (or evaluation) and *condensation*. The literature on MISs seldom refers to these functions let alone considers how to carry them out.

My experience indicates that most managers receive much more data (if not information) than they can possibly absorb even if they spend all of their time trying to do so. Hence they already suffer from an information overload. They must spend a great deal of time separating the relevant documents. For example, I have found that I receive an average of forty-three hours of unsolicited reading material each week. The solicited material is usually half again this amount.

I have seen a daily stock status report that consists of approximately six hundred pages of computer printout. The report is circulated daily across managers' desks. I've also seen requests for major capital expenditures that come in book size, several of which are distributed to managers each week. It is not uncommon for many managers to receive an average of one journal a day or more. One could go on and on.

Unless the information overload to which managers are subjected is reduced, any additional information made available by an MIS cannot be expected to be used effectively.

Even relevant documents have too much redundancy. Most documents can be considerably condensed without loss of content. My point here is best made, perhaps, by describing briefly an experiment that a few of my colleagues and I conducted on the Operations Research (OR) literature several years ago. By using a panel of well-known experts we identified four OR articles that all members of the panel considered to be "above average," and four articles that were considered to be "below average." The authors of the eight articles were asked to prepare "objective" examinations (duration thirty minutes) plus answers for graduate students who were to be assigned the articles for reading. (The authors were not informed about the experiment.) Then several experienced writers were asked to reduce each article to $2/3$ and $1/3$ of its original length only by eliminating words. They also prepared a brief abstract of each article. Those who did the condensing did not see the examinations to be given to the students.

A group of graduate students who had not previously read the articles were then selected. Each one was given four articles randomly selected, each of which was in one of its four versions: 100%, 67%, 33%, or abstract. Each version of each article was read by two students. All were given the same examinations. The average scores on the examinations were compared.

For the above-average articles there was no significant difference between average test scores for the 100%, 67%, and 33% versions, but there was a significant *decrease* in average test scores for those who had read only the abstract. For the below-average articles there was no difference in average test scores among those who had read the 100%, 67%, and 33% versions, but there was a significant *increase* in average test scores of those who had read only the abstract.

The sample used was obviously too small for general conclusions but the results strongly indicate the extent to which even good writing can be condensed without loss of information. I refrain from drawing the obvious conclusions about bad writing.

It seems clear that condensation as well as filtration, performed mechanically or otherwise, should be an essential part of an MIS, and that such a system should be capable of handling much, if not all, of the unsolicited as well as solicited information that a manager receives.

Assumption 2—The Manager Needs the Information That He Wants

Most MIS designers "determine" what information is needed by asking managers what information they would like to have. This is based on the assumption that managers know what information they need and want it.

For a manager to know what information he needs he must be aware of each type of decision he should make (as well as does make) and he must have an adequate model of each. These conditions are seldom satisfied. Most managers have some conception of at least some of the types of decisions they must make. Their conceptions, however, are likely to be deficient in a very critical way, a way that follows from an important principle of scientific economy: the less we understand a phenomenon, the more variables we require to explain it. Hence, the manager who does not understand the phenomenon he controls plays it "safe" and, with respect to information, wants "everything." The MIS designer, who has even less understanding of the relevant phenomenon than the manager, tries to provide even more than everything. He thereby increases what is already an overload of irrelevant information.

For example, market researchers in a major oil company once asked their marketing managers what variables they thought were relevant in estimating the sales volume of future service stations. Almost seventy variables were identified. The market researchers then added about half again this many variables and performed a large multiple linear regression analysis of sales of existing stations against these variables and found about thirty-five to be statistically significant. A forecasting equation was based on this analysis. An OR team subsequently constructed a model based on only one of these variables, traffic flow, which predicted sales better than the thirty-five variable regression equations. The team went on to *explain* sales at service stations in terms of the customers' perception of the amount of time lost by stopping for service. The relevance of all but a few of the variables used by the market researchers could be explained by their effect on such perception.

The moral is simple: one cannot specify what information is required for decision making until an explanatory model of the decision process and the system involved has been constructed and tested. Information systems are subsystems of control systems. They cannot be designed adequately without taking control in account. Furthermore, whatever else regression analyses can yield, they cannot yield understanding and explanation of phenomena. They describe and, at best, predict.

Assumption 3—Give a Manager the Information He Needs and His Decision Making Will Improve

It is frequently assumed that if a manager is provided with the information he needs, he will then have no problem in using it effectively. The history of OR* stands to the contrary. For example, give most managers an initial tableau of a typical "real" mathematical programming, sequencing, or network problem and see how close they come to an optimal solution. If their experience and judgment have any value they may not do badly, but they will seldom do very well. In most management problems there are too many possibilities to expect experience, judgment, or intuition to provide good guesses, even with perfect information.

Furthermore, when several probabilities are involved in a problem the unguided mind of even a manager has difficulty in aggregating them in a valid way. We all know many simple problems in probability in which untutored intuition usually does very badly (e.g., What are the correct odds that 2 of 25 people selected at random will have their birthdays on the same day of the year?). For example, very few of the results obtained by queuing theory, when arrivals and service are probabilistic, are obvious to managers; nor are the results of risk analysis where the managers' own subjective estimates of probabilities are used.

The moral: it is necessary to determine how well managers can use needed information. When, because of the complexity of the decision process, they can't use it well, they should be provided with either decision rules or performance feedback so that they can identify and learn from their mistakes.

[HINT: In deciding whether you agree or disagree with the author you may want to consider the definitions of *data* and *information* once more. When the author refers to some of the above items as information, is it really information or is it data?]

Assumption 4—More Communication Means Better Performance

One characteristic of most MISs which I have seen is that they provide managers with better current information about what other managers and their departments and divisions are doing. Underlying this provision is the belief that better interdepartmental communication enables managers to coordinate their decisions more effectively and hence improves the organization's overall performance. Not only is this not necessarily so, but it seldom is so. One would hardly expect two competing companies to become more cooperative because the information each acquires about the other is improved. This analogy is not as far fetched as one might first suppose. For example, consider the following very much simplified version of a situation I once ran into. The simplification of the case does not affect any of its essential characteristics.

A department store has two "line" operations: buying and selling. Each function is performed by a separate department. The Purchasing Department primarily controls one variable: how much of each item is bought. The Merchandising Department controls the price at which it is sold. Typically, the measure of performance applied to the Purchasing Department was the turnover rate of inventory. The measure applied to the Merchandising Department was gross sales; this department sought to maximize the number of items sold times their price.

Now by examining a single item let us consider what happens in this system. The merchandising manager, using his knowledge of competition and consumption, set a price which he judged would maximize gross sales. In doing so he utilized price-demand curves for each

---

*NOTE: OR stands for Operations Research. It is an academic subject area dealing with the application of mathematical models and techniques to business decisions.

type of item. For each price the curves show the expected sales and values on an upper and lower confidence band as well. (See the figure below). When instructing the Purchasing Department how many items to make available, the merchandising manager quite naturally used the value on the upper confidence curve. This minimized the chances of his running short which, if it occurred, would hurt his performance. It also maximized the chances of being overstocked, but this was not his concern, only the purchasing manager's. Say, therefore, that the merchandising manager initially selected price P_1 and requested that amount Q_1 be made available by the Purchasing Department.

In this company the purchasing manager also had access to the price-demand curves. He knew the merchandising manager always ordered optimistically. Therefore, using the same curve he read over from Q_1 to the upper limit and down to the expected value from which he obtained Q_2, the quantity he actually intended to make available. He did not intend to pay for the merchandising manager's optimism. If merchandising ran out of stock, it was not his worry. Now the merchandising manager was informed about what the purchasing manager had done so he adjusted his price to P_2. The purchasing manager in turn was told that the merchandising manager had made this readjustment so he planned to make only Q_3 available. If this process (made possible only by perfect communication between departments) had been allowed to continue, nothing would have been bought and nothing would have been sold. This outcome was avoided by prohibiting communication between the two departments and forcing each to guess what the other was doing.

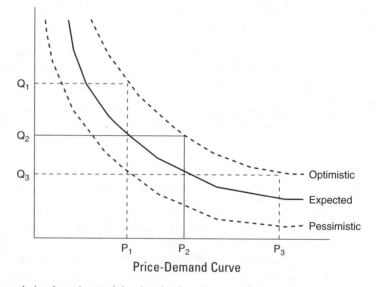

Price-Demand Curve

I have obviously caricatured the situation in order to make the point clear: when organizational units have inappropriate measures of performance which put them in conflict with each other, as is often the case, communication between them may hurt organizational performance, not help it. Organizational structure and performance measurement must be taken into account before opening the flood gates and permitting the free flow of information between parts of the organization.

Assumption 5—A Manager Does Not Have to Understand How an Information System Works, Only How to Use It

Most MIS designers seek to make their systems as innocuous and unobtrusive as possible to managers lest they become frightened. The designers try to provide managers with very easy access to the system and assure them that they need to know nothing more about it. The designers usually succeed in keeping managers ignorant in this regard. This leaves managers unable to evaluate the MIS as a whole. It often makes them afraid to even try to do so lest they display their ignorance publicly. In failing to evaluate their MIS, managers delegate much of the control of the organization to the system's designers and operators who may have many virtues, but managerial competence is seldom among them.

Let me cite a case in point. A Chairman of the Board of a medium-size company asked for help on the following problem. One of his larger (decentralized) divisions had installed a computerized production—inventory control and manufacturing—manager information system about a year earlier. It had acquired about $2,000,000 worth of equipment to do so. The Board Chairman had just received a request from the Division for permission to replace the original equipment with newly announced equipment which would cost several times the original amount. An extensive "justification" for so doing was provided with the request. The Chairman wanted to know whether the request was really justified. He admitted to complete incompetence in this connection.

A meeting was arranged at the Division at which I was subjected to an extended and detailed briefing. The system was large but relatively simple. At the heart of it was a reorder point for each item and a maximum allowable stock level. Reorder quantities took lead time as well as the allowable maximum into account. The computer kept track of stock, ordered items when required, and generated numerous reports on both the state of the system it controlled and its own "actions."

When the briefing was over I was asked if I had any questions. I did. First I asked if, when the system had been installed, there had been many parts whose stock level exceeded the maximum amount possible under the new system. I was told there were many. I asked for a list of about thirty and for some graph paper. Both were provided. With the help of the system designer and volumes of old daily reports I began to plot the stock level of the first listed item over time. When this item reached the maximum "allowable" stock level it had been reordered. The system designer was surprised and said that by sheer "luck" I had found one of the few errors made by the system. Continued plotting showed that because of repeated premature reordering the item had never gone much below the maximum stock level. Clearly the program was confusing the maximum allowable stock level and the reorder point. This turned out to be the case in more than half of the items on the list.

Next I asked if they had many paired parts, ones that were only used with each other; for example, matched nuts and bolts. They had many. A list was produced and we began checking the previous day's withdrawals. For more than half of the pairs the differences in the numbers recorded as withdrawn were very large. No explanation was provided.

Before the day was out it was possible to show by some quick and dirty calculations that the new computerized system was costing the company almost $150,000 per month more than the hand system which it had replaced, most of this in excess inventories.

The recommendation was that the system be redesigned as quickly as possible and that the new equipment not be authorized for the time being.

The questions asked of the system had been obvious and simple ones. Managers should have been able to ask them but—and this is the point—they felt themselves incompetent to do so. They would not have allowed a hand-operated system to get so far out of their control.

No MIS should ever be installed unless the managers for whom it is intended are trained to evaluate and hence control it rather than be controlled by it.

Required:

This assignment should be performed in groups of four to six people. As a group discuss the assumptions and contentions and come to a group consensus as to whether you agree or disagree with the author and why. Write a one-page report summarizing your group's conclusions and justifications. In addition, develop a one-sentence statement that describes what a good information system should have or should do in response to each assumption and contention.

2 CHAPTER

Modeling Business Processes

CHAPTER OBJECTIVES

The objective of this chapter is to help you understand how to analyze and model business processes and events. After studying this chapter, you should be able to:

- Describe a business process and identify the business processes of an organization.
- Identify the events that comprise a business process.
- Model operating events using the *REAL* concepts.
- Build and validate a *REAL* business processes model.

INTRODUCTION

In Chapter 1 we indicated that the first step toward enhancing a business professional's value is enhancing the role he/she plays in helping an organization define and improve its business processes. So what are business processes and how can they be designed to support an organization's objectives? How do we design information systems that collect, maintain, and process the data needed to generate the outputs required by management to effectively manage business processes in the information age?

There is no one answer to these questions. There are a variety of philosophies and methodologies that business analysts and information specialists use. Some people still argue that you must begin with a chart of accounts and use it as the foundation for designing any system structure to support accountants. Others argue that *semantic modeling,* which is an attempt to model real-world phenomena, is a better approach to meet the needs of demanding, sophisticated information age managers and information customers. In this text, we include examples of both approaches. However, this chapter illustrates a framework that is semantically based.

Some of you may be surprised to learn that many of the critical steps of building an information system have little to do with programming a computer. The process begins with identifying the need for a business solution, and acquiring a better understanding of the environment you plan to support and/or improve. If you want to help organizations define and improve their business processes, you need to incorporate all aspects of business processes—not just the financial aspects of some business activities. In this chapter, we discuss a method for acquiring this knowledge. We present additional analysis and design issues in Chapter 4.

Our analysis uses *semantic models*—models of real-world actions or phenomena. We use *REAL* business process modeling as a method to help you understand and model business processes. Much of the theory supporting our approach to identifying and describing business processes and events was first proposed by Bill McCarthy,[1] an innovative scholar in organizing business data to support a wide variety of information customers. During the late 1970s and early 1980s, McCarthy proposed an alternative architecture for organizing accounting data. McCarthy demonstrated that by capturing the essential characteristics of an operating event, multiple classification schemes could be supported, including traditional accounting information (e.g., financial statements that adhere to generally accepted accounting principles). The modeling method presented in this chapter is an adaptation of McCarthy's work.

BUSINESS PROCESSES

Before we begin modeling business processes we need a more precise definition of the terms we will use. Organizations, whether they are large or small, public or private, are formed to achieve objectives. You can find an organization's high-level objectives listed in their mission statement. To achieve their objectives, most organizations develop their vision and strategies.[2] They put a series of *business processes* in place to implement these strategies.[3]

In Chapter 1 we explained that every organization has three basic business processes: acquiring and paying for resources (e.g., financing, human skills, materials and supplies, and plant and equipment); converting resources acquired into goods and services for customers; and delivering goods and services to customers and collecting payment. We will now look at the activities of these business processes in more detail.

---

1 See W. E. McCarthy, "The REA Accounting Model: A Generalized Framework for Accounting Systems in a Shared Data Environment," *The Accounting Review,* July 1982, pp. 554–77, for a complete description of the underlying theory.

2 If you have not done so already, we recommend that you read "What is Strategy?" by Michael Porter before you proceed with analysis. You can find it in the November–December 1996 edition of the *Harvard Business Review.*

3 Some accounting textbooks use the term *accounting cycles* to describe business activities. Our discussion of business processes encompasses most of the activities detailed in "accounting cycle" discussions, but we will take a broader business perspective than most accounting texts.

Acquisition/Payment Business Process. The acquisition/payment process includes the activities involved in acquiring, paying for, and maintaining the goods and services needed by an organization. Objectives of this process include acquiring only those goods or services that an organization needs and can afford, receiving only those goods and services actually ordered, paying for goods and services actually received, properly maintaining goods acquired, and providing goods and services when needed. Organizations can acquire a wide variety of goods and services including:[4]

- Human resources (e.g., people's time and skills).
- Financial resources.
- Supplies.
- Inventories.
- Property, plant, and equipment.
- New ideas (e.g., research and development).
- Miscellaneous services (e.g., legal, power, telephone, protection, medical, financial, or custodial).

Conversion Business Process. The conversion business process focuses on converting goods and services acquired into goods and services for sale. Conversion processes across, or even within, organizations are very diverse and depend on the type of good or service being produced; the technology and resources utilized; restrictions of regulators, governments, society, or customers; and the preferences of customers and management.

The diversity of conversion processes makes it difficult to propose a single generalized conversion process. Assembling a toy car is vastly different from defending a client in court or discovering a cure for a crippling disease. Furthermore, any one organization may utilize more than one type of conversion process to generate unique goods and services for different customers. Nonetheless, at the heart of any conversion process is a sequence of activities that converts goods and services acquired into goods and services for customers.

Sales/Collection Business Process. The sales/collection business process includes the sequence of activities involved in delivering goods and services to customers for payment. Essentially, the sales/collection business process is the mirror image of the acquisition/payment business process. Whenever one entity acquires and pays for goods and services, another entity is selling the goods or services and receiving payment.

Although our analysis divides organization activities into discrete business processes, these processes are interdependent. For example, the ability to deliver a prod-

---

4 The more common types of acquisition/payment processes are those for human resources (personnel/payroll processing), financial resources, inventories, and fixed assets.

uct to a customer is dependent on the processes of acquiring and converting the resources used to create that product. It is important to remember that business processes are interrelated, but we differentiate them in an attempt to simplify our analysis. We will discuss the linking of business processes later in this chapter.

ARE ALL PROCESSES AND BUSINESS ACTIVITIES CREATED EQUALLY?

As you study organizations, notice that an increasing number of them prioritize their business processes based on the value of the process in achieving the organization's objectives. This makes sense because some business activities determine an organization's competitiveness in the marketplace while other activities might be classified as support activities. For example, how quickly a restaurant receives a shipment of inventory at the back door is probably not as important as how well they cook and serve the food. Certainly, the quality of cooking and serving is affected if ingredients are not acquired and maintained properly. But the activity of receiving goods is a support activity to other activities that provide a competitive advantage—cooking and serving high-quality food.

Due to the increased need for adaptability, effectiveness, and efficiency to remain competitive, most organizations find it essential to differentiate between the various business activities. Obviously, organizations must look internally at each of their functions and develop capabilities in each area. They must also effectively integrate and coordinate all business functions. However, in today's business world, an organization's performance is increasingly affected by the world around them. You might work for the most *internally* cost-effective organization you can imagine, but it might be an unsuccessful organization. Why? Perhaps the organization has competitors who better meet the needs of customers, do a good job of outsourcing[5] some business functions, or do a better job of creating effective strategic alliances with trading partners. To really understand and analyze an organization, it is important to understand more than internal operations and functions. You must look outside the organization at the industry, the suppliers, the customers, and all the other parties that effect organization performance.

To complete a more thorough "cradle to grave" analysis, many people use the value chain analysis originally proposed by Michael Porter.[6] Porter illustrated that each firm is a "collection of activities that are performed to design, produce, market, deliver, and support its product." Exhibit 2–1 displays Porter's generic value chain.

A *value chain* is defined as a set of business activities that add value or usefulness to an organization's products or services. The value chain is intended to show total value and consists of value activities and margin. Value activities are the physical and technological activities performed by an organization. Porter presented two types of value activities in

---

5 *Outsourcing* is when one organization finds another organization to perform some work. This is usually done when the outsourcing organization can't complete the work (e.g., they do not have the capacity or the expertise) or when they identify another organization that can complete the work in a more cost-effective manner.

6 M. Porter, *Competitive Advantage: Creating and Sustaining Superior Performance* (New York: Free Press, 1985); and *Competitive Strategy Techniques for Analyzing Industries and Competitors* (New York: Free Press, 1980).

E X H I B I T   2–1

Porter's Generic Value Chain

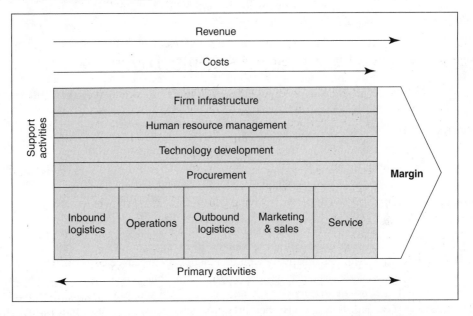

Michael Porter, *Competitive Advantage: Creating and Sustaining Superior Performance* (New York: Free Press, 1985).

his generic value chain: primary and support. *Primary activities* consist of the events that create customer value and provide organization distinctiveness in the marketplace. They are viewed as the critical activities in running a business. *Support activities* facilitate accomplishing the primary activities. Margin is the difference between total value and the cost of performing the value activities.

Porter's *primary* value activities include the following categories:

◆ Inbound logistics: activities associated with receiving, storing, and disseminating inputs to the products or services.

◆ Operations: activities associated with transforming inputs into the final products or services.

◆ Outbound logistics: activities associated with collecting, storing, and physically distributing the products or services.

◆ Marketing and sales: activities associated with providing a means by which customers can buy products and the means for inducing them to buy.

◆ Service: activities associated with providing service to enhance or maintain the value of the products or services.

Porter's *support* value activities include:

- Procurement: the function of purchasing inputs to the firm's value chain.
- Technology development: the know-how, procedures, or technology embedded in processes that are intended to improve the product, services, and/or process.
- Human resource management: activities involved in recruiting, hiring, training, developing, and compensating all types of personnel.
- Firm infrastructure: activities that support the entire value chain (e.g., general management, planning, finance, accounting, legal, government affairs, quality management).

Many people agree that this type of analysis is valuable because it forces you to understand both the internal operations of a firm as well as the forces and parties outside the firm that affect its ability to create value. The direct actions of an organization are only part of its overall value chain process. It is also important to look at external linkages, such as the activities of customers and suppliers, to understand the ability of an organization to create value. For example, some organizations may be more successful at creating value because they elicit quality responses from their customers and use the feedback to quickly change or upgrade their products. Other organizations may achieve success because they have worked effectively with their suppliers to reduce costs and improve the ability to respond to customer desires. A thorough value chain analysis stimulates your thought process by forcing you to understand all the activities that are strategically relevant to an organization, not just the portion of activities an organization controls or in which it directly participates.

BUSINESS PROCESS EVENTS

A *business process* is a series of activities intended to accomplish the strategic objectives of an organization. This definition implies that one process can be comprised of several activities. In our analysis, we will differentiate between an overall business process and the individual activities that comprise that process. We will use the term *event* to denote a single activity within a business process.

When business processes are well managed, they greatly enhance the organization's ability to achieve its objective of providing value to its customers. When they are not well managed, the organization sputters and limps along just like an automobile that is out of tune—a frustrating and less than ideal condition. To help us gain a deeper understanding of organizations, let's further divide each business process into three different event categories—operating events, information events, and decision/management events.

Operating events are the operating activities performed within a business process to provide goods and services to customers. We will exclude information processing activities and decision-making/management activities from this category. This is a broad definition, and we will refine it a bit later in our analysis. However, the definition of operating events must remain somewhat broad as it refers to a wide range of business activities. Exhibit 2–2 illustrates some operating events for a sample sales/collection business process. The exhibit shows one business process (delivering goods to customers and collecting payment) and the operating events that comprise the process (marketing goods, taking an order, shipping the goods, and collecting the customer payment).

Information events include three activities: *recording* data about operating events, *maintaining* reference data that are important to the organization, and *reporting* useful information to management and other decision makers. Recording events involve collecting data that describes operating events and storing the data in a *data repository* (e.g., a data warehouse, a database, or a file). Organizations also need to collect and keep current reference data about resources they own, external parties they do business with, and employees who work for them. We refer to these information events as *maintaining events*. Recording and maintaining information events create and keep current a repository of data that documents and describes an organization's business processes, including the people and resources associated with them. This data repository, or collection of data, is used to generate reports for information customers. The third type of information event, reporting, is the most demanding of the three. Reporting provides information and measurements to support organization activities such as planning, controlling, and evaluating.

Decision/management events are activities where management and other people make decisions about planning, controlling, and evaluating business processes. Examples include managing resources (e.g., human, financial, and physical), managing relationships with trading partners, developing a five-year business plan, deciding to design a new product or service, making a decision to close a branch office or open a new store, and making a decision to change vendors.

Operating events, information events, and decision/management events are presented as distinct categories, yet they are intertwined. (See Exhibit 2–3.) Decision/man-

EXHIBIT 2–2

Sample Sales/Collection Process Events

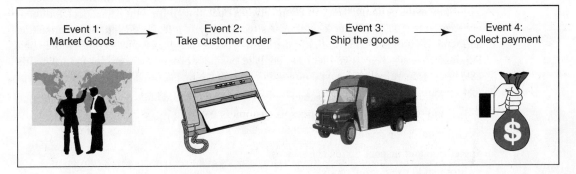

| Event 1: Market Goods | Event 2: Take customer order | Event 3: Ship the goods | Event 4: Collect payment |

EXHIBIT 2–3

Business Process Activities (Events)

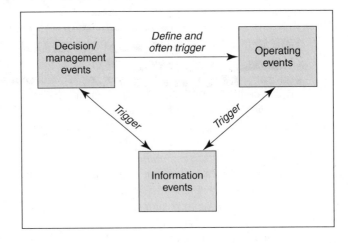

agement events define and often trigger operating events. Executing operating events triggers information events to record and maintain business data. Decision/management events also trigger the need for information reporting events when decision makers request information to support planning or evaluating business activities.

A word of caution before we proceed. We have found that students sometimes confuse operating events with information events. Remember that information events involve the use of data (e.g., collecting data that describes an operating event, reporting information to support the execution of operating events, or reporting information to support decision making or a management action). For example, the delivery of a product to a customer is an example of an operating event; recording data about the delivery and sending a bill are information events. Receiving a payment from a customer for goods and services provided is an operating event; recording data about the customer payment is an information event. A change in the location of a warehouse is an operating event; updating or maintaining the location of the warehouse in the data repository is an information event.

In manual systems, the distinction between operating, information, and decision/management events is somewhat clear-cut. As technology is introduced into an organization and work is automated, the ability to distinguish between these events becomes more challenging. To assist you as you learn to analyze business processes, consider the following examples. Regardless of the type of good or service being acquired, the following are typical operating events in the acquisition/payment business process:

- Request goods or services.
- Order goods or services.
- Receive and inspect goods or services.
- Store and/or maintain goods.

- Pay for goods or services.
- Return goods.

If you analyze a variety of acquisition/payment business processes, you will notice that some organizations may order the events differently, may use a subset of the events, or may add more detailed events. Nonetheless, the basic nature of the process is fairly stable across organizations and resources.

Although there is some diversity across the types of goods and services sold, the sales/collection process typically includes the following events:

- Receive an order for goods or services.
- Select and inspect goods or services to be delivered.
- Prepare goods or services for delivery.
- Deliver goods or services.
- Receive payment for goods or services.
- Accept customer returns of goods.

As with the acquisition/payment process, some organizations may order the events differently, may use a subset of the events, or may add more detailed events. Nonetheless, from an event perspective, the basic nature of the sales/collection process remains fairly constant across organizations and industries.

Finally, examples of some of the more general activities in the conversion process include:

- Assembling.
- Growing.
- Excavating.
- Harvesting.
- Basic manufacturing (e.g., metals, woods, and chemicals).
- Finished manufacturing (e.g., tools, instruments, and components).
- Cleaning.
- Transporting.
- Distributing.
- Providing (e.g., power, water, protection, and communication).
- Educating.
- Discovering (e.g., research and development).

As you read more about and visit businesses, you will invariably come across the term *workflow*. *Workflow* refers to jobs or tasks performed by members of a workgroup to achieve some objective. Some people use the term broadly to include the analysis of how a product or service flows from one person or business function to another. When defining a *workflow,* they might include a combination of operating, information, and decision/management events. Other people define *workflow* more narrowly and include only the movement and management of information among members of a workgroup. We will use the broader definition throughout this book.

EXTENDED ENTERPRISE BUSINESS PROCESSES

As we stated earlier in our value chain discussion, business processes are not only linked within an organization but business processes span organization boundaries. Some people refer to these as *extended enterprise business processes.*

Organizations have a growing number of extended enterprise business processes. For example, suppose you were analyzing the business processes for a supplier to automobile manufacturers with just-in-time inventory processes. The manufacturer only wants enough inventory on hand for one day's work (or sometimes even less). The supplier distributes and sells parts; they do not physically manufacture the cars. Would you consider activities of the automobile manufacturer's conversion process when modeling the supplier's business processes? In some cases, you should. If the supplier is a trading partner of the manufacturer, the supplier must know both what is planned and what has happened. Thus, the two company must share information across organization boundaries. Such sharing of information is increasingly present between shippers and their customers. Suppose you were modeling a company's acquisition/payment process. Carriers such as Federal Express and United Parcel Service allow customers to access their records to find out exactly where their packages are in the shipping process or use customer-generated data for processing orders.

Coordinating processes across organization boundaries requires us to view business processes in a multifirm context and understand an organization's entire value chain—not just the portion in which it directly participates. The *REAL* business process model discussed in this chapter can provide a conceptual basis for developing models of these processes that extend organization boundaries.

A BUSINESS PROCESS EXAMPLE

Let's use a simple example of a pizza restaurant to illustrate how to identify business processes, and differentiate between decision/management, operating, and information events within that process.

The boxed narrative on the following page describes a sales/collection business process for a small organization. The process helps Golden Pizza provide the best tasting pizza (prepared within 20 minutes) and the friendliest service in its marketplace. Read and reread the narrative and classify each activity as an operating, information, or decision/management event. After you have attempted this exercise, read on.

The decision/management events discussed in this example include:

- Analyze the Standish Market, Competitors, and Customers.
- Decide What Pizzas to Place on Golden's Menu.
- Determine if the Cooked Pizza Is Correct for the Customer Presenting His/Her Copy of the Order Form.

GOLDEN PIZZA

Tate runs the very successful Golden Pizza store in beautiful downtown Standish, California. Golden Pizza strives to provide the best tasting pizza (prepared within 20 minutes) and the friendliest service in Standish. Tate often spends time analyzing the Standish market, his competitors, and his customers. Tate makes decisions about pizzas to place on the menu. Customers place orders by telephone or in person at the store. Details of the order (type of pizza, quantity, drinks, price, etc.) are written on a sequentially numbered, multicopy order form. The amount of the sale is calculated, written on the order form, and told to the customer. The customer pays for the pizza, and the order taker writes Paid and details about the payment on the order copy (e.g., the type of payment and details about the check or credit card). A copy of the receipt is given to the customer. The customer is instructed to wait until his/her order number is called for pickup.

One copy of the order is given to the cook (Marty) so he knows the type and quantity of pizzas to make. Order forms are hung on a revolving wheel so Marty can scan each order while making the pizzas. Most orders stay on the wheel. Occasionally an order is knocked off the wheel and is either not filled or only partially filled. Because Tate promises customers they will have their pizza in 20 minutes or it is free, the cost of lost customer orders is "eaten" by Golden Pizza.

When an order is completed, it is boxed and the cook's copy of the order form is taped to the box. The customer presents his/her copy of the order marked Paid and the clerk compares the numbers on the two copies to make sure they are the same. The order copy taped to the box is saved for the accountant (Benjamin) to record and the pizza is given to the customer.

This example includes the following operating events:

- Receive Customer Pizza Order.
- Receive Customer Payment.
- Make Pizza.
- Box Pizza.
- Give Pizza to Customer.

These events define the process by which Golden Pizza creates value for its customers.

Both operating and decision/management events trigger information events. While reading the narrative, you might have thought there were very few information events. However, there are frequently more information events than operating or decision/management events. This is very common in traditional environments where all information processing is performed by hand. The list shown below does not even include the information processing Benjamin performs in the backroom to complete the traditional general ledger accounting. Collectively, the various operating events trigger the following information events:

- Record Customer Order.
- Calculate Order Amount.

- Mark Order Paid.
- Give Customer Copy of Order.
- Give Cook Copy of Order.
- Tape Order to Pizza Box.
- Remove Copy of Order from Box.
- Send Order Copies to Accounting.

The decision/management events might trigger the following information events:

- Generate a Customer Analysis Report.
- Generate a Report of Sales by Pizza Type.
- Generate a Gross Margin Analysis.
- Generate a Report of Lost Sales Due to the 20-Minute Guarantee.

While reading this example, we hope you considered opportunities for improving Golden Pizza's process. The key to improving the process is contemplating the "ideal" business process and then shaping the information events around the business processes. We will learn more about doing this as we work through this text.

Examples throughout this text, as with Golden Pizza, are not all inclusive, but they give a good starting point for learning about business activities and processes. Identifying operating, information, and decision/management events becomes easier with research and experience, but familiarity with business takes time and patience. Although this text can introduce the topic and provide a framework for understanding business processes, developing expertise requires more than reading this or any other single book. Understanding business processes comes from visiting actual organizations, reading the business press, talking with those involved in business processes, observing business processes where you work, and modeling the processes. We will now introduce a more formal modeling method to guide your analysis of organizations.

DEVELOPING A *REAL* BUSINESS PROCESS MODEL

REAL business process modeling[7] is a formal method of identifying and representing the essential characteristics that collectively describe business processes and events. The title *REAL* is an acronym for **R**esources, **E**vents, **A**gents, and **L**ocations. Preparing a *REAL* business process model requires you to identify *strategically significant business activities* and *essential characteristics about these business activities* (see Exhibit 2–4). This requires you to think like a business investigator or reporter and find answers to a variety of who, what, when, where, and why questions. As you analyze a business process, you find the essential characteristics of business events in the answers to the following:

---

7 See E. L. Denna, J. Jasperson, K. Fong, and D. Middleman, "Modeling Business Processes," *Journal of Information Systems,* Spring, 1994, pp. 43–54; and E. L. Denna, L. T. Perry, and J. J. Jasperson, "Reengineering and *REAL* Business Process Modeling," in *Business Process Reengineering: A Managerial Perspective,* ed. V. Grover and B. Kettinger (Harrisburg, Pennsylvania: Idea Group Publishing, 1996).

EXHIBIT 2–4

Essential Characteristics of Business Activities

- What happened?
- When did it occur?
- Who was involved and what roles did they play?
- What resources were involved and how much?
- Where did the event occur?
- What can go wrong during execution of the event?

What happened? This involves identifying the strategically relevant events within a business process. You should also strive to understand *how* each event is executed and *why* it is executed. This will aid in identifying opportunities for improvement.

When did each event occur? This involves determining each event's time of occurrence, relative to other events in the process, as well as the absolute time of an event. The absolute time of an event refers to the date/time stamp for an event and how long it took for an event to transpire.

What roles are performed and who/what agents perform the roles in executing each event? This involves identifying the parties (both internal and external to the organization) that participate in a significant way in executing each event.

What kinds of resources were involved and how much was used? This involves identifying the resource(s) that are increased or decreased as a result of each event.

Where did the event occur? This involves identifying the location of each event.

What can go wrong in executing the event? This involves identifying the risks associated with each event.

There is nothing magical about these questions. They sound a lot like the questions taught in a Journalism 101 course for writing a news story. For business analysis, the questions define the scope of what management can define, or change, when managing a business process (i.e., what happens, when, who is involved, what is involved, and where events occur). The *REAL* model helps us graphically display answers to these questions. In Chapter 4 we will show how the *REAL* model can be used to define the data needed about each event.[8]

Process information is graphically represented in a *REAL* model and supplemented with matrix worksheets. After you complete the steps in this chapter, your initial graphical model will display preliminary information about what events happened, what kinds of re-

---

8 More details about organization strategy and defining operating events and processes is available in L. Perry and E. Denna "Reengineering Redux," *Business Process Re-engineering & Major Organizational Change* (United Kingdom: Cornwallis Emmanuel Press, February 1995).

sources were involved, and what roles are performed and who/what agents performed the roles. Most graphical models will also display information about where the events occurred. Notice that all this information corresponds to Resources, Events, Agents, and Locations (*REAL*). Your matrix worksheets will include additional information about each of these characteristics, as well as information about when the event occurred, what can go wrong, and the how and why of each event. The model you develop following the steps in this chapter will be further enhanced and refined in Chapter 4.

The following six steps describe how to analyze a business process and develop your initial *REAL* model. To help you through these steps, we will use a simple case and present case checkpoints throughout our discussion.

McKELL'S RETAIL STORE

McKell's Retail Store has hired you to analyze their sales/collection process. Customers can purchase a variety of merchandise from McKell's. Each sale involves a customer assisted by a salesperson. The customer can buy one or more items of merchandise. McKell's sales force randomly assists customers (McKell's does not assign customers to specific salespersons); and each sale occurs at a specific register (McKell's has several registers). Individual items of merchandise are not uniquely identified. This means that McKell's does not assign a unique identifier to each white T-shirt sold, or each pair of size 9 white tennis shoes. The customers are allowed to pay with cash, check, or credit card.

STEP 1:
UNDERSTAND THE ORGANIZATION'S ENVIRONMENT AND OBJECTIVES

REAL modeling is an aid in analyzing an organization and its activities. The effectiveness and completeness of any model depends on how well you understand the organization being analyzed. Recall from Chapter 1 that helping businesses solve problems involves attention to many areas including strategy, culture, measurements, structure, and information technology. You need to gain insights that help you understand the organization at a high level.

Before concentrating on a particular business process, collect data and insights about the organization's objectives, industry, value chain, strategies, product lines, and customers. Pay attention to the organization's people, structure, technologies, and measurements. A better understanding of these factors will enhance your ability to evaluate business processes and identify processes and events that are not valuable, not competitive, and/or not meeting the objectives of the organization. As you analyze an organization, avoid getting bogged down in "how things have always been done" or "how we do things now." Don't be afraid to think creatively and innovatively as you perform your analysis.

STEP 2:
REVIEW THE BUSINESS PROCESS AND IDENTIFY THE STRATEGICALLY SIGNIFICANT OPERATING EVENTS

Analyzing an organization as a whole does not provide the necessary details. As a business analyst, you must analyze the organization at a more micro level. Begin by dividing the organization into its business processes. By analyzing one process at a time, you can more easily identify the operating events within each process. (We will explore the information and decision/management events later.) Examine the process from the business's perspective (rather than from the perspective of an outside party). During this step, you are trying to answer the what happened question listed in Exhibit 2–4 and give some insights into the how and why of each event.

In your *REAL* graphical model include the *strategically significant* operating events that comprise a business process. These are the operating events that the organization wants to plan, evaluate and execute/or control. Begin your *REAL* graphical model by representing events as rectangles with a descriptor inside the rectangle. Select terms that accurately describe each operating event. We suggest using an active voice to name events. Your description should reflect actions from the perspective of the organization you are modeling. For example, use Receive Customer Order, rather than Customer Order Is Received; and Hire Employee, rather than Employee Is Hired. We will *exclude* information events from our model during this part of the analysis. We will talk about these in detail in Chapter 4 and incorporate them into our model.

Make notes about the decision/management events on a *REAL* model worksheet (see Exhibit 2–5) as you document data about the how and why of each operating event. Four columns are provided: business objective, event trigger, business risks, and notes. An *event trigger* is the action that initiates the event. Sample triggers include a previous event, input from an external entity, a decision by an internal agent, or a business need. For example, in many organizations, the Ship Customer Order event should only occur if triggered by the existence of a valid approved Receive Customer Order event. A Receive Customer Order event of a pizza store (such as Golden Pizza) is triggered by a customer's decision to order pizza. A manager's decision to add personnel will trigger a Hire New Employee event.

Planning, executing and evaluating business processes are vehicles for implementing and supporting organizational strategies. Therefore, the why question is answered by defining where a particular event fits into the fabric of an organization's business processes and the event's relative importance in accomplishing the organization's strategy. During this step, document the why of an event in the objective column on the matrix. Some organizations may also label events as *primary* or *support*.

Be careful not to identify information events as operating events. To avoid this error, focus on the *essential characteristics about business activities* (see Exhibit 2–4). One method to determine if an activity is an operating event is to attempt to answer the Exhibit 2–4 questions about each event. If it is an operating event, you should be able to answer each question, particularly: What kind of resources were involved and how much was used? If, by chance, you mistake an information event (e.g., Print Customer Invoice) for

EXHIBIT 2–5

REAL Business Process Model Matrix

Event	Business Objective	Event Trigger	Business Risk	Notes

an operating event (e.g., Receive Customer Order), you will struggle to answer some of the questions. For example, you may be tempted to define a sales invoice (i.e., customer bill) as a resource, but an invoice is simply a document that includes data about an operating activity—not an organization resource. The sales invoice is an output document from the data repository containing the information about a Deliver Product/Service to Customer operating event.[9] If the answers to these questions are not obvious, you may be confusing information events and operating events. The same difficulty arises if you attempt to answer the questions about decision/management events.

Your accounting and economics training can also guide you in identifying operating events. Include the operating events that measure activities associated with the accounting definition of an *economic event.* For example, the receipt of goods from a vendor in exchange for a payment meets the definition of an accounting economic event—a purchase. Thus, an acquisitions/payment process should include the event that reflects the ownership transfer of the goods. Further, a process model should show event sets that display the increment in one resource group with a corresponding decrement in another resource group. This set of two operating events that include the increment and decrement of two resources

---

9 Recall from your financial GAAP accounting training that the delivery of a product or service to a customer in exchange for payment or a promise to pay meets the accounting definition of a *sale.*

is called *duality*—one event causes resource inflows while the other event causes resource outflows. For example, in modeling the acquisitions/payment process duality involves including an inflow of goods or services from a vendor event and also including a corresponding outflow event (such as payment to the vendor or a purchase return). In modeling the sales/collection process, duality includes a Deliver Product to Customer event and also a Receive Customer Payment event (and/or a Sales Return event).

An operating event is *strategically significant* if an information customer wants information to help him/her plan, execute, control, or evaluate that activity. The information customer serves as the final arbiter of value. The key to effective information customer support is not the *amount* of information provided, rather, the ability to provide accessible, useful, and timely information. *Strategically significant* events also include those that are regulated or mandated (e.g., Inspect Meat, Pay Taxes, or Perform Environmental Study). In most organizations, very few operating events fall under this category. Regulations usually specify information to be provided to regulatory or governmental agencies rather than specify the nature of an operating event.

Should your model include the extended enterprise business processes discussed earlier in the chapter? Focusing on events that are beyond your organizational boundaries may give you the feeling that identifying operating events is like the famous final exam question, Model the universe and give three examples. Where in the world do you draw the line? Our answer to all modeling questions relating to scope is What does the organization want to plan, execute, control, and/or evaluate? In this text, we will simplify life a bit and limit our scope. However, life is not so simple in the real world.

Finally, a frequently asked question is: How far do you go when decomposing business processes into operating events? The extent to which business processes should be decomposed into operating events is fairly simple: decompose the processes to the level organization members and leadership want to plan, execute, control, and evaluate. (Sick of that answer yet?) A useful guide is to decompose events to a level above which details about the business process are lost and below which details become minutiae. For example, selling mail-order merchandise might involve the following operating events:

- Receive Customer Order.
- Select, Inspect, and Package Merchandise.
- Ship Merchandise.
- Receive Customer Payment.

However, someone may rationally argue that the process actually involves just two operating events:

- Ship Merchandise.
- Receive Customer Payment.

So which is right? Frankly, the answer depends on the perspective of each individual. Because of the diversity of management styles and responsibilities, differences will exist across enterprises regarding the level at which organizations manage business processes and events. What you should realize is that processes can be described at various levels of abstraction. Typically, higher level abstractions tend to summarize a subset of lower level abstractions. For example, Ship Merchandise is an event that can be divided into a lower level description that includes Receive Customer Order; Select, Inspect, and Package Merchandise; and Ship Merchandise. Defining the level of detail requires all organization members to be involved. The danger in having management alone define a business process is they may overlook significant aspects of a process that are rather obvious to employees involved in executing the process.

McKELL'S RETAIL STORE CASE CHECKPOINT

Using the retail store example, McKell's has identified two events of interest: Sell Merchandise and Receive Customer Payment. Exhibit 2–6 illustrates the initial step in creating a *REAL* graphical model for McKell's.

Step Two initiated the analysis of the strategically significant operating events the organization wants to plan, execute, control, and evaluate. Specifying the event objective and trigger provide insights for understanding why and when the operating event occurs. Having identified relevant operating events and their objectives and triggers, you are ready to begin specifying several details about each event. Now we must focus on who, what, and where for relevant operating events.

EXHIBIT 2–6

McKell's Retail Store *REAL* Model: Step 2

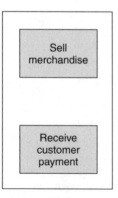

STEP 3:
ANALYZE EACH EVENT LISTED IN STEP 2 TO IDENTIFY THE
EVENT RESOURCES, AGENTS, AND LOCATIONS

Once you are confident you have identified the strategically significant operating events, the next task is to describe the essential characteristics of the events. As the term implies, *essential characteristics* refer to the characteristics that, if omitted, would render an inaccurate or incomplete description of the event. We will use the model developed during this chapter as the foundation for an information system. The data describing the characteristics of operating events will form much of the basis for generating outputs for information customers. The information customers use the output to plan, execute, control, and evaluate organization activities. Thus, if you omit part of the description of an event, you will not provide your information customers with data they might need in their operating and decision-making activities.

In this step, we will display information about the following questions:

1. What kinds of resources were involved?

At any point in time, organizations have an amount or *stock* of resources. An operating event affects that resource stock because an event involves the *flow* of a resource into the organization or a flow of resources out of the organization. Thus, an operating event description should include the types and quantity of resources involved. Sometimes identifying all the resources involved is fairly straightforward, but not always. For example, identifying groceries (the resource) involved in a sale at a grocery store is fairly obvious. However, you could also argue that several other resources are involved (e.g., the cash register, bags to package the groceries, and electricity to power the cash register). Including these additional resources would certainly provide a more accurate and complete picture of the event, but the refinement is small and immaterial. The guiding principle is to obtain enough detail so essential aspects of the event are not overlooked, but not so much detail that you become mired in minutiae.

2. What roles are performed and who/what agents perform the roles?

Another aspect of defining essential characteristics of operating events is identifying the agents involved and the roles they perform. Roles can range from internal responsibilities (e.g., salesperson, cleaning person, supervisor, or inspector) to external roles (e.g., customer or supplier). Roles can also involve responsibilities to grant authorization or approval, or to gain access to or custody of organization resources. Individuals, project teams, organizations, or programmable machines (such as robots or computers) can perform the roles. Those performing roles are called *agents*.

Events involving the exchange of resources between organizations always involve both internal and external agents, each performing a different role. For example, the internal role of a salesperson may be performed by a person or by a computer terminal that interacts with the external agent (the customer). Sample external agents include customers, vendors, and shipping *agents*.

Events internal to the organization involve an internal agent only (e.g., an inventory clerk for a warehousing event that picks goods and transfers them to the shipping dock).

3. Where did the event occur?

Lastly, where events occur is often an important element of their description. With information technology spread around the globe, events can occur anywhere and the customer's physical presence is not required for executing an event. Some people build *REAL* models and exclude the location objects in their graphical model. They choose to deal with "where" when they make decisions about systems design and implementation. When events can occur at multiple locations and management wants to collect data about each location, we suggest including a location symbol in your model. When you model smaller organizations that do not involve multiple locations (such a single grocer with one cash register), you may choose to omit the location objects from your model. Sometimes the location of an event can be derived from the location of the agents or resources involved with the event. You need only include locations that cannot be determined by referencing the event, resource, or agents.

Use rectangles with descriptors (as you did with the events) to add the agents, resource, and location (if any) to your graphical model. To help you draw your initial models in a somewhat standardized fashion, place the agents to the right of the events and place the resources and locations to the left. Make sure your graphical model includes at least one resource and one internal agent for each event. Events that are purely internal to the organization will not involve external agents; external events will involve at least one external agent. If you have a resource, agent, or location group that relates to more than one event, do not duplicate the rectangle. One rectangle can symbolize a class or group of resources, agents, or locations and one rectangle can be involved in more than one event. For example, if you are modeling a Place Order with Vendor event and a Receive Shipment from Vendor event in the same process model, you need only place one vendor rectangle on the diagram. Also, a resource box named cash can represent all instances of cash accounts. We will talk about distinguishing between specific occurrences or instances of the resources, events, agents, or locations that the rectangles represent in Chapter 4.

McKELL'S RETAIL STORE CASE CHECKPOINT

McKell's involves two operating events (Sell Merchandise and Receive Customer Payment), one internal agent (salesperson), one external agent (customer), two resources (merchandise and cash) and one location (register). Exhibit 2–7 adds resources, agents, and location to the model.

Next, you will further specify the essential nature of a process's operating events.

EXHIBIT 2–7

McKell's Retail Store *REAL* Model: Step 3

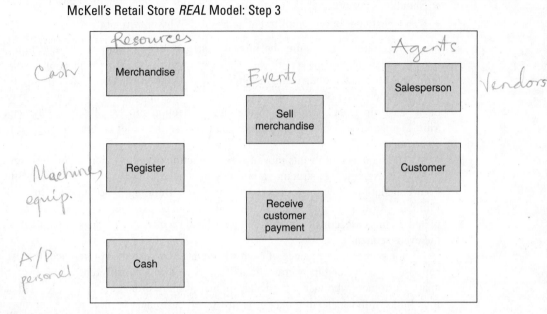

STEP 4:
IDENTIFY THE RELEVANT BEHAVIORS, CHARACTERISTICS, AND ATTRIBUTES OF THE EVENTS, RESOURCES, AGENTS, AND LOCATIONS

Remember we are trying to understand everything we can about the operating events and processes. The *REAL* concepts provide a vocabulary to guide this inquiry. In addition to identifying the events and related resources, agents, and locations, it is often helpful to identify additional characteristics to further describe operating events. For example, to understand the proper execution of an operating event, your analysis should answer the following:

♦ At what time or sequence in the process should the event occur?

♦ What are the exceptions to the "normal" ordering of events in the process?

♦ What is the proper authorization or approval to execute this event?

♦ What is a reasonable amount of resource associated with this event?

♦ What are the acceptable locations for executing this event?

In addition, the following questions illustrate how to derive additional valuable insight into the nature of the business process:

♦ What is an acceptable time period between events in a business process?

♦ How might the order of events vary by customer?

♦ Does the location from which goods are shipped matter?

◆ How many salespeople are assigned to each customer?

◆ Should a sales order clerk have custody of cash?

◆ Can a customer have two different addresses? Why or why not?

Make sure you acquire the information necessary to answer the question: When does this operating event occur? Recall that answering the: When? question involves determining an event's relative and absolute time of occurrence. The relative timing is determined by the sequence of events in a process. For example, some organizations may insist on a "cash up front" sequence in the sales/collection process: Receive Payment, then Ship Merchandise. Other organizations may reverse the order and provide credit to their customers.

The sequence of events may also be a function of the physical characteristics of the event. For example, constructing a building begins with Excavate Construction Site, then Pour Foundation. Then the events Lay Floor, Frame Building, Side Building, Install Rough Plumbing, Install Rough Electrical, and so forth can be executed until the building is completed. In this case, construction techniques, local regulation, and laws of nature determine the event sequence.

Sometimes the sequence of events is dictated by customer preference. For example, suppose a car dealership operates four sites located in four different cities several miles apart. Customers who visit a particular lot may want to order cars that are located at other lots. Initially, the dealership may have instructed customers to drive to the appropriate lot to pick up their cars. If enough customers cancel their orders or do not order because they don't want to drive to other lots, an astute dealership would change the process to reduce the loss of customers. Therefore, rather than requiring customers to pick up ordered cars, the dealer may initiate a new operating event called Transport Car. In the updated process, dealership employees drive ordered cars to the lots specified by the customers or even to the customers' homes. Adding a Transport Car event is management's attempt to meet the customer needs, and they will desire the information necessary to manage (i.e., plan, execute, control, and evaluate) the additional event.

Finally, as you investigate a process, think about what can go wrong. As you will learn from Chapter 5, all organizations face risks and management must identify and control material risks. Operating event risks result in errors and irregularities having one or more of the following characteristics:

◆ An operating event occurring at the wrong time or sequence.

◆ An operating event occurring without proper authorization.

◆ An operating event involving the wrong internal agent.

◆ An operating event involving the wrong external agent.

◆ An operating event involving the wrong resource.

◆ An operating event involving the wrong amount of resource.

◆ An operating event occurring at the wrong location.

Your *REAL* graphical model already displays some information that could help you identify examples of these risks. As you complete your analysis, make sure you acquire the knowledge necessary to identify specific examples of risks relating to each of these characteristics.

Use the business risk and notes columns in the business process model matrix (Exhibit 2–5) to document knowledge gained during this step. Other information not specific to a particular event (i.e., knowledge relating to a process as a whole) can be noted separately. We will frequently refer to the information recorded on this matrix during Chapter 4.

McKELL'S RETAIL STORE CASE CHECKPOINT

Reading this case highlights several characteristics of the business process such as:

- Each sale takes place at a specific register (location).
- Each sale involves only one customer (external agent).
- Only one salesperson (internal agent) is responsible for each sale.
- Each sale involves one or more items of merchandise (resource).
- McKell's merchandise items are not uniquely identified. Each instance of merchandise refers to a type or class of merchandise (e.g., size 12 white T-shirt, size 9 white tennis shoes, or size 5 leather gloves).
- The salesperson and customer do not have a direct relationship, because McKell's does not assign customers to specific salespersons. The customer and salesperson are related only through the sale.

While analyzing this event, you may document several additional characteristics, such as:

- Sales can only involve merchandise, not fixed assets.
- Sales cannot involve more (quantity) merchandise than McKell's has on hand.
- Sales cannot involve merchandise McKell's does not offer.
- Each sale must take place at only one register and the register identification must match an identification number on record.
- Each sale must include only one salesperson whose identification matches an identification number on record.

The next step involves defining how the resources, events, agents, and locations are related.

STEP 5:
IDENTIFY AND DOCUMENT THE DIRECT RELATIONSHIPS AMONG RESOURCES, EVENTS, AGENTS, AND LOCATIONS

Understanding the relationships among operating events and how each operating event fits into the sequence of a business process is important in understanding event characteristics, behaviors, and attributes. At this point, your graphical *REAL* model includes a variety of rectangles, but it does not display relationships. It simply lists the events, resources, agents, and locations. A user of your current model could not understand which resources are associated with which events, or which agents participate in which events. We show relationships by adding lines and diamonds between the resources, events, agents, and locations.

To update your model, complete three tasks. First, draw a line from each event to each resource, internal agent, external agent, and location associated with that event. On the line, add a meaningful term or phrase that describes the relationship between the objects. [Note: Some people draw a graphical model with a diamond at the midpoint of the relationship line. Using this method, you place the relationship descriptor inside the diamond. Your instructor will tell you which method to use.] Recall that you identified the resources, agents,

EXHIBIT 2–8

Template without Diamonds
Place Relationship Descriptions on the Lines

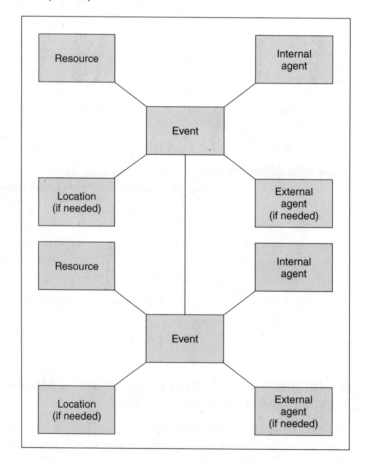

and locations related to each event when you completed Step 3. (You simply did not graphically represent these relationships on your model at that time.) When you complete this task, each event should adhere to one of the templates shown in Exhibits 2–8 or 2–9. Each event should have a line to at least one resource, one internal agent, one external agent (unless it is an internal event), and one location (if an explicit location is modeled).

Your second task in showing relationships involves graphically displaying events that are related to other events to show the required sequence of events in a business process. For example, the Order Goods from Vendor event should lead to the Receive Goods from Vendor event. This is also the time to graphically display duality between sets of economic events. For example, in the acquisitions/payment process, duality could in-

EXHIBIT 2–9

Template with Diamonds
Place Relationship Descriptions inside the Diamonds

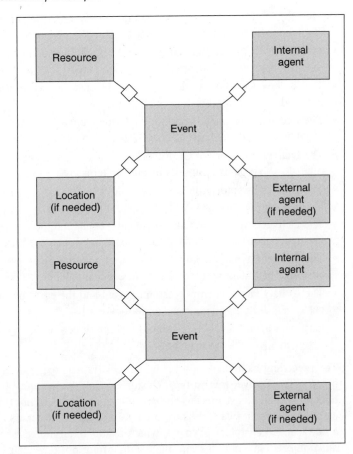

volve linking an inflow from the Receive Goods from Vendor event to one or more corresponding events like Pay Vendor and/or Return Goods to Vendor. In the sales/collection process, duality includes linking the Deliver Product to Customer event to the Receive Customer Payment event and/or the Receive Sales Return from Customer event.

Finally, your third task in showing relationships involves documenting direct relationships between pairs of agents, locations, and resources that exist *independently of an operating event.* For example, suppose an organization assigns customers to each new salesperson even if the salesperson has not participated in a marketing, order, or sales event with the customer. These two agents have a business link for evaluating the salesperson's performance. That relationship holds even if the salesperson never visits the customer (a marketing event) and the customer never orders any goods or services from the salesperson (an order event).

Consider an example of a sales/collection business process that consists of three strategically significant operating events: Receive Customer Order, Deliver Inventory to Customer (Sale), and Collect Payment from Customer:

- The Receive Customer Order event and the inventory resource are related—orders involve requests for inventory items.
- The Receive Customer Order event and the salesperson agent are related—*if* the salesperson executes the order (or receiving credit for the event).
- The Receive Customer Order event and the customer agent are related—orders are received from customers.
- The Receive Customer Order event and the Deliver Inventory to Customer (Sale) event are related—a delivery results from an order.
- The Deliver Inventory to Customer (Sale) event and the inventory resource are related—the organization sells inventory items.
- The Deliver Inventory to Customer (Sale) event and the customer agent are related— the customer takes delivery of the inventory items.
- The Deliver Inventory to Customer (Sale) event and the Collect Payment from Customer event are related—a sale should result in a cash receipt.
- The Collect Payment from Customer event and the Cash resource are related—a customer payment increases the cash resource balance.
- The Collect Payment from Customer event and the customer agent are related— customers are the source of customer payments.
- Customer agents and salesperson agents are directly related *if* each customer is assigned a specific salesperson.

The preceding examples only include direct (rather than indirect) relationships between objects. The Deliver Inventory to Customer (Sale) event and cash would not be listed as directly related objects because organizations receive cash *not* from the sale, but from the customer payment that results from the sale. If an event occurs between two events (e.g., a sale leads to customer payment, which results in an increase in cash), then the first and third objects (sale and cash in this example) are not *directly* related—cash and sale are linked or related via the third object (the customer payment). In addition, relationships are often context specific. For example, customer and salesperson are directly related *if* an organization assigns a specific salesperson to each customer. If, however, an organization has salespersons randomly assist customers during an event, the two are not directly related—they are only related via a sales event or a marketing event.

When completing this step, it is often helpful to document any important information about exceptions to these relationships as notes on your matrix. These data will prove useful in understanding and implementing business rules and operational controls as you design a process or a system.

McKELL'S RETAIL STORE CASE CHECKPOINT

Exhibit 2–10 illustrates the fifth step in creating a *REAL* model for McKell's. In this example, there are no direct relationships between resources, agents, and locations.

This step will prove very important as we learn to use our *REAL* model to develop information systems. Relationships describe associations between the *REAL* components that are used to document organization activities. Defining the relationships among the resources,

EXHIBIT 2–10

McKell's Retail Store *REAL* Model: Step 5

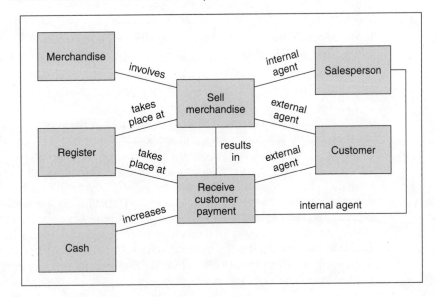

events, agents, and locations is critical to organizing a data repository and audit trail. What would happen if an organization stored a large amount of data, but had no idea how the data were logically related? For example, think about a telephone book that listed telephone numbers, names, and addresses but did not reveal which phone numbers went with which names and address. This step helps you avoid that problem. In Chapter 4 you will learn how to use model relationships to link various data items to create a variety of outputs. We have one final step before we shift our attention to such information systems issues.

STEP 6:
VALIDATE THE *REAL* BUSINESS PROCESS MODEL WITH BUSINESSPERSONS

Once an initial draft of the *REAL* model is completed, the next step is to validate the model's accuracy with businesspeople and repeat any necessary steps. Those who understand the details and objectives of the business process and events being modeled should perform the validation. Validation sessions should result in either confirmation of the model's accuracy or modification of the model. Modifications typically involve decomposing one or more operating events into more detailed operating events, or combining events.

Once a *REAL* model is created, does it need updating or maintenance? YES. The nature of business processes and events can change over time. More importantly, in today's fast-paced world, the nature of business processes and events often must change with time. The justification: That's the way we have always done it! is both inappropriate and dangerous in today's competitive world. An opportunistic competitor can quickly change the nature of the game. Once that happens a habit-driven organization is at a serious disadvantage and can die unless it changes its processes. Learning organizations are constantly searching for innovative ways to improve their business processes. Some people believe an organization's ability to learn may be "the single most important factor for creating a sustained competitive advantage."[10]

LINKING PROCESSES

Understanding the relationship between individual business processes is very important. Collectively, business processes result in the acquisition of goods and services, the conversion of acquired goods and services into goods and services for customers, the delivery of the goods and services to customers, and the collection or payment from customers. Although we often discuss business processes individually, they are intertwined. If you want to derive a model of an entire organization, you would complete the above six steps for each business process and link the various process models.

---

10 "Building Learning Infrastructures," *The Systems Thinker* (Cambridge, MA: Pegasus Communications, Inc., vol. 5, no. 3, April 1994).

Business processes are linked together in two ways: by sharing common resources or by an event in one process triggering an event in another process. For example, the Receive Merchandise event (part of the acquisition/payment process) and the Ship Merchandise event (part of the sales/collection process) are linked by the common resource merchandise. The Receive Merchandise event increases the quantity of merchandise on hand, while the Ship Merchandise event decreases the quantity on hand. Another example of a linking resource is cash. Cash is the resource involved in the Receive Payment event (in the sales/collection process) and provides funds to perform the Pay Vendor event (in the acquisition/payment process).

Alternatively, the sales/collection and conversion processes are closely linked by events. A Receive Customer Order event (part of the sales/collection process) may trigger the need for the Assemble Products event (part of the conversion process). Furthermore, Assemble Products events (part of the conversion process) may trigger Acquire Raw Materials events (part of the acquisition/payment process).

Although it is possible to link all the various processes together to form one model of the entire organization, be aware that the model can quickly become large and complex, even for a small organization. For example, consider the simple model presented in Exhibit 2–11. This partial *REAL* model illustrates how some of the operating activities from a variety of sample business processes are linked. The model also illustrates sample duality relationship sets from various processes (such as sale and receive cash, and purchase and pay cash). The duality relationship sets are denoted with increment and decrement labels.

CONCLUDING COMMENTS

Using only a few simple concepts we can develop rather complete models of business processes. The *REAL* concepts serve as a template for identifying and describing the essential characteristics of operating events. As you experiment with these concepts you will find that the essence of any business process, no matter how large, rests upon identifying and relating resources, events, agents, and locations.

Describing all the essential aspects of business processes requires a rich modeling language, such as the one introduced in this chapter. When system developers do not comprehensively model business activities as a basis for designing systems, there is a significant risk of producing a system that provides incomplete information. Incomplete information impairs the decision-making activities that rely on timely, complete, and accurate information.

To effectively learn *REAL* concepts you must apply them to real-world situations and explain and defend your conclusions to others. They are not learned by memorizing textbook definitions. Until you actually practice applying the material in this and remaining chapters, the concepts will be confusing, frustrating, and not well understood. You have to experience their effect, not just read about them.

In the next chapter we review system architectures that have been used to capture, process, and report data about these business processes. In subsequent chapters we en-

EXHIBIT 2–11

Partial *REAL* Diagram for Linked Business Process Example

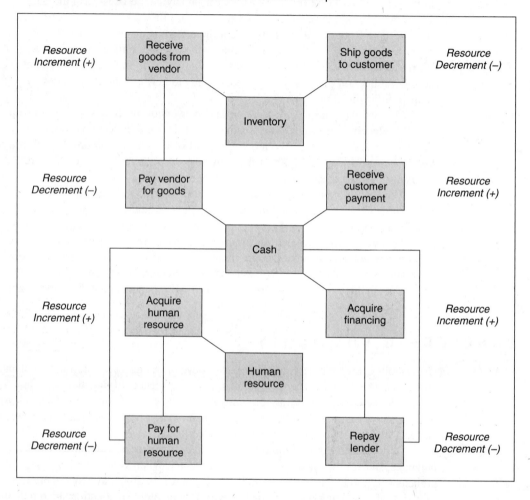

hance the *REAL* model and use it as the foundation for IT planning and design. This helps organizations shape IT applications around their business processes, enabling them to create a robust data repository and generate information to effectively support business activities—*in real time.*

Further Practice Using *REAL* Modeling

MULTIPLE BUSINESS PROCESSES

As we have already mentioned, learning how to do *REAL* modeling involves practice, not reading. Therefore, we would like to end this chapter with some additional *REAL* models of various business processes.

CHERRY BEE, INC.

Cherry Bee, Inc., is a small beekeeping operation located in Preston, Idaho. Each spring Marc, the owner, hires several beekeepers to manage and care for the hives owned by Cherry Bee. Marc pays these hive workers weekly during the spring, summer, and fall.

Marc purchases new supplies and materials for hive workers to use. The beekeepers go to the fields to check each hive, medicate each hive, clean any dead bees out of the hive, and add sugar water if the supply of honey in the hive is low.

Twice during the summer, hive workers extract honey from the hives. Then they go into the supply barn to strain the honey and package the finished product in a variety of different-sized containers. The finished honey is placed on shelves in the storage room. In the late fall, hive workers again check each hive, give them more medicine, and wrap the hives in black plastic to keep them warm during the winter.

Throughout the year, customers purchase honey from Marc at the Cherry Bee Store. Some commercial customers purchase the honey on account, while most customers pay cash. Marc purchases the supplies both on account and with cash from local vendors. The medicine, sugar, and black plastic are kept in the supply barn along with other supplies and materials, as well as the honey inventory.

This case includes a broad overview of the three major business processes. Can you identify the processes and the events in each process? This example includes two different types of acquisition/maintenance/payment processes: One for hiring and paying workers, and one for purchasing, storing, and paying for supplies and materials. Cherry Bee's conversion process involves checking the hives and extracting, straining, packaging, and storing the honey. Finally, a sales/collection process involves customers buying honey and Marc collecting cash for the sales either at the time of the sale or at some later date. Exhibit 2–12 categorizes the relevant events involved in each business process.

Next, you need to identify the management objectives, event triggers, resources (the what), agents (the internal and external who), and locations (the where) involved in each

E X H I B I T   2–12

Cherry Bee Business Processes

Labor Acquisition/Maintenance/ Payment Process	Supplies and Materials Acquisition/Maintenance/ Payment Process	Conversion Process	Sales/Collection Process
Hire workers Pay workers	Purchase supplies Pay for supplies Store supplies	Check hives Extract honey Strain honey Package honey Store honey	Sell honey to customer Receive payment for honey sold

event. You should have identified several agents including hive workers, vendors, customers, and Marc performing the roles of management, payables clerk, store worker, and cashier. Resources include supplies and materials, cash, human labor, hives, honey in process, and packaged honey. Locations include vendor store, Cherry Bee Store, supply barn, and fields. As you perform your analysis, do not forget that events that are completely internal to the organization do not include an external agent. After you have completed this step, compare your documentation to Exhibit 2–13. At this point, you may have found the management objectives and the event triggers tough, but this comes with more practice and business knowledge.

Finally, try using the information in Exhibit 2–13 to create *REAL* graphical models for each of the four business processes. You could create one comprehensive model that combines the four processes, but creating separate models is less confusing when you are just learning this new skill. Compare your models to Exhibit 2–14. How did you do? Hopefully okay, but just in case, let's try a few more simple cases.

SELLING A SERVICE

Let's try a service example to illustrate that resources can be both conceptual and physical. Services are not something tangible like a piece of merchandise. Providing services does not decrease the quantity on hand nor does it change the nature of the resource. To illustrate, imagine you are a customer representative responsible for the sales/collection process for a company that provides janitorial services.[11]

---

11 Other examples of conceptual resources include plans for future products (like architectural plans) or skills and capabilities of employees.

EXHIBIT 2–13

Cherry Bee Business Process Model Matrix

Event	Internal Agents	External Agents	Resources	Location	Business Objective	Event Trigger
Hire Workers	Manager (Marc)	Potential workers	Human labor	Cherry Bee store	Hire skilled, dependable workers at a fair rate ...	Need for labor
Pay Workers	Cashier (Marc), hive workers		Cash	Cherry Bee store	Pay only for services received, pay in a timely manner ...	Payment for services due
Purchase Mat. & Supplies	Purchasing agent (Marc)	Vendors	Materials & supplies	Vendor store	Have mat. & supplies on hand when needed, pay lowest prices ...	Need for mat. & supplies
Pay for Mat. & Supplies	Payables clerk (Marc)	Vendors	Cash	Cherry Bee or vendor store	Timely payment for supplies to maintain vendor goodwill ...	Purchase of mat. & supplies
Store Mat. & Supplies	Hive workers		Materials & supplies	Supply barn	Store materials & supplies in a safe, convenient location	Purchase of mat. & supplies
Check Hives	Hive workers		Hives, mat., & supplies	Field	Make sure hives are healthy and prepared for production ...	Beginning of spring
Extract Honey	Hive workers		Hives, honey, mat., & supplies	Field	Extract all the honey at the right point in time without waste ...	Hive full of honey
Strain Honey	Hive workers		Honey, mat., & supplies	Supply barn	Produce clean honey for sale ...	Extracted honey
Package Honey	Hive workers		Honey, mat., & supplies	Supply barn	Package honey in containers that promote a long shelf life ...	Honey was strained
Store Honey	Hive workers		Packaged honey	Supply barn	Store honey in a safe, convenient location until needed at store ...	Honey was packaged
Sell Honey	Store worker (Marc)	Customers	Packaged honey	Cherry Bee store	Sell quality honey for a fair price as quickly as possible ...	Customer enters store
Collect Payment	Cashier (Marc)	Customers	Cash	Cherry Bee store	Collect payments from customers in a timely manner ...	Sale of honey

Each day customers call to request a bid on work. You submit a bid to each customer who calls. If the customer accepts your bid, you create a contract stating the terms and conditions of the agreement (e.g., types of services to be provided, the cost of each, how often the services will be provided, and when payments are due from the customer). Once the customer signs the contract, teams of janitors provide the services and the customer begins making payments according to the terms and conditions of the contract. Your company employs a clerk to receive and process the payments.

EXHIBIT 2–14

Cherry Bee *REAL* Models (without relationship descriptors)

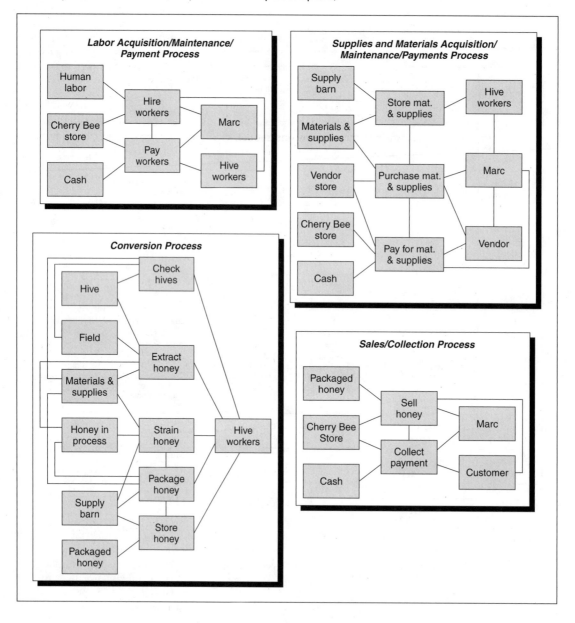

Did you identify the events in this scenario?

> Each day **customers call** to request a bid on work. You **submit a bid** to each customer who calls. If the customer accepts your bid, you **create a contract** stating the terms and conditions of the agreement (e.g., types of services to be provided, the cost of each, how often the services will be provided, and when payments are due from the customer). Once the customer signs the contract, teams of janitors **provide the services** and the **customer begins making payments** according to the terms and conditions of the contract. Your company employs a clerk to receive and process the payments.

Exhibit 2–15 displays a sample *REAL* model of this process. Notice how the resource is your services. Also, this scenario does not explicitly mention locations, so location objects are not included in this model. (Recall from the chapter that you will not always model locations separately.)

E X H I B I T   2–15

REAL Model of a Service Process (without relationship descriptors)

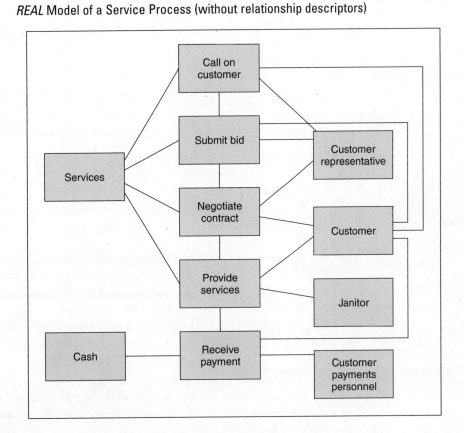

PROVIDING PUBLIC ASSISTANCE

This scenario is intended to remind you that business process modeling is not restricted to for-profit organizations. The concepts can be applied to processes in any organization, including various governmental agencies, charities, and foundations. One unique characteristic of not-for-profit organizations is that the recipients of goods and services are often not the people who pay for them.

> A shelter for abused women and children in your community provides temporary housing and food for women and their children who have been the victims of domestic violence. The following events occur between the time a victim enters and leaves the shelter.
>
> When a victim arrives, a receptionist greets her. A counselor interviews the victim, and assigns her to a room. A clerk in charge of inventory issues any necessary clothing and personal care items. The woman is free to use a stocked kitchen for daily meals during her stay. Each woman develops a plan of action, including immediate and long-range goals. A personal counselor helps the woman identify sources of available resources to achieve the goals. After a woman sets attainable goals and identifies sources for the resources needed to achieve her goals, she leaves the shelter.

A sample *REAL* model for this process is shown in Exhibit 2–16.

MAKING STEEL

Let's look at one final example. Imagine you are planning a steel making process. The steel manufacturing process converts raw iron ore into various grades of steel pipe, coil, and plate for sale to customers. The process should include the following events:

> *Bake.* This phase of the process bakes impurities out of raw coal in large ovens to make coke. Coke is approximately 97% pure coal. Because it is so pure it burns much hotter than regular coal.
>
> *Blast.* This phase uses the coke from the baking event to melt iron ore in large furnaces. The process results in metal slag (a waste product) that is skimmed off the iron ore.
>
> *Mix.* This phase mixes alloys with the pig iron in large furnaces that blow oxygen through the molten iron from the blasting event to make various grades of steel. The heat generated by blowing the oxygen allows the alloys and pig iron to bond to make steel that is poured into molds to form ingots.
>
> *Mill.* This phase shapes the steel ingots from the mixing phase into pipe, coil, or plate (the finished products) by a series of rolling and cutting operations. The finished products are then sold to customers.

A *REAL* model of this sample process is shown in Exhibit 2–17. One of the distinguishing characteristics of events in *REAL* models of conversion processes is that most events have both input and output resources. For example, the Blast event has coke and iron ore as inputs. The output resource is pig iron that becomes an input resource to the next conversion process

E X H I B I T   2–16

REAL Model of a Not-for-Profit Organization (without relationship descriptors)

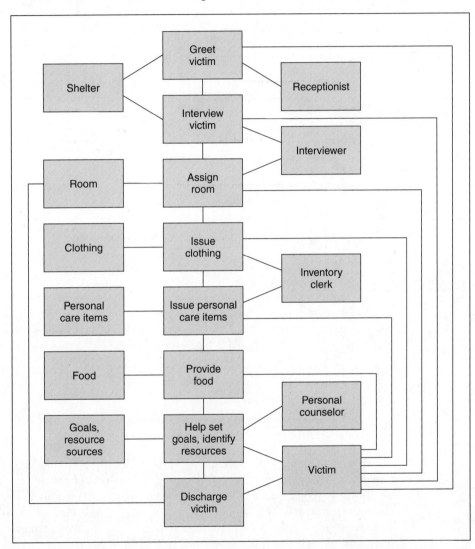

event, Mix Steel. Also, it is common to have several resources associated with one event. Notice how conversion process models identify the resources that must be acquired (e.g., coal,
limestone, alloys, and blast furnaces) as well as the resources that are sold (e.g., pipe, coil, and
plate). The organization needs an acquisition/payment process to acquire and pay for input resources and a sales/collection process to sell and receive payment from finished products.

EXHIBIT 2–17

REAL Model of a Steel Manufacturing Process (without relationship descriptors)

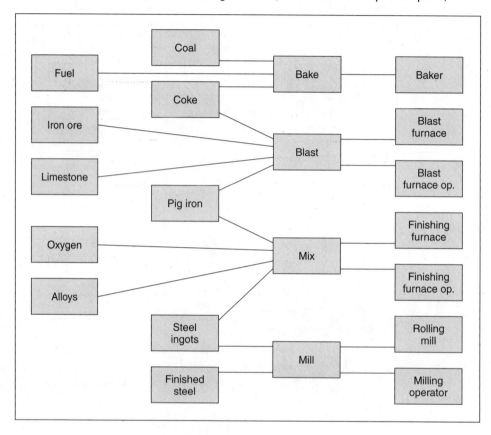

We could go on and on presenting *REAL* business process models, and we will present others in the remaining chapters of this book. However, you should realize we are simply describing common activities in your world. We cannot possibly introduce all the nuances and permutations of business processes in a text. The list is endless. All we are trying to do is get you familiar with a language for describing the world around you so you can learn more about business processes, their related information events, and the decisions associated with them.

We hope our discussion helps you observe various processes you use every day and that you begin to apply the concepts we have discussed to better understand and clarify the nature of business activities. Hopefully, our discussion will help you become more curious about an environment that is more important than the academic classroom—the real world.

CHECKLIST OF KEY TERMS AND CONCEPTS

acquisition/payment business process
business process
conversion business process
data repository
decision/management events
decomposing business processes
direct and indirect relationships
duality relationships
essential characteristics of business activities
extended enterprise business processes
information events
internal and external agents
linking business processes
operating events

primary value activities
REAL business process matrix worksheet
REAL business process model
REAL business process modeling
resource increment and decrement
resources
sales/collection business process
semantic model
semantic modeling
stock-flow relationships
strategically significant operating events
support value activities
value chain
workflow

REVIEW QUESTIONS

1. How can using a common language enable us to help organizations define their business processes?
2. What is a model? What are the strengths and weaknesses of modeling?
3. What is a business process?
4. What is a business event?
5. Describe the relationship between business processes and events.
6. What is an information process? How are information processes triggered?
7. What is the difference between a business process and an information process?
8. How are business and information processes related?
9. Describe three types of information processes.
10. What is a data repository?
11. List the three general types of business processes common to every organization.
12. Describe the acquisition/payment process. What are the organizational objectives of this process? List four sample acquisition/payment process events.
13. Describe the conversion process. What are the organizational objectives of this process? List four sample conversion process events.
14. Describe the sales/collection process. What are the organizational objectives of this process? List four sample sales/collection events.
15. Are the various business processes related or linked? Explain.
16. What is an extended enterprise process?
17. How do you determine the scope of a business process model?
18. Explain what is meant by a primary value activity.

19. Explain what is meant by a support value activity.
20. What is a learning organization?
21. How far do you go when decomposing business processes into business events?
22. List the essential characteristics that define business events.
23. How can the "why" of an event be answered?
24. What is *REAL* business process modeling?
25. List and describe the steps in *REAL* business process modeling.
26. What is the key to modeling business processes?

DISCUSSION QUESTIONS

1. Is it better to make one model of an entire organization or several smaller models of individual processes?
2. What is the difference between providing large volumes of information and providing accessible, useful information in a timely manner? Give an example of each.
3. Think about the company you work for or the school you attend. Is this organization a learning organization or a habit-driven organization? Provide evidence of your position.
4. Think of yourself as a resource specimen. Are you a learning individual or a habit-driven individual? Explain.
5. What are some advantages an accountant has over another business professional in modeling business processes? What are some disadvantages an accountant has in business process modeling?
6. Suppose you wanted to implement *REAL* business process modeling concepts when you enter the workplace. What obstacles and challenges would you expect to face?
7. Are some events outside organizational boundaries? Should information system designers focus on events that lie beyond an organization's boundaries?
8. All business organizations have at least three broad business cycles: acquisition/payment cycle, conversion cycle, and sales/collection cycle. In which of these cycles do each of the following activities belong? Explain your response.
   a. Delivering a new product to a customer
   b. Hiring new employees
   c. Paying for a new capital tool
   d. Assembling sub-components for a finished product

MINICASES AND OTHER APPLIED LEARNING

1. This case helps you identify operating events, information events, and decision/management events. For each of the following scenarios,

- ◆ Identify the operating events and related resources, events, agents, and locations.
- ◆ Identify any information events, including the type of event and the operating or decision/management event that triggered the information response.

    a. Gewirts, Inc. is a small manufacturing company that produces longboard skateboards to customer specifications. The company has several departments: Sales, Production, Customer Service, Accounting, and Data Processing. Sales-people occasionally call on the Data Processing Department for customer lists and buying trends. The Customer Service Department answers questions about orders and directs potential customers to the proper Sales representatives. Orders prepared by Sales representatives are sent to Data Processing to be entered into the computer system. Production obtains order information from terminals on the shop floor, manufactures the longboards, and sends the finished products to the customer. Because of the unique requirements of each longboard, the Production Department is responsible for purchasing raw materials and maintaining an adequate stock of materials and supplies. Accounting sends an invoice to the customer demanding payment as soon as the order is filled. Terms of the sale are net 30. Upon receiving the customer's payment, the Accounting Department pays the sales commission.

    b. On June 7, Quality Mart, a small retail grocer, realized it was low on several inventory items. Quality's purchasing clerk placed a large purchase order with Quick Groceries Company. The clerk added the order to the company's data file of outstanding purchase orders. On June 9, Quality received the inventory items, recorded the receipt, and placed the items on its shelves for resale. On June 11, Quality received an invoice (bill) from Quick Groceries. An accounts payable clerk used a computer program to compare the order, the goods received, and the vendor invoice. When she was satisfied that they matched, she recorded the purchase and increased the amount owed to Quick Groceries in accounts payable.

    c. A retail store customer takes his merchandise to the counter. The clerk scans the item's control tag to enter the price. The customer presents a credit card to *pay* for the merchandise and the clerk scans the credit card at his point of sale terminal to verify the payment. The customer then signs the credit card receipt and exits the store with his package.

    d. On March 10, a Huntoon Company sales order clerk received a phone order from Gibbs, Inc. for 20 pontoons. She entered the order data using an order entry software program. The order was added to the list of items to be moved from Huntoon's inventory warehouse to their shipping dock. When Huntoon's Shipping Department received the goods, they packed the order, shipped the goods, and recorded the shipment in the information system. In Huntoon's Billing Department, a billing clerk compared the Gibbs order with the shipping information received from the Shipping Department. Then, the billing clerk generated a sales invoice, which was mailed to Gibbs to request payment for the order, and increased Gibbs' accounts receivable balance.

2. K.L. Musical Instruments is a retail store that sells a variety of types of musical instruments. K.L. also has a repair shop to repair the instruments they sell. A purchasing agent is responsible for all purchases. A 30-day inventory of instruments is maintained. Most of the items purchased are bought through manufacturer's catalogs. Occasionally a manufacturer will send a sales representative to demonstrate a new instrument and the order will be placed through the sales representative. Shipment of all purchases is FOB destination and the manufacturer handles the payment of the freight. Several sales clerks are employed at K.L. They manage the store, assemble and display the instruments, service walk-in customers, make personal calls to some of the major accounts (such as schools with bands or orchestras), and deliver instruments sold to customers. Sales are made on account and for cash. Broken instruments are brought to the store by customers for servicing. A sales representative writes the repair orders. The instrument and repair order go to the Repair Department for service. Customers pick up the repaired instruments when they are completed. Occasionally the store will run low on cash and Krista, the owner, will make arrangements with the bank for a short-term loan. Krista and the store manager handle all personnel matters such as hiring, promoting, and firing. They also train the sales clerks. People in the repair shop are sent to special schools sponsored by the instrument manufacturers for training. A bookkeeper is employed to handle accounting and develop other reports required by management to operate the business.

Required:

   a. Group the operating events of K.L. Musical Instruments into the separate business processes using a format similar to Exhibit 2–12.
   b. Identify the information events described in this case. For each instance, define the event type (e.g., recording, maintaining, or reporting) and list the operating or decision/management event that triggered the information event.
   c. Perform the first five steps to create a *REAL* model for each of the business processes.

3. Coral's See-The-Reef, located on the Gulf of Mexico, is famous for its fast service. Coral's business is renting scuba and snorkeling gear. Coral needs someone to analyze her business and help her use that analysis to plan and design a new information system. Coral employs four fitting clerks, three rental clerks, and four cashiers. The fitting clerks enter equipment items and sizes and experience codes into the computer. The computer searches the rental inventory, by experience code, for the requested equipment. For example, a beginner is a code one, which tells the computer to locate the oldest equipment available in the requested size. If the requested size is unavailable, the fitting clerk is asked to change the size. Once the requested equipment is located, a duplicate rental invoice is printed. The rental clerk uses the second copy to retrieve the equipment. While this clerk gets the equipment, the customer pays the rental fee to a cashier. A deposit is added to the rental fee, and a code indicating the condition of the equipment is noted.

   When rental equipment is returned by a customer, it is checked in by a rental clerk who enters a condition code into the computer. If the difference between the return condition code and the rental condition code is one or less, the equipment is restocked and the deposit is returned. If the difference is greater than one, Coral determines a charge for excessive wear. The customer pays the cashier and the customer's deposit is returned. If the equipment is broken or lost, Coral estimates the value of the equipment and adds twenty percent. In the records, Coral transfers the damaged rental equipment to a sale inventory account. The customer then buys the equipment at the price set by Coral.

Cashiers also ring up new scuba equipment sales. Coral purchases any needed inventory and makes cash disbursements to vendors and employees. At the end of the year, Coral transfers any rental equipment to be sold to the sale inventory account.

Required:

 a. Group the business events of Coral's See-The-Reef into separate business processes using a format similar to Exhibit 2–12.

 b. Identify the information events described in this case. For each instance, define the event type (e.g., recording, maintaining, or reporting) and list the operating or decision/management event that triggered the information event.

 c. Perform the first five steps to create a *REAL* model for each of the business processes.

4. Go to a local restaurant. It can be any type, from fast-food to an elegant sit-down restaurant. Purchase and pay for a meal. Retain the receipt. As you are in the restaurant, keep a log so that you can answer the following questions about the restaurant's sales/collection process based on your experience (note: answer the questions from the restaurant's perspective).

 a. What is the name of the restaurant, and what type of restaurant is it?

 b. What happened?

 c. When did each event within the sales/collection process occur?

 d. What roles are performed and who (what agents) performed the roles in executing each event?

 e. What kinds of resources were involved and how much was used?

 f. Where did the event occur?

 g. What can go wrong in executing the event?

 h. What information is available on your receipt?

 i. Based on your answers to a–f above, identify the events as information (include the type), operating, or decision/management. For each information event, list the operating or decision/management event that triggered the information event.

 j. Perform the first five steps to create a *REAL* model for the restaurant's sales/collection process.

3
CHAPTER

The Traditional Accounting Information System Architecture

CHAPTER OBJECTIVES

The *objective of this chapter* is to enable you to analyze the traditional accounting information system (AIS) architecture. After studying this chapter, you should be able to:

* Describe the nature of the traditional accounting cycle and its relationship to business events.
* Describe the impact of IT on the traditional accounting system.
* Describe the limitations of the traditional accounting system architecture.
* Explain how the traditional architecture can limit accounting's ability to enhance its value.
* Describe an alternative accounting system architecture.

INTRODUCTION

In Chapter 1 we discussed the need for accounting professionals to change and the potential role IT can play in enabling changes. In Chapter 2 we analyzed organizational processes. As we continue we will first review some accounting and information system history and focus on the process by which accountants have traditionally processed accounting data both before and after the advent of information technology. We call this the *traditional accounting information system architecture.* Most organizations have implemented the traditional accounting information system (AIS) architecture.

We will then review how IT has been applied to the AIS and discuss several of the criticisms levied against the traditional architecture. We conclude the chapter by introducing an alternative basis for defining an organization's IT application architecture.

PACIOLI: THE FATHER OF TRADITIONAL ACCOUNTING

In about 1300 AD, some Italian accountants began using what we call *double-entry bookkeeping.* As Alfred Crosby suggests

> Merchants were driven to invent bookkeeping just as physicists were later driven to take up calculus. It was their only hope of knowing what was going on . . . The immediate significance of double-entry bookkeeping was that it enabled European merchants, by means of precise and clearly arranged records kept in terms of quantity, to achieve comprehension and, thereby, control of the moiling multitude of details of their economic lives. The mechanical clock enabled them to measure time, and double-entry bookkeeping enabled them to stop it—on paper at least.[1]

Luca Pacioli (pronounced Pa-chol-ee), a Franciscan monk who lived in Italy during the 1500s, is often called the father of double-entry bookkeeping. Crosby points out that Pacioli was not really the inventor, but was "the first accountant to combine his knowledge with Johann Gutenberg's technology[2] to instruct the world on the subject in print."[3]

Many people are unaware that Pacioli was a mathematician and author. He wrote such important works as *Summa de arithmetica, geometria, proportioni et proportionalita* (in 1494) and *Divina proportione* (1509). He was not an innovator, but a translator and compiler of popular books. The section of *Summa de arithmetica, geometria, proportioni et proportionalita* that dealt with bookkeeping (called "De computis et scripturis") was published in a large variety of languages and distributed in numerous countries in the 16th to 19th centuries.[4]

The traditional accounting information system is based upon what is typically called the *accounting cycle* and is based on the *accounting equation.* Although the ideas documented by Pacioli have been modified over the years, the essence of his original proposal remains intact.

At the heart of Pacioli's concept is a classification scheme known as the *chart of accounts.* The chart of accounts is used to classify and summarize financial measurements of an organization's assets, liabilities, and equity. Data organized and summarized using a chart of accounts are presented to users in the form of financial statements. The main financial statements include the income statement and the balance sheet. Data describing financial results of operations for a specific time period are summarized in an income statement, while data describing the financial position of the organization at a point in time are summarized in a balance sheet. Accounts summarized on the income statement are called

---

1 A. Crosby, *The Measure of Reality: Quantification and Western Society 1250–1600* (Melbourne, Australia: Cambridge University Press, 1997), pp. 202 and 208.
2 Gutenberg is credited with creating the technology that enabled authors to print books using movable type and a printing press.
3 Crosby, *The Measure of Reality,* p. 210.
4 Ibid., p. 215.

nominal (or *temporary*) accounts, while accounts summarized on the balance sheet are called *real* (or *permanent*) accounts.

CHART OF ACCOUNTS CODING SCHEMES

When developing a chart of accounts, most organizations use coding schemes. Coding uses letters or numbers in an abbreviated form to represent something. For example, "FL" is a mnemonic coding scheme—the two letters are used to represent the word *Florida*. Often charts of accounts are developed by combining two coding methods: block coding (a block of numbers used to represent a category) and group coding (subgroups of digits used to represent a meaning). For example, consider account 111 "Cash in Bank" and account 112 "Petty Cash." If all account numbers between 100 and 199 represent current assets, a block code identifies both of these accounts as current assets. If all cash accounts have 11 as the first two digits, a group-coding scheme would identify both accounts as cash accounts.

A sample chart of accounts is shown in Exhibit 3–1. Because each industry and each organization is different, so is each organization's chart of accounts. One compendium of sample charts of accounts and accounting procedures for a wide variety of industries is *The Encyclopedia of Accounting Systems.*[5]

Pacioli documented the double-entry, chart of account classification scheme used to record and store accounting data. Charles Sprague, an accounting scholar who codified much of contemporary accounting theory in the early 1900s, explained the nature of this process:

> Any occurrence [accounting transaction] must be either an increase or a decrease of values, and there are three classes of values [assets, liabilities, and equity]; hence there are six possible occurrences:
>
> **1.** Increase of Assets.
>
> **2.** Decrease of Assets.
>
> **3.** Increase of Liabilities.
>
> **4.** Decrease of Liabilities.
>
> **5.** Increase of Proprietorship [Equity].
>
> **6.** Decrease of Proprietorship [Equity].
>
> Balances of assets belong on the debit (left) side; therefore, increases are debits and decreases are credits. Balances of liabilities are credits; therefore increases of liabilities are credits and decreases are debits. Balances of proprietorship are credits; therefore increases of proprietorship are credits and decreases are debits. The result is six possible occurrences distributed as follows under debits and credits:

---

5 The *Encyclopedia of Accounting Systems,* 2nd ed., (Englewood Cliffs, NJ: Prentice Hall, 1974).

EXHIBIT 3–1

Sample Chart of Accounts

Account Title	Account Number	Account Title	Account Number
Current assets:		Long-term debt:	
Cash	110	Bonds payable	410
Accounts receivable	130	Stockholder's equity:	
Allowance for doubtful accounts	140	Common stock	510
Inventory	160	Capital in excess	520
Prepaid insurance	180	Retained earnings	550
Notes receivable	190	Revenue and expense summary	590
Property, plant, and equipment:		Revenues:	
Land	210	Sales revenue	610
Building	220	Interest revenue	620
Accumulated depreciation building	230	Rent revenue	630
Equipment	240	Expenses:	
Accumulated depreciation equipment	250	Purchases	710
Current liabilities:		Freight on purchases	720
Accounts payable	310	Purchase returns	730
		Selling expenses	740
		General and administrative expenses	750
		Interest expense	760
		Extraordinary loss (pretax)	770

Adapted from: T. R. Dyckman, R. E. Dukes, and C. J. Davis, *Intermediate Accounting* (Burr Ridge, IL.: Richard D. Irwin, 1993).

Debits (Entries on the left side)	**Credits** (Entries on the right side)
Increase of Assets	Decrease of Assets
Decrease of Liabilities	Increase of Liabilities
Decrease of Proprietorship (Equity)	Increase of Proprietorship (Equity)

. . . in every transaction at least two of the occurrences must appear . . . on opposite sides of the above list.[6]

When the accounts are in balance, the following equality is maintained:

$$\text{Assets} = \text{Liabilities} + \text{Owner's Equity}$$
$$A = L + OE$$

---

6 C. Sprague, *The Philosophy of Accounts* (Lawrence, KS: Scholars Book Co., 1907, 1908, 1972), pp. 23–24.

To keep the accounts in balance, Pacioli proposed a rigorous process for recording, maintaining, and reporting accounting data. Pacioli suggested the use of three books: the memorandum book, the journal, and the ledger. The memorandum book should include notations of every transaction, large and small, in whatever currency was being used and in as much detail as time and circumstance allowed. The journal was the source for the ledger, where the double-entry bookkeeping was done. It was in the ledger that the businessman could learn before anyone else whether he was a success or a failure. The process has been modified at times, but the underlying nature of the process remains essentially the same as when Pacioli first introduced it. The accounting equation is one of many possible models of an organization's economics. In and of itself, it does not keep the company economically viable or "balanced," nor does it ensure accuracy and completeness of the records. Rather, it provides one financially oriented view (or perspective) of the organization's activities and resources.

THE TRADITIONAL MANUAL ACCOUNTING INFORMATION SYSTEM AND THE ACCOUNTING CYCLE

A review of the basic accounting cycle will enhance your understanding of the traditional AIS architecture (i.e., the structure). However, our review of the traditional manual accounting system is not intended to be exhaustive. Our intent is to give an overview of its basic nature. We will refer liberally to an explanation of the accounting cycle provided by a group of accounting academicians in their book *Intermediate Accounting.*[7]

The accounting cycle illustrated in Exhibit 3–2 is a series of sequential steps leading to the creation of the financial statements. The cycle is repeated each reporting period (normally one year in length).[8] The first three steps in the accounting cycle require the largest amount of time and effort, and occur continuously throughout the period. The frequency of Step 3, posting, depends on the volume and nature of the recorded transactions. For example, firms with many daily cash transactions often post to the Cash account daily. Steps 4 through 9 generally occur only at the fiscal year-end. Step 10, reversing entries, is optional and occurs at the beginning of the next accounting period.

Inherent in the accounting cycle are mechanisms for reducing human error and keeping an organization's transaction data in balance (A = L + OE). Since human processors are limited in terms of memory and ability to organize and process details, the traditional accounting architecture segregates and summarizes details. This was necessary because, until only recently, all accounting data were recorded, maintained, and reported principally by hand with limited support from even primitive forms of information technology (e.g., adding machines and calculators). Before examining the impact of modern IT we will review the basic nature of each of the accounting cycle steps.

---

7 This section of the chapter is an abridgment of Chapter 3 of T. R. Dyckman, R. E. Dukes, and C. J. Davis, *Intermediate Accounting,* rev. ed. (Burr Ridge, IL: Richard D. Irwin, 1992).

8 Exhibit 3–2 applies to the preparation of all financial statements except the statement of cash flows, which requires additional input.

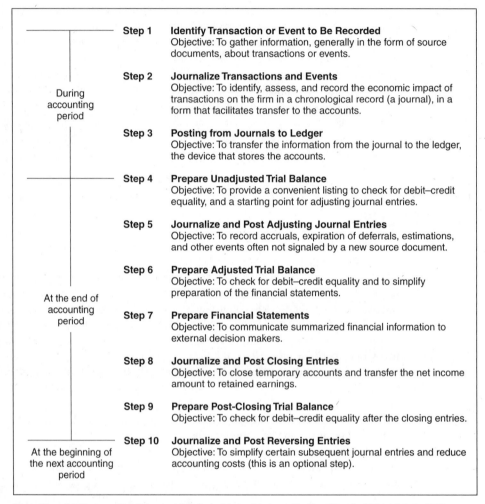

Adapted from: T. R. Dyckman, R. E. Dukes, and C. J. Davis, *Intermediate Accounting* (Burr Ridge, IL.: Richard D. Irwin, 1992).

Step 1: Identify Accounting Transactions to Be Recorded

The purposes of this first step are to *identify* the business events that can be considered accounting transactions and to *collect* relevant economic data about those transactions. Accounting transactions are the business events that cause a change in the organization's assets, liabilities, or owner's equity. These events include:

1. *Exchanges of resources and obligations between the reporting firm and outside parties.* These exchanges can be reciprocal transfers or nonreciprocal transfers. In a reciprocal transfer a firm *both* transfers and receives resources (e.g., sale of goods). In a nonreciprocal transfer the firm *either* transfers *or* receives resources (e.g., payment of cash dividends or receipt of a donation) or nonresources (e.g., stock dividends). Exchanges generally require a journal entry.

2. *Internal events within the firm that affect its resources or obligations but that do not involve outside parties.* Examples include recognition of depreciation and amortization of long-lived assets and the use of inventory for production. These events also generally require a journal entry.

3. *Economic and environmental events beyond the control of the company.* Examples include changes in the market value of assets and liabilities, and casualty losses. Only some of these events require a journal entry.

Other business events that do not meet the accounting test of affecting the organization's resources or obligations are essentially ignored while performing the accounting cycle. These events are "ignored" in that no data are captured about them in the accounting records. Accounting transactions that are difficult to measure precisely in financial terms are not journalized; rather they are reported in notes to the financial statements.

Accounting transactions are typically accompanied by a *source document* prepared by someone other than the accountant. In manual information processing environments, source documents generally use paper to record data about each transaction, the parties involved, the date, dollar amount, and other aspects of the event. Examples include sales invoices, freight bills, and cash register receipts. These documents are sequentially numbered to help uniquely identify each transaction. A separate transaction or source document does not signal certain events (e.g., the accrual of interest). Recording these transactions requires reference to the underlying contract or other source document supporting the original exchange of resources. Source documents are initially used to record transactions (Step 2). Source documents are subsequently used to trace and verify a transaction for evidence in legal proceedings and for audits of financial statements.

Step 2: Journalize Accounting Transaction Data

The purpose of this step is to measure and record the economic impact of transactions in a form that is consistent with the chart of accounts. Accounting principles that guide measurement, recognition, and classification of accounts are applied at this step. Traditional financial accounting texts are focused primarily on the proper classification and double entry recording of economic events.

Transactions are recorded in a journal—an organized medium for recording transactions in debit–credit format. A journal entry is a debit–credit recording of a transaction that includes the date, account names, account numbers, dollar amounts, and a description. A journal entry is a temporary recording; account balances are not changed until the information is transferred to the ledger accounts in Step 3.

Accounting systems usually have two types of journals: the general journal and several special journals. Non-repetitive entries and entries involving infrequently used accounts are recorded in the general journal. Repetitive entries are recorded in special journals. This helps organizations segregate or group transactions by transaction type. Typical special journals include a sales journal, cash receipts journal, purchases journal, cash disbursements journal, and payroll journal. If special journals are not employed, all transactions are recorded in the general journal.

Exhibit 3–3 illustrates an entry in a general journal. The credited accounts are listed below and to the right of the debited accounts. This entry records equipment financed with cash and debt. The *historical cost* principle requires the equipment to be recorded at the value of the resources used to acquire it. The posting reference and page number references are explained in Step 3.

Step 3: Post Journal Data to Ledgers

The process of transferring transaction data from the journals to individual ledger accounts is called *posting*. Posting reclassifies the data from the chronological format in the journal to an account classification format in the ledger—the device for storing information about each account.

Accounting systems usually include two types of ledgers: the *general ledger* and the *subsidiary ledgers.* The general ledger holds numerous individual accounts, grouped according to account type. Subsidiary ledgers support specific general ledger accounts that consist of many separate, individual accounts. They are used for accounts that normally require more detailed data (less summary) than are available in the general ledger. Sample subsidiary ledgers include the accounts receivable subsidiary ledger, accounts payable

E X H I B I T 3–3

General Journal Entry

	GENERAL JOURNAL			
				Page __J–16__
Date 2000	**Accounts and Explanation**	**Post. Ref.**	**Debit**	**Credit**
Jan. 2	Equipment	150	15,000	
	Cash	101		5,000
	Notes payable	215		10,000
	Purchased equipment for use in the business. Paid $5,000 cash and gave a $10,000, one-year note with 15% interest payable at maturity.			

subsidiary ledger, employee payroll subsidiary register, inventory subsidiary ledger, and a fixed asset subsidiary ledger. The accounts receivable subsidiary ledger groups transaction data by credit customer; the accounts payable subsidiary ledger groups transaction data by vendor; and so on. For example, a firm with a substantial number of accounts receivable customers will have one subsidiary ledger account for each credit customer. This gives a firm the ability to differentiate between the balances of each individual credit customer. Individual transactions are posted to subsidiary ledgers. Subsidiary ledgers are often updated (posted to) more frequently than the general ledger.

After a specified period of time (each week or month), the *totals* in each special journal are footed (summed) and posted to the appropriate general ledger accounts. The general ledger contains one summary ledger account per each account in the chart of accounts. This summary account is referred to as a *control account.* For example, the balance in the accounts receivable general ledger control account should be the sum of all the individual customer account balances contained in the accounts receivable subsidiary ledgers. In computing financial statements, only the control accounts are considered.

To illustrate the relationship between control accounts and subsidiary ledgers, assume that a firm's accounts receivable consists of three individual accounts with a combined balance of $60,000. The firm's general and subsidiary ledgers show the following balances in T account form:

GENERAL LEDGER

Accounts Receivable Control

$60,000

SUBSIDIARY ACCOUNTS RECEIVABLE LEDGER

Graphics, Inc.

$30,000

Digitax, Inc.

$20,000

Microtech, Inc.

$10,000

Exhibit 3–4 illustrates a section of a general ledger. This ledger depicts the status of selected general ledger accounts after posting the January 2 journal entry shown in Exhibit 3–3. Posting references (or folio numbers) are used in both the journal and ledger to ensure that an audit trail exists. An *audit trail* provides the capability to trace each individual transaction from its initial recording all the way through the accounting process to the financial figures published in the financial statements. Auditors should have the capability to reverse the process; trace the composition of the financial figures in the financial statements back to the individual transactions. An audit trail provides answers to these questions: Where did this item in the account ledger come from? To what account was this item in the journal posted?

EXHIBIT 3–4

Portion of a General Ledger

GENERAL LEDGER

		Cash			**Acct. 101**
1998			2000		
Jan. 1	balance	18,700	Jan. 2	J-16	5,000

		Equipment			**Acct. 150**
1998					
Jan. 1	balance	62,000			
2	J-16	15,000			

		Notes Payable			**Acct. 215**
			2000		
			Jan. 2	J-16	10,000

Posting references also serve to confirm that an entry was posted. For example, when the $5,000 cash credit from the general journal entry in Exhibit 3–3 is posted to the cash ledger account, 101 is listed next to the amount in the journal to indicate the account number to which the credit is posted. Similarly, in the cash ledger account, J-16 indicates the general journal page number from which this amount is posted. Cross-referencing is especially important for posting large numbers of transactions, detecting and correcting errors, and maintaining an audit trail.

Since some journal entries are ultimately posted to both the subsidiary ledgers and the control account in the general ledger, summing the subsidiary ledgers and comparing the total with the balance in the control account is necessary to check the validity of the duplicate data totals. This process is called *reconciling*. When the subsidiary ledger balance does not equal the general ledger control account balance, an investigation is necessary to determine which of the two totals is incorrect and make the necessary corrections.

Step 4: Prepare Unadjusted Trial Balance

An unadjusted trial balance is prepared at the end of the reporting period after all transaction entries are recorded in the journals and posted to the general ledger. The *unadjusted trial balance* is a list of general ledger accounts and their account balances. Exhibit 3–5 illustrates an unadjusted trial balance for Sonora, Inc., a fictitious retailing company, at the end of the fiscal year. This trial balance reflects Sonora's transaction journal entries recorded during the year and is used to illustrate the remainder of the accounting cycle.

The unadjusted trial balance is a convenient means for checking that the sum of debit account balances equals the sum of credit account balances. The unadjusted trial balance

EXHIBIT 3–5

Unadjusted Trial Balance Illustrated

SONORA, INC.

Unadjusted Trial Balance
December 31, 2000

	Account	Debit	Credit
Assets:	Cash	$ 67,300	
	Accounts receivable	45,000	
	Allowance for doubtful accounts		$ 1,000
	Notes receivable	8,000	
	Inventory (Jan. 1 balance, periodic system)	75,000	
	Prepaid insurance	600	
	Land	8,000	
	Building	160,000	
	Accumulated depreciation, building		90,000
	Equipment	91,000	
	Accumulated depreciation, equipment		27,000
Liabilities:	Accounts payable		29,000
	Bonds payable, 6%		50,000
Owners' equity:	Common stock, par $10		150,000
	Contributed capital in excess of par		20,000
	Retained earnings		31,500*
Revenues:	Sales revenue		325,200
	Interest revenue		500
	Rent revenue		1,800
Expenses:	Purchases	130,000	
	Freight on purchases	4,000	
	Purchase returns		2,000
	Selling expenses†	104,000	
	General and administrative expenses†	23,600	
	Interest expense	2,500	
	Extraordinary loss (pretax)	9,000	
	Totals	$728,000	$728,000

*January 1, 2000, balance (no transactions involved retained earnings in 2000).

†These broad categories of expenses are used to conserve space.

is the starting point for developing adjusting, closing, and reversing entries. For accounts with subsidiary ledgers, the account balance is first reconciled with the subsidiary ledger and only the control account balance is entered into the trial balance.

If the sums of debit and credit balances in the unadjusted trial balance are not equal, the error must be identified and corrected. Equality of debits and credits does not, however, imply the accounts are error-free. An unposted journal entry, an incorrectly classified account, and an erroneous journal entry amount are examples of errors that do not cause inequality of total debits and credits.

Step 5: Journalize and Post Adjusting Entries

A firm cannot prepare financial statements until adjusting journal entries are recorded. *Adjusting journal entries* are generally required when no source document exists to signal the need to recognize an event, or when a source document is not received in a timely manner. Many economic changes take place continuously with the passage of time (e.g., depreciation and interest). Frequent recording of such economic events is costly and less efficient than recording adjusting entries at the end of the accounting period.

Adjusting entries are also used to correct errors and to record changes in accounting estimates when new information becomes available. Adjusting entries generally record a change in a resource or an obligation and usually involve both a permanent and a temporary account. Source documents from earlier transactions are the primary information sources for adjusting entries.

Other examples of year-end adjusting entries include:

Recording deferrals: cash flows that occur *before* expenses are incurred or revenues are recognized.

Recording accruals: cash flows that occur *after* expenses are incurred or revenues are recognized.

Reclassifying account balances.

Recognizing inventory losses.

Accrual basis accounting requires these adjustments to reflect changes in resources and obligations under the revenue recognition and cost matching principles. Adjusting journal entries are recorded and dated *as of* the last day of the accounting period. They are recorded in the general journal and posted to the appropriate ledger accounts. Once adjusting entries are posted, the adjusted trial balance can be prepared.

Step 6: Prepare Adjusted Trial Balance

The adjusted trial balance lists all the account balances that will appear in the financial statements (with the exception of retained earnings, which does not yet reflect the current year's net income and dividends). The purpose of the *adjusted trial balance* is to confirm debit–credit equality, taking all adjusting journal entries into consideration. Exhibit 3–6 presents the adjusted trial balance for Sonora.

E X H I B I T   3–6

Adjusted Trail Balance Illustrated

SONORA, INC.
Adjusted Trial Balance
December 31, 2000

Account	Dr.	Cr.
Assets: Cash	$ 67,300	
Accounts receivable	45,000	
Allowance for doubtful accounts		$ 2,200
Notes receivable	8,000	
Interest receivable	100	
Inventory	90,000	
Prepaid insurance	400	
Land	8,000	
Building	160,000	
Accumulated depreciation, building		100,000
Equipment	91,000	
Accumulated depreciation, equipment		36,000
Liabilities: Accounts payable		29,000
Interest payable		500
Rent collected in advance		600
Income tax payable		20,000
Bonds payable, 6%		50,000
Owners' equity: Common stock, $10 par		150,000
Contributed capital in excess of par		20,000
Retained earnings		31,500
Revenues: Sales revenue		325,200
Interest revenue		600
Rent revenue		1,200
Expenses: Cost of goods sold	117,000	
Selling expenses	113,400	
General and administrative expenses	34,600	
Interest expense	3,000	
Income tax expense	20,000	
Extraordinary loss (pretax)	9,000	
Total	$766,800	$766,800

The account balances in the adjusted trial balance reflect the effects of adjusting journal entries. For example, the $400 balance in prepaid insurance equals the $600 balance in the unadjusted trial balance less the reduction caused by an adjusting entry. Account balances not appearing in the *unadjusted* trial balance emerge from the adjustment process. For example, the adjusted trial balance for Sonora includes several accounts resulting from adjusting entries: interest receivable, interest payable, rent revenue collected in advance, income tax payable, cost of goods sold, and income tax expense. Adjusting entries can also close account balances such as purchases, freight on purchases, and purchase returns.

Step 7: Prepare Financial Statements

The primary objective of financial accounting is to provide information that is useful to decision makers. The financial statements are the culmination of the accounting cycle. Financial statements can be produced for a period of any duration. However, monthly, quarterly, and annual statements are the most common.

The income statement, retained earnings statement,[9] and balance sheet are prepared directly from the adjusted trial balance. The income statement is prepared first because a net income figure is needed to complete the retained earnings statement.

The temporary account balances are transferred to the income statement, and the permanent account balances are transferred to the balance sheet. Exhibit 3–7 illustrates the current year income and retained earnings statements of Sonora.

The retained earnings statement explains the change in retained earnings for the period. If Sonora declared dividends during 2000, they would subtract the dividend amount on the retained earnings statement.

Exhibit 3–8 illustrates the current year's balance sheet. The ending retained earnings balance is taken from the retained earnings statement, not the adjusted trial balance.

Explanatory notes are included with financial statements to provide additional information that may prove useful to financial statement readers. Notes may include information about accounting transaction data that are somewhat subjective but important when assessing the financial well being of the organization. For example, financial statement users generally like to know about impending lawsuits, the estimated impact of natural disasters, the potential effect of political strife on remote operations, or a variety of other issues that have a potential impact on the financial health of the organization.

Step 8: Journalize and Post Closing Entries

Closing entries reduce the temporary accounts (e.g., revenues, expenses, and dividends) to a zero (closed) balance. Closing entries are recorded in the general journal at the end of the accounting period and are posted to the appropriate ledger accounts. Permanent accounts are not closed because they carry asset, liability, and owner's equity balances to the next accounting period. The Retained Earnings account is the only permanent account involved in the closing process.

---

9 A retained earnings statement or a statement of stockholders' equity generally is included in the complete set of financial
statements. However, they are not always considered to be part of the basic financial statements. In our example,
Sonora chose to report a retained earnings statement because no changes occurred in the contributed capital accounts
during the year.

EXHIBIT 3–7

Income and Retained Earnings Statements Illustrated

SONORA, INC.
Income Statement
For the Year Ended December 31, 2000

Revenues:		
Sales	$325,200	
Interest	600	
Rent	1,200	
Total revenues		$327,000
Expenses:		
Cost of goods sold	117,000	
Selling	113,400	
General and administrative	34,600	
Interest	3,000	
Total expenses before income tax		268,000
Income before extraordinary item and tax		59,000
Income taxes on income before extraordinary items ($59,000 × .40)		23,600
Income before extraordinary items		35,400
Extraordinary loss	9,000	
Less tax savings ($9,000 × .40)	3,600	5,400
Net income		$ 30,000

SONORA, INC.
Retained Earnings Statement
For the Year Ended December 31, 2000

Retained earnings, January 1, 2000	$ 31,500
Net income	30,000
Retained earnings, December 31, 2000	$ 61,500

Step 9: Prepare Post-Closing Trial Balance

A *post-closing trial balance* lists only the balances of the permanent accounts after the closing process is finished. (The temporary accounts have zero balances.) This step is taken to check for debit–credit equality after the closing entries are posted. Firms with a large number of accounts find this a valuable procedure because the chance of error increases with the number of accounts and postings. The Retained Earnings account is now stated at the ending balance and is the only permanent account with a balance different from the one shown in the adjusted trial balance.

EXHIBIT 3–8

Balance Sheet Illustrated

SONORA, INC.
Balance Sheet
At December 31, 2000

Assets			Liabilities		
Current assets:			Current liabilities:		
Cash		$ 67,300	Accounts payable		$ 29,000
Accounts receivable	$ 45,000		Interest payable		500
Allowance for doubtful			Rent collected in advance		600
accounts	2,200	42,800	Income tax payable		20,000
Notes receivable		8,000	Total current liabilities		50,100
Interest receivable		100	Long-term liabilities:		
Inventory		90,000	Bonds payable, 6%		50,000
Prepaid insurance		400	Total liabilities		100,100
Total current assets		208,600			
Operational assets:			**Stockholders' Equity**		
Land		8,000	Contributed capital:		
Building	$160,000		Common stock, par $10, 15,000		
Accumulated deprecia-			shares issued and outstanding	$150,000	
tion, building	(100,000)	60,000	Contributed capital in excess of par	20,000	
Equipment	91,000		Retained earnings	61,500	
Accumulated deprecia-			Total stockholders' equity		231,500
tion, equipment	(36,000)	55,000			
Total operations					
assets		123,000			
			Total liabilities and stockholders'		
Total assets		$331,600	equity		$331,600

Step 10: Journalize and Post Reversing Journal Entries

After the adjusting and closing entries are journalized and posted to the general ledger, the accounts are ready for the next period's transactions. Depending on the firm's accounting system and its accounting policy, reversing journal entries may be used to simplify certain journal entries in the next period.

At the beginning of the next period, the accountant may prepare and post *reversing entries* to compensate for the difference in timing between the occurrence of an actual economic reality, and the recording of the economic event in the accounting system. Reversing entries use the same accounts and amounts as adjusting entries but with the debits and credits reversed. These entries reverse adjusting entries made at the end of one period and prepare the accounting records for normal processing of business events in the new period. For example, an adjusting entry may be recorded on December 31 (at the end of the accounting period) to reflect wages earned (and expenses in that period) and a corresponding accrued wages payable. If the biweekly payroll is paid on January 6, the entire wages for the two-week period can be recorded as normal with a debit to wage expense *if* a reversing entry is made on January 1 to eliminate the wage payable and credit wage expense.

Audited Financial Statements

A publicly-owned enterprise whose stock is traded on a public exchange is required to publish its financial statements and distribute them to stockholders. Before the statements are released, however, a certified party must audit them. Organizations not required by statute to release their financial statements may still undertake audits in accordance with owners' directives or creditors' requirements, or as a matter of caution.

The purpose of a financial statement audit is to determine whether the statements fairly present the financial performance and position of the organization in accordance with generally accepted accounting principles (GAAP). Traditional auditing involves assessing the organization's business and information processing controls, sampling detailed data supporting each account, investigating the existence of key assets, assessing whether the records are complete, and a variety of similar activities. Most of this work is performed at the close of a reporting period. Assuming the auditor does not find any evidence of wrongdoing or improper record keeping, the financial statements are given a "clean opinion" and the statements are distributed to the information customers.

APPLYING INFORMATION TECHNOLOGY TO THE ACCOUNTING CYCLE

A careful review of the accounting cycle shows that it is both complete and complex.[10] During the first few hundred years of its use, one, or just a few, accountants could maintain an organization's accounting system. However, as organizations grew in size and complexity the dependence on human information processing and paper documentation became burdensome in three ways:

1. *Human error.* Regardless of how careful we try to be we humans are not very reliable as information processors. In fact, several features of Pacioli's accounting cycle were designed to detect human error by requiring various levels of summarized data and reconciling various sets of numbers.

2. *Human inefficiency.* Not only are we unreliable, humans are also not very efficient as information processors, especially in performing clerical tasks. Computers are much more efficient. This makes human information processing very expensive.

3. *Paper.* Manual accounting systems record, store, and communicate data and information using paper. This is expensive, not only because of the cost of the paper itself, but because of the cost to record, store, and use the data.

---

10 For further discussion and comparison of processing in manual and automated accounting information systems architectures, refer to Supplement B.

Furthermore, paper is easily destroyed and it is very difficult and expensive to have backup copies.

These same problems continue to confront organizations today. Although IT provides an opportunity to reduce the occurrence and cost of these problems, some organizations continue to use some manual processes along with their computerized processes for two reasons:

1. The technology does not exist, or is not sufficiently developed, to entirely computerize a process. Such circumstances are increasingly less frequent with the continued development of information technology.

2. The available technology is not yet cost effective. Although technological boundaries are being pushed back and continue to become more and more affordable, in some situations, the cost of applying technology is still too high. This, too, is becoming less frequent.

Many organizations have used information technology to replicate, or automate, the same processes they performed in manual systems.

> Double-entry bookkeeping did not change the world. It was not even essential for capitalism . . . Double entry bookkeeping was and is a means of soaking up and holding in suspension and then arranging and making sense out of masses of data that previously had been spilled and lost . . . Today computers compute faster than friar Pacioli would ever dream possible, but they do so within the same framework (accounts payable, accounts receivable, and all) as he did.[11]

Some may be tempted to ask what's so bad about simply automating the accounting cycle or any other information process that was designed to optimize manual system resources. Haven't organizations benefited significantly from doing so? Certainly organizations have reaped significant benefit from applying IT to the accounting cycle. For example, using IT has drastically reduced the number of accounting personnel (headcount); reduced dependence on manual, human information processing; and reduced the amount of paper used and the storage space for the paper in many organizations. However, simply automating the basic accounting cycle does not change the fundamental characteristic of the accounting architecture, nor does it eliminate the shortcomings that some people point out about the architecture.

CRITICISMS OF THE TRADITIONAL ACCOUNTING SYSTEM ARCHITECTURE

Is the traditional accounting system architecture the most efficient and effective structure to support professionals who are striving to play a key role in providing business solutions? Some people argue no because they feel that the architecture must evolve. As a student of

---

11 Crosby, *The Measure of Reality,* pp. 219 and 220.

an information profession, it is important that you understand the criticisms and weaknesses of the traditional architecture.

One criticism of the traditional architecture is a lack of integration across functional areas of the organization. Many organizations have separate systems for each functional area. This duplicates the number of journal entries and the amount of data stored within the systems. To illustrate, consider the following example of an international computer manufacturer that maintains a separate chart of accounts for its manufacturing and marketing divisions. Two ledgers are required in this organization because the manufacturing and marketing divisions have different criteria for reporting financial information. Manufacturing recognizes revenue when a product is shipped to a customer, while marketing recognizes revenue when the customer is billed for the product. The entire accounting process is automated.

Below is a description of the business events associated with shipping a computer and billing the customer. Below the event descriptions are the journal entries to record the transactions in the ledgers for both divisions:

Business Events:

December 15   Shipped a $300,000 computer to a customer.

January 10   Billed the customer $320,000, adjusting for the features added during installation.

Entries to Record the Computer Shipment:

On January 3rd, the following entries are posted to the ledgers to record the December 15 transaction. This is done as part of the month-end closing and reporting process:

On the Manufacturing Division ledger (Department 30):

Contra account	300,000	
Revenue		300,000
Trans-12	300,000	
Control account		300,000

On the Marketing Division ledger (Department 12):

Unbilled accounts receivable	300,000	
Contra account		300,000
Control account	300,000	
Trans-30		300,000

The Contra, Trans, and Control accounts offset one another during the corporate rollup process leaving the simple debit to Unbilled Accounts Receivable and a credit to Revenue.

Entries to Record the Customer Billing:

Billing occurs on the 10th of each month, but because posting only occurs monthly, the January 10 transaction is posted to the ledger on the 3rd of February as follows:

On the Manufacturing Division ledger (Department 30):

Contra account	320,000	
Revenue		320,000
Trans-12 account	320,000	
Control account		320,000

On the Marketing Division ledger (Department 12):

Accounts receivable billed	320,000	
Contra account		320,000
Control account	320,000	
Trans-30		320,000

Once again the Contra, Trans, and Control accounts offset one another during the corporate rollup process leaving the simple debit to Accounts Receivable Billed and a credit to Revenue.

Entries to Adjust for Revenue Recognition:

The problem at this point is that $620,000 has been recognized as revenue, not $320,000. To correct this, the original entries are reversed as follows:

On the Manufacturing Division ledger (Department 30):

Revenue 300,000		
Contra account		300,000
Control account	300,000	
Trans-12		300,000

On the Marketing Division ledger (Department 12):

Contra account	300,000	
Unbilled accounts receivable		300,000
Trans-30	300,000	
Control account		300,000

A total of 24 entries are used to record two simple events! These transactions do not take into account subsequent discounts, currency exchange rates, billing adjustments, or the possibility of value-added taxes for crossing international boundaries. You can see that the architecture is both cumbersome and costly. It is not difficult for the architecture to quickly get out of hand in promulgating hundreds of different ledger and subsidiary ledger systems to accommodate the variety of information and processing requirements across an organization.[12]

---

12 D. P. Andros, J. O. Cherrington, and E. L. Denna, "Reengineer Your Accounting System the IBM Way," *Financial Executive,* July/August 1992, pp. 28–31.

Let's step back and review the business process that leads to the recognition of this revenue.

A marketing representative visited a customer on a regular basis. After some months of effort, the customer ordered a mainframe on December 10. The Manufacturing Division released the mainframe for shipment to the customer, and the mainframe was shipped on December 15. On December 30, a marketing sales representative helped the customer install the new mainframe. During the session, the customer purchased and received $20,000 in product add-ons. On January 10, the customer was billed for the total cost of $320,000.

Within this process, the manufacturer has participated in a series of business activities: marketing products to a customer, taking a customer order, and delivering goods to a customer (i.e., shipping a mainframe computer and delivering add-ons to the customer).

How are these activities recorded and reported with traditional information systems architecture? A variety of systems exist within an organization to capture and report multidimensional data about business activities. The number of systems used often depends on how many different information perspectives, or *views,* people in the organization have when they want to manage business activities. For example, consider the following desired views of an order event:

- Production people want to know about the order to plan production processes.
- Marketing people want to know about the order to evaluate pricing, plan advertising campaigns, and target selling efforts.
- Personnel people want to know about the order to pay sales commissions.
- Executive management wants to know about the order to evaluate its impact on the organization.
- Investors and creditors want to know about all orders to assess the profitability of their investments and the likelihood of a return on their investment.

This is just a partial list of the possible diverse views. Not only are there a variety of different information customers interested in knowing about the order, each information customer's view of the order is different. Each class of information customers wants to know something different than others. The notion of multiple information views of the same phenomena is illustrated in Exhibit 3–9.

Traditionally, system designers have addressed the diversity of information customer needs by building a different system for each desired view. (See Exhibit 3–10.) Each system captures slightly different data about the same business event, with each system using its own classification scheme to select and record a subset of available data about the event.

You may wonder where the traditional accounting information system fits into this environment. The accounting system is one of the multiple systems that capture data about the business activities. However, the traditional AIS is unique in that it captures financial measurements about activities that meet the definition of an *accounting transaction.* In our example, the accounting system would capture data about the revenue recognition events (shipping the mainframe and selling add-on products). Since all the business activities in the process are handled by nonaccounting personnel, accounting entries are typically taken

EXHIBIT 3–9

Multiple Views of the Same Business Event

Personnel view

SALE

Production view

Marketing view

Investors and creditors
view (GAAP)

Executive view

from source documents that are prepared as part of the business activity. When the event meets the definition of an accounting transaction, an abbreviated version of the historical record of the transaction is recorded by accounting. As a result, data concerning the same business activity are maintained separately by accountants and nonaccountants; this leads to inconsistencies, information gaps, and information overlaps across the organization. Often, these multiple systems do not interface (communicate with each other) and duplicate data are stored in the various systems.

Although the intended effect is to accommodate the multiple views of information customers, the result is duplication in recording, maintaining, and reporting business data, added expense, and inconsistencies in the stored data. The burden is on the information customer to bridge the multiple processes, classification schemes, and data. More and more, information customers are faced with the challenge of *data certification:* Which system's output should we trust and rely on to support decision making?

The preceding discussion illustrates how an organization without integrated systems can prove very frustrating to information customers. Other characteristics of the traditional architecture are also criticized. Some of the most significant criticisms are summarized below:

EXHIBIT 3–10

The Proliferation of Accounting Subsystems

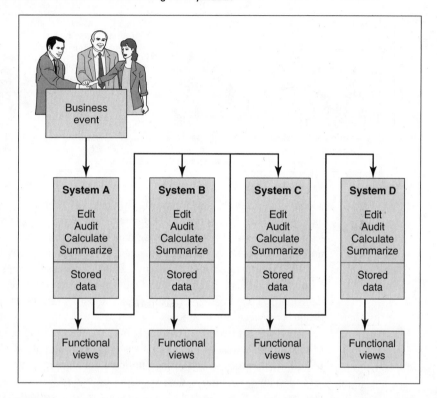

1. *The architecture captures data about a subset of an organization's business events (the accounting transactions).* Rather than gathering data about an entire business process, the traditional general ledger system focuses on what is often a small part of the entire process. As Exhibit 3–11 illustrates, not all business events are recorded in the traditional accounting system. An accountant identifies which events are to be recorded in the accounting system by asking whether the business activity affects the financial statements. If the answer is yes, documents that summarize the event are collected and used to input data into the accounting system. If the answer is no, the business activity is not recorded in the accounting system. However, data describing the activity are often recorded in one or more of the nonfinancial systems outside the accounting process.

2. *Data are not recorded and processed in real time (i.e., as the business activity occurs).* One of the subtleties of the traditional system architecture is that

EXHIBIT 3–11

Accounting Data: A Subset of Business Data

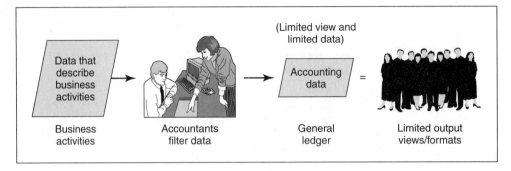

| Business activities | Accountants filter data | General ledger | Limited output views/formats |

account balances are never current. This is easily seen by the time lag on the example above. For example, the January 10 billing was not recorded in the ledger until February 3. Accounting data are generally recorded subsequent to, not simultaneously with, the occurrence of the business activity. In addition, the AIS architecture requires several offline[13] processing steps (posting, reconciling, adjusting, closing, and audit) before information is provided to decision makers. Postings, closings, and adjusting entries are necessary because the accounting process is not timely (i.e., the data in the accounting records do not reflect their current balances). Reconciling is necessary because of the duplicate data in the various systems. Reconciliation is needed to identify and certify which of the duplicate data are accurate.

Because accounting data are captured and processed days, weeks, or even months after the event occurs, accounting information for decision making is always late. The impact of information timeliness on the quality of information cannot be overstated. As Dyckman, Dukes, and Davis explain, "Accounting information should be made available to decision makers before it loses its capacity to influence decisions. Like the news of the world, stale financial information never carries the same impact fresh information carries. Lack of timeliness reduces relevance,"[14] and thereby its usefulness. Because information customers must make decisions all the time (in real time), not once every week or once a quarter, if information is not available from the accounting system, decision makers will go, and are going, elsewhere for information. As decision makers find other sources for needed information, the value of the accounting system and accounting information declines rapidly.

---

13 By *offline* we mean the information processing that can occur in the background while the business processes continue.
14 Dyckman et al., *Intermediate Accounting,* p. 44.

3. *The architecture stores and processes only a limited number of characteristics about accounting transactions.* Rather than capturing all available characteristics about an accounting transaction, the data captured in the traditional accounting system are only a subset of the descriptive data about business activities—primarily the date and financial impact of the transaction. Traditional accounting measurements are expressed in monetary terms: a practice that precludes the use of information on productivity, performance, reliability, and other multidimensional data being requested by today's information customers. Traditional accounting has tried to compensate for this by providing more and more footnote disclosures. However, without a more complete description of business activities, information customers are constrained in their ability to manage the business processes.

Because the accounting system only captures a debit/credit representation of the data (e.g., the date, account, and amount) for a subset of business events (the accounting transactions), it automatically narrows the type of information accountants can provide. Robert Eccles at the Harvard Business School recently observed the following regarding changes in the information decision makers are requesting:

> For years, senior executives in a broad range of industries have been rethinking how to measure the performance of their businesses. At the heart of this revolution lies a radical decision: to shift from treating financial figures as the foundation for performance measurement to treating them as one among a broader set of measures . . . Senior managers at one large, high-tech manufacturer recently took direct responsibility for adding customer satisfaction, quality, market share, and human resources to their formal measurement system. The impetus was their realization that the company's existing system, which was largely financial, undercut its strategy to focus on customer service.[15]

4. *The architecture captures and stores duplicate data in a highly summarized form.* In the traditional accounting model, source documents contain the detailed data about business activities. Some of these activities are recorded in the accounting system, and summaries of these transactions appear in the journals. Journal totals are summarized further as they are posted to the general ledger. This process duplicates data in the system—the same data are recorded several times with varying degrees of summarization. Once data are summarized or aggregated in the form of a special journal total or a general ledger account balance, they cannot be easily disaggregated. This limits information customers to the level of aggregation stored in the accounting system. Accountants can produce debit/credit information about individual transactions, totals by transaction types according to the predetermined time periods, and running ledger account balances. Alternative systems must be developed and maintained to provide other levels of aggregation.

---

15 R. Eccles, "The Performance Measurement Manifesto," *Harvard Business Review,* January–February 1991, p. 131.

This is not to say that summarizing data is wrong. Summarization is required for financial statement reporting. Rather, we must be cautious about using *one* particular aggregation method for one information customer group, and precluding other very different, but equally valid, aggregation levels for other information customers. We must respect and adapt to the individuality of information customers' decision processes and preferences, while also providing some standard measures of organizational results. These two objectives are not mutually exclusive.

5. *The architecture stores financial data to satisfy one primary view (perspective).* Rather than store accounting data in a way that supports a variety of views of the business, stored accounting data are organized around a chart of account structure primarily intended to produce financial statements. By retaining a chart of accounts classification scheme, we are asking users to decide up front what they think they might want to know about their business. Then we establish a classification scheme that stores summary data and limits the variety of output we can produce. This restricts management's ability to explore and analyze different perspectives of the data.

There is no convenient way for accountants to reclassify or reformat accounting data. Report flexibility is limited to selecting specific accounts with their account balances. To compensate for this problem, some organizations create dummy accounts, subsidiary ledgers, and contra accounts to supplement or "fix" the chart of accounts. Many also use separate charts of accounts for management accounting, tax accounting, manufacturing, marketing, corporate headquarters, and field offices. If our only objective is to present summarized financial statements, the chart of accounts classification scheme is adequate. But financial statement users are requesting other information that is difficult or impossible to extract from the chart of accounts structure.

Even if we were successful in developing a chart of accounts that satisfies information customer needs today, the requirements of information customers constantly change to respond to changes in the economic environment. Changing an organization's chart of accounts is no small task. It is not a simple matter of adding and/or deleting accounts and developing a new numbering scheme overnight and using it the next day. Changes in the chart of accounts affect the way information is recorded, posted, and closed to the trial balance as well as affecting the comparability of current transaction data with prior period transactions.

ARE THESE CRITICISMS VALID?

Criticism of the traditional accounting system architecture should not be interpreted as questioning the value of Pacioli's concepts, or the value of what accounting has done for the past 400 years. Pacioli's world was very different from ours. His was a world characterized by comparatively simple business organizations (both in terms of numbers of employees and types of responsibilities), simple information requirements (do we have more or less cash than when we started the business venture?) by a small number of information customers (primarily proprietors), simple and stable markets for goods/services (typically within a small geographic area), simple capital markets (if they existed at all), and a simple information technology (quill, inkwell, and parchment). Consider the following:

> Since the late 1980s, a quiet revolution has been building in corporate finance and accounting. More and more, companies are looking to their financial experts to act as business partners with operations managers and to dramatically reduce accounting and finance costs. However, changes in finance and accounting are still a generation behind operations management efforts that took root in the 1980s and are running hard just to keep pace.[16]

The criticisms we have presented simply highlight the difficulties of adapting the traditional accounting system architecture to a rapidly changing world. Today's business world is fast paced and more information intensive, and involves complex business transactions beyond Pacioli's wildest dreams. Recall from Chapter 1 that an information system is the infrastructure that produces information products for customers. As customers' demands and expectations of information change, information providers must update and create new information products. This requires the system infrastructure to evolve and change also.

Today's information customers are very demanding. They desire a larger variety of faster, customized information products delivered in a variety of modes. For example, many people now want their information system to produce a much broader array of information products such as balanced scorecards.

> A balanced scorecard is a set of measures that gives top management a fast but comprehensive view of the business. The balanced scorecard includes financial measures that tell the results of action already taken. And it complements the financial measures with operational measures on customer satisfaction, internal processes, and the organization's innovation and improvement activities—operational measures that are the drivers of future financial performance.[17]

Other people speak of information products yet to be developed:

> We have concentrated these past years on improving traditional information, which is almost exclusively information about what goes on inside an organization. Accounting—the traditional information system and the one on which most executives still depend—records what happens within the company. All recent changes in accounting—such as activity based costing, the executive scorecard, and economic value analysis—still aim at providing better information about events within the company. The new data produced by most new information systems also have that purpose . . . Increasingly, a winning strategy will require information

---

16 Thomas Walther, Henry Johansson, John Dunleavy, and Elizabeth Hjelm, *Reinventing the CFO: Moving from Financial Management to Strategic Management* (New York: McGraw-Hill, 1997), p. 3.

17 R. Kaplan and D. Norton, "The Balanced Scorecard—Measures That Drive Performance," *Harvard Business Review,* January–February 1992, pp. 71–79.

about events and conditions outside the institution: noncustomers, technologies other than those currently used by the company, markets not currently served, and so on. Only with this new information can a business decide how to allocate its knowledge resources in order to produce the highest yield. Only with such information can a business also prepare for new changes and challenges arising from sudden shifts in the world economy and in the nature and content of knowledge itself. The development of rigorous methods for gathering and analyzing outside information will increasingly become a major challenge for businesses and for information experts.[18]

The bottom line is that the traditional AIS architecture contains characteristics that inhibit accountants in providing valuable business solutions. Simply automating the accounting cycle has provided only limited benefits. More importantly, however, the traditional AIS architecture is often complex and costly, and it limits accounting's efforts to enhance its value.

The real question of concern to us is: Should the accounting architecture change to enhance the value of accounting? Remember in Chapter 1 we suggested three ways accounting can enhance its value to an organization:

Providing More Useful Information. Traditional accounting measures are expressed almost exclusively in monetary terms: a practice that precludes information on productivity, performance, reliability, and other multidimensional data that cannot be easily expressed in monetary terms. Traditional accounting system data are only a subset of the data about business activities. Capturing the date, account, and amount of accounting transactions is adequate to produce financial statements, but is inadequate from the enterprise perspective to provide the information needed for decision makers to manage an organization's activities.

Helping to Embed Real-Time Information Processes into Business Processes. Designing and implementing real-time information processes that execute business rules and gather business data as business processes occur presupposes involvement in an organization's business processes. This involvement enables accountants to provide meaningful, direct input into the design, development, and implementation of related IT applications. When accountants have little involvement in the actual business processes (which is where they can best control business process risk), they are constantly trying to control risk from a distance using primarily after-the-fact controls that do more to detect breaches of control than prevent them. This involvement results in accountants focusing their efforts on controlling information processing risk in the accounting system rather than controlling the actual business process or the systems that support the business process.

Helping Management Define Business Process Rules. To help management define business process rules presupposes involvement in an organization's business processes. By being removed from the process and paying attention to

---

18 P. Drucker, "The Future That Has Already Happened," *Harvard Business Review,* September–October 1997, pp. 20–24.

only a subset of the events in the process, the ac
associated with it, is often removed from the bus
allows accountants and process managers to drif
responsible for managing business processes ca
process with little or no input from accounting.
task separate from running the business. The se
on "accounting" rather than "business" proble
the organization's strategy, business processes, structure,
IT. This separation can foster unnecessary tension between process managem
and accounting. A better alternative is to develop an AIS architecture that enables
accountants to exercise influence over the development and implementation of
business rules throughout the business processes.

We are not the only authors promoting such ideas. Thomas Walther, Henry Johansson, John Dunleavy, and Elizabeth Hjelm, authors from a multinational business consulting firm (also referred to by some as a "Big Five" accounting firm), explain the importance of value creation as a new role for the OCFO (Office of the CFO).[19] The authors assert that many companies will require the CFO to offer the following:

- Insightful contributions to the strategy and planning process.
- Measures that focus and motivate the organization.
- Information and analysis that provides insight into how value is being created and how progress is being matched to strategic initiatives.
- Leadership of major financial initiatives.

Objectives such as these provide justification for changing the architecture of any information system that limits the potential of information providers in adding value to an organization.

We realize that some people will choose not to change from the traditional architecture. They may feel a change in the accounting architecture will reduce an organization's ability to adhere to GAAP (generally accepted accounting principles). It is important to remember that GAAP address the way financial statement information is *reported*. GAAP do not deal with or mandate the method of data collection, storage, or processing. Still others view the clerical procedures of classifying and recording journal entries, posting to a ledger, and generating a trial balance as integral parts of accounting. Such a perspective emphasizes the *how of accounting* rather than the *why of accounting*.

How do you prepare yourself to play an active role in enhancing the value of accounting information? First, you must understand all facets of traditional AIS design, including the criticisms levied against the architecture. Many of your clients will use the traditional systems architecture. However, you should also focus on being involved in creating new and innovative ways of combining accounting and IT to develop new business solutions. When you realize the traditional architecture can limit your ability to

---

19 Walther et al., *Reinventing the CFO*, p. 15.

enhance the value of accounting, you realize that changing the architecture is sometimes the key to enhancing value. Remember to separate the clerical mechanics—the accounting process supported by the traditional architecture—and "the way things have always been done" from the objectives of information age accounting. This will make it easier to objectively evaluate possible architectures and their ability to enhance your value as an information provider. It will also enable you to understand the evolving nature of information systems architectures.

THE EVOLUTION OF INFORMATION SYSTEMS DESIGN

Certainly Pacioli's original ideas were nothing short of brilliant in terms of proposing a method for recording, maintaining, and reporting economic data with a fairly primitive information technology. However, today's world and the profession's desire to move forward allow AIS designers to rethink the basic architecture of the AIS. Moreover, today's technology makes rethinking AIS possible.

A careful review of various accounting software products and information system architectures reveals that systems have evolved over time, and will continue to do so. McCarthy, David, and Sommer[20] present basic categories for information system evolution. The authors explain that most information systems are organized around one of three structures. The first is the classic accounting equation Assets = Liabilities + Owner's Equity. As we have discussed, this structure is based on the financial implications of economic events. This structure focuses on information accuracy and the rules that govern how and when transactions are recognized. The second structure is a hybrid one. It leverages the power of advancing technology resources. It has evolved beyond the traditional Assets = Liabilities + Owner's Equity structure, but retains much of the fundamental ties to bookkeeping conventions. Examples of this structure include materials requirement planning (MRP) systems and activity-based costing (ABC) systems. Systems that fall into the third system structure use Michael Porter's value chain analysis, introduced in Chapter 2, as the foundation. These systems do not limit scope to economic transactions, but strive to capture a wide range of information about all key business events.

The authors' 10 basic categories of information system evolution include:

Category 1—Lone Transactions. These systems capture a limited number of cash transactions to satisfy a limited number of information needs. An example is an electronic checkbook.

Category 2—Transactions and Obligations. These systems capture a limited amount of detail about cash and obligation transactions (such as loans and recurring payments). Examples include Quicken and Microsoft Money.

20 W. McCarthy, J. S. David, and B. Sommer, "The Evolution of Enterprise Information Systems," working paper, 1998. For a copy, you can contact W. E. (Bill) McCarthy at Michigan State University or Julie Smith David at Arizona State University.

Category 3—Bookkeeping. These systems are based on the Assets = Liabilities + Owner's Equity structure. They track transactions, summarize them, and generate reports that describe business assets and obligations.

Category 4—Multidimensional Accounting. These systems are also based on the chart of accounts but they can accommodate and process hundreds of general ledger codes. They can store more detailed transaction data than the bookkeeping packages. They can generate the traditional, summarized financial statements, but can also sort the accounts to answer other types of user queries.

Category 5—Modular Integration. These general ledger systems also support individual functional areas (such as manufacturing, training, and logistics) with automated processing modules. These modules are technically integrated with the accounting software, which means you can pass summarized data from the modules to the general ledger (and vice versa).

Category 6—ABC/MRP II. These systems include data about a variety of activities as well as data about activities both downstream and upstream from the manufacturing and conversion processes. These systems overcome some of the representation and integration problems of the first six categories.

Category 7—Enterprise Resource Planning (ERP). These systems break from the Assets = Liabilities + Owner's Equity scheme. ERP systems do not have the preparation of financial statements as their primary goal. Many ERP vendors stress an objective of inputting data only once and using it to generate various views. ERP vendors stress the process focus of their products. The software can span across functional borders, enabling integration of data and information flows. However, these systems are often inflexible and impose certain rules and processes on the organization. Successfully implementing these systems is often difficult and costly.

Given the massive interest ERP systems have generated over the past few years, we encourage you to investigate them further. Supplement B provides a list of ERP vendors. There is a large number of articles in the business and academic press that discuss this category of systems.

Category 8—Business Objects. These systems take advantage of object-oriented technology. They enable systems designers to more realistically model real-world phenomena and the characteristics and behavior of the phenomena.

Category 9—Semantic Theory of the Firm. These systems enable designers to explicitly represent an enterprise's full economic plan for creating customer value, including full information disclosure about all of the resources, agents, and locations of all events of interest. These systems, if implemented completely, could enable organizations to trace 100% of their economic processes from product inception to the final sale to the customer.

Category 10—Networked Enterprise. These systems have no technology limits (in terms of advances or high costs). They enable, at optimal levels, interorganizational coordination. These systems capture event information once, in real time, and make it available to all concerned parties. They support large groups of networked companies, some of which are connected in turn with individual customers.

The last few categories of systems are still in the development stages. They outline the development of future information systems architectures.

AN ALTERNATIVE INFORMATION SYSTEMS ARCHITECTURE: THE BUSINESS EVENTS–DRIVEN ARCHITECTURE

A few years ago, Thomas Johnson and Robert Kaplan, two well-known accounting scholars, observed:

> The challenge and the opportunity for contemporary organizations . . . is clear . . . systems can and should be designed to support the operations and the strategy of the organization. The technology exists to implement systems radically different from those being used today. What is lacking is knowledge. But this knowledge can emerge from experimentation and communication.[21]

Our intent is to empower you to experiment with the AIS architecture. Information technology should facilitate business objectives and goals rather than constrain or impose a certain form or structure to achieve them. Our objective is to develop IT applications that work toward solving business problems. The nature of specific IT applications is shaped by the IT application architecture.

The purpose of architectures in general is to define the general characteristics or style of a structure. The architecture guides the development of a plan or blueprint for a specific structure. Differing architectures result in very different plans. For example, Japanese architecture is quite different from Roman architecture that is quite different from Colonial architecture.

When architecture is applied to IT, it refers to the characteristics of how IT is used to capture, store, and use business data. The traditional AIS architecture is view driven; the desired views of business data shape how business data are captured, stored, and used. *View-driven IT applications* are designed to support specific functions (e.g., marketing, accounting, finance, or production) by providing a particular information perspective (called a *view*) to those who manage it. They are not intended to provide views of entire business processes that may span several organization functions.

Instead of shaping the AIS architecture around the seemingly infinite number of views about business processes and events, why not shape the architecture around the common thing that all the views are actually looking at—the business processes and events? By changing the orientation from user output views to business processes and events, designers can focus on collecting and storing data about the activities that underlie the wide

---

21 H. T. Johnson, and R. S. Kaplan, *Relevance Lost: The Rise and Fall of Management Accounting* (Boston: Harvard Business School Press, 1987), pp. 17–18.

variety of information customer views. This prevents the need for multiple systems that duplicate data storage and processing about the same business activities.

To add value to the organization as described above, the accounting information system must collect and store a larger set of data for all business events that are important to management. Multidimensional, detailed data must be recorded while the business event occurs, and query tools must enable information customers to access current information in real time. Rather than performing a clerical, filtering role, the accounting professional needs to be a business partner. The accounting professional thereby maintains the data store (an information warehouse), which is used to generate and deliver a wide variety of accounting information products in a variety of formats. These evolving systems facilitate user-defined output by making current information available in real time, at the user's request and specification.

Exhibit 3–12 illustrates an alternative generation of accounting information systems architecture, which we will refer to as an *event-driven architecture*. This architecture, which falls into Category 9 in the McCarthy, David, Sommer classification scheme discussed above, presumes that the nature of business processes and events shape how data are captured, stored, and used. By storing data that answer the five questions about an organization's business events (what happened, when, who was involved, what was involved, and where it occurred), an event-driven architecture can provide all the views of view-driven applications, without the data and process redundancy inherent in segregated, often

EXHIBIT 3–12

Event-Driven IT Application Architecture

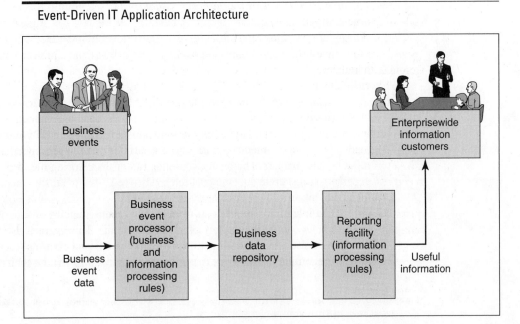

duplicate functional applications. Specifically, the architecture includes the following four characteristics:

1. *The architecture is based on business events (business activities) rather than information customer views.* Focusing on business events redefines the scope of accounting. Rather than selecting only those business events that change the company's assets, liabilities, or owner's equity, we select those business events that management wants to plan, control, and evaluate. Multidimensional measures of business activities are stored in a less aggregated form, enabling flexibility in reporting. This focus automatically forces an integration of the functional areas of an enterprise and enables the integration of both financial and nonfinancial data. This allows accountants to provide a more complete and representative picture of the organization they are trying to support.

2. *The architecture supports business process simplification and change.* Michael Hammer, the person most identified with the concepts of reengineering business processes, points out that although U.S. companies have made tremendous strides in restructuring and downsizing, most are still unprepared to operate in the 1990s. Despite enormous investments in IT, efforts to streamline and automate outdated processes have not yielded the dramatic improvements required to compete effectively in a global environment. Experience has proven over and over again that simply automating inherently inadequate processes and architectures will not solve business problems. Therefore, organizations must rethink processes and then apply IT.

3. *The architecture integrates all business data.* Data integration focuses on organizing all relevant data about all business events into one logical[22] information store instead of having a series of loosely integrated systems that often have information gaps and overlaps (e.g., the financial/nonfinancial paradigm). This single integrated store of data supports all information customer views.

   Business events form the foundation of the business *data repository*—an oft overused media term that typically means a big database. Effective integration of data does not imply simply applying database technology to inadequate data architecture. The key to data integration is storing consistent, reliable data that describe business events, rather than storing the data necessary to generate specific customer views (e.g., financial statements, management reports, or regulatory reports).

   Data integration reduces duplication and inconsistencies of data that arise when data are stored in a variety of separate systems. This characteristic (and the characteristic of integrating information processes and controls discussed next) is becoming increasingly important as organizations realign their people

---

[22] In computing, the term *logical* refers to what is seen by the user, rather than the physical attributes of stored data. This concept is discussed further in the supplemental chapters.

to work as team members on a common goal, rather than as distinct functional departments working somewhat independently of each other.

4. *The architecture integrates information processes and real-time controls.* When data are partitioned between financial and nonfinancial data (and any other type of partition), the number of processes quickly multiplies. Not only do you need two sets of recording, maintaining, and reporting processes, you also need processes, to reconcile the separate systems.

Process integration involves integrating the functional requirements of the three essential information activities—recording, maintaining, and reporting—and the controls required to reduce the related business and information processing risks. Particularly important is the integration of all requirements relevant to the recording of event data.

Process integration involves embedding the information system into the actual business process itself. Thus, information technology is used to record data and control the process during the execution of business events. The proper integration of processes can result in significant savings to the organization and can facilitate the reengineering of both business and information processes. One of the benefits of process integration is the identification of clerical processes that can potentially be automated, thereby shifting human efforts to nonmechanical, decision-oriented tasks.

CONCLUDING COMMENTS

The AICPA (American Institute of Certified Public Accountants) has acknowledged that "No matter how sound the financial reporting . . . *it is without value if the user does not perceive it to be sound.*"[23] Thus information providers must respond to meet the needs of their information customers. We realize it is difficult for some of you to envision or consider alternative system structures, especially when your training in accounting often relies so heavily on the traditional structure. However, it is critical that you adopt a philosophy that prompts you to keep your skills and knowledge base up to date. As Peter Drucker, a noted scholar has stated, "Knowledge is different from all other kinds of resources. It constantly makes itself obsolete, with the result that today's advanced knowledge is tomorrow's ignorance."[24]

Today's information users are critically evaluating information systems, and they are voicing their opinions. To many readers, Chapters 1 and 3 include many negative statements about the accounting profession; but we urge you to reconsider that view. Sometimes it is tough to accept criticism and even tougher to change. However, the accounting profession is aspiring to improve the services it provides to organizations and financial

23 *Meeting the Financial Reporting Needs of the Future: A Public Commitment from the Public Accounting Profession* (New York: American Institute of Certified Public Accountants, June 1993).

24 Drucker, "The Future That Has Already Happened," p. 22.

markets. Our interest in providing both criticisms and suggestions is to make accounting a stronger and more valued profession.

This review of the accounting profession and the evolution of the accounting system architecture is important in helping you understand the challenges facing accounting information system designers. Our discussion also introduced several characteristics that help improve system designs. Now it is time to begin focusing on analyzing, evaluating, and designing information systems.

CHECKLIST OF KEY TERMS AND CONCEPTS

Accounting cycle

Accounting equation

Accounting information system architecture

Accounting transaction

Adjusted trial balance

Adjusting entries

Assets

Audit trail

Balance sheet

Balanced scorecard

Block coding

Business events

Chart of accounts

Closing entries

Coding scheme

Control account

Data certification

Data repository

Double-entry accounting

Equity

Event-driven architecture

Financial statements

Generally accepted accounting principles
  (GAAP)

General journal

General ledger

Group coding

Income statement

Journal

Journal entry

Liabilities

Ledger

Nominal accounts

Luca Pacioli

Offline

Posting

Posting references

Real accounts

Real time

Reconciling

Retained earnings statement

Reversing entries

Special journals

Source document

Statement of cash flows

Subsidiary ledger

Trial balance

Unadjusted trial balance

View

View-driven IT applications

REVIEW QUESTIONS

1. List and briefly describe each of the information processing steps in the traditional accounting cycle.

2. Are all business activities recorded in accounting journals? Explain.

3. Name several examples of the various journals used by accountants. Why do organizations use multiple journals?

4. The book states that a journal entry is a temporary recording. Explain this statement.

5. Give examples of source documents and explain their general purpose.

6. Describe the process of posting.

7. List several examples of subsidiary ledgers. What is the purpose of subsidiary ledgers? How do they differ from the general ledger?

8. What is a control account?

9. Explain why reconciling is necessary in the traditional accounting architecture.

10. Describe the content and purpose of a "posting reference" column.

11. What is an audit trail? What purpose(s) does it serve?

12. Describe the audit trail in a traditional manual accounting system. For example, suppose you want to identify the items of equipment that are included in the balance for the "Equipment" account. How can you trace the balance in the "Equipment" account back to the individual transactions that form the balance?

13. How many accounts are in the general ledger? Explain your answer.

14. List the problems associated with dependence on human information processing and paper documents.

15. Why do some organizations continue to use both manual and computerized processing?

16. Does automating (i.e., replicating) traditional accounting processes solve the problems associated with manual accounting processing? Explain.

17. What is a view? Give three examples of a view.

18. What does "view-driven" mean?

19. How is focusing on business processes and events in designing information systems different from the traditional process of designing information systems?

20. List and explain each of the criticisms levied against the traditional accounting information architecture.

21. What is a balanced scorecard?

22. What is meant by the term data certification?

23. What is an information view?

24. Explain why systems designers have traditionally built multiple information systems within the same organization.

25. Compare and contrast the content of the data stored in accounting systems with data stored in non-accounting systems.

26. The chapter describes four characteristics of an event-driven architecture. Identify and explain each of the characteristics.

DISCUSSION QUESTIONS

1. Explain the difference in the data contained in the following: source documents, journals, subsidiary ledgers, general ledger.

2. Distinguish between an events-driven architecture and a view-driven architecture. Why does the chapter refer to the traditional accounting architecture as an example of a view-driven architecture?

3. Compare events-driven and traditional accounting system modeling. Specifically, do they seem to vary in terms of
   a. information customers they attempt to serve?
   b. assumptions about information customer's needs?
   c. objectives or goals of the resulting system?

4. Accounting specialties include financial accounting, auditing, cost/managerial accounting, and tax accounting. Does the traditional accounting system appear to facilitate one of the specialties more than the others? If so, could this hamper the ability of accountants to meet the objectives of providing useful information for all information customers who manage organizational operations?

5. Should accountants serve as information filters? What are the assumptions behind the accountant's role as an information filter?

6. What is an accounting transaction? How does it differ from a business event?

7. You have a friend who argues that if accounting processes were timely (performed in real time as business events occur) there would be no need for adjusting entries. Respond to her argument.

8. In governmental accounting, many entities want to measure the accomplishments of their programs by comparing the resources going into a program with the benefits flowing out. In fact, the Governmental Accounting Standards Board (GASB) has noted the limitations of general ledger structures for incorporating accountability measures and other critical data such as service efforts and accomplishments. Do you think the accounting system should help agencies measure the accomplishments of their service efforts, or do you think a separate system is needed? Justify your response.

9. Do Generally Accepted Accounting Principles (GAAP) mandate the use of general ledger–based accounting information systems? Explain your answer.

10. My accounts receivable subsidiary ledger lists the following customers:

Jane Fernin	$ 450.10
Marty Renquist	$1,451.60
Jeff Morton	$2,501.00
Rick Patterson	$ 994.70

The accounts receivable total in the subsidiary ledger is $5,397.40. However, the accounts receivable total in the general ledger is $5,947.80. Which of the two totals is correct? How would you go about identifying the error(s) in a traditional accounting system?

11. Refer to a sample trial balance where debits equal credits and the accounting system balances (in other words Assets = Liabilities + Equity). What is the purpose of a trial balance? What assurance does it provide for the organization? Which of the

following clerical errors would be revealed by developing a trial balance? Describe how the accounting system would normally identify the errors not revealed by developing a trial balance.

a. The accounting clerk posted the following adjusting entry to record depreciation for the year:

Depends on how much A/D

Accumulated Depreciation	$4,806	
Depreciation Expense		$4,806

b. The accounting clerk posted a $510 interest payment received from a note receivable as follows:

Interest Receivable	$ 610	
Cash		$ 610

c. The accounts payable clerk posted a $809 cash payment to a vendor when the goods were ordered (but not yet received) as follows:

Accounts Payable	$ 800	
Cash		$ 800

d. An accounts receivable clerk posted a $1,300 payment on account from a customer as follows:

Cash	$1,300	
Accounts Receivable		$1,330

e. The organization paid dividends and forgot to post any journal entry.

12. Select a friend who has an interest in business concepts, but is not an accountant. Without using the terms debits, credits, or chart of accounts, explain to him or her how to record a cash sale. Now explain, without using accounting jargon, why some accountants use debits and credits to represent transactions.

13. In Chapter 1, we presented comments Michael Hammer made about "reengineering" work. When organizations originally computerized accounting, did they "reengineer" or did they automate? Explain.

MINI-CASES AND OTHER APPLIED LEARNING

1. The Financial Accounting Standards Board (FASB) indicated that the traditional accounting information system design actually constrained standard setting in FASB Statement 95, "A Statement of Cash Flows." The Board received 450 comment letters, most from bank lending officers—accounting information users—who favored requiring the direct method for the cash flow statement. Corporation accountants, on the other hand, favored the indirect method due to excessive implementation costs. They appealed to the Board because they could not currently obtain gross operating cash receipts and payments directly from their accounting systems. The FASB decided to allow both the direct and indirect methods, largely due to design limitations of traditional accounting systems.

Required:

    a. Explain the limitations of the traditional accounting architecture that make it difficult to directly trace the cash flows of an organization.

    b. Did FASB respond properly to accounting's information customers? Justify your response.

2. An international corporation's acquisition of a fixed asset at one of their major production plants requires multiple systems and 45 days on average just to handle the record keeping activities. The multiple systems involved to record activities include:

- One system to handle all capital asset requests.
- A purchase order system used to select vendors and acquire (order) assets.
- A separate system to record the receipt of capital assets.
- A separate system to keep track of capital assets including original cost, location, and depreciation.
- The general ledger system.

Required:

Describe sample data possibly stored in each of the five systems. List as many instances as possible of duplicate data recording and processing.

3. Divide the class into seven project groups and assume the roles of the following individuals:

Group 1 Marketing Professional
Group 2 Production or Purchasing Manager
Group 3 Finance Professional
Group 4 Cost Accountant
Group 5 Financial Accountant
Group 6 Information Systems Manager
Group 7 Personnel Manager

Required:

Prepare a one-page summary of how your professional might respond if asked about the criticisms of traditional accounting systems that are presented in this chapter. Do you think your professional would agree or disagree with the criticisms stated? Defend your response.

4. Select a computerized general ledger package and analyze its features.

Required:

Compare the processing steps and data recorded with a manual accounting system architecture. When answering, consider the effect computerization had on the accounting cycle and on the types of documents used in a manual accounting system.

NOTE: To complete problems 5–9, your instructor must have ordered Arens and Ward, *Systems Understanding Aid* **or** *Systems Understanding Aid for Financial Accounting* **(Williamston, Michigan: Armond Dalton Publishers, 1990, 4th edition) for purchase from your bookstore. Complete the following in student project teams.**

5. Waren Distributing, Inc. has hired you as its accountant.

Required:

Complete the manual case set per the requirements on page 11 of the Instructions, Flowcharts, and Ledgers booklet.

6. Waren Distributing, Inc. has hired your project team to perform a general analysis of its manual accounting system.

Required:

a. Identify, summarize the contents of, and state the purpose(s) of all source documents, journals, and ledgers.

b. List the source documents, journals, and ledgers used in each cycle.

c. List and explain the origin, flow, and destinations of all source documents.

d. List and explain the various internal controls used by Waren.

e. Explain the time intervals of the steps in the various business cycles.

7. Waren Distributing, Inc. has hired your project team to perform a system analysis of its manual accounting system.

Required:

a. Chapters 3–6 of the *Systems Understanding Aid Reference* manual provide an overview of the controls used in a manual system. Review these controls to answer the following:

1. Concisely identify (label) the functions performed by each of the three Waren employees. Why have their duties been assigned this way? Identify three ways an employee might make an error or attempt to defraud the system and explain how each error or irregularity would be identified.

2. Cite two or three examples of proper authorization of transactions for the revenue cycle, expenditure cycle, and payroll cycle. For each example, explain how the authorizations are documented.

3. Explain the concept of independent checks on performance and its importance in a manual system. Cite two examples of independent checks on performance.

4. One internal control is the proper design and pre-numbering of documents and records. Why are documents pre-numbered?

b. Give examples and explain the use of three different methods of sequencing items in document files. What is the relevance of these methods?

c. For each cycle, explain which source documents are used to post directly to accounting journals.

d. Some documents that apply to the same transaction within the same cycle are attached together before filing. These documents represent part of the audit trail of a particular transaction. Describe the complete audit trail for the cash and sales balances listed on Waren's end-of-year financial statements.

e. Waren uses "special journals" to record routine transactions. What are the advantages of using this method over recording all transactions in a general journal? Which transactions would you record in a general journal? Since Waren uses journals and general ledgers, why do they need subsidiary ledgers?

f. Please explain the relative timing of posting data to the journals, subsidiary ledgers, and general ledger. What type of data is posted to the journals, subsidiary ledgers, and general ledger (e.g., document data, summary data from other records, etc.)? How often does Waren post to the general ledger? How is this posting documented?

g. Nancy Ford's initials are present on some ledgers. What process do they document? Should Adams perform this task? Explain.

h. Write a narrative to describe the process to locate a credit memo that has been previously issued to a specific customer.

i. Occasionally, Waren uses temporary files. Cite specific examples of these files and explain the business reason for their use.

j. Explain the coding scheme used in Waren's chart of accounts.

k. As of November 30, Waren's cash balance equaled $18,043.03. In the Cash general ledger, the letters "CR," "CD," and "PR" are repeated. What is the relevance of those letters?

l. Waren has decided to automate their accounting records as of the morning of December 26. Using the format of the Cash general ledger, show the proper calculation for their cash balance at that time.

8. Waren Distributing, Inc. has hired your project team to analyze its manual accounting system.

Required:

Use examples from the Waren system to illustrate each of the criticisms of traditional accounting system design noted in this chapter.

9. Ray Kramer recently decided that Waren Distributing should convert its accounting system to a computer driven system. Use a general ledger software package and the following December 199X trial balance to complete the conversion.

Waren Trial Balance
As of 24 Dec 199X

		Sub. Ledger	Debit	Credit
101	Cash		$ 34,778.15	
102	Accounts Receivable			17,529.00
	102.6 Bertram Appliance	$ 7,450.00		
	102.7 Fritter Appliance	4,560.00		
	102.8 Hanover Hardware	1,716.00		
	102.9 Reliance Electric	2,953.00		

	102.10	Saginaw Sales & Service	0.00	
	102.11	Okemos Housewares	850.00	
103		Allowance for Doubtful Accounts		$ 450.00
104		Merchandise Inventory	41,325.00	
105		Prepaid Expenses		
106		Marketable Securities		
107		Fixed Assets	14,766.00	
108		Accumulated Depreciation		2,745.20
201		Accounts Payable		0.00
	201.2	Chicago Office Supply	0.00	
	201.3	Super Electric Company	0.00	
202		Wages and Salaries Payable		
203		Federal Income Taxes Withheld		427.03
204		S.U.T.A. Payable		
205		F.U.T.A. Payable		
206		F.I.C.A. Payable		154.78
207		Federal Income Taxes Payable		
209		Notes Payable		
210		Interest Payable		
301		Capital Stock		20,000.00
302		Paid-In Capital		
303		Income Summary		
304		Retained Earnings		31,745.35
401		Sales		586,751.00
402		Sales Returns	31,430.00	
403		Sales Discounts	6,085.01	
404		Gain/Loss on Fixed Assets		
501		Merchandise Purchases	446,381.00	
502		Freight-In	8,511.00	
503		Purchase Returns		4,128.00
504		Purchase Discounts		7,937.85
505		Rent Expense	13,380.00	
506		Operating Expense	5,930.56	
507		Office Supplies Expense	3,702.72	
508		Depreciation Expense		
509		Wage and Salary Expense	27,853.91	
510		Payroll Tax Expense	2,666.86	
511		Federal Income Tax Expense		
512		Interest Expense		
513		Bad Debt Expense		
514		Cost of Goods Sold		
		Total	$ 654,339.21	$ 654,339.21

Required:

Using the general ledger software package:

a. Set up the necessary chart of accounts.

b. Enter the (December 24) trial balance amount for each account.

c. Enter the transactions for the last week of December.

d. Generate an income statement and balance sheet.

* Using some packages, you can omit the control account balances (accounts receivable and accounts payable) and enter only the subsidiary ledger amounts instead.

10. Dependability Inc. General Ledger Case

Dependability Inc. sells and scores questionnaires to companies to use primarily as an employment screening tool. The questionnaires measure a potential employee's dependability.

Customers who buy the questionnaires ask a job applicant to complete the questionnaire as part of the application process. They call the applicant's responses into Dependability's Analysis Center, using a toll-free number provided by Dependability Inc. Dependability's employees key the data into a computer. The results are immediately analyzed and a score is given to the customer. The customer uses the dependability score as part of the hiring decision.

Dependability Inc. has several part-time employees who work at the Analysis Center. Two employees are on duty at all times. They are not extremely busy, but experience shows that customer service is poor when only one employee is on duty. In addition to the part-time employees, there is one salesman (Joe D., considered a contract laborer) who is paid on a commission basis for questionnaires sold and scored, and one computer programmer/operator (Rebecca F.) who updates the computer programs to score the questionnaires and prepares customer month-end reports that summarize questionnaires scored during the month. Rebecca F. is paid as a contract laborer for the hours worked and amounts paid to her are recorded as Professional Fees.

The company is on a calendar year. Six months of operating data have been processed for 19X9. The account titles, account numbers, and account balances as of June 30, 19X9 are shown in Exhibit Dependability-1. Exhibits Dependability-2 through Dependability-5 show the subsidiary ledgers for accounts receivable, deposits/prepayments, accounts payable, and taxes payable.

During July the transactions contained in Exhibit Dependability-6 occurred. At July 31, an analysis shows that there were some payables that had not been recorded. Information about these are contained in Exhibit Dependability-7. Exhibit Dependability-8 contains some additional information about the company that you might find useful in advising management on their pricing policy.

Required:

a. Set up the accounting records of Dependability Inc. on a general ledger package. Enter the July transactions and required adjusting entries. Prepare financial statements at the end of July.

b. Management wants to know the minimum amount they can charge per questionnaire and still make money. They would like a recommended pricing structure with appropriate adjustments for quantity discounts. Also, one manager wants to know how much they have made on the Lightning contract. How would you determine this?

Exhibit Dependability-1
Trial Balance
June 30, 19X9

Account Number	Account Title	Debit	Credit
100	Cash	$ 53,564.54	
110	Accounts Receivable	18,660.80	
120	Deposits/Prepayments	1,170.00	
150	Capital Equipment	22,075.68	
160	Accumulated Depreciation		$ 22,075.68
200	Accounts Payable		4,458.20
210	Taxes Payable		668.88
300	Common Stock		300.00
310	Additional Paid-in Capital		2,700.00
320	Retained Earnings		38,007.48
400	Questionnaire Revenue		88,826.74
450	Interest Income		496.00
500	Telephone Expense	9,730.60	
510	Printing Expense	9,162.90	
520	Postage/Freight Expense	3,007.84	
530	Miscellaneous Expense	872.98	
540	Sales Commissions	3,000.00	
550	Travel Expense	52.00	
560	Professional Fees	8,835.20	
570	Wage Expense	22,193.28	
580	Rent Expense	2,500.00	
590	Payroll Tax Expenses	2,707.16	
	Total	$157,532.98	$157,532.98

Exhibit Dependability-2
Accounts Receivable—Subsidiary Ledger
June 30, 19X9

Invoice Number	Customer Name	Amount
290	Cyndees	$ 5,500.00
291	Lightning	1,965.00
292	Brickhouse	435.00
294	SoundsAlive	575.00
296	Lightning	2,670.00
297	Glassco	797.30
298	Brickhouse	790.00
299	Tracees	700.00
301	Brickhouse	75.00
302	Glassco	2,966.00
303	Fraziers	337.50
304	Brickhouse	50.00
305	Lightning	1,800.00
	Total	$18,660.80

Exhibit Dependability-3
Deposits/Prepayments
June 30, 19X9

Entity	Amount
US West	$ 670.00
AT & T	500.00
Total	$1,170.00

Note: These are deposits required to
install telephone services. However, this
account is also designed to include any
prepayments or deposits.

Exhibit Dependability-4
Accounts Payable—Subsidiary Ledger
June 30, 19X9

Supplier	Amount
Rebecca F.—Professional Services	$1,208.20
Lansdowne—June Rent	250.00
Joe D.—Sales Commission	3,000.00
Total	$4,458.20

Exhibit Dependability-5
Taxes Payable—Subsidiary Ledger
June 30, 19X9

Entity	Amount
State Tax Commission—Withholding	$ 162.30
Workers Compensation	70.00
Unemployment Fund	58.14
IRS—FICA & Fed. Withholding	290.94
State Tax Commission—Sales Tax	87.50
Total	$ 668.88

Exhibit Dependability-6
July Transactions—19X9

The following checks were written:

Date	Check Number	Payee	For	Amount
7	10131	Lansdowne	Rent for June–Oct.	$1,350.00
7	10132	Rebecca F.	Accounts Payable	808.20
7	10133	Federal Exp.	Postage/Freight	31.00
14	10134	Robert J.	Payroll	353.68
14	10135	Becky S.	Payroll	268.24
14	10136	Julianna G.	Payroll	315.12
14	10137	Stephanie F.	Payroll	341.58
14	10138	Bradley A.	Payroll	213.30
14	10139	Katherine C.	Payroll	242.94
25	10140	State Tax Com.	Taxes Payable	162.30
25	10141	Workers Comp.	Taxes Payable	70.00
25	10142	Unemploy. Fd.	Taxes Payable	58.14
25	10143	IRS	Taxes Payable	290.94
25	10144	State Tax Com.	Taxes Payable	87.50
28	10145	Federal Exp.	Postage/Freight	59.50
28	10146	AT&T	Telephone Expense	2,068.86
31	10147	Robert J.	Payroll	491.86
31	10148	Becky S.	Payroll	81.26
31	10149	Julianna G.	Payroll	425.44
31	10150	Stephanie F.	Payroll	374.46
31	10151	Bradley A.	Payroll	347.64
31	10152	Katherine C.	Payroll	252.20
31	10153	U.S. Sprint	Telephone Expense	82.04
31	10154	Federal Exp.	Postage/Freight	31.00

Note: The payment to AT&T is for telephone usage for the current month.

Note: The payroll payments recorded above are net of withholdings. The gross payroll, withholdings, and net pay are summarized below by payroll period. The amounts withheld from employees are recorded as Taxes Payable until they are remitted to the government agency.

Exhibit Dependability-6—continued
July Transactions—19X9

July 15, 19X9:

Employee	Gross	FICA	Federal Tax	State Tax	Net
Robert J.	$412.50	$31.56	$21.24	$6.02	$353.68
Becky S.	297.00	22.72	3.94	2.10	268.24
Julianna G.	360.24	27.56	13.40	4.16	315.12
Stephanie F.	396.00	30.30	18.78	5.34	341.58
Bradley A.	231.00	17.68	0.00	0.02	213.30
Katherine C.	264.00	20.20	0.00	0.86	242.94

July 31, 19X9:

Employee	Gross	FICA	Federal Tax	State Tax	Net
Robert J.	$605.00	$46.28	$50.12	$16.74	$491.86
Becky S.	88.00	6.74	0.00	0.00	81.26
Julianna G.	511.50	39.12	36.10	10.84	425.44
Stephanie F.	440.00	33.66	25.38	6.50	374.46
Bradley A.	404.24	30.92	20.00	5.68	347.64
Katherine C.	275.00	21.04	0.62	1.14	252.20

Exhibit Dependability-6—continued
July Transactions—19X9

The following invoices were prepared and mailed to customers:

Date	Invoice #	Customer	Amount
1	306	Peak	$5,850.00
10	307	Victory	470.00
10	308	SoundsAlive	575.00
12	309	Redeemer	364.00
12	310	Lightning	3,850.00
15	311	Glassco	1,340.00
15	312	Brickhouse	1,045.00

The following money was collected, by invoice, on the dates shown:

Date	Invoice #	Customer	Amount
1	299	Tracees	$ 700.00
15	291	Lightning	1,965.00
15	292	Brickhouse	435.00
15	294	SoundsAlive	575.00
15	297 & 302	Glassco	3,763.30
24	290	Cyndees	5,500.00
24	296	Lightning	2,670.00
24	303	Fraziers	337.50
24	306	Peak	5,850.00
31	308	SoundsAlive	575.00
31	298 & 301	Brickhouse	865.00
31	307	Victory	470.00

Exhibit Dependability-7
Adjusting Entry Information

1. Employer payroll taxes and payroll-related expenses (which are all recorded as Payroll Tax Expenses and Taxes Payable) are as follows:

   FICA & Medicare   7.65%

   Worker Compensation   .29%

   Unemployment—State   .5%

   —Federal   .8%

2. During the month Dependability Inc. had 20,000 questionnaires printed and mailed to various companies. Bills have been received for the printing and mailing, but they have not been paid by the end of the month. These are as follows:

Vendor	Amount
Print Services	$4,020.70
Mail Services	518.14

3. A bill has been received from Rebecca F. and Joe D. for Professional Fees and Sales Commissions, respectively:

Entity	Amount
Rebecca F.	$1,160.00
Joe D.	420.00

4. Part of the company's cash is in a money market account that earned interest during the month. The amount of interest earned was $166.66.

5. A telephone bill has been received from U.S. West for $248.78 but it had not been paid by the end of July.

Exhibit Dependability-8
Other Company Information

The number of questionnaires scored, by month, for the first seven months of 19X9 follow:

Month	Questionnaires Scored
January	1,292
February	1,574
March	1,746
April	2,346
May	2,896
June	3,540
July	3,824

The peak period of usage is during the latter part of the year as companies hire for the Christmas shopping season. Usage during September, October, and November is usually about 2 to 3 times the usage of January through April.

The Analysis Center is in a rented office. Rent until June was $500 per month. The first of June, the Analysis Center was moved into a new office, which only cost $250 per month. The rent payment during July was for the months of June through October.

The company buys telephone services from three suppliers; AT&T for the toll-free number, U.S. Sprint for outgoing long-distance calls, and U.S. West for the monthly access fee. The amount of the bill to AT&T is based on the number of calls received and the amount of time used.

The sales commission to Joe D. is 10% of questionnaire revenue on sales made by him. Not all companies using the product were contacted by Joe D.—several companies heard about the product from other companies and contacted Dependability Inc. directly. No sales commission is paid on these questionnaires.

The current price for each questionnaire varies between $7.80 and $11.50, depending on volume of usage and how successful the company was in negotiating with the client.

The Capital Equipment is primarily computer and telephone equipment. Even though it is fully depreciated, it is still reliable and adequate capacity for the next few years.

11. The past two decades have brought a proliferation of general ledger software packages and enterprise resource packages with various features, strengths, and weaknesses. Choose six accounting or enterprise resource packages (e.g., Peachtree, Great Plains Dynamics, Solomon, Platinum, BusinessWorks, AccPac, Oracle Financials, SAP, PeopleSoft, etc.). Obtain information about these six software packages either from their developer's website or from journal articles. Using the information you obtain, categorize each of the packages according to the continuum proposed by McCarthy, David, and Sommer.

Required:

 a. For each package, list the category (or categories if you believe a package overlaps two or more categories) in which you believe it best fits.

b. Explain which features of each package listed in (*a*) above caused you to categorize it as such.

c. Which categories on McCarthy, David, and Sommer's continuum are not covered by the software packages you examined?

d. Do you think any software packages exist that are in the categories mentioned in (*c*) above? Explain your speculation.

4

CHAPTER

Systems Analysis and Design of a Business Event–Driven System

CHAPTER OBJECTIVE

The objective of this chapter is to help you understand the key steps in analyzing and designing information technology (IT) applications.

INTRODUCTION

In Chapter 2 you learned that different views of an organization are merely different ways of looking at the organization's business activities. Chapters 2 and 3 illustrated the need to understand the business objectives and the organization's needs, rather than focus on a particular information view. In this chapter, we explain how to use the *REAL* business process model to analyze and design IT applications that support those responsible for defining and managing organization activities.

The material in this chapter is best learned by applying it. Therefore, we strongly encourage you to implement the concepts by using a software package of your choice.

ANALYSIS AND DESIGN OF A BUSINESS EVENT–DRIVEN IT APPLICATION

Designing quality IT applications requires a thorough understanding of the organization including its objectives, strategies, value chains, risks, and business processes.[1] Understanding an organization and the needs of its decision makers is the starting point for building

---

1 See Chapter 2 for a complete discussion of these concepts and how to gain this understanding.

effective information systems. The key to better information systems is not simply under-standing the *current* business operations and information processing, but understanding the organization's objectives and *desired* business processes. They serve as a guide to devel-oping systems objectives and requirements.

How do you move from a general understanding of the business to a detailed infor-mation systems design and implementation? As you might imagine, there are a variety of methods for analyzing and designing information systems. Our objective is to empower you with the analytical skills and philosophy needed to use any one of the available meth-ods and contribute insights that enhance the analysis and design process. We want you to understand how professionals move from a business need for information to creating the physical IT infrastructure that can provide that information. We will accomplish this by in-

E X H I B I T   4–1

Systems Development Process: Method One

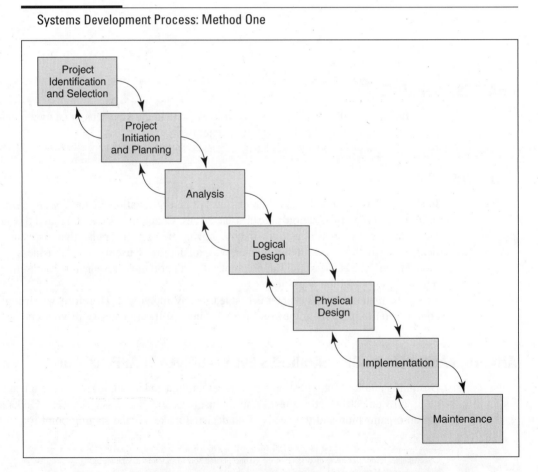

J. A. Hoffer, J. F. George, and J. S. Valacich, *Modern Systems Analysis and Design* (Reading, MA: Addison-Wesley, 1999).

troducing you to the steps of systems analysis and design and some of the variations in the analysis and design process.

To illustrate the variety of different systems analysis and design methods compare Exhibits 4–1 and 4–2. Exhibit 4–1 displays the steps of a systems analysis and design life cycle (SDLC) by J. A. Hoffer, J. F. George, and J. S. Valacich.[2] Exhibit 4–2 displays the systems development process presented by J. L. Whitten, L. D. Bentley, and V. M. Barlow.[3] There are other analysis and design approaches as well, including object-oriented analysis and design, prototyping, systems engineering, joint application design, participatory design, essential system design, and automating the SDLC using CASE tools. Each method has strengths and weaknesses and some companies use combinations of these methods. You need additional study in systems analysis and design, database design and management, and other topics to prepare yourself for a career as an information professional. In this text, we will introduce you to many of the key steps of systems analysis and design, but we will not provide an exhaustive study of the topic. We encourage you to take additional courses or undertake additional reading and self-study on these topics.

E X H I B I T   4–2

Systems Development Process: Method Two

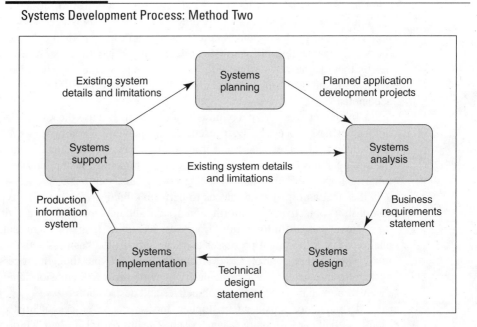

J. L. Whitten, L. D. Bentley, and V. M. Barlow, *Systems Analysis and Design,* instructor's ed., 3rd ed. (Burr Ridge, IL: Richard D. Irwin, 1994).

2 J. A. Hoffer, J. F. George, and J. S. Valacich, *Modern Systems Analysis and Design* (Reading, MA: Addison-Wesley, 1999).

3 J. L. Whitten, L. D. Bentley, and V. M. Barlow, *Systems Analysis and Design,* instructor's ed., 3rd ed. (Burr Ridge, IL: Richard D. Irwin, 1994).

This chapter introduces you to each of the following systems analysis and design phases, with emphasis on Phases I, II, and III:

logical models *physical models*

I. *The Analysis Phase*—determining systems requirements and structuring the requirements by creating process models, logical models, and conceptual data models.

II. *The Logical Design Phase*—developing the logical design of the database and designing forms, reports, interfaces, and dialogues.

III. *The Physical Design Phase*—designing physical files, databases, and programming instructions.

IV. *The Implementation and Maintenance Phase*—performing system coding, testing, installing, documenting, training users, supporting users, and maintaining the system.

PHASE I: SYSTEMS ANALYSIS

Step I-A: Defining Systems Requirements

After an organization has identified the need for a system project and has successfully made a business case to justify investing the time and funds necessary to undertake the project, a project team organizes and plans the work to be completed. The team considers the costs, benefits, feasibility, responsibilities, and project timeline. After completing these details they define the system requirements: What are the expectations of this system? What work and decisions will it support? What objectives will it help the organization to accomplish?

To answer these system requirement questions, we use the knowledge acquired during the business process analysis discussed in Chapter 2. Recall how we separated the operating and decision events from information processes. This enables you to think about the key operating and decision activities of the organization. In addition, you can determine the importance and value of each activity. Thus, your business analysis highlights the activities that an organization needs to perform effectively and efficiently in order to accomplish its objectives. An information system should support these activities.

Next, you add information processes, including data stores and data flows, to the analysis. The information processes and data support the business activities that management wants to plan, control, and evaluate. Do not limit your thought process to the current system environment. Consider the desired environment and envision innovative ways for the system to enable organization objectives and desired processes. *merchandise wholesale*

To illustrate, consider Christopher, Inc.'s revenue process. Christopher, Inc., provides baseball caps to major league baseball teams to sell in their ballparks. While analyzing their business process, Christopher's analysis team identified three key operating activities: receive orders from baseball teams (who are Christopher's customers), package and ship caps to the teams (the sale of merchandise), and receive payment from the teams. Exhibit 4–3 is a graphical *REAL* model of Christopher, Inc.'s key operating events, resources, agents, and locations that define the revenue process.

Christopher, Inc., *REAL* Model

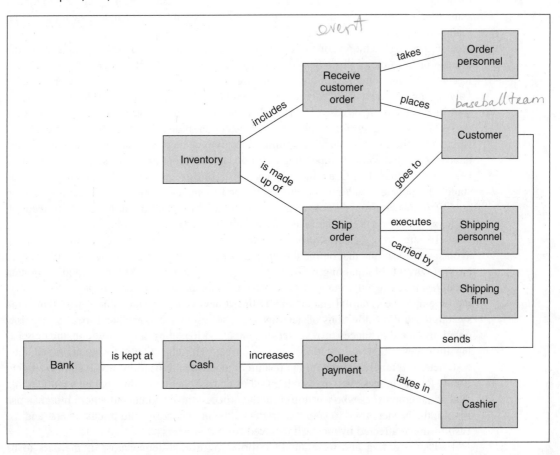

What processing instructions and data flows are necessary to support the operating and decision-making activities? When you strip away the complexities of an information system, you realize that it really includes two major components: (1) the data an organization chooses to record and maintain, and (2) the processing instructions used to record data, maintain data, and report useful information.

Generally, the workflow to support a business process involves three types of information events:

Recording operating event data.

Maintaining reference data about resources, agents, and locations.

Reporting useful information to information customers.

To plan a desired workflow that effectively and efficiently supports a business process you need to consider the data sources and destinations, the specifics of the information processing events, and the "route" data travels. To achieve this, you need to understand the operating event, decision need, or external stimulus that triggers each recording, maintaining, or reporting event.

Executing each operating event triggers the need to record descriptive data about the event. For example, a customer order of goods (an order event) triggers the need for a Record Customer Order information (recording) event. Recording operating event data involves capturing data about each operating event (e.g., time, participants, location, and resources involved). In the case of Christopher, Inc., part of the system requirements is recording each operating event: recording each customer order, recording each package and shipment to the customers, and recording each payment received from the customers. When data are captured while the operating event occurs, the recording process can execute business rules specified by management for each operating event. These rules are the guidelines, standards, policies, and/or procedures intended to increase operational and information quality by reducing such problems as errors, irregularities, and fraud. Ideally, the execution of the operating event and the related information process occur simultaneously.

To support a business process, a system must collect data about the resources, agents, and locations that define the operating events. The system must allow the data to be kept current. Maintaining reference data involves adding, deleting, or modifying data about resources, agents, and locations (e.g., changing products offered by a vendor; changing an employee's marital status; and adding a new vendor to the vendor list). Thus, the system must allow additions of new instances of resources, agents, and locations;[4] allow deletions of old instances of resources, agents, and locations, and allow updates to existing instances of agents, locations, and resources. The objective is to maintain accurate, complete, and timely data about the resources, agents, and locations involved in operating events for the process you are modeling. For Christopher, Inc., this includes maintaining data about employees who participate in the process, the customers to whom merchandise is sold, the carriers used to ship the products, the merchandise sold to customers, and the cash resource affected by the cash received from customers.

The recording and maintaining information events define most of the data to be stored in the system. The reporting information event generates outputs for interested parties. The reporting processes extract and convert stored data about events, resources, agents, and locations into information, and format the information for presentation to information customers. Reporting processes are used to generate views of the data to support people responsible for planning, executing, or evaluating the organization's performance. These views often consist of financial and performance measures and may take the form of hard-copy source documents, hard-copy reports, electronic data flows, or ad hoc queries. These data flows authorize actions, provide documentation to other business func-

---

4 An *instance* is one occurrence of an object. There are four types of objects: events, resources, agents, and locations. For example, one agent object is receiving clerks. One instance of receiving clerks is one individual employee, for example, Julie Esplin, who represents the organization in receiving payments from customers.

tions or to outside parties, and support both operational and strategic decision making. Data flows to information customers can be in a variety of forms like user-accessible data views on a computer screen, computer-generated data flows for electronic data interchange or electronic fund transfers, or the printing of hard-copy documents and reports.

The system for Christopher, Inc., should have the ability to create the data flows used by parties inside the company as well as data flows to communicate with parties outside the company. These data flows can take the form of electronic communications or paper documents and include data on customer orders, sales orders, shipments, sales invoices (billings), and customer payments. The system should also have the ability to generate standard reports (e.g., shipping analyses, sales figures, and timeliness of customer payments) as well as user-defined queries. Flexible system designs enable a large variety of user-defined system outputs.

conceptual logical physical model

Step I-B: Structuring Systems Requirements Using Process Modeling

Now that you have defined the work to be completed by a system, you begin to formalize that knowledge. In this step, analysts use process-modeling techniques to graphically represent the system requirements. Many analysts use data flow diagrams to graphically represent system requirements. An overview of data flow diagramming is presented in Supplemental Chapter A. (If you have not yet studied that material, we recommend you do so before proceeding.) Some analysis methods create several versions of data flow diagrams, including context data flow diagrams, data flow diagrams of the current physical system, data flow diagrams of the current logical system, and data flow diagrams of the proposed logical system. Often, each data flow diagram includes a thorough description of each data flow.

We will not focus on all of these data flow diagrams because several of them focus on the current system and current modes of information processing. We will focus on data flow diagrams of sample business event-driven systems.

To illustrate, let's continue with the Christopher, Inc., scenario. In their revenue process, Christopher, Inc., needs a system that enables communication with customers several times during the process (e.g., customers send in order data as well as payment data, and Christopher, Inc., sends back shipping, sales, billing, and payment data). Christopher, Inc., needs a system that allows them to send shipping data to their carriers and receive shipment confirmations from their carriers. Finally, Christopher, Inc.'s, systems should allow access by internal agents (such as management and other decision makers) to critical data and information.

How do we use all of our knowledge about Christopher, Inc., to graphically represent system requirements? One data flow diagram we could create is a *context diagram*—the highest level logical view of a system. As you will learn in Supplemental Chapter A, the circle represents computer processing (i.e., the execution of a group of computer instructions referred to as an *application*). Data flow diagrams use lines going into the circle to identify data recorded by the application and lines going out of the circle to identify output views provided by an application. Each of the flow lines (inputs and outputs) includes a label or name.

A context diagram shows a single high-level process, data flows, and the sources and destinations of the data that are *outside* the boundaries or scope of the system being analyzed. When creating a context diagram, you do not show the data stores and data flows *within* the boundaries of the system. Exhibit 4–4 shows a sample context diagram of Christopher's revenue process. Notice that the diagram gives a quick high-level overview of the major data flows into and out of the system by all parties involved. Also note how this diagram is consistent with the *REAL* model. The context diagram shows the external agents (customers and carriers) sending and receiving data flows. It illustrates the data flows to managers and other decision makers that do not directly participate in the business process, but require information about the process.

Since context diagrams are so high level and broad in scope, analysts often create more detailed data flow diagrams to show the processing modules that comprise the single process represented in the context diagram. For example, you could create a level 0 data flow diagram, as shown in Exhibit 4–5, to show the event processes (e.g., the customer order, packaging and shipping, and receipt of customer payment). A level 1 data flow diagram, as shown in Exhibit 4–6, provides details about each processing step included in the level 0 diagram (such as specific recording, maintaining, and reporting steps). You can continue to create more detailed data flow diagrams by taking each of these data flow diagrams and breaking the information processing steps into more minute detail.

As you create more detailed data flow diagrams, remember that each information process (recording, maintaining, and reporting) interacts with various data stores. Recording processes add record(s) to event data store(s), and refer to data stores for resources (the what), agents (the who), and locations (the where) associated with the event to verify and validate data collected about the operating event. For example, a Record Customer Order process might access an organization's order, product, customer, and salespeople data stores. Maintenance processes typically interact with individual data stores, because they are updating data about one specific agent, resource, or location. For example, a Maintain Customer Address process would access the customer data store. Reporting processes often interact with several data stores to generate desired outputs (e.g., a report of the hottest

E X H I B I T   4–4

Christopher, Inc., Context Diagram

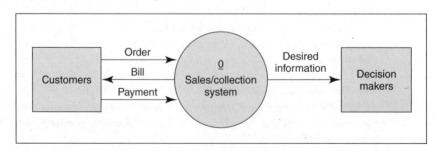

EXHIBIT 4–5

Christopher, Inc., Level 0 Data Flow Diagram

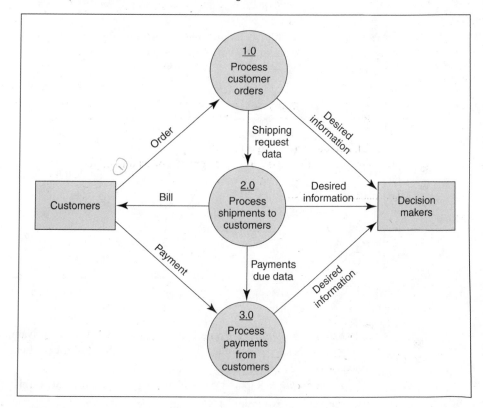

selling products sold last month in the Midwest region to customers over the age of 50 might draw from event data, customer data, and merchandise data).

Some analysts like to add more detail to context and other data flow diagrams, by providing the data elements that comprise the data flows on the diagram. We will refer to these data flow details as the *context dictionary*. Each entry in the context dictionary is separated from its definition by an equal sign (=) and is defined using the following set of symbols:

+   To connect elements of the definition

{ }   To identify repeating elements of the definition

For example, suppose you had a data flow diagram with five data flows: a sales invoice, a customer profile report, a product sales report, an accounting revenue query, and a sales-by-salesperson report. To clarify the details of the data flows, you could add the following context dictionary as a legend to the diagram:

EXHIBIT 4–6

Christopher, Inc., Level 1 Data Flow Diagram

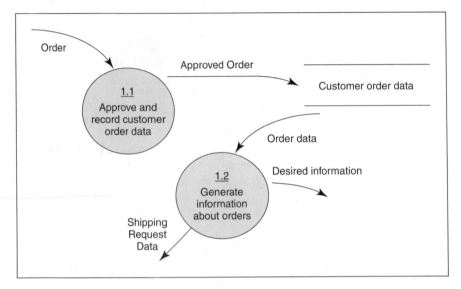

Sales-Invoice = Invoice # + Sale-Date + Register # + Customer Name + Salesperson Name + {Merchandise Name + Qty-Sold + Price + Item-Total} + Sale-Total

Customer-Profile = Report-Date + Name + State + Birth date + Telephone + {Merchandise Description + Qty-Sold}

Product-Sales = Report-Date + {Merchandise # + Merchandise Description + Qty-Sold + %Margin + $ Contribution}

Accounting-Revenue = Report-Date + Reporting-Period + Revenue for Reporting-Period

Sales-by-Salesperson = Report-Date + {Salesperson Name + {Merchandise-Description + Qty-Sold + $ Contribution} + Total Sales + Total Contribution

When you are creating data flow diagrams or work flows for a business process, how do you know how many recording, maintaining, and reporting processes you need for an IT application? You can use your *REAL* model and the context diagram as a guide.

♦ You need one recording process for *each* operating event object in the *REAL* model to collect data that describe and document the event.

♦ You need one maintenance process for *each* resource, agent, and location object in the *REAL* model to add, delete, or update data about each resource, agent, and location.

The number of reporting processes required for an application is a function of the number of perspectives or views required by information customers. At a minimum you will need one reporting process for each required output on the context diagram, but you should allow for ad hoc queries. Potential outputs include:

♦ Source documents: printed *or* electronic transmission of event data documentation.

♦ Preformatted reports: printed or electronic reports that are regularly used by information customers.

♦ Ad hoc, or user-defined, outputs: printed or electronic reports/queries/analyses that information customers design and request to provide a new view or a view that is rarely used.

Business event–driven IT applications are not bound to a particular set of views. Even relatively small IT applications can support several potential views. Maintain a customer service orientation and do not limit the number of potential reporting processes. Information needs change and the system must be flexible enough to provide a wide variety of views. For analysis and planning purposes, however, you should include all *needed* source documents and commonly used reports as shown on your context diagram.[5]

When using process-modeling techniques to create detailed models of a system, pay attention to detail and do not omit any important data flows or processing steps. These models are used to develop the logical models and the resulting physical system, and computers are only as complete and as effective as their instructions and data stores. In this age of high user expectations and desires for customized information, it is important to note that all possible output views are *not* restricted to views initially defined on the context diagram. When a data model is properly implemented, additional views are possible using ad hoc query tools. A flexible, comprehensive data repository can be used to generate a variety of views that were not anticipated during the modeling step—provided the data needed to generate a view are either stored in the data repository, or derivable from the data that are stored in the repository.

Step I-C: Structuring Systems Requirements Using Logical Models

After completing data flow diagrams that graphically show the flow of data to fulfill the system requirements, many analysts use logical models to represent the logic of the information processes denoted in the data flow diagram(s). Their objective is to produce structured descriptions and diagrams that enumerate the logic contained in each process denoted in the data flow diagram(s). Techniques used during this step include structured English, decision tables, decision trees, and state-transition diagrams or tables. We will overview the first of these techniques: Structured English.

Structured English is a code-independent way of communicating program logic. It is used to plan and document the steps of a computer instruction set (a program) without

---

5 Include only meaningful, useful reports. Do not include reports that an organization does not use, but simply generates because they have always had them. Also, carefully review paper source documents. In event-driven architectures, a goal of less paper is easily obtainable.

using a programming language. Structured English is used to define the detailed logic of each information process (see Exhibit 4–7). Unlike typical narrative descriptions, Structured English is a stripped-down version of English that focuses on conciseness and clarity to document the essence of an information process. Structured English eliminates:

Adjectives.

Adverbs.

Compound sentences.

Non-imperative expressions.

All but a limited set of conditional and logic structures.

Most punctuation.

Footnote type details.

So what is left? Structured English! Simply put, Structured English is a language that has a limited vocabulary and syntax. Structured English makes use of verbs (such as read, write, print, sort, move, merge, add, subtract, multiply, and divide). Nouns and noun phrases are used to describe data structures. The syntax of Structured English is usually re-

EXHIBIT 4–7

Structured English Example

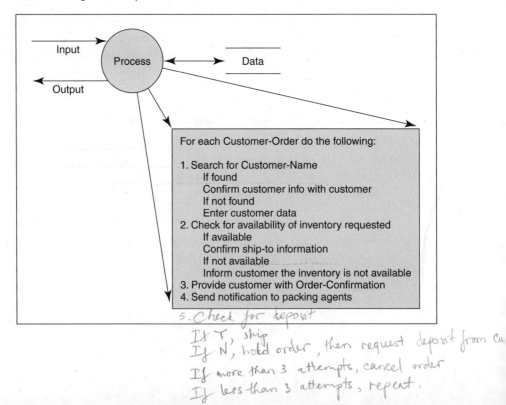

For each Customer-Order do the following:

1. Search for Customer-Name
    If found
    Confirm customer info with customer
    If not found
    Enter customer data
2. Check for availability of inventory requested
    If available
    Confirm ship-to information
    If not available
    Inform customer the inventory is not available
3. Provide customer with Order-Confirmation
4. Send notification to packing agents
5. Check for deposit
    If Y, ship
    If N, hold order, then request deposit from cu
    If more than 3 attempts, cancel order
    If less than 3 attempts, repeat.

stricted to three basic logic structures: sequence, choice, and repetition. By combining these three logical building blocks we can describe the details of any solution process and rules.

For example, suppose a processing step in a data flow diagram shows the need for computer instructions that search through customer files for people with birthdays in January. If a customer has a birthday in January, you want the computer to create a birthday card. If the customer's birthday is not in January, you want the computer to take no action. You want the computer to continue this search until all customer records are reviewed. Your Structured English instructions might look like:

> DO
> > READ customer records
> > BEGIN IF
> > > IF customer birthday month is January
> > > THEN GENERATE birthday card
> > > ELSE DO nothing
> > END IF
> UNTIL End of file

This is a great way for people who are not programmers to add value to this step in the analysis process. It also gives you a chance to think about the instructions that will ultimately result in programmed code.

In addition to including the logic for completing a desired task, this step provides an opportunity for thinking about ways information technology can be used to help reduce business and information risks.[6] Your processing instructions could include the logic necessary to reduce this risk. *Business event risk* results in errors and irregularities having one or more of the following characteristics:

> An operating event occurring at the wrong time or sequence.
>
> An operating event occurring without proper authorization.
>
> An operating event involving the wrong internal agent.
>
> An operating event involving the wrong external agent.
>
> An operating event involving the wrong resource.
>
> An operating event involving the wrong resource amount.
>
> An operating event occurring at the wrong location.

Information event risks include the risks associated with incomplete, inaccurate, or unauthorized recording, maintaining, and reporting information activities:

---

6 To reduce risks, you can include logic that helps detect, prevent, and/or correct errors and irregularities. Risks and controls are discussed in more detail in Chapter 5. Edit check logic is discussed in Supplemental Chapter D.

Recording risks include recording incomplete, inaccurate, or invalid data about an operating event. Incomplete data results in not recording all of the relevant characteristics about an operating event in the data stores. Inaccuracies arise from recording data that does not accurately represent the event. *Invalid* refers to data that are recorded about a fabricated event.

Maintaining risks are essentially the same as recording risks. The only difference is that the data maintained relate to resources, agents, and locations rather than operating events.

Reporting risks include data that are improperly classified, improperly summarized, provided to unauthorized parties, or not provided in a timely manner.

We have learned from experience that some students feel uncomfortable performing this step. Many of you have limited business experience, so how could you know the instructions a computer needs to effectively and efficiently support a business process? Frankly, the key to this step is to understand how an organization wants a business process executed. Experience and knowledge acquired during your business analysis (discussed in Chapter 2) are the keys to effectively completing this activity. To give you some idea of the processing steps involved in various tasks, refer to Tables 4–1, 4–2, and 4–3.

TABLE 4–1

Recording Instructions Sample Template
Used to Add Data to Event Data Stores

- This information process is triggered by the need to execute and document a business event. Invoke real-time business controls and verify that the organization activity adheres to prescribed business rules, policies, and business controls. (Access event, resource, agent, and location data stores as needed to perform these reviews.) Use edit checks and programmed business logic/rules to control the business risks associated with executing the business event.
- Collect event data from the data sources (e.g., the user, a source document, or electronic data communication).
- Invoke (real-time) information risk control. Check the data for accuracy, completeness, and validity. (Access the resource, agent, and location data stores that relate to this event to validate and verify data input.)
- If the input data does not meet the logic and control standards outlined, processing may be terminated. If processing continues, someone who is responsible for controls is notified of the exception. In some cases you may wish to allow someone to override controls. Any instances of overriding should also be communicated to the appropriate personnel.
- If the data are accurate, complete, and valid, processing continues according to the processing instructions, and data about the event are added to the appropriate event data store(s).

T A B L E   4–2

Maintaining Instructions Sample Template
Used to Update, Add, or Delete Resource, Agent, or Location Data

- This information process is triggered by the need to update data in a resource, agent, or location data store. Validate that the change is properly authorized and performed by an authorized user. Invoke real-time business risk control and verify that these changes adhere to prescribed business rules, policies, and controls. Use edit checks and programmed business logic/rules to control the business risks associated with executing the maintenance process. Access the resource, agent, and location tables needed to properly execute the update.
- Collect data from the data source(s) (e.g., the user, a source document, and electronic data communication).
- Invoke real-time information risk control. Check the data for accuracy, completeness, and validity. This step involves verifying that the individual or program attempting to modify the resource, agent, and location data adheres to prescribed business rules, business controls, and information controls.
- If the input data does not meet the logic and control standards outlined, processing may be terminated. If processing continues, someone responsible for controls must be notified of the exception. In some cases you may wish to allow someone to override a control. Any instances of overriding should also be communicated to the appropriate personnel.
- If the data are accurate, complete, and valid, they are processed (via any processing instructions) to update data fields in existing record(s), add new record(s), or delete record(s) in appropriate resource, location, or agent data stores(s).
- Since a maintenance program reflects a change in the status of an organization's resources, agents, or locations, it is often a good practice to initiate any needed action based on the change. For example, if an organization learns it can no longer purchase a certain inventory item for resale, it would be helpful to inform management about any back orders currently in the system for that inventory item. This could help the organization maintain good customer relations by providing them the ability to contact customers in a timely manner and suggest alternatives.

T A B L E   4–3

Reporting Instructions Sample Template
Used to Generate Queries, Documents, and Reports

- Access the user output request, along with any specifications or parameters. Validate that the user should have access to the requested information.
- Determine if a format is stored for the output. If so, access the format file. If not, allow the user to help specify a format or use a default format.
- Access necessary data from appropriate data stores (and process the data if necessary).
- Communicate the output to the screen, printer, or computer file and display it in the prescribed format.

Step I-D: Structuring Systems Requirements Using Conceptual Data Modeling

Thus far, we have discussed the process for determining what is required of an information system, techniques for representing the key processing steps of the desired system, and the data flows. Now it is time to focus on the specific data you want to capture to describe reality and generate needed outputs. We do this with a *conceptual data model*. Conceptual data models represent the entities or objects you want to collect data about, and rules about the meaning and interrelationships among these data objects.

To complete this step, most analysts use one of two modeling techniques: entity relationship (ER) or object oriented (OO). We use the ER technique in this book because we feel it is more suitable for introducing conceptual modeling to first-time modelers. However, we encourage you to learn more about OO methods as they are gaining prominence in systems analysis and design and are powerful for modeling business processes.

As the name implies, one of the key tasks involved in creating an ER diagram is to identify entities you want to collect data about. Often, *entities* are broadly defined as any person, place, object, event, or concept. For example, McFadden, Hoffer, and Prescott provide the following as examples of entities:[7]

Person: EMPLOYEE, STUDENT, or PATIENT

Place: STATE, REGION, or COUNTRY

Object: MACHINE, BUILDING, or AUTOMOBILE

Event: SALE, REGISTRATION, or RENEWAL

Concept: ACCOUNT, COURSE, or WORK CENTER

Each entity example cited above is often called an *entity group* or *entity type.* This is because each entity group represents a collection of individual entity *instances.* For example, Merchandise is an entity group. Individual instances of this entity type might include item 1, item 2, and item 3. Sales personnel is another example of an entity group. Sample instances might include salesperson 465 and salesperson 903. In our discussions throughout this text, we refer to an entity group when we use the term *entity*.

Entity types are represented on an ER diagram using a rectangle with an entity name inside.[8] The ER diagram also displays the relationships between entities. A *relationship* is an association between the instances of one or more entity groups of interest to the organization.[9] You denote relationships between entities by (1) drawing a line between the related entities with a diamond at the midpoint that is labeled with a semantic term that describes the relationship, or (2) drawing a line between the related entities with a semantic label that describes the relationship. Sound familiar? Time for us to confess that we have already introduced a portion of this step. If you review conceptual data models in various information systems texts, you will notice that the modelers are very broad in defining the

---

7 F. R. McFadden, J. A. Hoffer, and M. B. Prescott, *Modern Database Management* (Reading, MA: Addison-Wesley, 1999).
8 Some software tools, such as Oracle's Designer 2000, use rectangles with rounded ends.
9 F. R. McFadden and J. A. Hoffer, *Modern Database Management* (Menlo Park, CA: Benjamin Cummings, 1994), p. 128.

entities they include in a conceptual data model. In this chapter, we will once again use the work of Bill McCarthy to guide the creation of conceptual data models (as we did in Chapter 2 when we created graphical models of business processes). Thus, we will refine the definition of *entities* a bit and define them as operating events, and the resources, agents, and locations that are components of each operating activity. This allows you to use your *REAL* graphical model as the starting point for this step.

For traditional view-driven IT applications, conceptual data models focus on defining the structure of one or more *views* of the business. An event-driven data model uses the same notations as the view-driven data model, but the focus of the modeling effort is different. Rather than focusing on the various views of the organization, we focus on the *business activities* that compose the information represented in the views (the business processes).

As we discussed in Chapter 2, make sure you represent all the relationships between the entities in your model. This includes the relationships between each event and the corresponding agents, recourses, and locations; the relationships between the events; and the relationships between any resources, agents, and locations independent of an event occurring. The relationships in the *REAL* models you created in Chapter 2 can be refined. The model from Chapter 2 includes what we call binary relationships. *Binary relationships* are relationships between instances of two different entity groups. For example, an event (entity 1) is related to the resource (entity 2) affected by the event. Sometimes, analysts model recursive relationships (also known as *unary relationships*). A *recursive relationship* is the relationship between instances of a single entity group. For example, you could model a recursive relationship for the entity Employee, since an instance of the employee group manages one or more instances of the employee group. The graphical representation of a recursive relationship is illustrated in Exhibit 4–8. There is a third type of relationship, the *ternary relationship* that we will not discuss at this time.[10]

After you graphically represent the entities and relationships you want to include in a conceptual data model, you refine these relationships and use the results to guide the logical and physical design of your system. For example, if you plan to report data about an

E X H I B I T 4–8

Recursive Relationship Examples

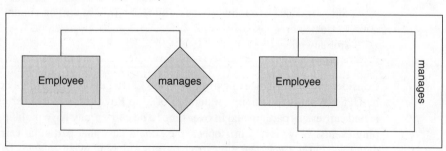

_____

10 A *ternary relationship* is a *simultaneous* relationship between three entity groups.

operating event, you must have the ability to link this event data with the data about the resources, agents, or locations involved in the event. To incorporate a complete, electronic audit trail into your information system, you also want the ability to link data stored about one event to data stored about the events that preceded and followed it.

Recognizing relationships among resources, events, agents, and locations is essential but is only a starting point. To link the data in your system, you must add precision to a model by defining the exact nature of the relationships. The business rules and characteristics governing the business process drive relationships between entities on a *REAL* model. Analysts use *cardinalities* to accomplish this task. The purpose of relationship cardinalities is to enrich our language for describing and more precisely representing business process rules. As the rules or characteristics governing the relationship change, so do the cardinalities.

Initially you may find the precision of defining cardinalities annoying, but with some blood, sweat, and a few tears, they become second nature. Without defining cardinalities, we cannot define the data structures used to store and link business data.

Relationship cardinalities have both maximums and minimums. To represent the minimum and maximum of relationship cardinalities we use the following notation:

Object 1   (minimum, maximum)——(minimum, maximum)   Object 2

Performing the following exercise derives the minimum and maximum placed beside object 1. Select one instance of object 2 (at random). Find the minimum number of instances of object 1 that are related to that one instance of object 2. Record it as the minimum cardinality next to object 1. Next, find the maximum number of instances of object 1 that are related to that one instance of object 2. Record it as the maximum cardinality next to object 1.

Repeating the exercise with a slight change derives the minimum and maximum cardinality placed beside object 2. Select one instance of object 1 (at random). Find the minimum number of instances of object 2 that are related to that one instance of object 1. Record it as the minimum cardinality next to object 2. Next, find the maximum number of instances of object 2 that are related to that one instance of object 1. Record it as the maximum cardinality next to object 2.

Have we adequately confused you yet? Let's practice using some relationships from Christopher, Inc., First let's examine the relationship between the Carrier agent entity and the Ship Product to Customer event entity.

Ship Products   (minimum, maximum)——(minimum, maximum)   Carrier (for
to Customer   any one Ship
(for any one   Products to
carrier)   Customer)

Consider any one instance of carrier from the Carrier entity group (e.g., one instance might be UPS). What is the minimum number of Ship Products to Customer events that the selected carrier has participated in over time? The carrier may have participated in zero shipping events. Why zero? Christopher, Inc., could have that particular carrier listed in their data files, but not yet used the carrier for any shipping event to date. This is possible because selecting a carrier and recording it in the database occurs before a shipment is made.

What is the maximum number of Ship Products to Customer events that the selected carrier has participated in over time? It could be 1, 2, 3, or thousands. We call this *many* and will use a * symbol to represent *many*. Thus our first set of cardinalities is:

Ship Products to Customer (for any one carrier)	(0, *)——(minimum, maximum)	Carrier (for any one Ship Products to Customer)

Let's get the second set of cardinalities. Consider any one instance of Ship Products to Customer from the Ship Products to Customer entity group (i.e., one instance is a single shipment of products). What is the minimum number of carriers that participate in a single occurrence of the Ship Products to Customer event? Christopher uses at least one carrier for each shipment. What is the maximum number of carriers that participate in a single occurrence of the Ship Products to Customer event? From our investigation, we find that Christopher, Inc., uses only one carrier for each shipment event. Thus our second set of cardinalities is:

Ship Products to Customer (for any one carrier)	(0, *)——(1,1)	Carrier (for any one Ship Products to Customer)

Getting better? Hold on and let's try a few more examples. Cardinalities are used to represent all relationships: event to resource, event to agent, event to location, event to event, agent to agent, resource to agent, and so on. Let's examine the relationship between two events in the Christopher, Inc., business process:

Ship Products to Customer	(minimum, maximum)——(minimum, maximum)	Receive Customer Payment

The cardinality between two event entities (e.g., Ship Products to Customer and Receive Payment from Customer) can describe the business rules governing two events. For example, let's suppose Christopher, Inc., requires customers to pay in full before anything is shipped and the entire order is delivered in one shipment. In addition, assume Christopher, Inc.'s customers are required to pay for each shipment separately. To get your first cardinality set, consider any one instance of Receive Customer Payment from the Receive Customer Payment entity group (one instance is a single payment for one order). What is the minimum number of Ship Products to Customer events that are related to any one Receive Customer Payment event? Zero. Christopher, Inc., requires payment before the shipment occurs. What is the maximum number of Ship Products to Customer events that are related to any one Receive Customer Payment event? One. Christopher, Inc.'s customers are required to pay for each shipment separately. Thus our first set of cardinalities is:

Ship Products to Customer	(0,1)——(minimum, maximum)	Receive Customer Payment

Now the second set of cardinalities. Consider any one instance of Ship Products to Customer from the Ship Products to Customer entity group (one instance is one shipment of products). What is the minimum number of Receive Customer Payment events that are related to any one occurrence of the Ship Products to Customer event? One. Christopher, Inc., requires payment before the shipment occurs. Notice how the minimum cardinality identifies the order of the events. A "1" on the minimum side of the cardinality indicates the object that comes first. What is the maximum number of Receive Customer Payment events that are related to any one occurrence of the Ship Products to Customer event? One. Christopher, Inc.'s customers are required to pay for each shipment separately. Thus our second set of cardinalities is:

Ship Products to Customer   (0, 1)——(1, 1)   Receive Customer Payment

Different business rules and policies affect the minimum and maximum cardinalities. Therefore, when a business rule or policy changes, you must update your cardinalities. This update can affect the composition and processing of your IT application, so use care when representing cardinalities. A subtle difference in a cardinality equation communicates a drastically different business process.

To illustrate, let's examine the same two event groups for Christopher, Inc., but change the business rules. What if Christopher, Inc., allowed customers to receive shipments on credit, and pay for several shipments in full with a single payment?

To get your first cardinality set, consider any one instance of Receive Customer Payment from the Receive Customer Payment entity group. What is the minimum number of Ship Products to Customer events that are related to any one Receive Customer Payment event? One. In this case we will assume that the customers do not prepay, but pay after the shipment occurs. What is the maximum number of Ship Products to Customer events that are related to any one Receive Customer Payment event? Many. Christopher, Inc.'s customers sometimes pay for several shipments with a single payment. Thus our first set of cardinalities is:

Ship Products to   (1, *)——(minimum, maximum)   Receive Customer
Customer   Payment

Now the second set of cardinalities. Consider any one instance of Ship Products to Customer from the Ship Products to Customer entity group. What is the minimum number of Receive Customer Payment events that are related to any one occurrence of the Ship Products to Customer event? Zero. Christopher, Inc., allows credit sales; thus they often ship before receiving payment. What is the maximum number of Receive Customer Payment events that are related to any one occurrence of the Ship Products to Customer event? One. In this case, we will assume that customers must pay for a single shipment in full with a single payment. Thus our second set of cardinalities is:

Ship Products to Customer   (1, *)——(0, 1)   Receive Customer Payment

Seems you are still with us, so let's push our luck and try one more example of changing the assumptions for two related entities. Suppose Christopher, Inc., decided to allow customers to receive shipments on credit, pay for several shipments with each payment, and make partial payments on shipments.

To get your first cardinality set, consider any one instance of Receive Customer Payment from the Receive Customer Payment entity group. What is the minimum number of Ship Products to Customer events that are related to any one Receive Customer Payment event? One. In this case we assume that the customers do not prepay but pay after the shipment occurs. What is the maximum number of Ship Products to Customer events that are related to any one Receive Customer Payment event? Many. Christopher, Inc.'s customers sometimes pay for several shipments with a single payment. Thus our first set of cardinalities is:

Ship Products to   (1, *)———(minimum, maximum)   Receive Customer
Customer   Payment

Now the second set. Consider any one instance of Ship Products to Customer from the Ship Products to Customer entity group. What is the minimum number of Receive Customer Payment events that are related to any one occurrence of the Ship Products to Customer event? Zero. Christopher, Inc., allows credit sales; thus they often ship before receiving payment. What is the maximum number of Receive Customer Payment events that are related to any one occurrence of the Ship Products to Customer event? Many, since customers often make partial payments on shipments. Thus our second set of cardinalities is:

Ship Products to Customer   (1, *)———(0, *)   Receive Customer Payment

Take a moment and consider the minimum cardinalities for these two entities. Ship Products to Customer has a minimum of one and Receive Customer Payment has a minimum of zero. What is the significance of these minimum cardinalities? Analysts often refer to the minimum cardinalities to determine whether an entity is mandatory or optional. An entity with a one minimum cardinality is often referred to as *mandatory,* while an entity with a zero minimum cardinality is often referred to as *optional.* In this case, an instance of Ship Products to Customer is mandatory while a corresponding instance of Receive Customer Payment is optional. When you are reviewing the minimum cardinalities of two related events, the minimum cardinalities can provide information about which event occurs first (i.e., the mandatory entity). If you are reviewing the minimum relationships between two other entity sets (such as a resource and an event, or an agent and an event), the minimum cardinalities reveal which entity is required or mandatory. For example:

Ship Products to Customer   (0, *)———(1,1)   Carrier

This reveals that an instance of Carrier must exist for Ship Products to Customer event to occur.

Hopefully, you are beginning to see how cardinalities affect what you expect to find in your resulting information system. Many people overlook the power of cardinalities as a tool to understand electronic audit trails, as well as the logic that should appear in information system processing instructions. The cardinalities represent how a business desires its business activities to occur; your information system should reflect this reality. To illustrate, put yourself in the role of an auditor who is collecting evidence and trying to determine whether business rules were followed. If you knew the following cardinality represented a desired business policy, would you expect to discover instances where shipments were executed and recorded in the information system prior to receiving a cash receipt?

Ship Goods to Customer   (0, 1)———(1, *)   Receive Payment from Customer

No. The audit trail should show the occurrence of a cash receipt prior to shipping the goods. How many cash receipts would you expect to find for any shipment? You could find many.

Lest you think we are finished with cardinality examples, let's practice using an example that illustrates how cardinalities are very dependent on the definition of the entity groups and instances included in a conceptual data model. This is important, yet a difficult concept for some students.

Consider two related entities: Merchandise and Ship Products to Customers. Christopher, Inc., sells baseball caps. They do not uniquely identify each baseball cap as an instance in their Merchandise entity group. Rather they consider an instance of Merchandise as one type or group of baseball caps (e.g., they consider all size 7 Atlanta Braves caps as one instance, all size 7½ Pittsburgh Pirate caps as one instance, and so on.)

Using this information, consider any one instance of Merchandise from the Merchandise entity group. What is the minimum number of Ship Products to Customer events associated with a single instance of Merchandise? Zero. The merchandise category must exist before it can be shipped. Christopher, Inc., may have some types of caps they have not yet sold and shipped. What is the maximum number of Ship Products to Customer events that involve the selected merchandise instance? Many—could be 1, 2, 3, or thousands. Remember an instance is not a single cap in this case, but a type or category of cap. Thus our first set of cardinalities is:

Ship Products to Customer   (0, *)———(minimum, maximum)   Merchandise

Now the second set of cardinalities. Consider any one instance of Ship Products to Customer from the Ship Products to Customer entity group. What is the minimum number of Merchandise instances that are involved in a single occurrence of Ship Products to Customer event? One, or there really is no need for a shipment! What is the maximum number of merchandise instances that are involved in a single occurrence of the Ship Products to Customer event? Many. A shipment could include several cap types. Thus our second set of cardinalities is:

Ship Products to Customer   (0, *)———(1, *)   Merchandise

What if resources are uniquely identified (e.g., large appliances, automobiles, or computers)? In this case, each instance of the Merchandise resource refers to one specific merchandise item.

Suppose Christopher, Inc., sells new automobiles. Consider any one instance of Merchandise from the Merchandise entity group. In this case one instance of Merchandise is a particular automobile with a unique vehicle identification number. What is the minimum number of Ship Products to Customer events that involve the selected merchandise instance? Zero. The automobile must exist before it can be sold and shipped and Christopher,

Inc., may have some cars they have not yet sold. What is the maximum number of Ship Products to Customer events that involve the selected merchandise instance? One. A new car should only be sold once. Thus our first set of cardinalities is:

Ship Products to Customer   (0, 1)———(minimum, maximum)   Merchandise

Now the second set of cardinalities. Consider any one instance of Ship Products to Customer from the Ship Products to Customer entity group. What is the minimum number of Merchandise instances involved in a single occurrence of Ship Products to Customer event? One, or there really is no need for a shipment. What is the maximum number of Merchandise instances that are involved in a single occurrence of the Ship Products to Customer event? Many, unless Christopher prefers to separate the sale and shipment of each car and make it a separate event. In that case, the maximum would be one. Thus our second set of cardinalities using the first assumption (i.e., multiple cars shipped during a single shipment event) is:

Ship Products to Customer   (0, 1)———(1, *)   Merchandise

When you model, always include the most instances that could occur (in both the minimum and maximum columns). If you model the higher order cardinalities, it allows your IT application to handle lower order cardinalities. For example, if you build a system using the relationship: _Sale but donot have merchandise in stock_

Sale   (0, *)———(1, *)   Merchandise

The information system can also handle:

Sale   (0, *)———(1, 1)   Merchandise

The first case denotes a sale with a maximum of many merchandise items, while the second case assumes only one item is sold during each sale. If you model the first case, your IT application can process the second case. If you model the second case, your IT application will need adjustment to enable correct processing of the first case.

Hopefully you are beginning to see that relationship cardinalities are powerful tools for representing management's policy governing operating events and processes. Later, we will use the cardinalities to define the data structures that store the business data. To help you practice what you have learned, Exhibit 4–9 displays a sample conceptual data model for Christopher, Inc., with cardinalities.

Before we leave cardinalities, we feel it is important to share some news. The world of systems analysis and design is not standardized. This means there is more than one way to perform or document any task. Recall that there are at least two different sets of symbols used in data flow diagramming. Chapter 2 discussed how some semantic models use a diamond to denote relationship labels while others do not. It should not surprise you that there are multiple notation sets for cardinalities. Exhibit 4–10 presents several pairs of notations that represent the same cardinality. On the left side of the exhibit the minimum cardinalities are represented with a 0 or a 1 on the left side on the relationship line and the maximum cardinalities follow to the right on the relationship line using 1 or an *. The

EXHIBIT 4–9

Christopher, Inc., *REAL* Model with Cardinalities

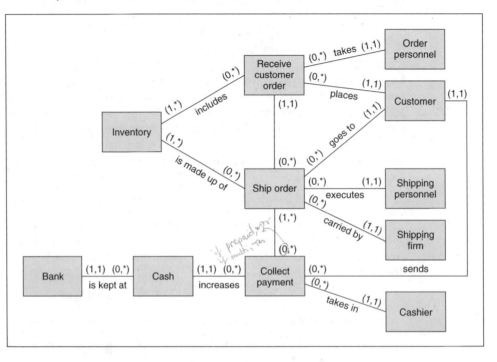

same relationships are shown on the right side of the exhibit using different notation. A minimum of zero is a circle around the line; a minimum or maximum of one is a 1 through the line; and "crow's feet" on the relationship line represent a maximum of many. Which is right? All of them. Choose a representation method and use it consistently throughout any project. Make sure you understand the concepts well enough so you can move from one technique to another with some ease.

If knowing that people use different notations to represent the same concept is not enough to make you scream in the night, the following might. Some authors and analysts use a technique that represents cardinality sets using a mirror image of the sets presented in this text. For example,

Sale   (0, *)———(1, 1)   Merchandise

would be represented as:

Sale   (1, 1)———(0, *)   Merchandise

Now you can understand how frustrating it is to present an overview of systems analysis and design without overwhelming you. Because there is no standard notation for cardinalities, we have selected one notation method and used it consistently throughout the text.

E X H I B I T 4–10

Different Notation to Represent Relationship Cardinalities

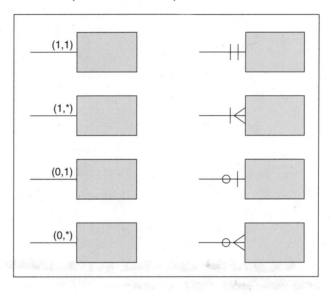

At this point in creating a conceptual data model, you have identified entities, identified the relationships between entities, and represented the nature of the relationships using cardinalities. Is your model complete? Many analysts would say no. Some analysts add entity attributes to their conceptual data model. An *entity attribute* is a property or characteristics that describe an entity. For example, attributes of the entity Student might include student ID number, Social Security number, last name, first name, street address, city, state, zip, and phone number. If you chose to represent attributes on your conceptual data model, the attributes are represented as labeled ovals, with lines connecting them to the corresponding entity group. Exhibit 4–11 presents an example of attributes for the Inventory entity.

Although you may feel we have overwhelmed you with details about conceptual data modeling, we have not come close to teaching you everything necessary to gain a deep understanding of conceptual data modeling. If you are interested in learning more about conceptual data models as they relate to systems analysis and design and/or database analysis and design, we would strongly encourage you to enroll in additional courses (or undertake self-study). You will find that the introduction we give in this chapter will serve you well in taking such a class but there is much more to learn.

Step I-E: Selecting a Design Strategy

During this step, systems analysts consider the various hardware, software, processing modes, and so on, that will be most effective and efficient in designing a system that fulfills the stipulated requirements.

Entity Attributes in an ER Diagram

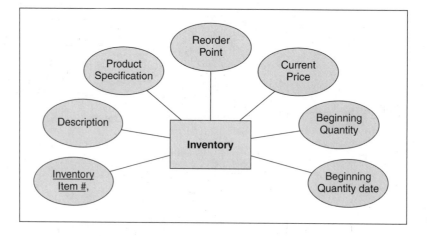

The concepts presented in this text are not dependent on a particular system design method or implementation technology. The architecture guiding these concepts can be implemented using a variety of technology platforms (both hardware and software). In fact these concepts have been implemented in organizations of all sizes using a variety of technologies. Although some development software has advantages over others, there is nothing inherent in the concepts presented in this text that is dependent on one particular type of technology.

Frankly, we will avoid a discussion of specific technology tools at this point because we want you to focus on thinking about the potential of information systems, rather than worrying about the trade-offs necessary for specific types of technology.

In this text, we illustrate how to build a business event-driven architecture using relational database technology. We chose relational database technology because of its availability and ease of use. For those already familiar with other implementation tools (e.g., C++, SmallTalk, Visual Basic, or ObjectVision), the specifics of how the data are structured may be different, but the basic nature of the concepts and the implementation steps presented in this chapter are the same. Common to all products is the requirement that you know how you want data structured and understand how you need to develop the recording, maintaining, and reporting processes. We believe the key to analyzing and designing the system is the knowledge of the business, not the particular technology used.

PHASE II: LOGICAL DESIGN

The work performed in Phase I provides an understanding of the processing requirement and data necessary to enable a system to fulfill its requirements. The logical design phase moves the analyst closer to actually creating the system's data stores and processing instructions.

Typically, the logical design phase involves several major components including designing forms and reports, designing interfaces and dialogues, and designing databases using logical data modeling techniques. In this chapter, we focus primarily on one portion of this phase, logical data modeling.

We use the conceptual data model as the guide to create logical models that we eventually use to create physical database objects. The challenge in defining an application's data repository is making sure the structure of the repository properly reflects the nature of the business process. If the structure does not reflect the business processes, IT is unable to enforce business rules and capture the appropriate business data. Defining data structures is yet one more step in using business rules to define the nature of the IT application. Although we use some IT terms, remember we are simply describing business rules and processes.

There are several logical modeling alternatives for structuring a data repository. Some details about the alternatives are available in Supplemental Chapter C. Without getting into a discussion of which structure is optimal, we describe how to translate a *REAL* model with cardinalities into a relational database structure.

The fundamental building block for relational database structures is a relation that will eventually become a table in a relational database. A *table* is a two-dimensional array having columns and rows. It is similar to a two-dimensional spreadsheet. Each column or field of a table is called an *attribute,* and each row of the table is called a *record.* Exhibit 4–12 shows an example of a table named CUSTOMER with sample data instances.

As you develop data structures, consider the role of the data relation; they will be used to create the data tables—the data sources and destinations used during application processing. The data tables will contain the recorded and maintained data that describe the essential components of an organization and its activities. These data will then be used to report information about and measurements of organization events, resources, agents, and locations. The event data tables will serve as the repositories for documenting the details about operating events. Thus, event data tables store transaction data—the information on source documents in traditional systems. Event data tables are much like expanded information age journals; they do not require the summarization and loss of detail required to record traditional accounting transactions. All the detailed documentation of business

E X H I B I T   4–12

CUSTOMER TABLE					
Customer #	**Last Name**	**First Name**	**Street Address**	**City**	**State**
1001	Bonds	Barry	25 Out of Here Blvd	San Francisco	CA
1002	Mays	Willie	24 Say Hey Avenue	Brooklyn	NY
1003	McGwire	Mark	62 Homerun Alley	St Louis	MO

activity data is available in the event data stores. Each instance in an event data table will include data about a separate event.

The resource and agent data tables include more updated and expanded information than the subsidiary ledgers of the traditional systems. Each resource data table includes data describing a corporate resource with a record for each instance of the resource. For example, an organization might have a resource data table for fixed assets, and each record will include data about a particular fixed asset or a fixed asset type. Each agent data table record will provide information about an internal or external person or entity (such as an employee, a project group, a customer, or a vendor) that participates in operating events.

The following describes the steps involved in defining a logical database design using relational database concepts.

Identify the Needed Relations

The first task in defining logical data structures is deciding how many relations are needed within the logical data repository. This decision is greatly simplified by reviewing the *REAL* conceptual data model and applying the following rule:

> *Each entity object (event, resource, agent, and location) in the* REAL *model becomes a relation.*

When you take the entities from your conceptual model and represent them in your logical model, this is called *mapping* (i.e., you map your entities into relations). If your data model had only the following objects:

Ship products to customers   (0, *)——(1, *)   Merchandise

You would have the following relations:

SHIP

MERCHANDISE

Identify the Key Attribute for Each Relation

Once relations have been identified, define the *key attribute,* or primary key, of each relation. The key attribute is the attribute that will uniquely identify each row of a table. You may have more than one attribute to choose from, and we refer to each of these as *candidate keys.* However, not every attribute of a relation can serve as the key attribute. For example, in the CUSTOMER table, the Last Name attribute would probably not work as the key attribute because many customers could have the same last name. City would probably not work because many customers could reside in the same city. Some attributes of customer could serve as key attributes but are difficult to manage using today's IT. For example, a customer's fingerprint, DNA pattern, retina pattern, or voiceprint might serve as a key attribute. Although each of these are possible candidate keys, some organizations find them fairly expensive to use with today's IT.

Until an object's inherent characteristics (e.g., a customer's fingerprint, DNA pattern, retina pattern, or voiceprint) can be used as key attributes, we create key attributes for each relation. Make sure each key attribute uniquely identifies each instance in an object relation. For example, you can create and assign a unique Customer # to each customer; assign a unique, sequential number to each event, and so on. To document the attributes (fields) included in a relation, include the attributes within parentheses after each relation name. The key attribute is listed as the first attribute and is underlined. Using the same data model and relations identified above, we can add the following key attributes:

SHIP (<u>Shipment #</u>,

MERCHANDISE (<u>Merchandise #</u>,

Linking the Relations

At this point you have identified separate relations that will become tables to house data about resources, events, locations, and agents, but you have not yet represented the relationships in the *REAL* model within your logical design. Therefore, the relations are not yet an accurate representation of the business, as represented in your conceptual data model. Unless your logical design includes a way to link data about the various entities, the resulting system cannot accurately store and report data about operating events and processes, and will not enforce the business rules defined during *REAL* modeling.

So how do you include the ability to link data about different entities in a logical model? For example, how will you link data about sales events and the salespersons and customers who participated in the sales? When you use the relational logical design, you link relations by placing the key attribute of one entity into the relation of the related entity. We refer to key attributes that are placed in another relation as *foreign keys* or *posted keys*. The sole purpose of foreign keys is to link relations so that the resulting relational tables can be used collectively to store business data and to generate useful information. The synergy created by linking the relations is a perfect example of the whole (the linked relations) being greater than the sum of the parts (the individual relations).

But which keys do you post, and where? There are rules that guide the linking of relations in the relational logical model. These rules are implemented by referring to the *maximum* cardinalities between two entities, as represented in your conceptual data model.

Linking Objects with Many-to-Many (*:*) Maximum Cardinality Relationships   The rule for linking objects with maximum cardinalities of many to many is:

Create a separate relation that includes the key attributes from both entity relations.

For example, the following relationship cardinality:

Ship products to customers   (0, *)———(1, *)   Merchandise

would be represented using the following relations:

SHIP	(Shipment #,
MERCHANDISE	(Merchandise #,
SHIP-MERCHANDISE	([Shipment #], [Merchandise #],

We use brackets ([ ]) to designate the Shipment # and Merchandise # as foreign keys in the SHIP-MERCHANDISE relation. Notice the Shipment # and Merchandise # combined also serve as the key attribute of the relation and are designated as such by underlining. We will elaborate on this later in the chapter.

Linking Objects with One-to-Many (1:*) or Many-to-One (*:1) Maximum Cardinality Relationships   The rule for linking objects with maximum cardinalities of 1 to many (or many to 1) is:

> *Post the key attribute of the object with the 1 side of the cardinality into the relation of the many (*) side of the cardinality.*

For example, the following relationship cardinality:

$$\text{Ship} \quad (0, *) \text{——} (1, 1) \quad \text{Customer}$$

would be represented using the following relations:

SHIP	(Shipment #, [Customer #],
CUSTOMER	(Customer #,

Once again, we use brackets ([ ]) to designate the Customer # as a foreign key in the SHIP relation.

The relationship between two event objects in a *REAL* model identifies the sequence of the events and impacts the creation of an electronic audit trail. When applying linking rules to relationships between two events, you may need to make an exception to enhance IT security. The exception occurs when you would normally post the primary key of the event that occurs second into the relation of the event that occurs first. Following the standard rule would leave a blank field in the first table and require the table to be subsequently opened to add the additional data as the business process occurs and data about the process are recorded. To prevent this, *create a separate relation that includes the key attributes from both event relations as was done with the many-to-many relationship.*

To illustrate, let's look at the following relationship between Order and Ship.

$$\text{Order} \quad (1, *) \text{——} (0, 1) \quad \text{Ship}$$

Normally, to link the two event relations you would simply place the key of Ship in the ORDER relation:

ORDER	(Order #, [Shipment #],
SHIPMENT	(Shipment #,

However, the Order event occurs before the Ship event in this case. The problem with the ORDER relation is that it has a very undesirable characteristic. Whenever a new ORDER record is created, we must leave the Shipment # blank because the order occurs before the shipment. Without going into all the reasons why this is undesirable, let us just say it complicates the process of capturing SHIPMENT data and also creates some unnecessary risk and control problems.

In this case an alternative way to link the two event relations is to create a third relation:

ORDER	(Order #, . . .
SHIPMENT	(Shipment #, . . .
ORDER-SHIP	([Order #], [Shipment #], . . .

Records for the resulting ORDER-SHIP table would be created when the SHIPMENT record is created thus eliminating the problem of having blank fields in the ORDER relation.

Linking Objects with One-to-One (1:1) Maximum Cardinality Relationships   To link relations with a 1-to-1 maximum cardinality, use the minimum cardinality to guide you. There are actually two options for cardinalities with maximums of 1:1:

> *Put the key attribute of the relation with a minimum cardinality of 1 (i.e., the mandatory one) in the relation with the minimum cardinality of zero (i.e., the optional one).*
>
> OR
>
> *Create a separate relation that includes the key attributes from both objects.*

For example, the following relationship cardinality:

Ship   (0, 1)———(1, 1)   Merchandise

could be represented using the following relations:

SHIPMENT	(Shipment #, [Merchandise #],
MERCHANDISE	(Merchandise #,

Or you can create a new relation

    SHIP-MERCHANDISE ([Shipment #], [Merchandise #],

Either of the two alternatives are appropriate when linking event relations to agent, resource, and location relations.

Avoiding Data Redundancy and Blank Table Fields

By using these rules to link relations we avoid relation structures that are arbitrarily restrictive. For example, imagine that instead of representing the relationship,

Sale   (0, *)———(1, *)   Merchandise

with the relations,

SALE   (Sale #,
MERCHANDISE   (Merchandise #,
SALE-MERCHANDISE ([Sale #], [Merchandise #],

you simply included three Merchandise #s as foreign keys:

SALE   (Sale #, [Merchandise-1], [Merchandise-2],
                              [Merchandise-3]),

The problem with this relation structure is that it cannot store data about a sale involving more than three items of merchandise, and if you sell less than three items of merchandise, you have blank fields. Such arbitrary structures are both dangerous and unnecessary if you follow the rules we have given to identify and link relations.

Creating a data relation to record the repeating data items of a many-to-many relationship greatly reduces duplicate data in your data repository. To illustrate, consider the many-to-many relationship between sale and inventory shown above. Documenting a sales event normally includes recording such items as the sale date, sales event number, sale terms, customer identifier, and salesperson identifier. It also includes information about the inventory items purchased by the customer. Notice that for each sale, there is one date, one sales event number, one set of terms, one salesperson, and one customer. Each of these can be represented in one record in the sales event data relation. However, there could be multiple inventory items, quantities, and prices listed for each sale. Some sales may have only 1 inventory item, but some may have 2 or 20. If you do not create a separate data structure for the Sale-Inventory relationship, duplication of data is introduced into the data relations. Consider the following relation with information about three sample sales events where Sale 1 includes three inventory items, Sale 2 includes two inventory items, and Sale 3 includes four inventory items.

SALES table (without a separate table for the Sale-Inventory *:* relationship):

Sales Event #	Date	Terms of Sale	Salesperson ID	Customer ID	Inventory Item #	Inventory Quantity	Price Each
1	2/5	2 10, net 30	4	3654	987	5	2.50
1	2/5	2 10, net 30	4	3654	785	4	1.75
1	2/5	2 10, net 30	4	3654	562	15	1.99
2	2/5	2 10, net 30	6	746	998	27	2.95
2	2/5	2 10, net 30	6	746	624	94	1.05
3	2/5	COD	8	2956	847	18	9.99
3	2/5	COD	8	2956	112	29	5.75
3	2/5	COD	8	2956	413	8	3.00
3	2/5	COD	8	2956	335	57	7.50

Now consider the same example with one SALES table and a separate table for the SALE-INVENTORY many-to-many relationship. Note the reduction in data duplication.

SALES Event Table

Sales Event #	Date	Terms	Salesperson ID	Customer ID
1	2/5	2 10, net 30	4	3654
2	2/5	2 10, net 30	6	746
3	2/5	COD	8	2956

Many-to-Many SALE-INVENTORY Table

Sales Event #	Inventory Item #	Inventory Quantity	Price Each
1	987	5	2.50
1	785	4	1.75
1	562	15	1.99
2	998	27	2.95
2	624	94	1.05
3	847	18	9.99
3	112	29	5.75
3	413	8	3.00
3	335	57	7.50

Defining Non-Key Attributes

Once you have linked the relations in your logical design, you are ready to add any additional attributes needed to generate the various views of the operating events and processes as defined by the system requirements. As you begin to add attributes to the various relations, plan for output views requested by information customers. Make sure to design your data relations so that you can store any data attribute inflows that document or describe events, resources, agents, or locations. If the data needed to generate the various views[11] are not stored in the resulting tables or derivable from data stored in the tables, information customers will not be able to obtain the needed views to support operations and decision making.

---

11 Do not forget about all the data needed to generate source documents, and formal and ad hoc reports.

Take care with challenging attributes. For example, some attributes are called *composite attributes*. Composite attributes can be decomposed into separate attributes. An example of a composite attribute is address. An address is actually composed of several separate attributes: street address, city, state, and zip code. You should represent the four separate attributes rather than lumping all the detail into one aggregated attribute. Another attribute type you should watch for is a *multivalued attribute*. A multivalued attribute can have more than one instance. For example, consider the skill attribute of the relation EMPLOYEE. An employee could have one skill, two skills, or many skills. You should use a separate relation to model multivalued attributes. The new relation would include the primary key of the relation (i.e., Employee number) and the multivalued attribute.

Employee Number	Skill

When defining relation attributes:

Each relation should include only those attributes that describe the entity represented by the relation.

Event relations should include attributes that describe and document an event and should not include data that describe the resources, agents, and locations of the event. Likewise, resource, agent, and location relations should not include event data, but should include only attributes that describe resources, agents, and locations, respectively. This may seem like common sense, but it has tremendous implications in the integrity of the data stored in the relations. One way to enhance the likelihood of data integrity is to minimize data redundancies in the relations.

Computer scientists refer to relations with minimal redundancies as *well normalized*. Although the concept of normalization is typically applied to relational database design, we have found it to be a useful concept to help organize data structures for other paradigms as well. The nontechnical interpretation of normalization is simply that each data attribute of a relation should describe only the object represented by the relation. Following the concept of normalization, relations should not include attributes that belong in relations representing other objects. For example, the CUSTOMER relation should include only attributes about customers while the MERCHANDISE relation should include only attributes about merchandise. The valid exception is foreign keys that link relations. Posted foreign keys introduce some data duplication into the relational model, but this is necessary to link the relations.

A second guideline for defining event-driven logical designs is:

Avoid including derivable non-key attributes in the relations.

Derivable attributes are information items that can be calculated using other data items, so there is no need to store them as relation attributes. For example, suppose you wanted to generate the following sales invoice:

Sales-Invoice = Sales-Invoice # + Sale-Date + Register # + Customer Name +
              Salesperson Name + {Merchandise Name + Quantity-Sold + Price
              + Item-Total} + Sale-Total

The Item-Total is derivable by multiplying the Quantity-Sold and Price of each type of merchandise sold. Furthermore, the Sale-Total is derivable by adding all the Item-Total amounts for the sale.

To self-test your ability to design the logical database, use Christopher's conceptual data model in Exhibit 4–9 and create the logical design. Check your work against the sample logical design presented in Exhibit 4–13.

Our discussion has provided only an overview of the intricacies of creating conceptual and logical models. For example, we did not include all of the rules for ensuring normalization of the relations in your logical model. Also, many people complete these steps differently. We have already told you about the different model choices (such as ER or OO) as well as the different representation methods and techniques. In addition, many modelers approach these steps from a different perspective. They include information products, such as invoices or checks, and information processes in their conceptual models. They choose to model information views, rather than business activities. Such approaches often require different steps to complete the models. For example, view-driven modelers must integrate various views before they move to the next step. Regardless of these choices, the next step in the process is to use the logical model to create a physical product.

THE REMAINING SYSTEMS ANALYSIS AND DESIGN PHASES: PHYSICAL DESIGN, IMPLEMENTATION, AND MAINTENANCE

In the physical design phase we create the physical files, databases, and programmed instructions. The implementation and maintenance phases of a systems project involve system coding, testing, installing, documenting, training users, supporting users, and maintaining the system.

Systems analysis and design is a potentially never-ending process. As business needs change, so do the needs for information systems to support the business. That is what makes this area so rewarding and challenging.

You may think you will not have the opportunity to build a physical system using the concepts presented in this text. However, you can build the next best thing: a *prototype*. An IT application prototype is a working, computerized model of an IT application plan. Prototyping is often used in a variety of fields to illustrate an idea. Rather than going straight from the blueprint to the final structure, architects will often build a model of the structure to help clients visualize the blueprint. Rather than constructing the building, then learning the client wanted something different, building a prototype allows you to make sure you understand the requirements much quicker and with less expense. An application prototype is similar to a model of a building constructed with cardboard, balsam wood, and other materials. It certainly is not anything you would actually move into, but it helps make sure you have captured the requirements before you complete the final structure.

Prototyping allows experimentation with the IT application. The final prototype often becomes the starting point for developing the application that an organization will implement. Therefore, the prototype serves as a final statement of business requirements for the IT application. Learning to develop IT prototypes is an important skill that allows you

EXHIBIT 4–13

Christopher, Inc., Sample Relations

Event Logical Structures (used to store documentation data about events)

Relation Name	Sample Attributes
RECEIVE CUSTOMER ORDER	Sales Order #, [Customer #], [Customer Order Representative Employee #], Date, Time, Shipping Instructions, Cancel by Date, Location of Order (e.g., phone, during sales call, fax, or mail)
SHIP ORDER	Invoice #, [Sales Order #], [Shipping Personnel Employee #], [Customer #], [Shipping Firm ID #], Date, Time, Shipment Tracking #, Sales Tax
COLLECT PAYMENT	Cash Receipt #, [Cash Account #], [Cashier Employee #], [Customer #], Date, Time, Amount Received, Electronic Funds Transfer #
ORDER/INVENTORY	[Sales Order #], [Inventory Item #], Quantity Ordered
SHIP/INVENTORY	[Invoice #], [Inventory Item #], Quantity Shipped, Price Each
SHIP/COLLECT PAYMENT	[Cash Receipt #], [Invoice #], Amount Applied to This Invoice

Resource Logical Structures (used to store reference data about resources)

Relation Name	Sample Attributes
INVENTORY	Inventory Item #, Description, Product Specification, Reorder Point, Current Price, Beginning Quantity, Beginning Quantity Date
CASH	Cash Account #, [Bank #], Type of Account (e.g., checking, savings, CD), Beginning Balance, Beginning Balance Date

Agent Logical Structures (used to store reference data about agents)

Relation Name	Sample Attributes
EMPLOYEE*	Employee #, Name, Street Address, City, State, Zip, Telephone #, Birth Date, Marital Status, Job code (e.g., order personnel, shipping personnel, cashier), Start Date, Salary, Comments
CUSTOMER	Customer #, Name, Street Address, City, State, Zip, Telephone #, Credit Rating, Credit Limit
SHIPPING FIRM	Shipping Firm ID #, Shipping Firm Name, Street Address, City, State, Zip, Telephone #, Contact Person, Rate Information
BANK	Bank #, Bank Name, Contact Person, Bank Street Address, City, State, Zip, Bank Phone #

*Alternately, Christopher would create separate logical structures for each type of employee (e.g., order personnel, shipping personnel, and cashiers).

to play an active role in specifying how an organization might use IT. Prototyping also forces precision in defining business requirements for the IT application. When prototypes are developed effectively, the IT application user should see minimal differences between the look and feel of the prototype and the final, installed application. All that should change is the performance and reliability of the final version of the application.

Think about all the analysis and planning you have done to this point. Students are often amazed that most of the work necessary to plan an effective IT application is done *before* you ever touch a computer to create programs or build actual databases. Software CASE (computer-aided software engineering) tools are available to help you model and plan the application, but these software tools cannot replace or compensate for a lack of understanding of the organization and its information customers.

It is time to implement the requirements we have defined to this point (which have been focused primarily on the structure of the data), and finish the definition of the processes. To allow students the opportunity to prototype an IT application, we typically use a relational database management system with a 4GL (fourth generation language) and a software tool for designing screens.

There are three parts to an IT application prototype:

- The data storage structures.
- The forms and reports used for the recording, maintaining, and reporting processes.
- The detailed logic underlying the forms and reports that implement the business and information process rules.

The physical tables are created from the relations in the logical model. The relations with their primary keys, foreign keys, and supporting attributes become tables and fields in the tables. For example, consider a relation named CASH with a primary key named Cash Account #, a posted foreign key named Bank #, and the following nonkey attributes: Type of account (e.g., checking, savings, CD, etc.), Beginning Balance, Beginning Balance date. This relation would be built as a physical table using some DBMS. The table, named CASH, would have the following fields: Cash Account #, a posted foreign key named Bank #, Type of account (e.g., checking, savings, CD, etc.), Beginning Balance, Beginning Balance date. The field Cash Account # would be denoted as the primary key field. This table would have one record for each cash account, and each record would include data in the attribute fields that describe the particular cash account.

The detailed logic for the forms and reports to support the recording, maintaining, and reporting processes can be documented using data flow diagrams. These diagrams are valuable in showing the interface between the processing instructions and the data tables. Identifying the tables that relate to each recording process is rather straightforward. The recording process accesses the tables representing each event object of the *REAL* model (the event table and any separate tables created for an event's many-to-many relationships) and all other objects (resources, locations, and agents) directly related to the event. Exhibit 4–14 illustrates a partial data flow diagram of the Record Order event. This recording process will add one or more records to the event table(s)—ORDER and ORDER-INVENTORY in this example. The arrow going from the process symbol to a data store

EXHIBIT 4–14

Linking an Order Recording Process with a Data Repository

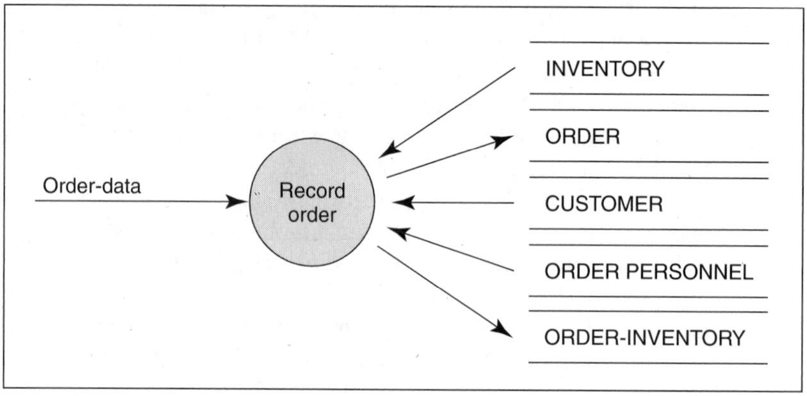

denotes writing data to a table. The process will also access data from the related resource, agent, and location tables to ensure that any business rules are followed and to enhance data validity and integrity. The arrow coming from a table into the process symbol denotes reading from a table.

Maintenance processes add, delete, or modify resource, agent, and location data stored in data tables. As Exhibit 4–15 shows, each maintenance process accesses a resource, agent, or location table undergoing maintenance. Maintenance processes will add one or more records, delete one or more records, or simply change the contents of one or more records. Recording processes may activate some maintenance processes. For example, a Take Order recording process may check the Customer file to verify customer data. If the customer is not found, the order process may invoke a maintenance process to add a new customer record.

Linking reporting processes to the data repository is similar to linking the recording and maintenance processes. As Exhibit 4–16 illustrates, the only difference is data is read from, rather than written to, the repository tables. The task is to identify which tables are needed to generate each desired output view. This can best be accomplished by studying the context dictionary that outlines the detailed contents of each report and the table relations to see where the individual data items are stored.

In this text, we do not demonstrate the specifics of developing a prototype using a particular software product for two reasons:

1. Event-driven prototyping is not dependent on any one technology. AIS faculty have a wide variety of appropriate preferences for a prototyping environment. For example, the three authors of this book prefer three different relational DBMSs for prototyping and we are beginning to use object-oriented tools for more advanced students. While each product has its strengths and weaknesses,

E X H I B I T   4–15

Sample Maintenance Processes and Data Access

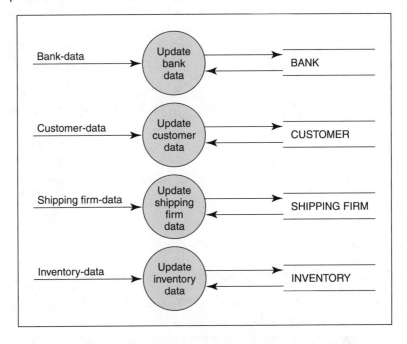

most environments provide adequate support for developing event-driven prototypes. We prefer focusing on the concepts that can be implemented using a variety of tools rather than adopting one particular tool that may soon be out of vogue.

2. Prototyping tools change so rapidly that it is impossible to include current information about any one product, let alone a variety of products. Therefore, we focus on defining the data and processes leaving you and your instructor to choose the technology for developing the prototype.

Regardless of the prototyping tool you choose, the following are typical steps in building an IT application prototype. The prototype will link the data pools, forms, and rules and allow you to test an actual (though perhaps scaled down) implementation of your application:

1. Build a table for each table defined by the *REAL* model.

2. Build a menu system that has the following choices:

Record Event Data.

Maintain Data.

E X H I B I T   4–16

Example of Generating a Sales-by-Salesperson Report

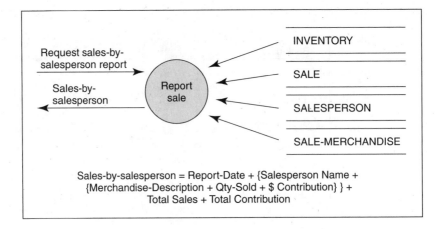

Sales-by-salesperson = Report-Date + {Salesperson Name +
{Merchandise-Description + Qty-Sold + $ Contribution} } +
Total Sales + Total Contribution

Reports.

Exit.[12]

3. Develop the necessary forms and procedures to collect event data and store the data in the appropriate tables.

4. Develop the necessary forms and procedures to maintain the resource, agent, and location tables.

5. Develop queries required to generate desired information.

6. Develop report formats for each report.

7. Write procedures to execute the queries and format the reports.

8. Link each recording, maintaining, and reporting form to the application menu defined in Step 2. Each form becomes a choice under the Record Event Data, Maintain Data, or Reports menu options.

If properly implemented, these steps facilitate the development of a business event–driven IT application prototype that can control the business process and perform the information processing required to support decision makers who are responsible for managing the process.

The look and feel of the prototype is an important factor governing how it is ultimately accepted. Take adequate time to make the presentation layer user friendly. You don't want evaluators to discard it because of appearance or because it is difficult to use.

---

12 A fifth menu option—online help—is necessary for final applications. In addition, you should complete system documentation including a user's manual, data dictionary, program flowcharts, and source code listings.

If the first impression is lacking, it is often difficult to get the user to give a prototype a second chance.

I'm Building a Prototype—But Am I on the Right Track?

Students often ask whether there are guidelines to determine whether they are on track in implementing the concepts outlined in this book. To aid you, we have put together some guidelines for developing prototypes:

- First, computers should display user-friendly interfaces. Input/Output screens should be designed to guide the user through the data acquisition and information delivery processes. In addition, user instructions and online helps can increase the probability of collecting accurate, complete, and timely data. When appropriate, designers should create format files for printed and displayed output. The look and format of information is often as important as the information itself.

- Second, when instructing a computer to access a data pool, the program instructions should specify details regarding where the data are stored, the format of the data pool, and which field(s) to access.

- Third, most processing code should begin only after reviewing and validating the accessibility of the computer user.

- Fourth, source data automation techniques, copying data from existing data pools, and having the computer automatically generate some fields, such as the date field or a sequentially numbered field, are methods to reduce human input error. Such techniques should be used whenever possible.

- Finally, programmers should ensure that proper backups and electronic audit trails are maintained at all times. We will discuss more about audit trails, backups, and other controls in Chapter 5 and Supplemental Chapter D.

A good IT application prototype should embody all the business requirements of the application. When it is handed to those who will develop the final IT application, you can say to the developers, "Don't change the business essence of the application." Using this approach, you remain in the driver's seat when it comes to defining the role IT will play in your organization.

CONCLUDING COMMENTS

Focusing on business processes and the events contained within them to build information systems reverses the traditional view-driven development process. Traditionally, system designers had limited technology and tools available to model, build, and implement information systems. This constraint affected the scope and content of the models and information systems. Organizations had to choose which limited portions of business processes they wanted to model, and the resulting models were usually crude representations of selected portions of the business processes.

Historically, systems were developed to satisfy a narrow reporting requirement. The process began by identifying the format of a desired system output, such as a report or document. A classification scheme was then designed to classify, accumulate, and summarize the data needed for the report or document. Often key organizational data were stored in a variety of systems. To coordinate subsystems, designers developed interfaces and reconciliation procedures. This resulted in a morass of poorly coordinated, view-driven systems that collectively are difficult to maintain and nearly impossible to modify. The information system, rather than serving as a support structure, a business enabler, or a strategic tool, becomes a business constraint. The effect of this architecture is significant when you consider that during the past decade businesses spent $1 trillion on information technology, but showed little gain in efficiency.[13]

For example, when initial accounting systems were developed, they modeled the accounting equation and generated financial statements. In this model, accountants served as an information filter. They screened and selected the information that came into the accounting system. The justification for this filtering role was that accountants, as the financial-statement experts, knew what information users wanted and needed. The general ledger and associated chart of accounts provided the foundation for this model and the data to be included in it. As we explained in Chapter 2, the resulting model is based on one view that guides (and ultimately restricts) data inputs, storage, and output. This is sufficient only if your dominant objective is to present financial statements according to GAAP. It is not sufficient if your objective is to develop and implement business process rules and provide useful information for all information customers throughout all functional areas of the organization. As we have discussed, today's organizations are adopting this objective.

How does this impact accounting information architecture? These changes are forcing an evolution in the analysis and design of accounting information systems as illustrated in Exhibit 4–17. Shifting to event-driven analysis has several consequences on traditional accounting information system. First, designers shift from modeling an output (GAAP statements) to modeling the underlying business activities. The resulting models map as much reality as possible into the information system. This shift does *not* prohibit organizations from preparing the traditional financial statements, it simply allows them to generate GAAP views, *and much more.* Second, if designers capture the essential characteristics of business events without favoring any particular classification scheme, the resulting system can use a single event description to support multiple views of the data. Information providers can generate current views (such as financial statements, management reports, and regulatory reports) and entirely new views to respond to changing requirements of information customers. Furthermore, information professionals can help respond to the challenges facing organizations: inefficient and ineffective business processes, unnecessary and burdensome organization structures, inadequate measurements to guide management, and ineffective uses of information technology.

---

13 "The Technology Payoff," Special Report, *Business Week,* June 14, 1993.

EXHIBIT 4–17

Evolution of AIS Modeling

	Stage 1: Manual systems	**Stage 2:** Automated systems	**Stage 3:** Event-driven IT applications
Resources	Manual	Information technology	Information technology
Process	Account cycle	Account cycle	Record, maintain, report business activity data
Data stores (files)	Journals and ledgers	Journals and ledgers	Business activity data integrated stores
Bias	Generate financial statements	Generate financial statements	Support planning, controlling, and evaluating activities of information customers

Now that you have studied an IT application design method different than the view-driven traditional architecture, we are prepared to talk about an extremely important topic for information providers and other business people—business and information process risk.

CHECKLIST OF KEY TERMS AND CONCEPTS

Ad-hoc report
Attribute
Binary relationship
Composite attribute
Conceptual data model
Context diagram
Derivable attribute
Foreign key
Instance

Key attribute
Linking rules
Maintenance information process
Maximum cardinality
Minimum cardinality
Multi-valued attribute
Non-key attribute
Normalization
Object

Output views	Relationship
Posted key	Relationship cardinality
Preformatted reports	Reporting information process
Primary key attribute	Source document
Prototype	Structured English
Prototyping	Systems analysis and design
Record	Systems development process
Recording information process	Table
Recursive relationship	Ternary relationship
Redundancy	Well-normalized relations

REVIEW QUESTIONS

1. What are the four systems analysis and design phases introduced in this chapter? What happens in each phase?
2. What is Structured English, and what is its purpose?
3. How do you determine how many recording, maintaining, and reporting information processes are needed in an IT application?
4. What are three types of outputs that users need?
5. Explain the structure and usefulness of a context diagram.
6. What does the "+" symbol denote when used in a context diagram? What do the "{ }" symbols represent?
7. What seven types of business event risks are discussed in this chapter? What are three main types of information event risks?
8. How are maximum cardinalities used when designing IT applications?
9. How are minimum cardinalities used when designing IT applications?
10. What does each record in an event table contain?
11. What does each record in a resource table contain?
12. What does each record in an agent table represent?
13. What does each record in a location table represent?
14. Explain the purpose of a primary key attribute.
15. Explain the purpose of a foreign key.
16. What are non-key attributes? List some examples of non-key attributes for a customer file.
17. Explain the rule to link a 1:1 maximum relationship cardinality.
18. Explain the rule to link a 1:* maximum relationship cardinality.
19. Explain the rule to link a *:1 maximum relationship cardinality.
20. Explain the rule to link a *:* maximum relationship cardinality.
21. What tables are needed to perform a recording information process?

22. What tables are needed to perform a maintenance information process?
23. What tables are needed to perform a reporting information process?
24. What are the three parts to an IT application prototype?
25. List the eight typical steps in building an IT application prototype.

DISCUSSION QUESTIONS

1. Why does the plan for an IT application begin with the *REAL* model?
2. How difficult is it to change the design of an events-driven IT application? Explain.
3. Is the following statement true or false? Explain your answer:
   When you finish your IT application, you will have only one table for each object.
4. Why are there exceptions to the linking rules for event relationships?
5. What does "well-normalized" imply?
6. What is a derivable attribute? Explain why the chapter states that you should not store attributes that are derivable.
7. How is data redundancy reduced when you use *REAL* modeling?
8. Is the following statement true or false? Explain your answer:
   Recording an event only involves adding one record to an event table.
9. Why do you need a separate table for an *:* maximum relationship cardinality?
10. Are the concepts presented in this chapter only useful for designing an IT application using relational data bases? Explain.
11. How does structuring systems requirements using logical models provide an opportunity for thinking about ways information technology can be used to help reduce business and information risks?
12. How can you determine whether you are on the right track in developing an IT application prototype?
13. Discuss the three stages of evolution of AIS modeling.
14. Use the following (partial) tables to answer the required questions:

Sales Event Table

Sales Event #	Date	Terms	Salesperson ID	Customer ID
1	11/5	2 10, net 30	4	2543
2	11/5	2 10, net 30	6	635
3	11/5	COD	8	1845

Sale-Inventory Table

Sales Event #	Inventory Item #	Inventory Quantity	Price each
1	876	10	1.25
1	674	8	0.875
1	451	30	0.995
2	887	54	1.475
2	513	188	0.525
3	736	36	24.995
3	001	58	7.875
3	302	16	8.00
3	224	114	8.75

Salesperson Table

Salesperson ID	Last Name	First Name
2	Cleaves	Mateen
4	Warrick	Peter
6	Peterson	Morris
8	Janakowski	Sebastian

Cashier Table

Cashier ID	Last Name	First Name
1	Weinke	Chris
2	Outzen	Marcus

Cash Receipts Event Table

Cash Receipt #	Date	Check #	Cashier ID	Sales Event #	Customer ID	Cash Account #	Amount Received
1001	11/6	11097	2	2	635	110146758	$178.35

Customer Table

Customer ID	Last Name	First Name	Address	City	State	Zip
101	Conrad	Chris	5629 Longfellow Dr.	Paragold	AK	65323
183	Anderson	Paul	674 Sunderland Lane	Sioux City	IA	63126
635	Padgham	Donna	1264 Algonquin Road	Mason	MI	48854
1845	Oliver	Andrew	8512 Bonita Dr.	Clearwater	FL	33051
2543	Cook	Carol	536 Secondary Ave.	Fremont	CA	75518

Cash Table

Cash #	Type of account	Bank Name
110146758	Regular checking	North First
1203948102	Payroll checking account	Credit Grantors

Inventory Table

Inventory Item #	Description
001	XL T-shirt
224	XL Sweatshirt
302	XXL T-shirt
451	Felt pennant
513	Ping pong ball
674	Golf ball
736	XL Polo shirt
876	Bumper sticker
887	Foam Football

Required:

a. What are the events, resources, agents, and locations that are included in the *REAL* model and used to design these tables?

b. Identify the key attribute of each table.

c. Identify the foreign keys of each table.

d. Is there an electronic audit trail represented in this scenario? Explain.

e. List the resources and agents involved in sales event #2.

f. List the resources and agents involved in Cash Receipt #1001.

g. Suppose you wanted to generate an invoice (bill) for customer # 2543 that lists the customer name and address, the salesperson name, and all other information about sales event #1, including the items sold. What tables would you need to generate the invoice? How would you link the records in the separate tables to generate the document?

h. Suppose you wanted to generate a report listing each customer name and the unpaid amount due from each customer. What tables would you need to generate the report? How would you link the records in the separate tables to generate the document?

i. Explain why we did not have to include the total sales amount as an attribute in the sales table.

j. If you need to record the following sale:
Sales event 4; on 11/10; COD terms; Salesperson 2; Customer 101; 30 units of item 887, for a total of $44.25.
What table(s) would you use? How many record(s) would you add to the table(s)?

k. If you have to maintain your records to reflect a change in Donna Padgham's last name and address, what table(s) would you use? How would you link the tables (if you need to use more than one)? How many record(s) would you add or modify to the table(s).

l. If you have to record the following cash receipt:
Cash receipt 1002; on 11/10; from customer 2543 to pay off sales event # 1; in the amount of $49.35 deposited into cash account # 110146758.
What table(s) would you use? How would you link the tables (if you had to use more than one)? How many record(s) would you add or modify to the table(s)?

MINI-CASES AND OTHER APPLIED LEARNING

1. Tom owns a small recreational trailer business in a suburban community located close to the mountains. The community is relatively small but growing at a fast rate. Tom's business is growing, not because of his effective sales style and personality, but by growth of the community. Currently, Tom's competition has been nearly nonexistent, but as the area grows he expects to encounter increasing competition.

Tom sells mostly trailers for vacationing and camping. When customers arrive on Tom's lot, they are greeted by a salesperson. The salesperson may show the customers the trailers on the lot, but the salesperson need not be present during the entire showing. Depending on customer preference, the salesperson will either take the customer on a tour or the customer may roam the lot freely, inspecting trailers at their leisure.

Since recreational trailers are fairly large-ticket items, customers will often leave the lot without making a purchase, only to return another day after making the decision to purchase a trailer. When a customer decided to make a purchase, the salesperson initiates a series of procedures to properly document the order and sale transaction. First, the salesperson determines the model of the selected trailer and offers the customer a list of options that correspond to the particular model. The customer may (1) purchase a trailer off the lot with no added features, (2) purchase a trailer off the lot with additional features, or (3) special order a trailer that is not currently on the lot.

In most cases, customers do not pay cash for their trailers. If, however, the customer pays cash, a simple sales contract is prepared and the customer drives off with his or her trailer. The majority of the customers use an installment method of purchase. Before an installment purchase is authorized, the customer's credit must be verified to determine creditworthiness.

With an installment purchase, an installment agreement is prepared in addition to the sales contract. Tom has arranged financing through a local bank for all installment sales. When an installment sale is made, the bank sends Tom a lump-sum payment equal to the price of the trailer. Instead of making payment to Tom, customers pay the bank plus interest. In either case, Tom receives a lump-sum payment for each trailer sold, whether that lump-sum comes from the customer or from the bank.

Once the credit is approved, the customer can take delivery of the trailer. This involves a delivery person who checks the trailer before delivering it to the customer. The customer may pick up the trailer or have it delivered by Tom.

Required:

Tom's Trailer Sales has identified the following events of interest: Customer Looks at Trailers; Customer Orders Trailer; Deliver Trailer; and Receive Payment.

  a. Identify the resources, agents, and locations associated with these events.
  b. List all direct relationships with cardinalities.
  c. Draw an *REAL* model with cardinalities.
  d. Create any needed tables, complete with key attributes, foreign keys, and non-key attributes. (Your instructor may require you to perform this step using a DMBS).
  e. List the recording and maintaining information processes needed for this sales/collection process. Give three examples of reporting processes for this case.
  f. For each information process listed in part *e,* draw a data flow diagram (similar to Exhibits 4–14 through 4–16) that displays the tables needed to perform the process.

2. Trinity Christian is a small religious organization located in the northeast region of the United States. Trinity holds weekly Sunday observance in church-owned chapels plus other religious events, such as Bingo, during the week. Trinity members are quite dedicated and regularly give contributions to their church.

Receiving donations is vital for the continuance of Trinity Christian. In fact, without member contributions, Trinity could not function as it currently does. Member donations pay for the maintenance and mortgage of local chapels as well as provide a small living allowance for the clergy.

Usually, donations are given directly to the clergymen, instead of the conventional "passing of the plate" as seen in other religious organizations. Donations are only received by authorized clergymen in sealed envelopes, provided by Trinity. Each envelope contains a donation slip that must be filled out and accompany each donation. The member fills out the slip, inserts one copy of the slip in the envelope and retains one copy for him or herself.

Received donation envelopes are opened at a later time, only when two or more clergy are present. The clergy count the donation and record the amount in a special ledger that documents donations by individual donors. After the donation is verified and recorded, two or more clergy must deposit the day's donations in a local bank. This deposit is made the same day (or the next day at the very latest) as the date of donation.

At the end of each year, the ledger is examined and account balances per donor are printed in report form and given to each individual donor as a means of confirming the donations received throughout the year.

Required:

Trinity Christian has identified the following events of interest: Receive Donation; Examine and Verify Donation; and Make Deposit.

    a. Identify the resources, agents, and locations associated with these events.

    b. List all direct relationships with cardinalities.

    c. Draw an *REAL* model with cardinalities.

    d. Create any needed tables, complete with key attributes, foreign keys, and non-key attributes. (Your instructor may require you to perform this step using a DMBS).

    e. List the recording and maintaining information processes needed for these entities. Give three examples of reporting processes for this case.

    f. For each information process listed in part *e,* draw a data flow diagram (similar to Exhibits 4–14 through 4–16) that displays the tables needed to perform the process.

  3. Maple Bluff Pharmacy sells prescription drugs and over-the-counter medications and supplies. All prescriptions and over-the-counter items are sold using a cash register. Each cash register retains a record of the transactions and who performed them on the cash register's journal tape. This information is subsequently entered into a computer.

Prescriptions received over the phone are taken by the pharmacist and recorded on a prescription slip. Also, prescriptions received over the phone are entered into a computer that matches the prescription with guideline dosage levels and instruction information and prints the necessary information for the prescription. After entering the prescription information into the computer, the prescription is filled and a hard copy of the prescription slip is filed numerically for future reference.

All sales items are paid for with cash, check, or credit card. On occasion, credit is extended to a customer, but he or she must be approved through the chief pharmacist. If credit is extended, a separate billing account is established. If a customer does not pay the bill within 120 days of the initial billing date, the account is turned over to a collection agency.

At the end of the day, cash in the register till is counted and compared with the total amount of credit card receipts, and account receivable slips. This check is performed by two employees in the safe room and is always monitored on camera. In addition, total cash receipts recorded in the computer are compared with the deposit totals each day before Deposits Express picks up the money for deposit.

Required:

Maple Bluff Pharmacy has identified the following events of interest: Process Prescription Order; Fill Prescription; Sell Merchandise; Receive Payment; Deposit Money.

   a. Identify the resources, agents, and locations associated with these events.
   b. List all direct relationships with cardinalities.
   c. Draw an *REAL* model with cardinalities.
   d. Create any needed tables, complete with key attributes, foreign keys, and non-key attributes. (Your instructor may require you to perform this step using a DMBS).
   e. List the recording and maintaining information processes needed for these entities. Give three examples of reporting processes for this case.
   f. For each information process listed in part *e,* draw a data flow diagram (similar to Exhibits 4–14 through 4–16) that displays the tables needed to perform the process.

   4. Dependability Inc.

Dependability Inc. sells and scores questionnaires that are used primarily as an employment tool. The questionnaires measure a potential employee's dependability. Customers who buy the questionnaires ask a job applicant to complete the questionnaire as part of the application process. Customers call the applicant's responses into Dependability's analysis center, where Dependability's employees key the data into a computer. The computer stores the raw data, analyzes it, and the results are given to the customer.

Companies begin using Dependability Inc. questionnaires through the sales efforts of Joe D. Joe's primary job is as a consultant on asset protection. He consults with a variety of companies, mostly retail, who have problems with employee dependability. He recommends Dependability Inc. products to those whom he thinks will benefit by their use. If the company agrees to use the questionnaires, Dependability Inc. assigns the company a number and gives the company a supply of questionnaires.

The company number is entered into the computers at the analysis center. Every time a company calls the center to have a questionnaire scored, they must provide their number. The computer uses the number to verify that the caller is a legitimate customer, to keep track of questionnaire usage, and to associate an applicant's questionnaire responses with a company.

Dependability Inc. has two different pricing policies depending on the type of customer:

1. **Up-front Sale.** At the time the company is provided a supply of questionnaires, they are billed the full price for those provided. For example, if 100 questionnaires are mailed to a customer and the agreed price is $5 each, they are sent a bill for $500. If the company fails to use any of the questionnaires, they bear the loss. This policy is generally used for clients with small usage.

2. **Billed for Use.** The company is billed a nominal fee (generally $.50 each) for the questionnaires shipped. At the end of each month, another bill is sent based on usage for the month. The price charged is often dependent on monthly usage, with a discount for large volumes, and is adjusted for the amount already paid. For example, if 300 questionnaires were scored during a month and the agreed price based on volume of use is $5 per questionnaire, the month-end statement would show $1,350 (300 * ($5.00 – $.50). This policy is used for clients with moderate to high usage because it relieves some of the penalty for lost or damaged questionnaires that are never used.

Computer-generated, month-end reports sent to the customer provide summary statistics on the questionnaires scored. The number of questionnaires used, as reported on the month-end report, is the amount charged under pricing policy No. 2. Monthly statements prepared by one of the part-time employees at the analysis center (who also acts as an accounts receivable clerk) remind customers of the amount due. Payments from clients are sent to the analysis center and are recorded and deposited by the accounts receivable clerk in the checking account of the company.

Required:

   a. Create a context diagram for Dependability, Inc.
   b. Create an *REAL* model with cardinalities for the sales/collection process.
   c. Create any needed tables, complete with key attributes, foreign keys, and non-key attributes. (Your instructor may require you to perform this step using a DMBS).
   d. List the recording and maintaining information processes needed for the sales/collection process. Give three examples of reporting processes for this case.
   e. For each information process listed in part *d,* draw a data flow diagram (similar to Exhibits 4–14 through 4–16) that displays the tables needed to perform the process.

5. Michelle's Collectibles is a small gift shop that specializes in high-demand collectible items. Michelle wants an IT application prototype for her sales/collection process and her acquisition/payment process. Both these processes are described below, along with the key reports and documents for each process.

   At least once a week Michelle surveys the merchandise on the store shelves and in the storage room in back to determine which items need to be re-ordered. Merchandise moves quickly through the store and Michelle is very concerned about having the merchandise her customers want.

   While taking inventory Michelle decides what to order and makes a note on the order sheet she has created. Once all items are noted she selects the vendors from whom she wants to order the various types of merchandise and places calls to the vendors. All vendors ship merchandise on Fridays and the truck usually arrives at Michelle's on Saturdays. When the truck arrives, each item delivered is checked against Michelle's order sheet to make sure only the items that have been ordered are included in the delivery. Each delivery does not always contain a complete order. Sometimes items are not delivered and require an additional delivery by the vendor. Michelle writes a check to the vendor to pay for inventory as it is received. As time permits, Michelle and her employees unpack the boxes received and either place the merchandise in the storage room or on the store shelves.

Customers enter the store throughout the day and select merchandise for purchase. Once customers have selected the merchandise they want to purchase, they take the items to the sales counter where the sales clerk calculates the total sale and requests payment from the customer. The customer can pay for the merchandise with cash, a check, or a charge card. Some customers have a credit account with the store. Michelle sends customers bills each month. A credit account must be paid in full by the end of the month. Customers are not allowed to make any more purchases until the end of the month account is paid in full.

During the acquisition/payment process, Michelle sends purchase order information to vendors (i.e., purchase order number, vendor information, buyer information, ship to information, date, total amount, and a listing of the item number, item description, quantity ordered, item price, and extended price for each item ordered). Michelle receives vendor invoices (bills) with an invoice number, date, vendor information, customer information, subtotal, tax, shipping charge, total purchase amount, and the item number, item description, item price, and quantity shipped for each item on the bill.

Michelle would like to generate the following documents reports to help her manage these processes.

Purchase Order Report for a period of time (including dates, item numbers, item descriptions, and quantities ordered).

Receiving Report for a period of time (including receiving report number, date, vendor information, item numbers, item descriptions, and quantities received).

Inventory Items Currently On Order Report (with the purchase order numbers, purchase order dates, vendor information, and the item numbers, item description, and quantities on order).

Account Status Report (with customer information, date, and balance due).

Billing statements (with customer information, date, time period, and balance due; a listing of each sale # and amount of each sale; and a listing of each cash receipt from the customer with the amount).

Sales Information Report (with customer information, and item number, item description, and quantity for each item sold).

Cash Receipts (with a date, time, salesperson information, subtotal, tax, total, and item description, item price, quantity, and extended price for each item).

Required:

    a. Prepare a context diagram for Michelle's sales/collection process.

    b. Create an *REAL* model with cardinalities for the sales/collection process.

    c. Prepare a context diagram for Michelle's acquisition/payment process.

    d. Create an *REAL* model with cardinalities for the acquisition/payment process.

    e. Create any needed tables, complete with key attributes, foreign keys, and non-key attributes. (Your instructor may require you to perform this step using a DBMS).

    f. List the recording and maintaining information processes needed for the acquisition/payment and sales/collection processes.

    g. For each information process listed in part *f,* draw a data flow diagram (similar to Exhibits 4–14 through 4–16) which displays the tables needed to perform the process.

    h. Draw data flow diagrams (similar to Exhibits 4–14 through 4–16) to display the tables needed to prepare the following reports:

    Purchase Order Report.

    Account Status Report.

    Inventory Items Currently on Order Report.

5

CHAPTER

Business and Information Process Rules, Risks, and Controls

CHAPTER OBJECTIVE

The objective of this chapter is to help you develop an information age control philosophy. After studying this chapter, you should be able to:

* Describe the relationship between risks, opportunities, and controls.
* Explain each of the components of an internal control system.
* Discuss weaknesses in the traditional control philosophy.
* Outline a control philosophy applicable to an information technology environment.
* Describe types of business and information process risks.

THE RELATIONSHIPS BETWEEN RISKS, OPPORTUNITIES, AND CONTROLS

Risks

A *risk* is any exposure to the chance of injury or loss. Every organization faces a multitude of risks. If a risk materializes, it threatens some aspect of the entity's operations, and more serious risks threaten the ongoing existence of the entity. Every day the news is filled with examples of risks that have developed into major losses, scandals, or total collapses of business organizations. *Threat* is another word some people use to describe these situations because they represent a probable evil, violence, or loss to the entity. The following is just a sample of the risks or threats that have plagued many companies:

* Unauthorized payments to influence the decisions of foreign government officials.
* Bad decisions by management to buy or sell subsidiary companies.

- Sexual harassment by members of top management.
- Faulty product design that causes costly recalls.
- Fabricating product quality tests to enhance the value of the company's stock.
- Invasion of a company's network by hackers through the Internet.

Every time one of these risks materializes, critics ask why. They criticize management for lack of due care. They criticize the auditors for not detecting the problem. Questions are always asked about how such a thing could happen within the organization and not be noticed by other people. Risks need to be identified and controlled, but these activities must be balanced with opportunities, objectives, and the cost of controls. Organizations need to balance operational efficiency with operational effectiveness. To the extent possible, information technology should be utilized to enhance both the efficiency and the effectiveness of controls as well as to reduce costs.

Opportunities and Objectives

Opportunity and risk go hand in hand. You can't have an opportunity without some risk, and with every risk there is some potential opportunity. Suppose you graduate from college and, rather than accepting employment with an established firm, you decide to open your own consulting firm to design and install information systems for small organizations. Some opportunities associated with such a decision are being your own boss, working when you want to work, accepting only the engagements you will enjoy working on, and unlimited profit potential. Some risks include having to work a 16-hour day to finish a job on time, producing poor quality work that results in client lawsuits, and not selling enough work to support your desired lifestyle.

People's objectives and the stated objectives of the organization impact both risks and opportunities. Conservative objectives that can be easily achieved require less risk. More aggressive objectives create greater risk as more difficult and complex activities are pursued to achieve them. For example, if your objective is to make a lot of money in your new consulting business, you will probably select a path of high growth. This will require you to hire other people and accept larger engagements. Some opportunities associated with this objective are more variety in the engagements you select, more specialization among your employees, greater personal flexibility, and higher profits. Some risks include hiring bad employees and losing a lot of money due to poor estimates and cost overruns on engagements.

Change creates opportunities. The world is constantly changing and change is often viewed in a negative light because it upsets the status quo. Work patterns change. Friendships are altered as people move to a new department, another company, or a distant city. Products and services that have been very profitable are no longer desired by the current set of customers. But with change come great opportunities. Information technology has been one of the biggest enablers of change in recent years. Each new generation of faster and cheaper computers, new software, and new telecommunications equipment all provide opportunities to do things we previously had not even thought about. New products and services are demanded. New skills are developed and greater profits may be generated from the new products and services. The people who are the most successful are those who are able to anticipate change, recognize the opportunities associated with it, and adapt very quickly.

In summary, change creates many new opportunities. The opportunities an organization seeks are guided by its objectives. But with every opportunity there is some element of risk. We seek to manage these risks by a system of controls.

Controls

A *control* is an activity we perform to minimize or eliminate a risk. The following are some of the risks we identified above in starting your own consulting firm and controls we could establish to minimize some of the risk.

Risk	Control
Having to work a 16-hour day to complete a project on time.	Have a second employee estimate the amount of time required to complete the project so a more realistic completion date can be negotiated.
Doing poor quality work and being sued by the client.	Have another employee review each system module for completeness and accuracy.
	Meet periodically with the client and have client personnel review the system to verify that it meets their expectations.
Not selling enough work to support desired lifestyle.	Perform a market study to identify the types of systems most companies want and to determine the demand for your type of systems.

The problem with controls is that implementation takes time and costs money. Frequently, there are multiple controls we could adopt for any particular risk and the controls differ in both cost and effectiveness. For example, to prevent poor quality work in your new consulting firm we have two controls listed above. Either control, or both of them, could be implemented. Having another employee review the system modules will take less time and cost less money than having periodic meetings with client personnel to have them review the system. However, it will probably be less effective. It is possible for the system modules, and even the entire system, to be correct and of high quality, but still not satisfy the client's needs. If we make an error in identifying what the client wants and needs the new system to do, we could develop a very good system but it would be the wrong system for that client. Periodic meetings with the client to have client personnel review the system would help avoid this mistake.

There are so many potential risks that it may seem overwhelming to try to control all of them. We should only focus on the most significant risks. The significance of a risk is determined by (1) its potential impact on the organization and (2) the likelihood of it occurring. (*Exposure* is a word some people use to describe the potential impact on the entity. Some people also use the term *risk* in a more narrow sense to describe the probability of a loss occurring. Risk, as with many words in the English language, has multiple meanings;

be careful to define your use of the term.) Risks that prevent an organization from achieving its objectives are very costly and may have a catastrophic impact on the ongoing viability of the entity. Materiality of risk, illustrated in Exhibit 5–1, is a function of:

1. The size of the potential loss and its impact on achieving the organization's objectives.
2. The likelihood of the loss.

As either the likelihood or size of the loss increases, the materiality of the risk also increases. The higher the materiality, the greater the need for managing the risk. In many situations these evaluations can only be measured in rough, order-of-magnitude amounts.

Organizations will typically live with low materiality risks because the cost of controlling all risk far exceeds the potential benefit. Management may chose to ignore risks that have a low impact and a low likelihood of occurrence. Controlling all risks to the point of eliminating all potential losses is quite unrealistic and unnecessary. In fact, a commitment to "zero risk" could leave an organization totally ineffective. Conversely, risks that have a high impact and a high likelihood of occurrence must be carefully controlled. The key is identifying and controlling the most *material* risks in a manner such that the *benefits* of controlling the risks exceed the *costs* of the controls, while the efficiency of the organization is balanced with effectiveness.

Business Risks

Too often our concept of risk focuses only on the loss of financial resources such as theft of cash by an employee, or paying the same vendor twice for the same purchase order. However, a risk is any exposure to the chance of loss or injury to the entity. While finan-

E X H I B I T   5–1

Materiality of Risk

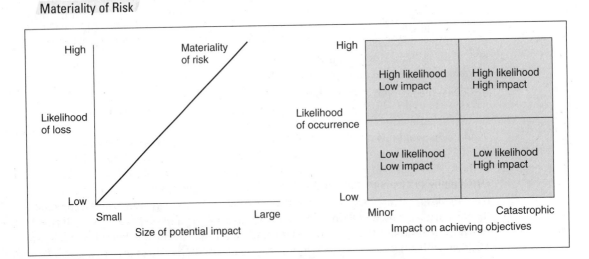

cial losses always injure the organization, they are not the only sources of injury. Businesses have many risks including strategic risks, decision risks, operating risks, and information risks as well as financial risks. All of these risks combined are what we will call *business risks.* Any of these risks can be equally damaging to the organization.

Strategic risks are risks associated with doing the wrong things. They include:

- Poor company vision.
- Failure to recognize the strength of a competitor.
- Lack of knowledge of government rules and regulations.

Decision risks are risks associated with making a bad decision. They include:

- Failure to recognize when a decision needs to be made.
- Failure to consider all relevant alternatives.
- Incorrectly evaluating available information on decision alternatives.

Operating risks are risks associated with doing the right things the wrong way. Examples include:

- Workers performing slow or sloppy work.
- Lack of safety standards in the manufacturing process.
- Errors in equipment settings that cause poor quality in a manufactured product.
- Failure to check product quality on a timely basis.

Financial risks are risks associated with the loss of financial resources or the creation of financial liabilities. Some financial risks are:

- Lack of physical controls over inventory.
- Extending credit to a customer who lacks the ability to pay.
- Allowing unauthorized people to write company checks to unapproved vendors.

Information risks are risks associated with information processing. Remember information processes include recording, maintaining, and reporting activities. Risks in these areas include:

- Developing incomplete or inaccurate information.
- Unreliable hardware or software.
- Failure to protect the system from hackers.

This should not be viewed as an exhaustive list of risk categories, but rather a sample of some of the more important risk categories. Organizations today must control all these risks.

Effective use of information technology can enhance controls and reduce their cost. By thinking differently about business rules and effectively applying information technology, organizations can increase their level of control at a reduced cost. The airline industry has done a masterful job of using technology to achieve this objective. Today, the most sophisticated form of transportation (air travel) is also the fastest and the safest. You have a higher probability of being struck by a car while crossing a street than dying in an airplane crash while flying across the Atlantic Ocean. Much of this has been achieved by using new technologies like radar, flight navigation systems, and advanced forms of communications as well as through advancements in aviation equipment and its maintenance.

Organizations must develop and implement a system of controls to manage the many risks they encounter. Accounting professionals refer to the rules, policies, and procedures that manage risks as the *system of internal control*. Without proper attention to such a system, the organization, as with a car, may be able to go fast but may also spin out of control. We will first discuss the components of an internal control system and then focus on a control philosophy that effectively uses information technology (IT) to implement controls.

INTERNAL CONTROL SYSTEMS

Internal controls encompass a set of rules, policies, and procedures an organization implements to provide reasonable assurance that (1) its financial reports are reliable, (2) its operations are effective and efficient, and (3) its activities comply with applicable laws and regulations. These represent the three main objectives of the internal control system. The organization's board of directors, management, and other personnel are responsible for the internal control system. The AICPA's *Statement on Auditing Standards No. 55* and *No. 78* have largely established our current standards for internal controls.[1] An important document in developing the current control philosophy was the report issued by the Committee of Sponsoring Organizations of the Treadway Commission (COSO).[2] Much of what follows came from these documents. The impact of this updated control philosophy on the accounting profession is only beginning to be realized. An AICPA Committee on Assurance Services has been organized to investigate the impact and to identify new opportunities for accountants.[3] Substantial changes are expected in the services public accountants offer as they provide new assurance services relating to business risks and controls.

As discussed earlier, there is a direct relationship between the entity's objectives and the controls required to achieve those objectives. The objectives of various organizations may differ widely, but all organizations must have objectives relating to accuracy of financial reporting, efficiency and effectiveness of operations, and compliance with applicable rules and regulations. Also, controls must be established over the activities of the entire entity and over each of its operating units and business functions.

The internal control system consists of five interrelated components: control environment, risk assessment, control activities, information and communications, and monitoring. We discuss each of these components in the following sections. The relationships between an entity, its objectives, and the five internal control components are illustrated in Exhibit 5–2.

---

1 Auditing Standards Board, American Institute of Certified Public Accountants, Statement of Auditing Standards No. 78, "Consideration of Internal Control in a Financial Statement Audit: An Amendment to SAS No. 55" (New York: AICPA, 1995).

2 "Internal Control—Integrated Framework" (New York: Committee of Sponsoring Organizations of the Treadway Commission, 1992).

3 Available only on the Internet at *http://www.aicpa.org/* under the subsection titled "Assurance Services."

EXHIBIT 5–2

Relationships among Components, Objectives, and the Entity

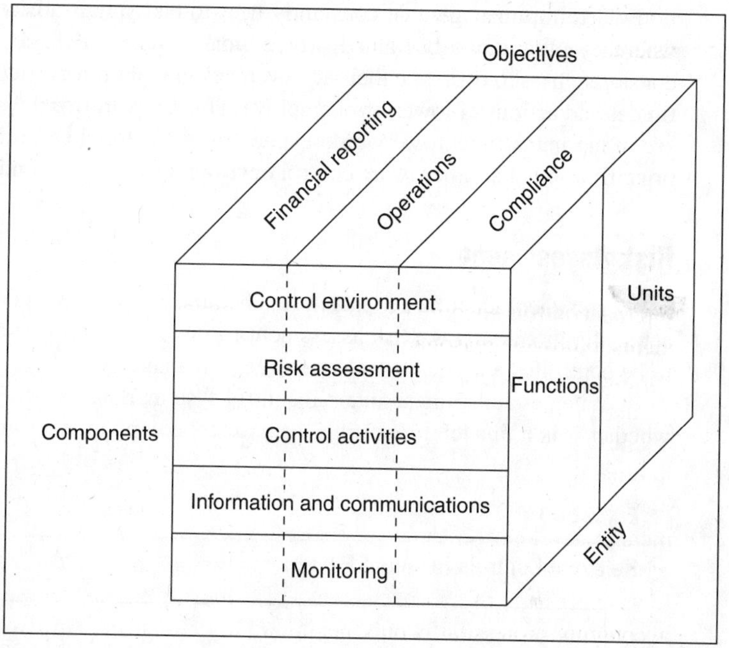

Control Environment

The *control environment* sets the tone of the organization, which influences the control consciousness of its people. This foundation provides discipline and structure upon which all other components of internal control are built. The control environment includes the following areas:

1. Integrity and ethical behavior.
2. Commitment to competence.
3. Board of directors and audit committee participation.
4. Management philosophy and operating style.
5. Organization structure.
6. Assignment of authority and responsibility.
7. Human resource policies and practices.

The attitudes and actions of top management largely determine the climate of an organization. Consider the environment of one organization whose top management has very high standards of moral and ethical conduct, is committed to hiring competent people and properly training them for their work, develops an organizational structure where the work of one person is checked by the work of another person, and is conservative in their management style and financial reporting. Contrast this with the climate of a second organization where top management constantly tries to take unfair advantage of their employees, where people are poorly trained, where work is poorly defined, and where management constantly tries to overstate their achievements and minimize their problems. Since the attitudes and actions of lower level employees typically mirror the attitudes and actions they see in top management, we would expect to find a strong control environment in the first organization but a rather weak control environment in the second organization.

Risk Assessment

Risk assessment identifies and analyzes the relevant risks associated with the organization achieving its objectives. Risk assessment forms the basis for determining what risks need to be controlled and the controls required to manage them.

When establishing an internal control system, risks associated with each objective—whether it is a financial reporting, operations, compliance, or any other objective—must

EXHIBIT 5–3

Relevant Controls for Audit Review

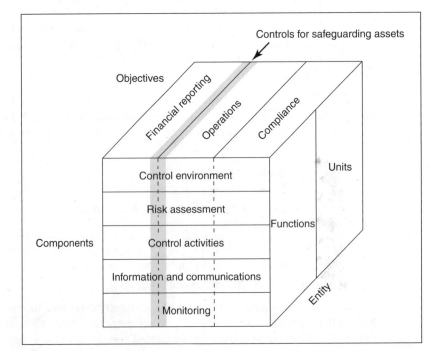

be considered. Some of the risks associated with the operations of the business include selecting a vendor who is dishonest, purchasing inferior raw materials, and an employee performing slow or sloppy work while on the job. Risk assessment is a much broader approach than that taken by the external auditor when performing an audit on the entity's financial statements. Since the auditor's opinion only relates to the fairness of external financial statements in presenting the results of operations and the financial position of the entity in conformance with generally accepted accounting principles, the auditor will only evaluate a small portion of the internal controls. For example, when the auditor evaluates internal controls over the unauthorized acquisition, use, or disposition of assets, only a few of the financial reporting and operating activities will be evaluated, as illustrated in Exhibit 5–3. Some of the specific controls the auditor will investigate to minimize risks associated with company assets include:

Risk	Control
An unauthorized employee gains access to cash.	A lock-box system for collecting cash.
An unauthorized employee manipulates the accounts receivable balances.	Passwords for limiting access to accounts receivable data files.
An employee takes inventory for personal use.	Physical controls to prevent unauthorized access to raw material inventory.

The risk considered by an independent auditor and the controls the auditor will require should be viewed as a *necessary* set of controls to be evaluated when issuing an opinion on external financial statements, but not a *sufficient* set. Some risks and controls that deal with the acquisition, use, and disposition of assets and that are very important to the success of a company, but that are of little interest to the auditor, include:

Risk	Control
Price of the product may be too low to make a fair profit.	Review product pricing decisions on merchandise held for resale to customers.
Price of the product may be too high and the company may not be competitive in the marketplace.	Establish guidelines to be followed in changing the price for any particular customer.
Quality of raw materials is not up to standard, resulting in an inferior product.	Review the quality of raw materials by an independent receiving clerk.
High product cost because raw materials are wasted while producing the product.	Issue only the budgeted amount of raw materials for the items to be produced.

Just because these risks and controls are not relevant to the auditor's opinion on the financial statements does not mean they should be ignored. The internal control system should place just as much emphasis on the efficiency and effectiveness of operations and compliance with applicable rules and regulations as it does on financial reporting.

Control Activities

Control activities are the policies and procedures the organization uses to ensure that necessary actions are taken to minimize risks associated with achieving its objectives. Controls have various purposes and may be applied at various organizational and functional levels.

Control Usage: Prevent, Detect, or Correct   Control activities may be classified by their use: whether they are used to prevent, detect, or recover from errors or irregularities. The purpose of each control is evident by its name:

- *Preventive controls* focus on preventing an error or irregularity.
- *Detective controls* focus on identifying when an error or irregularity has occurred.
- *Corrective controls* focus on recovering from, repairing the damage from, or minimizing the cost of an error or irregularity.

An *error* is an unintended mistake on the part of an employee while an *irregularity* is an intentional effort to do something that is undesirable to the organization. Often attention is focused too much on irregularities; however, more money is lost as a result of errors than is lost as a result of irregularities.

CASE IN POINT

Computer experts estimate that only 19% of data security losses (measured in dollars) are from dishonest or disgruntled employees while 65% are caused by errors and omissions. The errors and omissions are avoidable mistakes such as a clerk keying the wrong number without being prompted to double check the entry. Other items counted as losses are the loss of infrastructure due to power outages and natural disasters, 8%; water damage, 5%; and outsiders including virus writers, 3%.[4]

How the controls are used is very important because preventive controls are more desirable than other controls. We would prefer to prevent a problem rather than detect it and then have to incur the cost of recovering from the consequences. Nevertheless, other controls are needed to handle cases where preventive controls are not cost-justified or fail to prevent an error or irregularity.

Having a second clerk assist with each sale in an attempt to *prevent* theft of cash by the sales clerk is an example of a preventive control. The two clerks could *collude* with each other—act together through a secret understanding to conspire in a fraud—and this control would not prevent the theft. The possibility of *collusion* is a weakness in relying on the addition of people to prevent this type of error. To avoid the cash theft problem we could eliminate the use of cash entirely. Requiring all payments to be made with a credit card or through an electronic funds transfer can accomplish this. Scanning items sold and pricing them automatically by the cash register, along with a rule that requires a comparison of the cash in the cash drawer with total sales accumulated by the cash register during

---

4 L. Hooper, "For Data Security, Computer Virus is Least Problem," *The Wall Street Journal,* August 15, 1990, p. B1.

an employee's shift, is an example of a *detective* control. If the cash in the cash drawer does not equal total sales, we know the employee either pocketed some of the money, or made an error in giving change to a customer. An example of a *corrective* control is a policy of deducting the amount of a cash drawer shortage from the employee's pay. Such a policy may also serve as a preventive control.

Other categories of controls that are very important include segregation of duties, physical controls, information processing controls, and performance reviews. Notice there are overlaps in the control categories. For example, separation of duties and responsibilities, which we will discuss next, is both a preventive and a detective control.

Separation of Duties   Separation of duties structures the work of people so the work of one person is checked by the work of the next person as the next person performs his/her assigned tasks. Good separation of duties will have different people responsible for authorizing transactions, recording transactions in the accounting records, and controlling the assets. An example of a detective control is when the person recording a transaction in the accounting records verifies that the transaction being recorded was initiated by an authorized individual. A transaction initiated by an unauthorized person would not be recorded in the accounting records but would be reported to a supervisor. We will talk more about separation of duties in a minute.

Physical Controls   *Physical controls* include security over the assets themselves, limiting access to the assets to only authorized people, and periodically reconciling the quantities on hand with the quantities recorded in the organization's records. Assets such as cash, investments in stocks and bonds, and other liquid assets should be kept in a locked facility and the keys to the facility should be carefully controlled. Inventory should be kept in a separate room with controlled access. Proper authorization should be required for access to computer programs and data files. The people who are given custody of the assets are held responsible for them and they are accountable for any shortages between the quantities on hand and the amounts recorded in the accounting records.

Information Processing   *Information processing controls* are used to check accuracy, completeness, and authorization of transactions. The two broad groups of information processing controls are general controls and application controls. *General controls* cover data center operations, systems software acquisition and maintenance, access security, and application systems development and maintenance. Application controls apply to the processing of a specific application, like running a computer program to prepare employees' payroll checks each month. Application controls help ensure that transactions are valid, properly authorized, and completely and accurately processed.[5]

Performance Reviews   *Performance reviews* are any reviews of an entity's performance. Some of the more common reviews compare actual data to budgeted data or prior period

---

[5] See Supplemental Chapter D for a more detailed discussion of general controls and application controls.

data, operating data to financial data, and data within and across various units, subdivisions, or functional areas of the organization. An example of a performance review is comparing actual production costs of the current period with last period's production costs and budgeted production costs to identify any significant deviations. Any cost category that has a significant deviation should be investigated further to identify the cause. Another example is to compare the amount of sales within each region to the quantity of inventory shipped to that region to see if the ratio between sales and quantity shipped is about the same in all regions. If one region's ratio is low, you would want to investigate that region further to identify whether it was due to theft, damaged inventory, or some other explainable cause.

Information and Communication

The *information system* consists of the methods and records used to record, maintain, and report the events of an entity, as well as to maintain accountability for the related assets, liabilities, and equity. The quality of the system-generated information affects management's ability to make appropriate decisions in managing and controlling the entity's activities and to prepare reliable financial reports.

The information system should do each of the following to provide accurate and complete information in the accounting system and correctly report the results of operations.

1. Identify and record all business events on a timely basis.
2. Describe each event in sufficient detail.
3. Measure the proper monetary value of each event.
4. Determine the time period in which events occurred.
5. Present properly the events and related disclosures in the financial statements.

The *communication* aspect of this component deals with providing an understanding of individual roles and responsibilities pertaining to internal controls. People should understand how their activities relate to the work of others and how exceptions should be reported to higher levels of management. Open communication channels help ensure that exceptions are reported and acted upon. Communication also includes an organization's policy, accounting, and financial reporting manuals.

Monitoring

Monitoring is the process of assessing the quality of internal control performance over time. This is extremely important as most organizations are constantly changing their operations to meet new demands in the marketplace and capitalize on new opportunities. Monitoring involves assessing the design and operation of controls on a timely basis and taking corrective actions as needed. Management accomplishes the ongoing monitoring of activities by questioning reports that differ significantly from their knowledge of operations. Internal auditors or similar people also accomplish it through periodic evaluations to review internal controls, evaluate their effectiveness, report their results, and provide recommendations for improvement. Information from external entities is also valuable in monitoring internal controls. Complaints by customers or suppliers about billings or payments, reviews by various governmental agencies, and reports by external auditors all provide information on the adequacy of internal controls and how to improve them.

TRADITIONAL CONTROL PHILOSOPHY

Over the years, the accounting and auditing professions have developed a philosophy regarding risks and controls to guide the design, implementation, maintenance, and evaluation of internal control systems. Traditional control philosophy has been developed with the knowledge that *people* conduct the business activities and do much of the information processing, and that *paper* is used extensively to document, store, and transmit data. Payroll is a good example of this. Employees traditionally recorded their time on a time card. The time cards were forwarded to the supervisor for review and approval. Time from the time cards was then entered into the computer payroll program to calculate the employee's pay and prepare the paycheck. The computer also printed a payroll summary to document all employees' pay for the period.

Much of the traditional accounting and auditing control philosophy has been based on the following concepts and practices:

1. Extensive use of hard-copy documents to capture information about accounting transactions, and frequent printouts of intermediate processes as accounting transactions flow through the accounting process. Paper has been used extensively in recording, processing, and maintaining historical information. This is comforting to most people because they can see the flow of the process.

2. Separation of duties and responsibilities so the work of one person checks the work of another person. This works very well as long as people perform both the business activities and the information processes.

3. Duplicate recording of accounting data and extensive reconciliation of the duplicate data. Our current information systems are full of duplicate data. We have the same information about a sale event recorded on a sales invoice, in the sales journal, aggregated in the general ledger, and in a subsidiary ledger if the sale involved credit. Also, the Sales Department often has their own system to keep track of sales by product and by region. Plus, the Personnel Department may maintain some of the same sales data to accurately pay sales commissions to the salespeople.

4. Accountants who view their role primarily as independent, reactive, and detective. The concept of independence, which is critical to the attest function, has carried over into other areas of accounting. Accountants are often more reactive than proactive and more detective than preventive.

5. Heavy reliance on a year-end review of financial statements and extensive use of long checklists of required controls.

6. Greater emphasis given to internal control than to operational efficiency. Much of this is caused by the emphasis on the audit of external financial statements that orients the accountant's thinking on the financial controls that impact the accuracy of the financial statements.

7. Avoidance or tolerance toward advances in information technology. Even though the accounting function was the first to make extensive use of computers to automate accounting processes, accountants have not kept pace in exploiting the capabilities of IT.

Let's examine the soundness of these concepts and practices to see how valid they are today in a world filled with information technology. As we do we will develop several control concepts. At the end of the section we will present an updated control philosophy.

DEVELOPING AN UPDATED CONTROL PHILOSOPHY

Today, accountants and auditors are being criticized for their control philosophy. Some of the criticism is due to the implementation of centralized, compliance-based control structures. Much of the criticism is because the traditional control philosophy does little to address the impact of information technology (IT) on the risks associated with business operations, compliance with many rules and regulations, and information processes. The use of advanced IT exposes and magnifies the shortcomings of traditional internal control systems.

CASE IN POINT

During the 1980s, several large stock brokerage companies developed sophisticated computerized trading systems that allowed brokers to execute transactions much more quickly. While building these systems, no one would have ever imagined the potential embarrassment to one brokerage firm. One day a Solomon Brothers, Inc., clerk hit the wrong button on a program-trading terminal and sent a huge electronic sell order for as much as $500 million of stock just before the closing bell. The huge sell order, involving about 50 major stocks, caused virtual chaos on the Big Board floor in the closing minutes of trading, knock-ing the Dow Jones Industrial Average down by nearly 12 points, turning what had been a modest gain into a 1.57-point loss. "It happened in the last minute; the orders were peppered all over the place," said one stunned Big Board trader. "There was no inkling of it; all of a sudden it came in at 3:58 and 3:59 and it just rolled across the floor, all delivered by computer. This was a misguided missile." In a brief statement, Solomon said it "made an error" in executing a customer's order. Solomon expects to correct the error through market transactions over the next few days.[6]

How can accountants and auditors enhance their ability to help an organization identify and control business and information process risk? We need to develop a control philosophy that effectively integrates IT into the process in such a way as to protect and enhance the organization simultaneously. To accomplish this objective, we need to revise

---

6 W. Power and C. Torres, "Stock Drop as Solomon Clerk Errs," *The Wall Street Journal,* March 26, 1992, p. C1.

the assumptions and beliefs that underlie our control philosophy and our resulting system of internal controls.

The Developer Perspective

Control Concept 1: Accountants must become control consultants over the entire range of business risks with a real-time, proactive control philosophy that focuses first on preventing business risks, then on detecting and correcting errors and irregularities.

Most managers look to their accountants and auditors to identify and develop the internal control system. Accountants and auditors have traditionally used a standards-driven perspective that is particularly evident in independent, external audits. Most audits and auditing standards deal with detecting financial errors and irregularities at year-end. As we discussed earlier, the auditor only evaluates the controls necessary to render an opinion on the fairness of the financial statements and whether they conform to generally accepted accounting principles. Therefore, most of the controls dealing with business operations and regulatory compliance are not relevant to the independent audit of financial statements. We don't say this as a criticism of the traditional audit. This focus has allowed accountants to perform a valuable service in a cost-effective manner. However, when developing an internal control system, there is a need to break out of the *independent, reactive,* and *detective* modes and look at the business in a broader context. Greater emphasis needs to be placed on prevention, business operations, and regulatory compliance.

As we discuss risks and controls, remember our objective is to help you develop the skills necessary to design, use, and evaluate information systems. In this light, we view the accountant as a risk and control consultant to management. This requires an involved, proactive business perspective to aid in the design and implementation of business and information process rules that detect, prevent, and correct business risk. As a control consultant in today's business world, you need a real-time, proactive, control philosophy. Although the external auditor perspective and the control consultant perspective sometimes overlap, the risk and control consultant perspective is much broader and more useful when designing, implementing, maintaining, and evaluating business and information processes.

The Relationships between Risks and Specific Control Procedures

Control Concept 2: Use modern IT to achieve the objectives of recording, maintaining, and reporting information that is accurate, complete, and timely by:

- **Evaluating the risks associated with current business and information processes.**
- **Designing specific control procedures to manage the risks.**

The purpose and value of internal controls are to reduce exposure to risk. As a professional, your first task is to learn about a business and become trained in identifying potential risks. Next you develop business and information process rules to help your organization or clients reduce risk exposures. The key is to consider the risks first, then develop rules. Finally, the specific rules proposed as part of the control strategy will depend on various factors such as the environment, the size of the organization, the technology used, the ability of the employees, and the industry.

The reason for implementing specific control procedures is to reduce or eliminate the conditions that produce the risk. However, there is no one right combination of rules, and the mix can change over time as the organization's strategy, processes, structure, measurements, culture, and use of information technology changes. It is important to monitor the effectiveness of existing controls. Since control procedures are context specific, as new business and information processes are proposed, control objectives will remain constant, but the specific rules needed to achieve the objectives must change.

This approach is quite different from the more traditional approach that identifies the objectives of internal controls, then identifies lengthy checklists of control policies and procedures that are compatible with the traditional accounting system. Often, the risks that create the need for a specific control are a function of the architecture of the business and information processes. For example, independent checks on performance and separation of duties have traditionally been an important element of internal control. Let's examine these two rules to illustrate the problem of focusing on specific control procedures rather than identifying risks for a specific business context.

Independent Checks on Performance   Traditional accounting systems generally require one person to perform an independent check of another person's work by reconciling duplicate data in the system. Because accounting systems originally used human processors, the data were recorded twice to control for the potential risk of human error and to achieve the objective of accurate and complete data. The reconciliation was performed to validate the integrity of the duplicate data. Notice how the human processor created a risk of inaccurate data, and the control procedure to reduce the risk included duplicate recording and reconciliation of the duplicate data by human processors. Since this was necessary in a manual system, does this imply that all new systems should include duplicate data and costly reconciliation of the data? Not really! Yet many automated information systems still include duplicate data and reconciliation because processes intended to control risks that are specific to manual systems were replicated in an electronic data processing (EDP) environment that does not produce the same risks.

Separation of Duties   Traditionally, this control procedure structures activities such that the following responsibilities are assigned to different people: (1) authorizing transactions, (2) recording transactions in the accounting records, and (3) maintaining custody of assets. This procedure is implemented to reduce the opportunities for any one person to both perpetrate and conceal an error or an irregularity in the normal course of his or her work. For example, if one person has custody of inventory and also maintains the accounting records, the person could take some inventory for personal use and cover the shortage by an entry to the accounting records. The entry would reduce inventory, increase cost of goods sold, and use "Adjustment for damaged merchandise" as the explanation. This entry will maintain the balance between the inventory on hand and the amount of inventory recorded in the accounting records and no one will be able to detect the theft. However, by separating the authorization, record keeping, and custody of the assets, the person maintaining the accounting records would not be willing to make such an entry without instruction from the authorizing agent, and the authorizing agent would not give the instruction without evidence of damaged merchandise. If the person who has custody of the inventory takes some of it for personal use, there will be an imbalance between inventory on hand and the amount of inventory in the accounting records and the person charged with custody of the inventory will be held responsible for the shortage.

In a manual processing environment, it is useful to separate these responsibilities (custody, record keeping, and authorization) among different employees. However, IT applications challenge the need for this in some situations. With advances in information technology, much of what has traditionally been done by humans can now be done by the computer. For example, several organizations currently have one individual record business event data in real time as he or she conducts the business event. This directly challenges the traditional separation of duties concept by having the individual who executes a business event record all relevant business event data. How can an organization allow this and still have effective internal controls? Again, this is an example of how control procedures change with the environment. The importance of traditional separation of duties is diminished when modern information technology is properly utilized. Automated control processes can, in many cases, act in the role of a separate person and eliminate the risks of having one person perform what seem to be two incompatible activities.

CASE IN POINT

Most major retail stores now have integrated point-of-sale systems that contain built-in controls in the computer programs to allow one person to perform tasks that have traditionally been performed by several different people. As the sales clerk scans your purchases, the computer automatically determines the prices and totals the amount of the sale. The computer updates the company's cash balance for the cash sale and the inventory balance for the items sold. If the inventory balance falls below a minimum amount, the computer automatically orders replacement inventory from the supplier. Thus, one sales clerk has handled authorization (ordering replacement inventory from a supplier), record keeping (recording receipt of cash and reduction of inventory), and custody of assets (receiving the cash).

Precomputer systems typically had at least three people involved in the same transaction. A sales clerk assisted the customer, prepared a sales invoice, and entered the price of the items sold. A second person, a cashier, checked the accuracy of the pricing and the total on the sales invoice. This person generally received the cash. A third person monitored inventory amounts and reordered inventory as needed.

Should a lack of traditional separation of duties alarm us? The answer is maybe. Traditional separation of duties was implemented because it was feasible, both physically and economically in a manual processing system, to monitor employees and prevent innocent mistakes or purposeful harm to the organization. However, information technology can provide much of the observation capabilities that were previously performed by humans. As IT is increasingly embedded into business processes, we have a strategic opportunity to enforce business rules, policies, and procedures as the event is executed. Specifically, we can instruct IT to perform the following functions that were traditionally achieved by separation of duties:

- Facilitate the capturing of reliable business event data.
- Ensure the proper execution of management policy.
- Detect and more effectively prevent errors and irregularities.
- Provide increased control over organization resources.
- Perform independent checks on the execution of business events and the processing of information.

Separation of duties is still an important concept for developing a philosophy of internal control. However, the way the concept is applied differs in an IT environment. Perhaps we can update the concept to separating custody, authorization, and the ability to manipulate data and information. The specific duties that organizations need to separate are updated to reflect the updated resources used to design and operate systems.[7] Regardless of whether a check is performed by a person or by a machine, it is important to have a reasonable system of checks and balances in place.

The Ability to Protect and Enhance at the Same Time

Control Concept 3: Tailor control procedures to the business process in order to improve the quality of the internal control system while enhancing organizational effectiveness.

Today, most businesses are streamlining their operations, empowering employees, and eliminating tasks that do not add value. The objective of these efforts is to develop leaner, more efficient and effective organizations. Such efforts are compatible with the objective of promoting operational efficiency.

Unfortunately, some people view the objective of safeguarding assets as incompatible with promoting operational efficiency. Operating improvements often change both business and information processes. This obviously requires a reevaluation of internal control because you should not blindly apply traditional control policies and procedures to changed business processes. Yet some professionals feel that modifying internal controls compromises or diminishes their effectiveness and results in serious risk exposures. This type of thinking focuses on specific control procedures designed to evaluate internal controls, rather than focusing on risks and on designing context-specific procedures to control risks.

To illustrate, accountants are traditionally taught that a liability is not recognized until three documents—purchase order, receiving report, and vendor's invoice—have been reconciled. This review is considered necessary to detect whether (1) the goods were properly ordered, (2) the ordered goods were actually received, and (3) the vendor's bill is for

---

7 Supplemental Chapter D illustrates some separation of duties guidelines that are useful in a computing environment.

the proper amount. This reconciliation attempts to prevent the company from paying for something it did not purchase and receive. To someone who is trying to improve operational efficiency, this reconciliation is both costly and unnecessary. It results in a time lag between receiving the goods and formally recognizing a liability in the accounting records.

By altering the purchasing process and effectively using IT, an organization can implement a set of rules and controls to reduce or eliminate these risks. First, they can implement purchasing controls to reduce risks associated with placing an order. By requiring all orders to be computer generated, the computer can prevent ordering by an unauthorized person or ordering from an invalid vendor. Next, they can control the receipt of merchandise by having the computer confirm in real time that the goods received by a receiving clerk are the same as the items on the original purchase order. Using these controls, the organization can recognize the liability at the receipt of goods, allowing them to record relevant operational and financial data at the time of the business event. Matching the vendor's invoice and the items received can still be performed to assure that the purchasing entity and the selling entity are in agreement, but the process will not hamper the timely recognition of the liability, nor the timely control of each business event as it occurs.

By understanding an organization and the risks it faces, you can evaluate and design rules for a redesigned process based on their ability to control risk. To facilitate change and retain a high standard of internal control, identify the risks associated with the more efficient process and design control procedures to effectively reduce them. Do not allow specific control procedures to limit the potential of using technology to enable more efficient business operations. Rather, shape the rules to control the risks of the new process. Often the costs saved from an improved process allow us to be much more aggressive in controlling risk.

Information Technology Paradox: A Risk to Be Controlled or a Tool to Control Risk?

> **Control Concept 4: Accountants must become familiar with IT capabilities and risks and recognize the opportunities IT provides to prevent, detect, and correct errors and irregularities as decisions are made, operating activities occur, and information processes are executed.**

Innovative uses of information technology provide a strategic opportunity to help solve two fundamental business problems: support decision making and improve business and information processes. Unfortunately, the accounting profession is perceived as slow to recognize how quickly businesses are embracing information technology—dwelling too much on the risks of IT, rather than using IT as a tool to enable or enhance control.

Many people feel that powerful and complex computers increase risks because human judgment is bypassed, processing is concentrated, and data are stored in erasable and compressed forms. To be fair, using information technology certainly increases some risks. However, as Al Arens and Jim Loebbecke explain:

> Despite circumstances that may increase the potential for misstatements, well-controlled EDP (electronic data processing) systems have a greater potential for reducing misstatements. This

is due to the characteristic of uniformity of processing . . . and the potential for increased management supervision.[8]

Unfortunately, some auditors ignore the quality of an internal control system in an IT environment. Their evaluation consists of testing several individual transactions as they are processed through the computer system, or they may audit around the system altogether.[9] Either approach is shallow and expensive. Moreover, as organizations become more aggressive in their use of information technology to control risks, the approach of auditing around IT applications results in no independent assessment of the actual system of internal control embodied within the information system.

A better approach is to utilize technology itself to bring business and information process risk under control. Typically, the system of internal controls is an amalgam of procedures that attempt to prevent, detect, and correct risks. Auditors, because of the nature of the audit itself, have the reputation of focusing almost entirely on detective controls. Remember that the purpose of the audit is to express an opinion on the fairness of the financial statements for a prior period. However, the audit mentality has carried over to most of accounting. As we pointed out in Chapter 3, many accounting systems are not integrated with the execution of business processes. Therefore, when data finally reach the accounting system, the opportunity to prevent, or even detect, errors in a timely manner is past.

Accounting professionals must realize that the value of business and information process rules is in achieving *all* of the objectives of internal controls noted earlier—not just reliable financial reporting, but effectiveness and efficiency of operations, and compliance with applicable laws and regulations. An effective system of internal controls needs preventive, detective, and corrective controls. Once errors and irregularities are detected, the organization should focus on both correcting the impact of the error or irregularity, and developing preventive controls to ensure that the error or irregularity does not recur. When errors and irregularities are prevented, rather than detected and corrected, internal controls provide much greater value to the organization.

In short, what appears to be a paradox is not. Information technologies introduce new risks to an organization. Yet, a closer look reveals a risk trade: Automation replaces the risks of using human processors and paper storage methods, with the risks of using computer processors and electronic storage methods. Along with the new risks comes a tool that, when properly used, can increase the efficiency and effectiveness of achieving all the control objectives. The predominate factor in using information technology to reduce risk is a knowledge of business processes, the decisions that must be made, the information processes, and the capabilities of IT. The effective use of IT to prevent, detect, and recover from risk exposures is often limited by a lack of knowledge regarding IT capabilities or misconceptions regarding the impact of IT on the business, risk, controls, and auditing.

---

8 A. Arens and J. Loebbecke, *Auditing: An Integrated Approach,* 7th ed. (Upper Saddle River, NJ: Prentice Hall, 1997), p. 533.

9 *Auditing around the computer* is a term used to describe an audit where the auditor does not directly test the computer programs but draws inferences about their accuracy by examining inputs into the system and outputs from the system. If a program correctly handles a few known inputs, there is the presumption that it correctly handles all inputs. Typically, there is no direct evaluation of the program's built-in controls or its ability to handle exceptions.

IT is fast being embedded in an increasingly larger portion of business and information processes. This mandates the use of technology to control these processes. It also increases the difficulty of assessing the effectiveness of an organization's control structure without explicitly considering the information technology component of the system. If the accounting and auditing professions want to continue to play a key role in the design, use, and evaluation of information systems, they must have a correct understanding of modern information technology concepts and capabilities and be proficient in identifying, suggesting, implementing, and evaluating controls in today's organizations.

Information Processing Complexity

Control Concept 5: Processes that make extensive use of paper inputs and outputs and visible records of intermediate processes are not less risky than more complex, highly integrated systems. Highly integrated systems can be less risky provided they are properly constructed with the right controls built into them.

People have different attitudes about the complexity of information processing. Often people believe traditional information systems that possess characteristics inherent in manual information systems are much less complex than highly integrated information systems. Arens and Loebbecke contrast "noncomplex" (see Exhibit 5–4) and "complex" (see Exhibit 5–5) systems and indicate that this is not true.

> In noncomplex [traditional] EDP systems, there are often source documents in support of each transaction, and most results of processing are printed out. Thus, input, output, and to a great extent processing are visible to the EDP user and auditor. With greater volumes of data and more complexity this is no longer true.[10]

Obviously, familiarity with such a "less complex" environment creates the perception that such a system is easier to control and evaluate. The hardcopy documents of inputs, intermediate processes, and outputs provide some support for this perception. In actuality, the term *noncomplex* is misleading because such architectures actually consist of hundreds of loosely coupled, poorly integrated, noncomplex systems. As a result, many organizations are awash in a morass of poorly coordinated systems that possess the same weaknesses identified in Chapter 3.

CASE IN POINT

In 1979 IBM was using over 300 "noncomplex" applications to support their financial reporting requirements alone. In isolation, each system appeared very straightforward. However, these 300+ financial applications were fed data by thousands of other systems that provided the details of economic transactions. Attempting to maintain and control such an information system became nearly impossible and far more costly than necessary.

---

[10] Arens and Loebbecke, *Auditing: An Integrated Approach,* p. 532.

EXHIBIT 5–4

Traditional "Noncomplex" System

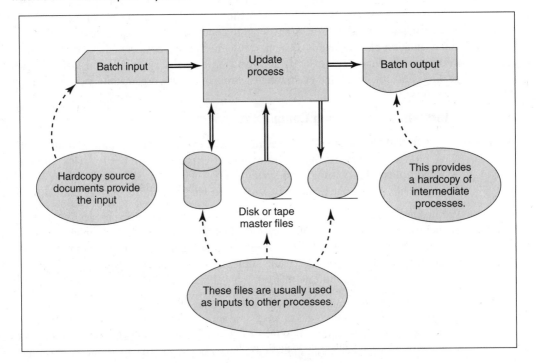

Different or *unfamiliar* should not be confused with *complex* and *risky.* Proper use of information technology can greatly simplify the business and information processes of the organization while also reducing organizational risk. It is detrimental to categorize systems with familiar, traditional characteristics and paper outputs as noncomplex and other designs as complex. In fact, the systems outlined in Chapter 4, although new and unfamiliar to many people are very simple. Business events have one recording process to capture relevant data and store it in a data warehouse. The data remain available with very little processing until they are accessed in a query for management and financial reports.

Visibility of Information

Control Concept 6: An electronic audit trail can be as effective as, or more effective than, a paper-based audit trail. The audit trail in an integrated, event-based system is often shorter and less complex than a traditional paper-based audit trail.

EXHIBIT 5–5

"Complex" Information System

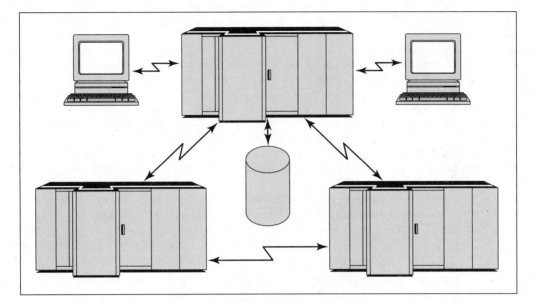

Traditionally, auditors have relied on the physical visibility of information in the form of paper to establish what is commonly called the *audit trail*. The traditional definition of the audit trail is the collection of documents that allows auditors to trace accounting numbers on the financial statements back to their origin (source documents), and vice versa. For example, the audit trail for Gross Sales on the income statement in a manual system would be the general ledger, the sales journals (and maybe the general journal), and the individual sales invoices (or other original documents to support journal entries). A paper audit trail was effective in manual systems because the primary medium for data flow and storage was paper. Doing away with the paper audit trail leaves some people with an uncomfortable feeling—they feel that because the audit trail is no longer physically visible, it does not exist.

While it is true that organizations may eliminate the use of paper documents in today's information systems, the ability to trace the flow of data can easily remain intact, visible, and real. In fact, the trail can be made more obvious than ever through proper systems design because data are not processed through a large network of loosely connected electronic and human processes. In IT applications that incorporate the concepts explained in Chapter 4, each data element about the resources, events, agents, and locations passes through a single recording process. Each report is the result of a single reporting process. Thus, the audit trail is maintained by individual transactions. Also, a variety of detailed data is available, often online, for audit analysis and evaluation.

CASE IN POINT

Some companies have a hard time getting rid of an electronic audit trail. People are information pack rats and the predilection to hoard is exceeded only by the ease with which computer users can copy and store data. Getting rid of data is sometimes a problem because hitting the delete key doesn't actually remove the data from the computer. The delete key only removes the file's name from the directory. The data remains on the disk until they are overwritten by new data. Experts estimate that a third of the average hard drive contains data that have been "deleted." This was a problem for PepsiCo, Inc., while defending a sexual harassment suit. Their attorneys' claim that sexual material was not stored in the workplace was questioned when Ontrack Data International sleuths discovered a strip-poker program on the company computer and testified that it had been intentionally deleted. That was enough to show that they had destroyed evidence and the judge subsequently increased the jury's verdict from about $450,000 to $1.7 million.[11]

Today's electronic audit trail is a map, consisting of both data and processes, that allows the organization to document system activities and test the integrity of a system's data and rules. This definition is useful for any type of system, manual or electronic. Like traditional systems, an electronic audit trail still consists of data and processes. The difference is the nonpaper form of the data, data flows, and processes. The burden is on us to familiarize ourselves with the data flows, processes, and storage mediums to review and validate the electronic audit trail.

Timing the Design and Implementation of Controls

Control Concept 7: Be actively involved during the design and development stages of a new or modified information system to help identify and implement controls in the system.

The timing and extent of involvement by accounting and auditing professionals in the design and implementation of information systems is an important issue. When should accountants and auditors evaluate the system—at the time of an independent audit of the financial statements or at the time the system is developed? Should they remain independent from systems design, and evaluate the design and suggest controls only after the system is in use; or should they consult with systems developers so rules to protect and enhance the organization can be built into the system during its design and development?

The answers to these questions are more obvious when we focus on the value IT can provide to an organization. IT provides value by:

1. Helping the organization to be much more proactive in preventing, detecting, and correcting errors and irregularities.
2. Facilitating, rather than inhibiting, continual improvement in business and information processes.

---

11 A. Markels, "The Messy Business of Culling Company Files," *The Wall Street Journal,* May 22, 1997, p. B1.

A real-time control mentality is required to realize these significant benefits. Rather than adding or "building on" control procedures after a system is developed and implemented, controls should be built into the system to allow detection, prevention, and correction at the point of each business activity.

CASE IN POINT

Today we have the technology available to include a chip within your computer that can monitor your work and the programs you run. Such a chip can have the ability to determine when you make a mistake or have difficulty performing a specific task within a selected application. The chip could prompt you on what to do or call the local help desk and report the problem to them. You might be surprised when you are at the height of your frustration in printing a report and the help desk calls and asks, "Are you having a problem printing from your computer?" They could then guide you in solving the problem.

The chip could also be used to keep track of which programs you use and report back to the maker of the software if you are connected through the Internet. Such a control would help eliminate much of the illegal use of software by people who do not have a legitimate license.

Pointing out weaknesses after an IT application has been developed is of limited value to an organization, especially when useful controls could have been built into the application and tested *before* the application was ever installed. Left unchecked, information technology will simply increase the risk exposure for the organization without providing the tools to mitigate risk. Preventing business event errors and irregularities requires controls to be built into the system's recording, maintaining, and reporting processes. As the Committee of Sponsoring Organizations (COSO) has argued:

> Internal control should not be viewed as something that must be superimposed on an organization's normal operating structure. To do so creates costs that can inhibit the organization's ability to compete. Internal control should be built into the infrastructure of an enterprise. When controls are integrated with operational activities, and a focus on controls has been instilled in all personnel, the result is better control with minimum incremental cost. Such integration avoids a superstructure of control procedures on top of existing activities. Whenever management considers changes to their company's operations or activities, the concept that it's better to "build-in" rather than "build-on" controls, and to do it right the first time, should be fundamental guiding premises.[12]

Evaluating the Internal Control System

Control Concept 8: Greater use of information technology provides the opportunity for new services that verify the adequacy of internal controls within the information system and the accuracy of queries in extracting desired information.

Internal control systems are typically reviewed by independent auditors at the time of the annual audit of external financial statements. Questions are being asked about the desirability of this practice. Should we retain the current emphasis on audited financial

---

12 *Internal Control—Integrated Framework.*

statements or should the emphasis be changed to audit the information system and the adequacy of its controls?

Information technology provides alternative information sources to those who traditionally relied on financial statements. For many years financial statements represented a large part of the information available to an enterprise's debt and equity investors. But IT is making other forms of information increasingly available. For example, investors can get up-to-the-minute data about companies through public and proprietary databases without waiting for quarterly or annual reports. These trends call into question the value of traditional financial statements and the auditors' opinion on them.

> Once capital suppliers have real-time access to an enterprise's database, they will have little interest in annual financial statements, and, by extension, auditor's opinions on them, issued well after the entity's fiscal year-end. What they might be far more interested in is real-time assurance from the auditor that either the information in the enterprise's databases is reliable or the system itself is highly likely to produce reliable data.[13]

Although this trend seems very threatening to many auditors, it opens up many new opportunities. One proposed service is an independent audit of the information system and the adequacy of its internal controls. Rather than expressing an opinion on the fairness of *financial statements* in accordance with generally accepted accounting principles, the auditor could express an opinion on the adequacy of the *information system* and its internal control procedures in capturing, storing, and presenting complete and accurate data about the organization's business events in accordance with generally accepted control practices. Such a service is being proposed by the Special Committee on Assurance Services of the AICPA:

> Systems quality assurance provides users with assurance that a system has been designed and operated to produce reliable data. System assurance involves testing the integrity of an information system. The CPA studies the system and analyzes the possible causes of defects in the data to determine if the system avoids them . . . [The proposed] model is quality-by-design and continuous improvement. For information systems to provide decision-makers with continuously reliable information, accountants must abandon the historical error-detection-and-correction model and move to a reliability-by-design model. This involves rigorous review and testing by the CPA.[14]

Another service might be assisting investors and creditors in extracting relevant information from the company's public database for their decision alternatives. The auditor could verify the accuracy of the investors' and creditors' queries in extracting the desired information.

Size of Business

Control Concept 9: Small organizations can have strong internal control systems by integrating controls into the information system and using IT to monitor and control the business and information processes.

---

13 R. K. Elliott, "What Is Ahead in the Assurance Function: The Future of Audits," *Journal of Accountancy* (New York: AICPA), September 1994.

14 Committee on Assurance Services, May 1998, http://www.aicpa.org/.

Based on traditional concepts of separation of duties it has been more difficult to establish an effective system of internal controls in small organizations because of their limited personnel and resources. However, when IT is properly used as part of the control environment, it is very feasible to develop a system that provides the necessary business and information processing controls. Even small businesses have the potential to greatly increase the effectiveness of their internal control system without incurring tremendous costs. Good internal control is not dependent nearly so much on having a lot of people as it is on developing an information age control philosophy and using IT intelligently.

UPDATED PHILOSOPHY OF INTERNAL CONTROLS WITH AN IT PERSPECTIVE

Earlier in the chapter we identified the concepts and practices that have guided our control philosophy. Many of these philosophies need to be modified substantially as we move into an information technology age. As we move from people processors to computer processors and from paper data storage and transmission to electronic data storage and transmission there are changes that must be made in our control philosophy. The following points summarize the changed philosophy.

1. Hard-copy documents should largely be eliminated. They are costly to both develop and maintain and they provide little benefit over an electronic version of the same information. In fact, because of size, storage cost, and inaccessibility, paper documents are becoming a liability.

2. Separation of duties continues to be a relevant concept, but IT can be used as a substitute for some of the functions normally assigned to a separate individual. Much of the control that has been spread across several individuals can now be built into the information system and monitored by information technology.

3. Duplicate recordings of business event data and reconciliation should be eliminated. Recording and maintaining the duplicate data and performing the reconciliation is costly and unnecessary in an IT environment.

4. Accountants should become consultants with a real-time, proactive control philosophy. Much greater emphasis should be placed on preventing business risks, than on detecting and correcting errors and irregularities.

5. Greater emphasis must be placed on implementing controls during the design and development of information systems and on more auditor involvement in verifying the accuracy of the systems themselves. Although the annual audit of the financial statements will continue to be a valuable service performed by external auditors, its relative importance will diminish as greater importance is placed on verifying the accuracy of the system itself and providing real-time reporting assurance services.

6. Greater emphasis must be placed on enhancing organizational effectiveness and internal controls must be adapted to remain strong. This does away with the checklist mentality and requires an evaluation of specific risks and the creation of controls to address those specific risks.

7. Information technology should be exploited to its fullest extent. This requires a concerted effort to understand both the capabilities and risks of IT. Modern IT should be used much more extensively to support decision processes, conduct business events, perform information processes, and prevent and detect errors and irregularities.

THE PROCESS OF DEVELOPING A SYSTEM OF INTERNAL CONTROLS

If you develop a control philosophy based on the key control concepts identified in this chapter, the process of developing an internal control system is rather straightforward:

1. Identify the organization's objectives, processes, and risks and determine risk materiality.
2. Select the internal control system—including rules, processes, and procedures—to control material risks.
3. Develop, test, and implement the internal control system.
4. Monitor and refine the system.

An event-driven system helps in both identifying and controlling risks. The next section explores risks and controls in an event-driven financial system and illustrates the thought process required to identify business and information processing risks and the appropriate rules to control them.

Risks and Controls in an Event-Driven System

An event-driven system provides a framework for classifying risks that builds upon what you have already learned about decision, business, and information processes. Acquiring the ability to identify risk requires knowledge of the business organization. Recall from Chapter 2 that the essence of an organization's operating events can be described by answering the following questions:

♦ What happens?
♦ When?
♦ Who is involved?
♦ What resources are involved?
♦ Where does the event occur?

In addition, business events trigger three types of information processes:

♦ Recording event data (e.g., recording the sale of merchandise).
♦ Maintaining resource, agent, and location data (e.g., updating a customer's address).
♦ Reporting useful information (e.g., preparing a report on sales by product).

We must now add the following question to our thinking process: What could go wrong?

Using these elements, we can build a taxonomy that classifies both desirable and un-desirable business events and information processes (see Exhibit 5–6). Notice how the straightforward nature of this system's architecture avoids many of the risks associated with a traditional architecture. Most of the risks associated with classifying and summarizing the event information and the risks of duplicate data and frequent reconciliation are avoided.

Operating Event Risks   Business event risk results in errors and irregularities having one or more of the following characteristics:

+ A business event occurring at the wrong time or sequence.
+ A business event occurring without proper authorization.
+ A business event involving the wrong internal agent.
+ A business event involving the wrong external agent.
+ A business event involving the wrong resource.
+ A business event involving the wrong amount of resource.
+ A business event occurring at the wrong location.

Our objective is to identify risks associated with operating events and control the risks (to the extent possible) at the time of occurrence. This usually requires embedding

EXHIBIT 5–6

Business and Information Processing Risks in an Event-Driven System

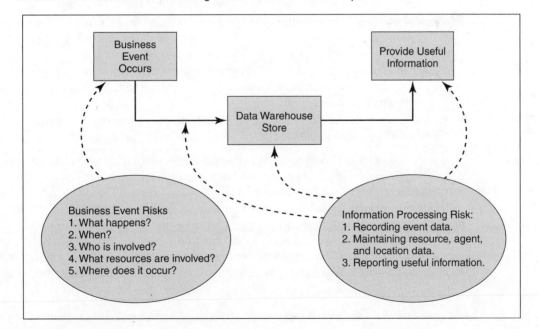

control procedures into the execution of the operating events. The rules, policies, and procedures associated with the events are then reviewed and mandated at the point and time of the activity. Because organizations are increasingly using technology to define and execute business processes, there is opportunity to achieve such real-time risk identification and control at low cost.

Your ability to identify or judge operating event risks results from your knowledge of an organization's business operations. While you may lack such knowledge at this point in your learning, the information in this text will help fill the gaps. Chapters 6 through 8 elaborate on business activities and processes and illustrate ways to use information technology to prevent, detect, and correct these errors and irregularities.

Information Processing Risks   Let's suppose you are able to control the risk associated with an operating event (i.e., the event was executed according to prescribed policies and procedures). The event triggers the need to record the activity in the information system—an information event. You now need to control the risk of recording the activity. Recall that the information processing objectives include recording and reporting accurate, complete, and timely data. Attempts to maintain the validity of data once it is inside the information system is referred to as maintaining *data integrity.*[15] Risks relating to information processing include:

- *Recording risks*—Include recording incomplete, inaccurate, or invalid data about a business event. Incomplete data result in not having all the relevant characteristics about an operating event. Inaccuracies arise from recording data that do not accurately represent the event. *Invalid* refers to data that are recorded about a fabricated event.
- *Maintaining risks*—Are essentially the same as recording risks. The only difference is the data relates to resources, agents, and locations rather than to operating events. The risk relating to maintenance processes is that changes with respect to the organization's resources, agents, and locations will go either undetected or unrecorded (e.g., customer or employee moves, customer declares bankruptcy, or location is destroyed through a natural disaster).
- *Reporting risks*—Include data that are improperly accessed, improperly summarized, provided to unauthorized individuals, or not provided in a timely manner.

Notice we do not include improperly classifying business event data as a recording error. Classifying business event data (including classifying debits and credits) is part of the reporting process.

Thus, it is necessary to review and analyze all recording, maintaining, and reporting processes of an organization to identify potential risks and design controls to reduce the risks. Although all information processing errors and irregularities are undesirable whenever they occur, they are particularly harmful when they occur during the recording and maintaining processes. Why? The answer is the old adage, Garbage in, Garbage out! If in-

---

15 Supplemental Chapter D lists several control measures used to increase data validity and maintain data integrity.

accurate, invalid, or incomplete data are either recorded or maintained, the result is erroneous reporting of all affected processes, regardless of the quality of the reporting process itself or the technology utilized. Furthermore, if the recording process also executes the management policy surrounding a business event, a faulty or illogical recording process can also introduce errors and irregularities into the execution of the business event itself.

Risk Management Opportunities for Information Professionals

Developing the ability to identify risks and create an effective system of internal controls takes time and actual experience. You will not find everything you need to know about risk in books. To become effective at designing internal control systems you must practice the principles we have outlined in this chapter. Those who implement these principles can enjoy a tremendous career in business, information processing, and information technology risk management.

We are proposing a very proactive, real-time control philosophy that uses IT as a control resource. Therefore, it should not surprise you that this philosophy has a significant impact on both accounting and IT professionals. Many professional accounting organizations that have provided audit services for years are reevaluating their own audit processes and services. They realize that auditing services must shift from being driven by regulatory requirements to being focused on adding value to organizations. There is a great opportunity for auditors to be involved in the actual development of IT applications, to provide audit assurances about the quality of the system itself, and to assist external users in obtaining special purpose information from company-provided databases. All this requires a management consultant control philosophy, as discussed in this chapter. As Steven M. H. Wallman, SEC Commissioner, observes:

> Accountants and independent auditors are the gatekeepers to the integrity of the markets. As forward looking changes . . . are explored and implemented, the auditor's role will become even more important. For example, such changes will cause an increased reliance on the internal controls and accounting decisions of the firm itself. Real-time information would be more of a nightmare than a dream without appropriate and increasingly reliable internal control mechanisms assuring the integrity of the information. Moreover, whole new fields of information disclosure and analysis will appear. Accounting will then provide, more than ever, the value added that permits the efficient allocation of resources that drives capitalism and underpins our democracy.[16]

In *Reinventing the CFO: Moving From Financial Management to Strategic Management,*[17] the authors provide the following guidelines with regard to the "new" fiduciary view of the profession:

---

16 Steven J. H. Wallman, "The Future of Accounting and Disclosure in an Evolving World: The Need for Dramatic Change, *Accounting Horizons* 9, no. 3 (September 1995), p. 90.
17 Thomas Walther, Henry Johansson, John Dunleavy, and Elizabeth Hjelm, *Reinventing the CFO: Moving From Financial Management to Strategic Management* (New York: McGraw-Hill, 1997), pp.14–15.

- Policies and procedures need to be revisited in terms of practicality and relevance, and revised as necessary.
- Controls should be built into processes as enablers and not imposed externally to the process as barriers.
- Cost and cycle time should be given high priority when building the fiduciary control environment.

To satisfy the business need for effective systems of internal controls, accounting professionals must work with developers of information systems to ensure business, information processing, and information technology risks are properly assessed and controlled. When this occurs, accountants, auditors, systems developers, and organizations as a whole can more effectively control the risk crisis.

CONCLUDING COMMENTS

Up to this point in the text, we have presented a number of topics to help you understand information systems, and help you become a more effective system user, designer, and evaluator. Let's overview our study thus far. Chapter 1 introduced information systems, the role and purpose of accounting information systems, and calls for change in the accounting profession. The first chapter also reviewed the accounting and information system professions, and stressed the need to merge the two professions to effectively use, design, and evaluate accounting information systems.

Chapter 3 reviewed the evolution of the design of accounting information systems, focusing on the general ledger and the accounting cycle. Understanding the general ledger design provides insights into some of the limitations accounting professionals have in producing the outputs desired by information customers. In summary, the structure of traditional accounting information systems has not been updated to take full advantage of the benefits gained by effectively using information technology. This chapter also examined the characteristics of redesigned, updated accounting information systems, and more importantly, it presented a challenge to accounting information professionals. The challenge is to effectively apply available resources to improve the ability of accounting to support organizations.

Chapters 2 and 4 provided a method for analyzing a business entity. The following chapters focus on individual business processes and illustrate many of these concepts further. Finally, it is time to begin applying the knowledge you have gained in the first five chapters of this text.

CHECKLIST OF KEY TERMS AND CONCEPTS

Application controls	Business event risk
Audit trail	Business risks
Business event controls	Checklist control philosophy

Collude/collusion
Control
Control activities
Control environment
Corrective controls
Data integrity
Detective controls
Error
General controls
Independent checks on performance
Information and communication
Information processing controls
Information processing risk
Internal control objectives
Internal control system

Irregularity
Materiality of risk
Monitoring
Objectives
Opportunity
Performance reviews
Physical controls
Preventive controls
Processing controls
Risk
Risk assessment
Risk materiality
Separation of duties
Statement of Auditing Standards (SAS) *No. 55 and No. 78*

REVIEW QUESTIONS

1. What is meant by a system of internal controls?
2. Distinguish between risk, exposure, and threat.
3. Describe the relationship between risk, opportunity, and objectives.
4. How do you determine the materiality of risk?
5. Should we attempt to control all risks? Explain.
6. Should an organization implement as many control procedures as possible? Explain.
7. Describe separation of duties and responsibilities.
8. Describe physical controls.
9. Contrast general and application controls.
10. Who is ultimately responsible for internal controls within an organization?
11. List the nine assumptions that underlie an updated control philosophy.
12. List and describe the five interrelated components of an internal control system.
13. Which type of control is needed more in today's risk environment: prevention, detection, or correction? Explain.
14. What role should specific control procedures or checklists play in determining if an environment is well controlled? Explain.
15. List the three types of duties that are separated using the traditional concept of separation of duties. How, if at all, should these be integrated in an IT processing environment?
16. What is the difference between "auditing around" versus "auditing through" the computer?
17. If organizations change from a manual system to a computerized system, do their internal control objectives change? Explain.

18. Define the term *audit trail*. How does the use of information technology affect the audit trail?

19. Is it necessary for an audit trail to be comprised of paper? Explain.

20. Describe in your own words the traditional control philosophy.

21. Is it better to build controls into an information system or add them to the system after it is built? Why?

22. True or False: "Control objectives are obtainable only in large organizations." Explain.

23. List the four steps in developing an effective system of internal control.

24. List seven variations of operating event risks.

25. Differentiate between information processing and operating event risks.

26. Explain the risks associated with recording information processes.

27. Explain the risks associated with maintaining information processes.

28. Explain the risks associated with reporting information processes.

DISCUSSION QUESTIONS

1. Why is it important to consider both the costs and benefits of an internal control policy, rule, or procedure?

2. Is risk 100% controllable? Explain your response.

3. Is it necessary to have different control philosophies in manual and information technology environments? Explain.

4. In general terms, what controls from a manual processing environment can we apply to a high-tech, computer environment? Explain.

5. A new auditor is in charge of an internal control evaluation. He decides to ask the organization's management for various types of documentation, then decide, based on his review of the procedures used to process the documents, whether the organization has a good system of internal control. Please comment on the strengths and weaknesses of this method of evaluation.

6. On January 1, CBU installed a new computer system for tracking and calculating inventory costs. On December 31, at closing, CBU's system reported inventory at $4.5 million for financial statement purposes. At midnight, the auditors performed a physical inventory count and found the inventory at $3.5 million. To correct the discrepancy, CBU's accounting staff processed an adjusting entry to reduce inventory by $1.0 million.

    The next day, two accountants were discussing the events of the previous night. Accountant A was proud of the audit and said it illustrated a benefit of having a good system of internal control. CBU had followed good internal control procedures by having a regular physical inventory count to safeguard a valuable organization resource. Accountant A was relieved that the problem was resolved: The financial numbers were corrected before they were reported. In short, he felt successful and thought CBU should feel fortunate to have his accounting staff as control advisors. Accountant B felt differently. She talked about the bad decisions that were made throughout the year based on the incorrect inventory numbers. She felt that she and the other accountants should have helped develop more timely and effective system controls.

Which accountant's philosophy is correct? How can you explain the diverse opinions? What policies or procedures, if any, should CBU develop to avoid such problems in the future?

7. You are studying for the CPA examination and find a discussion of the relationship between information technology and controls in your materials. The author argues that the use of information technology increases control risk and diminishes the audit trail. Explain why you agree or disagree with this opinion.

8. During spring break, you meet a student from another university. The two of you decide to meet later that evening to study for upcoming accounting information systems exams. The other student is taking a traditional class, and the two of you argue over the concept of separation of duties. Your new acquaintance states that regardless of the data processing environment, it is essential that an organization separate custodial, record keeping, and authorization functions. In addition, the student argues that accounting and information systems functions should be kept separate, and that all accounting data must be kept within the Accounting Department to assure data integrity for financial statements. How do you respond to your new friend?

9. What is a *real-time* control mentality? How does it differ from a traditional control mentality?

10. The chapter argues that organizations should develop "built-in" system controls. This requires organizations to design and implement controls during the systems development process. If an organization waits until after a system is built to design controls, these are referred to as "build-on" controls and are often more expensive to implement and less effective. The chapter also discusses how involved auditors and accountants should be in the design of internal controls. When does the chapter suggest auditors become involved in the design and implementation of internal controls? Is there a correlation between the timing of auditor involvement and built-in versus build-on controls? What impact does this issue have on auditor independence? Explain.

11. Respond to the following comment by an auditor:

The design of traditional accounting information systems are fairly uniform across organizations. Although the chart of accounts may differ, I can count on a consistent design in any company I audit. I know I can always find journals and ledgers and depend on the accounting cycle. That's not true with these event-driven systems. They tend to be customized to reflect the nature of the particular organization. Therefore, accounting systems design is more varied and that makes my job tougher. I don't see the need to allow organizations to implement any architecture other than the general ledger architecture. Do you?

MINICASES AND OTHER APPLIED LEARNING

1. For each of the following examples of minimum cardinalities (the maximum cardinalities are omitted), explain the business rule associated with the cardinalities and list the business risks of not following the business rule:
   a. Sale (0, –) and (1, –) inventory.
   b. Sale (0, –) and (1, –) cash receipt. *require cash receipt, before sale*
   c. Shipment (1, –) and (0, –) sale. *do not have sale until has shipment*
   d. Receipt of inventory (0, –) and (1, –) inventory order. *can't receive inventory until order*
   e. Salesperson (1, –) and (0, –) customer.
   f. Cash disbursements (0, –) and (1, –) purchases.
   g. Customer (1, –) and (0, –) sale. *customer but no sale*
   h. Purchase (0, –) and (1, –) vendor.
   i. Shipment (0, –) and (1, –) customer order.

2. Refer to Problem 1. Are these minimum cardinalities examples of situations that require internal control consideration? Explain. Do these cardinalities suggest a certain order or procedural rules for doing business? Explain.

3. A customer calls a mail order company to order merchandise. The order clerk takes the customer's name, mailing address, credit card number, and the merchandise numbers, sizes, colors, and quantities. After the order clerk hangs up, he or she verifies that the merchandise numbers given by the client are valid (that the company does indeed sell an item with that number) and checks with the Shipping Department on availability of the merchandise items.

Required:
   a. Identify the operating event risks in this environment.
   b. Develop a business rule or a control to reduce these operating risks.

4. ABC, a nonprofit company, recently decided to analyze its expenditures. During the analysis, ABC discovered that all orders for repair services always go to a company owned by the vice president's sister, and it has a reputation for high prices and poor service. During the analysis, ABC also discovered that many of its purchases for supplies were delivered to the vice president's home address.

Required:
   a. Identify potential operating event risks in the environment.
   b. Identify the business rules or controls necessary to reduce these risks.

5. A small company in New Jersey lost part of its office building lease. They decided to consolidate their inventory warehouse and shipping dock. Rather than taking up floor space with a separate inventory warehouse, the company stores its goods on the shipping dock for easy access by employees who load the goods on their trucks.

Required:
   a. Identify potential operating event risks for this activity.
   b. Identify potential information processing risks.

6. Perky Sports reconciles its cash registers at the end of the day against receipt information from the computer. When a sales clerk executes a sale, the items sold are scanned into the computer and the cash received is entered into the cash register. The computer automatically associates the price of each item sold with the item. Originally, the owner of the store counted all the cash in the registers each day, but now, due to increased time constraints, a night manager performs the reconciliation.

Required:

    a. Identify the operating event risks in this environment.

    b. Develop business rules or controls to reduce these business risks.

7. A private insurance company receives checks in the mail daily for premium payments. Two data entry clerks are responsible for entering all checks on the same day they are received. The data entry persons both work in the same office but on different computers. After the checks are entered they go to an accounting clerk who deposits them.

Required:

    a. Identify the operating event risks in this environment.

    b. Develop business controls to reduce these risks.

8. A consulting firm with 20 employees conducts business in its office and at various client locations. Consultants are responsible for tracking and reporting their own hours—both in total and by individual client, and their expenses. Some engagements may take weeks and expenses are reimbursed.

Required:

    a. Identify the operating event risks in this environment.

    b. Develop business controls to reduce these risks.

9. A truck driver for a food distributor loads his truck early in the morning according to the invoice purchase orders. He is responsible for picking up COD payments and, on his return trip, for picking up the inventory from major distributors. Currently the POs are handwritten by the floor manager the day before the delivery.

Required:

    a. Identify the operating event risks in this environment.

    b. Develop business controls to reduce these risks.

10. Consider the risks, both business and information processing, associated with each of the following events. Identify what could go wrong, the probability of it happening, and what controls might prevent, detect, or correct the problem.

    a. Deliver Product to Customer (includes pricing merchandise and preparing an invoice).

    Marty's Distributing Co. is a beverage distributor. A truck driver leaves the warehouse in the morning with a truckload of beverage and drives to each retail outlet on his route. After checking the quantity of beverage on the shelf, he adds more to fill the available shelf space and prepares an invoice for the quantity added.

The quantity and price are entered on the invoice; amounts are extended, and the total calculated. Only the invoice total is entered into the accounting system by accounting personnel.

b. Issue New Insurance Policy (includes review of the proposed policy).

The New Business Division of Personal Life Insurance Co. has the responsibility to review new policies sent to the home office by insurance agents. If the policy satisfies certain criteria relating to age, sex, medical history, and extracurricular activities (no skydiving or scuba diving), the policy is considered a "clean case" and issued automatically. If it does not satisfy the specified criteria, it goes through a more extensive review and underwriting process. The initial premium is sent to treasury for processing.

c. Cash Customer Check.

Wells Fargo bank has several branch offices throughout southern California. Any branch can process checks (and other transactions like deposits or mortgage payments) for any branch of the company. Suppose a person brings a check written to them for $850,000 on a Wells Fargo checking account at another branch and wants to cash it.

d. Pay University Research Assistants.

Each pay period each department of the university submits to the payroll office a list of research assistants and the number of hours they worked for the period. The list is prepared by a departmental secretary, signed by the department chair, and mailed to the payroll office by the department secretary. The checks are mailed directly to the research assistant by the payroll office.

e. Sell Merchandise to Customers.

Salespeople, whose pay is based on a percentage of gross sales, make all the sales of the company. The salesperson is free to set the price of items sold as long as they are above a specified minimum. A separate data entry person enters both sales quantities and sales prices into a computer.

11. Bob owns a small recreational trailer business in a suburban community located close to the mountains. The community is relatively small but growing rapidly. Bob's business is growing, not because of his effective sales style and personality, but because of the growth of the community. Currently, Bob's competition has been nearly nonexistent, but as the area grows he expects to encounter increasing competition.

Bob sells mostly trailers for vacationing and camping. When customers arrive on Bob's lot, they are greeted by a salesperson. The salesperson may show the customers the trailers on the lot, but the salesperson need not be present during the entire showing. Depending on customer preference, the salesperson will either take the customer on a tour or the customer may roam the lot freely, inspecting trailers at his leisure.

Since recreational trailers are fairly large-ticket items, customers often leave the lot without making a purchase, only to return another day to purchase a trailer. When the customer decides to make a purchase, the salesperson initiates a series of procedures to properly document the order and sale transaction. First, the salesperson determines the model of the selected trailer and offers the customer a list of options that correspond to the particular model. The customer may (1) purchase a trailer off the lot with no added features, (2) purchase a trailer off the lot with additional features, or (3) special order a trailer that is not currently on the lot.

In most cases, customers do not pay cash for their trailers. If, however, the customer pays cash, a simple sales contract is prepared and the customer drives off with the trailer. The majority of the customers use an installment method of purchase. Before an installment purchase is authorized, the customer's credit must be verified to determine creditworthiness.

With an installment purchase, an installment agreement is prepared in addition to the sales contract. Bob has arranged financing through a local bank for all installment sales. When an installment sale is made, the bank sends Bob a lump-sum payment equal to the price of the trailer. Instead of making payments to Bob, customers pay the bank plus interest. In either case, Bob receives a lump-sum payment for each trailer sold, whether that lump sum comes from the customer or from the bank.

Once the credit is approved, the customer can take delivery of the trailer. This involves a delivery person who checks the trailer before delivering it to the customer. The customer picks up the trailer or has it delivered by Bob.

Required:

Bob's Trailer Sales has identified the following events of interest: Customer Looks at Trailers; Customer Orders Trailer; Deliver Trailer; and Receive Payment. Identify potential operating risks and appropriate controls associated with each event.

12. First Assembly of Holy Christians is a small religious organization located in the Midwest.

First Assembly holds a weekly Sunday observance in church-owned chapels plus other nonreligious events, such as bingo, during the week. Members of First Assembly are quite dedicated and regularly give contributions to their church.

Receiving donations is vital for the continuance of First Assembly. In fact, without member contributions, First Assembly could not function as it does currently. Member donations pay for the maintenance and mortgage of local chapels as well as provide a small living allowance for the clergy.

Usually, donations are given directly to the clergymen, instead of the conventional "passing of the plate" as seen in other religious organizations. Authorized clergymen receive donations in sealed envelopes provided by First Assembly. Each envelope contains a donation slip that accompanies each donation.

The member fills out the slip, inserts one copy of the slip in the envelope and retains one copy for him- or herself.

Donation envelopes received are opened at a later time, only when two or more clergy are present. The clergy count the donations and record the amount in a special ledger that documents donations by individual donors. After the donations are verified and recorded, two or more clergy must deposit the day's donations in a local bank. This deposit is made the same day (or the next day at the very latest) as the date of donation.

At the end of each year, the ledger is examined and account balances per donor are printed in report form and given to each individual donor as a means of confirming the donations received throughout the year.

Required:

The First Assembly of Holy Christians has identified the following events of interest: Receive Donation; Examine and Verify Donation; and Make Deposit. Identify the operating risks and the controls associated with each event.

13. FootHill Pharmacy is located inside Country Square, a popular retail outlet. FootHill Pharmacy sells prescription drugs, using a cash register to record each sale. Each cash register retains a record of the transactions and who performed them on the cash register's journal tape. This information is subsequently entered into a computer.

Prescriptions received over the phone are taken by the pharmacist and recorded on a prescription slip. Also, prescriptions received over the phone are entered into a computer that matches the prescription with guideline dosage levels and instruction information and prints the necessary information for the prescription. After entering the prescription information into the computer, the prescription is filled and a hard copy of the prescription slip is filed numerically for future reference.

All sales items are paid with cash, check, or credit card. On occasion, credit is extended to a customer, but he or she must be approved through the chief pharmacist. If credit is extended, a separate billing account is established. If a customer does not pay the bill within 120 days of the initial billing date, the account is turned over to a collection agency.

At the end of the day, cash in the register is counted and compared with the total amount of credit card receipts, and accounts receivable slips. This check is performed by two employees in the safe room and is always monitored on camera. In addition, total cash receipts recorded in the computer are compared with the deposit totals each day before Wells Fargo picks up the money for deposit.

Required:

FootHill Pharmacy has identified the following events of interest: Process Prescription Order; Fill Prescription; Give Prescription to Customer; Receive Payment; and Deposit Money. Identify the business risks and appropriate controls associated with each event.

14. Honesty, Inc., sells and scores questionnaires that are used primarily as an employment tool. The questionnaires measure a potential employee's honesty and dependability. Customers who buy the questionnaires ask a job applicant to complete the questionnaire as part of the application process. Customers call the applicant's responses into Honesty's analysis center, where Honesty's employees key the data into a computer. The computer stores and analyzes the raw data, and the results are given to the customer.

Companies begin using Honesty, Inc., questionnaires through the sales efforts of Mark Hayes. Mark's primary job is as a consultant on asset protection. He consults with a variety of companies, mostly retail, who have problems with employee honesty and dependability. He recommends Honesty, Inc., products to those whom he thinks will benefit by their use. If the company agrees to use the questionnaires, Honesty, Inc., assigns the company a number and gives the company a supply of questionnaires.

The company number is entered into the computers at the analysis center. Every time a company calls the center to have a questionnaire scored, they must provide their number. The computer uses the number to verify that the caller is a legitimate customer, to keep track of questionnaire usage, and to associate an applicant's questionnaire responses with a company.

Honesty, Inc., bills the company in two parts. The company is billed a nominal fee (generally $.50 each) for the questionnaires shipped. At the end of each month, another bill is sent based on usage for the month. The price charged depends on monthly usage, with a discount for large volumes, and is adjusted for the amount already paid. For example, if 300 questionnaires were scored during a month and the agreed price based on volume of use is $5 per questionnaire, the month-end statement would show $1,350 [300 × ($5.00 − $.50)].

Computer-generated month-end reports sent to the customer provide summary statistics on the questionnaires scored. The number of questionnaires used, as reported on the month-end reports, is the amount charged. Monthly statements prepared by one of the part-time employees at the analysis center (who also acts as an accounts receivable clerk) remind customers of the amounts due. Payments from clients are sent to the analysis center and are recorded and deposited by the accounts receivable clerk in the checking account of the company.

Required:

Honesty has identified the following operating events of interest: Sell Questionnaires; Process Customer Orders; Ship Questionnaires; Score Questionnaires; Receive Payment; and Deposit Money. Identify the risks and controls that should accompany each event.

6

CHAPTER

The Sales/Collection Business Process

CHAPTER OBJECTIVE

The objective of this chapter is to introduce the sales/collection business process (also known as the *revenue process*). After studying this chapter, you should be able to:

- Identify the characteristics of the traditional sales/collection process and related IT applications.
- Describe weaknesses in the traditional sales/collection process and IT application architecture.
- Develop a *REAL* model of the sales/collection process.
- Suggest ways to improve the sales/collection process and its IT application.

INTRODUCTION

Throughout the first five chapters of this book we have discussed:

- The opportunity for accounting and IT professionals to increase their value (Chapter 1).
- The major business processes and how to analyze and model them (Chapter 2).
- The nature of traditional IT applications and their weaknesses (Chapter 3).
- The nature of event-driven IT applications and how to prototype them (Chapter 4).
- The nature of business and information processing risk and control (Chapter 5).

Now it is time to apply what you have learned to specific business processes. We will begin with the sales/collection process. The acquisition/payment process and other business processes are covered in the following two chapters. These three chapters will:

1. Review the purpose of the process.
2. Review the nature of the traditional process (with and without IT).
3. Outline the weaknesses of traditional business processes and IT applications.
4. Identify opportunities to enhance value.
5. Help define the ideal process.
6. Provide insights to help align business and information processes.
7. Provide useful measures about the process.

Although we will not include all the variations and complexities of traditional business processes and IT applications across all organizations, we will explore some of the major variations. When you complete Chapter 8, you should be able to analyze business processes and the IT applications used to support them and propose significant improvements to both. This ability will enhance your value to the organization. Once again, your mastery of this material depends more on how many times you apply it than on how many times you read it.

THE PURPOSE OF THE SALES/COLLECTION PROCESS

As you begin to improve a business process and its IT applications, you must clearly understand its purpose and importance. Too often, organizations modify a process or its IT applications without considering its strategic significance. Understanding processes and their related IT applications helps you avoid making unwise IT investments.

The sales/collection process is a series of operating events that collectively serve to attract customers, help customers select goods and services, deliver the goods and services requested, and collect payments for the goods and services. In addition, the process should:

♦ Minimize the amount of time between the selection of products and services and the collection of cash.

♦ Minimize the amount of cash that is not collected from customers for goods and services provided.

♦ Structure product quality and price to balance customer value and organization profitability.

The sales/collection process is often the only time the customer directly interacts with the organization. No matter how efficient the remaining organization processes are, if the sales/collection process does not function well, it is unlikely the organization will generate sufficient revenue to sustain itself. Generating revenue is the key to achieving growth and profitability. Organizations can produce an abundance of goods and create a variety of services, but the real test of value is whether someone will pay a price that covers the cost of goods or services and provides the organization with an acceptable return on invested funds. By the same token, if the organization has an outstanding sales/collection process, but produces poor-quality goods and services, the long-term ability of the organization to attract customers is questionable.

In for-profit organizations the interaction between the sales/collection process and other business processes is fairly straightforward. The number of units expected to be sold, adjusted for desired changes in inventory balances, determines the number of units that an organization will plan to produce in the conversion process. Planned production drives the amount of materials and other resources to be acquired in the acquisition/payment process, as well as personnel resources used and paid through the human resource process. This planning significantly impacts the financial resources the organization must secure and manage through the financing process.

In not-for-profit institutions (e.g., state and local governments), the revenue/collection and acquisition/payment processes are highly integrated because of the use of fixed budgets. The amount a governmental unit can spend, in many cases, is limited to the amount of revenue it collects. To carry out public policy, governments estimate their revenues and establish a spending plan by appropriating funds for specific programs such as infrastructure, administrative services, and capital outlays. Appropriations signify the amount the unit is authorized to spend to meet taxpayer needs.

Periodically, government decision makers compare actual and estimated revenues. If estimated revenues are too high or if economic conditions cause actual revenues to fall below the estimates, they revise their budgets. They also review their expenditures and liability commitments and update appropriations to compensate for the revenue shortfalls. Conversely, governments with projected revenue surpluses may update appropriations to take advantage of the increased revenues.

Legally, governments have a limited number of options for generating revenues. If governments raise revenues for a specific purpose, they must use those revenues for the declared purpose. To help governments demonstrate budgetary and legal compliance in these cases, government leaders need the ability to link certain revenue to the spending of that revenue.

AN OVERVIEW OF THE TRADITIONAL SALES/COLLECTION PROCESS

Let's begin our study of the sales/collection process by reviewing the traditional and automated sales/collection process. Then we will discuss more updated IT architectures. To help you with this study, refer to Table 6–1 for examples of some of the data flows traditionally associated with this process.

In a manual sales/collection process, paper is used as the primary means to capture and store business data and communicate information to information customers. Paper records also serve as the audit trail for documenting the process. Data about the sales/collection process are captured and maintained by various business functions that participate in the process. As a result, process data are scattered across various departments (e.g., the Sales Order Department, the Shipping Department, the Billing Department, and the Warehousing Department). Because no unit has a complete picture of the sales/collection data, various departments store duplicate data. Paper is also used to communicate authorizations between departments and to external parties.

In manual processes, organizations use multicopy forms or photocopy originals to create and distribute source documents. Source documents contain the detailed data about

TABLE 6–1

Sample Data Flows Commonly Associated with the Sales/Collection Process

Customer Order. A data flow originated by and sent from the customer. It typically includes data about the customer, where to ship the goods, order terms and conditions, the items the customer wants to order, and payment terms. The customer order is used to create the sales order.

Sales Order. A data flow created internally to document an order and the approval of an order. It often includes the same data items as the customer order. Copies of the sales order are used to communicate authorization to initiate other activities in the process (such as warehousing and shipping). Copies of the sales order are used as picking and packing slips.

Picking Slip. A data flow that is sent to the warehouse to authorize movement of ordered goods from warehousing to shipping. It is often a copy of the sales order. Stock-outs or other problems are noted on the picking slip.

Packing Slip. A data flow that is sent with the goods shipped to a customer. Often, the data flow is labeled with a "This is not a bill" message.

Bill of Lading/Shipping Notice. A data flow that describes the packages shipped, the carrier, the route, and customer information.

Sales Invoice (Bill). A data flow listing the merchandise, with prices, that have been delivered or sent to a buyer. It is a statement of money owed for goods or services supplied.

Remittance Advice. A data flow accompanying customer payment.

Deposit Slip. A data flow listing the monies physically transferred from an organization to a financial institution.

Customer Check. A data flow that authorizes the transfer of funds from the customer to the seller.

Open Sales Order. Orders are considered open after they have been approved. They remain open until they are shipped and billed. Thus, in a traditional system, an order could be shipped but still remain open until the billing process is executed.

Open Sales Invoice. Invoices are considered open once they are billed. They remain open until they are paid.

transactions and serve as supporting documentation for any subsequent information processing. Often, several departments retain copies of source documents to support their part of the process. For example, copies of invoices (the source document for a sale) are used to record journal entries that trigger the accounting cycle we reviewed in Chapter 3. Meanwhile, marketing, production, and other functions may keep a copy of source documents for their respective information processing.

Paper source documents are typically stored in filing cabinets (and some organizations use microfiche or document image scanning technology). Files of source documents and journals are often called *transaction files* while *master files* include the subsidiary ledgers, general ledger, and control accounts used by units within the Accounting Department (e.g., accounts receivable, inventory control, and general ledger).

Exhibits 6–1 and 6–2 illustrate most of the key data flows of the traditional manual sales/collection processes. They are not specific to one particular organization, but represent characteristics common to traditional sales/collection processes across organizations. The following explanation of the flowcharts is organized by operating events:

Take Order. The traditional process begins when a customer contacts the company to place an order.[1] The customer order typically includes data about the customer, where to ship the goods, the items the customer wants to order, and payment terms. The company receives the order and checks the customer files to see if the customer is a new or existing customer. Usually, this *customer order* is recopied onto a company's own *sales order* document. A copy of the sales order may eventually be used as a *sales invoice.* Having order data on a prenumbered internal document helps a company locate the data and avoid losing orders. This is important, because missing documents can signal unfilled or unauthorized transactions.

Approve Credit. A copy of the sales order is sent to the Credit Department for approval. Although it would be useful to access the inventory records to determine if items are available, this step is usually omitted in manual processes due to the amount of time and human effort required. If credit and other conditions of the order are approved, the Sales Order Department authorizes processing to continue. The Sales Order Department communicates this approval by sending sales order information to other departments. Sales order information is sent on a document, called a *picking slip* or *stock request document,* to the Warehousing Department. This document authorizes warehousing to pull the goods and move them to the shipping area. Another document called the *packing slip* is sent to the Shipping Department to communicate that goods are forthcoming from the Warehousing Department. Two copies of the sales order are sent to the Billing Department to inform them of the sale and for use in invoicing the customer after the goods are shipped. A copy of the sales order (the copy with Credit Department approval) is filed in the Sales Order Department with the customer's order document to create a customer order activity file. The file of customer orders is organized alphabetically (for ease in locating information by customer name). Finally, a copy of the sales order may be sent to the customer to acknowledge acceptance of their order.

Fill Order. Our focus now shifts to the Warehousing Department. Remember the Warehousing Department cannot act without authorization from the Sales Order Department. Authorization comes in the form of the picking slip or stock request document. Warehousing personnel pick the goods (noting any stock-outs or other problems on the picking slip) and transfer them to the shipping area. (If necessary, a *back-order* document is created for stock-out items.) A warehouse inventory subsidiary ledger[2] may be updated to reflect the goods taken out of inventory.

---

1 Marketing activities generally precede order placement but they are usually omitted on traditional process flowcharts.
2 In a traditional accounting system, each department may keep its own inventory records. These separate inventory records are not included in Exhibits 6–1 and 6–2.

EXHIBIT 6–1

Traditional Manual Sales/Collection Process Flowchart—Part I

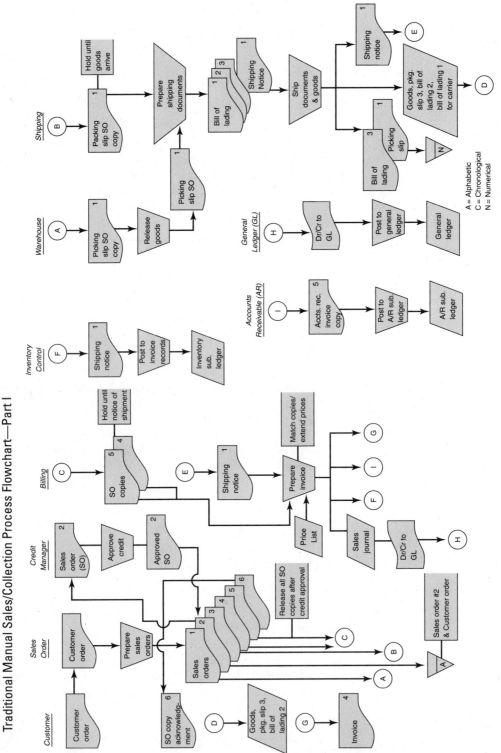

Exhibits 6–1 and 6–2 were prepared with the assistance of Dr. William Hillison, Arthur Andersen Alumni Professor, Florida State University.

EXHIBIT 6–2

Traditional Manual Sales/Collection Process Flowchart—Part II

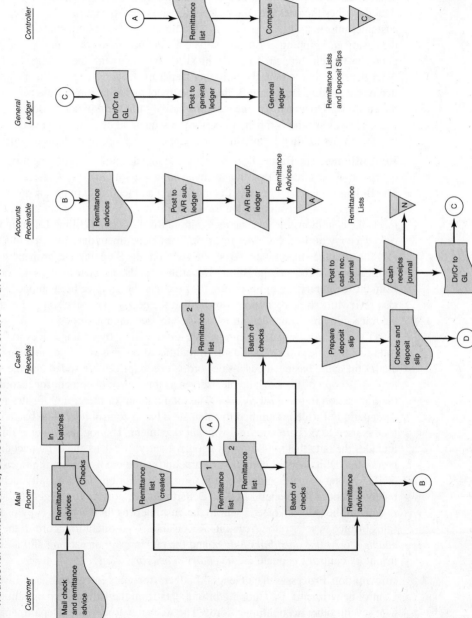

A = Alphabetic
C = Chronological
N = Numerical

Exhibits 6–1 and 6–2 were prepared with the assistance of Dr. William Hillison, Arthur Andersen Alumni Professor, Florida State University.

Ship Product. The Shipping Department is informed of the expected shipment by a copy of the packing slip from the Sales Order Department. As a control the Shipping Department compares the packing slip with the picking slip and the goods to be shipped. They pack the goods and select a carrier; they prepare a *bill of lading* (that describes the packages they accept for shipment, the carrier, the route, and customer information), keep a copy in the Shipping Department, and send a copy to the customer. Shipping personnel prepare a *shipping notice* to communicate that the goods have been shipped. The packing slip is included with the packaged goods. After the shipment is sent, the Shipping Department sends a copy of a shipping notice or the picking slip to the Billing Department as notification of the need to bill the customer. Documents in the shipping activity file are typically ordered numerically. This allows the company to perform a sequential or completeness check on the documents to identify missing documents or documents used out of order.

Bill Customer. The Billing Department is the first accounting department (with the exception of the Credit Department) involved in a traditional sales/collection process. The Billing Department reviews the transaction and records it in the accounting system. In traditional accounting, the transaction is recorded at this point because it meets the conditions for revenue recognition. Recall that the Billing Department received a copy of the sales order from the Sales Department that was filed in a temporary file until the shipping notice is received from the Shipping Department. Upon notification of shipment, the Billing Department pulls and reviews the sales order from the temporary file to make sure the products should have been shipped. They also review the shipping notice to verify that the goods have been shipped and that the transaction meets the definition of a sale for accounting purposes.

The Billing Department prepares a *sales invoice* by adding prices to the data found on the sales order document. In traditional processes, a sales invoice includes the same basic data as a sales order, except prices are added and the sale is totaled. A copy of the sales invoice serves as the source document for recording the transaction in the *sales journal.* The total amount of the group of sales invoices for a period of time is summed to calculate a batch control total. The batch control total is used to prepare a journal *voucher* document. The journal voucher document includes the data that you know as a journal entry: the date, the debit account number(s), the debit account name(s) and amount(s), the credit account number(s), the credit account name(s) and amount(s), plus a description. The journal voucher document is sent to the General Ledger Department for posting to the general ledger. A copy of the sales invoice is sent to the customer (as their bill). A copy of the sales invoice is sent to the Accounts Receivable Department to record in the *accounts receivable subsidiary ledger,* and the picking slip or packing slip is sent to inventory control to update the *inventory subsidiary ledger.*

Information Processes. The General Ledger, Accounts Receivable, and Inventory Control departments use shipping/billing data from the Billing Department to update several other accounting records. The Accounts Receivable Department uses a copy of the sales invoice to record invoice amounts in the customer's account in the accounts receivable subsidiary ledger. The Inventory Control Department reduces inventory balances in the inventory subsidiary ledger (for companies that use a perpetual inventory system) and assigns the goods sold to cost of goods sold. The General Ledger Department uses the journal voucher to record the total sale as a debit to Accounts Receivable and as a credit to Sales in the general ledger.

Receive Payment. At this point, the company waits for the customer to return payment. Often the sales invoice includes an additional page or section to be returned with the payment. The return portion, called a *remittance advice,* lists the customer's name, account number, and balance due. Generally, two people are assigned to open the mail to reduce employee fraud or theft. The employees document the payments by completing a *batch remittance list* that lists the source of each check and its amount. The amount of the check is compared with the amount on the remittance advice to verify their equality and the check is restrictively endorsed "for deposit only."

Information Processes. A copy of the batch remittance list is sent, along with the checks, to personnel in the Cash Receipts Department. A *deposit slip* is prepared to deposit the checks in the bank. The batch remittance list is used as a source document to record the cash received in the *cash receipts journal.* The totals are used to prepare a journal voucher that is sent to the General Ledger Department to update (increase) the General Ledger Cash account and (decrease) the General Ledger Accounts Receivable control account. The batch of remittance advices is sent to the Accounts Receivable Department where the customer's subsidiary ledger is updated to reflect the payment. The remittance advices are placed in customer files to document the customer payment. A copy of the batch remittance list is also sent to the controller to reconcile total remittances for the day to the bank deposit amount (recorded on a validated deposit slip obtained from the bank).

Organizations traditionally separate authorization tasks (performed by the Sales Order and Credit departments) from custody tasks (performed by the Shipping, Warehousing, Cashier, and Treasury departments) and recording tasks (performed by the accounting departments: Billing, Accounts Receivable, Inventory Control, and General Ledger). Recall that accounting systems strive for complete, timely, accurate, and properly authorized transaction data. Due to the duplication of data and the need for independent reviews of work performed by human processors, several additional controls are necessary in the traditional manual process.

First, clerks or supervisors perform independent reviews of other people's work, referred to as *independent checks on performance.* They often check the accuracy and completeness of prepared documents, records, and reports. Customers also provide an independent check on performance. Customers are sent acknowledgments, invoices (bills), and summary statements. Hopefully, they will contact the company when an error has occurred.

Second, properly designed documents encourage completeness and accuracy by enhancing data collection procedures. Documents are prenumbered to provide a unique identifier for each document. Often, documents are filed numerically, and someone performs a completeness or sequence check to identify missing documents. Missing documents can signal incomplete or omitted transaction data.

Batch totals are also used in traditional systems. Although batch totals sometimes fail to identify errors (e.g., when an accounts receivable subsidiary ledger batch total equals a general ledger Accounts Receivable Control account total, but several invoices and payments were posted to the wrong customer accounts or some items were not posted at all), they can identify some discrepancies (such as duplicate postings or transpositions). In this process, several batch totals are used. For example, the total of goods removed from the warehouse should equal the total of goods shipped. The total of credit sales invoices for a period should equal the increase posted to Accounts Receivable (in the subsidiary ledger and the general ledger) and to Sales Revenues (in the sales journal and the general ledger). Similarly, the total of cash remittances for a period should equal the bank deposit total, the increase posted to Cash (in the cash receipts journal and the general ledger), and the decrease posted to Accounts Receivable (in the subsidiary ledger and the general ledger).

Traditional processes create added information processing risks, namely duplication of data. Data duplication causes data certification problems. Periodically, the accounts receivable subsidiary ledger total is compared to or *reconciled* with the General Ledger Accounts Receivable Control account. Organizations should investigate and correct any discrepancies in a timely manner. Without this error correction, the organization does not know which balance is correct. The person who reconciles the account often initials the accounts to document that he/she performed the reconciliation.

AN OVERVIEW OF THE TRADITIONAL AUTOMATED SALES/COLLECTION PROCESS

Information technology has been applied to the traditional sales/collection process. What we present here is not specific to one organization, but represents characteristics common to traditional sales/collection processes across many organizations.

Typical IT applications automated the business and information process rules of the manual system. A traditional automated system is very similar to a traditional manual system; document flows are similar, as is the large amount of duplicate data. However, since authorizations and data access can be provided through computer screens there is a potential decrease in the amount of paper.

The manual and automated process flowcharts are very similar in terms of data stores and data flows. Basically, the physical design (as opposed to the logical design) was altered as manual processes and paper files (called *offline files*) were replaced with computer processes and tape or disk files (called *online files*). Like in the manual system, the data that support accounting entries are recorded and stored in other departments (such as Sales Order, Warehousing, and Shipping). The accounting system boundary is often defined as the ledgers and the journals that feed into the ledgers. As we discuss the automated process notice that the paper sales and cash receipts journals in a manual system have been physically changed to disk or tape transaction files. The paper inventory and accounts receivable subsidiary ledgers and the paper general ledger have been upgraded to disk or tape master files.

As you review the automated system flowcharts and the discussion that accompanies them, pay particular attention to the inputs, processes, and outputs. Input typically comes from a hard-copy document (the document symbols) and goes through one or more processes. Processes (represented by rectangles) store data in files (the tape or disk symbols) or prepare data in the form of a report (also a document symbol). Files may also be used as an input to a subsequent process.

Each computer-processing symbol denotes a computer program or programs that include a list of instructions for the computer. Each program can include screens for collecting data, edit checks on the data entered, instructions for processing and storing the data, security procedures (e.g., limiting access via passwords or user IDs), and steps for generating and displaying output. To understand the files and their use, it is important to consider their contents (their record layouts). Notice the relationship between the documents and files used for input and the files and documents generated as output. The input documents and the files must contain the data necessary to generate the desired output.

The content of the computer-readable files used in an automated system is similar to the paper files used in the manual system. Data collection and storage is still defined by the chart of accounts that govern this process: Sales, Sales Returns and Allowances, Sales Discounts, Cost of Goods Sold, Bad Debt Expenses, Marketing Expenses, Cash, Accounts Receivable, Allowance for Doubtful Accounts, and Inventory.

The automated sales/collection process can use batch processing (by accumulating a group of customer orders before processing) or online processing (by processing order information as it occurs). Let's examine a sample online system. Exhibits 6–3 through 6–8 display flowcharts of a traditional automated sales/collection process. Once again, it is important to refer to these flowcharts as you read the following narrative.

Order Entry. In the Sales Order Department (see Exhibit 6–3), the sales clerk enters customer order data into the system. Order data may be received by phone, by electronic mail, or by a hardcopy customer order. An edit routine checks characteristics of the input. The customer master file is accessed to verify the existence of the customer. If a customer record does not exist, a new customer record is added. A credit decision is made and the inventory master file is checked for availability of the items requested. If inventory is available or can be made available and the customer is judged a good credit risk, sales order data are recorded in the sales order transaction file called an *open sales order file*. An open sales order file includes the same data as the sales order document (data about the customer and the items ordered). Records are added to an open sales order file when an order is approved and the records are removed from the open sales order file when the order is shipped and billed. It is called an *open* file because it contains orders yet to be delivered (and ownership transferred) to the customer.

At this point, the customer order document (if there was one) is filed in an offline, paper document file, and a series of paper documents are printed. Many companies generate a hardcopy of the picking slip and send it to the Warehousing

EXHIBIT 6–3

Traditional Automated Sales/Collection Process Flowchart—Order Entry

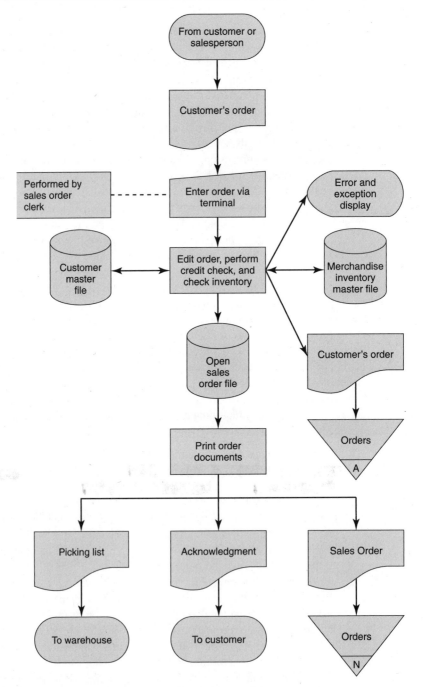

Source: Joseph W. Wilkinson and Michael J. Cerullo, *Accounting Information Systems: Essential Concepts and Applications,* 3rd ed. (New York: John Wiley & Sons, 1997).

Department. They may generate a copy of the sales order as an order acknowledgment for the customer. They may also produce hardcopy sales orders to maintain a paper file of sales orders, similar to what is maintained in a manual system.

Warehousing/Shipping. Warehousing receives the picking slip from the Sales Order Department. As in the manual system, warehousing personnel pick the goods, noting problems such as stock-outs, and transfer the goods to the shipping area. The Shipping Department (see Exhibit 6–4) receives the goods and the picking slip. The goods are packed, and the data about the packaged goods are entered into a *shipping transaction file.* This file contains the same data as the bill of lading and shipping notices used in manual systems. The *shipper/carrier reference file* (a file that contains data about the various shippers used by the company) is accessed. Data stored in the shipping transaction file are used to print the packing slip, bill of lading, and shipping notice. The packing slip is included with the shipped goods; one bill of lading is distributed to the carrier while a second copy is filed; and one copy of the shipping notice is distributed to Billing while one copy is filed.

Billing. The Billing Department (see Exhibit 6–5) accumulates a batch of shipping notices and prepares a batch total. Billing clerks use the shipping notice, customer master file, pricing reference file, and open sales order file to create a *billing transaction file.* The billing transaction file is the electronic version of the sales invoices generated in the manual system, and it serves as an expanded sales journal. As in the manual system, the Billing Department reviews the transaction (for control purposes) by verifying that there was a valid order (by examining the open sales order file) and a shipment (by examining the shipping notice). A billing procedure transforms the data from an order to an invoice by adding the prices.

Once the billing transaction file is compiled, various master files are updated and several hardcopy documents are prepared. Records from the open sales order file that have been invoiced are removed from the file (because they are no longer open orders) and are saved in a *sales history file.* Applicable customer records in the *accounts receivable master file* (the electronic version of the accounts receivable subsidiary ledger) are updated to reflect the credit sales. Records in the *general ledger master file* (the electronic version of the general ledger) for Cash, Accounts Receivable, Inventory, and Cost of Goods Sold are updated. The *merchandise* or *inventory master file* (the electronic version of the inventory subsidiary ledger) is updated to reflect the goods shipped. Records describing the invoices are added to the *open sales invoice file* (when a sale is invoiced it is reclassified from an order to a sale). These records remain in the open sales invoice classification until they are paid. [Notice how this process of taking records out of files and moving them to other files is similar to the manual process of removing paper documents from one paper file and storing them in a different paper file.]

Printed documents include a sales invoice that is used as a bill for the customer. The organization may print other summary data such as a hard-copy listing of the items invoiced, invoice batch totals, and a listing of the activity in the accounts receivable file. These summaries are compared to make sure that the total

EXHIBIT 6–4

Traditional Automated Sales/Collection Process Flowchart—Shipping

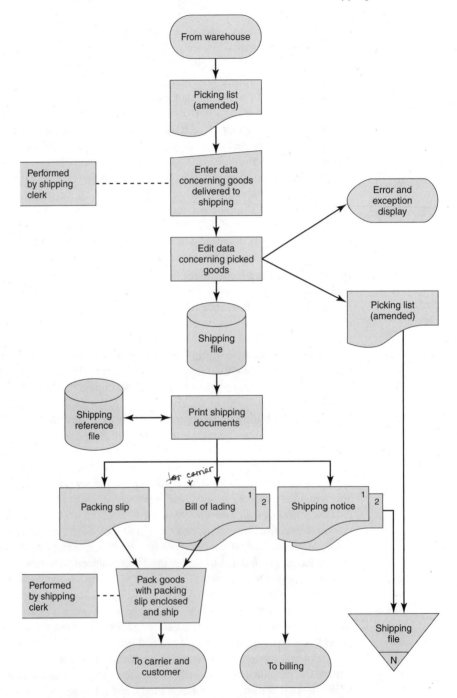

Source: Joseph W. Wilkinson and Michael J. Cerullo, *Accounting Information Systems: Essential Concepts and Applications,* 3rd ed. (New York: John Wiley & Sons, 1997).

Traditional Automated Sales/Collection Process Flowchart—Billing

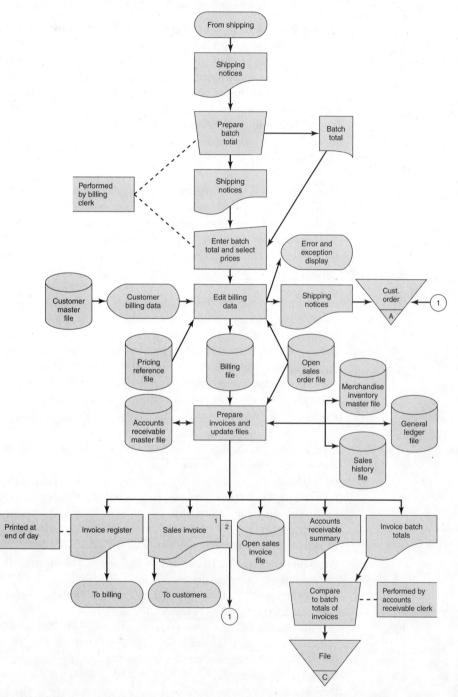

Source: Joseph W. Wilkinson and Michael J. Cerullo, *Accounting Information Systems: Essential Concepts and Applications,* 3rd ed. (New York: John Wiley & Sons, 1997).

change in accounts receivable is equal to the batch total of charge invoices processed during the period.

Notice the similarity between the accounts receivable master file, the general ledger accounts receivable record, and the open sales invoice file. The balances in all three of these should be equal. Why? They all contain duplicate data about the same totals; the information is simply summarized and formatted in different ways. The accounts receivable subsidiary ledger lists the amounts owed by customer, the open sales invoice file lists the amounts owed by invoice, and the general ledger accounts receivable record contains the balance due from all credit customers.

Remittance. When the customer pays the invoice amount (see Exhibit 6–6), the cash control procedures used in a manual system are applicable to the automated system. A mail room clerk totals the checks for a batch total. The cash receipt data and the batch total are entered into the computer. The computer performs edit checks on the data and errors are listed on an error and exception report. The computer references the accounts receivable master file and the open sales invoice file in performing the edit checks, but neither of these files is updated at this point. A *cash receipts transaction file* (the electronic cash receipts journal) is prepared. The computer prepares its own control total of the cash receipts for the day. This amount is compared with the manually prepared batch total prepared earlier and any discrepancies must be reconciled before processing continues. An exception and summary report is printed and sent to the Accounts Receivable Department along with a copy of the computer-prepared remittance list and the individual remittance advices. The checks and a copy of the remittance list are sent to the cashier.

Cashier. The cashier (see Exhibit 6–7) compares the checks with the remittance list and files the remittance list. Customer checks are combined with checks from other sources for deposit in the bank. Checks from other sources must be entered into the computer and added to the cash receipts file so that this file contains all the cash receipts for the period. A computer-generated deposit slip with two copies is prepared. The original and one copy accompany the checks in the deposit to the bank. The other copy along with a computer-printed cash receipts listing are sent to the accounting manager. A copy of the cash receipts listing is sent to accounts receivable and another copy is filed with the remittance list.

Accounts Receivable. The Accounts Receivable Department (see Exhibit 6–8) is responsible for updating the general ledger accounts (mainly Cash and Accounts Receivable), each customer's individual account in the customer accounts receivable file, and the open sales invoice file. Before these updates are performed several documents and files are compared as a control on the accuracy of the process. Information on the remittance list, remittance advices, exception and summary report, and customer reference files are compared. Any necessary corrections are entered into the computer, which performs edit checks on the entries using data contained in the open sales invoice file. The changes are added to the cash receipts file, which originated in the mail room and was updated by the cashier. Finally, the

EXHIBIT 6–6

Traditional Automated Sales/Collection Process Flowchart—Mail Room

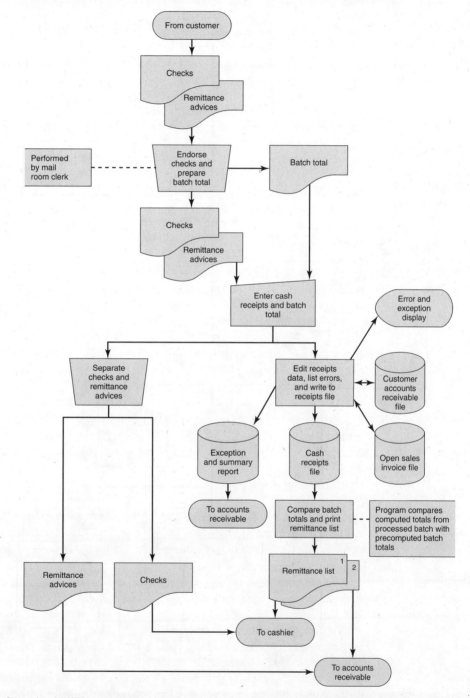

Source: Joseph W. Wilkinson and Michael J. Cerullo, *Accounting Information Systems: Essential Concepts and Applications,* 3rd ed. (New York: John Wiley & Sons, 1997).

EXHIBIT 6–7

Traditional Automated Sales/Collection Process Flowchart—Cashier

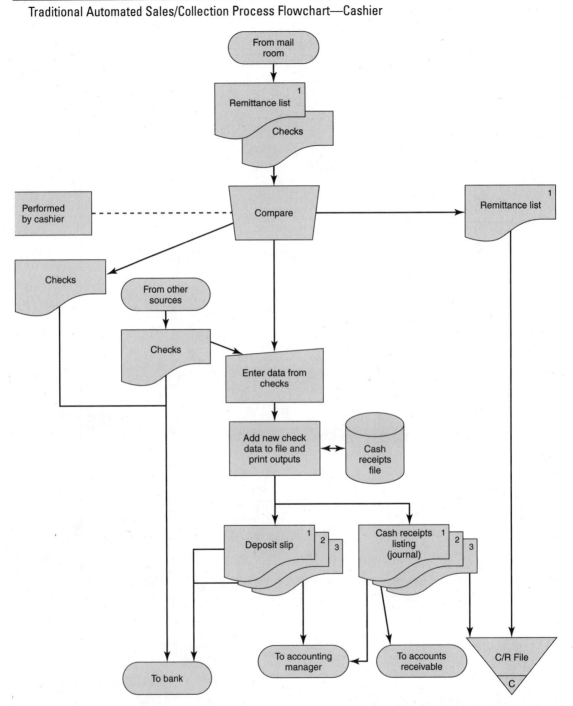

Source: Joseph W. Wilkinson and Michael J. Cerullo, *Accounting Information Systems: Essential Concepts and Applications,* 3rd ed. (New York: John Wiley & Sons, 1997).

EXHIBIT 6–8

Traditional Automated Sales/Collection Process Flowchart—Accounts Receivable

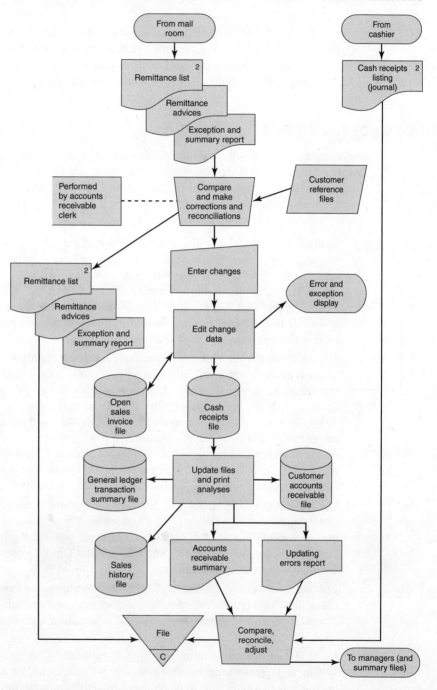

Source: Joseph W. Wilkinson and Michael J. Cerullo, *Accounting Information Systems: Essential Concepts and Applications*, 3rd ed. (New York: John Wiley & Sons, 1997).

cash receipts file is used to update the general ledger and the customer accounts receivable files. Paid invoices are removed from the open sales invoice file and written to the sales history file. An accounts receivable summary and an updating error report are printed, compared, and filed or sent to the appropriate manager.

CRITICISMS OF TRADITIONAL IT APPLICATIONS

One reason for reviewing the traditional sales/collection process and IT applications is to identify ways we can enhance the value of the process. In Chapter 3 we pointed out how certain characteristics of traditional IT applications limit our ability to enhance value. Our review of the sales/collection process should have clarified the points made in Chapter 3 regarding traditional IT applications:

Multiple Systems. Hopefully, this explanation of the sales/collection process helped you notice the large number of IT applications. A similar proliferation of applications exists in each functional area, including production, marketing, and finance. This IT application architecture results in tremendous duplication of both processing and data. Furthermore, it does little to improve the underlying business process. This use of departmentalized IT by function, called "stovepiped" use of IT, is often quite detached from the business process.

Subset of the Process. Instead of gathering a unified, broad range of data about all business events in the sales/collection process, each of the traditional IT applications capture, store, and process data about a subset of the events (for example, accounting systems capture only limited data about only the accounting transactions). Therefore, none of the applications provide an organizationwide view of this process. Information users interested in processwide views must select data from several applications in various functional areas and piece the data together to create their view. This requires the reconciliation of data across several applications that is time-consuming, costly, and often not achievable.

Untimely Processing. Accounting information captured in traditional accounting system architectures is untimely for two reasons. First, the accounting system does not capture data in real time. Second, a significant amount of processing must occur to transform accounting data into information. This often results in accounting reports being provided only monthly or quarterly.

Limited Characteristics. The traditional accounting system captures only limited characteristics about the events (e.g., date, account, and amount). Capturing only limited characteristics restricts the types of information accountants can provide to information customers.

Level of Aggregation (summarization). Data stored in the traditional accounting system are typically quite summarized. It is not uncommon for data about numerous sales and cash receipts to be recorded by only one entry for each day or week. For example,

Cash	1,000,000	
Accounts Receivable	200,000	
Sales for Store #234		1,200,000
Recorded sales for the month of May.		

When this level of aggregation is used, information customers are prevented from obtaining information necessary to answer a variety of questions (what happened, when, who was involved, what was involved, and where did it occur?). Details about the types of products sold, the customers involved, the salespeople, and so on, are buried in the one journal entry. The aggregation makes it impossible to answer many useful questions management might ask about the business process.

One View. Lastly, the traditional accounting system restricts users to only one view of the business—the financial view. The chart of accounts is used to classify data to support one primary view of the business. When more than one view is required, organizations build multiple financial systems to provide various views of the process. However, this strategy is inefficient and ineffective.

These characteristics of traditional sales/collection IT applications represent opportunities to enhance accounting's value, provided an organization is willing to change the architecture of the traditional accounting system.

OPPORTUNITIES TO IMPROVE THE PROCESS

Now that we have reviewed the traditional information processing associated with the sales/collection process, let's step back and look at the process from a broader business analysis perspective. There are several opportunities to improve the sales/collection process. In Chapter 1 we identified three opportunities for accounting and IT professionals to enhance their value:

1. Define rules to shape the business processes.
2. Embed IT applications in business processes to control the process and to capture and store detailed data in real time.
3. Provide useful information for decision makers to plan, execute, control, or evaluate the organization.

Focusing on each of these opportunities can significantly improve the sales/collection process. Understanding and defining a business process includes:

- Describing each event, what triggers the event, and the business rules associated with the event.
- Identifying business risks associated with each event.

The *REAL* framework aids in analyzing business events by highlighting *what* (the resources involved in the event), *who* (the internal and external agents), and *where* (the location) of each event. The events, agents, and resources involved in the sales/collection process will vary somewhat from organization to organization. This chapter overviews a *sample* variation of the sales/collection process. The general process discussed in this chapter can be easily adapted and applied to meet the exact requirements of any organization (e.g., nonprofit or governmental organizations, wholesalers, bartering arrangements, catalog sales, cash sales, retailers, service providers, prepaid sale activities, or manufacturers).

Information processes are triggered throughout the sales/collection process. Each business event triggers the need for a recording information process to collect data about the event. A change in the status of a resource, agent, or location triggers the need for a maintenance process to update resource, agent, or location data. The data collected and maintained during the recording and maintenance information processes are used to generate outputs via reporting information processes. The reporting processes are triggered by a request for information.

One item of great importance is the requirement that internal agents collect accurate and complete information about an event as well as various attributes about the related external agents, resources, and locations. For example, when salespeople make a sale, they have the responsibility to collect complete information about the products sold, services provided, customer attitudes, and related information. This is consistent with the philosophy that the person who represents the organization in conducting a business event has the responsibility to capture complete information about that event to satisfy the information needs of all information customers throughout the organization.

To embed IT into a business process you must define the data to be recorded and maintained and identify control logic to reduce the risks discussed in Chapter 5. Thus, the question left unanswered to this point is what are the events commonly found in the sales/collection process? The following is a collection of some of the more common business events. Along with a description of each event, we discuss the risks, and the information processes to record, maintain, and report entity data. Two important reminders before we begin the discussion. Because we discuss the activities in a sequential fashion, it may seem that the sales/collection process is linear. That is not necessarily true. Increasingly, business processes and the activities that comprise those processes are dynamic, rather than linear and static. Also, remember that the activities in this process are linked to activities in other processes. We are concentrating on one process at a time to simplify the discussion.

Marketing Event (Such as a Sales Call)

Event Description   The sales/collection process is actually triggered by a customer's decision to buy the organization's goods or services. In an effort to influence customer decision making, an organization plans, executes, and evaluates a variety of marketing events (e.g., a Sales Call, an Advertisement, or a Promotion) intended to inform customers about products and/or services and hopefully influence them to trigger the sales/collection process. Agents involved in the marketing effort include the sales and marketing persons (internal agents) and potential customers (external agents). The marketing event is triggered by the decision to publicize and promote the organization's resources (its goods and/or services). For illustrative purposes, we use the Sales Call as our primary marketing event.

Event Risks   Many of the risks associated with the Sales Call relate to the salesperson's efficiency. Some examples of risk include:

- Salespeople spending a lot of time with nontarget customers—people who never buy anything or don't buy enough to justify the time commitment of marketing personnel.
- Salespeople spending time doing unproductive things that do not influence potential customers.

For some organizations the information system can help salespeople identify desirable customers and help schedule their activities to minimize wasted time. The information system can also accurately report salespeople's activities. Merely recording and reporting the activities performed and the amount of time spent on each activity encourages effective use of time.

CASE IN POINT

Security control equipment is being used in retail stores at the cash register to prevent fraud and promote efficiency. The cash register and a video camera are connected to, and controlled by, a computer. The computer maintains a record of each transaction and the amount of time the clerk takes to execute it. All the clerk's activities are videotaped. The computer provides summary statistics at the end of each shift with unusual transactions, based on type or amount of time to execute, being highlighted. Security personnel can review the videotape of selected transactions to determine if fraud was present or if the employee needs additional training. The computer can directly locate the videotape of the transaction by the time it occurred, preventing the reviewer from having to fast forward and guess which is the specific transaction.

Other marketing event risks include ineffective use of marketing funds and expenses not being properly approved or approved by the wrong agent. The event may occur at an invalid or unauthorized location (e.g., a hotel where the organization pays a higher corporate rate). Also, marketing efforts may target the wrong product or market segment. Remember, event risks are activities that reduce the likelihood that an organization will fulfill their strategic or operational objectives with respect to the execution of a business event.

Event Recording   A marketing application and/or an expense tracking application capture marketing event data. An application to collect, edit, and store Sales Call event data should capture such data as the date, time, duration of the visit, products discussed, internal agents involved, and customer characteristics. Usually, it is important to record the location of the event and any other marketing effort that attracted the customer (e.g., a newspaper, a magazine, or another customer). Data about the marketing event should also be linked to data describing any goods and services the sales agent purchased as a result of the marketing event (e.g., travel, meals, and lodging).

RAL Data Maintenance   Complete documentation of this event includes a variety of resource, agent, and location (RAL) data pools: marketing personnel, customers, goods or services inventory, and possible listings of "acceptable" marketing locations. Any changes in the entities represented in these data pools require maintenance updates (e.g., adding a new salesperson, or updating a customer's address). This data can also assist with controlling the risks associated with this event or effectively executing it. For example, organizations could make notations in inventory item records such as "push this product for sales during the fall," or add notes to provide information about new products forthcoming or product upgrades.

Examples of Information Outputs   Marketing events such as Sales Calls have often been overlooked in most traditional accounting systems. Since a Sales Call does not change the composition of the company's assets, liabilities, or owner's equity, accountants have generally made no entry to record a Sales Call. Due to the emphasis on collecting data primarily for financial reporting purposes, the only consideration of the Sales Call in the traditional accounting systems has been as an administrative expense on the income statement. However, the Sales Call has the potential to provide information that is critical in meeting the objectives of the sales/collection process. Today, it is often possible to link marketing event data (and expenses) to the revenue generated by the marketing event. This analysis can provide feedback about the funds invested in marketing efforts.

   Information about customer preferences, how they became aware of the products and services, and other customer information is best collected during the Sales Call. Other analysis of marketing/sales call data with a potential impact on the bottom line are also useful. For example, suppose an accountant noticed that 75 percent of all salespersons traveling out of town stayed at a particular hotel chain. The accountant could provide valuable insight that could help the organization negotiate a new lower corporate hotel rate.

   Data collected about this event could be used to provide details for analysis of expense logs, salesperson productivity, markets, and customers.

Customer Order Event

Event Description   The next business event is usually a customer order for goods or services. A customer (the external agent) frequently sends the company an order for goods or services (the resource). Salespeople or customer service representatives (internal agents) may assist the customer and collect the order data. The organization determines whether they can fulfill their obligation by checking the availability of requested goods or services. The organization also determines whether to extend credit. These determinations are important because the company does not want to recognize the event as valid unless both parties can fulfill their part of the sales transaction (i.e., the company must have the ability to fill the order and the customer must have the ability to make payment). Once the customer order is approved, it becomes a valid sales order. Contrary to more traditional process assumptions, the price and terms of the impending sale may also be negotiated at this point in the process.

   Hopefully, an order can be traced to a Sales Call or other marketing efforts. Sales Calls and marketing efforts may occur before the salesperson obtains a customer order.

Sometimes the order will come during the Sales Call, but the two activities are separate business events even though they may occur at the same time. Linking the marketing efforts to the Customer Order event provides valuable information to evaluate marketing effectiveness.

Events often provide authorization for other events to occur. In the sales/collection process, the Customer Order provides authorization for warehousing and shipping activities. It is important to remember that the Order is not the key objective of this process. The objective is to deliver a product or service to a customer in exchange for payment.

Event Risks   Risks associated with this event include:

- Accepting an order from an undesirable or unauthorized customer (e.g., a bad credit risk, thus increasing bad debt losses).
- Taking an order for a product or service that is not currently sold by the company and can't be made available.
- Having an unauthorized person take the order.

These risks can be controlled declaratively within the system itself. For example, the IT application could be used to prevent an order from a customer who is not in the approved customer file. Procedures can be established to include only those customers in the approved customer file who are good customers and have an acceptable credit rating. The system can control the products or services sold by allowing only items on the "list of goods and services" to be sold, and by allowing them to be sold only by selected individuals. Finally, passwords and access codes can prevent unauthorized personnel from executing a customer order.

Event Recording   An order entry application program can execute and record a customer order, control the execution of the event, and accurately and completely record data about the event. The application used by customer service personnel should:

- Check for the existence of a customer. If it is a new customer, the program may allow the addition of new customers.
- Review and approve the customer's credit status (based on the credit policy of the organization).
- Check the validity of inventory requested, including type, quantity, and status.
- Collect complete and accurate event data including such items as date and time of the order, customer order number, a unique order identification number, the form of order (e.g., phone call, mail, or fax), customer information, shipping address, terms of the sale, credit card or other credit information, items and quantity requested, negotiated prices, salesperson identification, and sales order clerk identification.
- Note a back-order status when the goods or services requested are not immediately available.

The order entry program can also collect marketing data such as which catalog the customer is using, or how the customer heard about the company or its products. Productivity measures can also be collected and recorded such as the length of each order call or how long the customer had to wait on hold before an order clerk was available.

RAL Data Maintenance   The organization maintains data items regarding the agents, locations, and resources involved in the event. For example, organizations should update their files to reflect a change in customer addresses, add or delete salesperson records, and add or delete inventory items.

Examples of Information Outputs   Since the Order event provides authorization for warehousing and shipping activities, organizations need to provide data about approved orders to persons involved in these subsequent activities.

Since the order is not yet a sale per GAAP, financial data about this activity are not included directly on the financial statements. Does that mean it is not part of the accounting system and an accounting opportunity to provide value-added analysis? No! An accountant could use the open order data to forecast sales and cash receipts for a bank loan or for the financial markets. Data about the event are helpful in forecasting salesperson commissions. The event data also help measure sales order clerk and salesperson productivity. Information can also be provided about the link between marketing efforts and actual orders resulting from marketing expenditures.

Move the Goods from the Warehousing Area to the Shipping Area

Event Description   Sales order data for valid orders are communicated to warehousing personnel[3] so goods (the resource) can be picked from storage bins by warehousing employees (internal agents) and moved from the warehouse to the shipping dock. While the sales order activity was an authorization activity, warehousing is a custodial activity. Companies store their goods in warehouses for safekeeping (remember the control to safeguard the assets), and it is important to make sure that movements of goods from the warehouse are authorized (i.e., a valid sales order exists) and recorded. It is also important that the warehousing staff report any missing or damaged inventory items. For example, a sales order may have been approved because an information system showed 14 lawn mowers in stock. This number could be inaccurate if some are damaged or missing. Such inconsistencies make it necessary to periodically count the inventory and reconcile the quantity listed in the information system with the actual quantity on hand. When there is a discrepancy between inventory levels reported by the system and reality, it is important that the appropriate data flows are sent to decision makers in the acquisition and conversion processes. Remember, although we arbitrarily break the business processes and activities into separate chunks for analysis purposes, the business processes are intertwined, and they must execute in harmony to enhance the effectiveness and success of an organization.

---

3 Many organizations are eliminating the in-house warehousing function in an attempt to reduce costs and/or optimize the efficiency of this business process.

Event Risks   Risks associated with this activity include:

- Moving goods without an authorization (i.e., a valid sales order).
- Having an unauthorized agent move or release goods.
- Moving the incorrect inventory type or amount to shipping.
- Moving the goods to an incorrect or unauthorized location.
- Having employees take inventory items when the balances in the inventory system do not equal the actual quantity on hand.
- Having improper or inadequate physical safeguards over access to inventory, fire or other disasters, and inventory counts.

Event Recording   Organizations use an inventory management and control application to control and accurately record the movement of goods from the warehousing area to the shipping area. Documentation should include the date, time, a unique transaction number, warehousing clerk identification, quantity, and listing of items picked for movement. The event may change the status of an order to a *back order* if the items are not available. For example, if the system displayed that an item was in stock during the Customer Order event, but warehousing personnel find the item missing or damaged, warehousing personnel should adjust the inventory balances accordingly (following proper review and analysis procedures). In addition, an organization should inform the customer and others in the organization regarding the back-order status.

RAL Data Maintenance   Changes in the warehouse, warehousing personnel, and inventory items must be maintained. Sales order personnel should communicate canceled orders as soon as possible—before goods are moved to the shipping area, if possible.

Examples of Information Outputs   Warehousing provides information to shipping about resources to be shipped, noting any stock-outs or other problems. Queries or requested reports about this activity can include inventory status reports; back orders requested by warehousing; inventory loss, damage, or shrinkage during a period of time; production inputs; data to plan inventory purchases; warehousing and inventory holding costs; warehousing efficiency measures (such as the time between the customer order and the goods delivered to shipping for delivery); and analysis of warehousing personnel efficiency.

Ship Goods and/or Provide Services[4]

Event Description   Like Warehousing, Shipping is a custodial activity. When goods are delivered to the shipping area, they are packaged and readied for shipment. Generally, a

---

4 Although we provide a simple shipping event in this chapter, please be aware that the issues related to *distribution* are critical and often entail much more complexity than is represented in this discussion.

copy of a packing slip that summarizes the items on the sales order is included with the packaged goods. A carrier and route are selected to deliver the goods to the customer.

If an organization is providing a service rather than delivering a product, this event generally requires the active involvement of a trained employee. The organization must identify the nature of the service to be rendered and select an individual or group of individuals to perform the service. Services may be provided over an extended period of time by a variety of people. In addition, products may be delivered with the services. As the services are performed, the organization must record the people involved, any supplies or tools they use, and the amount of time spent on the project.

What is represented here as one event may constitute several events for a specific company. For example, some organizations will only ship a finished product, some will only provide a service, and some will do both. Some organizations may have various combinations for different customers. For example, a computer manufacturer, to serve one customer, may ship a new computer and let the customer install it and handle all conversion. For another customer, the organization may ship the computer, help the customer install it, and convert existing applications for processing on the new computer. Finally, other customers may call the same organization to repair a computer sold previously. Correctly understanding the business process for the company for which the data model and resulting IT application is being prepared is the key to developing an accurate data model and application.

The internal agent for this activity is the shipping or service agent; the exact designation of the position differs depending on the company's products or services. The carrier is an internal agent (if the organization provides the transportation) or an external agent (such as UPS or Federal Express). The customer continues as an external agent and the resource is the inventory of goods and/or services sold. The location of the goods is frequently an important component of this event to track the goods and interpret the FOB shipping point or destination terms.

Shipping and Service Activity Risks   Companies with an inventory of products or supplies for sale or for use in providing services have high risk with this event. Often, inventory items are very valuable and a variety of people, including both customers and employees, could be tempted to steal them. Service organizations must control the available time of service personnel. Wasting service personnel time or failure to bill for time spent in servicing customers is a loss to the company just the same as a loss of products or supplies. Other risks include:

* Having an unauthorized person ship the product.
* Having inventory items stolen from the shipping area.
* Shipping the item to the wrong customer or to an unauthorized location.
* Shipping the wrong product or the incorrect amount of product.
* Shipping without proper authorization (i.e., a valid sales order).
* Shipping poorly packaged products.
* Selecting a poor carrier or route.
* Losing sales due to untimely shipments.

The first two risks may be related. A person who steals from the company is frequently not authorized to have access to products, yet they take the products without recording a sale. Physical controls help reduce this risk by storing products within a controlled area and restricting access. However, people who are authorized to ship products are frequently those who steal them. Hiring honest employees and having them enter and exit through a specific door staffed by security guards helps reduce this risk.

Common information errors are failure to record, or incorrectly recording, a legitimate event. Failure to create a shipping or service data flow, manual errors in creating the data flow, or loss of a copy of the shipping or service data flow might account for this error. Integrating the system with the process and utilizing information technology to capture the event data in machine-processable form as the event occurs can help prevent these errors.

An information system can directly control several of these risks. The system itself can verify who ships products and to whom they are shipped. Passwords can prevent an unauthorized internal agent from gaining access to the system to ship products. Computer-generated access labels can prevent shipping products to the wrong customers, and product bar codes can help prevent shipping the wrong products.

Event Recording and RAL Data Maintenance   Shipping products or delivering services triggers two information processes. The first is to record the shipment of merchandise or the delivery of services, while the second is to bill the customer. The recording process triggers the billing process. We will discuss these two information processes separately.

Completely and accurately recording the delivery of goods and services to the customer includes recording such items as the date, a unique event number (such as a job number for a service contract or a bill of lading number for product shipments), a listing of the items and quantities shipped or used in providing the service, carrier and route information, shipping or service personnel, number and weight of packages, and customer and sale order identification. Data maintenance includes updating data about carriers, shipping or service personnel, customers, goods or services, canceled or changed orders, and shipping locations.

Shipments generate the need for shipping data flows, including the bill of lading and shipping notices. The bill of lading is a contractual shipping data flow to log the terms of the transfer of goods from the seller to the customer. Shipping notices may be sent to the customer to communicate information regarding order progress. Data about the shipping activity can provide information about the time between order and shipment, productivity of shipping personnel, movement or current location of shipments (for monitoring purposes), and carrier/route efficiency.

Once the goods are shipped, the company can bill[5] the customer and recognize the sale as revenue (if the revenue recognition rule conditions are met). Shipping goods and services triggers the information process of requesting payment from customers. The system can determine the proper charge and automatically generate a bill based on data about the shipment or the services. This method generally reduces the lag time between shipping/services (a business activity) and billing (a reporting activity triggered by the

---

5 The company should base the bill/sales invoice on the shipment—*not* the order.

shipping/service event). However, in some organizations, shipping or service personnel notify billing clerks regarding the shipment or the service, and a billing clerk reviews the transaction and initiates the system response.

Whereas the bill of lading and shipping notice data flows describe specific characteristics of the physical shipping activity, the sales invoice includes the data intended to measure the revenue generated by the economic exchange. Traditionally a billing clerk has the responsibility to pull the shipping and order information together and determine an appropriate amount to charge the customer. Complete and accurate billing data may include the date, job number or sales invoice number, amount of sale, items sold (including quantities and prices), sales tax, salesperson identification, customer identification, and billing clerk identification.

Information processing risks associated with this activity include neglecting to bill the customer, omitting part of the products or services provided in computing the bill, failing to bill customers for time spent by service personnel, billing at the wrong price, or billing the incorrect customer. Critical in preventing these errors is correctly recording prior events. If the services provided and products shipped have been properly recorded, the system can control the billing process and not allow a bill for an amount different from the value of goods or services provided, unless approved by a system-verified, authorized internal agent.

CASE IN POINT

Marty's Distributing Company is a distributor of alcoholic beverages and soft drinks. Under the precomputerized system, delivery people took a load of beer to a retail outlet and manually prepared a sales slip. There was no independent check on the accuracy of the amounts of beer recorded, the extension of quantity times price, or the summation of the total charge. At the time the computer was installed, the old system and the new system were operated in parallel for two months to verify the accuracy of the new system. During this time many errors were identified, and upon further investigation, it was found the delivery person had made all of them while preparing the sales ticket. The savings that the computer system generated by catching and preventing these errors more than paid for the computer system in less than one year.

Examples of Information Outputs   In addition to creating invoices, the shipping/billing data can be used to project cash flows and age accounts receivable (i.e., calculate the length of time that has passed on unpaid bills). The Providing Goods/Services event and the associated information processes affect several elements of GAAP financial statements such as inventory balances, accounts receivable, allowance for doubtful accounts, sales or service revenues, cost of goods sold, salary expenses (e.g., salesperson commission), and taxes payable for sales taxes.

Receive Customer Payment

Event Description   Payment may occur at the point of sale, the delivery of goods or services, or at some later date. Most customers use cash, check, or credit/debit cards to pay their obligations. Receiving cash is a custodial function. When the payment is received (hopefully in the form of a check, money order, or credit card payment rather than currency), company employees (internal agents) log the payment from the customer (the external agent), use the remittance advice to record the receipt, and deposit the funds (the resource) in the bank.

Due to the risk of loss, cash should be deposited at least daily, all employees who have access to cash should be bonded, and two employees should verify cash transactions. In addition to having customers mail or bring payments directly to the business, an organization can use the *lockbox method* or *electronic funds transfers* to collect customer payments. When the lockbox method is used, customers mail their checks to a post office address, and for a fee, a bank will pick up, total, and directly deposit the funds into the company's account. The bank then sends a copy of the deposit information and the remittance advices to the company. Electronic funds transfers reduce human involvement with cash by having customers electronically transfer funds from their bank account directly to the company's bank account. The form of payment is incidental to the occurrence of the event.

Event Risks   Cash is the most liquid of all assets and the one asset that is universally desirable. For this reason, organizations need to control who has access to cash. Electronic transfers of funds are desirable because they eliminate the need for employees to prepare receipts, record amounts received, and deposit cash into the company's bank account. The electronic transfer places the cash directly into the company's bank account and captures the cash receipt in machine-processible form. This is not only the most efficient cash receipt method, it also reduces many risks.

When cash is received in the mail, two people should open the mail. One person should take the money and prepare the deposit and the other person should send a receipt to the customer and record the receipt on the company's books. The system should compare the results of the two activities to verify their equality.

One control to reduce the risk of recording errors is a computer-processible remittance advice. If the customer pays the exact amount of the bill and returns the remittance advice with the payment, the computer can read the information on the remittance advice and know the amount of the payment and the customer information needed to correctly process the payment. The system should compare the amount of daily cash receipts with the total deposited in the bank account during the day. Each month, organizations should reconcile bank statements with internal cash records.

Organizations should also reduce the information risk of *lapping*. Lapping occurs when an employee steals cash from a customer payment and delays posting a payment to the customer's account. The employee uses funds from a subsequent customer payment to post to the first customer's account. This process continues by taking more cash and using subsequent customer payments to post as prior customer payments that were either stolen or used to post to a different customer's account. The records are always one or more customers behind in crediting payments to customer accounts. The employee who perpetuates the lapping scheme frequently tries to cover the fraud by writing off as uncollectible customer accounts that have actually been paid. Eventually, lapping becomes so difficult to hide that the perpetrator leaves the company or the lapping is detected.

Other information risks associated with receiving cash include failing to record a customer payment, accepting duplicate payments for the same invoice, crediting a payment to the wrong customer's account, and depositing a payment in the wrong cash account.

Event Recording   A cash receipt or cash management application program is used to record cash receipts from customers. Accurate and complete documentation should include date, cash receipt identifier (such as a unique remittance advice number), customer identification, amount received, employee identification (such as employees who count and deposit the cash), the account number where the cash is deposited, the location of payment (such as mail, or in person at the main office), and the check number of the payment. Some organizations link payments to specific invoices, while others simply apply payments to the outstanding balance.

The IT application should include the ability to receive a cash payment without linking it to a specific customer. For example, suppose someone sends a check but neglects to send the remittance advice and the name on the check does not correspond to the name of any customer account. The organization should be able to deposit the funds and tag the transaction as "unapplied cash" (a cash payment that was received but was not posted to a customer's receivable balance). If this occurs, the system should generate a listing of "unapplied cash" transactions and, as with all errors, they should be investigated and corrected as soon as possible. The IT application should also allow organizations to choose how they want to link customer payments to customer accounts. Two methods include specific invoice and balance forward. As the name implies, the specific invoice method involves matching payments to specific sales invoices. When organizations use a balance forward approach, they apply payments to a customer's total liability, rather than any specific invoice.

RAL Data Maintenance   Data maintenance includes the data stores for updating changes in customer, cash receipt employee, and cash account information.

Examples of Information Outputs   Data about cash receipts can be used to prepare a deposit slip and a listing of receipts (often called a *remittance list*). This activity affects the calculation of several GAAP financial reporting numbers such as accounts receivable, cash, allowance for uncollectible accounts, sales discounts, and cash flows from operations. Other activity reports include unapplied cash report, accounts receivable aging schedule, sales discounts not taken report, customer payment performance measures, timing of payments report, and mode of payment listing (e.g., cash, credit card, or electronic funds transfer).

Accept Returns and Approve Allowances

Unfortunately, goods and/or services are not always acceptable to the customer because they do not meet quality standards represented in the sale agreement or the product specifications of the customer. There are two options available to handle disagreements like these: The customer can keep the product/service and receive an adjustment or allowance in the price, or the customer can return the product/service (if it is possible to return the service previously provided). Returned products/services are the resources involved. The customer is the external agent and a sales manager is an internal agent.

The major risks associated with this event are making an unauthorized allowance to a customer's account, having unauthorized persons approve returns and/or allowances, and giving credit for returned merchandise when the merchandise is never received and/or placed in inventory.

Once again the system can control which internal agents are authorized to initiate allowances to a customer's account. Passwords can control access to this activity.

Physical controls are required to obtain the returned merchandise, move it into inventory, and prevent unauthorized access to inventory resources. Bar codes or identification numbers are useful to identify which merchandise has been returned, and the system can track who is responsible for the inventory.

Recognition of Uncollectible Accounts

An organization should carefully assess the customer's creditworthiness during the Sales Call and Accept Customer Order events. Scrutinizing a customer's payment ability is an important step in minimizing uncollectible accounts. In spite of credit reviews, some accounts become uncollectible.

Often, the accounts receivable clerk is the internal agent who identifies late accounts. The external agent is the customer. Sometimes the customer's location may not be known or they are not willing to talk to the accounts receivable clerk except through an attorney. When an organization receives legal documentation of inability to pay (such as bankruptcy papers), or fails to collect payment after extended efforts, the customer's account is normally written off as bad or uncollectible. The resource associated with this event is a complicated item because there is no tangible economic resource affected (such as cash or inventory). The uncollectible amount represents a loss in future cash flow that would have been collected had the customer paid. It reduces the accounts receivable calculation. It may be difficult to think of this as a "resource," but it does reduce income (a bad debt expense) and taxes payable to federal and state governments.

There are several risks associated with this event:

- Having an unauthorized person write off a customer's account.
- Approving the write-off of a customer's account with invalid or fraudulent justification.
- Selling additional goods or services to a customer who is not current with his/her payments or who has had previous uncollectible amounts.

IT could be used to prevent these risks. No person without a proper password or access code should be able to write off a customer's account. The IT application should also signal when a sale is being made to a customer who is behind in payments or who has a record of uncollectible accounts.

NEW ARCHITECTURES TO SUPPORT THE SALES/COLLECTION PROCESS

Organizations can significantly improve processes by following just one simple principle:

> **Embed IT into the business process so business event data are recorded and event/process rules are executed as each event occurs.**

The following examples illustrate this principle:

CASE IN POINT

Retail stores today use information technology to record data about a sale including the sales clerk, customer (if they use a credit card), items sold, when the sale occurred, and where the sale occurred. The technology captures more data while reducing the time to execute the business event (scanners can enter data much faster than someone keying in the data, and it requires someone with less skill). Furthermore, the technology consistently applies rules governing how merchandise is sold.

CASE IN POINT

UPS now captures all the data about package deliveries using a computer on which customers can sign their name electronically. Data about the delivery include the time the customer signs for the package, the delivery person's name, the person receiving the package, and where the package was delivered. Instead of having several pages of customer signatures that must be reconciled to delivery schedules at the end of each day, all the data are captured while the business events occur.

CASE IN POINT

Chevron has gas stations that allow customers to pay for gas at the pump. These "Fast-Pay" stations automatically bill the customer's credit card and eliminate the need for customers to pay a cash receipts clerk. All the data about the event Purchase Gas (e.g., customer's name, type of gas, quantity, pump location, and station location) are recorded while the customer is pumping gas, thereby reducing both the time the customer spends at the station and the number of employees needed to run a station. Many Fast-Pay Chevron stations have no employees on-site. Another benefit of these stations is the virtual elimination of nonpaying customers.

Each case illustrates the feasibility of recording business event data and executing business process rules as the event occurs. The trend toward applying IT as illustrated here continues to grow. Every day you can read about new IT applications that both simplify business processes and gather data about the business event while it occurs.

Embedding IT into the business process allows business and information processes to be improved simultaneously. Efforts to tune processes and IT applications should never end. Business processes are always changing and advances in IT enable processes to be modified and refined in ways we have not as yet imagined. A learning organization must expect, and even encourage, constant improvement.

Some organizations are beginning to reengineer their business and information processes to effectively use information technology. Some are using information technology to redesign the sales/collection process. Chapter F presents an overview of a phenomenon that is affecting a growing number of organizations: electronic commerce. In addition to electronic commerce, the trend is toward more enterprisewide information and embedding information technology into business processes. The following examples illustrate redesigned processes and the impact on organizations.

CASE IN POINT

Bell Atlantic Corporation examined their process for filling an order for telephone lines from a long-distance carrier. Their analysis revealed that because each department performed its own tasks before passing the job to the next department, each order passed through 25 hands before it was filled. Each step added time lags, costs, and potential errors to the process. The company studied each step in the process. By eliminating less relevant duties and assigning teams to follow a single order to completion, Bell Atlantic is able to fill orders in a few hours, rather than 15 to 25 days.

CASE IN POINT

Wal-Mart uses customer information from the sales floor to directly link sales activities and purchasing activities. Whenever a customer buys anything, the information goes directly—in real time—to the supplier's plant. The sale is automatically converted into a manufacturing schedule and delivery instructions including where, when, and how to ship replacement products.

Wal-Mart no longer deals with wholesalers. An analysis revealed that 20 to 30% of the retail price was used to pay for getting merchandise from a manufacturer's loading dock to a Wal-Mart retail store. Most of that cost was attributed to holding the inventory in three different warehouses: the manufacturer's, the wholesaler's, and Wal-Mart's. The process was reengineered to eliminate most of the costs by having the manufacturer ship the needed goods directly to the retail store.

CASE IN POINT

GTE has developed and implemented an Automated Work Administration System (AWAS) to dispatch telephone repair workers. Each repair worker is given a hand-held computer with a modem. These are stand-alone computers with programs to help the repair worker troubleshoot repairs from the job site, receive instructions from the main computer about the next repair job, store data about the current job, and report that data to the main computer.

The backbone of the system is a dispatch algorithm and a set of tables. The algorithm is an optimizer that knows where all employees are, their skills, and the work that needs to be done. It continually optimizes the factors and updates the schedule every two to five minutes for the entire dispatch center. A series of tables contain employees' skills and building characteristics. The system matches employee skills with the needs of the job and the characteristics of the building. With the new system, work is scheduled more efficiently, data on completed jobs are collected in machine-processable form, and workers have a tool that helps them perform their jobs better.[6]

---

6 Chris Sivula, "GTE's New Line on Customer Service," *Datamation,* May 1990, pp. 68–70.

CASE IN POINT

Hyatt Corporation, like other hotel chains, has a computerized reservation system. But Hyatt has a technological advantage—guests can make a reservation for any Hyatt in the United States by calling a toll-free number in Omaha, Nebraska, where an operator starts a bill, assigns a room, and even describes the view. On arrival, guests present their credit cards for verification and pick up their room keys. With every hotel having a 24-hour hookup to the Omaha center, operators can check guests in by remote control without having to navigate different systems. These common systems perform centralized functions like accounting that have previously been performed at each hotel. This results in savings of tens of millions of dollars. In addition to the dollar savings, guests spend less time in line.[7]

PROVIDING USEFUL MEASURES ABOUT THE SALES/COLLECTION BUSINESS PROCESS

Information from the sales/collection process can provide decision-making support for many information customers. Only a small portion of the required data about customers, competitors, and the economy is collected as a normal part of the sales/collection process. Some information about customer preferences and the effectiveness of marketing campaigns can be collected during normal sales calls. However, competitor products and services, economic trends, market size, market share, competitor benchmarking measures, and similar data must be obtained from outside sources or collected through independent studies. The following is a sampling of some of the information customers and information views supported by data from and about this process.

Top Management

Top managers are primarily interested in summary information for the sales efforts of the entire enterprise:

- Market share of company products compared to the market share of competitors.
- Trends in sales this year compared to prior years.
- Changes over time in key economic indicators compared to changes in the organization's sales, sales returns and allowances, and uncollectible accounts.

Marketing

The marketing function has a great impact on the sales/collection process and marketing personnel are among the dominant users of sales/collection information. The marketing area has primary responsibility for establishing pricing policy, price discounts, and credit terms.

---

7 Geoffrey Smith, "The New Realism in Office Systems: Computers Can't Take the Place of Good Management—But They Can Help," *Business Week*, June 15, 1992, pp. 128–33.

Most decisions concerning product design, styling, packaging, and product deletion fall under the jurisdiction of marketing. Marketing personnel also determine advertising strategy and develop advertising campaigns to promote specific products. Developing, evaluating, and administering the sales force fall within the responsibility of the sales function.

Information relevant to marketing includes:

* Amount and location of inventory in stock.
* Customer preferences and changes in those preferences.
* Cost to produce each product and to provide each service.
* Activity and success of each salesperson.
* Quantity and price of each product sold by salesperson, by customer type, and by geographic area.
* Detailed information on competitor's products, services, pricing strategy, and advertising campaigns.

Human Resource

The human resource function requires information about this process to effectively deploy an organization's workforce. The human resource function requires labor information so that they can determine workforce needs, oversee employee scheduling, initiate employee compensation, and conduct employee performance evaluations.

Production

The production area has the responsibility to maintain adequate stores of inventory on hand and produce a quality product. Projected and actual sales information is used extensively by production personnel to plan and adjust their schedules. Feedback from customers about product quality, defects, and warranty problems is valuable in adjusting product quality.

Finance and Accounting

Finance and accounting personnel complete information analysis to generate products for information customers both inside and outside the organization. The finance function of the enterprise must make decisions concerning the amount of cash available for short- and long-term investing and any cash needs that require additional financing. The balance due from customers, credit terms, and terms of payment provide vital information for making these decisions.

Accounting can provide and use information from the sales/collection process to generate a number of information products. For accounting, the sales/collection process contains the event that, for most companies, culminates the earning process. A *sale* is the point in the earning process when revenue is considered earned and reportable in public financial statements. The matching concept requires all costs associated with the goods and services sold during the period to be recorded as expenses in computing the period's net income. The sales/collection process contributes several important numbers for external reporting, including gross sales, sales returns, sales allowances, sales discounts, bad debt expense, and the accounts receivable balance. This process also affects the inventory balances.

Accounting uses information from this process to prepare management reports and financial statements. It can provide useful analysis such as economic value analysis, operating income, cash flows, project/product profitability measures, and sales backlogs. Accountants provide cost data on the individual products and services of the company, on inventory quantities and location, on customer credit standing, and on uncollectible accounts. An adequate (electronic or nonelectronic) audit trail must be maintained for auditors to verify the accuracy and reliability of each of these numbers. Additionally, accounting should ensure that adequate controls are in place to manage both business and information processing risks.

Are there opportunities for finance and accounting professionals to play a more critical role in the organization? In *Reinventing the CFO: Moving From Financial Management to Strategic Management,*[8] authors Walther, Johansson, Dunleavy, and Hjelm suggest ways that the CFO can become another "intelligent voice adding a different perspective to the decision making process." The authors suggest that finance people must provide:

- Strategic management and analysis (such as value chain and balanced scorecard type analyses).
- Management control measures that tie actions to corporate strategy and look more to the value chain and not merely the balance sheet.
- Cost management that is forward focused, provides relevant cost information, and creates an environment for cost control and even cost reduction. Accountants must not have a mind-set to simply cut costs, but to help manage costs relative to the value they provide.
- Effective and efficient management of financial processes.
- Support for the core business processes (i.e., the processes that are critical to run the organization).

As we discussed earlier in this text, the authors have noted the following trends in the finance function:

- Identifying only information that is predictive and actionable.
- Linking strategy to operations using key performance indicators.
- Simplifying key measures and reporting processes.
- Measuring across key processes throughout the business.
- Balancing financial and nonfinancial indicators.

---

8 Thomas Walther, Henry Johansson, John Dunleavy, and Elizabeth Hjelm, *Reinventing the CFO: Moving From Financial Management to Strategic Management* (New York: McGraw-Hill, 1997).

- Communicating key values through performance measures.
- Balancing strategic business unit or geographic performance against corporate results to establish managers' compensation.

To give you a better idea of some of the different types of value-added analyses that information age accountants can help provide, consider the following ideas from *Reinventing the CFO:* Accountants can suggest continuous improvement ideas relating to the sales/collection process, help identify key strategic issues and options related to this process (such as growth opportunities or key factors for successfully competing in a market, industry, culture, or environment), assess the contribution of a sales/collection process to overall organization performance, evaluate the sales/collection process with regard to how well the activities have helped the organization meet its strategic and operational objectives, create benchmarking data and metrics to compare the organization's process costs to industry or competitor costs, determine and measure the financial and operational key drivers of performance, complete analysis comparing organization performance to competitors, and/or measure actual performance against planned performance.

Is this list exhaustive? No. Try thinking about measuring trends and ratios such as total cycle time, downtime, sales and earnings growth, expense to revenue ratios, market share, customer satisfaction measures, order fulfillment speed, marketing cost per new customer, customer brand awareness and preferences, sales forecast accuracy, sales force productivity, sales cost to revenue ratio, number of new customers, order processing time, percentage of on-time shipments, number of customer complaints, new customer revenue, new product revenue, dollars saved from employee suggestions to improve the process, employee satisfaction with the process, employee productivity, sales per employee, asset turnover, sales to asset ratio, sales to working capital ratio, return on equity, cash flow to debt coverage, asset turnover, net trade cycle, days of inventory, days of receivables, accounts receivable turnover, days' sales outstanding, write-offs as a percent of sales, and number of customer inquiries/complaints as a percentage of the number of bills issued.

The purpose for presenting all of these examples and ideas is to get you to think like an information age business solution professional. We do not want you to limit your thinking to traditional bookkeeping and transaction processing issues, GAAP concerns, or financial analysis, for that matter. When you are trying to decide which data to collect, consider the data needed to perform these types of measures and analyses. Always look for opportunities to provide value-added information products. You may ask if there are established, optimal measures or techniques for measuring everything we have suggested. No. Additionally, you may ask whether you should always try to provide all of these analyses and measures in mass. Once again, our response is no. Don't simply generate a large amount of outputs. You will likely overwhelm your information customer and bury or overshadow the truly valuable information that is key to the success of a particular organization. These are the types of issues and decisions faced by today's business professional. Your willingness to tackle such issues and organization information needs provides many opportunities and challenges. We think such opportunities make life much more fun and exciting. We hope you share this sentiment.

AN EVENT-DRIVEN SALES/COLLECTION IT APPLICATION

Trying to digest everything we have covered in this chapter is a little easier when you step back and consider the big picture. To do so, let's review the sample sales/collection example used in Chapter 4 with the addition of the two events that management wants to plan, control, and evaluate; call on customer and prepare shipment.

Christopher, Inc., is the manufacturer and official supplier of patented glow-in-the-dark baseball caps. Major League Baseball granted a one-of-a-kind license to Christopher, Inc., and all of the major league teams purchase the caps from representatives of Christopher, Inc. These souvenir caps are only sold by major leagues inside major league baseball parks.

Christopher, Inc., employs six salespersons that visit and service teams in each division, one salesperson per division. Salesperson compensation is a commission on sales. Representatives of the major league teams can order caps via phone, mail, fax, or directly from their salesperson. After an order is verified and approved, the caps are moved from Christopher's warehouse and packaged for shipment. A shipping clerk readies the packages for pickup by United Parcel Service or Federal Express. As the shipment is recorded, Christopher's information system automatically generates an invoice and faxes a copy to the team office. This allows Christopher to recognize a sale as soon as the goods are shipped. All teams pay by electronic fund transfers. A cashier monitors and verifies electronic payments and applies them to a particular invoice (or invoices, if the team sent multiple payments with the same funds transfer). A *REAL* graphical model[9] of the sales/collection process for Christopher, Inc., is represented in Exhibit 6–9.

What type of information processing does Christopher, Inc., need to support this process? Christopher, Inc., wants to record data about the events in this business process—Call on Customer, Customer Places Order, Pick/Pack Inventory, Ship Order, and Collect Payment—to support decisions involved in planning, executing, and evaluating the process. Christopher needs data about the resources, agents, and locations involved in the process (e.g., cap inventory, customer, UPS, cash, salespersons, and other employees). Christopher's information system needs to generate a variety of outputs including customer orders, warehousing reports, products shipped, invoices, cash receipts, customer statements, sales summaries, and salesperson commission reports. Christopher also desires performance measures on the time between customer orders and shipment; the return on sales call expenses in total and by salesperson; the time between customer orders and warehouse processing; the time between warehouse processing and shipment; analysis of the time between invoicing and cash collections; and the time it takes clerks to enter data into the information system.

The computer instructions written to support this process would include the instructions needed to collect and store event data; the instructions needed to maintain data about resources, agents, and locations; and the instructions needed to generate the data flows, re-

---

9 Remember, the events, relationships, and so on, presented with this example are for a particular scenario with a particular set of assumptions. If the scenario or assumptions change, the specifics of the data model may also change. Also, this scenario focuses on events associated with the sales/collection process. Other events, such as Planning Production, or Acquiring Licensing Agreements, are viable, related events of other business processes.

EXHIBIT 6–9

REAL Model for Christopher, Inc. (without relationship semantics)

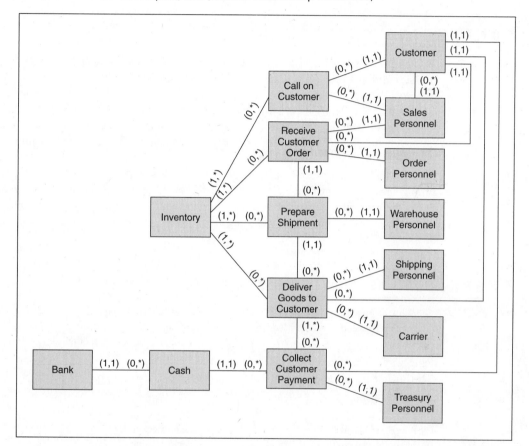

ports, and queries desired by users. The instructions should include business rule logic and both information and business controls. These include but are not limited to preventing or detecting the following:

- A shipment occurring without an authorized order.
- An order being approved without proper customer and credit review.
- An order being entered by an unauthorized employee.
- A shipment being sent to the wrong customer.
- A shipment containing incorrect or excess items.
- A shipment being sent to a non–major league address.

- ◆ A reimbursement for sales call expenses for a meeting at an unauthorized location.
- ◆ A cash receipt being credited to a customer without receiving the cash.

CONCLUDING COMMENTS

This chapter presented an overview of the sales/collection process and reviewed the nature of the traditional process and the use of IT in the traditional accounting system. We also reviewed the traditional process in the context of the criticisms discussed in Chapter 3. Analyzing the traditional process illustrates the opportunity for making significant improvements. By embedding IT in business and information processes, we can make significant improvements in the sales/collection process, and increase the value of accounting and IT professionals to the organization.

Other business processes are of equal importance to the sales/collection process. The following chapters introduce examples of additional business processes. Chapter 7 introduces the acquisition/payment business process, while Chapter 8 overviews some of the other key business processes including the conversion, financing, and human resource business processes.

CHECKLIST OF KEY TERMS AND CONCEPTS

Accounts receivable master file
Accounts receivable subsidiary ledger
Back order
Back-order document
Bill of lading
Bill of sale
Billing information process
Billing transaction file
Cash receipts journal
Cash receipts transaction file
Closed invoices
Credit memorandum or credit slip
Customer master file
Customer order document
Customer order event
Customer payment event
Customer statements
Deposit slip
Electronic funds transfer
General ledger master file
General ledger transaction file
Independent checks on performance
Inventory master file

Inventory subsidiary ledger
Journal voucher document
Journal voucher transaction file
Lapping
Lockbox method of collecting payment
Marketing event
Master file
Open sales invoice file
Open sales order file
Packing slip
Pricing reference file
Remittance advice
Remittance list
Return event
Sales/collection business process
Sales history file
Sales invoice
Sales journal
Sales order
Shipper/carrier reference file
Shipping event
Shipping notice document
Shipping transaction file

Transaction file
Turnaround document
Unapplied cash

Warehousing event
Write-off of uncollectible
accounts event

REVIEW QUESTIONS

1. List three objectives of the sales/collection process.
2. How is the sales/collection processes related to the conversion process, the acquisition payment process, and the financing process?
3. What is the difference between a customer order and a sales order?
4. Refer to Exhibit 6–1. Explain the data flow and purpose for each copy of the sales order document.
5. For a traditional system, identify the department or functional area that creates each of the following source documents:
   a. Sales order.
   b. Bill of lading.
   c. Shipping notice.
   d. Sales invoice.
6. In a traditional system, why does the Shipping Department notify the Billing Department of a shipment? Should the Billing Department use a sales order or a shipping notice to create an invoice? Explain.
7. Explain the difference between a sales order and a sales invoice.
8. Should the Sales Order Department distribute copies of the sales order before or after a credit check? Explain.
9. In a traditional system, at which points and in which departments does the accounting function execute control in the sales/collection process? Explain how the control is provided.
10. In a traditional system, identify the source document(s) used to post to the sales journal and the cash receipts journal.
11. In a traditional system, identify the source document(s) used to post to the accounts receivable (A/R) general ledger account and the A/R subsidiary ledger.
12. List all the accounting records updated in a traditional system to recognize a sale.
13. List all the accounting records updated in a traditional system to recognize a cash receipt.
14. Explain the difference between a remittance advice and a remittance batch list.
15. What is unapplied cash?
16. Describe the key components of separation of duties in a traditional sales/collection process. Be sure to include the nature of each duty listed (i.e., custody, recording, or authorization).

17. What are independent checks on performance?

18. Explain lapping.

19. What reconciliations are needed in a traditional sales/collection process?

20. What does it mean to "restrictively endorse" checks?

21. Describe the lockbox method of collecting customer payments.

22. What is an electronic funds transfer?

23. Describe a sample record layout for each of the following files in a traditional system:
   a. General ledger master file.
   b. Shipping transaction file.
   c. Shipping reference file.
   d. Accounts receivable master file.
   e. Open sales order file.
   f. Open sales invoice file.
   g. Billing transaction file.
   h. Merchandise inventory master file.
   i. Cash receipts transaction file.
   j. Pricing reference file.
   k. Customer master file.

24. Refer to Exhibits 6–3 through 6–8 and give the file name for each of the following:
   a. General ledger.
   b. Accounts receivable subsidiary ledger.
   c. Inventory subsidiary ledger.
   d. Sales journal.
   e. Cash receipts journal.

25. What is an open sale order? In a traditional system, when do records enter and leave the open sales order file?

26. What is an open sale invoice? In a traditional system, when do records enter and leave the open sales invoice file?

27. What are the uses of a numerical paper source document file?

28. During which event should an organization recognize revenue for an FOB shipping point sales transaction: Shipping Goods or Billing a Customer? Explain your response.

29. Identify sample resources, internal agents, external agents, and possible locations associated with each of the following business events:
   a. Marketing.
   b. Take Customer Order.
   c. Move Goods from Warehousing to Shipping.
   d. Ship Goods and/or Provide Services.
   e. Receive Customer Payment.
   f. Accept Returns and Approve Allowances.
   g. Write Off Uncollectible Accounts.

30. Describe the sales/collection process information requirements for each of the following information customers:
   a. Management.
   b. Marketing.
   c. Finance and Accounting.
   d. Human Resource.
   e. Production.

DISCUSSION QUESTIONS

1. Chapter 5 identified the following risks associated with each business event:

   ◆ A business event occurring at the wrong time or sequence.
   ◆ A business event occurring without proper authorization.
   ◆ A business event involving the wrong internal agent.
   ◆ A business event involving the wrong external agent.
   ◆ A business event involving the wrong resource.
   ◆ A business event involving the wrong amount of resource.
   ◆ A business event occurring at the wrong location.

   Give examples of each of these risks while executing the following events:
   a. Marketing.
   b. Take Customer Order.
   c. Move Goods from Warehousing to Shipping.
   d. Ship Goods and/or Provide Services.
   e. Receive Customer Payment.
   f. Accept Returns and Approve Allowances.
   g. Write Off Uncollectible Accounts.

2. Chapter 5 outlined the following risks associated with recording information processes:

   Recording incomplete, inaccurate, or invalid data about a business event. Incomplete data results in not having all the relevant characteristics about a business event. Inaccuracies arise from recording data that does not accurately represent the event. Invalid data refers to data that is recorded about a fabricated event.

   Give specific examples of recording risks associated with each of the following events:
   a. Marketing.
   b. Take Customer Order.
   c. Move Goods from Warehousing to Shipping.
   d. Ship Goods and/or Provide Services.
   e. Receive Customer Payment.

f. Accept Returns and Approve Allowances.

g. Write Off Uncollectible Accounts.

3. Give two examples of maintenance information processes that could be required for each of the following resources, agents, or locations:

   a. Customers.

   b. Employees.

   c. External (Shipping) Carriers.

   d. Cash.

   e. Inventory.

   f. Warehouses.

4. Refer to Exhibits 6–3 through 6–8. How many separate files contain customer data? List the files. Is this duplication reduced in an event-driven IT application? Explain.

5. Is there a natural ordering of events in the sales/collection process? If so, what is the natural order and how is it reflected in a *REAL* model?

6. Review the "Criticisms of Traditional Accounting Systems" section presented in Chapter 3. Discuss each of the criticisms and illustrate how an event-driven architecture overcomes these weaknesses.

7. Art by Tracy uses a traditional sales/collection system. Because data stores are currently segregated by business functions, the system uses hard copies of each of the documents associated with the process to disseminate information. Suppose you reengineer the process using an event-driven architecture. In the new design, you generate hard copies sparingly, usually to send to external entities. How does your system compensate for the lack of hardcopy documents that are considered essential in the traditional system? Does the lack of documents imply an audit trail deficiency? Explain.

8. What triggers or what authorizes each of the following events within a sales/collection process:

   a. Marketing.

   b. Take Customer Order.

   c. Move Goods from Warehousing to Shipping.

   d. Ship Goods and/or Provide Services.

   e. Receive Customer Payment.

   f. Accept Returns and Approve Allowances.

   g. Write Off Uncollectible Accounts.

9. In a traditional general ledger accounting process, accounting becomes involved during the billing phase, when a sale transaction occurs. How would you respond to a traditionalist who argues:

   Most of the data and processes discussed in this chapter are of no concern to accounting. The accounting function is concerned with the sale and collection transactions. These are necessary for us to post the sales, cash, inventory, and accounts receivable account information to the ledgers.

10. In some traditional accounting information systems books, students are taught to design systems with transaction files to replace journals and master files to replace

ledgers. For example, after automation the sales journal becomes the billing transaction file (a file that holds the data to generate the day's sales invoices), the cash receipts journal becomes the cash receipts transaction file (a file that contains remittance information), the accounts receivable ledger becomes an accounts receivable master file, and the inventory subsidiary ledger becomes an inventory master file. If you develop a sales/collection system based on the concepts discussed in this book, how do you compensate for the lack of journals? How do you compensate for the lack of ledgers? [Hint, refer to Chapter E if you need help here.]

11. The Kelly & Julie Company had a manual accounting system. When they had orders that were approved but not yet shipped and billed, they kept these sales order documents in a file called the *open sales order file*. When the sales order was shipped and billed, a clerk removed the applicable sales order document from the open sales order file and stored it in a closed sales order file. The sales invoice generated from the transaction was then placed in an open sales invoice file where it stayed until the payment was received from the customer. When the customer paid for the outstanding invoice, the sales invoice document was removed from the open sales invoice file and stored in a closed sales invoice file.

When Kelly & Julie automated their system, the new system emulated the manual processes. In the automated system, a clerk inputs customer orders into an open sales order file. The records remain in the open sales order file until the goods are shipped and billed. Then the records are removed from the open sales order file and posted to a sales order history file. A sales invoice record is created and posted to an open sales invoice file. When payment is received, the sales invoice record is removed from the open sales invoice file and posted to a sales invoice history file.

Although Kelly & Julie's new system is automated, did the business processes change? Explain why the two systems are so similar. Could you argue that an event-driven system replaces the physical open sales order and invoice files with a logical view of these files? Describe how such a system generates views of the open sales order and invoice files.

12. A traditional auditor is auditing an event-driven system and trying to collect audit evidence to support the sales figure on the financial statements. Normally, she uses paper sales invoices or sales invoice files as evidence. How would the auditor collect evidence in the event-driven architecture to verify the sales figure?

13. Mark & Sandra Business Consulting, Inc., known as MSBC, currently has the following files in their accounting system:
   a. A customer master file, which includes customer account numbers, names, and addresses.
   b. An accounts receivable master file, which includes customer numbers, names, addresses, and account balances.
   c. An open sales invoice file, which includes the customer and inventory data for billed credit orders that have not yet been paid.
   d. A general ledger file with all account balances, including total accounts receivable.

Please describe the relationship between these files. Does such a design include data redundancy? If the balances in the accounts are not in agreement, which one is correct?

14. Odlaw, the super accountant, is upset. A client is considering reengineering its sales/collection process based on the advice of a systems consultant. Currently, the client's billing clerk issues customer invoices only after reviewing the customer's sales order document to verify that there is a valid customer order and the shipping notice document received from the Shipping Department to verify that the goods were shipped. Odlaw likes this procedure because, as he says, "It is a sound internal control procedure and adheres to GAAP."

   The systems consultant suggested the client use an integrated data approach in this process to check for the existence of a valid order (on computer) before shipping, and automatically generate a sales invoice as soon as the shipping information is entered. Odlaw fears the lack of transaction review by the billing clerk will create internal control problems. Please prepare a memorandum to Odlaw to explain how the reengineered system can provide better control and more closely adheres to GAAP than the procedure currently in place.

15. Kathi likes the event-driven architecture and has decided to design a sales/collection system without an accounts receivable file. Can Kathi still generate the total accounts receivable for financial statement reporting? Does such a design violate GAAP? Explain.

16. Compare and contrast the audit trail of total sales reported on a financial statement by a traditional manual system, an automated general ledger system, and an event-driven system.

17. You are designing an event-driven system for a sales/collection process. Give examples of output you could generate to help *plan* each of the following events:
    a. Marketing.
    b. Take Customer Order.
    c. Move Goods from Warehousing to Shipping.
    d. Ship Goods and/or Provide Services.
    e. Receive Customer Payment.
    f. Accept Returns and Approve Allowances.
    g. Write Off Uncollectible Accounts.

18. You are designing an event-driven system for a sales/collection process. Give examples of output you could generate to help *evaluate the efficiency and effectiveness* of each of the following events:
    a. Marketing.
    b. Take Customer Order.
    c. Move Goods from Warehousing to Shipping.
    d. Ship Goods and/or Provide Services.
    e. Receive Customer Payment.
    f. Accept Returns and Approve Allowances.
    g. Write Off Uncollectible Accounts.

19. You are designing an event-driven system for a sales/collection process. Give examples of output you could generate to help *evaluate the performance of internal agents* involved in each of the following events:

a. Marketing.

b. Take Customer Order.

c. Move Goods from Warehousing to Shipping.

d. Ship Goods and/or Provide Services.

e. Receive Customer Payment.

f. Accept Returns and Approve Allowances.

g. Write Off Uncollectible Accounts.

MINICASES AND OTHER APPLIED LEARNING

1. LAIDBACKCO prides itself on sending customer sales invoices (the customer's bill) faster than any company in town. They send out invoices as soon as their customers call in their orders for services, rather than waiting for the services to be completed.

Required:

a. Identify potential business event risks.

b. Identity potential information processing risks.

2. Visit your library and find an article that describes a progressive or nontraditional sales/collection process system design.

Required:

Write a two-page report summarizing the design and explaining how it differs from traditional designs.

3. In project teams, visit a local organization and analyze their sales/collection process.

Required:

a. Flowchart their current process.

b. Prepare a data flow diagram of the process.

c. Prepare a *REAL* model with cardinalities of the process.

4. In project teams, identify a local not-for-profit organization in need of an improved IT application for their sales/collection process.

Required:

Analyze the process and develop an event-driven prototype for the process.

5. Lady Vol, Inc., sells mail order basketball equipment to commercial vendors. Customers place their orders by phone or by sending in a customer order form included in Lady Vol's merchandise catalog. A sales order clerk (answering the phone or opening the mail) takes or reviews the customer's order (e.g., item number, quantity, size, and color) and immediately checks the inventory availability. Customers use a company credit card or a preapproved line of credit to pay for their items. The clerk enters new customer data that is stored in a computerized customer master file, and the sales order data that is stored in a sales order transaction file. The sales order file includes all sales orders that have been approved but not yet billed or invoiced. The sales order clerk generates four hardcopy sales order documents using the data in the sales order file. One copy (called a *picking slip*) goes to the warehouse to help the workers select the items for shipment. One copy (called the *packing slip*) goes to the Shipping Department and is included in the cartons when they are packed for shipment. A third copy (called a *customer acknowledgment*) is sent to the customer, and a final copy is sent to the Billing Department.

The warehouse employees, upon receiving the picking slip, retrieve the items from storage and transfer them with the picking slip to the Shipping Department. If any of the items are not available or are damaged, the warehouse worker makes a note on the picking slip and notifies the Sales Order Department. The Shipping Department packages the items and selects a freight carrier for the order. A shipping clerk enters the packaging and shipping data into the computer in a shipping transaction file. The file is used to generate the shipping document (often called a *bill of lading*) and one copy is included with the shipment, one copy is filed in the Shipping Department, and one copy is sent to the Billing Department.

After the Billing Department receives the shipping notice, a clerk checks for a sales order and enters the billing data to a billing transaction file. A computer pricing reference file assigns prices to the shipped items, and a hardcopy invoice (the customer's bill) is printed and mailed to the customer. At this point, the general ledger is updated to reflect the sale, the accounts receivable master file is updated for any balance due, the sales order record is removed from the sales order file, and a sales invoice record is added to the sales invoice file. When credit customers pay their bills, they usually send a portion of their invoice called a *remittance advice*. A clerk deposits the checks in the bank and enters the remittance in a cash receipts transaction file. The general ledger is updated to reflect the cash receipt, the accounts receivable master file is updated, and the sales invoice record is removed from the sales invoice file and posted to a sales history file.

Required:

    a. Flowchart the process.
    b. Explain how this automated process differs from a traditional, manual process.
    c. Prepare a *REAL* model with cardinalities for this process.
    d. Using a software tool, prepare sample data attribute tables for the process.
    e. Identify source documents the process should provide. Using a software tool, prepare output screens to generate each of these source documents.

  6. The following describes the process to execute a credit sale at Willie's Furniture Store.

Sales clerks assist customers in locating and pricing merchandise. A sales clerk prepares a sales invoice with an original and three copies. If the merchandise on an invoice is priced differently than the list price, the sales manager must approve the price change with a signature. The third copy of the sales invoice is filed by the salesperson in a salesperson file.

The salesperson walks the customer and the remaining copies of the invoice to the Credit Approval Department where a clerk checks the invoice for mathematical errors. The credit manager evaluates the credit standing of the customer, and approves or rejects the application based on standard company policy. If the sale is approved, the credit manager marks "credit sale" on the invoice and returns it to the clerk. For credit-approved sales the second copy of the invoice is given to the customer. The Credit Approval Department keeps the original copy of the invoice in their files (filed numerically) and sends the other copy to shipping.

The Shipping Department uses their copy as a guide to pull merchandise and deliver it to the customer. The customer is asked to sign the invoice copy as evidence of delivery. The delivery person files the signed invoice copy by date.

Required:
   a. Prepare a context diagram for the process.
   b. Create a *REAL* model with cardinalities for the process.
   c. Create any needed tables, complete with key attributes, foreign keys, and non-key attributes.
   d. List the recording and maintaining information processes needed for these activities.
   e. For each information process listed in part *d,* draw a data flow diagram showing the tables needed to perform the process.
   f. Identify the business rules and business risks associated with each event.

7. Western Steel Company, located in Boulder, Colorado, produces steel for a variety of customers, including automobile manufacturers, construction companies, and the U.S. government. Western receives approximately 96% of its revenue from metal products and the rest from by-products such as oils, slag, and rare earth.

When customers order steel, an order clerk enters information into a computer that prepares a purchase order to track the order from production to collection of payment. If the customer's credit has been approved, production of the order begins immediately. If the customer is new, a credit check is performed.

After the order is filled, a tally count is made of the produced steel and the steel is shipped to the customer. If the steel is to be shipped by railroad, rail cars are checked for weight before shipping the order. The weight of the load is then compared to the order to ensure an accurate delivery. Accompanying the shipment is a computer-generated bill of lading and a copy of the purchase order.

Shortly after shipping an order, Western invoices the customer using prices on an approved price list. The invoice total is obtained by multiplying the quantity ordered and shipped by the standard price. Steel prices are set by the Sales Department, which determines competitive prices based on market conditions and cost information.

Customers send payments directly to a lockbox account in selected cities across the United States. The bank where a particular customer sends payment is located in the city closest to the customer's location. Western receives no payment, but Western receives a record of customer deposits from the bank maintaining the lockbox account. Accounting personnel maintain the billing and collection accounts, while the Credit Department issues credit to customers and follows up on past due accounts.

Required:

 a. Prepare a context diagram for the process.

 b. Create a *REAL* model with cardinalities for the process.

 c. Create any needed tables, complete with key attributes, foreign keys, and non-key attributes.

 d. List the recording and maintaining information processes needed for these activities.

 e. For each information process listed in part *d,* draw a data flow diagram showing the tables needed to perform the process.

 f. Identify the business rules and business risks associated with each event.

8. J&T Video Shopping Network

 Objective. The objective of this assignment is to help you learn how to query a database to obtain useful information.

 Background. J&T entered into the video sales business just six months ago and has experienced fair success. Several cable television stations have broadcast the program, which demonstrates name-brand products and flashes an 800 number for viewers to order items. J&T's product pricing is very competitive as inventories are purchased in very large quantities directly from manufacturers and overhead is minimal in comparison to retail outlets.

 This is a critical time in J&T's growth. National cable network time has recently been purchased and decisions need to be made on how to best use the expensive national air time. Some data have been collected and entered into relational tables as described below.

 Database. A complete database would consist of customer payment records, inventory purchases, and so on. However, the tables below will provide a representative exposure to relational databases and the power of a query language.

 The underlined field indicates the record's unique identifier. For example, every inventory item is referred to by its stock number. The table titled ORDR-ITM is necessary because inventory items have a many-to-many relationship with purchase orders. In other words, any particular item can be purchased by several customers while any one customer may purchase several items. Therefore, the individual items included in each purchase order are identified in the table ORDR-ITM. A partial *REAL* diagram for J&T video is shown in Exhibit 6–10.

Table Name	Fields
CUSTOMER	(Customer #, Name, Street Address, City, State, Zip, Age, Sex, Occupation . . .
ITEM	(Stock #, [Supplier #], Description, Unit Cost, Sales Price, QOH, Air Time . . .
ORDER	(P.O. #, [Customer #], [SSN], Date . . .
ORDR-ITM	([P.O. #], [Stock #], Qty . . .
SALESPERSON	(SSN, Name, Commission Rate)
SUPPLIER	(Supplier #, Name, Address, City, State, Zip . . .

EXHIBIT 6–10

Partial *REAL* Diagram for J&T Video

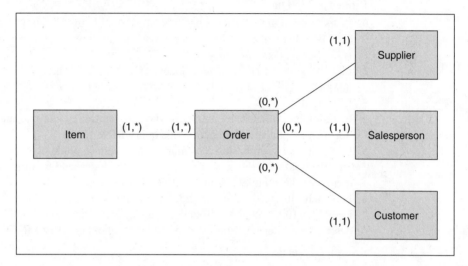

Copy of Files. To complete this assignment you need to obtain from your instructor a copy of the J&T files. These will be in a subdirectory titled J&T. Within this subdirectory you should have data for the first six months of operations.

As indicated above, decisions need to be made on how to best use expensive national air time. You have been asked to review data collected from J&T's first six months of operations. Answer the following questions by querying the database:

Simple Queries

a. List all customer names and occupations. (A solution to this query is in your J&T database as SIMPLE1.)

b. List the item description, profit per unit in dollars, and gross margin percent for each item. (A solution to this query is in your J&T database as SIMPLE2. Note the change in the "properties" by clicking the right mouse button with the pointer on the Gross Profit Percent field while in the Design View. The format has been changed to percent with 2 decimal places.)

c. List all female customers with their name and their age. (Name this query SIMPLE3.)

d. List each customer's name and occupation if their occupation is Housewife. (Name it SIMPLE4.)

e. List item description and quantity on hand (QOH) for each item whose QOH is less than or equal to 500. (Name this query SIMPLE5.)

f. List all item descriptions, percentage markup [(Price – Cost)/Cost] for each item, and potential profit by item for the quantity on hand [(Price – Cost) × QOH]. Sort the products in descending order by percentage markup. (Name this query SIMPLE6.)

Linked Table Queries

a. List supplier number 1010's name, state, and all items J&T buys from them. For each item list stock number, description, and unit cost. (A solution to this query is in your J&T subdirectory as LINKED1.)

b. List all the items Tracy Sheen (Sheen, Tracy) has sold. Include the item's stock number and description. (A solution to this query is in your J&T subdirectory as LINKED2.)

c. List all the customers, by name, to whom Joyce Bailey has sold merchandise. Sort them alphabetically. (Name this query LINKED3.)

d. List customers purchasing 5 or more of any item (include item description and quantity sold with the customer's name). Sort in descending order according to quantity sold. (Name this query LINKED4.)

e. List each salesperson's name and the total number of items each has sold (Hint: Use View/Totals to add a "Total" row and select Sum on Quantity.) Sort in descending order on Total Quantity Sold. (Name this query LINKED5.)

Complex Queries

a. Who is the target market for the aerobic exercise ware? Base your recommendation on age, sex, occupation, and quantity sold. Sort in descending order on quantity sold. (A solution to this query is in your J&T subdirectory as COMPLEX1.)

b. Which salesperson should receive the Outstanding Salesperson Award for the first few months of operations. Base the award on total gross margin for sales made by each salesperson. Your answer should show gross margin by salesperson in descending order. (A solution to this query is in your J&T subdirectory as COMPLEX2.)

c. What products are most attractive to housewives and, therefore, should be emphasized during afternoon air time? List occupation, quantity, and product description for items sold to housewives. Sort in descending order on quantity sold. (Name this query COMPLEX3.)

d. Which television salesperson personality should be used to sell item 102? Assume salespeople have equal air time with each product. Show in your answer table the salesperson's name, description of item 102, and the total quantity sold by each salesperson. (Name this query COMPLEX4.)

e. Management wants a report that shows product profitability per hour of air time. Note: Air time in the ITEM table is in minutes. List product stock number, description, and gross margin per hour of air time. (Hint: This will take 2 queries, one to identify total quantity of each item sold, and one to query that query to figure total gross margin per hour of air time. Format the new column and sort in ascending order on gross margin per hour of air time.) (Label these queries COMPLX5A and COMPLX5B.)

f. How much revenue was earned on Ferrari Toasters (stock #301) on PO1 #007? List on your answer table the PO# and product description in addition to the revenue earned. (Name the query COMPLEX6).

g. Calculate the historical cost-based value of each item in inventory and the total cost of inventory on hand at the end of the period. (Hint: You will need to have two queries; one to show the description of each item and its total cost, and a second to show only the total inventory value.) (Name these queries COMPLX7A and COMPLX7B.)

Required:

Turn in a printed copy of the query results and a copy of the SQL query itself for simple queries *c–f*, linked table queries *c–e*, and complex queries *c–g*.

9. NOTE: To complete problem 9, your instructor must have ordered the Arens and Ward, *Systems Understanding Aid* or *Systems Understanding Aid for Financial Accounting*, 4th ed. (Williamston, Mich.: Armond Dalton Publishers, 1995) for purchase from your bookstore.

   After reviewing the documentation in the *Systems Understanding Aid* package for the sales/collection business process, complete the following in student project teams.

Required:

a. Prepare a context diagram for the process.

b. Create a *REAL* model with cardinalities for the process.

c. Create any needed tables, complete with key attributes, foreign keys, and non-key attributes.

d. List the recording and maintaining information processes needed for these activities. Give three examples of reporting processes for this case.

e. For each information process listed in part *d,* draw a data flow diagram that displays the tables needed to perform the process.

f. Identify the business rules and business risks associated with each event.

g. Create an IT application prototype of Waren's sales/collection process. Input the test data and test your prototype.

10. The following assignment consists of four parts. Part 1 creates database tables. Part 2 creates forms and enters a small amount of data into them. Part 3 develops queries to obtain meaningful data from the database. Part 4 develops a partial income statement from the data in the database.

Part 1

The objective of this assignment is to teach you how to create tables for a database. The notes accompanying the assignment are for Microsoft Access 7 in Windows 95. Your instructor will provide similar notes if you use another database.

Canyon Adventure Equipment Company (CAEC) recently started business. CAEC sells a variety of biking, skiing, and camping gear from one local retail store. CAEC's mission is to provide customers with the best gear at the best price. The owner of CAEC would like to collect data on their operating activities in a relational database. Management will use this database to manage the business. You have been asked to develop this database for CAEC. (A partial *REAL* model for CAEC appears in Exhibit 6–11.)

A complete database would consist of tables such as customer payment records and sales returns. However, the tables below will provide a representative exposure to relational databases and a review of the procedures required to create tables and query tables of data.

Table Name	Fields
Customer	(<u>Customer#</u>, Name, Street, City, State, Zip, Gender)
Employee	(<u>Employee#</u>, Position, Name, Commission Rate)
Sale	(<u>Sale#</u>, [Employee#], [Customer#], Time, Date)
Item	(<u>Stock#</u>, [Category#], [Supplier#], Description, Sales Price)
Sale-Item	([Stock#], [Sale#], Quantity)
Supplier	(<u>Supplier#</u>, Name, Street, City, State, Zip)
Category	(<u>Category#</u>, Name)
Purchase	(<u>PO#</u>, [Employee#], [Supplier#], Date)
Purchase-Item	([PO#], [Stock#], Quantity, Unit Cost)

The <u>underline</u> indicates the record's primary key, and the brackets ([ ]) designate a foreign key. For example, every inventory item is referred to by its stock

E X H I B I T   6–11

Partial *REAL* Model for CAEC

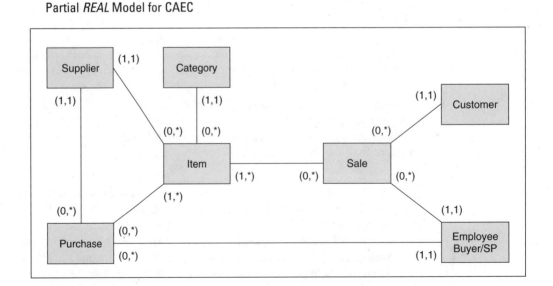

number. The table titled Sale-Item is necessary because inventory items have a many-to-many relationship with purchase orders. This means any particular item can be purchased by several customers while any one customer may purchase several items. Therefore, the individual items included in each sale are identified in the table Sale-Item. The same is also true for Purchase-Item.

Assignment:

Create a subdirectory called ACS. Create nine tables in the ACS subdirectory in a new database called CAEC. After creating the tables, establish the relationships between them as outlined in the *REAL* model in Exhibit 6–11.

The nine tables are those listed above. For uniformity, use the following field names and field types. Adjust the field properties to the field sizes and number types as indicated. (You make up and enter your own description.) Make the key field(s) the first field(s) in the table.

Attribute	Field Type	Field Size
Customer		
Customer#	Number	Long Integer
Name	Text	30
Street Address	Text	30
City	Text	20
State	Text	3
Zip	Text	10
Gender	Text	5
Employee		
Employee#	Number	Integer
Name	Text	30
Position	Text	20
Commission Rate	Number	Single—3 decimal places
Sale		
Sale#	Number	Long Integer
[Customer#]	Number	Long Integer
[Employee#]	Number	Integer
Time	Time/Date	Medium Time
Date	Time/Date	Short Date
Item		
Stock#	Number	Integer
[Category#]	Number	Integer
[Supplier#]	Number	Integer
Description	Text	30
Sales Price	Currency	

Attribute	Field Type	Field Size
Sale-Item		
[Stock#]	Number	Integer
[Sale#]	Number	Long Integer
Quantity	Number	Integer
Supplier		
Supplier#	Number	Integer
Name	Text	30
Street	Text	30
City	Text	20
State	Text	3
Zip	Text	10
Category		
Category#	Number	Integer
Category Name	Text	20
Purchase		
PO#	Number	Long Integer
[Employee#]	Number	Integer
Purchase		
[Supplier#]	Number	Integer
Date	Date/Time	Short Date
Purchase-Item		
[PO#]	Number	Long Integer
[Stock#]	Number	Integer
Quantity	Number	Integer
Unit Cost	Currency	

Notes for Microsoft Access: The main Microsoft Access commands to create a database and the tables include:

1. To create a new database: FILE/NEW DATABASE/BLANK/DATABASE/OK. Identify your ACS subdirectory, enter CAEC, and click CREATE.

2. To create tables: TABLE/NEW/DESIGN VIEW/OK. Enter field names, data types, adjust the field properties and description, and identify primary key (click on primary key field and select EDIT/SET PRIMARY KEY or click KEY button on tool bar). Save file (FILE/SAVE AS or click SAVE button on tool bar and enter the table name and click OK), and close the table.

   Note: When you want two primary keys in one table, click on one field. Then, holding down the control (CTRL) key, click on the second field and select EDIT/SET PRIMARY KEY or click on the KEY button on the tool bar.

3. Use the following directions to establish the relationships between the tables:

   a. In the Tables list of the Database window, click TOOLS, then RELATIONSHIPS. Add each of the tables listed in the Show Tables window to the Master Relationships window.

   b. Add the relationship between two tables by clicking on a primary key field in one table and dragging it to the foreign key field in the related table. A smaller Relationship window will appear when you release the mouse button.

   c. Verify the table relationships in the smaller Relationship window and the relationship type (one-to-many). Click on ENFORCE REFERENTIAL INTEGRITY, then click CREATE.

   d. Continue until all the relationships are identified, then close the Relationships window.

You don't need to turn anything in for this assignment. You will use these same tables for Part 2 and that assignment will show you have completed this assignment correctly.

Part 2

The objective of this assignment is to teach you how to enter data into a relational database using a form.

   a. Create single table forms for the following tables and enter the data listed below.

CUSTOMER						
Customer#	**Name**	**Address**	**City**	**State**	**Zip**	**Gender**
100	Smith, Jane	400 S. 623 W.	Provo	UT	84601	F
101	Vinto, Bill	329 N. 500 E.	Provo	UT	84600	M
102	Jackson, Marie	1200 N. 23 E.	Orem	UT	84607	F

EMPLOYEE			
Employee#	**Name**	**Position**	**Commission Rate**
8856	Benac, Bill	Buyer	0.07
4783	Woodfield, Leon	Seller	0.07
8954	Jesop, Janice	Seller	0.07

CATEGORY

Category#	Category Name
100	Tents
120	Backpacks
201	Downhill Skis

SUPPLIER

Supplier#	Name	Address	City	State	Zip
332	Mountainsmith	361 Redmond St.	Boulder	CO	56421
354	Sierra Designs	4971 South Mountain Ave.	Glendale	AZ	86347
802	K2	8 Fast Lane	Jackson Hole	WY	25896

ITEM

Stock#	Category#	Supplier#	Description	Sales Price
9	100	354	Sierra Designs Clip 3	$235.00
45	120	332	Mountainsmith Bugaboo	$160.00
67	100	354	Sierra Designs Clip Flashlight	$180.00
101	201	802	K2 Four	$549.00

The following Microsoft Access commands will help you create the form and enter the data.

1. Start Access and open the CAEC database: (FILE/OPEN database, change to ACS subdirectory, and select CAEC.)
2. Select forms design features: (FORMS/NEW/AUTOFORM: Columnar *and select the desired table* from the list arrow by Available Tables, then click OK.)
3. Save the form: (Click SAVE button, enter new form name if desired, and click OK.)
4. Enter data: (Type a field of data, press TAB or ENTER, and continue until all fields are entered. Pressing TAB or ENTER after the last field of data has been entered automatically saves the record in the file.)
5. When all records are entered, click on CLOSE button.
6. View your table to verify your data was entered accurately.

7. Print the form and the contents of the table: With the form highlighted in the Forms list of the Database window select the PRINT button or FILE/PRINT.

Note: If you find an error in the data in your table, use the form you created above to correct it. View the data in the table using the form. For the record with the error, double-click the field with incorrect data, correct the data, and press the TAB or ENTER key to move to other fields and correct them. Close the form when all errors are corrected.

Turn in a printout of each form you created and used for data entry.

b. Create a multiple-table form and enter the sale information given below.

Sale#	Customer#	Employee#	Time	Date	Stock#	Quantity
1	100	4783	3:20 PM	3/2/97	45	2
					45	2
2	101	4783	5:10 PM	3/3/97	45	1
					101	1
3	102	8954	12:20 PM	3/4/97	101	1

The following commands will help you create the form and enter the data.

1. On the Forms page, click the NEW button, select FORM WIZARD, and click OK.

2. From the Tables/Queries list select the Sale table. Click the >> button to select all fields. Don't leave this screen! Now select the Sale-Item table from the Tables/Queries list. Use the > button to select the Stock# and Quantity fields. Now click the NEXT> button. Make sure your data will be sorted by Sale and then Sale-Item. Also, select the FORM with SUB-FORMS option. Click NEXT>. Select the DATASHEET option. Click NEXT>. Select the style you would like and click the FINISH button. **Note:** It may be necessary for you to manually adjust the width of some of the fields. The field widths can be changed in the FORM DESIGN VIEW.

3. Enter sales data: Type a field of data in the form, press TAB or ENTER, and continue until all fields are entered. **Note:** You can enter multiple Stock#s and Quantities for each sale. After you complete the last item on the Sale#, click the next record button for a new Sale and click the SALE# box to move the cursor to that point and start entering another Sale. Access automatically saves the records in the table.

4. When all records are entered, click on the CLOSE button.

5. View your tables to verify your data was entered accurately.

6. Print the form and the contents of the table: With the form highlighted in the Form list window, click the Print button.

Turn in a printout of each form you created and used for data entry.

Part 3

The objective of this assignment is to teach you how to query a database to obtain useful information. CAEC needs to make many decisions concerning their operations. Among other things they want information about market demographics and product profitability.

To complete this assignment you will need to obtain the CAEC database from your instructor. It will have nine tables with data for the first few weeks of operations. The forms used to enter the data are also included. These are the same as you developed in Part 1 and Part 2 above except more data have been entered.

Answer the following questions by querying the database:

Simple Queries

a. List all customer names and gender in alphabetic order. A solution to this query is in your CAEC database as Simple_1_Query.

b. Calculate the total number of sales and the total number of items sold. A solution to this query is in your CAEC database as Simple_2_Query.

c. List all products where category# is 120. A solution to this query is in your CAEC database as Simple_3_Query.

d. Calculate the dollar amount of purchases made. Name this query Simple_4_Query.

e. Give the description and price of all items with a sales price greater than $500. Name this query Simple_6_Query.

Complex Queries

a. List supplier number 609's name and state and all items CAEC buys from them. For each item list stock number, description, and sales price. A solution to this query is in your CAEC database as Linked_1_Query.

b. Which category of products is most popular in Provo? List the city name, a count of items sold in each category in descending order, and the category name. A solution to this query is in your database as Linked_2_Query.

c. Calculate the total sales revenue for CAEC thus far. The solution provided with the database uses two queries. The first query selects price and quantity data from multiple tables. The second query answers the question using the data in the first query. A solution to this query is in your database as Linked_3a_Query and Linked_3b_Query.

d. Calculate the total cost of goods sold for CAEC thus far. Save the queries as Linked_4a_Query and Linked_4b_Query.

e. Sales commission for employees is a percentage of the sales revenue they generate. Calculate the total sales commission expense incurred thus far. This will take two queries to answer. Save the queries as Linked_5a_Query and Linked_5b_Query.

f. Which product category offers the highest percentage markup? The formula for calculating this is the average of ([Sales Price] – [Unit Cost])/[Unit Cost]. Show the average percentage markup by category in descending order. Save this query as Linked_6_Query.

Turn in the hard-copy printout of the query results for the queries you wrote.

Other Management Questions

Suppose you are the owner/manager of Canyon Adventure Equipment Co. Identify one management question you might have about the sales or purchase activity of the company. Then develop a query (or queries) to answer the question. Turn in the question you created and the solution to the query to answer the question.

Part 4

The objective of this assignment is to show you how financial statements can be generated without the use of a general ledger and journals. In the process, you will learn how to create a database report.

CAEC needs a partial income statement to apply for a bank loan. Your assignment is to generate a partial income statement using some of the queries you wrote in Part 3 above. The income statement must include the following: sales revenue, cost of goods sold, gross margin, and sales commission expense.

The following directions will help you create a Microsoft Access report.

1. Write a new query that consolidates all of the income statement items from previously written queries. Combine all the queries you want on the report into one query because a report can only run from one query.

Go to Query Design window for creating a new query. In the Show Table window select the QUERIES tab. Add the following queries to your new query: Linked_3b_Query, Linked_4b_Query, and Linked_5b_Query.

Double-click on the revenue, cost of goods sold, and commission expense fields to include these in your query. Gross margin must be derived from the revenue and cost of goods sold fields. Include the calculated gross margin field in your query. Save this query as Income_Statement_Query.

2. Now you are ready to create your income statement. Click on the REPORTS tab in the main window. Click the NEW button. In the New Report window choose the Income_Statement_Query. Also highlight DESIGN VIEW. Click the OK button.

In the Report Design window select VIEW and FIELD LIST to show the attributes of the Income_Statement_Query. With the FIELD LIST showing, click and drag each field to the position you would like it to be on the report. For each field there will be two boxes. The left label is the text title of the field. The right label is the data field where the actual data from the query will appear. To separate these boxes, select the field you want to adjust. Position your pointer over the large black square in the upper left corner of one of the boxes. In this position you can click and drag each box to the desired place. The text boxes can be edited to show the appropriate text for the report.

Use the label tool to create a title for the report in the header section. Activate this tool by clicking on the button with an **A** on it.

Turn in a printout of your report and a copy of the disk that contains your Income_Statement_Query and your CAEC income statement.

7

CHAPTER

The Acquisition/Payment Process

CHAPTER OBJECTIVE

The objective of this chapter is to review the acquisition/payment business process. After studying this chapter, you should be able to:

- Identify the characteristics of the traditional acquisition/payment process and related IT applications.
- Describe the criticisms of the traditional acquisition/payment process and the IT application architecture.
- Develop a *REAL* model of the acquisition/payment process.
- Identify opportunities to improve the acquisition/payment process and IT applications.

INTRODUCTION

The acquisition/payment process includes the business events associated with buying, maintaining, and paying for goods and services needed by the organization. This process includes acquiring raw materials, component parts, and other resources contained in finished products or services. It also includes acquiring, and paying for, a variety of other goods and services (e.g., utilities, supplies, insurance, repairs, maintenance, research, development, and professional and legal services). Acquiring property, plant, and equipment is very similar to the activities discussed in this chapter. However, because these acquisitions typically involve major resource commitments and a great deal more analysis and planning than do other acquisitions, they are frequently classified as a separate business process.

Processes that resemble the acquisition/payment process, but are more unique, include acquiring and paying for human resources, and financing capital. Business events associated with these activities are included in the human resource process and the financing process, respectively, and are discussed in Chapter 8.

In this chapter we discuss the strategy, objectives, and nature of the acquisition/ payment process, as well as opportunities to improve it. The chapter also reviews traditional designs for this process, and discusses elements of an event-driven IT application. We will not spend as much time comparing the traditional system with an event-driven system, nor will we explain the process in as much detail as we did for the sales/collection process in the prior chapter. You may perform these analyses on your own.

STRATEGY AND SCOPE OF THE ACQUISITION/PAYMENT PROCESS

The overall objective of the acquisition/payment process is to provide needed resources for the organization's conversion processes when they are needed. This objective can be broken into several sub-objectives:

- ◆ Purchase items from reliable vendors.
- ◆ Purchase high-quality items, or at least items of the desired quality.
- ◆ Obtain the items at the best possible price.
- ◆ Purchase only those items that are properly authorized and are for legitimate company purposes.
- ◆ Have resources available and in useful condition when they are needed by the company.
- ◆ Receive only those items ordered, and receive all the items ordered.
- ◆ Control items received so they are not lost, stolen, or broken.
- ◆ Pay for the items received in a timely manner to the appropriate party.

These objectives serve to shape the nature and scope of the acquisition/payment process. Over time the relative importance of each of these objectives will likely change as the organization responds to its environment. Therefore, changes in objectives and their relative priorities result in changes in the nature and scope of the acquisition process and the related IT applications. In this chapter, we first overview the acquisition/process, examining it from the REA (who, what, when, where, why) perspective. We follow with a review of the traditional architectures, both manual and automated, used to support the process.

AN OVERVIEW OF THE ACQUISITION/PAYMENT PROCESS

Organizations acquire a variety of goods and services. These include inventory, supplies, human labor, property, plant, equipment, and fixed assets. To describe the acquisition/ payment process, let's review some of the more common events that make up the process. Two important reminders before we begin the discussion. Because we discuss the activities in a sequential fashion, it may seem that the acquisition/payment process is linear. That is not necessarily true. Increasingly, business processes and the activities that comprise those processes are dynamic, rather than linear and static. Also, remember that the activities in this process are linked to activities in other processes. We are concentrating on one process at a time to simplify our analysis.

Request for Goods/Services (Monitor Need) Event

Event Description   The acquisition/payment process responds to an authorized individual's (internal agent's) requests for goods or services (resources) that are approved for use by the company. Monitoring various organization activities including production levels, sales levels, capital improvement plans, capital budgets, sales forecasts, or use trends and projections identifies the need for goods or services. This monitoring of levels, forecasts, and needs is a critical component of the purchasing process, and the information system should help by providing accurate, timely, and well-controlled information. Once a need is identified by an authorized individual (internal agent), a request is often communicated to an authorized buyer (internal purchasing agent). Alternatively, some organizations empower the authorized person who monitors the need to also execute the ordering process. These organizations often use technologies such as corporate debit cards to allow individuals to purchase goods or services (up to a certain dollar amount).

Event Risks   The main risks associated with this event are requesting items not actually needed; having unauthorized person(s) request goods or services; requesting the wrong type or amount of a good or service; receiving an authorized resource request from an inappropriate agent or location, and not requesting goods or services on a timely basis.

Event Documentation   The Request for Goods/Services needs to be documented and communicated to the buyer (purchasing agent) for review and potential approval.

RAL Data Maintenance   Organizations need to maintain current records of authorized goods and services and the various individuals who are authorized to monitor and request goods and services.

Examples of Information Outputs   Information users want the ability to produce various outputs from the information captured on this event including:

- Purchase requisitions.
- A list of requests made during the period.
- A list of requests outstanding (those not yet acted on by the buyer).
- A status report of goods or services (as support for monitoring need).

Authorize Purchase Event

In the sales/collection process, a critical component of the Customer Order event was the customer credit and order review. A similar review and authorization takes place in the acquisition/payment process.

Prior to ordering goods and services in many organizations, an Authorize Purchase event must occur. Authorization either precedes the request by allocating sufficient budget to a process owner, or follows each request if tighter control is desired. The purchasing clerks or buyers discussed in the Purchase Good/Service event communicate authorization to Receiving to take receipt of ordered goods or services. However, these agents often do not have the authority to execute orders unless they receive authorized requests.

Purchase Goods/Services Event

Event Description   In simple terms, a buyer (internal agent) reviews approved requests for goods or services (resources), selects a vendor (external agent), and negotiates the terms and conditions of the purchase. The buyer then places a purchase order for the requested items with a vendor. The selection of the vendor is based on several factors such as price, vendor performance, and quality. The buyer also communicates the open purchase order to the Receiving Department, which provides authorization to receive the goods or services upon delivery.

In reality, the purchasing decision is often a complex decision-making process. For example, sometimes organizations use a proposal process to select a vendor. In these cases, the organization puts out an RFP (request for proposal) as an invitation for vendors to bid for the right to fulfill purchasing needs.

It is important to remember that an order typically does not meet the accounting definition of *purchase*. Thus order data are not reported on financial statements.

Event Risks   Organizations need to implement controls to reduce the risk of poor vendor selection; ordering without a valid, authorized need; placing orders requested from unauthorized individuals or locations; ordering the wrong type, amount, or quality of a good or service; ordering at an inflated price or under bad terms; and ordering on an untimely basis, which can lead to increased organization costs (e.g., regularly paying extra for rush orders).

Event Documentation   IT applications should assist the buyer with reviewing the request including reviewing the agents authorized to request items and the goods or services authorized for purchase. The applications should also assist with selecting a vendor and completely and accurately recording the purchase order.

RAL Data Maintenance   Data stores should be updated to reflect any changes in resources authorized for purchase, changes in authorized buyers and persons authorized to request goods or services, and changes in vendors and resources offered by vendors.

Examples of Information Outputs   Data recorded by this event are used to create a variety of data flows including:

◆ Purchase orders.
◆ A listing of open purchase orders (approved orders not yet received and not yet recognized as liabilities).

- Orders approved and executed during the period.
- An aging of outstanding orders.
- Anticipated expenditures for cash planning (forthcoming cash disbursements based on outstanding open orders).

Receive Goods/Services Event

Event Description   Goods or services (resources) are received from a vendor (external agent) by authorized receiving agents (internal agents). Sometimes the person playing the receiver role (internal agent) is the same person that requested the goods or services. Receiving tangible goods is a bit different from receiving services but both focus on making sure that the goods/services received are those that were requested. After verifying authorization to receive the goods (via checking for a valid open purchase order), the goods or services are inspected and taken into the organization. Goods are transferred to the warehouse or the location where they will be used (such as a specific office building). Once goods/services are accepted, the organization typically recognizes a liability (i.e., the debt owed for the goods/services). When the vendor's invoice (the bill) arrives, the organization should reconcile the bill to the recorded liability, and contact the vendor if there is a discrepancy (e.g., the vendor's invoice does not reflect what was received or the agreed prices or purchase terms).

Event Risks   Organizations should guard against several risks related to this event, including receiving goods that were not ordered; failing to properly safeguard received assets; receiving the wrong type, amount, or quality of goods or services; receiving goods in poor condition; having unauthorized persons receive goods; and transferring goods internally to the wrong locations or to unauthorized persons.

Event Documentation   This event requires accurate and complete recording of the receipt of goods in a receipts event data pool and the inventory data pool. To authorize the receipt, there should be a valid open purchase order for the goods or services. Receiving clerks should record the time, location, type, quantity, and condition of the goods or services received and transfer them to the appropriate location. After the goods are received and verified, the organization can recognize a liability.

Some organizations choose to wait until they receive a vendor's invoice before recognizing a liability. At that point they reconcile the purchase order (proof that the goods were ordered), the receiving report (documentation of the receipt of goods), and the vendor's invoice. Waiting for the bill before reconciling the order with the receiving report and recording a liability can result in significant time lags between the actual completion of the business event (Receive Goods) and the recognition of the liability in the financial records.

Increasingly, organizations are streamlining this process to recognize the liability when the goods are received. Then when the vendor's invoice is received, the recorded receipt and liability are compared to the bill. Discrepancies should be resolved as soon as possible.

The receipt is recorded in a receipts event data pool and the inventory data pool. Liability data recorded for this event increase inventory levels, increase purchases, increase accounts payable, decrease open orders, and increase open payables.

RAL Data Maintenance   Organizations should keep current records regarding resources in stock or on order, vendors who supply goods or services, and authorized receiving agents.

Examples of Information Outputs   Data recorded by the Receive Goods/Services event are used to produce several data flows and reports. These include:

- Summaries and analyses of goods and services received.
- A listing of receipts during a period of time.
- A listing of purchases for a specified time period.
- A listing of aged payables.
- A listing of receipts per vendor.
- An analysis of vendor performance (e.g., the time it took to receive goods or services, and the condition or quality of the goods or services received).
- Back-order report.
- An inventory listing or status report.

Disburse Cash Event

Event Description   This business process typically concludes when, in agreement with an organization's cash management policy, an authorized financial manager (internal agent) disburses funds (resources) to the vendor (the external agent) to pay the liability. The activity is most often triggered by the liability due date. Check, debit card, or electronic funds transfer can be used to make the payment. All cash disbursements should be reviewed before payment to assure that the disbursement covers legitimate goods or services, including some special orders that require prepayment. When appropriate, discount periods and cash availability should be considered when deciding the amount and timing of the payment.

Event Risks   Organizations should guard against losing discounts without justification; paying for goods or services not ordered and received; paying the wrong amounts; paying late or failing to make a payment; paying the wrong party; and paying invoices more than once.

Event Documentation   The cash disbursement should be recorded in a cash disbursement event data pool. The data recorded for this event reduce cash levels, reduce accounts payable, and decrease open payables.

RAL Data Maintenance   To record and control this event, the system must maintain current data on cash availability and sources of cash, vendors owed, and agents authorized to disburse cash.

Examples of Information Outputs   Information users may request several outputs about this event including:

- Cash disbursed during a specified time period or to a particular vendor.
- An analysis of discounts used and/or discounts lost.
- A report of late payments or of required payments.
- A listing of open invoices (liabilities for received goods that have not yet been paid).

Purchase Return Event

Occasionally, purchased items are returned to the vendor for refund or credit. These returns should be authorized by an internal agent, and documented (including the shipment back to the vendor). The event should be monitored to assure that the organization receives a timely refund or credit.

DECISION SUPPORT REQUIREMENTS OF THE ACQUISITION/PAYMENT PROCESS

Traditional information customers for a typical acquisition/payment process include top management, buyers (purchasing personnel), receivers, accounting/finance, treasury, and vendors.

Top management desires summary information on the activities of this process to evaluate overall business effectiveness. Items of interest might include:

- Turnover of raw material components, average number of processing days contained in raw material inventory, and frequency and amount of downtime due to lack of component parts.
- Amount of obsolete, wasted, or stolen inventory.
- Purchase discounts available and purchase discounts lost.

The primary internal agents who perform the work of this process are buyers, receivers, and disbursement clerks. Each of these groups needs information to effectively perform their job.

To make wise purchase decisions, buyers (purchasing personnel) must know which items need to be purchased and information about vendors and their products and services. To a large extent, buyers rely on authorized people within the organization to request needed items. For example, a department manager may need a new piece of equipment to replace an existing machine that is down much of the time for repairs and maintenance. The department manager initiates the acquisition by preparing a purchase requisition.

Mathematical models such as economic order quantity (EOQ) and computer programs based on models such as materials requirement planning (MRP) are useful in identifying what will be needed for ongoing operations, when it will be needed, and how much to order. Selecting the vendor is perhaps the most critical aspect of the buying decision. To make a good decision the buyer needs information on the quality of vendor services, prices, and data about vendor performance.

Receiving clerks need information about goods and services on order. Enough information needs to be provided so that the receiving clerks do not accept items that were not ordered by the company. Providing too much information, however, has been known to encourage these people to steal excess items shipped by a supplier. Organizations should use care to provide adequate information and identify individual responsibility, as this is a point in the process where significant losses traditionally occur.

Treasury and finance have the responsibility to see that money is available to pay for items purchased, ensure that debts are paid, and correctly account for purchased items in financial reporting. Budgeting is used to plan cash flows for goods and services required in normal business operations and capital budgeting is used to help identify the amount and timing of cash needed to acquire long-term assets.

Accounting and finance uses acquisition/payment process information to prepare various management reports and financial statements. This process provides both raw materials and cost information to the conversion process for the development of products and services. It contributes many balances that are reported to external statement users, including inventory purchases; purchase returns, allowances, and discounts; property, plant, and equipment; selling expenses; administrative expenses; and accounts payable. Also, the amount of cash paid for these items is one element used in determining the cash balance.

Vendors provide information on their products and services for this process. The acquisition of a product or service is initiated by a purchase order. The vendor sends invoices and summary statements to the buyer to request payment.

To give you a better idea of some value-added analyses that information age accountants can help provide, once again consider the following list of ideas from *Reinventing the CFO*. These are continuous improvement ideas relating to the acquisition/payment process.

- Identify key strategic issues and options (such as key factors for successfully competing in a market, industry, culture, or environment).
- Assess the contribution of the acquisition/payment process to overall organization performance.
- Evaluate the acquisition/payment process with regard to how well the activities have helped the organization meet its strategic and operational objectives.
- Create benchmarking data and metrics to compare the organization's process costs to industry or competitor costs.
- Determine and measure the financial and operational key drivers of performance.
- Compare organizational performance to competitors, and/or measure actual performance against planned performance.

In addition, try thinking about measuring trends and ratios such as total cycle time, downtime, vendor satisfaction measures, days of inventory, days of account payables, days' supply of raw materials, purchase order preparation time, whether the resource request is necessary to fulfill strategy, whether the resource requested is the most effective resource to accomplish the task(s), and whether expenditures appear reasonable when evaluated against strategies and goals.

Once again, we concede that the key is finding the measurements and analyses that are important for your particular client or organization. In today's business world, there is no one static template, checklist, or tool set that a business solution professional will use to solve problems and add value. You need good analytical skills, an understanding of measurement theory, systems knowledge, and a good understanding of businesses in order to adapt, evolve, and achieve success.

TRADITIONAL MANUAL ACCOUNTING SYSTEM ARCHITECTURE

What are the information stores and data flows in a traditional manual environment? Exhibit 7–1 presents a partial overview of a traditional manual design used to support the purchase of inventory. Table 7–1 describes many of the data flows[1] and reports associated with the acquisition/payment process.

> **Purchase Requisition.** A department (such as Inventory Control) or an individual with a need for a good or service documents a request and sends a copy of a *purchase requisition* to the purchasing agent. The purchase requisition lists data about the inventory items requested, the requesting department, and the signature of the supervisor who approved the request. Possibly, the purchase requisition could list vendors who supply the items. A copy of this purchase requisition is kept on file and a copy is sent to the Purchasing Department.
>
> **Purchase.** Upon receiving the request, the purchasing agent reviews it and makes a decision to approve or not approve the requisition If the request is approved, an appropriate vendor is selected based on the vendor's prices, product quality, and past performance. Upon approval of the request and selection of a vendor, the purchasing agent creates a *purchase order* document. The purchase order identifies some of the same information as recorded on the purchase requisition (e.g., the requesting department and inventory data), as well as approval by the purchasing agent, vendor data, terms of the purchase, and prices of the goods. This document communicates authorization for the purchase both externally with the vendor and internally with various departments.
>
> To formally enter into a purchasing agreement, one copy of the purchase order is sent to the vendor. A second copy of the purchase order is sent to the requesting department to communicate approval. A third copy of the purchase order is sent to the Receiving Department to authorize them to take delivery of the goods when they arrive. This copy does not include the quantities of the goods ordered; it is referred to as a *blind copy of the purchase order.* Quantities are omitted to increase the likelihood that the Receiving Department will actually

---

1 These documents can take the form of paper or electronic communications.

EXHIBIT 7–1

Traditional Inventory Purchase Flowchart

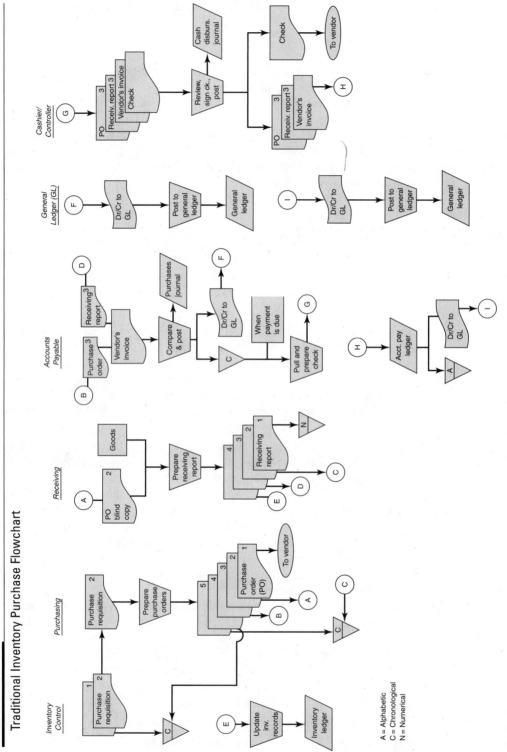

A = Alphabetic
C = Chronological
N = Numerical

This flowchart was created with the assistance of William Hillison, Arthur Andersen Alumni Professor, Florida State University.

TABLE 7–1

Data Flows and Reports Commonly Associated with the Acquisition/Payment Process

Purchase Requisition. An internal data flow requesting the purchase of specific goods or services. Various people throughout the organization use this data flow to request specific items. The Purchasing Department generally executes actual purchases.

Purchase Order. A data flow sent to a vendor as a formal request for the vendor to sell and deliver specified products or services at a designated price. Usually the Purchasing Department uses a purchase order to purchase goods and/or services from a vendor.

Receiving Report. A data flow used to summarize the receipt of raw materials or merchandise from vendors. The Receiving Department usually prepares the receiving report upon receipt of each shipment of goods.

Packing Slip. A data flow that is sent with the goods shipped to a customer. The vendor or supplier creates the packing slip.

Bill of Lading. A written receipt given by a carrier for goods accepted for transportation. The carrier that delivers or transports goods will usually give a bill of lading to the company shipping the items (vendor). The bill of lading relates to goods being shipped, but it is more applicable to the shipper (vendor) than to the receiver (purchaser).

Vendor's Invoice (Bill). A data flow listing the merchandise, with prices, that have been delivered or sent to a buyer. It is a statement of money owed for goods or services supplied. The vendor sends the invoice to the buyer as a request for payment for merchandise delivered or services provided.

Check. A data flow used to draw money from a bank account and transfer it to another entity. This is frequently used by the Treasury Department to pay for items purchased by a company.

Material Requirement Planning. Software program that identifies the raw materials required, and the timing of the requirement, to produce a specified number of subcomponents or units of a finished product. This planning is used to determine the amount of raw materials needed to meet production levels projected for the next time period.

Open Purchase Request. Purchase requests that have not yet been formally denied or upgraded to purchase order status.

Open Purchase Order. Purchase orders that have been sent to a vendor, but the items ordered have not yet been received *and* a liability has not yet been recognized. A copy of the purchase order is frequently maintained by Accounts Payable in an open purchase order file until the goods or services have been received.

Open Invoice or Voucher Payable. Bills related to purchases that have been approved for payment, but cash has not yet been disbursed to pay the liability.

Stock Status Report. A report on each inventory item sold by a company, including information about items out of stock, items below a minimum stock level, and item turnover analysis. Storeroom personnel generally use this report to identify inventory items that need to be requested.

Vendor Performance Report. This report summarizing each vendor's performance for a given period of time. Items on the report may include time between order and delivery, frequency of back-ordered items, quantity of merchandise received, and volume of purchases. The Purchasing Department uses this report to select the best vendor for a purchase order.

count the items when they are received. A fourth copy of the purchase order is sent to Accounts Payable for review of the completed transaction. A fifth copy of the purchase order along with a copy of the purchase requisition are kept in a file in the Purchasing Department as documentation of their purchasing activity.

Receiving. The next activity in the process occurs in the receiving area. When a delivery truck arrives, the Receiving Department expects the delivery based on the authorization (the blind copy purchase order) received from the Purchasing Department. The Receiving Department's role is to count and inspect the goods—a task they document on a *receiving report.* A receiving report lists items such as the inventory description, quantities received, and their condition. A copy of the receiving report and the blind copy of the purchase order are retained in the Receiving Department as documentation of the receiving activity. A second copy of the receiving report is sent to the Purchasing Department to keep them informed on the status of the purchase. A third copy of the receiving report is sent to the Accounts Payable Department to update them on the purchase. It is used later to review the validity of the transaction. A fourth copy of the receiving report is sent to Inventory Control to update the *inventory subsidiary ledger.* The goods are then transferred to a warehouse for safekeeping or moved immediately to the location where they will be used.

Accounting. Although a purchase has occurred, there is frequently a time lag in traditional accounting systems such that the liability is not recorded until a bill, called a *vendor's invoice,* is received from the vendor. When the vendor's invoice is received, the Accounts Payable Department reviews the related documents before approving the invoice for payment and recognizing the liability. Three documents are reviewed and reconciled: the purchase order (to confirm that a purchase was authorized by the Purchasing Department), the receiving report (to confirm that the goods were received), and the vendor's invoice (to confirm that the liability amount is correctly stated by the vendor). (A fourth document—the purchase requisition—is reviewed if the requesting department sends a copy to the Accounts Payable Department.) If there are discrepancies between the items ordered and received, the vendor is contacted. After the transaction is reviewed and the documents are reconciled, an accounts payable clerk records the invoice for eventual payment by recognizing the liability in the accounting records.

Once the Accounts Payable Department reviews the purchase and verifies the liability, the amount due is recorded in the *purchases journal* (if applicable) and the *accounts payable subsidiary ledger.* The Accounts Payable Department prepares a journal voucher that the General Ledger Department uses to update the Accounts Payable Control account balance, inventory balance, and total purchases in the *general ledger.*

Some organizations use a *voucher system* to organize liability records by vendor. Just as special journals help group similar transactions, a voucher system groups liabilities by vendor. When an invoice is received from a vendor, it is recorded on a *disbursement voucher* (also called a *payment voucher*). Each disbursement voucher lists all the invoices for a particular vendor. Thus, one document can give an overview of the amount due to a vendor rather than having to review all the individual invoices. Each disbursement voucher amount is recorded in a *voucher register*. So the total in the voucher register should equal the accounts payable subsidiary ledger total and the General Ledger Accounts Payable Control account balance.

In a paper system, the use of vouchers can reduce the number of checks an organization writes to each vendor. Instead of writing one check per invoice, the organization writes a check for the total liability listed on the disbursement voucher. Often, checks have a *check voucher* attached. The check voucher portion includes a description of why the check was written (e.g., a listing of the batch of vendor's invoices that support the summary data on the disbursement voucher).

Payment. When payment is due (the discount period is about to run out or the due date is near), organizations review and pay their liabilities. Many organizations maintain invoices payable in due-date order—often called a *tickler file*. Each day, a clerk reviews the file for invoices due and prepares the documents necessary to disburse cash. An accounts payable clerk pulls the batches of invoices, sorts them, and attaches other supporting documentation such as applicable purchase orders, receiving reports, and vouchers (if used). A copy of the check may be prepared (but not signed) by the clerk. The documentation is sent to the cashier for review. An authorized person (e.g., the treasurer) reviews the liabilities and supporting documentation and signs and mails the checks. The check totals are recorded in a *check register* or a *cash disbursements journal*. A journal voucher is prepared to update the General Ledger Cash and Accounts Payable accounts. The supporting documentation is sent back to Accounts Payable, where invoices are stamped paid, dated, and filed with the supporting documentation in a supplier file. The accounts payable subsidiary ledger is updated and a journal voucher is prepared for general ledger update of the Accounts Payable Control account.

Traditionally, organizations separate the authorization tasks (performed by the Purchasing Department and authorized individuals) from the custody tasks (performed by the Receiving, Warehousing, Cashier, and Treasury Departments) and the recording tasks (performed by the accounting functions: Accounts Payable, Inventory Control, and the General Ledger departments).

TRADITIONAL AUTOMATED ACCOUNTING SYSTEM ARCHITECTURE

Exhibits 7–2, 7–3, 7–4, and 7–5 illustrate a sample automated acquisition/payment process.

Purchase Requisition. Process activity begins in a requesting department, such as by an inventory clerk monitoring the quantity of inventory on hand in the inventory master file (Exhibit 7–2). Purchase requisitions for needed goods or services are created and stored in a requisition file and a copy of a purchase requisition is

EXHIBIT 7–2

Traditional Automated Acquisition/Payment Process Flowchart—Purchases

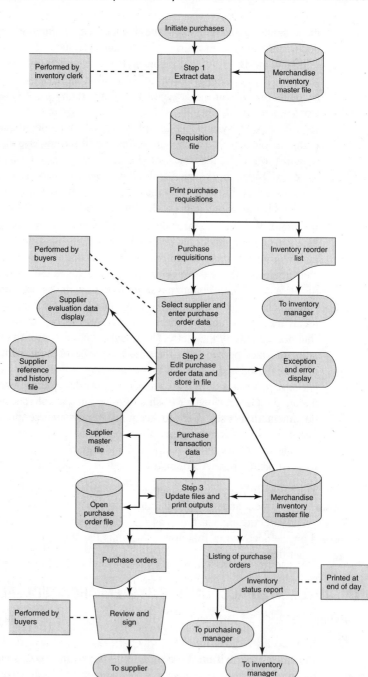

Source: Joseph W. Wilkinson and Michael J. Cerullo, *Accounting Information Systems: Essential Concepts and Applications,* 3rd ed. (New York: John Wiley & Sons, 1997).

printed and sent to the Purchasing Department. A request in the requisition file is considered an *open requisition* until it is denied or becomes a valid purchase order. A copy of the inventory order list is sent to the inventory manager.

Purchase. The Purchasing Department selects a supplier and enters the purchase data into a *purchase transaction data file.* An automated or manual process edits the purchase order data. During this phase, the *supplier master file* and the *supplier reference and history file* (files that contain data about the various vendors used by the company and their performance) and the *merchandise inventory master file* (a file that contains data about the various inventory items used by the company) are accessed. Edited data are used to update the supplier master file and the inventory master file, and the purchase order data are recorded in the *open purchase order file.* This file includes the same data as the purchase order document (data about the vendor and the items ordered). It is called an *open purchase order file* because records are added when an order is approved (when it becomes a valid purchase order). They are removed from this file when the purchase order is approved for payment (because at that time it is no longer classified as a purchase order, but as a purchase and a liability). Like the purchase order document, this file could be used to communicate authorization to other departments because the contents of this file are orders the Purchasing Department has approved for continued processing. At this point, a hard-copy purchase order is printed to mail to the vendor. Various summary reports are printed and sent to the purchasing manager and the inventory manager.

Recall that Purchasing needs to communicate authorization to several other departments, including the Receiving Department, the requesting department, and the Accounts Payable Department, for the process to continue. Depending on the sophistication of the design used, this communication could take place by electronically allowing access to the open purchase order file, or by printing purchase order copies and sending them to the departments. For example, the Receiving Department could get a hard copy of the purchase order with the quantities omitted (the blind copy). Alternately, the Receiving Department could electronically receive a limited view of the open purchase order file (with output that does not include the quantity field).

Receiving. The Receiving Department (Exhibit 7–3) receives a data flow from the Purchasing Department (electronically or via a hard-copy blind purchase order document). As in the manual system, they receive the goods (along with a packing slip), count them, and check the condition. This input is edited and recorded in a *receiving transaction file.* The *open purchase order file,* the *merchandise inventory master file,* and the *supplier history file* are updated to reflect items purchased, increased inventory, and vendor performance, respectively. The goods are transferred to the warehouse or an alternative authorized location. Data stored in the receiving transaction file are used to prepare a receiving report file or to print copies of the receiving report that are sent to stores and accounts payable. If needed, a back order is recorded.

EXHIBIT 7–3

Traditional Automated Acquisition/Payment Process Flowchart—Receiving

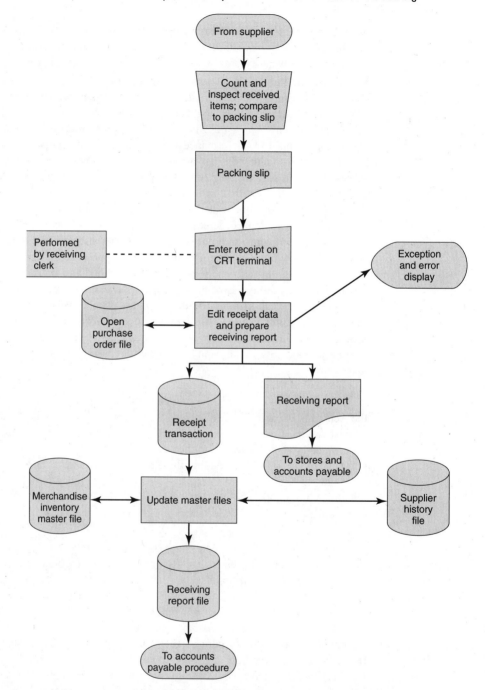

Source: Joseph W. Wilkinson and Michael J. Cerullo, *Accounting Information Systems: Essential Concepts and Applications,* 3rd ed. (New York: John Wiley & Sons, 1997).

Information Processing. When the vendor's invoice is received, the Accounts Payable Department (Exhibit 7–4) confirms that the items were ordered (by reviewing a hard copy of the purchase order or by accessing the open purchase order file) and prepares a batch total. The vendor's invoice is also compared to the receiving report and the order. When they are reconciled, a liability is recorded. The *accounts payable master file* is updated. Open purchase order records are removed from the open purchase order file and transferred to the history file. The liability is recorded in the *open vouchers file* (also called an *open invoice* or *payables file*) and a journal voucher record is created to update the *general ledger master file*. If a voucher system is used, disbursement vouchers are created and the voucher register is updated.

Payment. A cash disbursement clerk enters a request for disbursement data (Exhibit 7–5) and the computer extracts the due vouchers and accumulates a control total. The result of this process is a *due disbursement file*. Paid invoices are removed from the open voucher file and copied to a supplier history file. The accounts payable master file is updated and journal voucher information is recorded for updating the Cash and Accounts Payable accounts in the general ledger. Checks are prepared, reviewed, and signed, and a check register and disbursement summary may be generated. The cash disbursement clerk compares the batch totals from the beginning and ending of the process to verify process accuracy.

It is important to highlight a distinction between for-profit and government organizations with regard to the acquisition/payment process. Profit-oriented organizations that use a traditional general ledger retain purchase order data outside the accounting function. Acquisition data are not recorded in the traditional accounting system until the liability is formally recognized (after receiving the goods and comparing the purchase order, receiving report, and vendor's invoice). In governmental entities the purchase order is formally recorded in the traditional accounting system as an encumbrance. A debit to Encumbrances and a credit to Reserves for Encumbrances signify that the government has entered into a purchasing agreement that will ultimately lead to a liability and a cash disbursement. When the liability is formally recognized, the encumbrance is reversed (via a debit to the Reserves for Encumbrances and a credit to the Encumbrances account). To recognize the liability, government entities then record a debit to Expenditures and a credit to Vouchers Payable. An important output generated for government decision makers is *available appropriations*—equal to appropriations less all encumbrances and expenditures. This number represents the total amount the government has available to spend.

NEW ARCHITECTURES TO SUPPORT THE ACQUISITION/PAYMENT PROCESS

Some organizations are beginning to use information technology to reengineer the acquisition/payment process. The following examples illustrate process redesigns and the impact on the organizations.

Traditional Automated Acquisition/Payment Process Flowchart—Payables

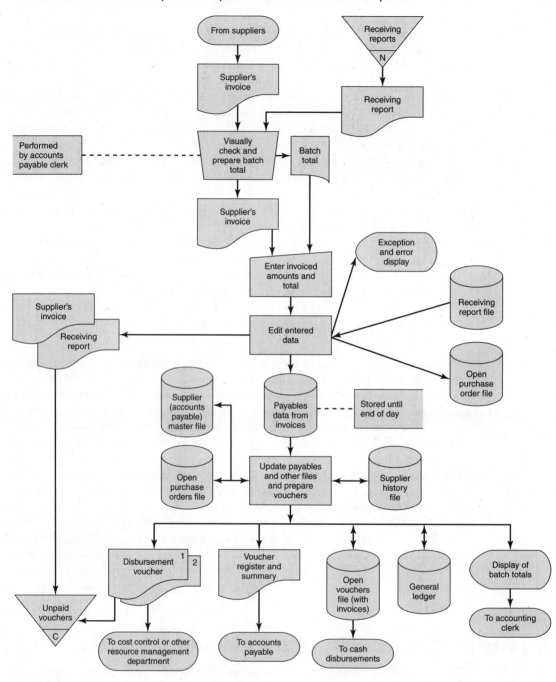

Source: Joseph W. Wilkinson and Michael J. Cerullo, *Accounting Information Systems: Essential Concepts and Applications,* 3rd ed. (New York: John Wiley & Sons, 1997).

EXHIBIT 7–5

Traditional Automated Acquisition/Payment Process Flowchart—Cash Disbursements

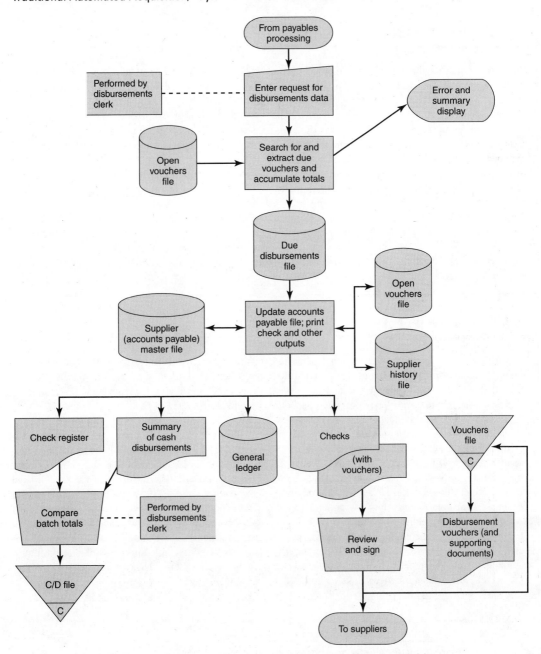

Source: Joseph W. Wilkinson and Michael J. Cerullo, *Accounting Information Systems: Essential Concepts and Applications*, 3rd ed. (New York: John Wiley & Sons, 1997).

CASE IN POINT

Ford used a traditional accounts payable process prior to reengineering. The Accounts Payable Department received a copy of the purchase order from the Purchasing Department, a copy of the receiving report from the Receiving Department, and a copy of the invoice from the materials supplier. Accounts payable personnel (consisting of 400 clerks) spent most of their time comparing the three documents and resolving discrepancies before issuing payment. Initially, Ford planned to automate the process and reduce headcount by 20%. Management satisfaction with the planned change diminished when they learned that Mazda employed just five accounts payable clerks. Ford decided to radically redesign the process by initiating "invoiceless processing." Now, Purchasing enters an order into an online database. Receiving verifies, validates, and controls materials receipts (in real time) by checking them against the open purchase orders in the database. If no open purchase order exists, the shipment is refused. If an open purchase order exists in the database, the receiving clerk enters relevant data about the items received, and the information system automatically matches the purchase data with receiving data. The system prepares the check, which Accounts Payable sends to the vendor. This process allows real-time control (control at the Order and Receive events, rather than during the accounts payable recording process) and integrates process review and recording. Ford also achieved a 75% reduction in accounts payable headcount.[2]

CASE IN POINT

IBM developed an integrated payroll and expense reimbursement system to pay more than 200,000 domestic employees. This system combined four separate processes (payroll, travel expense, miscellaneous expense, and time and attendance recording). The expense reimbursement portion of the old system is illustrated in Exhibit 7–6. IBM created an event-driven solution called NEDS (National Employee Disbursement Solution). Now, all business events that require reimbursement are considered claims. An employee submits claim data directly into the computer. The computer edits and audits the claim data as it is entered. For example, the computer will not accept the claim if the data are not complete or if the claimed amounts are outside predefined limits for the nature of the travel. Management reviews and approves the claim electronically and the system deposits the reimbursement amount directly into the employee's bank account with an EFT payment. The modified system is illustrated in Exhibit 7–7.

NEDS eliminated 80% of the employees assigned to build, maintain, and use prior reimbursement systems. The 17 systems supporting the traditional reimbursement processes have been replaced by one business solution—NEDS. Overall, NEDS and related changes will save IBM almost $300 million during the next 10 years. This savings does not include any of the benefits resulting from management's ability to use information from the system to negotiate contracts with travel and lodging providers and to monitor the value and effectiveness of travel.[3]

---

2 Michael Hammer, "Business Process Reengineering: Don't Automate, Obliterate," *Harvard Business Review,* July–August 1990, pp. 104–12.

3 D. P. Andros, J. Owen Cherrington, and E. L. Denna, "Reengineer Your Accounting System the IBM Way," *Financial Executive,* July–August 1992, pp. 29–33.

EXHIBIT 7-6

Traditional Reimbursement Process

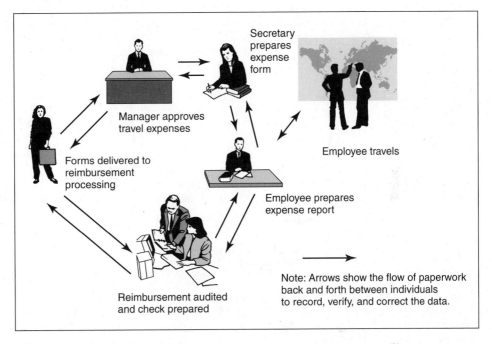

Secretary prepares expense form

Manager approves travel expenses

Forms delivered to reimbursement processing

Employee travels

Employee prepares expense report

Reimbursement audited and check prepared

Note: Arrows show the flow of paperwork back and forth between individuals to record, verify, and correct the data.

To enhance the efficiency of the purchaser/supplier relationship, many companies require or encourage the use of electronic data interchange (EDI), a form of electronic commerce. EDI is the electronic transmission of business data flows (data) between or within organizations in a structured, machine-retrievable format. EDI transmission differs from a fax or unformatted electronic mail. EDI is typically batch related, rather than interactive, and is predominantly used for business-to-business, rather than business-to-consumer, communications.

EDI can replace the physical exchange of paper documents between trading partners during the order, delivery, invoice, and payment phases of the process (see Exhibit 7–8). Paper documents commonly replaced by EDI include purchase orders, picking slips, advance shipping notices, freight bills, order acknowledgments, receiving discrepancy reports, invoices, remittance advices, deposit slips, and even checks (if an organization uses electronic funds transfers or electronic payments between the companies' bank accounts).

EDI communications often require specialized hardware and software. The electronic data flow is called a *transmission set,* and the format adheres to some specified standard such as ANSI X12 (American National Standards Institute) or EDIFACT (Electronic Data Interchange for Administration Commerce and Transport). A communications inter-

EXHIBIT 7–7

IBM's NEDS (National Employee Disbursement Solution)

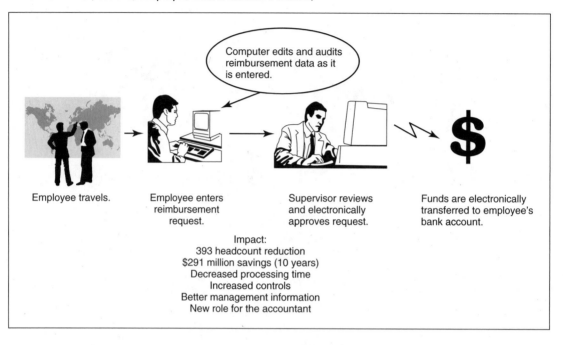

Computer edits and audits reimbursement data as it is entered.

Employee travels.

Employee enters reimbursement request.

Supervisor reviews and electronically approves request.

Funds are electronically transferred to employee's bank account.

Impact:
393 headcount reduction
$291 million savings (10 years)
Decreased processing time
Increased controls
Better management information
New role for the accountant

face gives a computer the ability to transmit and receive transaction sets. This EDI interface moves data to and from the appropriate application software. The application software then uses the EDI transaction set data as the input for internal processing.

There are a variety of transmission methods. Companies can communicate with each other directly (a relationship that requires compatible hardware and software) or they can use an independent network service. Virtual private networks (VPN) allow point-to-point communication. The third-party providers, known as *value-added networks* or *VANs,* allow users to interconnect with each other's networks regardless of the type of equipment they use. The trend is toward using the Internet as the EDI communications network. This is known as *EDI Lite.* EDI Internet transmissions typically use the MIME (multipurpose Internet Mail Extension) protocol.

Systems designers must consider risks and controls when developing EDI systems. Organizations should implement procedures to ensure that each EDI transmission is accurate, complete, and verified for transmission authenticity. EDI systems should include proper error detection and correction procedures, and limit access to EDI transmissions and organization data pools. The electronic audit trail should be complete and viable, including proper authorization and control of orders and payments. EDI partners should have appropriate documents (perhaps legal) to substantiate and validate the electronic commu-

EXHIBIT 7–8

EDI Data Flows

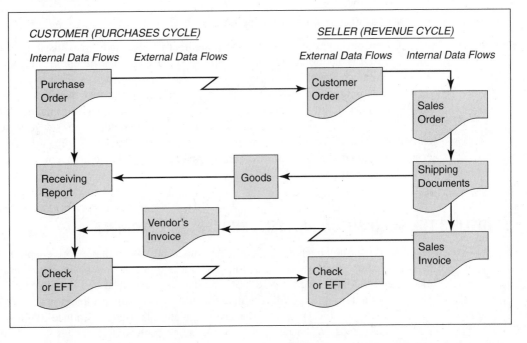

nication arrangement. In addition, it is important to retain manual signatures on file to support the electronic data flows that include electronic, rather than manual, signatures.

Installing an EDI system can simply automate a traditional process and not really change an organization's business and information processes. However, innovative applications of EDI and other forms of electronic commerce can result in significant process redesign. In either case, EDI is often credited with reducing the amount of clerical work and shortening the process time associated with the acquisition/payment and sales/collection processes.

EDI can reduce processing expenses by reducing manual preparation of documents, paper and mailing costs, and errors. Organizations have cited other EDI benefits including:

- Improved customer relations and service.
- Improved production scheduling.
- Better cash management.
- Improved inventory management.
- Lower inventory costs.
- Improved data access.
- Reduced order lead times.

- Reduced occurrences of out-of-stock items.
- Improved information on price changes and product availability.
- Reduced labor costs.
- Better accuracy in ordering, shipping, and receiving.

Companies engage in an increasing number of electronic transmissions of data. A cousin to EDI is electronic funds transfers (EFT). EFT uses a different set of standards to control the transmission of financial resource data. Many entities use EFT to pay a variety of financial obligations. In some jurisdictions, organizations that incur a certain dollar amount of estimated tax payments must transfer their payments electronically. Additionally, many governmental agencies are developing ways to deliver their services electronically. Some agencies are implementing electronic benefit transfer (EBT) systems for governmental entitlement programs. These systems authorize, deliver, redeem, reconcile, and settle various benefit claims.[4]

MODELING THE ACQUISITION/PAYMENT PROCESS: AN EXAMPLE

The Manufacturing Division of Christopher, Inc., (introduced in previous chapters) will be used to illustrate the acquisition/payment business process. This business process, *REAL* model, and the table structures to store the data are described and illustrated below. We also present a description of the computer instructions to support this process.

Christopher, Inc., monitors the level of materials used to produce its glow-in-the-dark baseball caps. When necessary, an inventory control clerk requests goods for purchase. A purchasing supervisor reviews the requisition and approves or denies the request. If the request is approved, a purchasing clerk orders the goods from the appropriate vendor. When goods are received, a receiving clerk verifies the content and quality of the goods and transfers the shipment to the storage area until they are requested by production. Christopher records a liability upon receipt of goods. When a hard copy of a vendor's invoice is received, an accounts payable clerk verifies the invoice with receipt information and the vendor is contacted to resolve discrepancies. Consistent with the payment terms, a cashier disburses funds to the vendor.

The acquisition/payment process for Christopher, Inc., is represented in the *REAL* model shown in Exhibit 7–9.[5] Christopher, Inc., records data about each event (Order Request and Review, Order Goods, Receive Goods, and Disburse Payment). Data are maintained about the resources, agents, and locations involved in the process (materials inventory, cash, vendors, inventory control clerks, purchasing review supervisors, purchasing

---

4 For more information, refer to the United States Office of Technology Assessment report, "Making Government Work, Electronic Delivery of Federal Services," November 1993.

5 Remember, the events, relationships, and so on, presented with this example are for a particular scenario with a particular set of assumptions. If the scenario or assumptions change, the specifics of the data model may also change. Also, this scenario is focusing on events associated with the acquisition/payment process. Other events, such as planning production or acquiring licensing agreements are viable, related events of other business processes.

EXHIBIT 7–9

Christopher, Inc., Acquisition/Payment *REAL* Model (without relationship semantics)

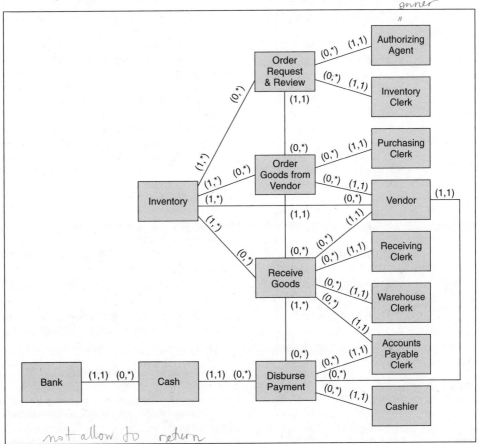

clerks, warehousing employees, accounts payable clerks, receiving clerks, and cashiers). Christopher's information system can prepare a variety of outputs (reports, queries, and documents). Reports include inventory items below their economic order quantity, inventory items on hand in the warehouse, materials received during a specified period of time, amount of cash disbursed, which vendors have not been paid, and vendor information. Christopher, Inc., may also desire performance measures on such items as the time between purchase orders and receipts, the number of requests submitted versus the number of requests denied, an analysis of purchase discounts lost, the time between inventory requests and when orders are placed, or the time between receipt of goods and movement of goods to warehousing for safekeeping.

The tables supporting the *REAL* model for Christopher, Inc.'s acquisition/payment process would likely include the following:

Event Logical Structures: (used to store documentation data about events)

Table Name	Sample Attributes (by no means an all-inclusive set)
PURCHASE REQUEST	Purchase Request #, [Inventory Control Clerk Employee #], [Reviewing Supervisor Employee #], Date, Time, Special Requests or Comments
ORDER GOODS	Purchase Order #, [Vendor #], [Purchasing Clerk Employee #], [Purchase Request #], Date, Time, Shipping Instructions, Cancel by Date, Location of Order (e.g., phone, fax, or mail), Shipping Expenses, Sales Tax, Order Confirmation Number
RECEIVE GOODS	Receipt #, [Employee # of Accounts Payable Clerk comparing a vendor's invoice and receipt information], [Purchase Order #], [Receiving Clerk Employee #], [Vendor #], [Warehousing Employee #], Date, Time Received, Vendor's Invoice #, Shipping Cost, Sales Tax, Time Transferred to Warehousing
DISBURSE PAYMENT	Check #, [Cash Account #], [Cashier Employee #], [Vendor #], [Accounts Payable Clerk Employee #], Date, Time, Amount Disbursed
REQUEST/INVENTORY	[Purchase Request #], [Inventory Item #], Quantity Requested, Product Specifications
ORDER/INVENTORY	[Purchase Order #], [Inventory Item #], Quantity Ordered, Negotiated Cost Each
RECEIVE/INVENTORY	[Receipt #], [Inventory Item #], Quantity Received, Cost Each, Condition Comments
RECEIVE/PAYMENT	[Receipt #], [Check #], Amount applied to this invoice, Purchase Discounts Applicable, Purchase Discounts Taken

Resource Logical Structures: (used to store reference data about resources)

Table Name	Sample Attributes
INVENTORY	Inventory Item #, Description, Product Specification, Reorder Point, Current Price, Beginning Quantity, Beginning Quantity Date
CASH	Cash Account #, [Bank #], Type of Account (e.g., checking, savings, CD), Beginning Balance, Beginning Balance Date
INVENTORY/VENDOR	[Inventory Item #], [Vendor #]

Agent Logical Structures: (used to store reference data about agents)

Table Name	Sample Attributes
EMPLOYEE[6]	Employee #, Name, Street Address, City, State, Zip, Telephone #, Birth Date, Marital Status, Job Code (e.g., inventory control clerk, purchase request review supervisor, receiving clerk, accounts payable clerk, warehousing clerk, and cashier), Start Date, Salary, Comments

---

6 Alternatively, Christopher, Inc., could have created separate structures for each type of employee (e.g., data pools for purchasing employees, accounting and finance employees, warehousing employees, and receiving employees).

Table Name	Sample Attributes
VENDOR	<u>Vendor #</u>, Name, Street Address, City, State, Zip, Telephone #, Contact Person, Comments
BANK	<u>Bank #</u>, Bank Name, Contact Person, Bank Street Address, City, State, Zip, Bank Phone #

The computer instructions to support this process are designed to control collecting and storing event data; maintaining resources, agents, and locations data; and generating data flows, reports, and queries desired by users. The instructions should include business rule logic for both information and business controls. These include (but are not limited to) preventing or detecting the following:

- Initiating a purchase order without an authorized request.
- Approving a purchase order without proper review.
- Having a fictitious employee approve a purchase order.
- Having a warehousing or receiving clerk delete or modify a purchase order.
- Accepting a shipment containing incorrect items.
- Accepting a shipment of inferior goods.
- Accepting a shipment without an approved purchase order.
- Disbursing cash without a corresponding receipt of goods.
- Disbursing a different amount of cash than the cost of goods received.
- Disbursing cash to an invalid or fictitious vendor.

CONCLUDING COMMENTS

The sales/collection process and the acquisition/payment process are only two examples of common business processes. To complete our study of business processes, Chapter 8 will introduce three additional business processes: the human resource process, the financing process, and the conversion process. Both the human resource process and the financing process are special cases of the acquisition/payment process discussed in this chapter.

CHECKLIST OF KEY TERMS AND CONCEPTS

Accounts payable master file	Check register
Accounts payable subsidiary ledger	Check voucher
Acquisition/payment process	Disburse Cash event
ANSI X12 standard	Disbursements data transaction file
Authorize Purchase event	Disbursements/payment voucher
Blind copy of a purchase order	EDIFACT
Cash disbursements journal	EDI communications interface
Check	EDI Lite

EDI transmission set
EDI value-added networks (VANs)
Electronic benefits transfer (EBT)
Electronic data interchange (EDI)
Electronic funds transfers (EFT)
General ledger
General ledger master file
Inventory master file
Inventory subsidiary ledger
Material Requirements Planning (MRP)
MIME (Multipurpose Internet Mail Extension)
 protocol
Open (invoice or voucher) payables file
Open purchase order file
Open purchase requisition
Purchase order document
Purchase Goods/Services event
Purchase requisition document

Purchase Return event
Purchases history file
Purchases journal
Receive Goods/Services event
Receiving report document
Receiving report transaction file
Request Goods/Services event
Stock status report
Supplier history file
Tickler file
Value Added Network (VAN)
Vendor master file
Vendor performance report
Vendor's invoice
Virtual Private Network (VPN)
Voucher register
Voucher system

REVIEW QUESTIONS

1. List eight objectives of the acquisition/payment process.

2. How is the acquisition/payment process related to the conversion process, the sales/collection process, the human resource process, and the financing process?

3. What is the difference between a purchase requisition and a purchase order?

4. Refer to Exhibit 7–1. Explain the data flow and purpose for each copy of the purchase order document.

5. For a traditional system, identify the department or functional area that creates each of the following source documents:
   a. Purchase requisition.
   b. Purchase order.
   c. Receiving report.
   d. Disbursements voucher.
   e. Voucher register.
   f. Check.
   g. Voucher.

6. In a traditional acquisition/payment process, at what points and in which departments do the accountants execute control? Explain how the control is provided.

7. Identify for a traditional acquisition/payment process the source document(s) used to update the purchases journal and the cash disbursements journal.

8. List all the accounting records updated in a traditional acquisition/payment system to record a liability.

9. List all the accounting records updated in a traditional acquisition/payment system to recognize a cash disbursement.

10. Explain the difference between a disbursements voucher and a voucher register.

11. What is the purpose of a tickler file?

12. What is a blind copy of a purchase order? What purpose does it serve?

13. Describe the key components of separation of duties in a traditional acquisition/payment process. Be sure to include the nature of each duty listed (i.e., custody, recording, or authorization).

14. What reconciliations are needed in a traditional acquisition/payment accounting information system?

15. Describe a sample record layout for each of the following files in a traditional system:
    a. Vendor master file.
    b. General ledger master file.
    c. Open purchase order file.
    d. Receiving report transaction file.
    e. Accounts payable master file.
    f. Open invoice or vouchers payable file.
    g. Cash disbursement data transaction file.
    h. Merchandise inventory master file.
    i. General ledger/journal voucher transaction file.

16. Refer to Exhibits 7–2 through 7–5 and give the file name for each of the following: the general ledger, the accounts payable subsidiary ledger, the inventory subsidiary ledger, and the cash disbursements journal.

17. What is an open purchase order? In a traditional system, when do records enter and leave the open purchase order file?

18. What is an open invoice or voucher payable? In a traditional system, when do records enter and leave the open vouchers file?

19. Which event more likely enables an organization to recognize a liability: Receive Goods or Receive Vendor's Invoice? Explain your answer.

20. Identify the resources, internal agents, external agents, and possible locations associated with each of the following business events:
    a. Request Goods/Services.
    b. Purchase Goods/Services.
    c. Receive Goods/Services.
    d. Disburse Cash.
    e. Purchase Return.

21. Describe the information required by each of the following in performing their role in the acquisition/payment process:
    a. Management.
    b. Purchasing.

c. Accounting.

d. Treasury and Finance.

DISCUSSION QUESTIONS

1. Chapter 5 identifies the following risks associated with each business event:

   ◆ A business event occurring at the wrong time or sequence.

   ◆ A business event occurring without proper authorization.

   ◆ A business event involving the wrong internal agent.

   ◆ A business event involving the wrong external agent.

   ◆ A business event involving the wrong resource.

   ◆ A business event involving the wrong amount of resource.

   ◆ A business event occurring at the wrong location.

   Give examples of each of these risks that could occur while executing the following events:

   a. Request Goods/Services.

   b. Approve Purchase.

   c. Purchase Goods/Services.

   d. Receive Goods/Services.

   e. Disburse Cash.

   f. Purchase Return.

2. Chapter 5 identifies the following risks associated with recording information processes:

   Recording incomplete, inaccurate, or invalid data about a business event. Incomplete data result in not having all the relevant characteristics about a business event. Inaccuracies arise from recording data that do not accurately represent the event. Invalid data refers to data recorded about a fabricated event.

   Give specific examples of recording risks associated with each of the following events:

   a. Request Goods/Services.

   b. Approve Purchase.

   c. Purchase Goods/Services.

   d. Receive Goods/Services.

   e. Disburse Cash.

   f. Purchase Return.

3. Give two examples of maintenance information processes that could be required for each of the following resources, agents, and locations:

   a. Vendors.

   b. Employees.

c. Cash.

d. Inventory.

e. Warehouses.

4. Is there a natural ordering of events in the acquisition/payment process? If so, how is this ordering reflected in a *REAL* model?

5. Explain what triggers or authorizes each of the following events within an acquisition/payment process:

a. Request Goods/Services.

b. Approve Purchase.

c. Purchase Goods/Services.

d. Receive Goods/Services.

e. Disburse Cash.

f. Purchase Return.

6. Compare and contrast the acquisition/payment process for a current asset such as cash, an operating asset such as supplies, and a long-term asset such as a building.

7. Refer to the Christopher, Inc., example included in this chapter. Explain how each of the following is generated. In each case, if more than one table is used, explain how the tables are linked.

a. Total purchases for a financial statement.

b. An open purchase order report.

c. An open payables report.

d. Purchase order document.

e. Voucher register.

f. Total accounts payable for a financial statement.

g. A listing of the accounts payable subsidiary ledger.

h. An accounts payable aging report.

i. A receiving report.

j. A purchases journal (i.e., a purchases transaction report).

k. A cash disbursements journal (i.e., a cash disbursement transaction report).

8. How do you compute the cost of inventory on hand for financial statement purposes using an event-driven system? How does the costing assumption affect the calculation? Do you need more than one system if you want to use a weighted-average inventory figure for financial statement reporting purposes and a LIFO figure for tax purposes? Explain.

9. How do you compute a cash balance for financial statement purposes when using an event-driven system?

10. Compare and contrast the audit trail of total purchases reported on a financial statement in a traditional system, an automated general ledger system, and an event-driven system.

11. Compare and contrast the audit trail of the cash amount reported on a financial statement in a traditional system, an automated general ledger system, and an event-driven system.

12. Suppose you are designing an event-driven system for an acquisition/payment process. Give examples of output you could generate to help *plan* each of the following events:
    a. Request Goods/Services.
    b. Approve Purchase.
    c. Purchase Goods/Services.
    d. Receive Goods/Services.
    e. Disburse Cash.
    f. Purchase Return.

13. Suppose you are designing an event-driven system for an acquisition/payment process. Give examples of output you could generate to help *evaluate the efficiency and effectiveness* of each of the following events:
    a. Request Goods/Services.
    b. Approve Purchase.
    c. Purchase Goods/Services.
    d. Receive Goods/Services.
    e. Disburse Cash.
    f. Purchase Return.

14. Suppose you are designing an event-driven system for an acquisition/payment process. Give examples of output you could generate to help *evaluate the performance of internal agents* involved in each of the following events:
    a. Request Goods/Services.
    b. Approve Purchase.
    c. Purchase Goods/Services.
    d. Receive Goods/Services.
    e. Disburse Cash.
    f. Purchase Return.

15. Visit your library or search the Internet for examples of organizations that have adopted EDI. In small groups, discuss whether the organizations cited used EDI to automate their business processes or whether EDI was used to reengineer their business processes. In addition, discuss the reason why the organizations cited decided to use EDI, and make a list of the positive and negative comments about the use of EDI.

16. Discuss the difference between the acquisition/payment processes of for-profit and government organizations. In a government that uses an event-driven architecture, what event is used to calculate encumbrances? What event is used to calculate expenditures? What events are necessary to calculate available appropriations?

MINICASES AND OTHER APPLIED LEARNING

1. A receiving department clerk at your company is dating a customer order clerk. Often, the customer order clerk likes to take long lunches and forwards her calls to the receiving department clerk. The receiving department clerk only has access to the

purchase order system, so he inputs the forwarded orders using the purchase order screen. When the customer order clerk returns, the receiving clerk reads her the information, and then deletes the purchase orders.

Required:

   a. Identify potential business event risks.
   b. Identity potential information processing risks.

2. UNREAL Company prides itself on good internal control. The Purchasing Department screens and processes all purchase requisition requests from the various departments. The purchase requisition data is stored on computer in a purchase requisition file. If a purchase requisition is approved by management, the Purchasing Department creates a purchase order record to add to their purchase order file, and sends a hard-copy purchase order document to a vendor with a reputation for low price and quality service. A blind copy of the purchase order is sent to the Receiving Department and the Accounts Payable Department.

   When the ordered goods are delivered to UNREAL Company, the Receiving Department checks for an existing purchase order, counts the goods, and documents the delivery on a receiving report. These data are entered into the computer and stored in a receiving report file.

   When UNREAL Company receives the vendor's invoice (UNREAL's bill), a clerk in the Accounts Payable Department reconciles the purchase order, receiving report, and vendor's invoice to ensure that the goods were ordered and received, and the vendor's invoice is correct. If the three documents agree, the vendor's invoice is approved for payment and the transaction is entered into the general ledger. The purchase order record is removed from the purchase order file and a vendor's invoice payable record is added to the vendor's invoice payable file. The amount due to the vendor is also increased in the accounts payable subsidiary file.

   A cashier issues a check within the purchase discount period if UNREAL's cash flow permits. The payment is recorded in the general ledger. A cash disbursement record is added to the cash disbursements file. The vendor's invoice payable record is removed from the vendor's invoice payable file. The amount due to the vendor is reduced in the accounts payable subsidiary ledger; and the vendor's invoice is stamped paid. However, if a discrepancy exists between the three documents (the vendor's invoice, the purchase order, and the receiving report), the accounts payable clerk must investigate the discrepancy before approving payment and recognizing the liability.

Required:

Using traditional control philosophy, discuss whether UNREAL Company has a well-controlled environment. Specifically, do they have adequate separation of duties to safeguard their assets? Do they have adequate documents to support a good audit trail?

3. Refer to Problem 2. UNREAL Company has decided to hire you as a financial system specialist. You decide to redesign the process as follows:

All departments are connected to an online purchasing system that is encoded with the logic and controls used by the purchasing department personnel. The system allows departments that need inventory to enter most orders for automatic processing. The system verifies a need for goods, uses an expert system to identify an appropriate vendor, and electronically sends purchase order information to the appropriate vendor. Humans in the Purchasing Department only process large or unusual orders. When the ordered goods are delivered to UNREAL Company, the Receiving Department verifies the existence of an order by checking the computer files. If a valid order exists, a clerk documents the delivery using scanning equipment to enter receipt data into the computer system. The computer system disburses an electronic funds transfer to the vendor's bank account in the amount needed to pay for the items received at the price ordered.

Required:

    a. Is there a conflict between safeguarding UNREAL's assets and the desire to improve processing efficiency? What are the benefits of reengineering the process? How would you respond to someone who argues that the reengineered process has a diminished audit trail?

    b. List and describe the specific information processing risks related to this process.

  4. Odlaw, the super accountant, is upset once again. Another of his clients is considering reengineering their acquisition/payment process based on the advice of a systems consultant. Currently, Odlaw's client has an accounts payable clerk who approves vendors' invoices for payment only after reviewing and reconciling the purchase order, receiving report, and vendor's invoice. The clerk reviews the purchase order to verify that there was a valid order, the receiving report to verify that the goods were received, and the vendor's invoice to verify the bill is correct. Odlaw likes these procedures because, as he puts it, "they are sound internal control procedures and adhere to GAAP." The systems consultant recommends Odlaw's client use an integrated data approach in this process, check for the existence of a valid order (on computer) at receipt, and automatically approve payment for the goods as soon as they are received (the payment approval is based on the quantities received and their price). Odlaw fears the lack of transaction review by the accounts payable clerk will cause serious internal control problems.

Required:

Prepare a memorandum to Odlaw on the adequacy of the controls in the reengineered system and how closely they adhere to GAAP.

  5. Tri-Fork, Inc.—Acquisition/Payment Process. Tri-Fork, Inc., manufactures and sells switch boxes for computer networks. The switch box has about 10 parts or subcomponents and a few screws and wire. An inventory of these items is maintained by a group of supply clerks. When the quantity of an item gets low, the clerks initiate a purchase requisition. The production manager reviews and approves each purchase requisition before it goes to the Purchasing Department. The two items the production manager checks are the quantity to be ordered and the part or subcomponent specifications.

      Selection of the vendor is made by a buyer in the Purchasing Department who prepares and sends a purchase order to the selected vendor, usually the vendor offering the lowest price.

Goods are received by receiving clerks who count the items received and prepare a receiving report. The Accounts Payable Department assembles a packet containing a copy of the purchase order, a copy of the receiving report, and the vendor invoice. They pay the vendor the invoice amount. The same documents are sent to accounting to update the accounting records.

A review of the process has identified several problems:

a. The production people complain about having to work with inferior parts and subcomponents. The manager of the Production Department says he identifies the correct specifications for each item, but the purchasing agents say they have no information on vendor quality to improve their selection process.

b. Production was held up for two days when they ran out of a subcomponent and had to rush-order a few days' supply. A large order, at a very favorable price, was "in-process" but the production delay was more costly than the price savings.

c. A review by an outside consultant of paid invoices shows that several vendors have been <u>overpaid</u> due to pricing, extension, and footing errors on the invoices.

d. The supply clerks complain that the quantity of parts and subcomponents they receive is different than the quantity requested. Management is not sure where to look for the problem or who they should investigate.

e. Accounts payable is frequently short of cash and cannot take advantage of cash discounts on large purchases. Payment clerks say they don't have good information on the timing of purchases or payments.

Required:

Management has asked you for a recommendation on each of the above items. If you feel you lack necessary information, identify the information you need and how you would go about obtaining it. If your recommendation differs depending on whether their system is manual, traditional computer based, or events driven, identify what you would do in each situation.

6. Happy Eddie's is a small used car dealership conveniently located in the suburbs of Knoxville, Tennessee. Eddie buys, sells, and trades trucks and both small and large automobiles. Eddie has four salespeople besides the individuals mentioned in the following narrative.

Purchases. Eric, the assistant sales manager and Eddie's son-in-law, purchases automobiles from people in the community. A 3 × 5 card is completed on every newly purchased automobile; written on the card are the serial number, make, year, mileage, when purchased, and any comments on the features or the condition of the automobile. The newly purchased automobile is then routed to Eddie's daughter, April, who manages the Service Department.

Trade-Ins. All trade-ins are also handled by Eric. The amount of the trade-in agreement is based on the make, year, mileage, and condition of the trade-in. All this information is contained in a trade-in agreement that is completed by Eric and the customer. The trade-in is then submitted to the garage for any necessary maintenance or repair work.

Parts and Service. Eddie operates a Parts Department for the convenience of the Service Department. The service employees requisition every needed part. The cost of these parts is accumulated on the service ticket. The Service Department only handles automobiles that belong to the dealership (including trade-ins) or automobiles that are covered by Happy Eddie's warranties. Other individuals seeking service are referred to Happy Eddie's Garage down the street. A job sheet is completed for every car admitted to the Service Department. The job sheets are sequentially numbered and contain the serial number of the automobile, a description of the automobile (make and year), and the customer's name (Happy Eddie's is the customer name for trade-ins and purchases of used cars from customers).

Sales. Eddie's wife Beverly handles all automobile sales. Beverly and the customer complete a sales agreement that includes the customer's name, information on the automobile, price, and method of payment. Eddie allows people he trusts to finance the purchase directly through the dealership with installment payments. Those he does not know or cannot trust must finance their purchase personally or, with the help of Beverly, through Maclay National Bank. The terms of any installment loans financed directly through the dealership are included in an installment loan agreement that is completed at the time of purchase.

Warranty Sales. Beverly is also responsible for warranty sales on certain vehicles. Warranties range from 3 to 24 months and from 5,000 to 20,000 miles depending on the condition of the automobile. All the information relative to the warranty sale is included on a warranty contract completed at the time of the sale.

Melanie Gail is the administrative assistant who is responsible for all office functions including cash receipts, cash disbursements, loan payment reminders, and daily bank deposits.

Required:

   a. Prepare a context diagram for each process.

   b. Create a *REAL* model with cardinalities for each process.

   c. Create any needed tables, with key attributes, foreign keys, and non-key attributes.

   d. List five recording and maintaining information processes needed for these activities.

   e. For each information process listed in part *d,* draw a data flow diagram that displays the tables needed to perform the process.

   f. Identify the business rules and business risks associated with each event.

   g. Create an IT application prototype for this company. Develop and input sample test data to test your prototype.

  7. In project teams, visit a local organization and analyze their acquisition/payment process.

Required:

    a. Prepare a one- to two-page description of the process.

    b. Flowchart their current process.

    c. Prepare a data flow diagram of the process.

    d. Prepare a *REAL* model with cardinalities of the process.

  8. In project teams, identify a local nonprofit organization in need of an IT application for their sales/collection process.

Required:

Analysis the process and develop an event-driven prototype for it.

  9. PCA Company purchases over $10 million of office equipment per year under its "special" ordering system. Individual orders range from $5,000 to $30,000. "Special" orders are orders on low-volume items that have been included in an authorized user's budget. Department heads include in their annual budget requests the types of equipment and their estimated cost. The budget, which limits the types and dollar amounts of office equipment a department head can requisition, is approved at the beginning of the year by the board of directors. Department heads prepare a purchase requisition for the Purchasing Department. PCA's "special" ordering system functions as follows:

Purchasing. Upon receiving a purchase requisition, one of five buyers verifies that the person requesting the equipment is a department head. The buyer selects the appropriate vendor by searching various vendor catalogs on file. The buyer phones the vendor, requests a price quotation, and gives the vendor a verbal order. A prenumbered purchase order is processed with the original sent to the vendor, a copy to the department head, a copy to receiving, a copy to accounts payable, and a copy filed in the open requisition file. When the Receiving Department orally informs the buyer that the item has been received, the buyer transfers the purchase order from the unfilled file to the filled file. Once a month the buyer reviews the unfilled file to follow up and expedite open orders.

Receiving. The Receiving Department receives a copy of the purchase order. When equipment is received, the receiving clerk stamps the purchase order with the date received, and, if applicable, in red pen prints any differences between quantity on the purchase order and quantity received. The receiving clerk forwards the stamped purchase order and equipment to the requisitioning department head and orally notifies the Purchasing Department.

Accounts Payable. Upon receipt of a purchase order, the accounts payable clerk files the purchase order in the open purchase order file. When a vendor invoice is received, the invoice is matched with the applicable purchase order, and debiting the equipment account of the department requesting the items sets up a payable. Unpaid invoices are filed by due date and, at due date, a check is prepared. The invoice and purchase order are filed by purchase order number in a paid invoice file, and the check is forwarded to the treasurer for signature.

Treasurer. Checks received daily from the Accounts Payable Department are sorted into two groups: those over $10,000 and those $10,000 and less. Checks for $10,000 and less are machine signed. The cashier controls the key and signature plate to the check-signing machine and maintains a record of usage. The treasurer or the controller signs all checks over $10,000.

Required:

    a. Without reference to the case described above, summarize the objectives of an acquisition/payment system. (That is, if it is a good acquisition/payment system, what characteristics will it have?)

    b. Identify weaknesses in PCA's acquisition/payment system described above.

    c. If your intent was to defraud PCA's acquisition/payment system, who would you want to be and how would you commit the fraud without it being detected?

10. **Business Overview.** E&M Carpet Cleaning is a family-owned carpet cleaning franchise of a large international carpet cleaning chain. Ervin and Mary Hogan (employees #3000 and #3001, respectively) recently purchased the franchise and are busy building a client base.

    Personnel. Erv and Mary employ three individuals: Salvador Anned, Shane Dean, and Mitch Ade (employees #3002, #3003, and #3004, respectively), who help with the cleaning. When there is enough business, two crews are formed. These crews are supervised by Erv and Salvador.

    Initial Estimate. When a new customer calls to request services, Erv is responsible for evaluating the client's situation and giving an estimate. Since E&M Carpet Cleaning has customers that request cleaning on a regular basis, all estimates are recorded for future reference. Many factors enter into E&M's pricing scheme (type of carpet, size of rooms, location of building, time of day that access to the building can be obtained, etc.), so if any factors change, Erv performs a new estimate for the client. Otherwise, the same estimate is referenced several times. [Unless otherwise specified, a client's mailing address and the location of the job are the same.]

    Employee Services. Erv and Mary each draw a set salary of $250 per week. Other cleaning employees (including supervisors) are paid an hourly rate. Salvador is paid $6 per hour, while Shane and Mitch each receive $4 per hour. Employees' starting and ending times are recorded by a time clock. Erv and Mary purchase all supplies and equipment. Mary also disburses payment for all bills and payroll. The last purchase (prior to June 5, 199x) was #227.

    Job. Employees are assigned to jobs according to a schedule of ordered jobs. Mary usually makes job assignments each morning. When a job is completed, the supervisor fills out a job sheet listing the equipment used and the employees and supervisor who worked on the job. This information is turned into Mary at the end of the day.

    Cash Receipts. Erv and Mary require most customers to pay by cash. When a job is completed, the supervisor is responsible for the client's payment. All cash receipts are given to Mary. However, a few customers are allowed to charge jobs. Often these customers will send in their payments, but occasionally Mary must bill the customer. [As of June 5, 199x, no E&M customers had outstanding balances and E&M had no accounts payable.]

Fixed Assets and Other Information. As of June 4, E&M owned six cleaning machines, numbered 6000 through 6005. They were purchased on January 2, 199x, for $132.99 each. Erv estimates that each has a two-year life with no salvage value. E&M also owns two vehicles. A used van was purchased on January 3, 199x, for $21,000 cash. Mary estimates that the van will have a three-year life with no salvage value. A new truck was purchased on May 20, 199x, at a cost of $17,500. E&M took out a two-year, 8% note for $5,000 to pay off the truck and the first payment was due on June 20, 199x. Mary estimates the truck will have a five-year life with no salvage value. As of the end of business on June 4, 199x, E&M had a $9,247.10 cash balance in account #4958678 at Ukiah Savings and Loan (946 Bankers Lane, Cambridge, CA).

E&M Cleaning Transactions List

1. June 5, 199x—Erv completed an estimate for Fillmore Office Building, customer #153. Job #5000 was scheduled for 6/6/9x. Estimate information is:

Est #	Location	Room	Size	Hours	Charge
4000	2344 Main St.	230	9 × 12	1.5	$ 30.00
	Cambridge, CA	235	18 × 22	2.0	55.00
		130	25 × 30	3.0	75.00
		147	20 × 28	2.5	60.00
			Total	9.0	$220.00

2. June 5, 199x—Mary purchased brushes from vendor #702, Hoover Machines (19 Commercial Blvd., Venture, CA): 2 bristle head brushes @ $10.50 each, 10 buffer mop heads @ $8.90 each, and 3 buffer wax heads @ $5.89 each. They were paid on CD #8000 with check #257 for $127.67.

3. June 5, 199x—Erv completed an estimate on a convention center owned by customer #154, Eastbrook Complex (mailing address: 783 Wymount Street, Venture, CA) and scheduled job #5001 for 6/6/9x. Details of the estimate are as follows:

Est #	Location	Room	Size	Hours	Charge
4001	378 Gujarati	1015	10 × 15	1.5	$ 30.00
	Cambridge, CA	1050	35 × 40	4.0	130.00
		1100	12 × 20	2.0	50.00
			Total	7.5	$210.00

4. June 6, 199x—Received completed job card.

Job #	Date	Start	End	Employee #	Equipment #	Supervisor #
5000	6/6/9x	8:05	10:30		6000, 6001	3000
		8:05	10:30	3002	6002, 6003	
		8:05	10:30	3003		
		8:05	10:30	3004		

5. June 6, 199x—Received completed job card.

Job #	Date	Start	End	Employee #	Equipment #	Supervisor #
5001	6/6/9x	12:45	14:45		6000, 6001	3000
		12:45	14:45	3002	6002, 6003	
		12:45	14:45	3003		
		12:45	14:45	3004		

6. June 6, 199x—Mary received payment of $220.00 from Fillmore Office (job #5000) on CR #7000. She also received payment of $210.00 (job #5001) from Eastbrook on CR #7001.

7. June 6, 199x—Erv performed an estimate for Akeem Young's residence (customer #155) and scheduled job #5002 for the afternoon of 6/7/9x. Estimate information is:

Est #	Location	Room	Size	Hours	Charge
4002	1215 Siles	Living	16 × 22	2.5	$ 50.00
	Filmore, CA	Bedroom	9 × 12	1.0	30.00
		Bedroom	15 × 20	2.0	50.00
			Total	5.5	$130.00

8. June 7, 199x—Received completed job card.

Job #	Date	Start	End	Employee #	Equipment #	Supervisor #
5002	6/7/9x	8:30	11:45		6004, 6005	3000
		8:30	11:45	3002		

9. June 7, 199x—Erv provided an estimate for a new customer (#156): Coldwell Bank of Fillmore. He scheduled job #5003 for 6/9/9x. Estimate information includes:

Est #	Location	Room	Size	Hours	Charge
4003	71 N. Main St	10	15 × 23	2.5	$ 50.00
	Cambridge, CA	Main	50 × 50	5.0	130.00
			Total	7.5	$180.00

10. June 8, 199x—Received payment of $130.00 from Young for job #5002 on CR #7002.

11. June 8, 199x—Mary purchased 10 gallons of White Sands cleaner @ $9.75 per gallon from vendor #703, Chemical Haven (969 Live Oak Dr., Fillmore, CA) on CD #8001 and check #258 for $97.50.

12. June 8, 199x—Erv completed an estimate for customer #157, Sunray Corporation (mailing address: 124 Bay Street, Cambridge, CA). Estimates #4004 through #4006 were scheduled for 6/12/9x as jobs #5004, #5005, and #5006, respectively. Estimate information is:

Est #	Location	Room	Size	Date Scheduled	Hours	Charge
4004	9732 Oakdale Filmore, CA	Six rooms	32 × 40	6/12/9x	6.0	$130.00
4005	23 Valley Rd. Filmore, CA	Five rooms	30 × 35	6/12/9x	4.0	110.00
4006	378 Main St.	400	18 × 25	6/12/9x	2.5	60.00
				Total	12.5	$300.00

13. June 9, 199x—Received completed job card.

Job #	Date	Start	End	Employee #	Equipment #	Supervisor #
5003	6/9/9x	9:05	11:15		6000, 6002,	3000
		9:05	11:15	3002	6005	
		9:05	11:15	3004		

14. June 9, 199x—Mary received payment of $180.00 from Coldwell for job #5003. She used CR #7003.

15. June 10, 199x—Erv did an estimate for customer #158, Mackey Construction (mailing address: 46758 East Tennessee Boulevard, Pillsburg, CA), to clean carpets in a house just painted. Job #5007 was scheduled for 6/12/9x. Estimate information is:

Est #	Location	Room	Size	Hours	Charge
4007	900 London Pilsburg, CA	Five Rooms	36 × 50	5.5	$140.00

16. June 12, 199x—Mary used the following time card information for the week ended June 10 to calculate and disburse payroll:

Check #	Amount	CD #	Employee #	Date	Start	End
259	$250.00	8002	3000	6/5	8:00	12:00
				6/6	7:30	15:30
				6/7	8:00	13:50
				6/8	9:15	12:30
				6/9	8:30	13:15
				6/10	10:15	11:30
260	$250.00	8003	3001	6/5	8:00	16:00
				6/6	8:00	16:00
				6/7	8:00	16:00
				6/8	8:00	16:00
				6/9	8:05	13:30
261	$ 97.50	8004	3002	6/6	7:45	15:30
				6/7	8:05	12:15
				6/9	8:25	12:45
262	$ 29.47	8005	3003	6/6	7:50	15:15
263	$ 42.00	8006	3004	6/6	7:51	15:15
				6/9	8:15	12:50

17. June 12, 199x—Mary received the following completed job cards:

Job #	Date	Start	End	Employee #	Equipment #	Supervisor #
5004	6/12/9x	8:35	10:09		6000, 6001,	3000
		8:35	10:09	3002	6002	
		8:35	10:09	3004		
5005	6/12/9x	11:00	12:07		6000, 6001,	3000
		11:00	12:07	3002	6002	
		11:00	12:07	3004		
5006	6/12/9x	13:30	15:25		6000, 6002	3000
		13:30	15:25	3004		
5007	6/23/9x	13:00	15:15		6001, 6003	3002
		13:00	15:15	3003		

18. June 12, 199x—Mary received payment from Sunray for jobs #5004, #5005, and #5006; amount $300.00 on CR #7004.

19. June 13, 199x—Mary received payment from Mackey for job #5007; amount $140.00 on CR #7005.

20. June 14, 199x—Mary placed advertisement in Venture County Journal (4967 Elm Street N., Venture, CA; vendor #704). The advertisement will run from June 19 through 21. She used CD #8007 and check #264 for $45.50.

21. June 15, 199x—Erv completed an estimate on the Eastbrook Complex, customer #154. Job #5008 was scheduled for 6/16/9x. Estimate information is:

Est #	Location	Room	Size	Hours	Charge
4008	738 Wymount	831	18 × 25	3.0	$ 60.00
	Venture, CA	838	20 × 24	3.0	65.00
		845	27 × 35	4.0	105.00
			Total	10.0	$230.00

22. June 15, 199x—Mary purchased another cleaning machine (#6006) from Hoover Machines, using CD #8008 and check #265 for $139.95.

23. June 15, 199x—Nix Realty (mailing address: 782 North Main St., Fillmore, CA; customer #151) called to have a living room and two bedrooms cleaned at Wilshire Apartments, #203 (Address: 1247 Hillgrove Avenue, Cambridge, CA). Estimate #3998 had been completed on June 2 (32 × 34, 4.0 hrs, $110). Job #5009 was scheduled for 6/16/9x.

24. June 16, 199x—Steve Jones (Address: 567 Dover Way, Fillmore, CA; customer #152) called to have three rooms cleaned. Erv had performed estimate #3999 on June 2 (25 × 32, 4.0 hrs, $110). Job #5010 was scheduled for 6/16/9x.

25. June 16, 199x—Mary received the following completed job cards:

Job #	Date	Start	End	Employee #	Equipment #	Supervisor #
5008	6/16/9x	8:20	12:05		6003, 6004,	3000
		8:20	10:00	3002	6005	
		8:20	12:05	3003		
5009	6/16/9x	13:15	14:30		6003, 6004,	3000
		13:15	14:30	3003	6005	
		13:15	14:30	3004		
5010	6/16/9x	12:10	12:10		6000, 6001	3002
		12:10	12:10	3004		

26. June 16, 199x—Received $110.00 from Nix Realty for job #5009 on CR #7006. Also received $110.00 from Steve Jones for job #5010 on CR #7007.

27. June 17, 199x—Received $10.00 from Steel Recycling on CR #7008. Erv took some old machine parts to the scrap yard.

28. June 19, 199x—Paid the following utility bills to vendors #705 and #706:

Ventura Electric (94 5th Ave., Venture, CA), CD #8009 and check #266 for $175.21. Southern Cal Water (1 Old St., Venture, CA), CD #8010 and check #267 for $43.38.

29. June 19, 199x—Received an order for job #5011 from First Christian Church (Address: 538 Callie Spring Dr., Pillsburg, CA; customer #150) to clean their fellowship hall. The job was scheduled for 6/20/9x based on estimate #3397 (50 × 50, 6.5 hrs, $140.00) performed by Erv on June 1.

30. June 19, 199x—Received the following time card information for the week ended June 17th to calculate and disburse payroll.

Check #	Amount	CD #	Employee #	Date	Start	End
268	$250.00	8011	3000	6/12	7:45	16:10
				6/15	9:00	10:30
				6/16	8:00	15:55
				6/17	10:15	12:45
269	$250.00	8012	3001	6/12	8:00	16:00
				6/13	8:00	16:00
				6/14	8:00	16:00
				6/15	8:00	16:00
				6/16	8:00	16:00
270	$ 77.50	8013	3002	6/12	7:45	16:00
				6/16	8:10	12:50
271	$ 39.33	8014	3003	6/12	12:45	15:30
				6/16	8:05	15:10
272	$ 48.33	8015	3004	6/12	8:10	15:45
				6/16	10:15	14:45

31. June 19, 199x—Received payment of $230.00 from Eastbrook for job #5008 on CR #7009.

32. June 19, 199x—Paid $175.00 for accounting services. Check #273 written to vendor #707: Arthur Whinney (One Valued Services Lane, Fillmore, CA) using CD #8016.

33. June 20, 199x—Received completed job card.

Job #	Date	Start	End	Employee #	Equipment #	Supervisor #
5011	6/20/9x	9:20	11:35		6005, 6006	3000
		9:20	11:35	3002		

34. June 20, 199x—Erv performed an estimate for a new customer (#159), Southern California Realty (mailing address: 308 Jefferson, Ukiah, CA). Job #5012 was scheduled for 6/21/9x.

Est #	Location	Room	Size	Hours	Charge
4009	7344 Kilroy Circle Ukiah, CA	Nine Rooms	55 × 65	12.0	$425.00

35. June 20, 199x—Made $228.43 truck loan payment to Ukiah Savings and Loan on CD #8017 and check #274. $166.67 was applied to the note principal.

36. June 20, 199x—Erv did maintenance work on cleaning machine #6002. He also changed the oil on the van and truck.

37. June 20, 199x—Two checks were prepared and sent by Mary: CD #8018 and check #275 for $10.67 to Hoover Machines for machine part; CD #8019 and check #276 for $20.31 to Bob's Hardware (95467 Main St., Cambridge, CA; vendor #708) for oil and filters to change oil on vehicles.

38. June 21, 199x—Received completed job card.

Job #	Date	Start	End	Employee #	Equipment #	Supervisor #
5012	6/21/9x	8:45	13:10		6000, 6002,	3000
		8:45	13:10	3002	6006	
		8:45	13:10	3003		

39. June 21, 199x—Charged $500.00 on account at vendor #709, Dan's Ford (8511 Tallahassee Tiger Sharks Lane, Cambridge, CA) for van repair. The repair will not extend the life of the van.

Required:

    a. Prepare a context diagram for each E&M process.

    b. Create a *REAL* model with cardinalities for each E&M process.

    c. Create any needed tables, complete with key attributes, foreign keys, and non-key attributes.

    d. List the recording and maintaining information processes needed for these activities.

    e. Give at least three examples of reporting processes.

    f. For each information process listed in part *d,* draw a data flow diagram that displays the tables needed to perform the process.

    g. Create an IT application prototype for E&M. Input the *transaction* data to test your prototype.

    h. List the business rules applicable to this organization. Explain how to incorporate each rule in an application prototype.

    i. What additional cost and expense information would you recommend that E&M track to enable them to better calculate job costs and set prices? Explain.

NOTE: To complete problems 11 and 12, your instructor must have ordered Arens and Ward, *Systems Understanding Aid* or *Systems Understanding Aid for Financial Accounting* (Williamston, Mich.: Armond Dalton Publishers, 1990, 4th edition) for purchase from your bookstore. Complete the following in student project teams.

11. Review the documentation in the Systems Understanding Aid Package to complete this assignment.

Required:

    a. Prepare a context diagram for Waren's acquisition/payment process.

    b. Create a *REAL* model with cardinalities for Waren's acquisition/payment process.

    c. Create any needed tables, complete with key attributes, foreign keys, and non-key attributes.

    d. List the recording and maintaining information processes needed for these activities.

e. Give three examples of reporting processes.

f. For each information process listed in part *d,* draw a data flow diagram that displays the tables needed to perform the process.

g. Identify the business rules and business risks associated with each event.

h. Create an IT application prototype for Waren's acquisition/payment process. Input sample data to test your prototype.

12. Waren Distributing has hired you to experiment with an event-driven system. They want you to learn how financial statements can be generated without the use of a general ledger and journals (i.e., traditional accounting reports become one view of the data). As you complete the assignment, notice there are no accounting processes, (e.g., summarizations or classifications to bias the data or alternative views of the data).

Your professor will supply you with some supplemental information and several databases that contain all the data necessary to develop the income statement, statement of changes in retained earnings, and the balance sheet for Waren Distributing, for the year ending 199x. However, your assignment is to develop only part of the income statement and part of the balance sheet. Be sure to structure your queries so they will accommodate an ongoing business. Your queries, except for the dates, should be accurate for use in future years.

Required:

a. Produce an income statement from sales through gross margin for the year ended 31 December 199x. The revenue, cost of goods sold, and gross margin sections of the income statement should appear in good form for a retail establishment. Make sure the cost of goods sold section shows each item making up the cost of goods sold (e.g., beginning inventory, purchases, and freight-in).

Submit a printed copy of your partial income statement and a disk containing any programming, queries, and database tables.

b. Produce the asset portion of the balance sheet as of 31 December 199x. The current assets and noncurrent assets sections with appropriate totals should appear in good form for a retail enterprise.

Submit a printed copy of your partial balance sheet and a disk containing any programming, queries, and database tables.

CHAPTER

Other Business Processes

CHAPTER OBJECTIVE

Prior chapters have reviewed the sales/collection and acquisition/payment processes. The objective of this chapter is to introduce three additional business processes: the human resource process, the financing process, and the conversion process. After studying this chapter, you should be able to:

- Identify the characteristics of other traditional business processes and related IT applications.
- Identify the weaknesses of the traditional processes and their IT application architecture.
- Develop *REAL* models of the various business processes.
- Identify opportunities to improve the business processes.

INTRODUCTION

Business processes can be broadly categorized into the acquisition/payment process, conversion process, and sales/collection process. Prior chapters provided an overview of the sales/collection process and the acquisition/payment process. The acquisition/payment process may be very broadly defined to include not only raw materials, inventory, and supplies used in normal business activities, but also human resources, financial resources, property, plant, and equipment, and anything else the organization acquires from external suppliers. However, most businesses find it easier to segregate these more specialized acquisition activities and study them as separate business processes.

The conversion business process is perhaps one of the most complex because it varies so much from one organization to the next. Selling goods and services and collecting cash for one company is very similar to selling goods and services and collecting cash for any other company. The same holds true for buying and paying for resources used by the organization. All these business processes are fairly similar across companies. However, the conversion process is quite unique for each company as they attempt to differentiate their products and services from their competitors.

This chapter introduces three additional business processes: the human resource process, the financing process, and the conversion process. Both the human resource and financing processes are special cases of the acquisition/payment process. Therefore, you should see several similarities in these processes. With each process we will review its objectives, nature, and the information typically used to plan, execute, control, and evaluate significant business events.

As you study these business processes, remember there are many variations from one organization to the next. To include even a few of the variations would make the chapter very long and unduly complex. Therefore, we focus on the most significant business events and the process you should follow when you study a particular organization's business processes. Be sure you understand the main business processes and how they fit together. Focus first on identifying operating events, resources, agents, and locations and their relationships. This knowledge will help you identify information users, decision requirements, and needed measurements.

HUMAN RESOURCE BUSINESS PROCESS

Strategy and Objectives

The primary objective of the human resource process is to provide the human labor and expertise that an organization needs to function efficiently and effectively. People who work for a company are generally considered the company's most valuable assets. Some of the more important responsibilities of the human resource process are to identify human resource needs, hire people to fill those needs, train the people to function effectively in their assigned jobs, evaluate employee performance, pay employees for work performed, and handle employee terminations and retirements. These as well as other human resource activities are spread across several functional areas of the organization including human resources, accounting, finance, production, and security.

Accounting has traditionally focused on the payroll aspect of the human resources process. Traditionally, the system that accounting uses to account for and pay employees is entirely separate from the systems that personnel uses to hire, evaluate, train, and terminate employees or the systems that finance, production, or other areas use to track employees. To review the human resource process, we begin by examining the traditional manual payroll process and then the computerized payroll process traditionally used by accounting. Finally, we will outline an event-driven process that integrates the payroll activities with other significant events required to manage human resources.

Traditional Manual Payroll Process

The traditional manual payroll process uses an extensive amount of paper to capture, convey, store, and report information. Exhibit 8–1 depicts a typical manual payroll process for a manufacturing company that uses a job order cost system. The process begins in the personnel function when an employee is hired. The Personnel Division hires the employee, authorizes a rate of pay, and collects information about marital status and number of dependents for payroll deduction purposes. As employees arrive and leave work they record their hours on *time cards* with Timekeeping to show the time they arrive and leave. As they work during the day, employees record on *job time tickets* the amount of time they spend working on individual jobs. The job time tickets are reviewed by the production supervisor and transferred to Timekeeping to be reconciled with the *time cards*. If employees properly punch in and out, accurately record time worked on job tickets, and have no wasted time between jobs, the total time on the job time tickets should equal the time recorded on the time cards.

Cost Accounting uses the job time tickets to post labor costs to job order cost sheets. This provides an important link between the human resource process and the conversion process, which we will discuss shortly. Labor, along with materials and overhead are the major inputs to the conversion process. The cost of labor and other inputs is used as a basis to value work in process as well as finished products.

The Payroll Division verifies pay rates and calculates deductions for such items as Social Security taxes (FICA), federal and state income taxes, as well as net pay. These amounts are recorded on a *payroll register* that the Accounts Payable Division uses to prepare a *payroll voucher* to authorize a transfer of funds to the payroll checking account. Most organizations use a separate bank account, called an *imprest account,* to pay employees. A check for total net payroll is written by the cashier and deposited into the *imprest payroll account* at the bank. The cashier also prepares individual checks on the imprest payroll account for employees, which are distributed personally or electronically to employees. In some companies, an employee, called a *paymaster,* distributes paychecks to each employee.

This process has several key data flows and control points. Key data flows include the job time tickets, time cards, payroll register, pay voucher, and checks to the imprest payroll account and to individual employees. There are also several important control points. One control that is not shown on traditional flowcharts involves someone in Timekeeping observing employees as they punch in and out of work to verify that employees punch their own time card and only their own time card. This prevents an employee from punching in and out for a friend who is not able to attend work that day. The timekeeping employee is also responsible for controlling time cards between check-in and check-out times to prevent employees from manipulating their own or someone else's time card. Controls include a review of the job time tickets by the factory supervisor and Timekeeping's reconciliation of the job time tickets and the time cards. Such reconciliations and reviews can identify errors or discrepancies. For example, if an employee is able to bypass the timekeeping control and punch in for a friend, it is generally difficult to post time to jobs for the friend during the

EXHIBIT 8-1

Traditional Manual Payroll Process Flowchart

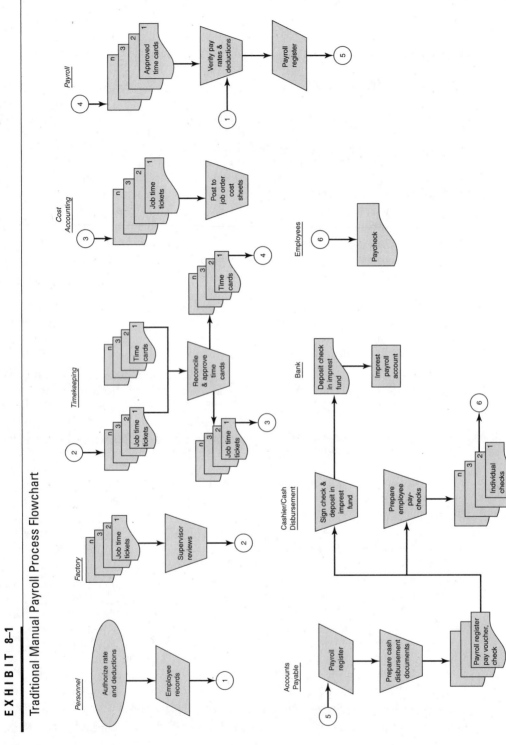

day without a supervisor discovering it. Finally, the separation of duties between the various departments is also important in a manual system. By only paying employees who have been hired by Personnel and who have worked time that has been approved by a supervisor, people are prevented from entering fictitious employees on the records and paying them for time they did not work. Authorization duties (performed by Personnel) are separated from record-keeping duties (performed by Timekeeping, Payroll, Accounts Payable, and Cost Accounting) and custodial activities (performed by the cashier).

Traditional Computerized Payroll Process

The basic substance of most payroll processes did not change substantially when they were initially computerized. Exhibit 8–2 illustrates a typical computer-based batch payroll process. The Personnel Division initiates the process by hiring employees and collecting personal and payroll data about them. These data, as well as subsequent changes to the data, are entered into an *employee payroll master file*. This important file contains data about the employee's pay rate, marital status, exemptions, and pay and deductions for the year to date. Organizations should properly prepare, review, and approve data prior to entry into this file. Access to the file must also be controlled. Someone could obtain substantial gain by manipulating their own or an accomplice's pay rate or federal or state income tax withholdings.

A time ticket, or similar recording process, continues to serve as input to the payroll process. Time and attendance are determined by calculating the time between when employees enter work and when they leave work (as well as the department they work in for a process costing system or the jobs they worked on for a job order costing system). A payroll clerk prepares some type of batch total early in the process, preferably as soon as the time tickets are first accumulated. The batch total could be the number of employees who worked (a record count), the total hours worked (a "financial" total), or the total of the employees' identification numbers (a hash total). The batch total is used to verify the accuracy of the payroll process. For example, if a record count were used for the control total, we would expect the number of checks printed by the computer to equal the record count. If total hours worked were used, we would expect the total of the hours paid on the summary report generated by the computer to equal total hours worked.

Information from the time cards is converted by the Data Processing Department to computer-processable form by a key-to-disk or similar process. During this process a variety of edits are performed. These may include limit and reasonableness tests to verify that the hours worked are within limits and reasonable for each employee's classification. They may also include validation tests to see that the employee's number is a valid number or completeness test to verify that all necessary data to pay an employee have been entered. Any errors or exceptions are reported on an exception and summary report.

Payroll, for most companies, is most efficiently processed in batches because most employees are paid at the same time, such as weekly, bimonthly, or monthly. Typically, the payroll process is most efficiently performed by a sequential process that requires the transaction data (e.g., hours worked by employee) to be in the same sequence as the

EXHIBIT 8–2

Traditional Automated Payroll Process Flowchart

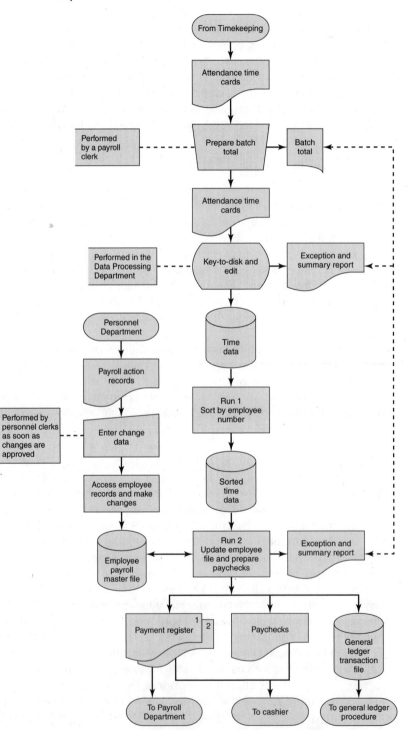

employee payroll master file (usually sequenced by employee identification number). To facilitate this sequential processing, the time card data are sorted by employee number prior to updating the master file and preparing the paychecks. This sorting puts the time data (the transaction data) in the same order as the employee file (the master file). The sorted time card data and the employee payroll master file are the inputs into the process to calculate employee's gross pay, deductions, and net pay. The year-to-date earnings on the master file are updated, a payroll register is printed in duplicate, paychecks are printed for each employee, an exception and summary report is printed, and information to update the general ledger is printed to a general ledger transaction file.

Notice how several of the same data flows used in the manual system are also used in the computerized batch process. Also, many of the controls are the same. Observing employees punch in and out of work is still a timekeeping function. Supervisors still review the allocation of employee time to the jobs. There continues to be about the same separation of duties between Personnel, Timekeeping, Factory, Accounting, and cashier so the work of one area checks the work of other areas.

A control group executes one added control in a computerized system. This group of people has the responsibility to review the activities of the Data Processing Department. For the payroll process, the control group receives the batch totals and the two exception and summary reports. They compare the batch totals with information on the exception and summary reports to verify that data have not been added or lost during processing. They follow up on errors and exceptions to identify their cause and see that appropriate corrections are made. For example, if an employee has time card data, but is not listed as a valid employee in the master file, the control group will want to know why. Also, if an employee has 90 hours of work in a week, the control group will want to see if it is legitimate, why someone is working so many hours, or how 90 hours was recorded when the person actually worked less hours.

Information Needs in the Human Resource Business Process

As previously stated, the human resources process involves more than payroll activities. Let's examine some of the key business events associated with the *entire* human resource process including headcount approval, hiring, training, assigning, compensating, evaluating, and terminating/retiring employees. Information is needed to effectively plan, execute, control, and evaluate these activities.

Approve Headcount   In many organizations approved headcount is a key tool for controlling labor costs. For example, in one well-known computer software company, a supervisor wishing to increase headcount must prepare the necessary paperwork to identify and justify the need for a new position. There is an extensive review process that requires the division manager, area controller, and executive vice president to approve the request. Only when all these approvals are obtained can the position be opened for hiring.

Hire Employees   Organizations continue to need professional, support staff, and technical personnel in today's competitive, advanced business environment. Individuals agree to work in exchange for wages, benefits, and other rewards. Hiring is the process of matching the skills and interests of people with the needs of the organization. Important in the hiring process is an accurate description of the organization's needs. Not only must accurate projections be made of the number of individuals needed, but also organizations must develop job descriptions and skill requirements associated with each job position. Those responsible for the Hire Employees event use the job descriptions and skill requirements as a basis for selecting new hires.

Train Employees   Accurate job descriptions and proper screening for new hires can minimize initial job training. Nevertheless, changes in organizations and job requirements make retraining current employees an ongoing process. Training requires an understanding of the current knowledge and skills of the people to be trained, identifying the desired skills and knowledge, and a program to provide what is currently lacking. Maintaining a record of each employee's training can provide important information in assigning employees to new jobs.

In a world of rightsizing and downsizing, are personnel and training costs viewed differently? In *Reinventing the CFO: Moving From Financial Management to Strategic Management*[1] authors Walther, Johansson, Dunleavy, and Hjelm point out that there is a new paradigm with regard to personnel costs and training. They explain that traditionally some organizations considered administration and support workers as costs to be cut. The value-driven mentality sees them as "resources to be trained."

Today, organizations also provide training in varied topics not directly related to enhancing specific job skills. These include awareness of sexual harassment, multicultural issues, and other human and legal issues.

Assign Employees   Part of management's responsibility is to organize and direct the work of employees. Organizing involves identifying the activities to be performed, structuring the activities into jobs, and positioning the jobs into departments, project teams, or divisions. Competent individuals who have the skills, abilities, and training necessary to perform them must fill the jobs. To effectively assign people to jobs, management must receive information on the operating events that must be performed, the skills required to perform them, and the skills, abilities, and training of each employee.

Downsizing, restructuring, and process reengineering directly affect today's workforce. Entire business processes may be restructured to accomplish the same objective more efficiently and effectively. Each operating event within a business process is evaluated to determine if it is necessary. Similarly, the tasks associated with each event are evaluated. A critical question is often asked: Is information technology available to perform this event, or facilitate the performance of this event? The primary objective of reengineering is to eliminate non–value-adding business events, streamline those that remain, and use information technology to the extent possible to efficiently achieve the desired objective.

---

1 Thomas Walther, Henry Johansson, John Dunleavy, and Elizabeth Hjelm, *Reinventing the CFO: Moving From Financial Management to Strategic Management* (New York: McGraw Hill, 1997).

Compensate Employees   A variety of methods are used to compensate employees and the information system must record, maintain, and report information about all of them. Monitoring and measuring personnel compensation are complex and data-intensive activities.

Employee compensation may come in the form of salary, commission, salary plus commission, rate per hour, or rate per piece (based on units of work). Most managers and top-level executives are paid a salary and perhaps a bonus depending on the profitability of the company. Manual-type work is typically paid by the hour with a premium rate for overtime hours. Overtime pay may be computed on a daily basis (any time over eight hours per day), or on a weekly basis (any time over 40 hours per week). Many sales jobs have commission pay based on the amount sold. This may be complicated by a base salary with commissions for sales in excess of a specified minimum amount. Finally, pay for some factory workers is based on units produced, while pay for other workers may have a base salary, plus a piece rate per unit manufactured.

To accurately pay employees, the information system must accumulate and provide information on the employee's activities used to calculate compensation. For some employees, time may be most critical; for other employees, some measure of performance, such as sales dollars or units manufactured, will be most critical.

In addition to regular pay, employers must measure and calculate other forms of pay, employee benefits, and deductions. Additional forms of pay include overtime pay, comp pay, vacation pay, and sick pay. Employees can also participate in a variety of benefit options and deductions, including cafeteria benefit plans, retirement plans, pre-tax plans for childcare and medical expenses, and tax-deferred savings plans. An organization's information system must record and maintain data relating to all these options for each employee.

Most of the information required to compensate employees is collected as an attribute of the operating event itself. For example, when a salesperson makes a sales call and obtains an order, one of the order's descriptive attributes is the salesperson responsible for the sale. This information is available in the integrated database, and can be extracted to calculate gross sales by salesperson and used to calculate sales commissions.

In addition to the check the employee receives, there are a multitude of other reports and checks that need to be prepared relative to payroll. Employers are responsible to act as an agent of federal and state governments to withhold estimated amounts for federal and state income taxes and FICA taxes. The employee may authorize other payroll deductions (e.g., union dues and government bonds), that the employer must account for and report. There are several other taxes that the employer must pay beyond those that are withheld from the employee. Employer taxes vary from state to state, but most include a matching amount for FICA, unemployment taxes for both the state and federal governments, and worker's compensation. Each payroll-related deduction or employer tax has a report, and usually a required payment, associated with it.

Evaluate Employees   Performance evaluations serve several important functions in an organization:

- They provide a basis for recognizing and rewarding performance.
- They guide personnel actions such as hiring, firing, and promoting.

- They provide individuals with information for their own personal development.
- They identify training needs for the organization.

Quality performance evaluations should focus both on behaviors and productivity. Behaviors reference more subjective qualities like attitude, dependability, mental alertness, flexibility, judgment, and appearance. Measures for these items are usually obtained by a questionnaire survey of managers and/or peers. Productivity measures focus on outcomes: what was actually produced, how long something took to complete, or percentage of items with defects. These measures are developed as a by-product of an event-driven system. As an operating event is performed, the system records the amount of time it takes. The output of each event is also recorded, as is the quality of the output. All of these can be related to the internal agents who perform the event. The results are valuable measures for performance evaluations.

Terminate/Retire Employees Terminate Employees is the most undesirable of all operating events. Unfortunately, this has become an important event as many companies attempt to downsize or rightsize. Effectively performing each of the aforementioned events is important in avoiding problems with this event. Doing a quality job of hiring and training employees can reduce the likelihood of having to subsequently terminate them. However, if an employee is to be terminated, there must be good justification for that action and it must be properly documented. Performance measurements and evaluation reports outlined above are critical in this process.

Above and beyond the information that is required to perform the events of the human resource process, there are mandated reports that must be filed with outside organizations and agencies of the government. The following are two examples:

- The Equal Employment Opportunity Act (1972) prohibits discrimination on the basis of race, religion, sex, or national origin. A commission was set up to enforce this act. Employers must be able to show that their hiring practices do not discriminate, or, if they do discriminate, they must be able to show that the discrimination is due to job-related characteristics.
- The Occupational Safety and Health Act (1970), OSHA, requires employers to provide employees with a safe working environment, free from health hazards. It also requires employers to maintain a record-keeping system that monitors and reports job-related injuries and illnesses. OSHA may conduct workplace inspections and give citations and penalties for failure to comply with the requirements of this act.

Events, Agents, and Resources for the Human Resource Process

A sample graphical *REAL* model for the human resource process is illustrated in Exhibit 8–3. The model divides Approve Headcount into two events. A supervisor proposes a headcount adjustment, which is reviewed and approved or rejected by a planning committee. The hiring officers of the company handle the actual hiring of a new employee. Em-

EXHIBIT 8–3

REAL Model of the Human Resource Business Process

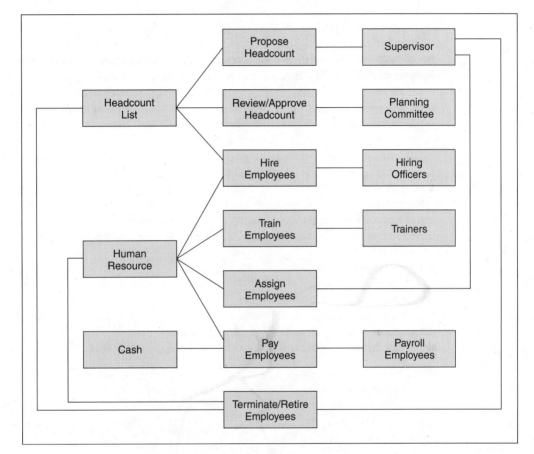

ployees are trained by various trainers and assigned to specific jobs by the supervisors. A payroll clerk pays employees for the work they perform. For the company illustrated in this exhibit, the supervisor has the responsibility for terminating or retiring employees.

FINANCING BUSINESS PROCESS

The financing business process provides the capital resources an organization needs to fund all aspects of its operations. A substantial portion of cash is used to fund two of the business processes we have discussed already: the acquisition/payment process and the human resource process. Much of the cash available to the financing process comes from the sales/collection process. However, other financing alternatives are occasionally used. The relationships among financing and other business processes are illustrated in Exhibit 8–4.

Strategy and Objectives of the Financing Business Process

The objectives of this process are to have the liquid funds needed to run the business, but to not let cash sit idle. By having sufficient cash on hand or available the company can buy in quantity and obtain more favorable prices. They can take advantage of cash discounts. When a supplier or vendor has a tight cash position, they will frequently give special discounts to customers who pay in cash. Having cash available to pay obligations on time and being able to pay in cash gives an organization a great deal of power.

Cash by itself does not earn money; in fact, it generally loses money due to inflation. Certain receivables, such as accounts receivable, do not earn any interest. Therefore, organizations should minimize the levels of idle cash on hand and collect receivables as quickly as possible and convert these assets into assets that earn interest or grow in value over time. Effective cash management policies and procedures can enhance the overall return for a company. Some of the more common policies and procedures are summarized below:

> Billing customers immediately after a product is provided or a service is performed.

EXHIBIT 8–4

Sample Process Relationships

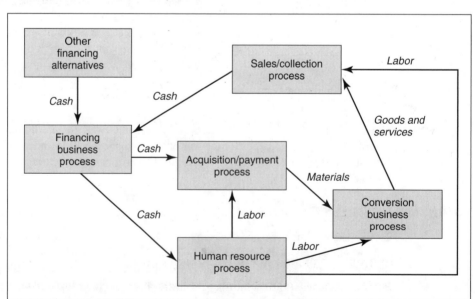

Keeping cash in accounts that earn interest. Checking accounts for corporations typically do not earn interest. To compensate for this, corporations should have a money market, interest-bearing account and transfer cash between the checking account and the money market account (keeping enough in the checking account to cover checks outstanding, but no more).

Planning the amount of time that checks will be in the mail and held by suppliers and not putting cash into the checking account until checks are expected to clear the vendor's or supplier's bank.

Having customers mail remittances to deposit boxes located in cities where mail is delivered more quickly. For a fee, a financing institution will manage the deposit lockbox and deposit funds in the account of the company to minimize the amount of time the check is in the mail.

Hedging foreign currency transactions where necessary to minimize foreign exchange losses. International operations and the handling of foreign exchange is an art in itself. A transaction with a foreign company may be stated in either dollars or the foreign currency. If it is stated in the foreign currency, there is a potential gain or loss when money is finally paid or received, depending on the change in the values of the two currencies. Hedging is one option to reduce an exposed foreign currency position.

Organizations can obtain necessary funds from a variety of sources. An organization can obtain funds from owners by selling common stock or requiring additional owner investments for a proprietorship or a partnership. For a corporation, there is the option to sell additional classes of stock such as class B common or preferred stock. Bonds may be issued or money may be borrowed on an open note or a mortgage from a lending institution. A company can sell any asset, but the most commonly sold assets are short- and long-term investments. Short-term investments are typically acquired during times when excess cash is on hand, and these are the most likely assets to be sold when additional cash is needed. Notes and/or accounts receivable may be *factored* (sold). In any given situation, some combination of these alternatives may be used to obtain the necessary funds.

Organizations can invest excess cash from operations in a variety of options including:

- Short- and long-term investments in financial instruments of other companies.
- Money market accounts that bear interest.
- Certificates of deposit (CDs).
- Treasury notes.

Rather than investing excess cash, the company may decide to reduce debt, purchase assets rather than lease them, or return money to owners through dividends or withdrawals.

Information Needs in the Financing Process

Information is needed to achieve the objectives outlined above and reduce the risks inherent in this process. There are several risks associated with the financing process including:

Investments may lose money. If money is invested in common stocks of other companies, the value of the stock may decrease due to a variety of reasons, most of which are out of the control of the investing company. A good information system will provide real-time information on the actual return on various investments to assist in making timely buy/sell decisions.

Cash flow estimates may be inaccurate and money may be required at a time when there are no liquid funds available. A good information system will provide accurate information on the amount of cash needed for normal operations and the amount of cash available for investment purposes.

The return on investment may be superficially low if an organization keeps too much cash on hand or in other liquid assets. The return on more liquid investments (e.g., money market accounts or certificates of deposit) is frequently much less than can be earned on longer-term investments in other assets (e.g., stocks and bonds). Timely information on cash needs and returns on investments is necessary to maintain a balance between liquidity and profitability.

Cash is the most liquid of all assets and the one asset most dishonest people like to steal. There are a number of risks associated with theft or misappropriation of cash and other liquid investments. Organizations should *bond*, or insure, people who have access to cash and other liquid assets. The information system must have built-in controls to accurately account for cash and liquid investments and maintain a record of responsibility to minimize the chance that these assets will be stolen or misappropriated.

What are some of the examples of value-added financial analyses you can perform? You can measure return on equity, cash flow to debt coverage, interest coverage, projected growth in earnings per share, dividend payout ratios, price-earnings ratios, market to book ratios, return on assets, return on investment capital, economic profit, economic value-added analyses, total shareholder return, and balanced scorecard analyses.

Events, Agents, and Resources in the Financing Process

The financing process includes the business events associated with obtaining the necessary cash to operate the business, effectively managing available funds, and wisely investing excess cash.

Exhibit 8–5 contains a graphical *REAL* model for a sample company that we will use to illustrate the resources, events, agents, and locations in a representative financing process. The exhibit models the Equity Company, a partnership that borrows money from lending institutions or sells short-term investments as necessary to meet all its short- and long-term cash needs.

Equity Company's Accounting Department is responsible for maintaining the cash balance and projecting cash receipts and disbursements for the next quarter. Accounting sends a monthly report to the Finance Department summarizing expected cash flows. The bottom line of the report is the amount of additional cash needed to meet normal operations, or the amount of cash available to pay existing notes or invest in short-term securities.

EXHIBIT 8–5

Sample Equity Company Financing *REAL* Model

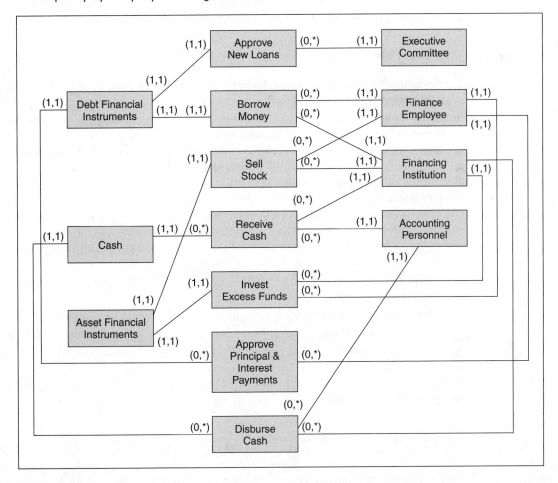

Equity Company's executive committee must approve new loans. The Finance Department negotiates the loan with a financing institution and secures the necessary approvals from the executive committee. The Finance Department is also responsible for making short-term investments and paying both principal and interest on borrowed funds. Accounting makes the actual payment, but Finance tracks the notes, including the required interest payments and maturity dates, and sends a request for payment to Accounting.

Equity Company's resources are cash and various debt and asset financial instruments. Examples of debt financial instruments are notes payable, bonds, or mortgages. Asset financial instruments could include stock certificates, certificates of deposit, Treasury notes, mutual funds, options, and derivatives.

Equity's internal agents are the executive committee, finance employees, and accounting employees. Financing and investing institutions such as banks and brokerage firms are the external agents. The operating events include Borrow and Pay Loans, Buy and Sell Stock, and the approvals required for these activities.

CONVERSION BUSINESS PROCESS

The operating events required to convert raw inputs into finished products or services are contained in the conversion process. The inputs and outputs of the conversion process and its relationships to the other processes are shown in Exhibit 8–6. Materials and equipment are provided through the acquisition/payment process and labor is acquired through the human resource process. Finished products and services are the outputs of the conversion process, and they are sold through the sales/collection process.

The operating events of the conversion process differ from company to company and across industries. Each conversion process is rather unique. Even for companies with similar goods or services, the conversion process may be differentiated by the specific activities that management wants to plan, execute, control, and evaluate.

Many manufacturing entities have the most extensive conversion processes. Exhibit 8–7 illustrates in T account form the flow of resources in a manufacturing operation.

Manufacturing processes can be broadly categorized into two types: job costing and process costing.

Job Order Costing. Companies that use job costing have a diversified product line in which products are produced in batches, with each batch representing a unique product. Examples of job costing include car repairs, printing, and home

E X H I B I T 8–6

Sample Conversion Process Data Flows

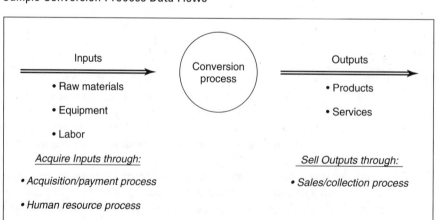

EXHIBIT 8–7

Flow of Resources—Manufacturing Process

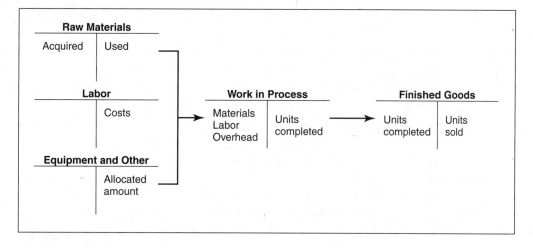

construction. The job is frequently initiated at a customer's request and the customer's specifications identify the characteristics of the job. Costs are accumulated by job, allocated equally to the individual units produced by that job, and reported according to each job.

Process Costing. Companies that use process costing produce a homogeneous product continuously. Examples include cement, petroleum products, flour, beer, and steel. Costs are accumulated by operating event, cost center, or department for a given period of time. These costs are assigned to individual units according to the number of equivalent whole units produced during the time period. Reports are generally prepared according to the way costs are accumulated (e.g., by operating event, cost center, or department).

Assigning manufacturing costs to units produced in both job costing and process costing is an averaging process: simply divide the manufacturing costs (accumulated either by job or by business event) by the number of units produced. This cost is used by accountants to value ending inventories of work in process and finished goods, and cost of goods sold during the period.

Since none of the operating events in the conversion process involve outside agents, they are all what might be classified as *internal discretionary events*. We could have just one business event that we call *convert* and let that represent all the activities required to convert raw inputs into finished products. However, that does not adequately provide managers with the detailed information they need to effectively plan, control, and evaluate their area of responsibility. Therefore, we divide the conversion process into meaningful activities that represent operating events.

Information Customers and Their Needs

The typical information customers for the conversion process include top management, production personnel, accountants, and auditors. There are no external information customers associated with the conversion process. External entities receive information about the conversion process through public financial statements prepared by accountants.

Top management is concerned with summary data that reflect the overall success of the conversion process. Such success often involves measures of efficient and effective production processes and effective or appropriate pricing structures. The type of information that management requests includes:

♦ Number of units produced and the cost per unit this period compared with prior periods.

♦ Percentage of defective units, reasons for the defects, and what is necessary to prevent future defects.

♦ Potential demand for products or the backlog of orders along with the number of units in finished goods inventory and planned production for the next period.

Production personnel should have a significant input in identifying operating events and structuring the system such that it provides information to plan, execute, control, and evaluate individual activities within the production process. Planning production includes identifying what to produce, when to produce it, and how it is to be made. Information provided by the sales/collection process is critical in determining what to produce and when. Expected demand for individual products, including colors and styles, and the desire changes in quantities in inventory are used to determine which specific products to manufacture and when to schedule production. Both engineering and research and development are useful in deciding the most efficient way to make the product.

Production personnel also have the responsibility to control and evaluate the production process. Standards for time, cost, and quality help them control and evaluate the process. The standards, based on historical data or engineering studies, provide a baseline estimate to compare against actual results. A quality information system should constantly monitor results in all three areas and provide immediate feedback so corrective action can be taken to prevent long periods of inefficient production or production of defective units.

Accountants and auditors are responsible for tracking manufacturing costs, assigning them to units produced, and verifying that adequate controls are in place to safeguard the assets. The conversion process must provide financial accountants with several key numbers, including raw material inventory balance, ending work in process, finished goods inventory, and cost of goods sold.

Conversion process activities also affect the decisions and information needs of the human resource process. The human resource function of the organization requires information about open job positions, job descriptions, and skill requirements to have the needed people available and properly trained.

The authors of *Reinventing the CFO*[2] discuss the changing paradigm in cost management that relates to the conversion process. They point out:

> The traditional cost-cutting mentality sees production workers being replaced with automation. The value-driven cost-management paradigm sees them in need of optimization through technical support.

> The traditional cost-cutting mentality simply sees expenses ripe for cutting. The value-driven cost-management paradigm sees cost drivers that help focus process improvement efforts.

> The traditional cost-cutting mentality focuses on price and variances. The value-driven cost-management paradigm looks at quality, time, service, vendor partnerships, and then price.

Designing an information system that supports the complexities and intricacies of a conversion process requires a careful analysis and a detailed understanding of the objectives of the process. Traditionally, organizations generated multiple systems to support the conversion process. In fact, organizations often developed financial accounting systems and a variety of separate cost/managerial accounting systems. By using a *REAL* model to design an event-driven system, organizations can derive financial statement information and other information needed to support a variety of programs (including activity-based costing, quality management, just-in-time inventories, and material requirements planning).

Events, Agents, and Resources in the Conversion Process

Since the conversion process is unique to each entity, a specific example will be used to illustrate this process. Nicol's Bottling Company manufactures a line of glass bottles that are sold to several distributors of sparkling water. Three factors are identified as critical to successfully manufacturing a bottle:

- Control costs of operations, including raw materials, labor, and other manufacturing costs.
- Maintain and increase worker productivity while minimizing breakage and defective bottles.
- Keep plant equipment in good repair.

Management would like to receive information on these items to effectively plan, execute, control, and evaluate the process.

The bottle manufacturing process is continuous and involves the following steps:

1. Heat the glass compound.
2. Pour the hot glass compound into bottle molds.

---

2 Walther, Johansson, Dunleavy, and Hjelm, *Reinventing the CFO*, pp. 88–89.

3. Remove the molds, inspect the bottles, and remove any glass spurs.

4. Package the bottles for shipment.

Exhibit 8–8 contains a *REAL* model for Nicol's Bottling Company. The four key operating activities in the manufacturing process are the operating events. The agents are all internal. The resources include raw materials and supplies, equipment, work in process, and finished goods.

Let's examine the conversion process and the event-driven solution to see how management is able to obtain the information they need to effectively plan, execute, control, and evaluate each event. For each of the operating events, the information recorded by the system includes the time the event starts and stops, the resources used, the number of units of product involved, and the internal agent or agents.

Cost of Operations   Because we know each resource used during each event and the number of units produced, we can easily calculate and report the conversion cost. We can calculate cost in a variety of ways including the cost by event for a period of time,

E X H I B I T 8–8

Nicol's Bottling Conversion Process *REAL* Model (without relationship semantics)

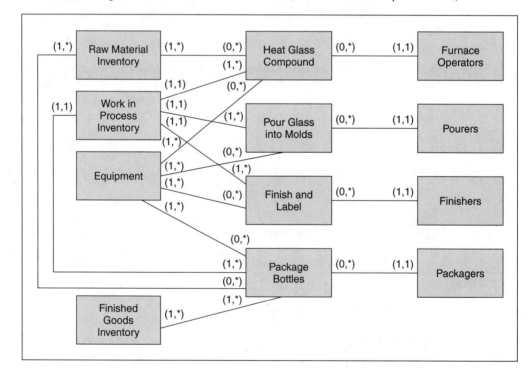

cost per unit produced, or the cost of individual inputs such as labor cost per unit, material cost per unit, and other cost per unit. By capturing other data about the conversion process such as the heat of the glass compound, time between heating and pouring, and time between pouring and labeling, we can identify relationships between various aspects of the conversion process, cost, and quality. For example, we may find we have more breakage and lower quality as the length of time between heating and pouring increases.

Worker Productivity   By knowing which workers worked on each event, the amount of time involved, and the quantity and quality of the work accomplished, we can provide a variety of reports on worker productivity. For example, we can develop a report that shows by pourer the amount of hot glass poured, the number of bottles produced, the amount of waste, and the average time per bottle. By reviewing this report we may find greater waste associated with certain pourers and decide additional training is needed or to rotate work assignments due to pourer fatigue.

Equipment Repair   Knowing which pieces of equipment are used for which business events, the amount of time they are used, and the number of units produced will help plan equipment repairs, maintenance, and replacements. Performing timely preventive maintenance can prevent much of the equipment repair. By also capturing data on date and type of machine repair and maintenance, reports can be provided on a regular basis showing equipment usage since they were last serviced and an approximate date for the next scheduled maintenance.

RELATIONSHIPS AMONG BUSINESS PROCESSES

To facilitate discussion, we divided organization business activities into separate business processes. We further divided business processes into smaller pieces (events) to make the analysis, design, development, and implementation of the information system more manageable. However, it is important to remember that the business processes that comprise an organization's total activities are interrelated. Let's step back and take a look at an organization from a macro-, rather than a microperspective.

To illustrate the interrelationships among business processes, consider the following generic model of key events, resources, and agents for an entire business:

Event	Resource	Agent
Acquire Financing	Financing instruments	Employees Investors Creditors
Acquire Resources to Produce Goods/Services	Inventory	Employees Vendors
Acquire Employee Services	Employee resources	Employees

Event	Resource	Agent
Acquire Property, Plant, and Equipment	Property, plant, and equipment	Employees Vendors
Convert Resources to Finished Goods/Services for Sale	Inventory	Employees
Sell Goods/Services	Inventory	Employees Customers
Receive Cash	Cash	Employees Customers Creditors Investors
Disburse Cash	Cash	Employees Vendors Creditors Investors

Exhibit 8–9 presents a graphical representation of this model. Keep in mind that we are viewing the business at a very high level. When we do, there are not a large number of events, resources, or agents. External agents include investors, creditors, vendors, and customers, while the internal agents include employees. The financing instruments may include stocks, bonds, notes, or similar ownership interests or debt securities. Our resource of goods and services is used very broadly to include all the resources that are bought, developed, or available for sale. Longer-term assets are included in the property, plant, and equipment resource. We have separated out cash in this example because it is the common link between several business processes, but it, like property, plant, and equipment and other resources, could be included in a single goods and services resource. Cash received from the sale of products and services is used to acquire more resources and produce and sell more goods and services.

The eight business events listed above have, for the most part, been discussed as separate business processes in this text. The Acquire Financing event constitutes the financing process; the Hire Employees event constitutes the human resource process; and the Build Products event is the conversion process. The sales/collection process and the acquisition/payment process each have two events in Exhibit 8–9: Sell Goods/Services and Receive Cash, and Purchase Resources and Disburse Cash, respectively. The human resource process spans all the other business processes because all the processes must be conducted by employees who are hired, trained, assigned, and paid through the human resource process.

The financing process and the conversion process are key processes because of how they link the other processes (as shown in Exhibit 8–4 earlier in the chapter). One of the first and sometimes most difficult events is acquiring financing. The financing process is a link between the sales/collection process, the human resource process, and the acquisition/payment process. Cash is the common resource that links them.

Managing the link between the business processes is extremely important. For example, the amount of cash that is expected to be collected from the sales/collection process, and the amount of cash that is expected to be paid by the human resource and acquisi-

EXHIBIT 8–9

Generic Overview of an Entire Business

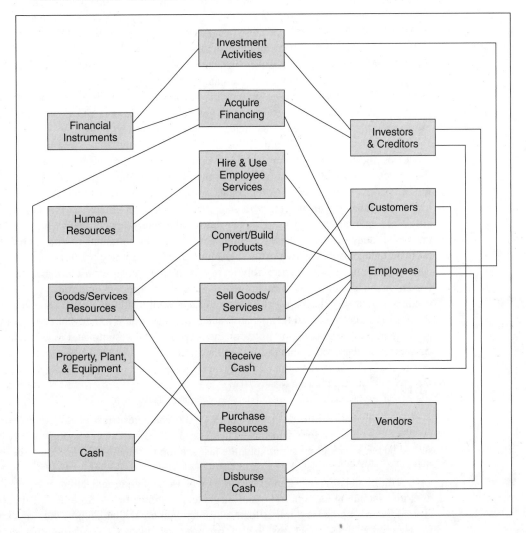

tion/payment processes is critical to the financing process. If anticipated receipts exceeds disbursement, financing responds by seeking possible investments to effectively place available cash to maximize the return to the organization. When anticipated disbursements exceed receipts, financing must liquidate investments or find other financing sources to obtain the needed funds. Cash is the common resource, but information about the current and planned cash flows and cash needs is critical in effectively managing each process.

The conversion process provides a link on the other side of the human resource process, the acquisition/payment process, and the sales/collection process. Inputs into the conversion process include labor (provided by the human resource process), and materials, equipment, and supplies (provided by the acquisition/payment process). The outputs of the conversion process are the goods and/or services available for sale that are the input to the sales/collection process. The resource provides the primary link between each process, but information about the current and anticipated needs for each resource is critical to effectively managing other processes. Anticipated sales trigger the need for conversion to produce goods and services. Based on the amount of goods/services to be produced, the human resource process must secure the necessary people and the acquisition/payment process must secure the necessary materials, supplies, and equipment.

The most efficient organizations have the best flow of information between the processes and the least amount of idle resources both within and between the processes. For example, raw material is a primary resource that links the acquisition/payment process with the conversion process. Some organizations have an entire function associated with inventory management. Inventory management handles raw materials from the time they are purchased until they are used in production. In recent years companies have recognized the tremendous costs associated with holding substantial amounts of raw materials. The costs include an opportunity cost associated with having money tied up with an asset that does not generate revenue and rarely increases in value, cost of obsolescence, and risk of theft or breakage. Entire systems have been developed to reduce or eliminate inventory. An event-driven system that captures data about each event in all the business processes, stores the data in a disaggregated format, and makes them available to relevant users throughout the organization alleviates the need for these specialized systems and makes relevant information available on demand.

CONCLUDING COMMENTS

This chapter has outlined the objectives and characteristics of additional business processes commonly found in most business organizations. Even though we have presented business processes separately, the last section of the chapter discussed the integration between the processes.

Traditional systems support the functional areas of an organization. In this text, business understanding and analysis (and ultimately systems architecture design) is centered around business processes rather than the functional areas that support the processes. By focusing on business processes, the information systems can support these processes and can evolve as the business processes change and require updated system support.

CHECKLIST OF KEY TERMS AND CONCEPTS

Bonding employees	Debt instruments
Cash management policy	Downsizing
Conversion business process	Employee payroll master file
Cost of operations	Equal Employment Opportunity Act

Factoring accounts receivable
Financing business process
Financing instruments
Finished goods
Headcount approval
Human resource business process
Imprest bank account
Job costing
Job time tickets
Liquid assets

Occupational Safety and Health Act
Paymaster
Payroll register
Pay voucher
Process costing
Reengineering
Rightsizing
Time cards
Work in process
Worker productivity

REVIEW QUESTIONS

1. What is the primary objective of the human resource business process?

2. Identify the three most important internal controls in a manual payroll business process. Why are these the most important?

3. List and briefly describe the key data flows in a manual payroll business process. Which data flows are added or deleted when the traditional payroll process is computerized?

4. What is the difference between payroll tax withholdings and employer payroll taxes? Identify examples of each type of tax.

5. What is an imprest checking account and why is it used for paying employees?

6. What are the key business events associated with the human resource business process?

7. What is the primary objective of reengineering business processes?

8. What role do performance evaluations serve in an organization?

9. What variables should be evaluated when completing performance evaluations? Which of these variables can be obtained from a "good" information system?

10. Describe the Equal Employment Opportunity Act (1972). How does it impact the design of the human resource information system?

11. Describe the Occupational Safety and Health Act (1970). How does it impact the design of the human resource information system?

12. What are the objectives of the financing business process?

13. Describe an effective cash management policy. What does it entail?

14. Describe a lock-box system and explain why it is used.

15. What types of funding sources are used in the financing business process?

16. What are the risks inherent in the financing business process?

17. Describe the key business events associated with the financing business process.

18. What are the inputs and outputs of the conversion business process?

19. Explain the difference between job order and process costing.

20. Who are the primary information customers of the conversion business process?

21. Why is inventory management so important for an organization?

22. Why do the conversion processes from one organization to the next differ so widely?

DISCUSSION QUESTIONS

1. Why are people considered the most valuable assets by some organizations?

2. What types of fraud can occur in the payroll business process? How can this fraud be prevented?

3. Describe separation of duties and responsibilities in a traditional manual payroll process. What types of errors and irregularities can be prevented by this separation?

4. Describe edit checks performed by the computer when the traditional payroll process is computerized. What types of errors and irregularities can be identified by these checks?

5. Why is payroll processed using a sequential batch process? Is this more efficient than an online, real-time process? Explain.

6. Describe the most likely content of an employee master file.

7. Describe the role of the control group for a computerized batch, sequential payroll process. Would you want the control group to control dissemination of all outputs from the payroll process? Why?

8. How can an event-driven system increase an organization's effectiveness in achieving its objectives in the human resource business process?

9. Describe the Assign Employees event in the human resource business process. What type of information is needed to perform this event effectively?

10. Describe the Evaluate Employees event in the human resource business process. What type of information is needed to perform this event effectively?

11. Describe the Terminate Employees event in the human resource business process. What type of information is needed to perform this event effectively?

12. Identify alternatives for obtaining additional cash in the financing business process when expected cash receipts are less than cash disbursements. Which of these is most desirable for short-term needs? Which is most desirable for long-term needs? Explain.

13. Describe separation of duties and responsibilities in a financing business process. What types of errors and irregularities can be prevented by this separation?

14. What types of fraud can occur in the financing business process? How can this fraud be prevented?

15. Describe the Invest Excess Funds event in the financing business process. What type of information is needed to effectively perform this event?

16. Describe the Approve Principal and Interest Payments event in the financing business process. What type of information is needed to effectively perform this event?

17. How are costs accumulated and reported under job costing? How are costs accumulated and reported under process costing? Why are these different?

18. Describe three key users of information about the conversion business process and the type of information they want.

19. How can an event-driven system increase an organization's effectiveness in achieving its objectives in the conversion business process?

20. If you had to rate the human resource, conversion, and financing business processes in terms of importance to an organization's success, which process would receive the highest rating and which would receive the lowest rating? Why?

21. What other business processes are most closely linked to the human resource business process and how are they linked?

22. What other business processes are most closely linked to the conversion business process and how are they linked?

23. What other business processes are most closely linked to the financing business process and how are they linked?

24. How can an event-driven system increase an organization's effectiveness in achieving its objectives in the financing business process?

MINICASES AND OTHER APPLIED LEARNING

1. Visit your library or access an information network to research derivatives and other innovative financing instruments.

Required:

Prepare a written summary of your findings. Include a discussion of the risks associated with these instruments and suggest ways an information system can help manage these risks.

2. As a group, visit a local company to gain an understanding about its personnel/payroll system.

Required:

   a. Write a one- to two-page description of the system.
   b. Identify and describe the forms, data flows, and reports they use. Be sure to include IRS forms 940 and 941 along with other quarterly payroll tax reports.
   c. From your description, develop a context diagram for the personnel/payroll system and a *REAL* graphical model that shows the significant events and their related resources, agents, and locations.
   d. Describe how the accounting data are used, if at all, in evaluating performance.

3. C-Short Company is a manufacturing entity with a very large investment in capital equipment. Newly invented computerized robotics equipment has the potential to significantly reduce manufacturing costs and improve product quality. The cost of the new equipment is $.6 million. C-Short Company does not have that much cash

available and cash flow projections indicate that this amount of cash will not be available in the near future.

C-Short is organized as a corporation. A condensed balance sheet at the end of the most recent year is as follows: (000s omitted)

Assets

Cash	$ 200
Accounts receivable	400
Inventory	600
Short-term investments	100
Long-term equity investments	600
Long-term notes receivable	800
Property, plant, and equipment	9,400
Intangible assets	400
Total	$12,500

Liabilities & Owner's Equity

Current liabilities	$ 1,000
Mortgages on land and buildings	2,500
Bonds—11%, 15-year convertible	2,500
Common stock & paid-in capital	3,000
Retained earnings	$ 3,500
Total	$12,500

Current interest rate for an 8-year note is 8 percent.

Required:

    a. Prepare an exhaustive list of alternatives for securing or acquiring the equipment or obtaining the cash needed to acquire the new equipment. What are some of the advantages and disadvantages associated with each of the alternatives?

    b. Which three alternatives would you recommend the company pursue? Why?

    c. What additional information, besides that listed above, would you like to have in making your decision and where would you expect to obtain it?

4. What control policies and procedures in a production information system would provide the best protection against the following errors? *Protection* is used broadly here to include prevent, detect, and correct.

    a. A stock clerk stole items from the raw materials stock room. Two clerks are employed but since the company runs two shifts, only one clerk is on duty at any one time.

    b. A production employee stole partially completed items from the work-in-process inventory. The items were sitting on a cart in the aisle after the polishing process was completed.

c. Production workers continued to produce the product even though its quality was below standard. The company uses a process cost system.

d. Containers with lids in which finished products are stored are always used in pairs. Also containers and lids are always purchased in pairs. However, the inventory records consistently show more lids than containers.

e. After the inspector finished inspecting the finished goods (a batch of chairs in a job costing system) he entered "20" good chairs, rather than "200" good chairs. The original job order specified 220 chairs. This created an error in both finished goods inventory and the amount of scrap for the job.

f. Production workers in a process costing system posted some of their time to Department A that they actually spent working in Department B. The workers don't like the manager of Department A and they want to get him fired.

5. Wilco Research Co. performs scientific research projects for a variety of companies around the world. The president has given you copies of the last two years' financial statements and asked you to help him determine why the most recent year's results were so disappointing, especially when they had plenty of work and all of the projects seemed to be profitable.

The company uses a job cost system. Each job is labor intensive and requires two to four months to complete. Other than direct labor, the only other cost directly traceable to a project is project materials, but on average they are only about 20% as large as direct labor. All other costs are included in various overhead accounts. No overhead, however, is charged to individual jobs. They are simply listed on the income statement as an operating expense. A review of the financial statements showed the following:

a. Direct labor compared to project revenue is in line with the company's bidding policy ($3 of revenue for each $1 of labor), which suggests that the projects were completed within the budgeted amount of time.

b. General Salaries (an overhead account) increased substantially. General Salaries contains the labor cost of the scientific researchers for time they do not charge to a specific project.

c. Laboratory Supplies (an overhead account) also increased substantially. This contains the cost of supplies not traceable to specific projects.

Required:

What are some of the important questions you would ask the president about the company's operations and information system to help identify the source of the poor performance? Relate your questions specifically to the company's information and management system over the conversion process.

6. Moroni Turkey Processing Plant—Measuring, Evaluating, and Encouraging Employee Productivity. The farmers of Moroni, Utah, joined together several years ago to organize a cooperative to improve their standard of living. The cooperative has three entities: Moroni Hatchery, Moroni Feed Processing, and Moroni Turkey Processing. Farmers who join the cooperative own the companies and share in the profits, if any, from their business activities. But equally important, the cooperative provides a business opportunity that has great earning potential, more than a dairy farm or growing hay and grain. The Hatchery manages a flock of turkeys that provide the eggs to be tended, hatched, and sold to the farmers. Farmers buy feed for their flock from the Feed Processing plant. When the birds are mature, they are killed, processed, and frozen by the Turkey Processing plant. They sell the processed birds under the Norbest label in retail stores.

The processing plant is a very large facility with about half the space for processing the birds and half the space as freezer storage for the processed birds. The processing portion of the plant has a chain-drawn line running through it in a circular motion. Birds are brought to the plant for processing and are hung on the line, about 18 inches apart, by their feet. As the line with birds hanging in it moves through the plant, the workers process the birds. This requires several steps including: killing, removing the feathers, removing the innards, cutting out any bruised meat, washing, inspecting, reinserting parts of the innards, tying the feet, wrapping in a plastic cover, and fast freezing. Some critical elements of the processing include the following:

- Farmers must take birds off feed 24 hours before processing so the birds have nothing in their digestive system at the time of processing. Birds lose a lot of weight when they are off feed for this period of time; it takes about a week for a bird to regain the weight it loses during this "fast." Therefore, once the farmer and the processing plant decide to process a flock of birds, the entire flock must be processed regardless of the amount of time required.

- The U.S. government pays meat inspectors to inspect each bird. This provides an independent and uniform check on quality.

- Some of the people who work in the processing plant are the farmers and their spouses and children, but they are in the minority. The Personnel/Payroll Department hires many other locals, but they cannot meet the labor needs of the plant. Perhaps half or more of the labor force are migrant workers who come to Moroni, Utah, for the processing season and live in mobile homes in a trailer park.

- Federal law requires the processing plant to pay overtime at $1\frac{1}{2}$ times the normal rate for time worked over 8 hours each day. Workers know that an entire flock of birds must be processed once the processing has begun. Therefore, the workers have an incentive to work slow, break a machine whenever possible, and perform similar activities to lengthen the workday. They don't have to work as hard, they have more frequent breaks, and they make more money.

- If one machine along the line is broken, the entire line must stop until the machine is fixed. While the machine is being repaired, all the line workers take a break. However, a bird cannot be on the line more than a specified amount of time (like 2 hours). If a machine is broken and it takes more than the maximum amount of time for repairs, all the birds must be removed and processed as mink feed. The return on mink feed is much less than if the birds can be sold as "human" feed.

◆ Workers can cause a machine failure by overloading it or sticking their knife into its gears.

◆ The manufacturing system collects very good information about individual birds as they are processed. To accurately pay the farmer, the system records each bird's sex, weight, and grade. The grade is either A, B, C, or D based on the amount of bruised and damaged meat. This information is passed to the Accounting Department and used as a basis to pay each farmer.

◆ Some birds take longer to process than other birds depending on their sex, weight, and grade. For example, a hen is easier to process than a tom because it is smaller and usually does not have as much bruised meat. Lightweight toms naturally weigh more than hens, have more bruised meat, and take more time for processing. Heavyweight toms are the largest; they typically have the lowest grade and take the longest time to process. The manufacturing system has good historical records on what was processed each day. This includes the farmer's name, the flock's sex, average weight, average grade, and the amount of time required for processing. In addition they know exactly how many birds were processed in each flock as well as the grade and weight of each bird. Typically, one flock will be all hens, all lightweight toms, or all heavyweight toms.

◆ The financial systems of the processing plant are not well integrated. That is, the Personnel Department has their own system to keep track of employees and the time they work. Summary data are passed to the Accounting Department, who writes the individual payroll checks and handles payroll taxes. The manufacturing process records information about the birds as they are processed and summary information is passed to Accounting to pay the farmers for their flocks. The manufacturing records are very accurate and very detailed as indicated above.

◆ Management of the processing plant controls the speed of the line. If they want to go faster, they can speed up the line. However, the workers must be able to accurately process the birds as they pass on the processing line. If they don't, the government inspectors will not approve the birds. Unapproved birds must be reworked or processed as scrap. When the workers don't like the speed of the line, they stick a knife in a machine to break it so they can take a break. Government inspectors can go much faster than the line typically moves, so they are not the bottleneck in the process.

◆ Worker attitude is a major problem. Workers are paid according to the amount of time worked—the longer they work, the more they are paid. Management of the processing plant knows the workers can do much more but they have not found the right incentive to bring about a change in attitude.

Required:

a. What is Moroni's underlying problem? Is it a cultural issue, a strategy problem, or due to poor management of people or structure, poor use of information technology, or bad measurements? (See Chapter 1 for a review of these issues.)

b. The management of Moroni have come to your for recommendations on what to do and how to go about it. What would you recommend?

7. **Personnel/Payroll Business Process.** The following personnel/payroll problems are taken from real-life situations. Unfortunately, adequate controls were not in place to prevent or detect the weaknesses. For each situation, identify the control or controls that should have prevented, detected, and helped recover from the problem:

a. A departmental secretary had the responsibility to prepare a payroll summary (including name, Social Security number, and hours worked during the period) for research assistants employed by the Chemistry Department of the university. The information for the payroll summary was taken from each research assistant's time card. Once prepared, the payroll summary was reviewed by the department chair and forwarded to the Payroll Department where checks were prepared and mailed to each research assistant. The departmental secretary defrauded the university by adding her name, Social Security number, and hours worked to the list of research assistants after the department chair had reviewed and signed the payroll summary. This happened every pay period for several months before it was detected.

b. A payroll computer programmer for a major hospital defrauded fellow employees by manipulating the program used to prepare Form W-2s at the end of the year. The programmer subtracted $1 from the total amount of federal income tax withheld from each employee and added it to his own federal income tax withholding (about $2,000). The total amounts for the year still balanced and were consistent with the total quarterly amounts reported to the IRS. The problem was discovered when a janitor, who had saved every pay stub throughout the year, totaled the federal income tax withholding for the entire year and found it was $1 different than reported on his Form W-2. Investigation of his complaint led to the discovery of the manipulation.

c. Employees in the Field Division of Del Monte Corp are paid by the hour with overtime for any time over 8 hours a day. Suppose you work in this division and after finishing your normal work for the day (5:00 PM), your supervisor sends you to mow the hay in a particular field in Fairview, Idaho. Upon arrival, you recognize the field as being owned by the supervisor. Obedient to the assignment, you connect the mower to the tractor and mow the field. Several hours later (10:00 PM) as you are leaving the field, the supervisor meets you and instructs you to put the time on your daily time card, which you always fill out manually at the end of the week. (Each day you are working in a different field; fields don't have time clocks; and your time card gets mutilated if you carry it around all week). You realize that by doing this, you will be paid overtime by the company for mowing the supervisor's field.

8. **Database Project.** The objective of this assignment is to develop a variety of evaluation measures for the conversion process of a service organization (a CPA firm). The conversion business process is where most companies distinguish their products and services from their competitors, yet we struggle in developing good information to evaluate the effectiveness of the process. Below is a short description of the conversion business process and its relationship to the personnel/payroll and sales/collection business processes for a CPA firm:

Forest & Kappa, CPAs, bills clients based on a fixed rate engagement fee that is determined at the time the engagement is secured. The engagement fee is based on the estimated number of hours required to complete the engagement (e.g., an audit) and the billing rates of the personnel (auditors) expected to perform the work. Care is taken in planning the engagement so it can be completed at a minimum cost, while ensuring quality work. Therefore, staff-level employees perform most of the detailed work and managers and partners perform reviews and handle client relations. This takes advantage of the experience of the managers and partners as well as the lower rates of the staff and senior-level people. An audit plan, developed at the time the firm bids on the work, is used to estimate the number of hours required by each level of auditor involved with the engagement. Audit plans are subsequently used to assign people to audits and individual tasks on an audit.

As auditors perform various audit tasks they record their time in the information system. (A *REAL* model of Forest & Kappa's processes is shown in Exhibits 8–10 and 8–11.) The supervisor has access to the information system to review the amount of time spent on various audit tasks. Information in this system is used to evaluate the profitability of the engagement fee, pay employees for their services, and evaluate performance. Only part of the system has been developed and information on only three audits has been entered into the system. However, management wants to get some idea of how the data within the system might be used to evaluate the firm's success on a particular audit, evaluate individual performance in completing audit tasks in a timely fashion, and evaluate the accuracy of their budgeted time for individual audit tasks. An assistant has prepared two queries and two reports that are included with the database, but additional work is needed.

Required:

(Your instructor may want you to complete this assignment in small groups.) Obtain the Microsoft Access database from your instructor to use in completing this assignment. Use the queries and reports provided with the database and other queries and reports you develop to evaluate Forest & Kappa's results of operations for the three audits entered into their database. The types of questions the managing partners want answered are summarized below. Summarize your results in memo form (not to exceed two pages plus any exhibits or charts).

a. The success of the firm in completing the audit as expected.

b. The performance of individual auditors.

c. The accuracy of the amount of time budgeted for various audit tasks.

EXHIBIT 8–10

Forest & Kappa, CPAs: Sales/Collection Process Model

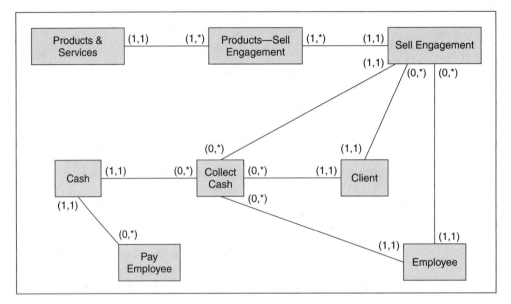

Note: The three clients for which audits have been performed are PC Palace, American Precision, and Granite Gold. The firm has 16 employees (see the EMPLOYEE table) and has 21 audit tasks that may be performed on each audit (see the AUDIT TASK table). Notice how a prompt has been entered in the "criteria" field of the Audit Time Analysis query so the user can evaluate multiple audits. You may want to use the same concept to evaluate employees and audit tasks. Notice also that the process models shown in Exhibits 8–10 and 8–11 show the intermediate tables to handle the many-to-many relationships between various entities.

9. The payroll and personnel function represents a large expense for many companies, especially the auditing divisions of accounting firms. Clients are frequently billed based on staff, manager, and partner involvement in the audit. Firms bill clients based on a predetermined rate for each person involved. For example, a company bills a partner's hours at a substantially higher rate than it bills the staff's hours. Partners also trade employees to work on different projects for different clients. Careful tracking and planning go into each audit to maintain both audit quality and the lowest possible cost to the client.

For each client engagement, an audit plan is developed to identify the type and quantity of hours necessary to complete each audit step. For example, the audit plan might specify 30 hours to count warehouse inventory. Each week auditors record their time on a time and expense report and submit it to the audit supervisor. The supervisor

EXHIBIT 8–11

Forest & Kappa, CPAs: Conversion Process Model

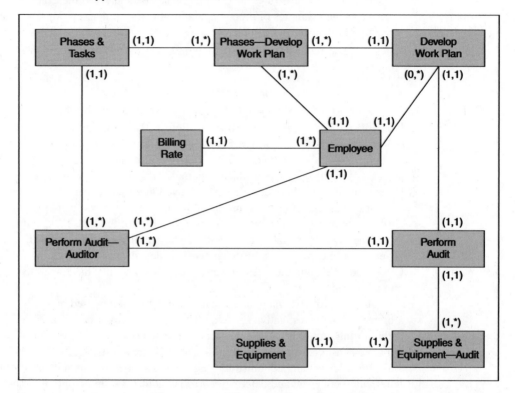

compares the actual time to the budgeted time in the audit plan. The time and expense reports are then submitted to the Payroll Department who prepares paychecks for the auditors. Each week the Payroll Department calculates pay based on a yearly salary and overtime for each employee. In addition, the Payroll Department must track deductions for state and federal taxes, FICA, insurance, a 401(K) plan, flex plans, and so on. Once the deductions are withheld, the net pay is deposited into the employee's checking account or a check is issued in the name of the employee.

Required:

   a. Prepare a context diagram for the process.
   b. Create a *REAL* model with cardinalities for the process.
   c. Create any needed tables, complete with key attributes, foreign keys, and non-key attributes.
   d. List the recording and maintaining information processes needed for these activities.

  e. For each information process listed in part *d,* draw a data flow diagram that displays the tables needed to perform the process.

  f. Identify the business rules and business risks associated with each event.

  g. List specific examples of processing control rules for determining event data accuracy, validity, and completeness in this process.

10. Refer to the scenario presented in Problem 9.

Required:

  a. Develop a prototype using a DBMS.

  b. Develop sample test data to check the accuracy of your prototype.

11. Recently, the Federal Bureau of Investigation (FBI), the Central Intelligence Agency (CIA), and the Internal Revenue Service (IRS) formed a special task force to crack down on illegal aliens who commit monetary crimes against the U.S. government and do not pay taxes on their illegal incomes. This special task force, known as the Federal Intelligence Service (FIS), has enjoyed great success and has generated huge revenues from collecting taxes on illegal income. This success can largely be attributed to the combined resources and specialties of the FBI, CIA, and IRS.

   The FIS's tremendous revenue-producing ability has caused the U.S. government to demand more FIS agents. This demand coupled with the FBI's, CIA's, and IRS's unwillingness to supply additional agents, has forced the FIS to hire new agents.

   The FIS follows many of the same hiring procedures used by the aforementioned investigative agencies. The FIS carefully screens each applicant before hiring him or her using physical endurance tests, interviews, polygraph tests, written exams, background checks, and psychological tests.

   Interviewers and administrative agents form a review committee to study the information collected and determine which candidates to hire. Only the most qualified candidates are hired. The committee chooses the best candidates and sends the candidates' files to the Office of Personnel Management, which hires the candidate, completes employment arrangements and paperwork, and establishes a start date. Salaries are nonnegotiable since the government predetermines salary levels for entry-level investigative agents.

   Agents are paid monthly, according to their pay scale, after deducting involuntary as well as voluntary deductions. Each year, on the anniversary of employment, each agent's supervisor conducts a performance evaluation. The supervisor completes a performance evaluation form that is stored in the agent's file and used later to determine promotions and pay raises.

   Agents discontinue employment in one of three ways: being terminated, quitting, or retiring. In some cases, a supervisor dismisses an agent as a result of the performance evaluation if sufficient evidence of misconduct or negligence exists to support the termination. Agents occasionally quit the agency to pursue more attractive employment options. Agents are eligible for retirement after 20 years of service, regardless of which agency (FBI, CIA, or IRS) initially employed them or where they are currently assigned. Agents may elect to remain with the FIS after 20 years but must retire by age 55. Retired agents receive retirement benefits until they die.

Required:

   a. Prepare a context diagram for the process.

   b. Create a *REAL* model with cardinalities for the process.

   c. Create any needed tables, complete with key attributes, foreign keys, and non-key attributes.

   d. List the recording and maintaining information processes needed for these activities.

   e. For each information process listed in part *d,* draw a data flow diagram that displays the tables needed to perform the process.

   f. Identify the business rules and business risks associated with each event.

   g. List specific examples of processing control rules for determining event data accuracy, validity, and completeness in this process.

12. Refer to the scenario presented in Problem 11.

Required:

   a. Develop a prototype using a DBMS.

   b. Develop sample test data to check the accuracy of your prototype.

13. The Department of Buildings (DOB) is responsible for constructing all federal buildings. This includes constructing entirely new buildings and additions to existing buildings. DOB does not perform any of the work itself but hires contractors to erect the buildings. Funding for construction projects comes from the federal agency requesting the new building or building addition.

     When a federal agency desires the addition or construction of a new building, the agency submits a building plan to DOB for approval. DOB reviews each building plan, studies its feasibility, approves or disapproves the plan, provides an estimate of the cost of approved plans, and returns the approved or disapproved building plan to the originating agency. A committee of eight managers meets each week to review and approve/disapprove new projects. A project is approved by a majority vote. Agencies with a rejected building plan may modify their original plan and resubmit it to DOB for additional consideration.

     Agencies with approved building plans contact DOB to initiate the construction or modification of a building. DOB completely handles the construction from the moment the requesting agency contacts DOB until termination of the project. DOB first drafts the project requirements using the approved building plan, then solicits bids for the given project. As each bid proposal is received, a DOB secretary photocopies and files the proposal. DOB receives bids from contractors for a minimum period of two months.

     After the bidding period, DOB carefully evaluates each bid proposal. DOB selects a contractor not by a lowest bid criterion, but by a best value measurement. This measurement is a composite score based on such factors as quality of prior work, ability to meet deadlines, and reputation. The bid selection committee, comprised of a different set of eight managers, selects the preferred contractor by a majority vote. After a contractor is selected, DOB negotiates and finalizes a contract.

Required:

a. Create a *REAL* model with cardinalities for the process.

b. For each business event listed above, identify the business risks associated with it and the business rules that could be implemented to address the risks.

14. The Department of Buildings (DOB) is responsible for maintaining and restoring all federally owned buildings. DOB does not perform any of the work itself, but hires contractors to restore and maintain U.S. government buildings. Funding for periodic maintenance and restoration comes from DOB's allocated budget.

DOB continually monitors the condition of federal buildings. Every year, DOB inspects each federal building and prioritizes building repairs. DOB then studies the alternatives to restore the building to suitable condition. A committee of eight managers meets each week to select the best alternative. Alternatives are selected by a majority vote. Any restoration project in excess of $100,000 must first be approved by the Department of Internal Affairs.

DOB completely handles building maintenance and restoration from the moment a building is constructed until its demolition. Before any new restoration project, DOB first drafts the project requirements, then solicits bids for the project. As each bid is received, a DOB secretary photocopies and files the proposal. DOB receives bids from contractors for a minimum period of two months.

After the bidding period, DOB carefully evaluates each bid proposal. DOB selects a contractor not by a lowest bid criterion, but by a best value measurement. This measurement is a composite score based on such factors as quality of prior work performed, ability to meet construction deadlines and specifications, and reputation. The bid selection committee, comprised of a different set of eight managers, selects the preferred contractor by a majority vote. After a contractor is selected, DOB negotiates and finalizes a contract with the contractor.

Required:

a. Create a *REAL* model with cardinalities for the process.

b. For each business event listed above, identify the business risks associated with it and the business rules that could be implemented to address the risks.

15. After retirement, Glen & LeRae opened a retirement center for the young at heart. The facilities at the retirement center include tennis courts, a golf course, a swimming pool, and similar recreational facilities. They sponsor off-site activities as well. Residents are free to come and go as they please.

Employee Assignments. Employees are hired to help residents and perform other necessary tasks. Several employees watch the pool and other athletic facilities to make sure everyone is safe. Other employees prepare meals, perform janitorial duties, and take residents on off-site activities as requested. Most residents prefer to use the center's van for off-site activities, thus avoiding the hassles of driving.

LeRae handles all the office and bookkeeping chores, such as cash receipts, cash disbursements, and supply purchases. LeRae has an assistant who is responsible for admitting and releasing residents, and scheduling volunteers. Glen supervises the employees and assists the residents.

Dining Area. The dining area is available to guests, as are all center facilities. Residents' meals are included in their monthly fee. However, guests are required to pay for their meals. For this reason, the menu includes prices. A chief cook supervises other cooks and orders the food.

Medical Facilities. A medical facility and a full-time nurse are available 24 hours a day. There is also an on-call doctor for emergencies. Medical expenses other than the nurse and on-call doctor are paid by residents. Nurse and doctor expenses are included in the residents' bills. Monthly check-ups by a nurse are required. These appointments are recorded on the computer to assure that all residents are examined.

Expectations. LeRae expects the computer system to record where and on what task an employee's time is spent. She uses this information to access the efficiency of the center and to decide when to hire additional employees. Of course the computer system will handle all basic business functions as well.

Required:
   a. Create a *REAL* model with cardinalities for the process.
   b. For each business event listed above, identify the business risks associated with it and the business rules that could be implemented to address the risks.

16. Deep in the heart of America's Rust Belt on the bank of the Ohio River lies Smokem Steel Mill. Smokem Steel Mill (SSM) produces steel in many different sizes, shapes, and grades. SSM uses a combination job order and process cost system to account for its processes.

Process Oriented. SSM, like other steel mills, manufactures steel through a series of processes. The mill transforms raw materials into steel by subjecting the raw materials to a series of processes. Each process is applied in a department that is specifically tooled for that type of work. The department processes are applied to mass quantities of raw materials and work in process. Work in process progressively becomes closer to a finished product as it passes through the different departments. Some characteristics of the steel (e.g., strength, purity, and shape) can be adjusted according to a particular order.

Job and Production Scheduling. The production of steel at SSM is coordinated by a job schedule. The job schedule determines when each job should begin each process. Jobs are begun by placing them on the job schedule. Jobs are placed on the job schedule in one of two ways:

   1. A customer places a steel order through an SSM salesperson.
   2. The amount of inventory in finished goods drops below acceptable levels.

These two methods are reflective of the way finished goods (steel) can be sold.

1. Steel is sold to the customer who placed an order.

2. Customers who have not placed orders can buy directly from SSM finished goods inventory. However, they may purchase only those items that have *not* been produced for a specific customer order.

Based on job orders and desired inventory levels of raw materials, a purchasing agent orders needed raw materials.

Materials can be received by truck, train, or barge from different transport companies. SSM has a critical need to keep accurate records of all material shipments received, as well as records of the supplier and the transport company. Management uses this information to evaluate suppliers and transport companies.

Department Processes. Every department adds raw materials and/or partially processes steel to the manufacturing process. Raw materials become work in process as they enter the manufacturing process. This work in process moves from department to department until it becomes a finished product.

Equipment and employees are assigned to one department only. A supervisor in each department is responsible for the work performed.

Cash Flows. All employees are paid a salary every two weeks. For effective control over cash, SSM has hired cashiers to handle cash receipts and disbursements. Cashiers are separated into cash receipt cashiers (CRC) and cash disbursement cashiers (CDC). Operating expenses are paid as incurred.

Required:

    a. Create a *REAL* model with cardinalities for the process.

    b. For each business event listed above, identify the business risks associated with it and the business rules that could be implemented to address the risks.

CHAPTER

Business Solutions, Change, and the Solution Professional: Challenges and Opportunities

CHAPTER OBJECTIVE

The objective of this chapter is to place the contents of this book into the larger framework of building business solutions. After studying this chapter, you should be able to:

+ Explain the nature of integrated business solutions.
+ Explain the principles of managing change.
+ Describe the opportunities confronting today's accounting and IT professionals.

INTRODUCTION

The concluding chapter of most texts attempts to tie together loose ends and deliver a nicely wrapped package. We do not intend to do that. Instead, we want to open a few more doors to potential options and opportunities and encourage you to ponder possible linkages to other disciplines.

During the 1980s the American Assembly of Collegiate Schools of Business (AACSB) sponsored a study by Porter and McKibbin on management education. The results of the study were published in a report entitled *Management Education and Development: Drift or Thrust into the 21st Century.*[1] According to the study, one of the primary criticisms of management education is the insufficient emphasis on integration across functional areas. The primary issue is whether the typical business school curriculum provides "sufficient

---

1 L. W. Porter and L. E. McKibbin, *Management Education and Development: Drift or Thrust into the 21st Century* (New York: McGraw-Hill, 1988).

attention to both the need to and the means to use specialized functional knowledge in an integrated approach to the increasingly complex, fast-changing, and multidimensional problems of contemporary business."

Students, faculty, and managers often specialize in a functional area like accounting, marketing, finance, systems, *or* organizational behavior and largely ignore the other areas. Such a narrow focus creates a stovepipe mentality in which people focus on *accounting* or *marketing* rather than *business* problems. This mind-set deemphasizes the relationship of accounting to strategy, business processes, organization structure, IT application architecture, or nonfinancial measurements.

Throughout this book we have discussed how accountants can enhance their value by:

* Defining rules to shape and control business processes.
* Embedding information processes into business processes and executing rules over the business process while capturing and storing detailed data about business processes in real time.
* Providing useful information to decision makers for planning, executing, controlling, and evaluating business processes.

These objectives represent a radical expansion of the scope of accounting. In this chapter we want to go even further by framing the future of accounting in the context of business solutions and change management.

THE NATURE OF BUSINESS SOLUTIONS

Many approaches have been advanced to solve business problems with only limited success. Some solutions emphasize the positioning of products and services to capitalize on an organization's strengths and opportunities. Some approaches emphasize stewardship responsibilities by redesigning the organization around self-managing teams. Other approaches recommend new technology and/or systems such as executive information systems (EIS) or Enterprise Resource Planning (ERP) systems. Still other approaches try to solve business problems by changing an organization's culture.

Each of these and other solutions provides some benefit, but most have provided only marginal success. This unending stream of approaches has left some people and organizations disappointed, divided, and even disabled. They are disappointed because of overpromised and underdelivered solutions; divided along functional boundaries, product lines, or solution disciplines; and disabled because people have given their best efforts but have had limited success in correcting the problems. As a result, many people are less eager to try something new. They seem convinced that nothing can fix their problems and they resist future changes to protect themselves from further frustration and exhaustion.

What do we know about developing solutions to business problems? Experience shows that successful business solutions adhere to the following principles and characteristics:

- First, solutions must integrate five key components:
  — Business processes and events.
  — Business strategy.
  — Organization structure and individual stewardship responsibilities.
  — IT architecture.
  — Measurements.
- Second, the solution must be aligned with the organization's culture.
- Third, solutions must constantly adapt to a complex, changing world in real time. There is no such thing as a permanent, integrated business solution.

Exhibit 9–1 presents the solution components. As this exhibit illustrates, business processes and events are closely related to an organization's strategy, structures, IT architecture, and measurements. The business processes serve as the foundation for defining effective business solutions but business processes must be integrated and aligned with other solution components. To this point, this text has primarily discussed the relationship between an organization's business processes and IT application architecture. Let's review this relationship as well as the other relationships of the solution framework.

Business Processes and Strategy

Translating strategic objectives into effective business process design is challenging. The lack of a clear definition of business processes has been the principal cause of a long-standing disconnect between strategy formulation and implementation. *REAL* modeling provides a method for making this important connection by focusing on business processes

EXHIBIT 9–1

Template for Building Business Solutions

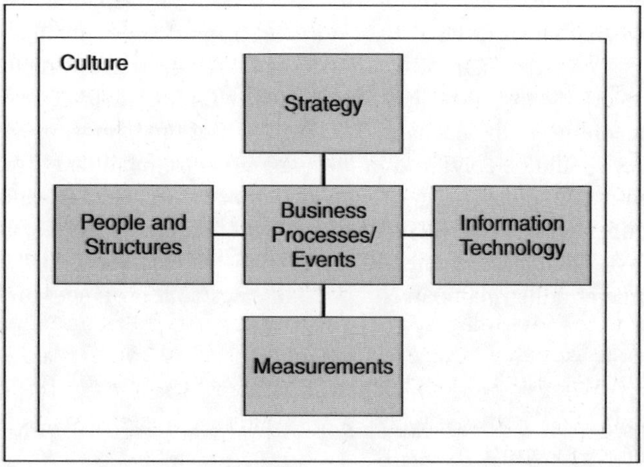

and emphasizing their role in achieving strategic objectives. Defining business processes improves strategic thinking by providing a precise way to think about what a business does and what it should do in the future.[2]

Linking and aligning strategy and business processes provide a framework for prioritizing business processes and events as an organization strives to create value. In the final analysis, the customer is the final arbiter of value. The events and processes that directly support the products and services demanded by customers are those that are most important. Everything else an organization does should support the events that create customer value. In this light, strategically significant business events are often classified as follows:

1. *Core business events.* Events that create distinctiveness for the business in the marketplace.
2. *Support events.* Events that facilitate the core business events.

Organizations should work to eliminate events and related information processes that do not fit into one of these categories.

Business Processes and Organization Structures/Individual Stewardship

Some organizations are experimenting with alternative organization structures, but most organizations are still structured along functional boundaries (e.g., production, accounting, information systems, marketing, or finance). These stovepiped organization structures cause gaps and overlaps of responsibilities for business processes. Gaps and overlaps can result in process management being uncoordinated, overcoordinated, or nonexistent.

For example, the typical order management cycle originates in the *Marketing Department* where orders are generated. A clerk in the Customer Service Department handles order entry. The Production Department and the Shipping Department typically handle product manufacturing and product shipping. Billing and collection is the responsibility of the *Finance Department.* Finally, the Service Department handles any postservices for product repair or warranty work.[3]

An alternative to a functional organizational structure is to align the structure according to the business processes. *REAL* models define stewardship responsibilities according to the business processes. Using this philosophy, the stewardship responsibilities should be contained in the same organizational unit. For example, the roles for order entry, shipping, and collection as outlined on a *REAL* business model of the sales/collection process would all be contained within a single organization structure. This enables the organization to seamlessly manage all interactions with a customer from order to cash receipt rather than parceling out all sales/collection activities to a variety of functionally

---

2 L. T. Perry and E. L. Denna, "Reengineering Redux," *Business Process Re-engineering & Major Organizational Change,* February 1995.

3 B. P. Shapiro, V. K. Rangan, and J. J. Sviokla, "Staple Yourself to an Order," *Harvard Business Review,* July–August 1992, pp. 113–22.

separate areas. The stewardship defined in the *REAL* model represents roles that can be filled by individuals or by teams reporting to a single business process owner who reports to a multiple process owner (see Exhibit 9–2). A business process–driven organization structure focuses on shaping the structure around the work to be performed throughout all the business processes.

Our experience has shown that the most efficient way to manage a process and make sure it is properly planned, controlled, and evaluated is to organize the process events and their respective stewards within one organization structure. Otherwise, the process and its supporting systems will eventually become arbitrarily divided among management or functional groups, resulting in "turf wars" as well as gaps and overlaps in managing the separate events within the business process.

Business Processes and IT Architecture

Business processes also serve as a foundation for developing an IT application architecture that overcomes the weaknesses of the traditional IT architecture such as a myriad of duplicate or overlapping systems that do not interface (as discussed in Chapters 2 and 3). A business event–driven IT application architecture encourages organizations to support business events and processes with a simpler, more integrated architecture comprised of three information process categories as illustrated in Exhibit 9–3. Business event data are

EXHIBIT 9–2

Organization Structure Based on Business Processes

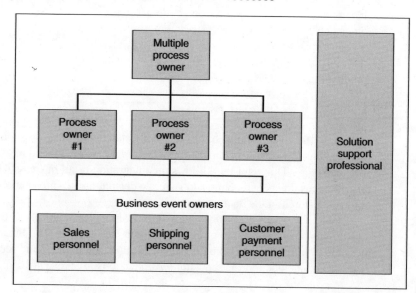

EXHIBIT 9-3

IT Application Architecture: Record, Maintain, and Report

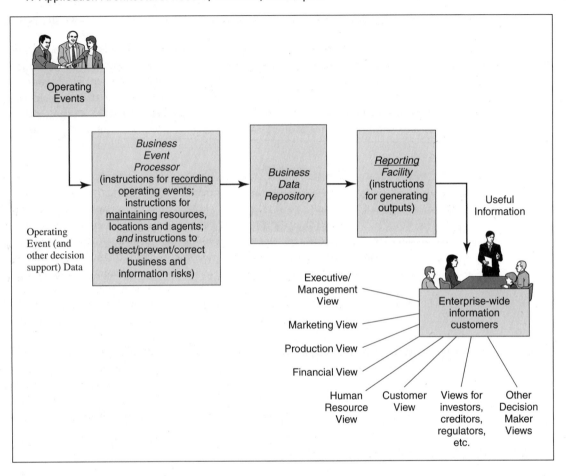

captured as the event occurs and business rules and controls are applied to verify the accuracy and completeness of the data. Captured data are stored and maintained in the business repository. This repository allows the integration of all business data. Authorized information customers can define and generate desired useful information (within the scope of the data stored in the data repository).

Output views of the business can range from financial analyses, to production schedules, to customer profiles, to employee productivity reports. The breadth of information available to information customers is dependent on the number and scope of the business process data included in the repository. Applications in an event-driven architecture are a collection of recording, maintaining, and reporting rules that govern how data and information are captured and reported.

Business Processes and Measurements

Traditional business measurements are generally aligned to functional boundaries. Since each function is typically involved in only a portion of a business process, functionally focused measurements provide only partial views of business processes. Furthermore, because the functionally driven systems have significant gaps and overlaps in stored data and processing, an organization can only capture partial, overlapping, or even competing views of the business process. The definition of traditional accounting information is often too narrow, due to the emphasis on financial reporting measurements driven by GAAP.

An event-driven architecture provides decision makers with a clean slate upon which they can rethink the measurements they use in their decision-making activities. Focusing on business processes can result in a fundamental shift in the types of measurements an organization uses to plan, control, and evaluate its business processes. A business process focus calls attention to cycle times, resource utilization, employee productivity, how business processes and activities are related, and resource availability and needs. Often, traditional views do not provide information that enables an organization to effectively manage its business processes. An event-driven IT application architecture makes such measurements both possible and affordable. For example, rather than looking at estimated cost variances, organizations can examine the actual costs of business events over time to identify trends.

In summary, when developing a business solution, you need to first obtain an understanding of the business processes and then consider all solution components. We often refer to solutions that follow these principles as *event-driven business solutions.* Switching to a new architecture requires a paradigm shift for many people. Change is often difficult for everyone involved, so let's discuss the challenges of managing change.

THE NEW BUSINESS CONSTANT: CHANGE

This text has argued that organizations should anticipate the need to update their information and business processes in this dynamic business environment. *Change* in a broad sense is a planned or unplanned response to pressures and forces. The need to change is now the norm. With change comes the challenge of change management. Managing change cannot be trivialized and must be considered while defining, developing, executing, and evaluating new ways of doing things. Change management is a long and tedious process. Although many changes can be planned and anticipated, often change brings unanticipated, even unintended, impacts and implications. Changes in political systems, economies, technology, and societal preference over the past 10 years have provided ample evidence of our dynamic world. As science fiction writer Isaac Asimov once explained:

It's easier to foresee the automobile than the traffic jam, the atom bomb than nuclear stalemate, the birth control pill than women's liberation. Put another way, the march of technology is inexorable and, to some extent, predictable. But the resulting corporate organizational and managerial ramifications are much harder to imagine.

Some individuals or organizations proceed with a change until the people involved with the change resist it. The problem with this reactive posture is that by the time the negative reaction is exhibited, it is typically too late to do anything about it. Those who develop and implement innovative business solutions should understand the impact of change on human behavior and principles for managing change.

Types of Organizational Change

Organizational change can be classified according to its scope and depth.[4]

- *Developmental change* is the improvement of an existing system. If for some reason the current system does not measure up to its expectations, organizations make fine tuning–type changes to bring it in line with expectations.
- *Transitional change* is the implementation of a known new state. Current ways of doing things are replaced with a new process. The key here is that the old system is replaced with a new system and the new system is developed prior to implementation. This type of change typically involves several steps, such as design, development, pilot tests, and phased-in operations.
- *Transformational change* is the emergence of a new state. It is a radical change where you essentially trash what exists for something new, but what is new is not yet known. The new state becomes known over time as the organization reconceptualizes its mission, culture, critical success factors, form, and leadership.

Determining the type of organization change required is critical. Both the depth and complexity of implementation grow as you move from developmental, to transitional, to transformational change. Most information systems changes would be classified as *developmental* or *transitional* changes. Because of reporting requirements and management's constant need for information, rarely can an organization discard its current information systems and let a new system emerge out of the chaotic death of the old system.

Some important questions to ask when determining the type of change best suited for an organization include:

1. How far do we want to go? Is this too far or not far enough?
2. What type of result do we want: short term or long term?
3. How much change can the organization absorb in one change and cumulatively?

---

4 Linda Ackerman, "Development, Transition or Transformation: The Question of Change in Organizations," *OD Practitioner,* December 1986, pp. 1–8.

4. Can the changes contemplated be presented positively? If not, why?

5. What happens if we don't change?[5]

Deciding When to Change

The decision about when to change is as important as what to change and how much to change. There are several strategies:

- Change when things are going well. Organizations that make this choice are leaders who anticipate pressures on the horizon and make change as a matter of foresight and preparation. Companies that adopt this philosophy truly believe that if they are not routinely changing themselves they risk complacency and stagnation.

- Change when results are mixed. These changes are made when there are some problems but they are not life threatening. Situations arise that management feels need attention, but the need is not pressing. For example, "It would be nice to know which machines require timely maintenance." or "If I knew how much set-up time was required with each product I could better manage production scheduling."

- Change demanded by a full-fledged crisis. For example, some changes are required to avoid a loss of competitive advantage, loss of major customers, or to satisfy a new reporting requirement by the Financial or Governmental Accounting Standards Board.

Deciding when to change requires a careful balance. Waiting until a crisis demands change often is more expensive as deadlines place demands on development schedules that would not be required with more advanced planning. Waiting until a crisis exists may indicate a more fundamental problem in the organization, such as inattentiveness to problems and unwillingness to introduce change to confront a situation. Making change before a "problem" or "crisis" exists is equally difficult. Many people have the attitude If it isn't broke, then don't try to fix it! Creating an artificial crisis by crying wolf may work in the short run, but people see through this strategy and lose confidence in leaders because of the leaders' dishonesty and deceitfulness. Deciding when to change requires a keen sense of timing and leadership.

Managing Change and Creating a Common Vision

One of the most important factors in implementing change is developing a common vision of the finished "product." To do this all members of the organization need to understand the problem being addressed, the approach to solving the problem, and the final product to be developed. People must understand the "problem" or threat and buy into the need for a solution.

Few things create greater uncertainty and resistance within organizations than individuals not knowing the reason and extent of a change. Management should make every

---

5 Todd Jick, *Managing Change: Cases and Concepts* (Burr Ridge, IL: Richard D. Irwin, 1993), p. 3.

effort to prevent any surprises by informing all affected parties in an effort to minimize or reduce the resistance to change. People must understand what needs to be done, the part they will play, and how to perform their assigned tasks. Envisioning the end product includes developing expectations well grounded in reality.

Once the problem is identified and communicated, the change project scope, depth, pace, and implementation strategy must be determined. *Scope* refers to the size of a project and what will and will not be included within the project. When you define *scope* you draw a boundary line that delineates what the project will and will not accomplish. *Depth* refers to the number and magnitude of changes. *Pace* refers to the speed with which the change is designed and implemented. The implementation strategy choices include implementing the change all at once, phasing in over an extended period of time, running a parallel system with the existing system, or implementing a pilot project in some small portion of the organization.

Change managers must also consider factors related to organization culture, participation, and performance evaluation.

Organization Culture   Each organization has a unique culture that distinguishes it from all others. Changes should support rather than challenge the organization's culture. Proper use of information technology should not presuppose an organization culture or structure. Quite the opposite, the technology should allow an organization to choose the culture and structure it desires.

Participation   Allowing people to participate in identifying the problem, the solution approach, and the final product is the most powerful technique for creating a common vision and the support to achieve it. People become committed to what they help develop.

Before attempting a change, management must carefully analyze the capabilities of those participating in the change process. If the organization's people are technically weak and grounded in traditional ways of thinking and operating, initiating a significant change involving technology will require much more careful planning and creative thinking than in organizations with technological expertise.

Equally important is ensuring widespread representation throughout the organization during the change process. Participants should represent various organization stewards and responsibilities. Favoring one particular type of participant over another can cause dysfunctional behavior on the part of those who feel left out or uninformed.

Performance Evaluation   Because changes often alter people's responsibilities, organization and system changes often impact the way individual performance should be measured and evaluated. Unless the performance evaluation process is updated, changes may obscure personal performance, thus creating disincentives for supporting the proposed changes.

When people don't understand and agree on the problem, the change effort, or the approach to solve the problem, and share a common vision of the finished product, they are likely to resist any efforts of management to move them toward a desired end. This resistance is usually manifested in some type of dysfunctional behavior.

Dysfunctional Human Behavior   People react to change based on how it affects them personally. While some people are unaffected by a change, other people must change what they do, how they perform their work, who they work with, and even their informal associations within the organization. When people conclude that a change has a negative effect on them, their behavior can become quite dysfunctional and their actions can endanger themselves and the enterprise. Most dysfunctional human behavior is manifest in one, or more, of three ways:

> *Aggression* involves any attempt by an individual or group to damage the organization or its information system. For example, when several manufacturers introduced robotics technology into the assembly line, employees in these organizations saw the robots as a threat to their long-term employment stability. As a result, they did several things to sabotage the move. Some employees poured drinks on the computer keyboards, while others "accidentally" knocked computers off their stands making them crash to the floor. This ruined several workstations used to control the robots and drove up the cost of the technology.

> *Projection* involves any effort to blame the system for problems that people face. Systems, whether computerized or not, are often blamed for everything from ordering too many items of a particular product to losing an order altogether. You have no doubt had the experience of making a restaurant reservation by telephone and, upon arriving, found that they had lost your reservation for your family and 15 friends. "Our computer must have lost your reservation," is the typical response.

> *Avoidance* involves any attempt to avoid using the system. For example, in recent years several large banks became concerned about inconsistencies in the application of loan approval policies across loan officers. Some banks used expert systems to standardize the approval process and assist loan officers in evaluating loan applications. During the development process, however, only a few loan officers were involved. The new system made loan officers little more than glorified data entry clerks. As a result, loan officers avoided the system altogether and reverted back to the old process. The bank eventually pulled the system and made substantial modifications to cater to the preferences of its loan officers although hundreds of thousands of dollars had been spent on the system.

Changing current processes, responsibilities, or uses of information technology spawns most dysfunctional behavior. Properly managing the process of defining, developing, executing, and evaluating processes, people, and technology is the key to minimizing the dysfunctional behavior of the people affected by the change.

Responsibilities for Managing Change

We suggest a division of responsibilities for managing change among management, employees, and IT specialists:

Management Should:

◆ Openly support efforts to continually improve all aspects of the organization.

◆ Determine timing for enterprisewide changes.

◆ Approve suggestions for improvement.

◆ Monitor progress of approved changes and ensure that measurement systems are adjusted quickly.

◆ Assist in resolving problems resulting from change.

Employees Should:

◆ Commit to continual individual and organization improvement.

◆ Actively participate in suggesting and implementing changes.

◆ Demand creative solutions to business and information problems.

Change Agents (those who guide or develop the business solutions) Should:

◆ Understand the impact of IT as a change agent.

◆ Deal with problems in a timely and effective manner.

Following suggestions such as these increases the likelihood of successfully cultivating a culture of continual improvement and facilitating an organization's efforts to continually improve. Change management is a complex and challenging field. As a business professional, it is important that you be aware of this. We encourage you to seek out some of the numerous change management references to learn more about it.

THE FUTURE OF ACCOUNTING, IT, AND BUSINESS SOLUTIONS

This book does not contain many of the conventions of traditional accounting system architecture for a very good reason. The authors of this text believe that accounting is primarily concerned with two objectives:

1. Providing useful information (measurements) to support decision making.
2. Helping organizations identify and control risks with business and information processes.

Unfortunately, these two objectives are often lost when studying an accounting system architecture based on debits, credits, and other artifacts (e.g., journals, ledgers, and charts of accounts). We realize that the two objectives do not include the word *accounting*. Yet, these objectives describe the goals of most information professionals. The artificial boundaries and labels given to information (such as *accounting information* versus *management information* versus *executive information* versus *marketing information*) are going away and being replaced with one label: the information needed to more effectively execute and evaluate the various activities of an organization.

In this text, we have attempted to provide a look at both the past and the future. An understanding of the past is important in understanding current and future directions. An idea of where things are headed makes you better able to take advantage of changes and new opportunities.

We have outlined new opportunities for information professionals. Organizations need help in using IT to provide useful information and to control business and information processes. However, to do so will require significant change in traditional system architectures and the skill set of those who develop and use IT solutions.

Businesspeople who are responsible for planning, influencing, and evaluating an organization's business processes need the assistance of professionals who understand strategy, organization structure, process, measurement, and IT/information system issues. These skills are no longer divided arbitrarily among accounting, information systems, finance, organization behavior, and other disciplines. Instead, they must be integrated (as illustrated in Exhibit 9–4) into a single set. We believe accountants and other information professionals can prepare themselves to become the solution professionals of the information age.

Gary Sundem, past president of the American Accounting Association summarized accounting's current situation when he wrote:

> Accounting finds itself in a position similar to that of the railroads earlier this century. If
> we define our product narrowly, such as providing rail transportation, demand is likely to

EXHIBIT 9–4

IS Professionals Provide Integration and Structure

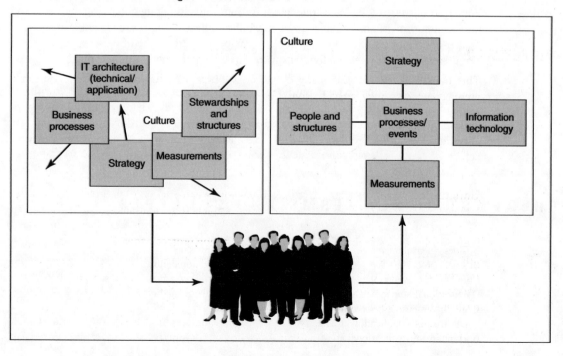

decrease. If we define it broadly, such as transporting goods, demand will increase. But to define accounting broadly, as production and communication of economic information, we have to recognize changes in the desirable characteristics of information that give it value. I have concerns that not only are we not recognizing these changes, but we do not have a system that motivates such recognition. On the other hand, the role of information in society is becoming more important, so providers of the right kinds of information may produce one of the most valuable and hence best selling products in the future. For accountants to continue to sell their services at premium prices, they must be the producers of "state-of-the art" information.

This and similar observations make it clear that accounting, and therefore the accounting system, must and will change. Although it is clear that the profession will change, the question is whether individual professionals will change. Throughout this book, we have laid a foundation for learning that helps accounting professionals deal with the issues raised by Sundem, the AICPA, and countless others. Rather than predicting the decline of a profession, this book is about increasing the value of accounting during an exciting, evolutionary period in the profession. As AICPA Chair Robert Mednick suggested, accountants can become "premier information professionals in a world of electronic commerce and virtual global trade," but the time to begin the rigorous preparation is now.

SEIZE THE DAY!

We began this text by laying a foundation for innovative thinking about accounting as an information profession. We sincerely believe the profession has never faced a time with greater opportunities. We hope this book has helped identify some of those opportunities. Today's organizations need individuals who can develop business solutions that coordinate strategy, processes, structures, measurements, and the use of IT. Organizations can no longer afford specialization without integration. Specialists need to understand how their skills interact and integrate with the skills of other specialties. There is great opportunity in developing and maintaining a set of skills that allow you to coordinate the components of business solutions. Professionals who seize the day will see their value blossom as never before.

CHECKLIST OF KEY TERMS AND CONCEPTS

Business data repository (data warehouse)	Managing change
Business measurements	Measurements
Business processes	Organization culture
Core business events	Organization structures and stewardship
Dysfunctional human behavior	Stovepipe mentality
Event-driven business solution	Strategy
Event-driven IT application architecture	Support events
Integration across functional areas	

REVIEW QUESTIONS

1. What do Porter and McKibbin say has been an area of weakness for business schools in general?
2. What is the problem with a stovepipe mentality (a focus on functional areas of business) and what aspects of the business should be integrated?
3. How can an accountant enhance his/her value within an organization?
4. What effect have overpromised and underdelivered solutions had in some organizations?
5. What are the essential components of an effective business solution?
6. List the guiding principles for developing an effective business solution.
7. What role does understanding an organization's business processes play in implementing a solution framework?
8. How does understanding an organization's business processes enhance strategic efforts?
9. What is a core business event? Give an example.
10. What is a support event? Give an example.
11. What should an organization do with the events that do not fall into the core business event or support event categories? Why?
12. What is business event–driven IT application architecture?
13. Describe the primary focus of an event-driven business process in terms of business measurements.
14. Identify and describe the three types of organizational change.
15. Describe the three strategies for determining when to make an organization change.
16. Describe scope, depth, pace, and implementation strategy when planning and enabling change.
17. How is most dysfunctional behavior manifested?

DISCUSSION QUESTIONS

1. If management education lacks emphasis on integrating functional areas, how could the education process be changed to incorporate an integrated focus?
2. How can an accountant break down the walls between the functional areas within an organization and help align the functional areas to focus on achieving the overall organizational objectives and strategies?
3. Why have so many approaches to business solutions emerged within the past decade and why have so many of these solutions failed?
4. Who is the final arbiter of value? Why? What implications does the final arbiter of value have on an organization's business processes?

5. What would an organization look and feel like if it was aligned by business processes instead of by functional areas?

6. How can an organization prevent its IT strategy and overall business strategy from diverging?

7. Describe one alternative to aligning an organization's structure along functional boundaries. How is this alternative better or worse than aligning an organization's structure along functional boundaries?

8. Most systems projects would be classified as what type of organizational change? Why?

9. Why is waiting until there is a full-fledged crisis to make an organizational change a poor strategy?

10. What are the problems and benefits of making an organizational change when things are going well?

11. Why is a vision of the final product one of the most important factors in implementing change? How can an organization help its members create a vision of the final product?

12. How should business solution professionals and management manage change?

13. If you wanted to implement significant change within an organization, how would you go about doing it?

14. Why is participation in planning and implementing an organizational change so important?

15. What do you think the role of the accountant should be?

MINICASES AND OTHER APPLIED LEARNING

1. Visit your library or access an information network to locate articles that discuss examples of how organizations are managing change.

Required:
Prepare a written summary of your findings.

2. Visit your library or access an information network to locate articles that discuss examples of how organizations are redefining their structure.

Required:
Prepare a written summary of your findings.

3. Visit your library or access an information network to locate articles that discuss the AICPA's Vision Project.

Required:
Prepare a written summary of your findings and the impact you expect the project to have on the profession.

4. Susan Green was the bookkeeper for Marty's Distributing Co., a distributor of Budweiser and Miller beers. Being a rather small company, all of the daily accounting work could be performed by one employee. In addition to Susan, there were five men who ran the warehouse and delivered the beer. Marty was the president and owner of the company. When he was not jogging or skiing, he supervised the warehouse/delivery men as well as the front office.

For several years profits have been very good and sales have grown faster than industry averages. Marty's times at cross-country ski races and road races have dropped steadily and have reached a point where he is a consistent winner. Life seemed good except for the pressure he was receiving from the breweries to computerize his accounting system. With strong encouragement from them and a little guidance from a CPA friend, Marty bought a new IBM computer and accounting software to accompany it.

Only one day was required to set up the hardware, install the software, and convert the files. Sue seemed surprised the morning the CPA walked into her office carrying the new computer. However, she only complained a little as he rearranged her office to make room for the computer. The software company provided two days of training on their system; one on the same day the computer was delivered and another about a week later. Marty hung around the office to observe the first day of training. Sue seemed to have a hard time learning how to run the computer and enter the data. She seemed to have a mind block. Even at the end of the day she had difficulty correctly loading a floppy disk in the disk drive. As a result, the decision was made to run the manual and computer systems in parallel for one month to verify the accuracy of the new computer system.

Things did not go well during the month of parallel processing. Sue constantly complained about either not having enough time to run both systems, or that she did not understand how to run the computer system. To keep things up to date, Marty started to run the computer system by himself. It only took him three or four hours each day, but those were the hours he generally spent skiing or jogging. Suddenly, life was not so great anymore.

Marty found that much of the three or four hours spent on the accounting system was devoted to identifying discrepancies between the computer and manual results. When the error was located, it was almost always in the manual system. Therefore, Marty's confidence in the new computer system increased significantly.

At the end of the month, Marty was ready to scrap the manual system and go entirely with the computer system. Sue wasn't quite ready. Marty went back to skiing and jogging and Sue went on with the manual system. When Marty saw that the computer system was falling behind, he again spent personal time to catch it up. He also spent time with Sue to make sure she understood how to run the computer system. He also sent her to more training by the software company and to a two-day computer training session sponsored by IBM.

After two more months, many more hours of Marty's time keeping the computer system up to date, and many more hours helping Sue understand what she was supposed to do, Marty was at the height of his frustration. "Sue should know how to run the system, but she doesn't seem to want to do it. I can do all the accounting work on the computer in a few hours each day, but she cannot even do it in her normal eight-hour workday. What shall I do about my problem?" asked Marty.

Required:

    a. In retrospect, how should Marty's Distributing Co. have handled the computerization of their accounting system?

    b. What would you recommend at this point?

5. Jeans, Inc., manufactures and sells denim jeans to retail outlets. Suppose you work in the Information Systems Department of Jeans, Inc., and your most recent assignment is to work with a cross-functional team to modify the payment system for manufacturing employees. Information about the current production and payment systems, the proposed system, and your assigned roll on the team is outlined below.

    Manufacturing workers currently perform a single task repeatedly. These are special tasks like sewing pockets or zippers, or attaching belt loops using specialized machines like a pocket setter, a fly stitcher, or a belt looper. Workers' pay is calculated using a piecework system according to the amount of work each worker completes. The partially processed jeans flow from one specialized task to the next. As a result, there are piles of partially processed jeans at each workstation. This causes the dollar value of work in process to be fairly high at all times. Speed in garment making, and the amount of a worker's pay, relates directly to a worker's skill and stamina for the grueling, repetitive motions of joining and stitching fabric. One negative aspect of the current process is the number of work-related injuries caused by workers pushing to make piecework goals. Management has a great desire to increase productivity, reduce the monotony of the current systems, and cut the number of repetitive-stress injuries.

    The new system will organize employees into groups of 10 to 35 workers who will share the tasks of making jeans. The new structure is designed to allow self-managing teams. The teams are free to design the layout of their machines, assign people to each task, and rotate the tasks among team members to avoid the repetitive nature of the old piece-rate system. The team concept is designed to free workers from having to "park their brains at the factory gate" and enable them to better manage themselves and to devise better, safer sewing practices. Each sewing team will produce finished pairs of pants every day and will be responsible for the quality of the finished product. One of the benefits of this system is that it will reduce, or entirely eliminate, the work in process. All the workers in the team will be paid according to the total number of pants the group completes and the finished quality of them. Another of the hoped-for benefits of the proposed system is an increase in productivity from the smaller work groups and the peer pressure higher producers will put on lower producers.

    The information systems of the company need to be modified to capture data on group performance rather than individual performance. The system will need to keep track of the members of each team, the number of pants produced each day, and the number and type of defects in the finished product.

Required:

    a. Top management has determined they want to move off the old piece-rate system to the new team-based system. The team to which you have been assigned has been given the task of implementing the change throughout the organization. You are to attend a meeting later in the day to decide how the change should be implemented and each person is to make a 5-minute presentation on his or her views about an implementation plan. Write and briefly explain the key points of your proposed implementation plan. To what extent do you think the employees should be involved in the decision to adopt the new team-based system and how it will be implemented? What type of employee training should be included?

    b. Evaluate the proposed change from an employee's perspective. Is the proposal appealing to you? Why or why not? Are there any weaknesses in the proposed team-based system? What is your responsibility, if any, as a member of the implementation team to voice these concerns?

6. Levi Strauss & Co. instituted a team-based system for manufacturing their famous denim jeans six years ago. The team-based plan replaced a piece-rate production system that had been in place for many years. Under the team-based plan employees were organized into groups of 10 to 35 workers who shared the tasks of making jeans. The team structure allowed the teams to be self-managed. Teams were free to design the layout of their machines, assign people to each task, and rotate the tasks among team members. The team concept was designed to empower workers, to enable them to better manage themselves, and to devise better, safer sewing practices. Each sewing team produces finished pairs of pants every day and is responsible for the quality of the finished product.

    The team-based system eliminated all work in process inventory. Also, the turnaround time (i.e., the time from when an order is received to when the products are shipped to retail customers) improved from nine weeks to seven weeks. However, there are several significant disadvantages with the system:

- Productivity declined 23 percent in the first year of the team-based system. Even though productivity has improved since then, it is still 7 percent below the old piecework level.
- Even though workers were given seminars on team building and problem solving, most teams have not been able to maintain cordial working relationships. Peer pressure on slower workers is intense and often dysfunctional. For example, one seamstress had to restrain a co-worker who had picked up a chair and was about to throw it at a woman who constantly needled her about slow work.
- Divvying up the work of absent team members often led to trouble. During one such dispute an 11-year veteran says a teammate threatened to kill her. According

to a police report, the teammate had previously taken a stress leave, during which time she thought about wanting to tie up her co-worker, shoot her in the head, and watch her die.

- Workers were inadequately trained to fill their empowered roles and broadened responsibilities. Workers lacked training on issues like balancing workflows or spotting quality problems.
- The team concept created inequities in employee compensation. Wages of the top performers fell (from around $8.75 to $7.00 per hour) and the wages of lower skilled workers often increased.
- The climate of the organization has changed substantially in the last six years. Levi was once classified as one of the best companies to work for, by management gurus and by magazines like *Working Mother.* Now the stress of working at Levi is so bad employees say they feel relieved when they are terminated. According to one employee, "I hate teams. Levi's is not the place it used to be."[6]

Top management feels a need to make a change. One option is to close the factory and contract the work with offshore factories that may be able to perform the work cheaper. Another option is to rework the production process and the payment system.

Required:

a. How could a such a great company with bright people and hard workers make what appears to be such a bad decision in switching from the piece-rate system to the team-based system?

b. How should management have handled the change to the team-based plan? Should employees be involved in making the next change? If so, how?

Organizational and Program Flow charts

macro - overall

micro - detailed

---

6 This and Minicase 5 are based on an article written by Ralph T. King, Jr., "Jeans Therapy: Levi's Factory Workers Are Assigned to Teams, and Morale Takes a Hit," *The Wall Street Journal,* May 20, 1998, p. A-1.

Flowcharts and Data Flow Diagrams

James Rinaldi

SUPPLEMENT OBJECTIVE

The objective of this supplement is to introduce two types of documentation tools: flowcharts and data flow diagrams. After studying this supplement, you should be able to:

* Describe and prepare flowcharts describing the information system and the documents and procedures used in the system.
* Describe and prepare data flow diagrams depicting the flow of data through the system.

FLOWCHARTING

Purpose and Description

Often, it is necessary to document details about an information system. You could produce a voluminous written narrative describing the who, what, when, and where of the system. However, there is a concise alternative. *Flowcharting* is used to graphically document information systems. Pages of narrative describing system processes and data/document flows can be succinctly summarized using a simple flowchart. Unlike more conceptual tools, flowcharting focuses on the physical aspects of information flows and processes. The objective of this portion of the supplement is to help you develop the skills necessary to prepare and interpret flowcharts.

Flowcharts are used to describe an entire information system or some portion of it. The entire information system contains input into a manual and/or computer process and some type of output. The output may be distributed to users to aid in decision making or retained and subsequently used as input into another process. *Systems flowcharts* are used to illustrate the entire information system. Sometimes a flowchart will focus on some aspect of the system, such as the documents used in the system and the procedures performed on them or the hardware used in a computer processing environment. Other flowcharts focus entirely on the logic of computer programs that process the input data, maintain data files, and prepare reports.

The different types of flowcharts are as follows:

Systems flowcharts show the entire system configuration, including the documents, data flows, and processes of a system.

Document/procedure flowcharts show the creation, flow, and destinations of documents within a system and the procedures performed on them.

Hardware flowcharts show the hardware configuration of a system.

Program flowcharts show the logic and processing steps of a computer program.

To manually create flowcharts, you can draw freehand or use a flowcharting template that can be purchased for a few dollars. However, there are a variety of easy-to-use flowcharting packages on the market today. This supplement and text deal primarily with systems and document/procedure flowcharts.

The Basic Elements of Systems/Document Flowcharts

Document flowcharts consist of three simple graphical elements that can be combined to represent various types of physical information flows and processes:

1. Symbols.
2. Flow lines.
3. Areas of responsibility.

[handwritten: Origin – start   termination – finish]

The documents and processes of information systems can be illustrated by linking various symbols together as shown in Exhibits A–1, and A–2. Compare the following explanation of each process with its flowchart before we discuss the detailed conventions for preparing flowcharts.

> Exhibit A–1 illustrates the typical document flow in a manual accounting system. Employees throughout the organization begin the accounting process as they record transaction information on various source documents. Generally, there are multiple copies of the documents. In this example, the source document has an original and two copies. The original is given to the external agent participating in the transaction, the customer. The first copy (document 2) is filed numerically according to the document's sequential number in a permanent file in the organizational unit where the transaction took place. The second copy (document 3) is sent to the Accounting Department for recording. After the transaction is recorded in the appropriate journal and posted to an applicable subsidiary ledger, that copy of the source document is filed numerically in a permanent file within the Accounting Department. After a specified period, information from the transaction journal is posted in the general ledger; the general ledger is used to prepare adjusting and closing entries; a trial balance is used to verify the balance of the ledger prior to preparing financial statements that are distributed to investors and creditors.
>
> Exhibit A–2 illustrates the typical flow of documents in a sales collection process. The sales clerk begins the process by preparing a sales invoice. When preparing the sales invoice, part of the clerk's responsibility is checking the customer's credit. The sales invoice has three parts; part 1 is filed numerically in a permanent file within the sales area, part 2 is given to the customer, and part 3 is sent to the accounts receivable clerk. When payment is received from the customer, a cash receipts clerk endorses the check for deposit and prepares a remittance advice with three parts. Part 1 is given to the customer, part 2 is filed numerically in a permanent file in the cash receipts area, and part 3 is sent to the accounts receivable clerk. The accounts receivable clerk records information from the invoice and the remittance advice in the appropriate transaction journals (e.g., sales journal and cash receipts journal), updates the accounts receivable ledger, and files each document numerically in a permanent file within the accounting area.

Flowcharting symbols and methods can vary widely across professions and organizations. There is no one set of generally accepted flowcharting principles and symbols. The flowcharting conventions and symbols we present in this supplement are representative of those most commonly used.

EXHIBIT A–1

Document Flow in a Manual Accounting System

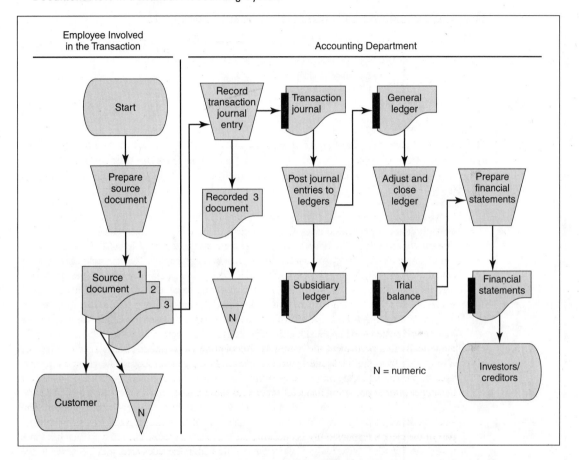

Flowcharting Element 1: Symbols   A variety of symbols are used to represent the physical aspects of the document/data flows and processes of an information system. Since flowcharts illustrate the physical features of a system, there are various symbols in each category. For example, there are at least four storage symbols, and the one chosen depends on the physical characteristics of the storage medium (e.g., whether it is a paper file, a disk file, or a tape file). The following describes some of the more frequently used symbols in flowcharting.

Input and output: documents   The document symbol is used for all types of paper source documents that are processed by the system (e.g., checks, invoices, ledgers, journals, and reports). The name of the document is entered on its face (see symbol A in Exhibit A–3).

EXHIBIT A–2

Sales/Collection Document Flowchart

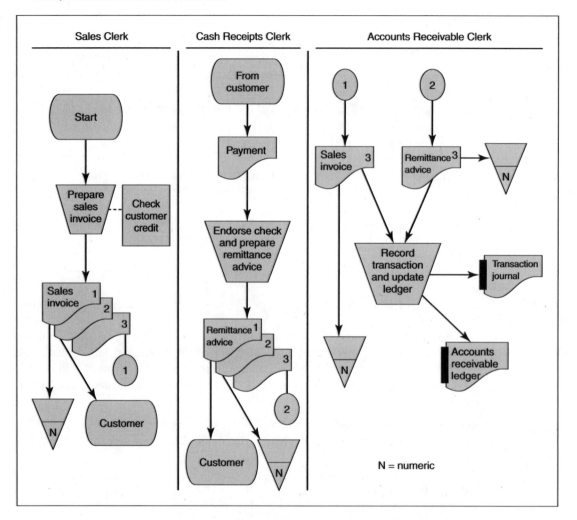

A document used to store information, such as a journal or ledger, as opposed to a document that is processed, such as a check or invoice, can be distinguished by darkening the left-hand edge of the symbol (see symbol B in Exhibit A–3).

Multiple copies of a document can be shown in two ways, depending on the situation being described. The overlapping approach staggers symbols for each copy of the document. Each document is also numbered. The numbers may be arranged in a sequence that best fits the flow of documents from that point of the chart. This method is well suited for

EXHIBIT A–3

Flowchart Symbols: Documents

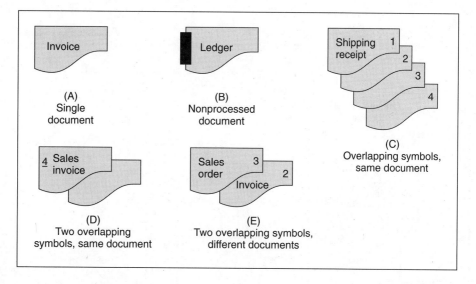

flowcharts having different copies of the document flow to different processes or responsibilities (see symbol C in Exhibit A–3).

The two-overlapping approach uses only two symbols for all copies of the document, regardless of the number of copies. The number of copies of the document in the group is noted in the upper left-hand corner of the document (see symbol D in Exhibit A–3). This method is well suited for flowcharts having all copies of the documents flow to the same process or responsibility (see symbol E in Exhibit A–3).

Input: on-line computer device (keyboard or terminal)   This symbol is used to describe the entry of data into a computer through an online terminal/keyboard (see symbol A in Exhibit A–4).

Terminal display   This symbol (see Exhibit A–4) is used to show a computer terminal display. It is often used in conjunction with the online computer device symbol to show data being entered into a computer process using an online terminal.

Input and output: I/O   The input/output symbol is used to display records and master files (such as the journals and ledgers used in accounting) (see symbol C in Exhibit A–4). A description of the input/output is entered on the face of the symbol.

Processing   The manual process symbol indicates a manual operation (such as completing forms or verifying amounts) often performed on, or with a document (see symbol D in Exhibit A–4). There are two machine processing symbols: one for online computer processing (see symbol E in Exhibit A–4) and one for offline processing or processing

EXHIBIT A–4

Flowchart Symbols

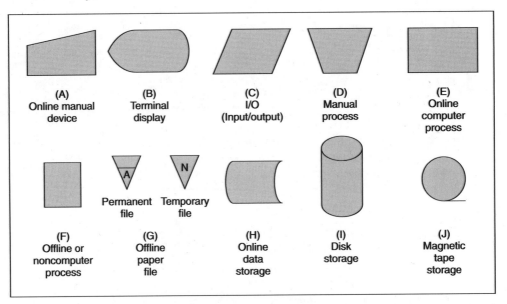

performed by a machine other than a computer (see symbol F in Exhibit A–4). A description of the operation is entered on the face of the symbol.

Storage files A manual system offline storage symbol represents any storage of paper documents (e.g., file cabinet, safe, or shelves). Two types of files exist—temporary and permanent. A temporary file is a storage device for documents that will be involved in subsequent processing. A permanent file is often distinguished by a horizontal line across the top of the symbol. The method of document order or organization is denoted using an A (alphanumeric), N (numeric), or C (chronological) (see symbol G in Exhibit A–4). Whenever abbreviations or codes are used, you should place a legend on your flowchart to assist readers.

There are various computer-storage symbols, including an online storage file symbol, disk-storage file symbol, and magnetic tape–storage file symbol (see symbols H, I, and J in Exhibit A–4). A description of the file contents is entered on the face of the symbol.

Terminal or system exit/entry This symbol is used to indicate the beginning or ending point of the process represented on a flowchart. It is also used to display system entry or exit of data (see symbols A and B in Exhibit A–5).

On-page connector On-page connectors allow document flows to be bridged within a single page of the flowchart. Each connector is numbered within a page. An arrow pointing to a connector identifies the other connector on the same page where the document

EXHIBIT A–5

More Flowchart Symbols

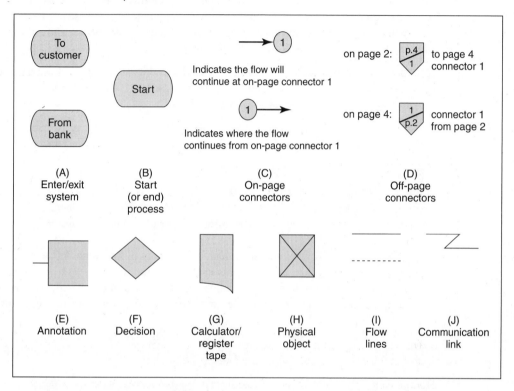

flow continues. An arrow pointing away from the connector identifies the connector from which the flow is continuing (see the symbols labeled C in Exhibit A–5).

Off-page connector   Rarely do document flowcharts fit on one page. Off-page connectors are used to connect multiple pages of a document flowchart. Shown within the off-page connector symbol is the page number that the flow continues to (or from which the flow came) and a connector number (see the symbols labeled D in Exhibit A–5).

Annotation   This symbol is used to include important supplementary information or explanations that are difficult to describe graphically within the flowchart itself (see symbol E in Exhibit A–5).

Decision   Sometimes in a system, the course of action depends on making a decision or choice. For example, if a clerk's task is to review a document for completeness, the next action would depend on deciding whether the document is complete. Suppose that if the document is complete, the clerk files the document. On the other hand, if the document is incomplete, the clerk sends the document back to the user department. A decision symbol (see symbol F in Exhibit A–5) would display the decision, and a description of the decision would appear in the symbol (e.g., Is the document complete?). Two labeled flow lines would exit from the decision symbol to illustrate the indicated course of action. In this case, a line labeled with yes (yes the document is complete) would lead to a paper offline file, while a line labeled no (no the document is not complete) would show the document flowing back to the user department.

Calculator or register tape   This symbol is used to represent the output from a process that provides a summary of calculations such as totaling a batch of cash receipts or sales, or calculating discounts (see symbol G in Exhibit A–5).

Physical (nondocument) objects   This symbol is used to denote any physical object that may accompany a document flow (e.g., merchandise, supplies, and products) (see symbol H in Exhibit A–5).

Flowcharting Element 2: Flow Lines   Flow lines are used to connect the symbols on the document flowchart. A solid line indicates actual physical flow of a document or object. A dotted or dashed line indicates flow of information rather than the physical document (see symbol I in Exhibit A–5).

Arrows are used when the document or information flow is not left to right or top to bottom. The assumed flow of documents and information is from top to bottom and from left to right. As long as this flow is followed, arrows are not required. Arrows must be used when there is a counterflow. However, there is nothing wrong with using arrows on all flow lines.

Some flowcharts also display communication link symbols (see symbol J in Exhibit A–5). This symbol is used when telephone lines, microwave towers, or satellite transmitters are used to transfer data.

Flowcharting Element 3: Area of Responsibility   Areas of responsibility are displayed to enable the flowchart reader to clearly identify changes in responsibility as the documents flow through the system. They are represented on flowcharts by segmenting and labeling columns (see Exhibits A–1 and A–2). On Exhibit A–1, two areas of responsibility are displayed (the employee and the Accounting Department), while Exhibit A–2 displays the responsibilities of three clerks.

Areas of responsibility may be departments, sections within a department, or individual employees within a department. Judgment must be used in choosing the level of subdivision that one column should represent. For example, in a small company, the Billing Department might be represented by one or more pages.

Preparation Conventions

Several techniques have been developed to guide the preparation of a flowchart. The main objective of these techniques is to enhance the readability, and thereby enable the validation, of the flowchart.

Left to Right, Top to Bottom   A page in a book is read from top to bottom and from left to right. Similarly, a flowchart is most easily understood if the same convention is followed. Therefore, when preparing a document flowchart, begin in the upper left-hand corner and work from left to right and from top to bottom.

All Documents Must Have an Origin and Termination   A flowchart must clearly indicate where a document is introduced into a system and where it is permanently filed or leaves a system. Each copy of a document must flow to one of the following:

1. A permanent file symbol.
2. A symbol denoting an exit from the system.
3. An off-page connector.

Following this convention ensures that the progress of every document has been observed and documented from "cradle to grave." Whenever the final destination of a document is unknown, an annotation symbol is used to indicate that additional investigation is required.

Keep Flowcharts Uncluttered   A flowchart is an important analytical and design tool. However, great amounts of detail reduce a flowchart's ability to communicate. For this reason, to the extent possible, observe the following rules:

1. Place areas of responsibility with the most frequent interchange adjacent to each other to avoid long arrows.
2. Enter narrative on charts only within symbols.
3. Avoid using narrative to explain what is already adequately described by the flowchart itself.

Make Sure the Progress of a Document Is Clear   Diagram a document before and after a process is performed, when entering or leaving a file, and on entering or leaving a page. Also, if a document is altered (e.g., updated, signed, or approved), change the name of the document to indicate its current status. For example, notice in Exhibit A–1 the flow of the source document. It is created by the manual process Prepare Source Document. Copy 1 is given to the customer, and copy 2 is filed. Copy 3 is sent to the Accounting Department, where information from the source document is recorded in the transaction journal. Copy 3 is then filed numerically in a permanent file.

Make Sure Your Flowchart Is Complete: Represent Each Input, Process, Output, and Storage Step   When flowcharting a process, make sure you include all the major steps in the process. It is often helpful to remember that systems are simply a combination of inputs, processes, outputs, and storage of data.

The Basic Elements of Hardware and Program Flowcharts

Hardware flowcharts show the hardware configuration of a system. When drawing a hardware flowchart, the same symbols are used, but they are used to represent physical pieces of computer hardware. Therefore, the document symbol is used to represent a printer, the magnetic tape symbol represents a tape drive, a disk symbol represents a disk drive, a computer process symbol represents a central processor, and an offline process symbol represents auxiliary hardware like an optical character reader. The type of hardware is recorded on the face of the symbol.

Program flowcharts depict the detailed logic of a computer program. Only five symbols are used in program flowcharting: input/output (see C in Exhibit A–4), process (see E in Exhibit A–4), decision (see F in Exhibit A–5), start/end (see B in Exhibit A–5), and flow lines (see I in Exhibit A–5). As always, a description of the logic is recorded on the face of the symbol.

Summary

Following the preceding instructions can guide the development of an effective flowchart for analyzing an information process or system. The flowchart is one of the easier types of documentation for information customers and management to understand. Often, auditors use system, document, and procedure flowcharts to understand business and systems controls in an environment.

Although many individuals and organizations still use flowcharts, their usefulness is limited. The primary weakness of the flowchart is that it is tied to physical information flows and system characteristics that hide the procedural essence of the system. Some flowcharts are full of data and processing artifacts because they are tied to an outdated information technology. Therefore, any effort to propose a new system that takes advantage of current information technology requires the conceptual aspects of the system to be documented and designed. Data flow diagrams are a useful tool for documenting the conceptual aspects of an information system.

DATA FLOW DIAGRAMS (DFD)

A second documentation tool is the data flow diagram (DFD). Data flow diagramming symbols are used for a variety of system analysis purposes, including graphically displaying the logical flows of data through a process. Unlike flowcharts, which represent the physical components of an information system, data flow diagrams can provide a more conceptual, nonphysical display of the movement of data through a system. Data flow diagrams disregard such things as organizational units, the computer on which the data are processed, and the media on which the data are stored. The movement of data across offices or departments within a particular system environment is not represented.

There are four different categories of data flow diagrams:

- Data flow diagrams of the current physical system.
- Data flow diagrams of the current logical system.

- Data flow diagrams of the new or proposed logical system.
- Data flow diagrams of the new or proposed physical system.

Both logical and physical diagrams use the same set of symbols. The logical diagrams show the conceptual flow of data without including any references to the physical characteristics of the system. The physical diagrams, on the other hand, include labels that describe physical attributes of the system, such as labeling worker or job titles, department names, and the names or descriptions of the technology used to process and store the data.

Data Flow Diagram Symbols

Data flow diagrams include four symbols: process, data inflow sources and outflow sinks (destinations), data stores, and data flow lines. Like flowcharting, there are variations on some of the symbols. For example, two standard symbol sets are those developed by Gane and Sarson[1] and DeMarco and Yourdon[2] (see Exhibit A–6). We will use the DeMarco and Yourdon symbols in this text.

Process   Circles[3] are used to represent processes that take data inflows and transform them to information outflows (see symbol A in Exhibit A–6). The circle contains two labels. The first label is a process number (explained later) and the second is a process name.

Data Sources and Sinks   Rectangles (or squares) represent data (inflow) sources and (information outflow) sinks (see symbol B in Exhibit A–6). The rectangle is labeled with the name of the data source or sink/destination (e.g., Customer, Vendors, Government Agency). The sources and sinks play an important role in the data flow diagram. The sources and sinks are agents external to (i.e., outside the scope of) the system represented on the diagram. They delineate the boundaries of the system.

Data Stores   Two parallel straight lines[4] are used to display a store or collection of data (see symbol C in Exhibit A–6). Some people refer to data stores as *data at rest*. A description of the data store contents is entered on the symbol. Data stores are used anytime it is necessary to store the output from a process before sending it on to the next process.

Data Flow Lines   Data flow lines display the route of data inflow and information outflow (see symbol D in Exhibit A–6). They can be straight or curved lines. The data flow is generally labeled with the name of the data (e.g., customer order, bill, financial analysis) and the arrow indicates the direction of the data flow.

---

1 C. Gane and T. Sarson, *Structured Systems Analysis* (Englewood Cliffs, NJ: Prentice Hall, 1979).
2 T. DeMarco, *Structured Analysis and Systems Specifications* (Englewood Cliffs, NJ: Prentice Hall, 1979); and E. Yourdon and L. Constantine, *Structured Design* (Englewood Cliffs, NJ: Prentice Hall, 1979).
3 Some use rectangular boxes with rounded corners.
4 Some use a rectangular box that is open at one end.

EXHIBIT A–6

Data Flow Diagram Symbols

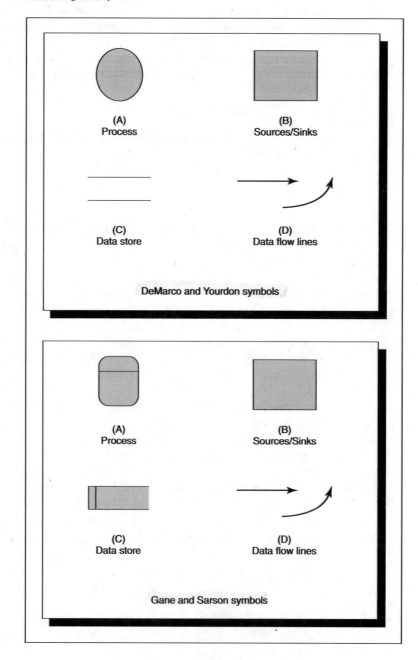

Constraints

As with any documentation tool, there are some conventions that should be followed. The following data flow diagramming rules are recommended by Hoffner, George, and Valacich. Exhibit A–7 graphically displays several of the rules described below. We will use these rules in this text.

General Rules

1. All processes should have unique names. If two data flow lines (or data stores) have the same label, they should both refer to the exact same data flow (or data store).
2. The inputs to a process should differ from the outputs of a process.
3. Any single DFD should not have more than about seven processes.

Process

4. No process can have only outputs. (This would imply that the process is making information from nothing.) If an object has only outputs, then it must be a source.
5. No process can have only inputs. (This is referred to as a *black hole.*) If an object has only inputs, then it must be a sink.
6. A process has a verb phrase label.

Data Store

7. Data cannot move directly from one data store to another data store. Data must be moved by a process.
8. Data cannot move directly from an outside source to a data store. Data must be moved by a process that receives data from the source and places the data in the data store.
9. Data cannot move directly to an outside sink from a data store. Data must be moved by a process.
10. A data store has a noun phrase label.

Source/Sink

11. Data of any concern to the system cannot move directly from a source to a sink. It must be moved by a process. If data flows directly from a source to a sink (and does not involve processing) then it is outside the scope of the system and is not shown on this system's DFD.
12. A source/sink has a noun phrase label.

Data Flow

13. A data flow has only one direction between symbols. It may flow in both directions between a process and a data store to show a read before an update.

Data Flow Diagramming Rules

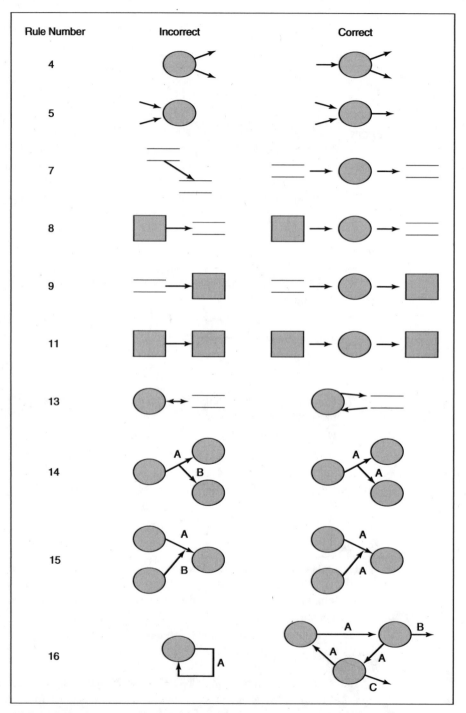

J. Hoffner, J. George, and J. Valacich, *Modern Systems Analysis and Design* (Reading, MA: Benjamin/Cummings, 1996), p. 321.

To effectively show a read before an update, draw two separate arrows because the two steps (reading and updating) occur at separate times.

14. A fork in a data flow means that exactly the same data goes from a common location to two or more different processes, data stores, or sources/sinks. (This usually indicates different copies of the same data going to different locations.)

15. A join in a data flow means that exactly the same data comes from any of two or more different processes, data stores, or sources/sinks, to a common location.

16. A data flow cannot go directly back to the same process it leaves. There must be at least one other process that handles the data flow, produces some other data flow, and returns the original data flow to the originating process.

17. A data flow to a data store means update (i.e., delete, add, or change).

18. A data flow from a data store means retrieve or use.

19. A data flow has a noun phrase label. More than one data flow noun phrase can appear on a single arrow as long as all of the flows on the same arrow move together as one package.

Levels of Data Flow Diagrams

Data flow diagrams are divided into levels to keep their size and complexity manageable.

Context Diagram   The highest level of data flow diagrams is the context diagram. Refer to Exhibit A–8 for a context diagram of a sample sales/collection system. A single system is represented on a context diagram and it provides the scope of the system being represented. The system under investigation is identified in a process symbol in the center of the diagram labeled with a 0. Sources and sinks (destinations) of data and information are also shown. Thus, the context diagram shows one process (representing the entire system) and the sources/sinks that represent the boundaries of the system. The data flow lines into

E X H I B I T   A–8

Context Diagram Example

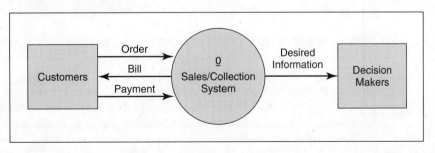

EXHIBIT A-9

Level-Zero DFD Example

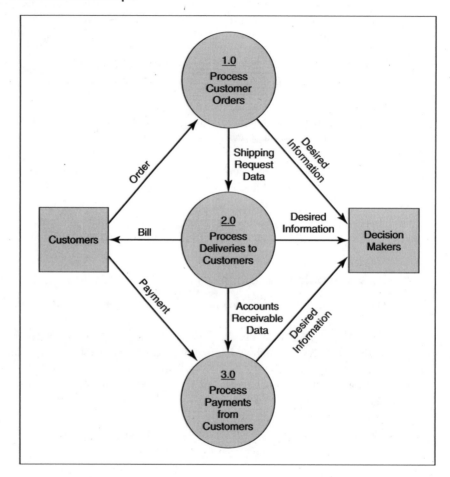

the process represent the input data to the system (provided by sources), and the data flow lines from the process represent the output information from the system (going to the sinks).

Subsequent Level DFDs   The process identified in the context diagram is divided into the more detailed processes performed within the system. The next level under the context diagram is called *level zero* and depicts only the very high level processes of the system. Each of the level-zero processes may be subdivided into more detailed processes in subsequent levels of DFDs. When you take the processes on a data flow diagram and divide each into more detailed (sub)processes, this is referred to as decomposition. When you have decomposed the system processes into the most detailed levels (referred to as the *low-est level DFDs*), the resulting DFDs are called primitive DFDs.[5]

Each process in a zero-level DFD is labeled sequentially, with a number followed by .0. For example, if a zero-level DFD includes four processes that comprise the system represented in a context diagram, the processes on the zero-level DFD are labeled as 1.0, 2.0, 3.0, and 4.0. The .0 identifies this as the level-zero DFD. For example, Exhibit A–9 is a level-zero DFD of the context diagram represented in Exhibit A–8. It shows that the sample sales/collection system has three main high-level process categories:

◆ Process customer orders (labeled as 1.0).

◆ Process deliveries to customers (labeled as 2.0).

◆ Process payments from customers (labeled as 3.0)

Suppose you wanted to show more detail about the processes represented in Exhibit A–9. You could create a level-one DFD for each process. Exhibit A–10 provides a sample level-one DFD for process 1.0 of Exhibit A–9. It shows that the "process customer order" process is made up of two processes (e.g., "approve and record customer order data" and

E X H I B I T   A–10

Level-One DFD Example

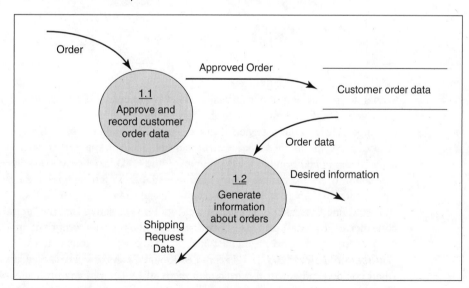

---

5 Refer to page 335 of J. Hoffner, J. George, and J. Valacich, *Modern Systems Analysis and Design* (Reading, MA: Benjamin/Cummings, 1996), for a list of rules on determining when the primitive DFD level is achieved. This text is also a good source for advanced data flow diagramming concepts and rules.

EXHIBIT A–11

Level-Two DFD Example

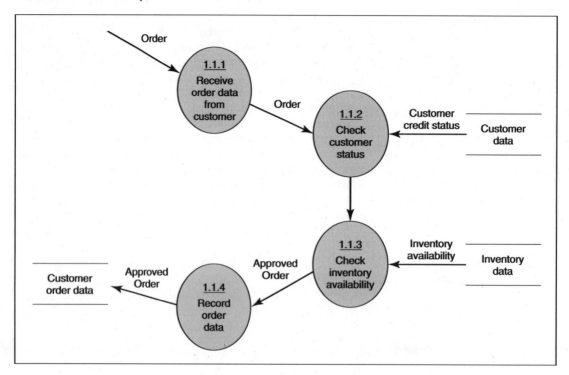

"generate information about orders"). The two processes are labeled as 1.1 and 1.2, respectively. The first digit refers to the corresponding level-zero process number. The second digit refers to the assigned level-one process number. Notice that you can omit the source/sink symbols (in this case customer and decision makers) on more detailed, lower level DFDs. In addition, notice that the level-one DFD has the same system input and output data flows as the corresponding level-zero DFD. When such related DFDs are consistent in showing inputs and outflows, they are said to be *balanced* DFDs.

Exhibit A–11 shows a sample level-two DFD. It shows that the "approve and record customer order data" process shown on Exhibit A–10 is comprised of four processes ("1.1.1 receive order data from customer," "1.1.2 check customer status," "1.1.3 check inventory availability," and "1.1.4 record order data"). As noted earlier, additional levels of detail could be provided in subsequent levels of DFDs. For example, if "check customer status" is complex and there are several subprocesses required to complete this process, process 1.1.2 could be divided into subprocesses on a level-three DFD, labeled as 1.1.2.1, 1.1.2.2, 1.1.2.3, and so on.

COMPARING FLOWCHARTS AND DATA FLOW DIAGRAMS

As noted earlier, a primary difference between data flow diagrams and flowcharts is the representation of the physical and logical characteristics of a system. Flowcharts are biased toward representing the physical characteristics of the system, while data flow diagrams can omit the physical system attributes. To illustrate this difference, suppose you wanted to document the data flows in the following manual system scenario:

> A supervisor in the factory collects the time cards from workers in her department and reviews the calculation of total hours for the week. She sends the time cards to Accounting Payroll, where a clerk uses them to record weekly wages in the individual employee earnings record, then files the time cards alphabetically.

Exhibit A–12 displays flowchart and data flow diagram documentation segments of this activity. Now suppose the activity remains constant, except that the Accounting Payroll Department automates its process using magnetic tape. Refer to Exhibit A–13 for updated documentation. Now suppose that everything still remains constant, except that the Accounting Payroll Department decides to upgrade to magnetic disks (see Exhibit A–14).

Notice anything unusual? The flowchart documentation had to change twice to reflect the changes in the physical components of the information system. However, the data flow diagram did not change because the basic conceptual flow of data in the system did not change—only the physical characteristics of the devices used in routing and storing the data changed. Thus, the data flow diagram provided a better documentation of the underlying data flows and processes in the system. Although not as detailed, the data flow diagram helps the reader focus on information, rather than technology.

CONCLUDING COMMENTS

This chapter has presented an overview of both flowcharting and data flow diagramming. Some organizations and consultants have developed their own diagramming techniques. Whether you use flowcharting, data flow diagrams, or a proprietary diagramming tool is really a matter of choice and dependent on what you are trying to analyze or design. Diagramming tools combine the efficiency of graphics and rigor of rules to communicate the nature of the process being modeled. It is important for analysts to develop the skills to both read and create documentation of information and business processes using tools such as flowcharts and data flow diagrams.

CHECKLIST OF KEY TERMS AND CONCEPTS

Areas of responsibility	Context diagrams
Balanced DFD	Data flow diagrams
Constraints	Data flow diagram symbols

EXHIBIT A–12

Comparative Example—Version 1

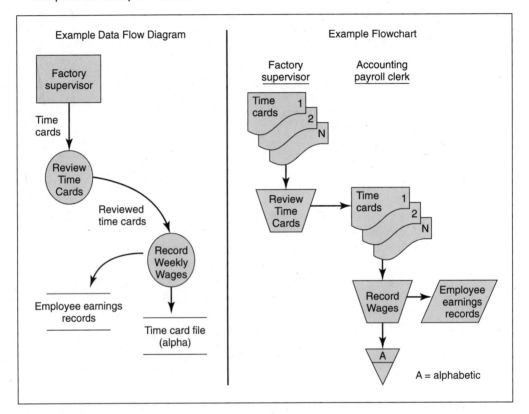

Decomposition of DFDs	Hardware flowcharts
Document/procedure flowcharts	Level-zero DFD
Flowcharts	Primitive DFD
Flowchart conventions	Program flowcharts
Flowchart symbols	System flowcharts
Flow lines	

REVIEW QUESTIONS

1. Draw the flowcharting symbols and describe the use of each.
2. List and define the various types of flowcharts.
3. What are the three basic elements of flowcharts?

E X H I B I T   A–13

Comparative Example—Version 2

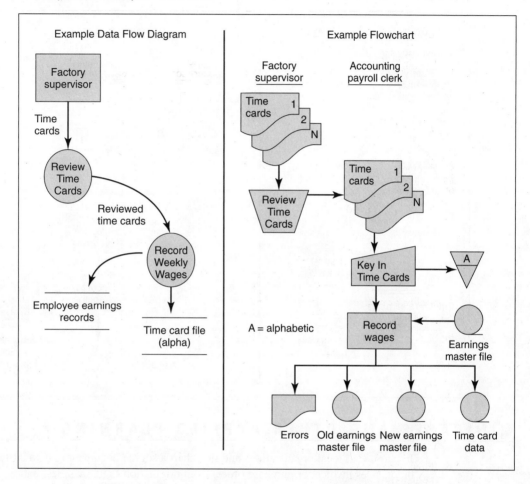

4. What are the important flowcharting conventions or techniques you should follow to make a flowchart easier to understand?

5. Draw the data flow diagram symbols and describe the use of each.

6. List and explain the various levels of data flow diagrams.

7. What are the important conventions or techniques you should follow when drawing a data flow diagram?

8. Explain the difference(s) between data flow diagrams and flowcharts.

EXHIBIT A–14

Comparative Example—Version 3

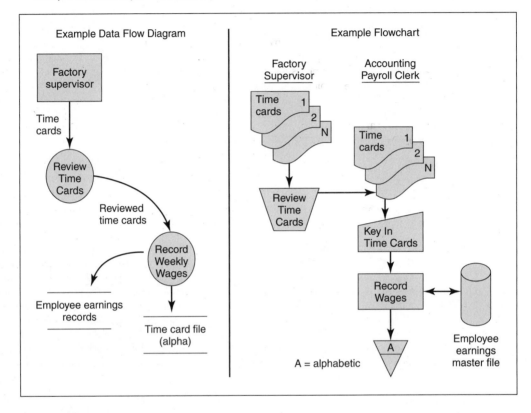

Example Data Flow Diagram · Example Flowchart

MINICASES AND OTHER APPLIED LEARNING

1. In pairs, visit local organizations and flowchart a source document (e.g., a customer order, sales invoice, or purchase order) from origination to its final destination. Also, flowchart a task performed by one of the organization's clerks. In class, exchange your flowchart with another team and write a narrative of their flowchart. Prepare a written or verbal critique of how well the other team interpreted the flowchart your team prepared.

2. The following describes the process to execute a credit sale at Willie's Furniture Store.

Sales clerks assist customers in locating and pricing merchandise. A sales clerk prepares a sales invoice with an original and three copies. If the merchandise on an invoice is priced different than the list price, the price change must be approved with a signature by the sales manager. Copy 3 of the sales invoice is filed by the salesperson in a salesperson file.

The salesperson walks the customer and the remaining copies of the invoice to the Credit

Approval Department where the invoice is checked for mathematical errors by a clerk. The credit manager evaluates the credit standing of the customer, approves or rejects the application based on standard company policy, and marks "credit sale" on the invoice along with the results of the credit evaluation. Invoice copy 2 of a credit-approved sale is given to the customer. The Credit Approval Department keeps the original copy of the invoice in their files (filed numerically) and sends the other copy to shipping.

The Shipping Department uses their copy as a guide to pull merchandise and deliver it to the customer. The customer is asked to sign the invoice copy as evidence of delivery. The delivery person files the invoice copy by date.

Required:

- *a.* Prepare a document/procedure flowchart for the process described above.
- *b.* Prepare a logical data flow diagram for the process.

3. Motor Building Industry (MBI) Incorporated develops and manufactures natural gas–powered motors. Capital tools are the larger, more-prominent assets of the organization. Because of their long life and significant value, considerable attention is devoted to their acquisition and use. The following procedures are used in acquiring capital tools for MBI, Inc.

A capital tool is defined as any individual item that costs over $10,000. Capital tools must be requested by a department manager and reviewed and approved by the capital tool planning committee. The department manager prepares a purchase request and a copy (which is filed numerically) and sends the original copy to the planning committee. The planning committee reviews all purchase requests and decides whether to approve the tool request. The committee remits disapproved purchase requests to the requesting manager and forwards approved purchase requests to MBI's Purchasing Department.

Approved capital tools are purchased by the purchasing department manager. Using the approved purchase request, a purchasing agent prepares a purchase order and a copy for each order. The original is filed numerically and the copy is sent to MBI's Receiving Department. Each tool is assigned to only one purchasing agent, and the assignment is made according to the vendor from whom the tool is intended to be purchased. Several vendors are assigned to each purchasing agent to establish a personal relationship with the vendor and secure a more favorable price because of their knowledge of the vendor.

Receiving clerks at the dock receive the tools, inspect them, match the tool to a purchase order, complete a receiving report, and route the tool to the department that originally requested it. Receiving clerks send the receiving report to the Treasury Department and file a copy alphabetically. Purchase orders are filed numerically. Occasionally, tools are received that were never ordered. Even though the number of these items is relatively small, sorting them out and returning them occupies a major portion of the receiving clerk's time.

The Treasury Department is informed of capital tools received by the receiving report. They pay vendors monthly for the items invoiced by the vendor during the month. An elaborate matching process is required to verify that the price paid is the same as the price negotiated by the purchasing agent.

Required:

- *a.* Prepare a context diagram for the system.
- *b.* Prepare individual data flow diagrams to represent each of the following: Record

Purchase, Maintain Buyers, and Prepare Approved But Not Yet Purchased Report. You can omit process numbers for this exercise.

c. Prepare a flowchart of MBI's tool acquisition process (excluding the payment process) described above.

4. The Warehouse Club is a small merchandise discount store that sells everything from grocery items to automotive parts. The Warehouse Club is able to secure low prices by buying in bulk and by operating out of a leased warehouse. In addition, only paid members are allowed to shop at a Warehouse Club location. The following is a description of the yearly member renewal process.

At or near the first day of each month, an accounts receivable clerk queries the membership database to identify those whose membership expires during the following month. For example, on January 1 a query is executed to identify memberships that expire during February. A membership renewal list is printed for use in preparing individual invoices and for documentation.

Using the computer and the membership renewal list, an accounts receivable clerk prepares each individual invoice for members. This process automatically updates accounts receivable records. The computer prints two copies of the invoice. The original invoice is sent to the customer and the invoice copy is stored numerically in a filing cabinet. The membership list is also stored in a filing cabinet but is filed according to the date.

When payment checks are received, they are immediately processed. First, a copy is made and stored alphabetically in customer files. Next, account receivable records are updated and customers are given another year of shopping privileges. Finally at the end of the day, checks are endorsed and deposited in the bank.

Required:

a. Prepare a flowchart of this process.

b. Prepare a logical data flow diagram for this process.

5. Convenient Computing Associates (CCA) operates a mail-order operation and sells a vast array of computer products and accessories. The following is a description of Convenient Computing's collection process:

The policy of CCA is to collect all accounts receivable as quickly as possible. CCA encourages prompt payment by sending reminder statements at the end of each month and calling customers whose balance is more than 30 days past due.

On the last working day of the month, the accounts receivable clerk prints a statement for each customer showing a balance due on their account. Statements are automatically generated by a computer that maintains the accounts receivable files and records. The original statement is mailed to the customer and a copy of the statement is filed alphabetically according to customer last name.

On the 15th and the last day of the month, the accounts receivable clerk prints an open accounts receivable aging report by customer. The clerk calls all customers with invoices more than 30 days past due. The purpose of the call is to verify the accuracy of the invoice data. If the information is correct, a polite reminder is given to encourage prompt payment. The open receivable report is marked with the clerk's initials and the date the call was made, and filed by date when all calls are complete.

Required:

　　a. Prepare a flowchart of this process.

　　b. Prepare a logical data flow diagram for this process.

6. Wiltex Research is a company that performs energy research on a contract basis for major oil and chemical companies. The following narrative describes the process to acquire materials for research projects.

A project manager determines the materials needed for a project and purchases them from a vendor. A purchase order is completed by the project manager for each piece of materials. A catalog price is used, or the vendor is contacted by telephone to determine the price. The purchase order has an original and two copies (copy 1 and copy 2).

The project manager sends the purchase order to the project supervisor for approval/disapproval. The project manager writes approved or disapproved on the purchase order, signs it, and returns it to the project manager. The project manager sends the original copy of approved purchase orders to the vendor, sends copy 1 to the accounting clerk, and files copy 2 in a permanent project file (ordered numerically by project number). Disapproved purchase orders are thrown in the garbage can by the project manager.

The accounting clerk files copy 1 in a temporary file (numeric by PO number).

The project manager receives and inspects materials sent from the vendor and compares them to the packing slip. The packing slip is sent to the accounting clerk as evidence that the materials have been received. The accounting clerk matches the packing slip with the copy 1 of the purchase order and prepares a check (which has an original and one copy).

The check is attached to the packing slip and copy 1 of the purchase order and is sent to the project supervisor for a signature. Once signed, the entire set of documents is returned to the accounting clerk who sends the original copy of the check to the vendor, and files the copy of the check with the supporting documentation attached to it in a permanent file (ordered numerically by check number).

Required:

Prepare a flowchart of this process.

An Overview of the General Ledger Architecture

SUPPLEMENT OBJECTIVE

The objective of this supplement is to review several systems terms and concepts, and overview some basic features of the traditional general ledger architecture. After studying this chapter, you should be able to:

- List and describe various file types.
- Describe how a computer stores and accesses data.
- Describe various processing methods.
- Explain the difference between physical and logical file structures.
- Describe how computers search for data.
- Describe the processing and audit trail of an automated, batch general ledger.
- Describe the processing and audit trail of an automated, online general ledger.

OVERVIEW OF BASIC SYSTEMS TERMS AND CONCEPTS

File Types

Files are used to store data and processing instructions. Each file is given a name and saved on a storage medium like a hard disk, floppy disk, or CD-ROM. An example of a file is a word processing document created using Microsoft Word. The two types of files computer users use most often are *executable files* and *data files*. Executable files usually have an .exe extension. Data files are used to store anything from transaction data to business reference data to a word processing or a graphics document. Often files are referred to by their type or content. Types of data files used in traditional systems include master files, transaction files, history files, reference files, and suspense files.

Master files contain balance data or the status of an entity at a point in time.[1] In traditional accounting architectures, ledger files are examples of master files because they contain chart of account balances (accounts that represent assets, liabilities, and equities). Subsidiary ledgers are also master files because they contain information about such things as vendors, credit customers, inventory, assets, or employees. Master files do not contain event or activity data, but their balances are updated by such data. For example, general ledger master files are periodically updated by journal transaction data.

Transaction files or *activity files* contain activity data.[2] In traditional accounting

---

1 In Supplemental Chapter E we explain that business event–driven system master files are resource, agent, and location data stores.

2 In Supplemental Chapter E we explain that business event–driven system master files are event data pools that store detailed data about business activities.

architectures, these data are used to update the balance in the master files. The data normally stored in journals in a traditional accounting system are examples of transaction files. They contain the activity data used to update the running balance listed in the subsidiary and general ledger master files. Batches of source documents are also examples of transaction files.

History files or *archive files,* as the name suggests, contain inactive past or historical data. Examples could include general ledger files from 1985–97, previous year balance sheets, or income statements.

Reference files contain referential data such as a listing of the chart of accounts, tax rate schedules, or customer price lists.

Suspense files are awaiting some action to complete their processing. Examples include journal transactions awaiting processing until posting time occurs, or records identified as incomplete or erroneous that need correction and reentry for processing (e.g., a payment by a customer who is not listed in a customer master file).

Storage and Access of Data in a System

Originally, all IT application data were stored and accessed sequentially. *Sequential storage* implies that records are stored one after another in some order (by account number, alphabetically by customer's last name, or another specified order). Retrieving data in a sequential file implies that all data be read in sequential order to find a particular record. To illustrate, suppose you purchase a cassette tape containing one of your favorite songs. The songs are stored sequentially (one after another) on the tape. To listen to your favorite song, you must fast forward or rewind (search the songs one after another) to *sequentially access* the desired song—there is no faster access option. Some storage mediums like tape cartridges and open reel tapes require sequential storage and sequential access of data.

With the invention of disk technology, alternative storage and access methods were introduced. Today, direct-access or random-access methods dominate information technology use. Direct- or random-access storage allows each record to be stored and subsequently retrieved on the file storage medium without reading all the records that precede it in the file. In reality, the data may be stored in a "random" order, but the computer maintains an index or a randomizing technique to keep track of the location of each record. *Direct access* allows the computer to retrieve any record requested by the user, regardless of its physical position in a file. There is no need to sequentially search all or part of the other records stored on the storage device. A direct-access device is like using a phonograph record, a CD player, or a DVD device; you can move the phonograph arm or the CD reader directly to your favorite song without having to listen to or fast forward through the other songs on the album or CD.

The *indexed sequential access method (ISAM)* combines the characteristics of both a sequential and an indexed file. Records are stored sequentially in groups or in blocks of data with an *index* (i.e., a table of contents) of addresses for each group of records. The file can be processed sequentially, but the index can also be used to directly identify the location of one group of records. Using ISAM, an index of storage locations is read into memory. The index lists the memory locations of each group of records. The computer identifies the group containing the desired record and retrieves the data group from the storage medium. Since the records in the group are stored sequentially, the computer reads through the group of records to locate the desired record. To use our music-media example, the songs would be stored in sequential order as before, but accessible through an index. To find your song, the computer searches the index table to decide in which data group your song was stored. The computer would go to the memory address listed in the index, and retrieve the group of songs. It would sequentially search the group until it located the beginning of your song. Although ISAM combines sequential and direct-access methods, it requires a great deal of maintenance to keep the index updated and to retain the sequential order of the records. There are also storage devices that use indexed direct-access methods to retrieve data.

Sequential storage is used in paper, tape, or disk storage mediums. Tape storage devices allow sequential access only. Direct access is possible in disk or paper storage mediums.

Processing Methods

The timing of processing reveals when activity data are posted to update computer master files. Thus the processing method affects the timeliness of data stored in master files. Processing is often identified by type: batch, online, real-time, or report-time processing.

Batch processing accumulates transaction data for a period of time to collect a *batch,* or group, of transaction data. Then all of the transactions in the transaction file are posted to the master file in one processing run. Therefore, processing (i.e., updating of the master file) occurs after a group of transaction data is collected. Processing involves merging the data in the transaction file with the current master data to create a *new, updated* master file. Thus, with batch processing, transaction data may not be entered in the computer system until some time after a business activity occurs, and master files may be updated even later. The only time the master file is accurate and up to date is immediately after a batch of transaction data has been processed.

Online processing means the computer-input device is connected to the CPU so that master files are updated as transaction data are entered. *Real time* denotes immediate response to an information user; transaction data are entered and processed to update the relevant master files and a response is provided to the person conducting the business event fast enough to affect the outcome of the event. Although they sound similar, online and real-time processing can differ. Real-time processing updates master files as a business activity occurs, while online processing updates master files whenever transaction data are entered (which may *not* be when a business activity occurs). Real-time processing generally requires an online input device.

Report-time processing means the data used to generate the requested report are processed as the report is created. *Report-time processing* is a term used primarily in event-driven systems and it is similar to real-time updating. Most event data are stored in a detailed or disaggregated form and the relevant data are selected, processed, and any master files are updated as the information customer's report is generated.

Due to the sequential access limitations of tape, tape storage mediums always use batch processing. Disk storage mediums can handle batch, online, or real-time processing.

Physical and Logical File Structures

Files have a *physical* structure and a *logical* structure. The *physical* structure relates to where the data are physically stored on the storage medium. Each file contains a certain amount and form of data and they are located at some physical memory location on the storage device.

The term *logical* refers to what the processor or user sees. The *logical* structure relates to the order of the data for processing purposes. For example, suppose a user wanted to update a file that has a sequential physical structure. This suggests that the data are physically stored on tape or disk one record after another according to some specified order (such as alphabetically). If you printed the records as they are physically stored, the physical order (how they are actually stored) and the logical order (what the user would see on the printout) would be the same. However, suppose a user wanted to sequentially process and print (in alphabetical order) a randomly stored data file. A randomly stored data file can have records stored in a seemingly chaotic fashion. In this case the physical and logical structures are very different. Nevertheless, the computer can take the randomly stored data (the file's *physical structure*) and create a list in alphabetical order for the processor or the user to see (the file's *logical structure*).

Inconsistency between the file's physical and logical structure happens more often than you may realize. If you could physically see the contents of a disk that contains a spreadsheet file, you would realize that the file is stored in chunks on various tracks and sectors of the disk (the file's physical structure). However, when you retrieve the spreadsheet file, you are presented with a worksheet consisting of cells in rows and columns (the file's logical structure) in the desired order. The point to remember is that sometimes what computer users see is an illusion that is managed by the technology devices.

Computer Data Searching

How does a computer locate a particular record or a particular group of records? Each record normally has a data field called a *key attribute* (also known as a *primary key*) that uniquely identifies it and distinguishes it from other records in the file. The key attribute is created at the time the record is initially stored in the file. When a computer user requests a particular record, he/she must identify its *key*. The computer searches the file and compares the key input by the user with the keys of records in the file to locate a record or records that match the input key.

A *secondary key (nonprimary key attribute)* can identify a record as part of a group; thus searching on a secondary key can locate a group of records with some common characteristic. To illustrate, consider the data contained in a college student file. Each record in the file would likely contain the following fields: Name, Social Security Number, Address, Major, GPA, and Credit Hours Earned. In this example, a student's Social Security number could be used as a primary key. It is a unique identifier because each person has a different Social Security number. If a user searches for records with a 123-45-6789 Social Security number as the primary key, the computer would locate information about one student (the student with that Social Security number). If a user wanted to search on a secondary key, such as students with an accounting major, the computer search would yield information about a group of students (all those with the accounting major). Name is also a common secondary key, as two or more students could have the exact same names.

If a computer is searching a tape file for a record with a specific primary or secondary key, the computer must look at each record one after another (sequentially) to locate and retrieve a record. If the computer uses a direct-access device (such as disk), the computer can go directly to the desired record, without having to review all preceding records.

A REVIEW OF THE TRADITIONAL MANUAL GENERAL LEDGER ARCHITECTURE

Manual processes rely heavily on paper documents and records, flows of paper documents through the system, and specialization of labor. Chapter 3 discusses the manual general ledger architecture.

In a manual system, paper carries the data, information, and special documentation such as proof of approvals and authorizations. Thus, manual systems generate an audit trail using a large amount of paper and paper files. Source documents serve as the repository for the detail transaction data. They are also used to communicate needed data from one person to the next and to document authorization for the transaction. Each document has a unique identifying number (e.g., its primary key). Files of source documents are organized or sequenced by one of many methods, including:

* By date/chronologically.
* Alphabetically.
* By document number/sequentially.

You can also merge the sequencing methods (e.g., file items by number within date). The method chosen depends on how you want to locate or retrieve the data. For example, organizing the documents in a file by document number allows a department to perform a completeness check or sequence check to identify if any documents are missing. Organizing documents by date could help highlight items requiring attention or action. Organizing paper documents alphabetically can help locate customers or vendors more easily.

Traditional systems collect and store data by business function, so there is duplicate data retained in various departments (such as the Sales Order Department, the Shipping Department, the Billing Department, and the Warehousing Department). Paper is used to communicate data and authorizations between departments and functions and to external parties. This requires multiple copies of most documents.

Manual systems employ batch processing. Each source document is a *transaction record,* and each document file is a *transaction file.* Each function or department retains transaction files that document the work or activity they have performed. The documents relating to a particular transaction comprise a portion of the audit trail. In the traditional accounting architecture the source documents provide the activity details that support summary data postings to journals and ledgers. The journals used in the accounting departments are also *transaction files* that contain accounting summary data. The system's *master files* include the subsidiary ledgers and the general ledger used by various accounting departments.

TRADITIONAL AUTOMATED GENERAL LEDGER ARCHITECTURE

The basic architecture of the accounting system did not initially change when IT was applied. General ledger (GL) applications simply automate the manual accounting system. Automated general ledger systems still include source documents, journals, ledgers, a trial balance, and, of course, the financial statements themselves. Some source data, the ledgers, and journals are in computerized form (tape and disk) rather than paper form. The posting and mathematics are performed electronically rather than manually. Although the number of human errors, the number of clerical personnel, and the dependence on paper is substantially reduced, automation of the traditional accounting system process does not take full advantage of the capabilities of information technology.

Computer applications of the traditional accounting process mirror the manual processes that preceded them. A traditional automated GL system is very similar to a traditional manual GL system. Rarely does automation of the accounting system affect the nature of an organization's source documents, accounting records, and information processes. Document flows are similar to the manual systems, as is the large degree of data duplication. Since authorization and data flows can be accomplished by paper or by access to a computer screen, there is sometimes a decreased amount of paper flows in an automated system.

The manual and automated processes are very similar in terms of data stores and data flows. Basically, the physical design of the system (rather than the logical design) was altered as manual processes and paper files were replaced with, or supplemented by, computer processes and tape or disk files. As in the manual system, the data that support accounting entries are recorded and stored in other departments (such as Sales Order, Warehousing, and Shipping). The accounting system boundary is often defined as the ledgers and the journals that feed into the ledgers. The paper journals used in the manual system have been physically changed to disk or tape transaction files. The paper subsidiary ledgers and the paper general ledger have been upgraded to disk or tape master files.

What are some of the changes in automated GL systems? There are examples of procedural differences between manual systems and some automated GL systems. For example, some automated systems allow users to input source document data online, rather than waiting for batch input. Other systems provide improved coordination of the subsidiary ledger with the general ledger control accounts. Rather than treating them as two duplicate pools of data, some automated GL systems use the summation of the subsidiary ledger to compute the total for the general ledger control account. In other automated GL systems, users can generate interim financial statements, rather than waiting until the end of the period. Finally, some of these systems allow users to close the books without having to create and post closing entries.

Exhibits B–1 and B–2 show sample flowcharts of processing journal input to a general ledger.[3] Exhibit B–1 illustrates batch processing using tape, and Exhibit B–2 illustrates online processing using disk.

Each computer-processing symbol on the flowchart (i.e., the rectangle) denotes a

---

3 Refer to Supplemental Chapter A for a review of flowchart documentation methods.

EXHIBIT B–1

Tape Batch Processing Example

Step 1: The data are entered into the computer system.
Input: A batch of journal vouchers (journal entries).
Process: Transfer of data from paper to tape.
Output: A tape of unsorted journal entry transaction data.

Step 2: The transaction data are sorted to order the data in the same ordering scheme as the primary key of the master file (in chart of accounts order). This step is needed because of the sequential posting procedure.
Input: A tape of unsorted journal voucher data.
Process: Sort all the journal entries in chart of accounts order.
Output: A sorted tape of journal transaction data.

Step 3: The transaction data are posted to the master file.
Input: The sorted tape of journal voucher data and the current general ledger master file.
Process: Update the balances in the current general ledger master file to reflect journal entry data, and perform edit routine to identify journal vouchers with errors or incomplete information.
Output: The sorted journal vouchers, the current (now "old") general ledger master file, a new (current) general ledger master file, and an error and exception list displaying all the journal vouchers that could not be processed due to errors. If necessary, the old master file and the transaction file can provide backup copies for the new master file.

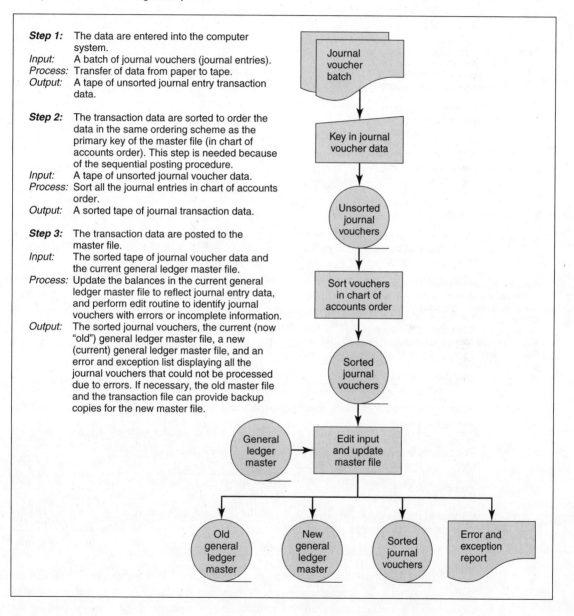

EXHIBIT B–2

Disk Online Processing Example

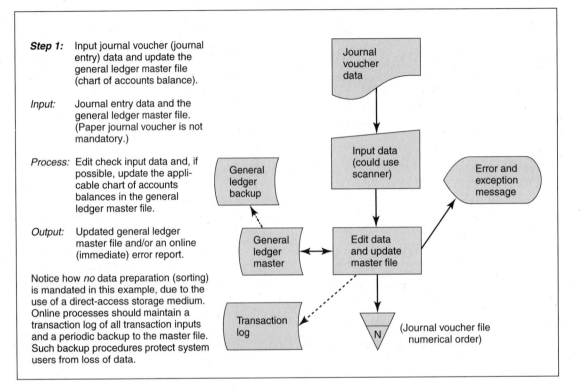

Step 1: Input journal voucher (journal entry) data and update the general ledger master file (chart of accounts balance).

Input: Journal entry data and the general ledger master file. (Paper journal voucher is not mandatory.)

Process: Edit check input data and, if possible, update the applicable chart of accounts balances in the general ledger master file.

Output: Updated general ledger master file and/or an online (immediate) error report.

Notice how *no* data preparation (sorting) is mandated in this example, due to the use of a direct-access storage medium. Online processes should maintain a transaction log of all transaction inputs and a periodic backup to the master file. Such backup procedures protect system users from loss of data.

Journal voucher data

Input data (could use scanner)

General ledger backup

Error and exception message

General ledger master

Edit data and update master file

Transaction log

N (Journal voucher file numerical order)

computer program or programs that include a list of computer instructions. Each program can include edit checks (which analyze the data and identify items that require review or correction), screens for collecting data, help screens to prompt the user, instructions for processing and storing the data, security procedures (e.g., limiting access via passwords or user IDs), and steps for generating and displaying output. The flowchart also includes both electronic and paper data flows. To understand the files and their use, it is important to consider their contents (known as their *record layouts*). The contents of the paper files used in the manual system and the computer-readable files used in an automated system are very similar.

Exhibit B–1 provides an overview of a batch general ledger process. Recall that the traditional manual GL process consists of determining if an activity meets the definition of an accounting transaction, creating a journal entry summary of the activity, posting the journal entry to a journal (and data to a subsidiary ledger, if applicable), then posting the journal to the ledger. The journal entry (in Exhibit B–1) is written on a source document that is called a *journal voucher.* Journal vouchers are keyed into the computer. When the batch of transactions is keyed into the computer, you have an unsorted transaction file. *Unsorted* refers to the fact that the transactions are not in any particular order. Can you guess the record layout of the journal voucher transaction file? It contains the items normally associated with a journal entry (such as journal voucher number, date, account numbers, debit amount, credit amount, and description). The journal number serves as the primary key, differentiating one journal entry from another.

The journal entry transaction file will be used to update the general ledger master file. The general ledger contains such data as the chart of accounts number, account name, the balances, the normal balance notation (e.g., debit or credit), beginning balances, year-to-date debits, and year-to-date credits. The GL contains a record for each chart of accounts. The chart of accounts number serves as the primary key for the records in the file. Because tape can only be read one record after another sequentially, the journal entry transaction file is sorted to put the journal entry data in the same order as the file to be updated (the general ledger master file). The sorted transactions are used to update the account balances in the master file. For each transaction record, the computer searches for a match between the transaction file record (the chart of accounts number of the account being debited or credited) and the general ledger master file record chart of accounts number to identify a particular account for update. When the search keys of the transaction record and the master record match, the balance in the general ledger master file account is updated by the journal entry amount recorded in the transaction file. Notice how not all data in the transaction file are copied to the master file; only the balances are updated. The entire process yields four outputs: a copy of the general ledger prior to the update, a copy of the transaction file, a copy of the general ledger after update, and a copy of the error and exception report. An *error and exception report* lists the journal entries that could not be processed due to errors.

The documentation of the journal entry is still contained only in the journal voucher transaction file. So the audit trail in this automated environment emulates the manual audit trail:

Source documents → Journal voucher transaction file → Ledger master file

Exhibit B–2 illustrates an online accounting process. The journal entries (recorded on journal vouchers[4]) are entered into the system and the computer performs a search to locate the accounts (in the general ledger chart of accounts) affected by the journal entry. These accounts in the GL master file are updated and stored in the same general ledger master file. Then the paper journal voucher documents are filed.

Notice the transaction log and the general ledger backup file in Exhibit B–2. The transaction log has the same file format as the journal voucher transaction file in the batch-

---

4 This process does not require paper input. The journal entry data could be entered directly into the computer.

processing example. The general ledger files also have essentially the same file format as the general ledger file used in the batch-processing example. The transaction log is needed to create an electronic audit trail of the journal entries. The second copy of the general ledger is needed for backup. The paper journal vouchers can serve as the audit trail and part of the systems backup, but imagine what would happen if you did not create an electronic transaction log. You would have no electronic data to document the changes in the balances of the general ledger accounts and you would not have any electronic backup to reconstruct the general ledger master file if it was destroyed or became corrupted!

Notice that once again the automated system audit trail emulates the manual audit trail:

Source documents → Transaction log → Ledger master file

General Ledger Software Packages

Several general ledger accounting software packages are available in the market. General ledger packages differ in terms of features and scope. Most are comprised of a series of modules, and many users add on modules that can be purchased to make the general ledger information more useful. Sample GL software modules include:

- The general ledger.
- Accounts payable.
- Accounts receivable.
- Order entry/invoicing.
- Payroll.
- Reports.
- Inventory stock control.
- Purchase control.
- Job costing.
- Fixed assets.

General ledger vendors are working to adapt their products to changing user desires and needs. In fact, one vendor states that its products do not just process debit and credits, but are designed to support all financial information flows. *Accounting Technology,* a trade publication, recently ran an article that presented the history of accounting general ledger software.[5] When you read about trends and developments in GL packages,[6] the vendors often mention the following types of advances:

- Flexibility.
- Network/client server capability.

---

[5] M. Cohn and R. Bellone, "Looking Back: History of Accounting Software," *Accounting Technology,* January 1997, pp. 19–36.
[6] For a discussion of the features of the "new generation of general ledgers" see S. McKie, "The New Breed of Power-Packed GLs," *Controller Magazine,* January 1998, pp. 24–29.

- Graphics base.
- More look-up ability.
- Ability to drill down to detail.
- Data mining ability.
- More user-defined output.

Other, more complex packages include capabilities such as the ability to interface with the Internet or intranets; the ability to interface with electronic commerce systems; the ability to support and process multinational transactions, the ability to be accessed through the web.

Accounting software packages fall into categories ranging from low-priced products for small organizations, to midpriced products for medium-sized organizations, to enterprisewide applications for the large multinational organizations. These large systems, referred to as *enterprise resource planning,* ERP, *systems,* are often enterprisewide system architectures with financial modules as one component of the integrated package.

Although studies have been done to determine their popularity,[7] the package chosen for a particular business should be based on how well the package fits the organization's needs not on the package's popularity. To learn more about these packages, check out some of the following URLs of companies that produce accounting software packages:

ERP Software Vendors

http://www.baan.com

http://www.cai.com

http://www.geac.com

http://www.jdedwards.com

http://www.oracle.com

http://www.peoplesoft.com

http://www.sap.com

Other Accounting Software Vendors

http://www.accountmate.com

http://www.accpac.com

http://www.aicpa.org/sc/software.html

http://www.champbiz.com

http://www.cougarmtn.com/

http://www.cyma-systems.com

http://www.daceasy.com

http://www.dpro.com/

---

[7] For example see D. Prawitt, M. Romney, and S. Zarowin, "A Journal Survey: The Software CPAs Use," *Journal of Accountancy,* 184, no. 5 (November 1997), pp. 52–66; and D. Keeling, "A Buyer's Guide: High End Accounting Software," *Journal of Accountancy,* December 1996, pp. 43–52.

http://www.flexi.com/

http://www.gps.com

http://www.intuit.com

http://www.lawson.com/

http://www.macola.com/

http://www.myob.com

http://www.navision-us.com/

http://www.onewrite.com

http://www.osas.com/

http://www.peachtree.com

http://www.platsoft.com/

http://www.realworldcorp.com/

http://www.sbt.com

http://www.scala.com

http://www.solomon.com

http://www.sota.com

http://www.sqlfinancials.com/

http://www.stateoftheart.com

http://www.taascforce.com

http://www.u-a-s.com/

We suggest you take some time and view their home pages on the Internet. You will no doubt come across several of these packages, or packages like them, during your career.

CONCLUDING COMMENTS

Today's information systems students should learn about the evolution of accounting information systems designs. This involves learning about the various architectures of accounting systems: the traditional manual system, the traditional automated system, and business events–driven designs. Chapter 3 presented an overview of the accounting cycle and general ledger concepts that guide the development of both the traditional manual and traditional automated architectures. This supplement complements that discussion by describing, in greater detail, the form and content of data flows and processing in both systems.

CHECKLIST OF KEY TERMS AND CONCEPTS

Batch processing
Direct access
Error and exception report

Field
File
History or archive file

Index	Record
ISAM	Reference file
Journal voucher	Report-time processing
Key attribute	Secondary key
Logical structure of a file	Sequential access
Manual traditional general ledger architecture	Sequential storage
	Sequential storage
	Suspense file
Master file	Traditional automated general ledger architecture
Online processing	
Physical structure of a file	Transaction log
Primary key	Transaction or activity file
Random storage	Transaction record
Real-time processing	

REVIEW AND DISCUSSION QUESTIONS

1. What is stored in computer files?
2. Define *master file*. Give an example of a master file.
3. Do master files contain event or transaction data? Explain.
4. Define *transaction file*. Give an example of a transaction file.
5. Define *history file*. Give an example of a history file.
6. Define *reference file*. Give an example of a reference file.
7. Define *suspense file*. Give an example of a suspense file.
8. How are records ordered in a sequential file?
9. Describe the process a computer uses to locate a record using sequential access.
10. How are records ordered in a random storage file?
11. How do you locate a record using direct access?
12. What is ISAM? Explain how records are stored and accessed using ISAM.
13. Describe batch processing.
14. Describe online processing.
15. Describe real-time processing.
16. Describe report-time processing.
17. Are online and real-time processing the same? Explain.
18. Are real-time and report-time processing the same?
19. Explain what is meant by a file's physical structure.
20. Explain what is meant by a file's logical structure.
21. What type of processing is typically used in a manual accounting system?
22. What constitutes a transaction record in a manual general ledger system?
23. What constitutes a transaction file in a manual general ledger system?
24. Prepare the record layout for a journal voucher.

25. What would be a good primary key for a journal voucher or a journal voucher transaction file? Why?

26. What would be a good primary key for a general ledger master file? Why?

27. Why do you sort a transaction file before you update a master file on tape when using batch processing?

28. Prepare a record layout for a general ledger master file.

29. Describe the contents of an error and exception report.

30. Are all journal voucher transaction data copied into the general ledger master file? Explain.

31. Describe the audit trail in a traditional manual general ledger architecture.

32. Describe the audit trail in a traditional automated general ledger architecture.

33. What is the difference between a transaction file and a transaction log? What are the similarities and differences between the two?

Data and Database Management Systems (DBMSs)

4 types of database

SUPPLEMENT OBJECTIVE

The objective of this supplement is to introduce database management systems (DBMSs). After studying this supplement, you should be able to:

- Describe the difference between file-oriented and database environments.
- Describe a DBMS.
- Identify various types of DBMS software.
- Describe common features of a DBMS.
- Describe how DBMSs are used.

FILE VERSUS DATABASE ENVIRONMENTS

Computer processing involves two components: data and instructions (programs). Data used by programming instructions are often accessed in either of two ways:

1. A user can supply input data directly.
2. A computer program can access data stored on a secondary storage medium (e.g., a hard drive, network file server, CD, disk, or tape).

Conceptually, there are two methods for designing the interface between program instructions and data. In the past, organizations developed each application independent of the other. A specific data file was created for each application. Creating such a one-to-one relationship between an application program and data files is called *file-oriented processing*. An alternative approach is *data-oriented processing*. While file-oriented approaches mandate a one-to-one relationship between programs and data files, data-oriented approaches create a single data repository to support numerous applications. With a data-oriented approach, a data pool is created and a variety of programs access needed data from the shared data pool.

The disadvantages of file-oriented processing include redundant data and programs and varying formats for storing the redundant data. To illustrate, suppose you want to design data and instructions to complete three tasks: (1) record customer orders, (2) maintain a customer mailing list, and (3) record customer shipments. A file-oriented approach would have three application programs—one for each task—and each program would access a separately prepared data file for a total of three separate data files. Consider the following files with a partial listing of the fields for each file:

- Order file: Order Number, Date, Customer Number, Customer Name, Customer Address, Inventory Items Ordered, Quantities Ordered.
- Mailing list: Customer Number, Customer Name, Customer Address.

- Shipment file: Date, Shipment Number, Order Number, Customer Number, Customer Name, Customer Address, Inventory Items Ordered, Items Shipped.

Notice the duplication in these separate files. Customer Name, Customer Number, Customer Address, Order Number, and Inventory Items Ordered are all stored in two or more files. In addition, the format for similar fields may vary because the programmer used inconsistent field formats. This often occurs when different programmers develop the various programs and files. For example, the Customer Number in the mailing list file may be formatted as a five-character numeric field, while Customer Number in the shipment file may be formatted as an eight-character alphabetic/numeric field.

Redundancies in data and programs are both inefficient and problematic. Data redundancies create data inconsistencies as data across the applications are changed or updated. For example, a change in a customer's address by an application recording sales data will not automatically update the customer's address recorded in the application used to generate customer invoices for mailing. Consider the implications of a change in our sample files, such as changing a customer's name. This update requires three separate file maintenance programs and data inconsistency will result if they are not executed properly and in a timely manner.

In file-oriented environments, application developers create a large volume of duplicate computer code to perform similar tasks in all the separate applications (e.g., opening and closing files, performing queries, and developing security functions). As a result, developing and maintaining business applications is expensive and difficult. The business and information processing risks associated with developing and maintaining duplicate data are also increased.

For our previous example, a data-oriented approach would design a data pool that would include the following data items:

- Customer items: Customer Number, Customer Name, and Customer Address.
- Order items: Order Date, Order Number, Inventory Ordered, Quantities Ordered, and Customer Number.
- Shipment items: Shipment Date, Shipment Number, Order Number, Customer Number, Items Shipped, and Balance Due for Shipment.

Programmers would write three application programs: record orders, record shipments, and maintain the mailing list. Each program would access the common data pool for the desired data. Notice how this structure reduces the instances of data redundancy and the potential for data inconsistency. Data maintenance is also reduced. Changes in a data item, such as changing a customer's name, require only one update.

A data-oriented approach allows programmers and users to use the same pool of data to create various views of the same data. For example, to generate output, the program code would select the applicable items to generate records of orders, order documents, order reports, customer mailing lists, shipping documents, shipping reports, and a wide variety of user-requested outputs.

E X H I B I T   C–1

Database Architecture

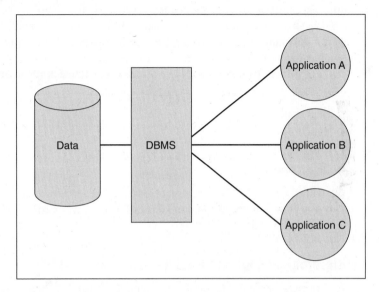

In file-oriented environments, programmers develop physical files to record data and generate output for each desired view of the data. In data-oriented environments, programmers develop an integrated data store to record data, then select applicable data items from the common data file to create a variety of logical outputs (views).[1] Exhibit C–1 illustrates database architecture.

WHAT IS A DATABASE MANAGEMENT SYSTEM (DBMS)? ✓

A DBMS is the resource available to define and manage data structures in an information system. DBMS software was originally developed to simplify and enhance the value of an organization's data by reducing data and programming redundancy, inconsistent data formats, and data inconsistencies. A DBMS environment allows the development and maintenance of a data repository that is independent from application programs. Such flexibility enables database users to create and maintain IT applications that capture, maintain, and report data while shielding application developers from the physical structure and maintenance of the data repository. Today's DBMS technology is the result of several years of development that has spawned various types of DBMS software.

---

1 *Logical* refers to what the user sees, rather than what physically exists on the file storage medium.

TYPES OF DBMS SOFTWARE

DBMS software differs in the features offered to users and developers. One of the critical differences between DBMS software packages is their ability to create and manage *logical* data structures (i.e., the way the data are conceptually organized). How the DBMS software implements and manages the relationships between data is key in determining the features it can offer.

DBMS software packages use a variety of architectures to organize and access data, including:

- Hierarchical
- Network
- Relational
- Object oriented

We will discuss how data are organized and accessed in each of these methods. We will also overview how the various models differ in terms of complexity, flexibility, and computational demands.

Hierarchical Logical Structures

As the name implies, hierarchical databases (also called *tree databases*) organize and search data using the structure of a family tree. Each record of the hierarchical structure may have multiple "child" records that are subordinate to it. In other words, the child record is "owned" by and accessed through the "parent" record. For example, in Exhibit C–2 student records are subordinate to (or owned by) course records. A single record describes each course with a course number and section number; the course owns students who are described by student records that are subordinate to the course record. An alternative method of representing the relationship between courses and students in a hierarchical structure is to have multiple course records that are subordinate to a student record, so that each student owns a record for each course he or she is taking. However, you must make a choice as to which of these scenarios you want to model in this environment.

Choosing which records are superior and which records are subordinate depends in part on storage efficiency as well as on the quantity and types of queries you anticipate. Because the hierarchical structure can model only 1:1 and 1:* maximum cardinalities, this restricts the usefulness of the hierarchical database structure. However, there are cases when the hierarchical structure is acceptable. For example, hierarchical structures are commonly used to organize accounting data when a chart of account structure is used. When you decompose financial statements, for example, the hierarchical structure of the data is rather obvious (see Exhibit C–3).

Hierarchical structures are fairly restrictive in terms of access. The access path is from parent to child. They are also computationally demanding because of the links that must be maintained between the parent and child records.

EXHIBIT C–2

Sample Hierarchical Structure

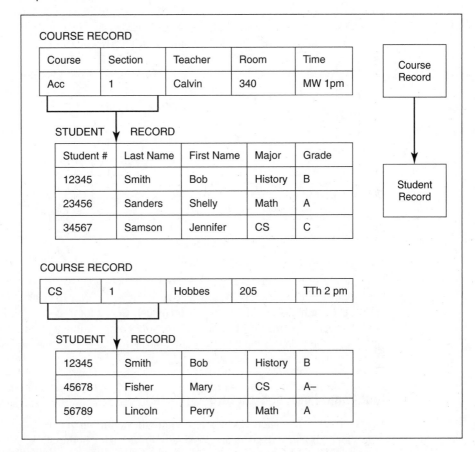

Network Logical Structure

Network structures overcome many of the limitations of the hierarchical structure. While the hierarchical structure has only one superior record for one or more subordinate records, the network structure allows any number of superior records to be related to any number of subordinates (and vice versa). The distinction between parent and child records is eliminated. Using a network structure, student records could be subordinate to course, and course records could be subordinate to student records *at the same time.*

Originally, simple network structures could model 1:1, 1:*, and *:1 maximum cardinalities. Later, complex network models were developed to model 1:1, 1:*, *:1, and *:* maximum cardinalities. As a result, network structures have a great deal more flexibility

EXHIBIT C–3

Accounting Data in a Hierarchical Structure

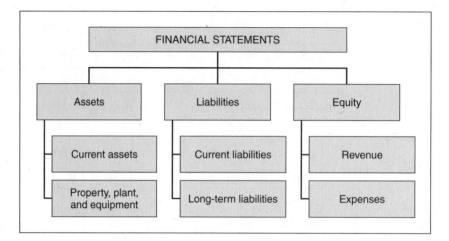

than flat file or hierarchical structures. However, network DBMS software is fairly complex because you must know the physical structure of the data to be able to search the database. This is a major roadblock to nontechnical users adopting network DBMSs. As you might expect, network DBMS software is more computationally demanding than hierarchical structures due to the need to maintain the links between the superior and subordinate records.

Relational Logical Structure

Both hierarchical and network models require the definition of cardinalities as the database is developed because the data are physically linked using addresses or pointers to superior and subordinate records to generate logical structures. This makes database design complex, and limits the ability to change or update desired output views in a timely manner.

One of the more popular types of database technologies today is based on the theory of relational math (set theory).[2] Relational databases organize and store data in two-dimensional tables consisting of rows and columns. For example, a table listing names and telephone numbers is shown in Exhibit C–4. The table is arranged in columns, which are called *attributes,* or *domains,* and *rows,* which are called *records* or *tuples.* Each row of information in a table is called an *instance.* One of the table fields is a unique identifier field (the *key attribute* or *primary key*). Normally, each table contains:

---

2 Supplemental Chapter B describes the evolution of database models (the assumptions of which characterize (DBMSs) in
    more detail.

EXHIBIT C–4

A Sample Relational Table

Name	Telephone Number
Maureen Rodriguez	485-5215
Steve Anderson	268-9615
Cheryl Gibbs	377-3216
Lyn Hoggan	226-5476
Scott Kirkham	321-9512
Karrie Eaquinto	462-6387
Jim Stice	373-6733

1. Data items about a particular group of people, resources, locations, or business activity type.[3]
2. Data items (usually key attributes) that are used to combine or link tables.

The relational approach to designing databases allows more flexibility. By introducing some limited duplication into the data pool, users are able to create relationships and logical structures ad hoc, rather than having to predefine relationships as the database is created. A change in the database does not require rewriting all the application program codes. Like the network model, relational databases can incorporate all of the types of maximum relationship cardinalities.

Rather than physically linking data, relational models make use of logical tables to model structures. Relationships among tables are represented by common data values in the tables. Data from different tables can be combined by matching a data item common to both tables. Examples of linking relational tables are presented in Chapter 4.

Each table contains data about a specific entity (for example, a business activity, resource, or agent). Sometimes, separate tables are created to include the relationship or link between two tables. Exhibit C–5 demonstrates such table organization. The Customer table contains only data items about customers (e.g., Name, Telephone, and Balance fields). The Sale table contains only data items about a sale (e.g., Invoice Number, Date, and Customer fields). The Product table contains data about inventory items maintained by the company (e.g., Item Number, Description, Price, and Cost fields). Finally, the Product-Sale table contains data items that describe the quantity of items sold in each sale (e.g., Invoice Number, Item Number, and Quantity fields).

The power of relational DBMS software is the ability to maintain several tables of related information that can be accessed by several different information customers in

---

3 Putting only data items about a particular entity or object into a data table is known as *normalization*. A table is in normal form if it only contains items that describe the main theme or focus of the table (e.g., customers, sales orders, or inventory) plus any fields needed to link the table with other tables. Chapter 4 further discusses data table construction and normal form.

EXHIBIT C–5 *Parent child Relationship*

Examples of Relational Tables

	CUSTOMER			SALE	
Name	**Telephone**	**Balance**	**Invoice #**	**Date**	**Customer**
Nicol	123-4567	123,456	213	01Sep99	Nicol
Benjamin	852-7412	365,412	214	01Sep99	Charisse
Tate	951-3578	214,569	215	02Sep99	Benjamin
Charisse	357-4563	456,321	216	02Sep99	Tate
Marty	632-1587	124,682	217	03Sep99	Marty
Sariah	145-9687	975,632	218	03Sep99	Sariah
McKell	875-6891	112,002	219	04Sep99	McKell

	PRODUCT				PRODUCT-SALE	
Item #	**Description**	**Price**	**Cost**	**Invoice #**	**Item #**	**Qty**
1	Rocket	215	100	213	1	2
2	Violin	250	75	214	2	1
3	Bat	35	22	215	2	1
4	Doll	56	12	216	4	5
				217	3	2
				218	4	1

many different ways. For example, the data items from the various tables illustrated in Exhibit C–5 could be used to calculate accounts receivable by totaling the balance due for each customer. As well, the tables could be used to summarize what each customer purchased during a month, to calculate the average time between a sale and a related cash receipt, and to calculate total sales for the income statement.

One of the great advantages of the relational structure is its ability to simplify the organization of complex sets of data. In comparison to hierarchical and network structures, relational databases are fairly straightforward both in terms of organizing and searching the data. The drawback of relational DBMSs is they are computationally very demanding primarily because of the ad hoc search capability. Therefore, when tables in a relational database begin to exceed tens of millions of records (even on the largest computers), hierarchical or network structures and related software prove to be much more efficient than the relational model.

Object-Oriented Structure

A more technologically sophisticated model than the relational model is the object-oriented database structure. Objects contain both data as well as methods (i.e., instructions for processing the data). The major advantage of object-oriented (OO) structures is their increased flexibility to represent very complex data structures that capture the essence of complex objects existing in reality. Using object technology, programmers can model and implement complex data types such as voice, video, and audio. A current popular trend in database development is the attempt to overcome the limitations of relational database methods by combining the relational approach with object technology concepts. Using object technology to supplement relational database models is referred to as ORDMS (object relational database management systems). Although OO structures have several conceptual advantages over the other structures, it is much more computationally demanding (meaning it requires heavy use of computing resources) than even the pure relational structure. Today, there are a limited number of pure object-oriented database applications in use. However, as technology improves, the frequency of object-oriented applications will increase.

OTHER FEATURES OF A DBMS

A database administrator (DBA) is often hired to coordinate data management activities such as approving both the physical contents and user views of the database. DBMS packages have a variety of features, including:

- Data definition commands, which are used to set up the data structures and define user data views of the data. These are known as *logical views* or *schemas.*
- Data manipulation commands, which are used to add, delete, and update data in the structures.
- Data query commands, which help users ask questions about the data.[4]
- Forms generators, which are used to design the format and look of desired screens and forms.
- Report generators, which are used to define the format and look of desired output.

Additionally, DBMS environments provide management and security features. Many packages include a user interface designed to aid programmers and users with the processes of data definition, data queries, and application design.

DBMS (AND FILE) DOCUMENTATION

Database and file contents are documented at the record or data item level. Exhibit C–6 illustrates the relationships between common terms used to describe various components of a database. The *database* generally consists of many *files* and each file contains many

---

4 Popular data query tools include QBE (query by example) and SQL (structured query language). Using QBE, a grid or replica of an empty record is displayed and the user types search criteria in the applicable columns. SQL, on the other hand, is an actual program language that you can use to directly interact with data, or you can embed SQL commands in programs that access and process data. Some DBMSs include both methods (e.g., defaulting to QBE and offering SQL capabilities as an option). SQL3 is the structured query language standard for object relational databases.

EXHIBIT C–6

File Structure Relationships

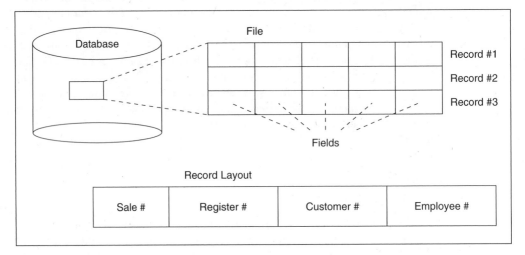

records. For example, one file in the database may be a TakeOrder file that contains data on all the Take Customer Order events. Each event represents one record. Within each record there are many *fields* of data called *data items,* with each data item representing one *attribute* about the entity. In the TakeOrder file, each record (in this example an event) is called an *entity* and there are various attributes to describe that entity. One of the attributes is the customer's name and it is recorded in one field of the record.

Documenting files by records, using a *record layout,* is consistent with the way data are processed in more traditional processing environments—data files are processed record by record. A *record layout* details the record structure, including record field names, the width of each field, and the type of data stored in each field (e.g., numeric, alphanumeric, or date).

Since database data items are shared by numerous applications, database documentation, called *data dictionaries,* document data item, rather than record level, detail. Data dictionaries include information about the database and data items in the database. Data dictionaries provide a catalog of data item information such as name, description, data type, date created, name of person who created it, data representation, data range, list of applications using it, and the person(s) authorized to view or change the data item.

DBMS ANALYSIS AND DESIGN

Much of the work to develop a database and the programs associated with it is completed during the analysis, planning, and design stages of a system. A central objective in analyzing and designing the database is to identify the set of data needed to document business activities (e.g., financing, selling, purchasing, or marketing) and provide information about parties (e.g., customers, vendors, or employees) and resources (e.g., cash, services, or inventory) involved in the business activities. This has been and will continue to be the key to effectively creating useful databases (i.e., databases that support both operational and strategic decision making).

Architecture plans include an overview of such DBMS components as:

- The specific data items and structures needed.
- The attributes of each data item.
- The primary identifier for each data structure.
- A method for linking related data items and structures (which requires an understanding of data/object relationships).
- Needed business and information controls.
- Needed help screens and help functions.
- Input/output screens, report formats, queries, and documents.
- Computer instructions needed to perform recording, maintenance, and reporting tasks.

To create a physical and logical data environment, the developer begins by using data definition commands to create the data structures. This includes specifying all needed data items (fields), primary key (the unique identifier), data type (such as date, alphanumeric, numeric, graphic, video, animation, picture, or audio),[5] field width of each data item, any data item default values, and any data item constraints or validation rules. The developer also specifies how data items and structures are related.

Next, the developer creates input/output screens (for collecting or displaying data), queries, reports, and document formats. To create programmed computer instructions, the developer uses macros or application languages included in the DBMS or some other language that is able to interface with the data. These instructions use the DBMS data manipulation commands to write code for recording and maintaining data.

At this point, the developer has created a data structure, and is ready to enter actual data into the structure. Programmers can directly input data into the data structures, or they can test their macros, forms, and programs to input the initial pool of data. After initial data are entered, and the organization wants to use the environment during actual business activities, data recording, maintaining, and reporting are accomplished by accessing the data structures, I/O screens, report and query formats, and other programmed instructions developed for users. Perhaps the most useful component of the database environment is the query commands that allow users to generate a variety of desired outputs, ad hoc. Thus, users are not limited to a specific collection of preprogrammed instructions to generate output.

If an organization uses database technology to develop a system, you cannot assume

---

5 Data items could also be objects linked to or embedded from other applications, such as a spreadsheet graph or a word processing document.

that an efficient, nonduplicate data-oriented environment is created. Some programmers, due to their desire to automate existing processes, simply recreate their file-oriented data processing environment using a DBMS. Many accounting environments that use DBMS technology still store and process data in files that mirror the files that existed in file-oriented manual accounting systems.

DATA WAREHOUSES

In many current database environments, users are limited in the types of ad hoc queries they can effectively execute. In some cases, this is due to the limitations of DBMS technology. In other cases, this is due to the structure of the databases, data included in the database, and the use of available technology. Thus in some environments, databases have been narrowly defined for capturing, maintaining, and reporting the data and information for supporting day-to-day business operations. In these environments, databases are the key component of the online transaction processing system (OLTP).

Organizations also need access to information that will help them more effectively perform analysis and decision making on matters that are not simply operational in nature. They desire access to high-level data views or snapshots of trends and summaries of organizational performance over a period of time. An increasing number of IS developers are advocating the use of data warehousing technology to satisfy this need for what is called *online analytical processing* (OLAP).

Data warehouses contain data from operational databases, as well as data from other, often external, sources. The objective is to capture and make available the knowledge and information viewed as critical for analysis and decision making. After the desired data are collected from internal and external systems, the data are combined and duplicate, invalid, and unneeded data are removed. The data are aggregated (i.e., summarized) and organized by dimension and/or subject area. Unlike operational databases that are ever changing to reflect changes in the state of an organization, data warehouses provide summary data as of a certain point in time. Data warehouse users can mine the data and "slice and dice" it to generate desired outputs. The creation and management of a data warehouse is a complex process that has grown out of the desire to have access to more than operational data. Once again, users are sending a signal that they need enterprisewide information views of an organization to support all levels of analysis and decision making.

CONCLUDING COMMENTS

Database technology and DBMSs are powerful tools to make systems development and use much more efficient. Some organizations are supplementing databases that contain operational data with data warehousing techniques. Significant changes have been made in approaches to database design during recent years and it will likely continue in the future. Data integration will be a key in reengineering business processes and developing solutions to business problems. As the limitations of database technology evaporate, we believe organizations will increasingly combine all relevant data about business events, financial and nonfinancial, into a common information storehouse (be it physical or logical). This will result in a complete integration of enterprise information, providing the information required in the decision-making process.

CHECKLIST OF KEY TERMS AND CONCEPTS

Attribute	Key attribute ✔
Database Administrator (DBA)	Logical data structures ✔
Database Management System (DBMS) ✔	Logical views of data ✔
Software	Network structure ✔
Data definition commands	Normalization
Data dictionary	Object-oriented file structure ✔
Data manipulation commands	Online analytical processing (OLAP) ✔
Data-oriented processing environments	Online transaction processing (OLTP)
Data query commands ✔	Primary key ✔
Data Warehouses ✔	QBE—Query By Example ✔
Domain	Record
Entity	Record layout
Field	Relational logical file structure
File ✔	Report generators
File-oriented processing environments	Schema
Form generator	SQL—Structured Query Language ✔
Hierarchical logical file structure ✔	Tuple

REVIEW AND DISCUSSION QUESTIONS

1. Compare and contract file-oriented and data-oriented processing environments.
2. What is a DBMS? Is there more than one type? Explain.
3. Describe the tree or hierarchical logical structure. What types of maximum relationship cardinalities can it model? Why is it restricted to these relationships?
4. Describe the network logical structure. What types of maximum relationship cardinalities can it model? How can it handle these relationships?
5. Describe the relational logical structure. What types of maximum relationship cardinalities can it model? How can it handle these relationships?
6. What is an object-oriented structure?
7. True or False: "There is no data redundancy in relational structures." Explain.
8. List and describe five features of a DBMS.
9. Is a Data Base Administrator a person or software? What does it do?

10. What is the difference between QBE and SQL?
11. Explain the structure and purpose of a record layout.
12. Explain the structure and purpose of a data dictionary.
13. Describe the DBMS analysis and design process.
14. What are data warehouses?
15. Compare and contrast an online transaction processing (OLTP) system and an online analytical (OLAP) processing system.

Sample Electronic Data Processing Controls

Useful cho practice

SUPPLEMENT OBJECTIVES

Chapter 5 introduced business and information process risk and the philosophy of a system of internal controls. However, Chapter 5 did not cover the specific controls to be included in the internal control system to minimize or prevent individual risks. Part of developing a system of internal controls is identifying specific controls to minimize the likelihood that errors and irregularities will occur; and, if they do occur, to minimize the loss from their occurrence.

The objectives of this supplement are to review the control philosophy and identify some of the most important controls to minimize risk. After studying this supplement, you should be able to:

1. Identify what contributes to a strong control environment.
2. Identify specific controls to prevent, detect, or recover from risks associated with:
   a. Operating activities.
   b. Information processes.

REVIEW OF CONTROLS PHILOSOPHY

Every entity, whether it is a business organization, governmental agency, or not-for-profit entity has some stated objectives. Entities are established to do something for someone. They might be organized to make money, provide public services, or administer an estate. There are many opportunities available to these entities to achieve their objectives. With each opportunity, there is some risk. The risks may be: *strategic*—doing the wrong things; *decision*—failure to make a needed decision or selecting a poor alternative; *operating*—doing the right things the wrong way; *financial*—losing financial resources or creating financial liabilities; or *information*—making errors in recording, maintaining, and reporting activities. We refer to these and similar risks as *business risks*. Although all these risks must be managed, we will focus primarily on operating, financial, and information risks.

The operations of an entity can be subdivided into several business processes. Some of the more common business processes include sales/collection, acquisition/payment, and conversion. An organization will perform many operating activities in each of these business processes. Some of the operating activities associated with the sales/collection process are taking a customer order, picking the merchandise, packaging and shipping the items, and collecting payment from the customer. The risks associated with these and other processes are frequently called *operating activity risks*. Therefore, an *operating activity risk* involves any undesirable outcome associated with providing goods and services to customers while an *information processing risk* includes any undesirable outcome associated with recording, maintaining, or reporting information. An example of an operating activity risk is the possibility that a cash receipts clerk will pocket some of the money received while accepting a customer's payment. This is also a *financial risk* because it represents a loss of cash—a financial resource. An information processing risk is the possibility that the clerk will incorrectly record the amount of cash received.

Controls are established to manage or minimize risks. All the controls combined constitute the *internal control system.* Therefore, the internal control system of an entity is comprised of a set of rules, policies, and procedures to provide reasonable assurance that (1) its financial reports are reliable, (2) its operations are effective and efficient, and (3) its activities comply with applicable laws and regulations. In developing a system of internal controls, the first thing you should do is identify things that can go wrong while executing an operating activity or an information process (the risk), and estimate both the cost associated with each risk and the probability of the risk occurring. The reason we begin with this analysis is to focus our controls in areas where they will do the most good. Since controls are costly, it does not make good business sense to develop controls for things that won't happen, or for things that if they do happen, will not cost much money or have much impact. However, organizations should use care when analyzing the costs and benefits. Sometimes the benefits are understated.

CASE IN POINT

Four out of five United Kingdom (UK) organizations have suffered an IT security breach in the past few years according to a recent survey. Despite the reliance of many organizations on IT, data security is still seen by many as a "grudge buy," because the benefits of having software and systems security are largely invisible. No one likes paying for a service they can't see.

Acts of software piracy, fraud, hacking, and sabotage are costing UK's information technology market billions of pounds every year. That figure is rising fast. According to the survey, the total annual cost of these breaches exceeds 1.2 billion pounds. Much of the loss is preventable, yet the losses are on the increase. The naive attitude of it will never happen to me is still prevalent in the mind-set of many companies.

When it comes to the much-hyped art of hacking, the traditional image of the acne-blemished teenager in his bedroom surfing the digital waves of large multinational organizations just does not hold true. According to the survey, "You are far more likely to be hacked into by your own staff than by outsiders." In one such case a giant IT company employed a youth with no IT knowledge or experience. Within a year, he had developed considerable knowledge about Unix and gained unauthorized access to many supervisory privileges. Not only did he create many unauthorized super-user accounts for himself but also he deleted vital files and directories. On discovery it took the IT support and corporate security teams 30 days to investigate the incidents, which ended up costing the company 33,000 pounds.[1]

After identifying risks and their materiality, the next step in developing an internal control system is to identify a control, or a set of controls, that will *prevent, detect,* or *correct* what could go wrong. The most desirable controls are those that prevent an error or irregularity, but they are frequently the most difficult and costly to implement and main-

---

1 M. Lynch, "Don't Get Caught Out! Companies Should Implement Security Systems to Protect Their Information Systems," *Exe,* May 1994, p. 20.

tain. If we cannot prevent something from happening, we at least want to know it has happened (detect it) and be able to recover from it (correct it).

The last step in developing an internal control system is to implement the rules, policies, and procedures that can be cost justified. Generally, there are several controls that can help prevent, detect, or recover from a business risk, but every control has a cost. For example, if we want to prevent a sales clerk from pocketing some of the proceeds from a sale, we could require two sales clerks to be involved with every sale. (Even then the two employees could collude and defraud the company, thus minimizing the effectiveness of this control. But the risk of collusion is much lower than the original risk.) The cost of this control is the cost of the second employee. In deciding whether a second employee is cost justified, we must estimate the probability of an employee taking money and the amount he/she might steal. If the cost of the added employee is less than the loss from cash theft, it will be cost beneficial to add a second employee. Where we have several controls to select from, we place greater emphasis on those that prevent the problem, than on those that detect the loss or help us recover from it.

When you analyze the cost of controls, do not simply examine the financial costs, but the cost in terms of operational effectiveness as well. Some costs are the negative effects of reductions in operational effectiveness. For example, an organization that reduces all risks may be more efficient, but may become a less effective competitor in the marketplace. Thus, it is important to balance efficiency and effectiveness when evaluating control strategies.

An internal control system consists of five interrelated components: control environment, risk assessment, control activities, information and communication, and monitoring. Each of these components was introduced in Chapter 5. The objective of this supplement is to review each of these components and identify specific control activities that can be applied to minimize risk. As you read and study this chapter, remember that it is not a comprehensive listing of all controls. This is a dynamic and exciting time. As organizations and environments change, new controls are necessary. Innovative organizations and consultants are regularly developing and implementing new and updated control policies and procedures.

CONTROL ENVIRONMENT

definition control process

The control environment sets the tone of the organization and influences the control consciousness of its people. The control environment encompasses several areas, but the integrity and ethical values of the organization as a whole, management's philosophy, and how the organization treats its people are some of the most important.

Integrity and Ethical Values

Integrity is represented by the honesty and moral character of the people within the organization and their commitment to moral principles. People have high moral character when they do the right things for the right reasons. Integrity and ethical values are essential elements of a control environment. The effectiveness of controls cannot rise above the integrity and ethical values of the people who create, administer, and monitor them. Integrity and ethical behavior are the products of the entity's ethical and behavioral standards, how they are communicated, and how they are reinforced in practice.

Controls that can help improve the integrity and ethical values of the organization include:

Hire honest people. There are a variety of pencil and paper honesty tests available to measure people's honesty. However, something as simple as asking people in a job application interview, "Are you an honest person, and if you are hired, can we count on you to be totally honest in your dealing with the company, fellow employees, and our customers?" establishes an expectation of ethical conduct within the organization.

Establish a code of conduct. Every organization should have a code of ethical conduct. It need not be long, but it should identify what is and is not appropriate conduct within the organization. Because of the increased sensitivity about what is and is not ethical, the discussion process associated with developing the code is frequently as important as the code itself.

Have a violations review committee. Every entity should have a committee to review employee's complaints about inappropriate conduct within the organization. When appropriate, the identity of the complaining employee should be kept anonymous.

Review company practices and rules. Periodically, the company's practices should be reviewed to determine if there are any incentives and temptations to encourage people to engage in dishonest, illegal, or unethical acts. For example, sometimes the pressure to achieve performance goals is so great it causes employees to fabricate operating data.

Organizations should continually review their rules and decide whether they are rational, defensible, and effective. Unfortunately, too many organizations have too many picky rules. These include rules that are arbitrary, irrational, and unworthy of support and obedience. People will comply with irrational rules when there is adequate surveillance and punishment. But the threat of punishment does not contribute to moral development; indeed, it tends to inhibit the internalization of ethical behavior. Rewarding good behavior is better than threatening punishment to influence behavior, since rewards avoid the resistance and rebelliousness that accompany punishment.[2] Once rules are established that contribute to the productivity and effectiveness of the organization, managers have the responsibility to explain the importance of the rules and lead by example. When this is done, organizations can be quite successful in implementing some rather demanding rules.

---

2 David J. Cherrington and J. Owen Cherrington, "How to Stop Lying, Cheating, and Stealing," *Executive Excellence,* July 1990.

Impact of Management's Philosophy on the Control Environment

In addition to the honesty and integrity of the people within the organization, management's philosophy can either contribute to or help prevent, a high-risk environment. Frequently, there are no specific controls that can be applied to management's philosophy, but if it contributes to a high-risk environment, it creates a need for greater controls over the more detailed operating activities. Questions that may be asked to identify a high-risk environment include:

> Is the organization committed to hiring competent people who possess the knowledge and skills needed to perform their assigned jobs?

> Does management have a conservative or reasonable approach in accepting business risks and in reporting the financial results of operations?

> If there is a board of directors, are there outside representatives on the board?

> If the entity has an annual audit of their financial statements, does it have an audit committee to oversee the audit?

> Does the company have a well-defined organizational structure with appropriate division of duties and responsibilities and identified reporting relationships so that important activities are planned, executed, controlled, and monitored on a timely basis?

> Do people understand the company's policies and practices, what they are responsible for, and to whom they report?

> Has management developed a culture that emphasizes integrity and ethical behavior?

If the answers to these and similar questions are yes, the organization would be classified as having a very favorable control environment. In such an environment, the need for extensive, detailed controls will be lessened because errors or irregularities would be identified and corrected in a timely manner. For example, errors and irregularities will be minimized in an entity that is well organized with appropriate division of duties and responsibilities, well-established reporting relationships, and a climate of honesty and integrity. However, even if the entity is well organized with appropriate division of duties and responsibilities and reporting relationships, if the culture condones dishonesty, errors and irregularities will frequently not be noticed or not be reported.

Human Resource Policies and Practices

People are frequently the most important assets of the organization. However, if they are not the right people and if they are not managed properly, they may become more of a liability than an asset. *Human resource policies and practices* relate to hiring, orienting, training, evaluating, counseling, promoting, compensating, and terminating employees.

Sound personnel practices are essential in controlling both operating activities and information processes. This is becoming increasingly important as organizations empower employees in an attempt to streamline operations and cut costs. The quality of an organization's employees directly influences the quality of the goods and services provided to the customers. Generally speaking, competent, trustworthy employees are more likely to help the organization create value.

Little can be done to completely stop employees who are determined to embarrass, harm, or destroy an organization. Occasionally, employees join together to inflict errors or defraud the system. This is called *collusion.*

The following controls can help ensure success in hiring and retaining quality employees:

Check the background of each applicant. Regardless of the position in the organization, take time to perform a background check on the applicant before offering a job. Many organizations have suffered significant losses at the hands of individuals who have had a history of incompetence, fraud, or other dishonest acts. Checking references, résumés, scholastic records, and similar information will minimize the possibility of hiring an incompetent or dishonest employee.

Bond people in critical positions. Bonding is a form of insurance that protects against losses by dishonest employees. To bond an employee, the company pays a fee to a bonding company. The bonding company will perform a background and character check on the employee and if they are satisfied, they will "bond" the employee. This means that if the employee subsequently steals from the company, the bonding company pays the loss but retains the right to prosecute the employee for the loss. Although a defensive measure that may foster a feeling of distrust with employees, bonding is often a very wise business practice for key employees who have the potential to participate in material errors or irregularities. Moreover, some industries are required to bond certain individuals to comply with legal requirements.

Explain organization policies and procedures. Training sessions should be conducted for all new employees to inform them of the organization's policies and procedures. *Policy and procedure manuals* should be available to describe (1) what is and is not appropriate conduct at work; (2) what is considered confidential information; and (3) safety procedures.

Define promotion and personal growth opportunities. Organizations should provide opportunities for personal growth to all employees. Regular reviews of each employee's performance are an essential element of this process. Employees should clearly understand the nature of the review and the standard used to evaluate them. In addition, each employee should have the opportunity for continuing education to keep abreast of changes within his/her specialty and the fast-changing technological world that will certainly affect both the individual and the organization.

Define procedures for terminating employees. If a key employee announces he or she is leaving the organization, management should be notified immediately. A checklist should specify employee *exit policies and procedures.* The checklist should include recovering all organization resources issued to the employee, terminating the employee's access to the information system, and revising distribution lists that include the employee's name. Lastly, an *exit interview* can help determine the exact reason for the termination, remind the individual of confidentiality agreements, and identify potential problems with the work environment.

Provide well-defined work schedules. Scheduling people's work assists in separating incompatible functions. The work schedules should assign specific, compatible responsibilities to each employee (based on their training, skill level, and expertise), communicate a time budget for performing responsibilities, and ask employees to account for their time and periodically report on their progress. Failure to complete assigned duties and resolve issues in a timely manner should be investigated. Work schedules should include *rotation of duties* and *required vacations.* The same job should not always be assigned to the same employee but should be rotated among qualified employees. Every employee should be required to take a two-week vacation every year. These controls prevent one person from covering up any errors or irregularities by continuously being in charge of one task or set of tasks.

RISK ASSESSMENT

Risk assessment is a process of identifying things that can go wrong and the probability of their occurrence. There are no exhaustive checklists identifying all the things that can go wrong. People with criminal minds work on expanding these checklists all the time. They are looking for weaknesses in the system and identifying ways to take advantage of a weakness for personal gain, without being caught. Failure to identify these weaknesses before they are identified by people with criminal minds often results in significant losses.

We are not only concerned with the potential loss from fraud but also with unintentional errors. Remember that losses due to unintentional errors are much higher than losses from intentional irregularities. Risk assessment must cover both the intentional irregularities to defraud the company and the unintentional errors all employees make during the normal course of business.

Some of the important areas you should investigate during the risk assessment phase include:

Where has the company incurred losses in the past and how much has been lost? A historical analysis of where errors and irregularities have occurred in the past provides a good list of potential future losses and information to assess both the probability and the magnitude of the loss. Reports from the internal auditors provide valuable information on prior losses and their causes. Reported differences between the physical quantities of assets on hand and the amounts recorded in the accounting records identify which assets have had shortages in the past.

Where have similar companies incurred losses and how much have they lost? Much can be learned from another company's mistakes. This type of information can be directly obtained from the company or through published literature. Consultants who have had significant exposure to a variety of companies are frequently hired to perform a review of a company's operations and identify areas of exposure.

Ask employees where errors and irregularities are most likely to occur. Most employees are honest and want to do a good job. They know where errors and irregularities have occurred and have not been reported, and they know where irregularities could occur and not easily be detected. Many employees are in a situation where they could defraud the company without being detected, but they don't because of their honesty and loyalty to the company. They can not only identify the areas of risk, but also identify controls to reduce the risk.

Once we have identified things that can go wrong and their likelihood of occurrence, we need to identify and implement specific controls to help prevent, detect, or recover from the errors and irregularities. This is the topic of our next section.

CONTROL ACTIVITIES

Control activities are the policies and procedures the organization establishes to verify that activities are properly performed. They help ensure that necessary actions are taken to address the risks identified in the preceding discussion. Control activities have various objectives and are applied at various organizational and functional levels.

We can classify control activities by their use (i.e., whether they are used to prevent, detect, or recover from errors or irregularities). *Preventive controls* focus on preventing an error or irregularity. *Detective controls* focus on identifying when an error or irregularity has occurred. *Corrective controls* focus on recovering from, repairing the damage from, or minimizing the cost of an error or irregularity. An *error* is an unintended mistake on the part of an employee while an *irregularity* is an intentional effort to do something that is undesirable to the organization.

Control activities relevant to the information processing activities of an entity may be broadly classified into three areas: separation of duties, physical controls, and information processing controls.

Separation of Duties

Separation of duties structures the work of people so the work of one person checks the work of another person. Separation of duties is a preventive control for both errors and irregularities. Traditionally, organizations tried to separate (1) the authorization of transactions in the accounting records, (2) the recording of transactions, and (3) the custody of assets. This separation was an attempt to reduce the opportunity for one person to both perpetuate and conceal an error or regularity in the normal course of his or her work. As these concepts are applied to a data processing environment that uses information technology, there are some specific functions to separate. Let's explore this in more detail.

Separate Accounting and Information Systems from Other Organization Functions

Many scholars agree that accounting and information systems are support functions and should have organizational independence from the departments that use their information and perform the operational activities of the organization. This does not mean that accounting and information systems should not actively support and help other functions. It implies that to the extent possible, the organization should ensure that:

> *A user department initiates all transactions. User departments* are the organizational units that perform the operating activities of an entity, such as a Purchasing Department which purchases raw materials, a Marketing Department that markets services, or a Production Department that produces finished products. They use the services of accounting and information systems that have the responsibility to capture and store relevant data and provide useful information. User departments should initiate all business transactions. For example, the Purchasing Department should initiate all transactions relating to the purchase of goods and services. The Accounting and Information Systems Departments should never initiate or modify such a transaction.

> *User departments authorize new business application software and changes to current application software. Application software* are the programs that process the business events of the organization, such as process a sale transaction or prepare employee paychecks. A formal written authorization from the owner/user department should accompany any new or modified software. For example, the Personnel Department should generally initiate a change in the payroll program to reflect new pay rates or new withholding tax rates. Information systems people should not be allowed to modify application software without prior authorization from a user department.

> *Custody of assets resides with designated operational departments.* The only assets accounting and information systems should have are those required to perform their work. All operational assets like inventory or investments in stocks and bonds should be in the appropriate user department.

> *Errors in transaction data should be entered on an error log, referred back to the user department for correction, and followed up on by the control group.* Errors in recording business event data should be prevented to the extent possible. But accounting and information systems personnel should not be allowed to correct errors in the transaction data identified during a processing run.

Separate Responsibilities within the Information Systems Function

Some functions within the information systems areas are incompatible and ideally separate.[3] When possible, organizations should separate the following functions from each other:

---

3 It is difficult to separate some of these functions in environments with high levels of end-user computing and autonomy.

Systems analysis—analyzing the information and processing needs and designing or modifying the application software. Those who complete this task are called *systems analysts.*

Database administration—integrating the data requirements of analysis and design to maintain an enterprise data resource. The person who is responsible for the database is called the *database administrator.*

Programming—writing computer programs to perform the tasks designed by analysts. Individuals who perform this job are called *computer programmers.*

Operations—running the application programs (designed by systems analysts and written by the programmers) on the computer. The people who perform and oversee this task are called *computer operators.*

Information systems library—storing programs and files when not in use and keeping track of all versions of data and applications. A *librarian* is the person responsible for doing this. The library itself should be separate from the computer operating area and located in a secure facility.

Data control—reconciling input and output, distributing output to authorized information customers, and monitoring the correction of errors. Individuals responsible for this job are called the *data control group.* The data control group does not correct the errors; they refer them back to the user department for correction and follow up to make sure they are corrected and processed by the accounting and information systems groups.

The most critical separation is between developing business application software and any of the other functions. Since systems analysts and computer programmers develop business application software, they should not be allowed to operate the applications with live business data nor be given access to the applications once they have been approved for business use. Both analysts and programmers have detailed knowledge of the programs and the data processed by the program. By allowing these people to gain access to the programs or the data, they can make unauthorized changes in either the programs or the data and profit by the changes.

Systems analysts, programmers, and database administrators should not operate the computer or have access to programs or the database after an application has been tested and turned over to the computer operating personnel. As well, computer operators and other data processing personnel should not have access to any of the details of the logic of the programs or the structure of the database. This would give them the information they need to modify the programs or data for their own benefit.

Programs and data should be secured in the library and checked out only to authorized individuals. This library function separates the custody of the information assets from those who operate the applications. As data custodian, the librarian prevents unauthorized personnel from accessing data.

The librarian should not have access to the computer equipment to operate programs or change the data. If this was possible, the librarian could make unauthorized changes to the programs or the data and profit by the change.

Requiring the data control group to be organizationally independent of computer operations helps ensure that processing is performed correctly and data are not lost or mishandled. The data control group oversees the activities of all the other people from a control perspective.

Lastly, organizations should rotate jobs among operations personnel to avoid having any single operator always overseeing the operation of the same application. Whenever possible, two qualified people should be on duty in the computer room while applications are running, whether batch or online. The system should maintain a copy of all commands entered by operators through the computer console (commonly called a *console log*) and the data control group should routinely review logs to check for suspicious or unauthorized activities by operators.

Physical Controls

Internal control + examples on control activitie list duty & explanation

Physical controls encompass the physical security of the organization's assets and records, authorization to access computer programs and data files, and periodically counting the quantities of physical assets and comparing them with amounts shown on financial records.

Physical Security of Assets and Records   The assets and sensitive records of the organization should be protected and only released to, or accessed by, authorized individuals. Many of these are simple controls such as separate storage rooms, locks on doors and filing cabinets, and surveillance people. For example, employees should be required to enter and exit from work through a designated area and a security person should observe employees as they enter and exit. The identity of the person should be verified and any unusual items that are brought to, or taken from work, should be examined.

Physical access controls prevent unauthorized access to the computer devices themselves. Typically, large systems or file servers are housed in a locked room that is entered only with a combination lock or a key. When unauthorized personnel or others gain access to the physical devices, they can seriously disrupt operations or even destroy the devices themselves.

Access Controls—Computer Programs and Files   When IT is embedded in the business and information processes, individuals who execute business events must gain access to the technology to execute business and information processes. Unauthorized access to the system represents a tremendous risk to the organization. Preventing unauthorized access to the system is critical. Controlling access is particularly important when the system has online, real-time transaction processing capabilities.

Access controls restrict unauthorized access to the system itself, to physical devices, and to data in the system. With the enormous stores of valuable information being amassed by organizations, maintaining reliable access controls is as essential as safeguarding any physical resource of the organization. This is so important that most database management software (DBMS) packages and some communications software packages (such as local area network or telecommunications software) include security procedure modules.

Access controls restrict unauthorized access into the system. They can be subdivided into physical access controls, system access controls, and data and application access controls. Physical access controls are handled by using separate rooms to store equipment and data with access restricted by locked entry and surveillance people as discussed above. System access controls and data and application access controls are discussed next.

System access controls   System access controls are used to prevent unauthorized access into the system. Data communication lines with online access to the computer and its data make physical access controls inadequate. Organizations must control who obtains access to the system through an online terminal or by data communication lines. Typical access controls involve the use of passwords and an access control matrix.

A *password* is a unique identifier that only the user should know and is required to enter each time he/she logs onto the system. Passwords, however, are no panacea. Unless passwords are formally assigned, routinely changed, and protected from use by other people, they will quickly get into the wrong hands and provide unauthorized access to the system.

CASE IN POINT

Surveys show that most passwords are "no-brainers" for hackers trying to break into a system. The most common password is the user's own name or the name of a child. The second most common password is *secret*. Other common passwords in order of usage are:

- Stress-related words such as *deadline* or *work*.
- Sports teams or sports terms like *bulls* or *golfer*.

- *Payday*.
- *Bonkers*.
- The current season (e.g., *winter* or *spring*).
- The user's ethnic group.
- Repeated characters (e.g., "bbbbb" or "AAAAA").
- Obscenities or sexual terms.[4]

The *access control matrix* identifies the functions each user can perform once they gain access to the computer. It controls what data and programs the user may access. For example, only a limited number of individuals will be allowed access to payroll data. Some users will only be allowed to read the data, while other users will have the right to both read and update the data.

Other system access controls include *voice recognition, fingerprint identification, retina patterns, digital signatures, personal identification numbers (PINs),* and *identification or plastic cards.*

---

4 L. Light, "Up Front—The List: Hackers' Delight," *Business Week,* February 10, 1997, p. 4.

C A S E   I N   P O I N T

Active-badge technology can authenticate potential users. Users carry a badge that transmits a weak radio signal that is picked up by special receivers when people wearing a badge come within a designated range (generally several feet). The advantage of this approach is that the authentication is automatic, with no action on the part of the user and with no need for physical contact between the badge and the sensor.

The most secure level of authentication involves some unique and unforgettable aspect of an individual's body. In the past, biometrics authentication was based on comparisons of fingerprints, palm prints, retina eye patterns, signatures, or voices. More recently, a system that recognizes keyboard-typing patterns has been developed. Another new technology can reportedly read infrared facial patterns using only a simple video camera for image capture.[5]

Systems software should limit the *number of user attempts* to access the system. This may vary from nonrecognition of the user's name, to turning off the terminal, to keeping the ATM card after three unsuccessful attempts.

Organizations can also use *terminal identification codes* to prevent access by unauthorized terminals over communication lines. A host computer can require a terminal to electronically transmit its identification code that identifies it as an authorized terminal and defines (and limits) the type of transaction a terminal user can perform. The host computer compares the identification code it receives from the terminal with a list of approved terminal identification codes to verify that it is an approved terminal.

C A S E   I N   P O I N T

The strongest protection against unauthorized access to a network is the "token" system, which authenticates a user through a hardware device combined with a log-in password process. The "smart cards" make the network tougher to crack by incorporating a randomly generated, one-time-only password code. Like a bankcard, the smart card works in sync with the host system to authenticate access. But instead of a single code or PIN, the card generates a random code, which can change every 60 seconds, and is read into the system. If the code matches the software on the host, access is granted. Some cards can be configured with information such as areas of the network that the user is entitled to access. Elaborate ones may include an "electronic eye" on the card, which captures the resemblance of the user, reads it into the system, and allows it to be viewed by the network manager.[6]

Data and application access controls   Data and application access controls maintain the integrity and privacy of data and processes within a computer system. They should prevent loss, destruction, or access of data and applications by unauthorized personnel.

---

5 R. Kay, "Distributed and Secure," *Byte,* June 1994, p. 165.
6 D. McKay, "Network Managers Face Formidable Challenge," *Computer Dealer News,* July 13, 1994, p. 29.

An *information system library* should be used to store critical program documentation, data files, and programs when they are not in use. A *librarian* should be responsible for the library and the library should be physically inaccessible to unauthorized people. Lists of authorized personnel and the extent of their authorizations should be maintained and verified using identification techniques and procedures described above.

Organizations should deliberately destroy confidential data that are no longer needed. For example, it is advisable to *shred sensitive hard-copy printouts* before they are discarded. *Thoroughly erase* data on diskettes, magnetic tapes, or disk packs, rather than simply remove the file address from the file directory.

Encryption is used to protect highly sensitive and confidential data. Encryption is a process of encoding data entered into the system, storing or transmitting the data in coded form, and then decoding the data upon its use or arrival at its destination. This prevents unauthorized access to the data while it is stored or as it is transmitted. Our information age has sharply increased our need for cryptography. Cryptography helps prevent penetration from the outside, protects the privacy of users, and ensures the integrity of communication. It can also increase assurance that received messages are genuine.

Confidentiality, the benefit most often associated with cryptography, is obtained by transforming (encrypting) data so that they are unintelligible by anyone except the intended recipient. Integrity is a security service that permits a user to detect if data has been tampered with during transmission or while in storage. Closely related to integrity is authenticity, which provides a user with a means of verifying the identity of the sender of a message.

CASE IN POINT

A brief look at communication systems explains the importance of cryptography in achieving security. Telephony is an excellent example. The only way to provide a secure voice path between two telephones at arbitrary locations is to encrypt the words spoken into one and decrypt them as they come out of the other. Public-key cryptography makes it possible for the two phones to agree on a common key known only to them without the mediation of a trusted third party. The users simply establish the call, push a button, and wait a few seconds for the phones to make the arrangements.[7]

Reconcile Physical Quantities with Recorded Quantities   Periodically, the physical assets should be compared with the assets recorded on the financial records. Auditors generally require a physical count of inventory on hand to compare with the amount reported on the financial statements. The same idea should be applied to other assets:

> At the end of each sales clerk's shift the amount of cash in the cash drawer should be counted and compared with the sales total from the cash register for the employee's shift.

---

7 S. Landau et al., "Crypto Policy Perspective," *Communications of the ACM,* August 1994, p. 115.

Fixed assets such as computer equipment should be tagged with identification numbers and assigned to specific employees. At least annually an inventory clerk should compare what each employee actually has with what they have been issued.

Property, plant, equipment, and inventories of all types should be counted and the quantities compared with the financial records. Any differences should be reconciled. Frequently this identifies errors and irregularities that would never be detected otherwise.

CASE IN POINT

Cook & Campbell, a construction firm for residential homes, was surprised to find they had one more vacant lot on their financial records than they actually owned at the end of their first year of operations. Upon closer examination they found they had constructed a home on one of the vacant lots and sold it without recording the sale of the lot on the financial records. The lot had actually been sold with the home, but the value of the lot was not included as they priced the home and it was not shown as an expense on the income statement. The anticipated $15,000 profit on the speculative home actually turned into a $20,000 loss as they corrected their mistake.

Information Processing Controls

Information processing controls check the accuracy, completeness, and authorization of transactions. Two broad categories of information processing controls are general controls and application controls.

General Controls   General controls include all controls over data center operations, access security, systems software acquisition and maintenance, and application system development and maintenance.

The information systems functions of an organization should be administered by a high-level person (e.g., a chief information officer or CIO) who reports to the president. An IS Steering Committee, composed of several other key officers of the organization, work with the CIO to develop a plan that identifies the strategic use of information technology within the organization and prioritizes the development of individual components.

The responsibility for all aspects of the information systems functions of the organization falls under the CIO. This individual has the responsibility to see that there is adequate separation of duties and responsibilities, adequate access security, and that the operations of the data center are properly controlled as we have discussed above. The other general controls of acquisition, development, and maintenance of both systems and application software are discussed in the next sections.

Development and maintenance of systems and application software   *Systems software* are the computer programs that make the computer hardware run. They include the operating system, DBMS, software to network several computers and handle the transmission of data between them, and various utilities programs to back up files. *Application software* are the programs that process the business events of the organization such as the acquisition of goods and services and the production of finished products. Because of the high cost to develop custom software, there is a growing trend to purchase both systems and application software and modify them as necessary to meet the needs of the organization. Care must be taken in specifying the requirements of the software, analyzing available software to see which package best meets the requirements, modifying the software as necessary, and testing individual applications and the entire system to make sure it processes the data accurately.

User departments are generally responsible for developing the list of software requirements. People from the user departments, the systems analysts, and the programmers work together to identify potential software packages in the market and compare their features with those desired by the organization. When modifications are required, the systems analysts design the changes and the computer programmers write the code to make the changes. *Test data* are generally used to verify that the programs and the entire system work correctly. Test data are a set of business events to test every logic path within the programs. The correct results from running the test data are developed independently from the system being tested and are compared with the results obtained when processed by the new system. If the new system correctly processes the test data, we assume it has been modified correctly. The data control group is responsible for reviewing the testing and the test results to verifying that they are adequate and that the system is ready for use.

This same process must be followed every time a modification is required in a program. The request comes from the user department. Systems analysts design the change, programmers write the code, test data are used to verify that the program functions properly, and the data control group verifies the program is ready for use. Once the modification is complete, it is turned over to the operating people and controlled by the systems librarian.

Controls over developing and maintaining a system are very important. The way a system is developed is as important as how it is operated in preventing errors and irregularities.

CASE IN POINT

You may not know it, but software can kill. Eugene Smith of Doylestown, Pennsylvania, was declared dead by software. A driver's licensing database insists he died in a traffic accident (probably as a result of a data input error). He has spent nearly three years trying to get reinstated through Pennsylvania's computer system. But the software is designed so that once you are dead, you stay dead.[8]

Financial losses because of software defects are an international problem. As institutions become dependent on electronic funds transfers, the software itself becomes more complex. Individual programmers have taken advantage of this complexity by concealing code

---

8 R. Riehle, "Killer Software: Program Errors Can Kill People, Both Figuratively and Literally, Making Structured Software Engineering Essential," *HP Professional,* February 1994, p. 54.

in programs that transfer minute amounts from individual transactions to their own accounts. What's the true magnitude of the financial shrinkage due to faulty software? No one knows.

CASE IN POINT

Sometimes a software defect is intentional. For example, a Manhattan software contractor was fined $25,000 for putting a "bug" in the software of a law firm. According to the judgment, the contractor put a statement in the program to make it abort when the system reached case number 56789. He planned for the system to fail so the law firm would retain him to fix it for a hefty fee. The law nabbed him. But another consultant earned $7,000 to repair the software.[9]

       If an organization has poor controls over developing and maintaining its systems, the likelihood of it creating an effective system of internal controls is rather low. Experience has shown that separating some accounting and information processing functions and implementing adequate documentation controls is important for managing systems development and maintenance.

Application Controls Application controls apply to the processing of individual applications. These controls help ensure that transactions are valid, properly authorized, and completely and accurately processed. Our discussion of application controls will be divided into data input controls, processing controls, and file controls.

Data input controls Some of the most important controls are those dealing with the accuracy and completeness of data as the data are entered into the computer. None of the information processing controls or file controls can correct for inaccurate or incomplete input data. The accuracy of the input data is checked by event processing rules, data entry verification, and several edit checks.

       Event processing rules. Event processing rules should be built into the system to verify that prescribed business rules are followed when executing an event. Recall our modeling of business rules associated with events, resources, and locations from Chapters 2 through 4. Some examples of the rules included:

> It is all right to have a customer without a sales event, but it is not permissible to have a sales event without a customer (a 1 and 0 on the minimum side of the relationship between customer as an external agent and the Take Order event).

Take Order (0,*)   (1,1) Customer

> Products can be shipped (Ship Product event) only after a valid order has been taken (Take Customer Order event).

Ship Product (0,*)   (1,*) Take Customer Order

---

9 *Ibid.*

Each order can have one or more types of inventory associated with it and each inventory type can be involved in none to many orders (a 0 to 1 on the minimum side, and a many-to-many on the maximum side of the relationship between Take Customer Order event and Inventory resource).

Take Customer Order (0,*)   (1,*) Inventory

Event processing rules allow IT to verify the sequencing of business process events, verify whether all of the relevant components of an event are considered, and embed business rules into the applications. For example, would you, as company controller be willing to allow an order without a customer? Of course not! A customer is required for a valid order. Therefore, your application should verify that a customer is associated with each order.

Event processing rules and other programmed business logic can help organizations *detect* errors or irregularities, and can sometimes help *prevent* errors. To illustrate detection, consider a mail order company that does not normally have prepaid sales and very rarely incurs cash sales. Should the information system allow processing a cash receipt without having previously processed a corresponding sale? Perhaps, *but* the key is that such an occurrence might signal or *detect* a possible error. The IT application should identify the potential error. An investigation could reveal that the customer is paying for the same invoice twice (the customer's error), or that a sale was not recorded in the system (the organization's error). The latter reveals a breakdown in the execution of the organization's process rules, and timely corrective measures are critical. Rules could then be embedded in IT applications to prevent such errors in the future.

Event processing rules can also help *prevent* errors or fraud. If an IT application supports the execution of the business event, the rules governing the event and the data describing it can be executed and recorded in real time. The system can note activities that represent exceptions to prescribed rules, send exception messages to a responsible person for review, or prevent the execution of the activity. For example, is a shipment necessary to record an order? No, an order event should precede the shipping event. Is an order necessary to execute a shipment? Yes! The authorization for a shipment is the existence of a valid order. Without a valid order, the shipping event should not be executed. An IT application could deny the execution and recording of a shipment that is not supported by a valid order. If shipping personnel can only generate shipping labels through the system, the likelihood of shipping merchandise without an order is reduced significantly. If an organization uses IT to record events *after* they occur, the system's ability to prevent errors and irregularities is substantially reduced; it can only *detect* rather than *prevent* the potential errors and irregularities.

When an error or exception is flagged during a process rules check, the user or a supervisor is notified of the problem using *exception reporting*. When process rules are performed in real time, the user is alerted immediately, often via an error/exception message displayed on the computer screen. Alternately, some exceptions are written to an error/exception report, which is printed at periodic intervals. The data control group should review and resolve the potential errors and exceptions as soon as possible to enhance data validity and ensure accurate information on a timely basis.

These and similar business rules that are identified while analyzing the business process and building the process models must be built into the system to check the accuracy and legitimacy of the events as they occur and as they are entered into the system.

Data entry verification. As event data are entered into the system they must be checked to verify the accuracy of the record being updated and the accuracy of the data itself. Two controls often applied in this area are closed-loop verification and key verification.

> *Closed-loop verification* helps the user verify that the correct record is being processed and updated. It does this by using one input data item to locate the record to be updated and displaying other data about the record so the data entry person can verify the correctness of the record. For example, if a sales order clerk enters a customer number for a customer buying merchandise on account, the computer uses the number to locate the customer record, then displays additional customer data (such as name and address) on the computer screen. This way the user can verify that the correct customer record is being updated.
>
> *Key verification* (also called *rekeying*) keys input data twice. The first data entry clerk enters the data and a second entry clerk reenters the same data. The computer compares the data entered on the second keying operation with the original data and highlights any differences. The second entry clerk verifies and corrects any differences.

Edit checks. *Edit checks* are incorporated into computer instructions to verify and validate the completeness, reasonableness, and/or accuracy of data. Edit checks can help reduce both operating risk and information processing risk. Their use is not limited to one type of risk or circumstance. The following is an overview of some of the edit check logic used in information systems.

Sample field edit checks. There are several edit checks that can be used to check the accuracy, reasonableness, and completeness of one field of input data. For example, a customer's account number represents one field of data, while the amount of an order represents another field of data.

> *Check digit.* A formula can be used on an account number, part number, or similar standard number to calculate a check digit. The check digit is appended to and maintained as part of the number (usually as the last digit). For example, suppose we want a five-digit account number (including the check digit) and the first four digits of the account number (based on style, division, color, and product type) are 1534. A check digit formula is used to add the fifth digit. There are several check digit formulas, and one rather simple, but less than adequate, formula adds the account number digits and extracts the second digit of the sum. The resulting account number using this formula is 15343 (the 3 is the second digit of $1 + 5 + 3 + 4 = 13$).
>
> *Completeness check.* A completeness check verifies that all critical field data are entered. It checks for missing data or blanks.

Default value. Default values set the field contents to a prespecified (default) value. In some cases the default values may be overridden, while in other cases they may not.

Field or mode check. A field or mode check verifies that the entered data type is the appropriate mode for a field. For example, if a field is declared as a text or an alphanumeric field, the data input should be alphanumeric (letters and numbers). Other field modes include numeric, date, logical, counters, memo, and embedded objects (such as video, audio, or graphics).

Range (limit) check. A range check compares entered data to a predetermined acceptable upper and/or lower limit. Data are not accepted without special authorization if the data fall outside the specified limits.

Validity/set check. A validity check compares entered data against prespecified data stored within the computer to determine their validity. For example, to determine the validity of a user identification number, the computer would compare the entered primary key of the user to a stored list of valid user numbers.

Sample record edit checks. The next level of edit checks examines an entire record, generally a record in the file being updated by business event data. Some of the more common record edit checks are:

Master reference check. A master reference check verifies that an event/transaction record has a corresponding master record to be updated. An error occurs when there is no corresponding master record for the transaction record. For example, there is an error if you input a sale for a customer not currently included in your customer data files.

Reasonableness check. Reasonableness checks verify whether the amount of an event/transaction record appears reasonable when compared to other elements associated with each item being processed. For example, if an employee is coded as a clerk, it is probably unreasonable that her pay per week is $5,000. Note that a reasonableness check is not the same as a limit check. It might be reasonable for the president to have a weekly check of $5,000. The reasonableness of the pay is based on the relationship between position (clerk versus president) and the amount of the pay, not a fixed dollar amount.

Referential integrity. Referential integrity is a safeguard to ensure that every posted foreign key attribute relates to a primary key attribute. For example, suppose you have two tables: a Salesperson table and a Sales event table. Since the two tables have a relationship (a salesperson participates in each sale), you must include the primary key attribute of the Salesperson table (e.g., salesperson number) in the Sales event table; salesperson number is a foreign key attribute in the Sales event table. You want to invoke referential integrity to ensure a link between the two tables. Referential integrity prevents writing a sale in the Sales event table without a valid salesperson number from the Salesperson table. It also prevents deleting a salesperson from the Salesperson table as long as the salesperson has sales in the Sale event table.

Valid sign check. The valid sign check is used to highlight illogical balances in a master file record. For example, a negative balance for the quantity on hand for a particular item in inventory is a likely error.

Sample batch edit checks. The next level of edit checks is for an entire batch of events or transactions. Sometimes business events can be grouped into batches for a period of time, such as one day, and processed together. Controls are needed to make sure none of the events are lost, no unauthorized events are added, and that all events are in the proper sequence and correctly processed.

Sequence check. A sequence check verifies that the records in a batch are sorted in the proper sequence. For sequential processing (which is frequently used with batch processing), the transaction records must be sorted in the same order as the master file's primary key. A sequence check can also be used to highlight missing batch items (such as a missing check).

Transaction type check. A transaction type check verifies that all transactions included within the batch are of the same category or type. For example, we would not want the addition of a new customer to be confused with the addition of a new employee.

Batch control totals. When transactions are processed in batches, each batch should be dated and assigned a unique batch number. Batch control totals are used to verify that all transactions within a batch are present and have been processed. They verify that no transactions were added or deleted during processing. There are several types of control totals. Let's use a record that includes a customer number field and an invoice amount field to illustrate three types of control totals: hash, financial/numeric, and record control totals.

- ◆ *Hash control total.* A hash control total is the sum of an attribute in a file that has no real meaning or use. For example, the sum of the customer number field of all the records in a batch is a meaningless number for purposes other than as a control total. But if it is calculated when the batch is first assembled, the computer can recalculate it after the records have been entered for processing. If the computer-generated sum is the same as the original amount, we have some assurance that all records were accurately processed. If they are not the same, one or more transactions may have been either added or deleted from the batch.

- ◆ *Financial/numeric control total.* A financial control total is the sum of a financial field, such as the invoice amount, of all records in a batch. Usually this is a meaningful numeric or financial field. For example, the total of the invoice amounts is meaningful because it represents the increase in accounts receivable and it is useful to evaluate the effectiveness of those taking orders for the day.

◆ *Record control total.* A record control total is a total of the number of records in a batch. So if a batch contains 46 records, the record count is 46.

All the control totals can be used to verify batch input, processing, and output. For example, suppose a clerk enters 46 customer invoices totaling $14,678.93 in charge sales into a computer file. Also assume that the sum of the customer account numbers on the invoices is 738476846. Once these records are entered into a batch transaction file, the file should include 46 records (the *record count*), the customer number field should total 738476846 (a *hash total*), and the sum of the invoice amount field should total $14,678.93 (a *financial total*). When the records are processed to update the customer receivable master file, the update run should show that 46 records were affected, and the accounts receivable total should increase by $14,678.93.

Notice that batch totals do not identify errors in individual records. Batch totals only highlight errors in the group as a whole. Batch totals do not ensure that individual records are updated correctly. For example, if the total of an accounts receivable subsidiary ledger equals the total in a general ledger accounts receivable control account, this does not signify that the posting to the individual customer accounts are correct. It only indicates that the same total amount was posted; some individual items could have been posted to the wrong customer's account!

Processing controls Information processing controls are designed to verify that event, resource, agent, and location information are recorded and maintained accurately, completely, and in a timely manner. They also help ensure the information on reports is complete, properly summarized, and reported to the appropriate people.

Process controls verify that the input data are properly recorded in the database and any balances maintained within the system are properly updated. Many of the program development and maintenance controls, data input controls, and edit check controls identified above are also used as process controls. The following examples illustrate the application of these controls to verify process accuracy.

Test data to verify that computer programs function properly are an important element in verifying the accuracy of information processing. Once a program is correctly written and tested it is very reliable in performing the same operations again and again.

Closed-loop verification is used when the input data are being processed in an online, real-time mode. For example, closed-loop verification is used to make sure the customer account being updated is accurate. Because of the mode of processing, this serves as an input and a process control.

Edit checks on the record and batch level are also used as process controls. For example, a reasonableness check when used in a sequential batch process is a process control. As a transaction is being processed, the computer can compare one element of input with the master record to see if it appears reasonable. If it does not, an error is recorded on the error log. An example of this is a sales order process. Selling 10 computers to a customer with an occupation listed as housewife would not seem reasonable and the transaction would be printed on an error report. If however, the sales clerk was entering the transaction by an online, real-time process and the sales clerk attempted to execute such a transaction, the computer could perform the reasonableness check as the data are entered and highlight the unreasonableness. In this case it is an input control.

As you can see, many online, real-time controls become process controls when the mode of processing is shifted to batch processing. This explains why real-time processing helps organizations prevent errors more easily than organizations that perform batch processing after a transaction has already occurred. With batch processing, error detection is more common than error prevention.

One of the benefits of an event-driven architecture is the simplicity of data storage and processing. Most event data are stored in a raw, unprocessed form. Processing consists of recording the individual characteristics and attributes about each business event. Most classifications, summarizations, and balances are developed as part of the reporting process. This is much more streamlined and less complex than a traditional processing environment where you have to control not only the input but also a complex posting process to perform classifications, summarizations, and balance calculations. Processing in an event-driven architecture is very simple; it is a direct recording of the event attributes. This allows our controls to be much more straightforward. The key to control is making sure the event record is being recorded in the correct file in a timely, complete, and accurate manner. Then we accurately report this data per the request parameters of the information customer.

File controls   Devices or techniques are available to verify that the correct file is being updated and to prevent inadvertent destruction or inappropriate use of files. Some of these controls include the following:

> *External file labels* (as simple as stick-on labels) identify a storage media's contents. They also help prevent someone from inadvertently writing over the contents of the disk or tape.
>
> *Internal file labels* record the name of a file, the date it was created, and other identifying data on the file medium to be read and verified by the computer. Internal labels include *header labels* and *trailer labels*. Header labels are a file description recorded at the beginning of a file. Trailer labels mark the end of a file and contain control or summary data about the contents of the file.
>
> *Lockout procedures* are used by database management systems to prevent two applications or users from updating the same record or data item at the same time.
>
> *The read-only file designation* is used to mark data available for reading only. The data cannot be altered by instructions from users, nor can new data be stored on the device.
>
> *File protection rings* allow data to be written on a magnetic tape. When the ring is removed, the data on the tape are protected from being accidentally overwritten.

Data loss and file reconstruction capability. Regardless of the controls taken to secure the computer and prevent problems, files are occasionally lost and programs are occasionally destroyed. Therefore, it is necessary to maintain *backup* or *duplicate copies of current data files, programs, and documentation.* At least one set of backup copies of all these items should be stored at a location that is physically removed from the computer facilities. Organizations should develop a policy concerning how long to retain backup copies. The length of time will depend on the managerial and regulatory requirements of the enterprise. The purpose of backup copies is to allow an enterprise to reconstruct its data should a disaster strike and cause a loss or corruption of data. The basic task is to retain copies of reference (resource, agent, and location) data and event data for use in reconstructing any lost data.

File reconstruction involves reprocessing the event or business activity data against the master resource, agent, or location reference data. Organizations typically update data in either a batch mode or a real-time mode.

Batch process file reconstruction. Batch processing collects a group of event and maintenance data for a period of time (such as a day) before the master reference files are updated. Processing updates the current version of the master reference file to create a new master reference file as illustrated in Exhibit D–1. When the next batch of event and maintenance data (for say the next day) are ready to be processed, the new master reference data of the prior run becomes the current master reference data for the new run.

The backup and file reconstruction procedure generally used with batch processing is known as the *grandparent-parent-child* approach. At least three generations of both event/maintenance data and master reference data are maintained (see Exhibit D–2). If the current version (the "child" copy) of the master reference file is destroyed or lost, the organization can reconstruct it by rerunning the appropriate event/maintenance data against the prior copy of the reference data (the "parent" copy). If a problem occurs during that reconstruction run, there is one more set of backup data to reconstruct the parent. The parent is then used to reconstruct the child and processing continues normally.

Batch processing often uses checkpoint controls for applications that take an extended amount of time to process. Some batch processing runs take as long as six to eight hours to run and if a problem occurs during processing you don't want to have to start again at the beginning. *Checkpoints* consist of data and program "snapshots" that are taken periodically during batch processing. If a hardware failure occurs during a long processing run, the system can resume processing at the last checkpoint, rather than at the beginning of the run.

Real-time process file reconstruction. Real-time processing updates master reference data with new event and maintenance data as the new data are captured as illustrated in Exhibit D–3. As the event or maintenance data are processed to update the master reference data, they are also recorded in a separate *transaction log*. This log is a critical part of the reconstruction process.

File reconstruction procedures must be developed for real-time processing. The transaction log and a periodic copy of the master reference file are the keys to file reconstruction. Periodically the master reference file is duplicated on a backup medium such as disk or magnetic tape. Copies of all event and maintenance data are stored on a *transaction log* as they are entered into the system. At least three generations of both the event/maintenance data and the master reference data are maintained as with batch processing. If the master reference file is lost or destroyed, the first-generation backup copy is

E X H I B I T   D–1

Batch Processing

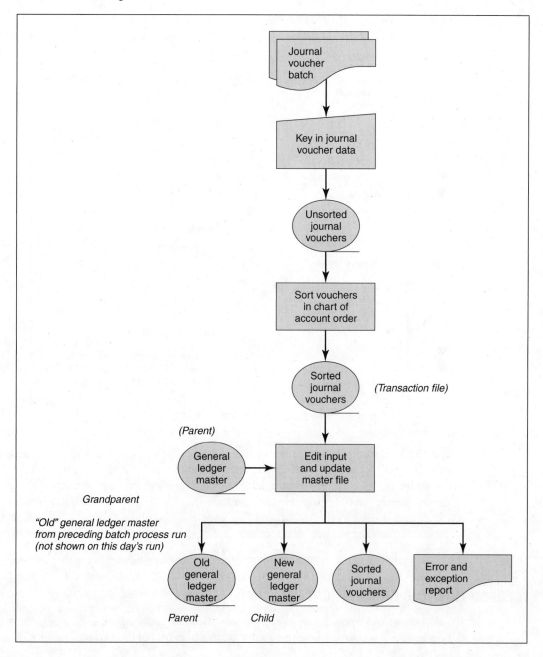

EXHIBIT D–2

Batch Process File Reconstruction

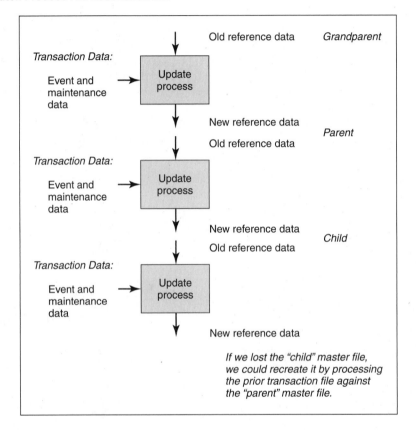

If we lost the "child" master file, we could recreate it by processing the prior transaction file against the "parent" master file.

updated for the activity on the transaction log since the copy of the master reference file was made (see Exhibit D–4). Once the master reference file is updated, processing continues normally. The three generations allow for additional errors in reconstructing the file. If the first generation is destroyed in reconstructing the file, the second generation master reference file is used to reconstruct the first generation master reference file. The backup copies of both the master reference file and the transaction log should be stored at a remote site.

INFORMATION AND COMMUNICATION

Information and communication are the identification, capture, and exchange of information in a form and time frame that enable people to carry out their responsibilities. The in-

EXHIBIT D–3

Real-Time File Processing

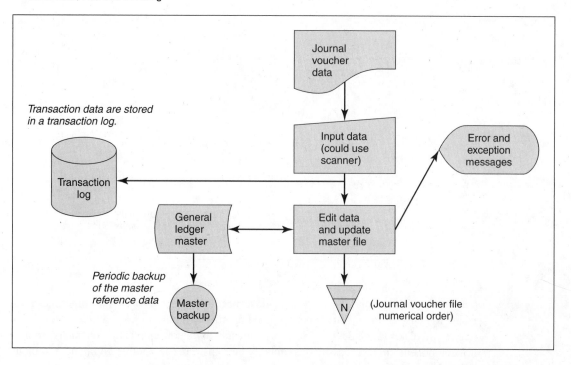

formation system captures, processes, and reports information to people throughout the organization. Most of the controls relative to the information system and the communication of data to responsible individuals have been covered in prior sections of this supplement. There are, however, three additional controls that relate to the information system and they are hardware controls, documentation controls, and computer virus protection.

Hardware Controls

Hardware controls relate to protecting the physical pieces of hardware and making sure they operate correctly.

Protecting against System Failure   Until we have a fail-safe technology, we must guard against possible failures in the computer hardware and its power source, as well as protect system hardware from the environment. Such failures can result in the interruption of business operations and the loss of data.

As a preventive measure, organizations should properly maintain computer equipment and facilities, and operate equipment in an appropriate physical environment

EXHIBIT D-4

Real-Time Master File Reconstruction

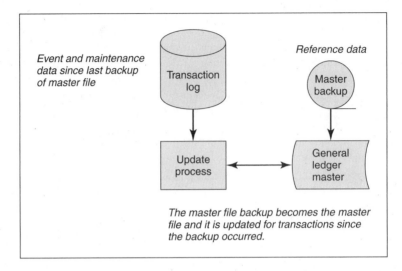

Event and maintenance data since last backup of master file

Transaction log

Reference data

Master backup

Update process

General ledger master

The master file backup becomes the master file and it is updated for transactions since the backup occurred.

(environmental controls). For larger systems, specially prepared rooms are sometimes necessary to house computer equipment. Some organizations have *backup system components* (e.g., extra disk storage devices, extra printers, and extra communication channels) so that if a component fails, processing can quickly be transferred to another component without interrupting the flow of processing for an extended period of time.

Not only can computer components fail, but the power source for the components can also fail or provide an irregular power supply. The loss of power shuts down the entire operation and any data in temporary storage will be lost. Protection from the loss of power is usually provided through the use of special battery units called *uninterruptable power supplies (UPS).* These devices provide battery support and sound an alarm when power is interrupted. This allows needed time to stop computer processes and back up data and instructions (programs).

An irregular power supply can damage or destroy the computer hardware. Sudden and dramatic increases in power are called *power surges* or *spikes.* Protecting against surges or spikes involves the use of a *surge protector* or *line conditioning.* Conditioning power lines is sometimes provided by utility companies, but can also be provided by a simple and relatively low cost, device called a *surge protector.*

Built-in Hardware Controls Several controls are built into the hardware components to verify the accuracy of data processing. An *echo check* is used to verify the accuracy of data communications among various pieces of hardware. An echo check retransmits data back to the sending device for comparison to the original data. If what is transmitted back is not the same as what was initially sent, the valid communication is sent again.

A *parity bit* is an extra bit appended to a transmitted byte to verify the transmission's validity. The parity bit is used for parity checking. The parity bit is a 1 or a 0 depending on the sum of the bits in each byte and whether the machine uses an odd or even parity pattern. For example, if a computer uses an even-bit parity, the sum of the 0s and 1s of the nine bits should equal an even number. Thus, if a 01001100 byte were to be transmitted, a parity bit of 1 would be appended. The nine transmitted bits are 010011001, which results in an even parity $(1 + 1 + 1 + 1 = 4$, an even number). Some machines use an odd-parity pattern, meaning the sum of the nine digits should equal an odd number.

Documentation Controls

Documentation is a term used for the paper that describes the programs, systems, and procedures used in a data processing environment. A great deal of paper is generated while analyzing information needs, designing an application, and writing computer programs. Documentation is used to describe different aspects of an information system. Standardized documentation helps control the development, operation, and maintenance of a system. There are several types of documentation as well as several tools to describe a system or a program within the system.

Supplement A discusses two tools for documenting the flow of documents and information in a system: flowcharts and data flow diagrams. Flowcharts and data flow diagrams are used in a variety of ways to describe how an application works, the files supporting an application, the sequence of steps to operate an application, a sequence of organization activities, or the flow of data through a system.

There are several types of documentation including the following:

1. *Procedural documentation* defines the management policies relating to the information systems function. This includes personnel standards and procedures for documenting, testing, and operating applications.

2. *Systems documentation* defines the purpose of a specific application and describes the application's relationship to files, inputs, and outputs. Part of systems documentation includes a flowchart of what the application does, inputs to the application, outputs from the application, and descriptions of the application files, error messages, and controls.

3. *Application documentation* describes the inner workings of an application. Application documentation includes a flowchart of program logic as well as written explanations about the computer program itself.

4. A *user manual* describes how to use an application. It describes the specific procedures required to execute the application, enter data, generate reports, and recover from errors while the program is being executed.

5. An *operator manual* is used when applications run on a large computer with a number of dependent users. In large computer systems, the program is actually run by an operator but used by various other people. The operator manual

describes which files are needed to run the application, any setup procedures, procedures for correcting errors during operations, and how much time is required to run the program.

6. *Data documentation* includes data dictionaries and record layouts. The *record layout* details the structure of a record within a file, including field names, the width of each field, and the type of data stored in each field (e.g., numeric, alphanumeric, and date). Since items in a database are shared by numerous applications, database documentation, called *data dictionaries,* highlight data item, rather than record level, details. Data dictionaries provide information about the database and data items in the database. Data dictionaries include for each data item such information as name, type, range, source, and list of applications that use it, and the person(s) authorized to view or change the data item.

7. *Operating documentation* to review all aspects of system usage. Organizations should maintain and review documentation that details systems operations and use. This is normally accomplished by various logs that include *application program change logs, system access logs, system use logs, operator/console logs, system data and program library access logs, and error logs.* Some sophisticated software packages (such as local area network software or client-server software) include procedures that can generate operation logs. However, it is critical that you understand that simply having documentation or generating operations logs is *not* an adequate control! The *control* comes from monitoring the logs and using them to prevent, detect, or correct errors.

CASE IN POINT

A northeast manufacturing company narrowly lost a $1 billion project after a rival broke into its network of Unix workstations and learned what it planned to bid. The intrusion was detected only because an auditing system had been installed on the network to log system access. But by then it was too late; the company had already lost the contract. "Tens of billions are lost this way each year," claims Bill Malik, research director with the Gartner Group, Inc. For the most part, companies aren't admitting security breaches on their client-server systems; many others don't even know about the problem. If the northeast manufacturer hadn't checked its auditing system access log, for example, it simply would have chalked up the lost bid to bad luck.[10]

Each organization should ensure that all documentation is complete, accurate, and only accessible to those who have a legitimate need to see it. When documentation falls into the wrong hands, unauthorized changes can be made to the system, resulting in significant errors or irregularities.

10 T. Groenbeldt, "How Secure Is Your System?" *Information Week,* October 24, 1994. p. 64.

Documentation helps users learn to operate the information system and is used by analysts and programmers to plan modifications or improvements to it. Without adequate documentation, users, developers, and auditors must invest a tremendous amount of additional time to learn how a system works.

CASE IN POINT

Recently, a large university found it had no documentation for an alumni information system. The system maintained alumni addresses, donation commitments, and prior donations. Several students had developed it over a period of several years and taught the new student employees how the system worked before they graduated. Eventually, those managing the system failed to hire a student in time to be trained before the prior student graduated. Because the system was not documented, several students had to be hired to learn how the system operated. Having no documentation resulted in unnecessary expense and delay in operating and modifying the system.

Computer Viruses Protection

One of the most dysfunctional human behaviors is using information technology to harm the organization. Computer viruses are one example of this. A *computer virus* is a computer program that alters the performance of the system or its computer files. Some viruses are rather harmless; however, a growing number of computer viruses inflict great harm. *Computer virus detection programs* have been developed to constantly monitor the system to see if any viruses are present and to eliminate them.

CASE IN POINT

In the summer of 1977, Thomas J. Ryan wrote and published a book that became an instant cult classic for computer hackers. *The Adolescence of P-1* chronicled the fictional development of the world's first virus—a program that moved from computer to computer, taking control of the operating systems of 7,000 computers. When this book first appeared, it was regarded as good science fiction. A mere 11 years later, a Cornell graduate student turned the experience into reality when he developed a program that ran amok: It jumped into the world's largest computer network and began taking control of the connected machines. The program was designed to both hide itself (fortunately the design had a bug) and defend itself against removal. It could also adapt to at least two radically different computer architectures. It spread like wildfire. The number of systems infected? 6,200.[11]

Today an entire industry has grown out of the need to prevent, detect, and correct computer viruses. Estimated losses due to computer viruses exceed hundreds of millions of dollars. Although technology is providing some relief, it cannot completely control dysfunctional human behavior.

---

11 J. McAfee, "The Virus Cure," *Datamation,* February 15, 1989.

CASE IN POINT

To Dark Avenger, his viruses are his passport. No one seems to know what he's avenging, but it's believed he started out as a computer science student at the University of Sofia in Bulgaria. "The American government can stop me from going to the U.S., but they can't stop my virus," he boasted to one virus researcher. His darkest contribution isn't a virus at all, but a tool kit he calls the Mutation Engine. It lets viruses change their appearance and internal structure as they spread, making them difficult to find. He's also written a kind of schizoid virus. The fast-acting version actively searches for targets, spreading and replicating itself on the host system and any other system connected to it. A time-released variant slowly and almost invisibly eats away at data on a disk so it's unlikely you'll notice until it's time to kiss your data goodbye.[12]

MONITORING

The system of internal controls must be constantly evaluated and updated. As the organization changes and as information technology changes so do the business risks. New technology brings with it new risks that most people don't even consider.

CASE IN POINT

One day a state's welfare payment system suddenly showed a $15 million shortage. An investigation showed the $15 million left the fund by a direct wire transfer to a Swiss bank account. It was withdrawn from the Swiss bank on the day of the deposit and the account was immediately closed. Further investigation showed the cause of the direct wire transfer was a small section of code (written in machine language) in the welfare payment program that checked to see if today's processing date was the same as a specified date. If they were the same, the $15 million was transferred. The person who had written the program had ceased working for the state agency about a year before the fund transfer, and was believed to be living in Switzerland. This type of fraud was not possible before welfare payments were processed by computer and before the existence of direct wire transfers of funds.

How do you stay current? This chapter has introduced a portion of the control and security concepts and terms related to systems environments. For example, as more organizations use communications strategies involving the Internet, intranets, extranets, electronic data interchange, electronic commerce, and so on, professionals must strive to stay familiar with the terms and concepts that describe information security. There are a number of resources available to provide a glossary, introduction, and/or overview of relevant terms and concepts. To illustrate, consider the following segment of a glossary available at *http://www.securityinfo.com*. Table D–1 includes just a small sample of the glossary contents. It is presented to convince you that this text (which may appear to include too much information at times) is only an introduction to information systems and business concepts.

---

12 C. Sandler, "Virus, They Wrote: People Who Write Computer Virus Software Programs," *PC Computing,* September 1994, p. 206.

You need to refer to other more specialized and comprehensive resources to learn more. We hope the following list makes you curious enough to check out the rest of the glossary and bookmark it and other similar web sites for use as valuable resources.

TABLE D–1

Selected Glossary Terms from www.securityinfo.com

Security Term	Definition
ACL	Access control lists are typically comprised of a list of principals, a list of resources, and a list of permissions.
Address spoofing	A type of attack in which the attacker steals a legitimate network (e.g., IP) address of a system and uses it to impersonate the system that owns the address.
Application gateway firewall	A type of firewall system that runs an application, called a *proxy,* that acts like the server to the Internet client. The proxy takes all requests from the Internet client and, if allowed, forwards them to the Intranet server. Application gateways are used to make certain that the Internet client and the Intranet server are using the proper application protocol for communicating. Popular proxies include Telnet, ftp, and http. Building proxies requires knowledge of the application protocol.
Asymmetric algorithm	An encryption algorithm that requires two different keys for encryption and decryption. These keys are commonly referred to as the *public* and *private keys.* Asymmetric algorithms are slower than symmetric algorithms. Furthermore, speed of encryption may be different than the speed of decryption. Generally asymmetric algorithms are either used to exchange symmetric session keys or to digitally sign a message. RSA, RPK, and ECC are examples of asymmetric algorithms.
Certification authority (CA)	A trusted agent that issues digital certificates to principals. Certification authorities may themselves have a certificate that is issued to them by other certification authorities. The highest certification authority is called the *root CA.*
Data diddling	An attack in which the attacker changes the data while en route from source to destination.
Data integrity	The reasonable assurance that data are not changed while en route from a sender to its intended recipient.
Data privacy	The reasonable assurance that data cannot be viewed by anyone other than the intended recipient.
DES	Data encryption standard; the most common encryption algorithm with symmetric keys

T A B L E D–1 *(continued)*

Security Term	Definition
Dictionary attack	A form of attack in which an attacker uses a large set of likely combinations to guess a secret. For example, an attacker may choose 1 million commonly used passwords and try them all until the password is determined.
Digital certificate	A structure for binding a principal's identity to its public key. A certification authority (CA) issues and digitally signs a digital certificate.
Digital signature	A method for verifying that a message originated from a principal and that it has not changed en route. Digital signature is typically performed by encrypting a digest of the message with the private key of the signing party.
DSA	Digital signature algorithm; this algorithm uses a private key to sign a message and a public key to verify the signature. It is a standard proposed by the U.S. government.
Eavesdropping	An attack in which an attacker listens to a private communication. The best way to thwart this attack is by making it very difficult for the attacker to make any sense of the communication by encrypting all messages.
Kerberos	A third-party trusted host authentication system devised at MIT within Project Athena. The Kerberos authentication server is a central system that knows about every principal and its passwords. It issues tickets to principals who successfully authenticate themselves. These tickets can be used to authenticate one principal (e.g., a user) to another (e.g., a server application). Moreover, Kerberos sets up a session key for the principals that can be used to protect the privacy and the integrity of the communication. For this reason, the Kerberos system is also called a key distribution center (KDC).
Man-in-the-middle attack	An attack in which an attacker inserts itself between two parties and pretends to be one of the parties. The best way to thwart this attack is for both parties to prove to each other that they know a secret that is only known to them. This is usually done by digitally signing a message and sending it to the other party as well as asking the other party to send a digitally signed message.
Masquerading	An attack in which an attacker pretends to be someone else. The best way to thwart this attack is to authenticate a principal by challenging it to prove its identity.

T A B L E D–1 *(continued)*

Security Term	Definition
Packet filter	A type of firewall in which each IP packet is examined and either allowed to pass through or rejected. Normally packet filtering is a first line of defense and is typically combined with application proxies for more security.
Private key	A key that belongs to a principal and is never revealed to anyone. It is used by a principal to decrypt messages that are sent to it and are encrypted with the principal's public key. It is also used to encrypt a message digest sent by the principal to anyone else. This provides nonrepudiation, as anyone can use the principal's public key to decrypt the digest and be sure that the message originated from that principal.
Public key	A key that belongs to a principal and is revealed to everyone. In order for everyone to trust that the public key really belongs to the principal, the public key is embedded in a digital certificate. The public key is used to encrypt messages that are sent to the principal as well as to verify the signature of a principal.
Replay attack	An attack in which an attacker captures a message and at a later time communicates that message to a principal. Though the attacker cannot decrypt the message, it may benefit by receiving a service from the principal to whom it is replaying the message. The best way to thwart a replay attack is by challenging the freshness of the message. This is done by embedding a time stamp, a sequence number, or a random number in the message.
S-HTTP	Secure hyper text transfer protocol; an extension to the HTTP protocol to protect the privacy and integrity of HTTP communications.
S/MIME	Secure multipurpose Internet mail extensions; a protocol for sending secure e-mail.
Secret key	A key used by a symmetric algorithm to encrypt and decrypt data.
Secure Single Sign-On (SSSO)	Secure single sign-on (SSSO) satisfies three synergetic sets of requirements. From an end-user perspective, SSSO provides a single user ID and a single password to log on once and gain access to all resources that one is allowed to access. From an administrative perspective, SSSO allows management of all security-related aspects of one's enterprise from a central location. This includes adding, modifying, and removing users as well as granting and revoking access to resources. From an

TABLE D–1 *(continued)*

Security Term	Definition
Secure Single Sign-On (SSSO) *(continued)*	enterprise perspective, SSSO provides the ability to protect the privacy and the integrity of transactions as well as engage in transactions that are auditable and nonrejectable.
Smart card	A tamper-resistant hardware device where sensitive information can be stored. Typically a smartcard stores the private key(s) of a principal. Smart cards can also be used to encrypt or decrypt data on the card directly. This has the desirable effect of not exposing the private keys, even to the owner of the key. Smart cards are password protected; in order for an application to use the keys and functions of a smart card, the user must enter the correct password to open the card.
SSL	Secure socket layer; a standard for establishing a secure communication link using a public key system.
Symmetric algorithm	An algorithm where the same key (a secret key) can be used for encryption and decryption.
Trusted gateway	Trusted gateways are firewalls that use very secure operating systems. These operating systems are typically rated B1 or better according to the *Trusted Computing Base Evaluation Criteria* (the "orange" book). The firewall system itself is divided into three software compartments: that which interacts with the Internet, that which interacts with the enterprise, and a trusted gateway that mediates communications between the other two compartments. The operating system prevents applications that run in one compartment from accessing resources outside of that compartment. Any application that runs on the Internet compartment (e.g., a Web server) can only have access to resources in the Internet compartment (e.g., public HTML pages), or else it must use the trusted gateway to ask for information from the enterprise compartment.

CONCLUDING COMMENTS

Chapter 5 introduced you to the importance of understanding organization risks and developing a real-time, proactive control philosophy. This supplement provides some specific examples of controls that are available to reduce organization risks. Some of the control examples cited are useful for preventing errors and irregularities, while others are helpful in detecting and correcting errors and irregularities.

Just as change has become a constant feature of organizations and IT, the need for creativity and innovation in developing and identifying control procedures to reduce risks is becoming consistent across organizations. We believe accounting and auditing professionals can meet this need, but they must realize that the set of tools they use requires constant review and update to reflect the changing nature of organizations. Also, the tools used to protect an organization against material risk must not hamper attempts to promote operational efficiency and effectiveness.

CHECKLIST OF KEY TERMS AND CONCEPTS

Access control lists (ACL)
Access control matrix
Access controls
Address spoofing
Application documentation
Application gateway firewall
Application program change logs
Asymmetric algorithm
Backup system components
Batch control totals
Batch edit checks
Bonding
Business/operating event controls
Certification authority (CA)
Check digit
Checkpoints
Closed-loop verification
Collusion
Completeness check
Computer viruses
Console log
Data and application access controls
Data dictionaries
Data diddling
Data documentation
Data encryption standard (DES)
Data integrity
Data privacy
Default value
Dictionary attack
Digital certificate
Digital signature
Digital signature algorithm (DSA)
Eavesdropping
Echo check

Edit checks
Encryption techniques
Environment controls
Error/exception reporting
Error logs
Event processing rules
External file labels
Field edit checks
Field (mode) check
File controls
File protection rings
Financial/numeric total
Grandparent-parent-child reconstruction
Hardware controls
Hash totals
Header labels
Information processing controls
Information systems library
Internal file labels
Kerberos
Lockout procedures
Man-in-the-middle attack
Masquerading
Master reference check
Operating documentation
Operator/console log
Operator manual
Packet filter
Parity bit
Passwords
Personal identification numbers (PINs)
Physical access controls
Private key
Public key
Procedural documentation

Range check

Read-only file designation

Reasonableness check

Record count

Record edit checks

Record layouts

Referential integrity

Rekeying (key verification)

Replay attack

Secret key

Secure Hyper Text Transfer Protocol (S-HTTP)

Secure Multipurpose Internet Mail Extension (S/MIME)

Secure Single Sign-On (SSSO)

Secure Socket Layer (SSL)

Sequence check

Smart card

Surge protector

Symmetric algorithm

System access controls

System access logs

System data and program library access logs

System documentation

System use logs

Terminal identification codes

Trailer labels

Transaction-type check

Trusted gateway

Uninterruptible power source

User manual

Valid sign check

Validity (set) check

REVIEW QUESTIONS

1. Define each of the terms in the above *Checklist of Key Terms and Concepts.*
2. Differentiate between an operating activity risk and an information process risk.
3. What is the objective of a system access control?
4. List five examples of system access controls.
5. What is the objective of a physical access control?
6. What is the purpose of an information systems library?
7. Explain the purpose of encryption techniques.
8. When is exception reporting displayed to the user? Explain.
9. Give an example of closed-loop verification.
10. How do check digits help ensure that field contents are valid?
11. Give an example of a completeness check.
12. What is the objective of a completeness check?
13. Give an example of a field or mode check.
14. Give an example of a range/limit check.
15. What is the objective of a validity/set check?
16. What is the objective of a master reference check?
17. Give an example of a reasonableness check.
18. Explain referential integrity.
19. Give an example of a valid sign check.
20. What is the purpose of a sequence check?

21. Explain a transaction-type check.
22. List and explain three different types of batch control totals.
23. How do internal and external labels provide file control?
24. What is the objective of a lock-out procedure?
25. How do read-only file designations and file protection rings protect file contents?
26. To protect data on magnetic tape, should the tape file protection ring be off or on?
27. Describe the grandparent-parent-child file reconstruction procedure. What type of processes typically use this type of backup and file recovery procedure?
28. How are checkpoints used in batch processing?
29. Describe the file reconstruction procedure for online, real-time processing. What type of processes typically use this type of backup and file recovery procedure?
30. Explain the usefulness of each of the following types of documentation:
    a. Procedural documentation.
    b. Systems documentation.
    c. Application documentation.
    d. User manuals.
    e. Operator manuals.
    f. Data documentation.
31. Contrast data dictionaries and record layouts.
32. List five examples of operating documentation.
33. The chapter cites four examples of hardware controls to prevent system failure. Which of these are preventive controls? Which are corrective controls?
34. Give and explain two examples of built-in hardware controls.
35. List six policies and procedures that can reduce the risks associated with hiring and retaining quality employees.
36. Why do organizations bond employees?
37. List four policies that help ensure that accounting and information systems professionals are organizationally independent from other functions.
38. What six information systems functions should an organization separate? Of these, which are the most critical to separate? Why?
39. What is a computer virus?

DISCUSSION QUESTIONS

1. This supplemental chapter lists six information systems functions that an organization should separate. Is it difficult to separate these functions in environments where end-user computing is increasingly prominent? Explain.
2. Why do we have computer viruses?

3. After today's batch processing, the master file is current with all data through 5:00 PM. In the evening, the master file tape is accidentally used as a backup tape for a real-time processing system. Describe the process necessary to recover the batch processing master file.

4. This supplement discussed a completeness check. Should all fields always have data recorded in them? Explain.

5. A clerk leaves his desk and someone loads a virus into the clerk's computer system. Give examples of system access and physical access controls that could have stopped this from happening.

6. A computer operator loads a data tape. She first checks the tape's external label. Should she do more to ensure data security? Explain.

7. This supplement explained that emphasis is often placed on the technical characteristics of an IT application (e.g., the response time, user friendliness, and user interfaces). However, we suggested that it is also important to evaluate whether IT applications adequately support and ensure the proper execution of business activities, and help prevent and detect organization risks. Which is more important: the technical issues relating to an IT application, or the business/control issues? Justify your response.

8. A clerk at Noname University has just keypunched this semester's student tuition payments. When the items were given to her for data entry, the clerk was told that there were 2,000 records, totaling $2,000,000, and that the sum of the last four digits of the students' Social Security numbers was 11,714,703. When she finished the data entry, the keypunch machine verified that she had entered 2,000 records, totaling $2,000,000, and that the sum of the last four digits of the students' Social Security numbers was 11,714,703. What type of a batch total is the sum of the student digits? What type of a batch total is the number of items she entered? What type of batch total is the sum of the tuition payments? Can the clerk use these batch totals as assurance of good data input? Explain.

MINICASES AND OTHER APPLIED LEARNING

1. A shipping clerk is about to ship goods to a customer.

Required:

Give specific control or edit check examples that could be used to:
   a. Prevent this business event from occurring at the wrong time or sequence.
   b. Prevent this business event from occurring without proper authorization.
   c. Prevent an invalid internal agent from executing this event.
   d. Prevent the shipment from going to an invalid external agent.
   e. Ensure that the proper resources are used in this event.
   f. Ensure the proper amounts of resources are used in this event.
   g. Ensure the event involves valid locations.
   h. Ensure the event is recorded completely.

i. Ensure the event is recorded accurately.

j. Ensure the event data recorded are valid.

2. A computer operator at the local data processing center decides to visit work on a Monday evening. She has a key to the outside door, and since there is no key required for the computer room, she simply walks into the computer room. The operator, who is really one of the nation's most notorious computer programmer/hackers (having been convicted five times for manipulating various firms' data files), opens the documentation bookcase, located in the corner of the computer room. In the bookcase she finds the procedural documentation, the systems documentation, user manuals, application documentation, and operator manuals. She examines the documentation to understand the payroll program and to find the location of the payroll files. She accesses the information systems library, which is available to all computer operators at all times, accesses the payroll program, reprograms it, and runs a payroll job that creates one electronic funds transfer (to a new account opened by the operator under an assumed name). On Tuesday, the operator transfers the funds to a Swiss bank account and does not show up for work.

Required:

Prepare a summary that details any internal controls violated in this situation.

3. Visit a computer software store or find advertisements to research three computer virus software detection applications.

Required:

Write a brief description of the software packages. Include in your description whether the packages detect and correct viruses, or whether they simply scan and detect viruses.

4. Visit your library, use the Internet, or use Lexis/Nexis to locate two articles: one documenting a case of an organization's problem with viruses and one article detailing how to control and safeguard against viruses.

Required:

Write a one-page summary of each, and be prepared to make a five-minute oral presentation on each of the articles.

5. In groups, visit a data processing department. Review the different types of documentation used in the organization. Try to find examples of each of the documentation types listed in the chapter.

Required:

Write a brief summary of your findings.

6. Write the procedural documentation for hiring and retaining quality employees as cashiers at your favorite video store.

7. Identify the department or agency that manages the local area network at your college. Invite an agency or department representative to your class to discuss how the following risks are controlled:

   a. Unauthorized system access.
   b. Power failures or surges.
   c. Loss of data and files.
   d. Computer viruses.
   e. Hardware failures.

8. Review the user documentation for the DBMS you are using for class projects.

Required:

Prepare a report that documents how the following controls are implemented: (Note: You may find more than one method for each control.)

   a. Systems access.
   b. Completeness check.
   c. Default value.
   d. Embedding business event rules.
   e. Field check.
   f. Range or limit check.
   g. Validity check.
   h. Referential integrity.
   i. Valid sign check.
   j. Closed-loop verification.

9. Consider the following from *The Wall Street Journal:*

> A former Lotus Development Corp. product manager says that Lotus typically found 5,000 bugs per product. It fixed serious flaws before shipment but ignored or put off fixing minor bugs such as a pixel that was colored differently from screen to screen.
>
> Bugs in software regularly have alarming consequences . . . just ask Dan Beckner, who uses accounting software from PeachTree Software to run his Eldridge, N.Y., radio and security devices business. In July, he recorded the sale of a video camera that cost him $325; the software not only failed to warn him he was out of stock but also miscalculated the camera's cost at $4,567,896. Mr. Beckner's company is small, "so that error was obvious," he says. But others were insidious. Upon double-checking his data, he found several small cost miscalculations. If he hadn't found the errors, he would have underestimated his taxes and underpaid the Internal Revenue Service.[13]

Required:

Write a summary suggesting ways that organizations developing new software can protect themselves from faulty software.

10. Consider the following summary of a *Business Week* commentary:

> Which is more accurate, humans or machines? Although technology is capable of 100% accuracy, some stores average as low as 85% accuracy, according to investigators who are researching the accuracy of scanning technology. Retailers argue that the systems are more accurate than human clerks and many retailers argue that the accuracy issue is being blown out of proportion.

---

13 J. E. Rigdon, "Frequent Glitches in New Software Bug Users," *The Wall Street Journal,* January 18, 1995, p. B1.

Retailers say the problems are primarily attributable to the failure to enter data into scanner computers, especially when prices change.[14]

Required:

Write a memo suggesting specific control polices and procedures that retailers could implement to reduce this problem.

---

14 "Maybe We Should Call Them 'Scammers,'" *Business Week,* January 16, 1995, p. 32.

APPENDIX D–1

Templates for Event Processes

In Chapter 5, we discussed some of the details about developing, recording, maintaining, and reporting processes for an IT application. In Chapter 6 and this supplement, we have suggested that these information processes should include business event and information processing controls designed to reduce business event and information processing risks. Often emphasis is placed on the technical characteristics of an IT application (e.g., the response time, user friendliness, and user interfaces). In addition to these issues, it is important to evaluate whether IT applications adequately support and ensure the proper execution of business activities. In addition, IT applications should, to the extent possible, help prevent organization risks. In cases where prevention is not possible, the application should help detect and correct errors and irregularities.

There are numerous ways to implement input, processing, and edit check controls in applications developed using today's IT resources. The following templates provide a reference for understanding how edit checks and similar programming logic affects the recording, maintaining, and reporting applications discussed in Chapter 5.

RECORDING INSTRUCTIONS TEMPLATE—USED TO ADD RECORDS TO EVENT DATA POOLS

1. This information process is triggered by the need to execute and document a business event. Invoke real-time business control and verify that the organization activity adheres to prescribed business rules, policies, and business controls. Use edit checks and programmed business logic/rules to control the *business risks* associated with executing the business event. Access the event, resource, agent, and location tables needed to properly execute the event.

2. Collect event data from the data sources (e.g., the user, a source document, or electronic data communication).

3. Invoke (real-time) *information risk* control. Check the data for accuracy, completeness, and validity.[15] To complete this step, it is necessary to access the resource, agent, and location data pools that relate to this event and use data from them to aid in validating the input.

4. If the input data do not meet the logic and control standards outlined, processing may be terminated. If processing continues, someone who is responsible for controls is notified of the exception. In some cases you may

---

15 To perform such review and exception reporting, many programmers use edit check and business control logic during system processing. Examples of this logic were illustrated earlier in this supplement.

wish to allow someone to override control. Any instances of overriding should also be communicated to the data control group.

5. If the data are accurate, complete, and valid, processing continues according to the processing instructions, and data about the event are stored in a record(s) added to the appropriate event data pool(s).

MAINTAINING INSTRUCTIONS TEMPLATE—USED TO UPDATE, ADD, OR DELETE[16] RESOURCE, AGENT, OR LOCATION RECORDS

1. This information process is triggered by the need to update data in a resource, agent, or location data pool. Validate that the change is properly authorized and performed by an authorized user. Invoke real-time *business risk* control and verify that these changes adhere to prescribed business rules, policies, and business controls. Use edit checks and programmed business logic/rules to control the business risks associated with executing the maintenance process. Access the event, resource, agent, and location tables needed to properly execute the update.

2. Collect data from the data sources (e.g., the user, a source document, and electronic data communication).

3. Invoke real-time *information risk* control. Check the data for accuracy, completeness, and validity. This step involves verifying that the individual or program attempting to modify the resource, agent, and location data adheres to prescribed business rules, business controls, and information controls.

4. If the input data do not meet the logic and control standards outlined, processing may be terminated. If processing continues, someone responsible for controls must be notified of the exception. In some cases you may wish to allow someone to override a control. Any instances of overriding should also be communicated to the data control group.

5. If the data are accurate, complete, and valid, they are processed (via any processing instructions) to update data fields in existing record(s), add new record(s), or delete record(s) in appropriate resource, location, or agent data pool(s).

6. Since a maintenance program reflects a change in the status of an organization's resources, agents, or locations, it is often a good practice to initiate any needed action based on the change. For example, if an organization learns it can no longer purchase a certain inventory item for resale, it would be helpful to inform management about any back orders currently in the system for that inventory item. This could help the

---

16 Use the delete option wisely. Any critical information should be backed up before deletion from active data pools.

organization maintain good customer relations by providing them the ability to contact customers in a timely manner and suggest alternatives.

REPORTING INSTRUCTIONS—USED TO GENERATE QUERIES, DOCUMENTS, AND REPORTS

1. Access the user output request, along with any specifications or parameters. Validate that the user should have access to the requested information.
2. Determine if a format is stored for the output. If so, access the format file. If not, allow the user to help specify a format or use a default format.
3. Access necessary data from appropriate data pools and process the data (if necessary).
4. Communicate the output to the screen, printer, or computer file and display it in the prescribed format.

The Changing Nature of Journals and Ledgers

goes w chap 9

adventure of acct system

SUPPLEMENT OBJECTIVE

The objective of this supplement is to explain how changing the accounting information system architecture does not diminish the ability to provide the records commonly associated with the traditional accounting (general ledger) cycle. This "proof of concept" is critical to evaluate whether alternative designs can effectively support external financial reporting. After studying this supplement, you should be able to:

♦ Understand that debits and credits can take more than one form.

♦ Describe differences in data and processing in traditional and events architectures.

♦ Describe data reporting in an events architecture.

♦ Understand that journals and ledgers can be logical data views as well as physical data files.

♦ Evaluate alternative AIS architectures based on objective criteria.

WHERE ARE MY DEBITS AND CREDITS?

This text has introduced accounting system design concepts that do not rely on charts of accounts, debits, and credits as the foundation. To assess whether an alternative system architecture is viable to meet the needs of information customers, it is important to focus *not* on whether the alternative emulates the traditional mode of processing and data storage, but whether it is able to accomplish the desired objectives of the traditional architecture, *and much more.* This requires you to understand the needs of end users of accounting information, as well as the capabilities and required outputs of the traditional accounting process.

For example, to support the sales/collection process using a traditional general ledger architecture, most data are recorded during two activities: while billing the customer (after the shipment has occurred) and after receiving a customer payment. Billing customers generates debits to accounts receivable, credits to sales, debits to the cost of sales, and credits to inventory. Receiving customer payments results in debits to cash and credits to accounts receivable.

These recordings and subsequent summarizations are performed primarily for financial reporting purposes. Accounting wants to report several things: customers owe more money (i.e., an organization has generated sales revenue that has not been paid); sales revenue has increased; expenses associated with generating revenue have increased; and the organization has less inventory. For cash receipts, an organization wants to report that they have more cash, and people owe them less money (i.e., customers paid for their sales).

Let's examine portions of the tables that store events data and verify whether these reporting objectives are still accomplished in an events architecture that does not include explicit debits, credits, journals, or ledgers. Assume an organization begins the period with $500 of inventory and $200 of cash. Since this is the beginning of the period, there are no sales and no cash receipts. First, let's "book" a sale using sample relational event-driven tables rather than charts of accounts. Assume the organization sells $125 of inventory for $175 on credit and that the sale data are documented in the Sales event data table and the Sale-Inventory event data table. The event table calculations would reveal the following information:

Sales Table	Sale-Inventory Table	Collect Payment Table
$175 revenue	$125 worth (cost) of Item #s sold	$0

Does the organization have data that would reveal the same information as a corresponding debit to accounts receivable and a credit to sales? Is the accounting equation still intact with debits equaling credits? The answer to both questions is yes. Debits and credits are used to denote equal increases and decreases in components of the accounting equation. The effect of a debit to accounts receivable and a credit to sales is still present since a sale that has no corresponding payment (documented in the Collect Payment table) results in a simultaneous increase in accounts receivable and sales. The information in the Sales table shows an increase of $175 to revenue (i.e., a *credit* to sales). Since there is no corresponding payment for that sale, the amount the customer owes (i.e., the sales minus cash receipts, also known as the *accounts receivable*) is also increased, or *debited,* by $175.

How can you accomplish this without a chart of accounts or table called accounts receivable? Recall that event-driven architectures are defined by actual business events as illustrated in Exhibit E–1. Often, people confuse accounts in a chart of accounts with business events. Accounts receivable is not a business event—it is an amount derived by comparing two events. Accounts receivable is included in an organization's chart of accounts because there is a timing difference between two business activities—the recognition of sales revenue and the collection of cash for that revenue.

Suppose the customer later pays $100 of the amount due. Does the organization have a *debit* to cash and a *credit* to accounts receivable? Let's review the updated status of the events documented in the tables:

Sales Table	Sale-Inventory Table	Collect Payment Table
$175 revenue	$125 worth of Item # sold	$100 cash receipt

The organization now has a *debit* to cash (via the $100 increase to the cash balance) and a *decrease* (credit) to accounts receivable (Sales minus Cash Payments has now decreased by $100). Notice the event tables also document an increase in the cost of goods sold (the needed *debit*), and by identifying the item sold in the Sale-Inventory Table we can reduce the number in inventory when calculating inventory levels (the *credit* to inventory).

EXHIBIT E–1

Event-driven architectures defined by actual businesses

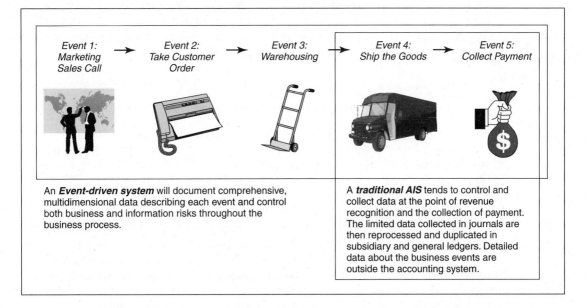

| Event 1: Marketing Sales Call | Event 2: Take Customer Order | Event 3: Warehousing | Event 4: Ship the Goods | Event 5: Collect Payment |

An **Event-driven system** will document comprehensive, multidimensional data describing each event and control both business and information risks throughout the business process.

A **traditional AIS** tends to control and collect data at the point of revenue recognition and the collection of payment. The limited data collected in journals are then reprocessed and duplicated in subsidiary and general ledgers. Detailed data about the business events are outside the accounting system.

It is no accident that the events-driven process of documenting business activities can yield the same information as a journal entry. Double-entry accounting and the chart of accounts (concepts conceived before the introduction of advanced information technologies) were developed as a method to help humans summarize and manage large volumes of data about business phenomena. Journal entries are nothing more than summary data about selected business activities, data that are routinely captured in an organization's primary information system. The processes of posting to journals and then to ledgers are extra steps that were necessary in the past due to limited technology options. Using today's technology, we are no longer constrained by human resources, thus we can devise alternative architectures that allow us to derive data directly from massive volumes of detailed data, without having to perform additional labor-intensive clerical steps and summarizations. The events-driven architecture provides an alternative for achieving more efficiency and less data duplication—rather than automating traditional manual processes. Such an architecture allows organizations to decrease their reliance on separate physical accounting system architectures while expanding the type of financial and nonfinancial analysis accountants can perform.

At this point, you may question whether alternate architectures violate generally accepted accounting principles (GAAP). Isn't a separate general ledger system, similar to the traditional accounting cycle, required? The answer is no. GAAP identifies how financial statement information is *reported*. GAAP does not specify the methods for data collection, storage, or processing.

HOW DATA CAN BE STORED AND DERIVED IN AN EVENTS ARCHITECTURE

In the events-driven architecture, control and information processing is accomplished by creating a logical view of the physical data, which usually corresponds to accessing the event, and corresponding resource, agent, and location data—so once again the *REAL* acronym guides the logic of the process. To illustrate, consider the following sample tables that could be designed to model a revenue process.

Sample Event Logical Structures:
(used to store documentation data about events)

TABLE NAME	SAMPLE ATTRIBUTES
SALES CALL	Sales Call #, [Salesperson Employee #], [Customer #], Date, Starting Time, Ending Time, Meeting Location, Meeting Expense, Meeting Details
CUSTOMER ORDER	Sales Order #, [Salesperson Employee #], [Customer #], [Customer Service Representative Employee #], Date, Time, Shipping Instructions, Cancel by Date, Location of Order (e.g., phone, during sales call, fax, or mail)
MOVE INVENTORY	Picking #, [Sales Order #], [Warehouse Clerk Employee #], Date, Time Started, Time Completed, Time Released to Shipping Area
SHIP MERCHANDISE	Bill of Lading #, Invoice #, [Picking #], [Shipping Clerk Employee #], [Customer #], [Carrier ID #], Date, Time, Shipment Tracking #, Packaging Information, Shipping Cost, Sales Tax, Salesperson Commission
COLLECT PAYMENT	Cash Receipt #, [Cash Account #], [Cashier Employee #], [Customer #], Date, Time, Amount Received, Electronic Funds Transfer #
ORDER/INVENTORY	[Sales Order #], [Inventory Item #], Quantity Ordered
MOVE/INVENTORY	[Picking #], [Inventory Item #], Quantity Picked
SHIP/INVENTORY	[Bill of Lading #], [Invoice #], [Inventory Item #], Quantity Shipped, Price Each
SHIP/COLLECT PAYMENT	[Cash Receipt #], [Invoice #], Amount Applied to This Invoice

Sample Resource Logical Structures:
(used to store reference data about resources)

TABLE NAME	SAMPLE ATTRIBUTES
INVENTORY	Inventory Item #, Description, Product Specification, Reorder Point, Current Price, Beginning Quantity, Beginning Quantity Date
CASH	Cash Account #, [Bank #], Type of Account (e.g., checking, savings, CD), Beginning Balance, Beginning Balance Date

Sample Agent Logical Structures:
(used to store reference data about agents)

TABLE NAME	SAMPLE ATTRIBUTES
EMPLOYEE	Employee #, Name, Street Address, City, State, Zip, Telephone #, Birth Date, Marital Status, Job Code (e.g., salesperson, shipping clerk, cashier), Start Date, Salary, Comments
CUSTOMER	Customer #, [Salesperson Employee #], Name, Street Address, City, State, Zip, Telephone #, Credit Rating, Credit Limit
CARRIER	Carrier Id #, Carrier Name, Street Address, City, State, Zip, Telephone #, Contact Person, Rate Information
BANK	Bank #, Bank Name, Contact Person, Bank Street Address, City, State, Zip, Bank Phone #

These sample tables document five business activities.[1] The sales call is documented in a single table. The order, movement of inventory, shipment, and collect payment events are each documented in two tables. The primary event tables include one record per event for all the nonrepeating items describing an event, and the second tables (e.g., the Order/Inventory, Move/Inventory, Ship/Inventory, and Ship/Collect Payment tables) reflect any many-to-many relationships between the events and a resource, agent, location, or other event. Each of these many-to-many tables includes one or more records relating to a single occurrence of an event. Notice how the event table(s) includes a posted key for each agent and resource involved in the activity. For example, the Customer Order and Order/Inventory tables include a unique identifier for the order (the event); the salesperson and customer service representative (the internal agents); the customer (the internal agent); the inventory items (the resources); and the location of the order when linked. This is no coincidence because these tables are based on logic derived from a *REAL* model, and they allow us to link event tables with other tables to develop an almost unlimited number of output views. Also notice how event keys are posted to subsequent event tables to generate a complete audit trail throughout the business process.

To illustrate a crude example of events-driven application processing, consider the following examples of storing and retrieving data, beginning with recording a cash receipt. A cash receipt is a payment from a customer for an invoice. To record the cash receipt the application accesses the Collect Payment, Ship/Collect Payment, Customer, Employee, Cash, and the Ship Merchandise data tables. One record documenting the receipt is added to the Collect Payment data table and a record is added to the Ship/Collect Payment data table for each invoice paid by the cash receipt. The program produces a screen to collect all the relevant data items. In addition to edit checks (e.g., completeness of the information and validity of the program user), the program checks whether the input customer number is valid (this is done by searching for the customer's number in the Customer data pool). The program alerts the person entering the data if he or she is recording a cash re-

---

1 In this example, the data that describes the shipment (the point of sale in this example) and the data that measures the value of the goods sold are combined in the ship event tables.

ceipt for a customer who has no outstanding invoices (this is checked by searching the records of sales invoices that have not been paid). If this occurs often, it signals a potential internal control problem (i.e., the need to verify that all sales are being recorded). After the customer and sales invoice numbers are verified, the program stores the remittance advice data in the event data tables.

How would you produce a sales invoice? A sales invoice is a document that reflects the sale of inventory by a salesperson to a customer. Thus, the needed data are stored in the Ship Merchandise, Inventory, (Salesperson) Employee, Customer, and Ship/Inventory tables. The related keys linking the data tables facilitate access to the data needed to generate the document.

Suppose you want to add an inventory item (or salesperson employee) to your files. The IT application would instruct the computer to access the Inventory data table (or Employee data table), add a blank record, and present a data input screen to the user to collect all the data items for storage in the appropriate table(s). Next, the computer should perform edit checks on the data (e.g., field checks, completeness checks, and checking to see if the inventory item already exists in the data table). Finally, the computer records each valid data item into the corresponding record field, then saves the updated data table. This process stores the data for future use.[2]

To prepare a listing of open sales orders, you create a query that lists all orders that have not been shipped and billed. Would a query of open sales invoices resemble the query needed to generate an accounts receivable total, an accounts receivable listing, or an accounts receivable aging? The answer is yes. Although the actual data items displayed by the query may differ, both open sales invoices and accounts receivable measure the same business activities: Sales that have not been paid. Unlike the traditional file-oriented approach, which maintains separate data files for each type of report, the events approach derives reports, queries, and other output from a common set of business activity data pools.

Although the preceding example illustrates an alternative way of storing and generating traditional accounting transaction data, it illustrates only one iteration of creating and using relational database tables. A designer could create other versions of the tables, or he or she could use other types of technologies (such as object-oriented techniques) to implement events-driven system concepts. The example is not intended to show you *one* particular physical system alternative, but to illustrate that traditional accounting data can be derived from operational data stores, allowing organizations to experiment with a variety of system architectures.

WHERE ARE MY JOURNALS AND LEDGERS?

In a traditional accounting system architecture, most sales/collection process data are recorded in the sales and cash receipts journals (or transaction files), the accounts receivable and inventory subsidiary ledgers (or master files), and the general ledger.

---

2 If you wanted to update, rather than add, an inventory or salesperson record, you would simply access the appropriate record and make any authorized changes.

Are journals and ledgers lost when you move to an events architecture? Again, the answer is no. They become logical output views rather than physical files. To understand this, consider the definition and role of a journal. It is a summary of business event data; thus, you should be able to derive journals from event tables. For example, a sales journal is an output that includes a portion of the data in Sales event table(s), and a cash receipts journal is an output which includes a portion of the Cash Receipt event table(s).

Subsidiary ledger and general ledger account balances are also summaries of event data. How could you calculate an accounts receivable figure for the balance sheet? As we explained earlier, since accounts receivables are sales that have not been paid by some point in time, the total customer payments [in the Collect Payment event table(s)] would be subtracted from total sales in the Sales event table(s) to generate an accounts receivable balance normally contained in the general ledger. If a report summarizing the accounts receivable subsidiary ledger is required, formatting the output to list the same information by customer is easily accomplished.

How would you calculate gross sales for an income statement? Since income statement figures measure activity over a period of time, you would total the sales data recorded in the Sales event table(s) between a specified beginning and ending date.

Other income statement and balance sheet items are derived in a similar manner. Balance sheet items disclose account balances at a point in time, so queries should produce financial measurements through a particular date. Income statement numbers represent activity over a period of time, so queries should specify a beginning and ending date, and calculate a financial measure of the activity that occurred during that time. Calculating financial statement figures requires knowing the applicable GAAP rules and definitions for each item reported on the financial statements and developing queries that derive data that fit GAAP criteria. Some measurements are derived from event tables based on actual, observable business activities, and some measurements (such as depreciation, allowances, or goodwill) are derived from event tables based on business activities that are not directly observable and are approximated or calculated.

Contrary to traditional architectures that maintain separate physical structures for data, journals, subsidiary ledgers, general ledger, and other specialized reports, the events architecture maintains detail data for relevant organization activities, and the outputs and other reports are generated from the detail data. This reduces data duplication and aggregation, and provides a new spectrum of potentially useful information.

OTHER DIFFERENCES IN THE EVENTS ARCHITECTURE

There are numerous implications of changing to an alternative architecture such as an events-driven design. These include:

- Storing a broader spectrum of data and data types to document business activity.
- Reducing the duplicate data and the number of physical files.
- Creating a per transaction audit trail rather than an aggregated, functional audit trail.
- Reducing the amount and time of processing.

Our earlier discussion has illustrated some of these differences, but let's examine them in more detail.

A primary benefit of an events-driven architecture is the simplicity of data storage and processing. Recording involves accessing the data pools representing each entity of the *REAL* model directly related to the event, and recording the event attributes. Each maintenance process captures and edits data about various resources, agents, or locations and stores the data in the appropriate tables. From a control perspective, it is important to make sure the event or maintenance data are being captured, edited, and stored in a timely, complete, and accurate manner. Because no further posting or summarization is needed once the data are captured, any information processing risks associated with traditional processing are eliminated. During a reporting process, data are accessed from the appropriate tables, rather than reprocessing the event details and storing the summary as a separate file that is then used to support further processing. From an events perspective, reporting involves identifying which tables are needed to generate a view and then performing the appropriate processing steps to produce the view.

To illustrate, refer to Exhibit E–2. This exhibit provides a template of both traditional[3] and events-driven processing steps. The traditional model, has a two-step process:

Step One

Input:	Transaction source data.
Process:	Perform edit checks and store data to transaction/journal file.
Output:	Data recorded in journal/transaction file.

Step Two

Input:	Journal/transaction file.
Process:	Post to files and generate printed documents and summaries.
Outputs:	Transaction records transferred from an open file to a closed history file.
	Records added to a new open file.
	Balances updated in subsidiary ledgers.
	Balances updated in the general ledger.
	Hard-copy documents (often includes one paper copy for filing).
	Hard-copy printouts of summary data that are stored in electronic files.

An events-driven architecture requires only one process:

Step One

Input:	Event source data (validated by and linked to previous events).
Process:	Store event data in event table(s), execute business and information control, and exception reporting.

---

3 These are based on the traditional processing flowcharts presented in Chapter 6.

EXHIBIT E–2

The Processing Steps to Produce the View

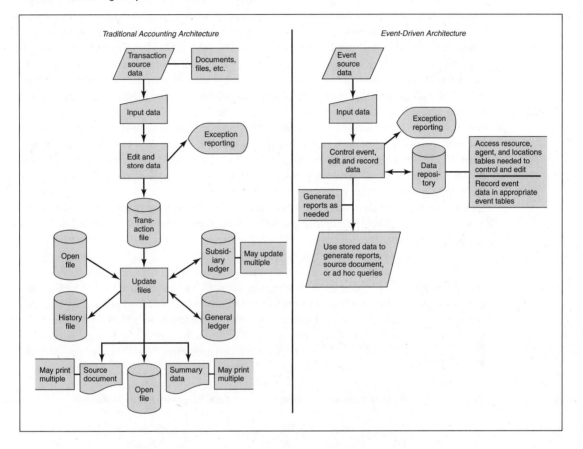

Outputs: Data recorded in the event data repository.
            Online queries and printed outputs generated as needed.

Step One in both environments is similar. However, the event environment promotes real-time control at each point in the business process and collects a variety of multidimensional data to describe the business activity. The critical difference between the two environments is the elimination of the intermediate processing steps of the traditional architecture. Step Two involves posting, data storage, and reporting processes that create data duplication, supplemental processing, and numerous physical files. In addition, it complicates the process of maintaining, certifying, and reporting duplicate data. Step Two posting and data storage processes are eliminated and replaced by reporting information processes in the events architecture.

The two architectures also create different versions of the audit trail. The traditional audit trail is often fragmented across various stores of data housed in different functional areas throughout an organization. For example, the supporting documentation for total sales on the income statement consists of monthly postings from the sales journals to the general ledger sales account. The amounts posted from the sales journals may represent entries from aggregated batches of sales. Even if each sale is documented with a corresponding journal entry, the details of the sale are not evident until you locate the sales invoice that was used to record the sale entry. To link this to the shipment and order that generated the sale requires you to go outside the accounting system and piece together what is often a myriad of documents and electronic files.

Now consider an audit trail in an events environment. Suppose the auditor wants a detailed list of all sales. This can be easily provided from the data contained in the sales event table. Because the related events, resources, agents, and locations are incorporated into the REAL model, the auditor can click on any sale, and the system can use the data table links to retrieve the corresponding shipment and/or order information for each selected sale. If the auditor wants to verify the customer who took part in the sale, the system can use the appropriate link to provide information about the customer (or any other agent or resource).

The events system allows additional flexibility not possible in a traditional architecture. To illustrate, let's consider two examples that require separate systems and/or separate processing in a traditional environment: accrual- versus cash-basis accounting and LIFO versus weighted-average inventory costing. You may have heard people say that they keep two sets of books: one for financial reporting and another for taxes. In the events architecture, the same pool of data can generate both costing methods. It only requires reporting processes based on the appropriate query parameters. To illustrate, consider the following abbreviated event tables:

Purchase of Inventory Event				Sale-Inventory Event Table	
1/6	16 units	$24.00		1/30	5 units
2/7	25 units	$32.50		2/28	17 units
3/30	10 units	$14.00		4/30	4 units
4/24	47 units	$70.50			

To derive a first-quarter inventory balance based on a weighted-average method, the query would calculate the inventory balance based on the average costs of the remaining inventory. To calculate the inventory balance using the LIFO method, the query would calculate the amount based on the assumption that the remaining items were the first items purchased. This provides the potential to truly match costs with the revenues they generate.

An events-driven system also provides the flexibility to compare cash-basis versus accrual-basis accounting using the same data. Suppose the totals in sales and cash receipts tables for January 1 through January 31 equaled:

Sales Event Table Total	Cash Receipts Event Table
$1,467,958.47	$1,256,876.98

Using accrual accounting, January revenues equal $1,467,958.47. Using cash-basis accounting, total revenue would be based on the cash receipts of $1,256,876.98. As these examples illustrate, there is no need for multiple systems or duplicate files to generate a variety of measurements and outputs, even if the measurements and outputs are based on different assumptions.

In addition to eliminating the need for numerous clerical tasks (e.g., reconciliations and journal/ledger postings), the events architecture eliminates the need for closing entries, reversing entries, and adjusting entries. Accruals are automated and can be updated to allow current, real-time reporting.

This architecture enables accountants to change their focus from clerical tasks to more value-added, real-time control and decision support. The events structure provides increased opportunities for accountants to perform analyses that support decisions that impact the bottom line. For example, rather than simply viewing marketing expenses as an item to be reported on the income statement, accountants could analyze the effectiveness of sales calls (in the aggregate or by individual salesperson) by linking sales call data to order information and measuring the productivity of the sales force. The opportunity to help an organization become more effective is limited only by *imagination,* rather than an incomplete or inflexible application architecture.

CONCLUDING COMMENTS

In this text we have suggested that accountants should evaluate alternative accounting information system architectures as a means of enhancing their value. Any alternative architecture should be evaluated using objective criteria. Any alternative AIS design must provide an infrastructure that enables accountants to meet various objectives. First, the architecture should support, not constrain, efforts toward operational excellence while also documenting organization activities. Second, the architecture must provide complete details and descriptions of organization activities. Third, data collection and reporting must occur in real-time rather than days, weeks, or even months after the fact. Fourth, the architecture must support preventive controls addressing business and information process risk rather than detective information process controls that do little to reduce business process risk. Fifth, the architecture should support a shift in accounting's role from simply reporting traditional measures to enhancing the measures used by an organization to plan, execute, and evaluate business events and processes. Finally, the architecture should allow accountants to derive GAAP reports and provide a complete, detailed electronic audit trail that links each event in a business process, rather than fragmenting the audit trail across a variety of different applications scattered across organization functions.

Although alternative architectures are now viable and are used by a variety of organizations, there is a major obstacle that will keep many organizations from success-fully changing the nature of their AIS architecture: the resistance of humans to change. People become accustomed to doing things in a certain way. Even those willing to con-sider change often focus on how technology can accelerate a traditional process rather than on how technology can enable an alternative approach to improve the process. Thus, when given an opportunity to rethink how to improve task performance, it is difficult for some people to separate the task objective from the traditional task process.

Ultimately, the true benefit of rethinking business and information processes is de-ciding how best to meet user information needs—independent of the technology and struc-ture traditionally used to perform tasks. To successfully change the AIS architecture, ac-counting professionals must separate the clerical mechanics—the traditional accounting cycle process supported by the traditional accounting information system design—from the objectives of accounting. To that end, it is time to begin rethinking the accounting process and evaluate alternative methods on the basis of the ability to best serve the user. As a business student, you should understand traditional architecture processing (whether manual or automated) but you must also learn to use and evaluate alternative architectures based on what they help an organization to accomplish, rather than whether the architec-ture automates traditional accounting processes intended for a world with limited infor-mation technologies.

Information Technology Components

SUPPLEMENT OBJECTIVES

The objectives of this supplement are to review the business impact of information technology (IT), summarize the basics of IT hardware, and introduce a different approach to learning and staying current on IT hardware and software. After studying this supplement, you should be able to:

- Describe the impact of information technology on organizations.
- Identify and describe the components of information technology.
- Explain the objectives of technology advancements for each IT component.
- Describe the characteristics of an optimal information technology.
- Describe ways by which an accounting professional can stay abreast of IT advancements.

INTRODUCTION

In this supplement, we present the first of a two-part study of information technology (IT). Reviewing basic elements of information technology is becoming increasingly difficult. As soon as you understand one product or concept, new and improved versions are created. Within the next few years, people will use new and innovative technologies in ways we currently cannot imagine.

So how do we study an ever-changing topic such as IT? Our approach rests on three assumptions. First, technology is ever changing. A critical part of becoming and remaining a valuable information professional is staying current with IT resources throughout your career. You must always strive to gain the knowledge of what is happening in the marketplace and what technology issues your clients are facing. Second, IT personal-productivity skills are essential for today's professional. These include proficiency in using tools such as spreadsheets, word processors, presentation graphics, Internet usage, communication, and databases to enhance your personal efficiency and effectiveness. Finally, studying IT is more productive when it is done from the perspective of identifying IT's usefulness, application, and impact. One of the attributes of successful business professionals is the ability to articulate and understand the broader implications of technology, and its impact on the decisions made by an organization. Our approach focuses your attention on IT's power and use, rather than on the technology itself.

We are well aware of the diversity of students' backgrounds with respect to information technology. For those with a strong technology background this supplement will help you define the potential benefits of technology for an organization. Others of you will also learn new terminology and new concepts.[1] We hope we help every reader enhance their

---

1 Two examples of good (free) Internet technology dictionaries are located at http://www.techweb.com/encyclopedia and http://wombat.doc.ic.ac.uk/foldoc/index.html.

ability to see IT from a business perspective and not be overwhelmed by the technology. We encourage you to invest the additional time to improve what we call your "strategic, conceptual" understanding of information technology. As you increase your familiarity and understanding, remember to focus on how technology affects organizations, and how the use of technology can help accounting professionals produce and deliver more valuable information.

THE IMPACT OF INFORMATION TECHNOLOGY

We are constantly amazed at the effect information technology (IT) has had, and continues to have, on individuals and organizations. Anticipating the impact of information technology is becoming more difficult. As Ralph Carlyle observed:

> Science fiction writer Isaac Asimov once said that it's easier to foresee the automobile than the traffic jam, the atom bomb than nuclear stalemate, the birth control pill than women's liberation. Put another way, the march of technology is inexorable and, to some extent, predictable. But the resulting corporate, organizational, and managerial ramifications are much harder to imagine.[2]

We are in the midst of an era of significant innovation in the business world due in part to the impact of information technology. When used appropriately, technology can affect how an organization plans, executes, and evaluates its processes. At a minimum, technology should be viewed as an *enabler*—a resource tool that, *if applied effectively,* can help an organization meet its objectives. Technology can enable significant change in an organization's strategy, processes, organization structure, individual roles and responsibilities, measurements, and even the organization's culture. Some impressive organizations have learned to view technology as more than an enabler. They are learning to use technology as an effective strategic weapon. Therefore, understanding the nature and use of IT in solving business problems is becoming increasingly important for anyone who wants to be involved in solving business problems and taking advantage of opportunities in the marketplace.

Despite all the "enabling and strategic tool" hype, remember that the application of technology in businesses does not automatically guarantee a positive experience or an optimal outcome. We are still learning how to integrate strategy, people, structures, business processes, measurements, and technology. The outcome of their integration depends on how effectively the technology is implemented and used by an organization.

EXAMPLES OF THE STRATEGIC USE OF INFORMATION TECHNOLOGY

Discussing the strategic use of IT could fill a book. Generally speaking, the strategic use of IT affects organization effectiveness, efficiency, and innovation by eliminating, automating, enhancing, and enabling business processes. The following examples illustrate just a few of the many ways IT is affecting organizations, including developing new products or services,

---

2 R. Carlyle, "The Tomorrow Organization," *Datamation,* February 1, 1990, p. 22.

improving decision maker effectiveness, and enabling change. Notice how in each example it is the impact of technology, rather than the specific technology, that is the key to success.

Developing New Products or Services

Many companies capitalize on technology innovations to develop new, or to revitalize existing, products and services.

CASE IN POINT

Speech recognition software allows computers to talk with humans. Recent advances in the software enable it to recognize what people say with more than 95% accuracy. The software has tremendous potential for a variety of business applications. For example, voice recognition software is widely used for collect calls: Will you accept? Yes or No? AT&T estimates a $100 million a year savings in operator time. Also, every second shaved off the average connect time by using telephone-automated directory-service attendants— the kind that ask you What city? and then hand you off to an operator—leads to $1 million in industry-wide savings a year.

UPS normally hires temps in its call centers at Christmas time to handle customer questions about package deliveries. Last Christmas they purchased voice recognition software in the "low six figures" instead of temporary employees. Unaided by humans, the software responds by voice to customer's inquiries on the whereabouts of their parcels. By not adding staff, they recovered their initial investment in one year. Operating costs are about one-third what the company would have had to pay workers to handle the same number of calls.[3]

Sometimes, a company that does not capitalize on new technology to develop new, or revitalize existing, products and services can suffer negative or adverse consequences.

CASE IN POINT

How long does it take a new computer technology to wreck a 200-year-old publishing company with sales of $650 million and a brand name recognized all over the world? Not very long.[4]

Such is the story of Encyclopedia Britannica. Since an encyclopedia on a CD is priced lower than hard-bound books, Encyclopedia Britannica's sales force (over 2,000 people strong) did not want to change to a new technology that would lower sales

commissions. Their story was similar to IBM's and Western Union's. In the 1980s, IBM's powerful mainframe sales force did not acknowledge the potential of the microprocessor. Over a century ago, Western Union turned down Alexander Graham Bell's offer to sell them his patent for the telephone. Western Union thought the purchase would jeopardize their large investment in telegraph equipment.

---

3 N. Gross, P. C. Judge, O. Port, and S. H. Wildstrom, "Let's Talk: Speech Technology Is the Next Big Thing in Computing," *Business Week,* February 23, 1998, pp. 60–72.

4 G. Samuels, "CD-ROM's First Big Victim," *Forbes,* February 28, 1994, pp. 42–44.

Increasing Decision Maker Effectiveness

Providing better information, improving the decision process, or automating the decision process altogether can support decision making. We are seeing explosive growth in the use of information technology to support all levels and aspects of decision making. This trend will continue to push back the boundary of what is possible and justifiable. One of management's biggest decisions is how to price products. IT has opened a new set of pricing options.

CASE IN POINT

Coca-Cola is asking the question: Why should the price of a can of Coke be the same all the time? Would people pay more for a cola fix on a sweltering summer day than they would on a cold, rainy one? The answer may be provided by "smart" vending machines that will be hooked up to Coke's internal computer network, letting the company monitor inventory in distant locales—and change prices on the fly. Consumers might balk if Coke's prices suddenly rise. But they might be willing to buy a cold soda on a chilly day if the vending machine flashed a special promotion, say $.20 off—the digital equivalent of the blue-light special. There is a revolution brewing in pricing that promises to profoundly alter the way goods are marketed and sold. In the future, marketers will offer special deals—tailored just for you, just for the moment—on everything from theater tickets to bank loans to camcorders. It will be done through the Internet, corporate networks, and wireless setups to link people, machines, and companies around the globe.[5]

Marketing Goods and Services

Even small businesses can now use the Web to give them the reach of a huge conglomerate. Going online eliminates many of the traditional barriers to entering a national or a global market.

CASE IN POINT

Before Perry and Monica Lopez decided to peddle hot sauce on the World Wide Web, their clientele was limited mainly to the neighborhood around their Hot Hot Hot store in Pasadena, California. Today they get customers from Switzerland, Brazil, New Zealand, and other faraway spots. Their 300-square-foot store is now a global company with their home page generating an active business.

More companies are gearing up to take orders and payments over the Web. A recent study found that 22 of 30 big corporations surveyed plans to offer online transactions by next year, or about double the number now.[6]

---

5 A. E. Cortese and M. Stepanck, "Good-bye to Fixed Pricing? How Electronic Commerce Could Create the Most Efficient Market of Them All," *Business Week,* May 4, 1998, pp. 70–84.

6 J. Carlton, "Think Big: The Net Gives Small Businesses a Reach They Once Only Dreamed of," *The Wall Street Journal,* June 17, 1996, p. R27.

WHAT ACCOUNTING INFORMATION PROFESSIONALS SHOULD KNOW ABOUT INFORMATION TECHNOLOGY

A fair question to ask is, Why do I need to know anything at all about technology? Let's once again think about the role of professional accountants as presented in the CPA Vision Project[7] and review the top five competencies and the top five services of the accountant:

National Top Five Core Competencies

- ◆ Communications skills.
- ◆ Strategic and critical thinking skills.
- ◆ Focus on the client and market.
- ◆ Interpretation of converging information.
- ◆ *Technologically adept—able to utilize and leverage technology in a way that adds value to clients and employers.*

National Top Five Core Services

- ◆ Assurance.
- ◆ Management consulting.
- ◆ Financial planning.
- ◆ International.
- ◆ *Technology—provide services in technology application, system analysis, information management, and system security.*

In fact, the AICPA's information technology mission is to enable all members to provide value to their clients and their employers through effective application of current, emerging, and future information technologies. The AICPA's objective is to have the business community "think CPA" when it thinks business solutions and, specifically, think *business solutions through technology.*[8]

Technology affects how organizations operate, what accounting and other information systems professionals do, and how management, financial, and IT professionals interact. Accountants do not need a degree in electrical engineering or computer science to become very sophisticated technology users and application experts. Advances in technology have made it possible to dedicate more time to professional and business issues and less time to technology issues, while still being an effective technology user. Therefore, what all accounting program graduates need is what we call a *strategic, conceptual understanding of information technology.*

A strategic, conceptual understanding of information technology focuses on:

1. The functions of each IT component.
2. The objectives of technology advancements for each IT component.
3. The potential business impact of new technology.

---

7 For more information, see http://ww.cpavision.org.
8 For more information, see http://www.aicpa.org.

Understanding the concepts behind the technology helps you use, evaluate, and control technology more effectively. Without a conceptual understanding, the technology may be misunderstood and thereby employed ineffectively or even inappropriately. More importantly, a strategic, conceptual understanding of technology encourages you to concentrate on applying and using technology to achieve business purposes and avoids getting mired in engineering details.

THE FUNCTION OF INFORMATION TECHNOLOGY COMPONENTS

Today's information technology actually had its beginnings as far back as 1830 when Charles Babbage first hypothesized a gear-driven analytical engine for solving numerical problems. Although Babbage never actually built his dream, he began a series of advances in computational technology that has resulted in creative applications and products in today's marketplace.

Technological applications differ in terms of their capacity, price, and size; however, they have the same basic components: input, output, processor, memory, storage, communication channels, and instructions. These various components (shown in Exhibit F–1) are common to all computers and to manual information systems as well. Whether you are preparing financial analyses manually or with a computer, the same basic components are used. A variety of computer components and devices are available to perform various func-

EXHIBIT F-1

Components of Information Systems

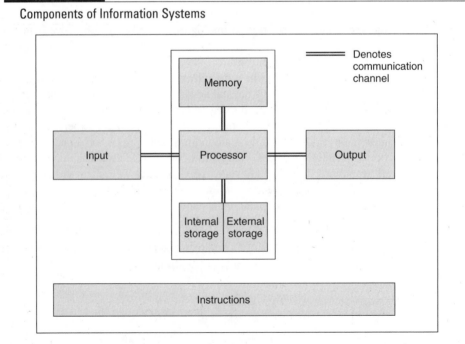

tions. For example, Exhibits F–2 and F–3 illustrate various components used to support an accounts payable clerk.

The function and purpose of each device shown in Exhibit F–2 is quite straightforward. The input/output box (input device) is used to collect the input data (input) in the form of documents to prepare (process) a check for a supplier. After the documents are sorted in alphabetical order on the desk (memory), a calculator (coprocessing device) is used by the clerk (the primary processor) to calculate (process) what is owed to each vendor. When the clerk verifies (process) the documents for a specific supplier, a check (output) is written (process) using the pen and checkbook (output devices). The supporting documents and the check stub are stapled together and filed in the file cabinet (storage device). The Accounts Payable Manual (instructions) guides this entire process.

In a computerized environment, various devices are used to perform the same basic functions that might be performed manually. The difference is the speed, reliability, flexibility, and potential processing volume. The components of a computerized information system (shown in Exhibit F–3) are divided into two groups: physical *hardware devices* (input, processor, memory, storage, channel, and output) and *software* (instructions). Although hardware devices are the most visible, the software is actually what makes the computer useful. In and of itself, the hardware is nothing more than a very expensive paperweight or conversation piece. However, without the computer hardware, the software would be equally useless.

EXHIBIT F–2

Manual Information System Components

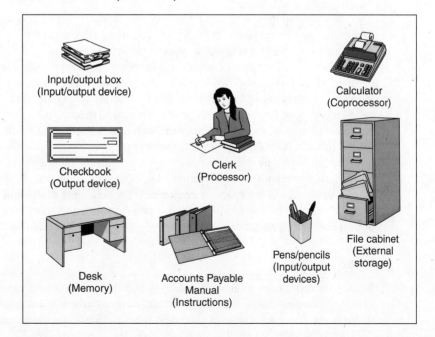

Input/output box
(Input/output device)

Calculator
(Coprocessor)

Checkbook
(Output device)

Clerk
(Processor)

Desk
(Memory)

Accounts Payable
Manual
(Instructions)

Pens/pencils
(Input/output
devices)

File cabinet
(External
storage)

EXHIBIT F–3

Components of a Computerized Information System

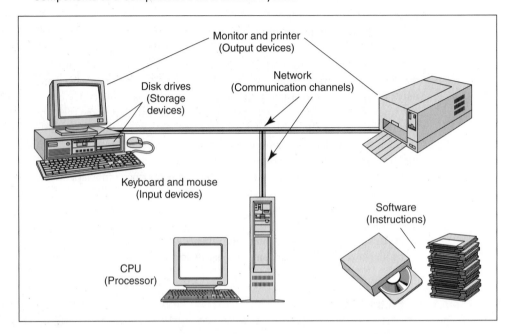

When computers were first introduced, most processing was performed in a separate Electronic Data Processing (EDP) Department, using large and very expensive computers. As a business activity occurred, a clerk recorded the activity data on a paper, called a *source document.* Batches of the source documents were given to the Data Processing Department. Data processing clerks, often called *keypunch operators,* entered the data from the source documents and verified the data by entering it a second time. The second entry, called rekeying or key verification, was performed to reduce errors during data entry. The input was processed, the EDP Department stored the data, and the resulting output was delivered (usually on reams of computer paper) to user departments.

Today, such a model of computer input, processing, and output is dated. Computing takes place throughout an organization's locations, at customer and supplier locations, or even in the homes of organization employees. The following discussion will acquaint you with the purpose, business value, and direction of advancements of each technology component used by organizations.

Input

Input devices are used to enter instructions into the computer and to collect and prepare data for processing. To provide useful output, a computer must have reliable input data and instructions. Using a garbage can analogy, when the input is garbage, so is the output.

Organizations strive to input complete, accurate, and timely information. To meet these objectives, many new input devices are being developed to replace the keyboard, which has traditionally been used to enter most data. More natural forms of data entry, such as speech, hand signals, or writing are now being used. Development trends include entering business data at the time and location of the activity (to enhance data timeliness), reducing human intervention (to increase completeness and accuracy), and entering more types of data (to increase documentation completeness).

Examples of input devices range from the traditional keyboard to the more natural forms of input. More natural forms include pointing devices (e.g., mice, track balls, and light pens), microphones for speech input (used with speech recognition software), optical character recognition (OCR) devices (e.g., scanners, optical character readers, and bar coding), video cameras, digital cameras, magnetic strip readers, smart card readers, scanners, magnetic ink character recognition (MICR) devices, telephones, image processing, touch-sensitive screens, and PEN-based computing.[9] For example, some long distance customers activate their phone calling card via voice recognition. Exhibit F–4 shows a variety of input devices available today.

EXHIBIT F–4

Computer Input Devices

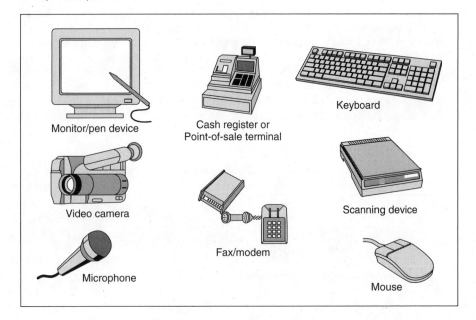

Monitor/pen device

Cash register or
Point-of-sale terminal

Keyboard

Video camera

Fax/modem

Scanning device

Microphone

Mouse

---

9 MICR machines read magnetic ink characters such as those applied to checks and deposit slips. OCR machines can recognize printed characters. PEN computing uses a stylus to enter handwriting and other marks into the computer.

OCR and MICR devices are often used to improve the efficiency and accuracy of certain information processes. For example, most utility companies utilize *turnaround documents* that customers return with their payments. Turnaround documents are generated by the organization (e.g., a customer bill) and are used as input to process customer payments—the customer "turns around" or returns a portion of the bill to the company with payment (hence the name *turnaround*).

Input devices are making significant contributions toward innovations in business and information processes and improving process control. The following case illustrates how input devices can be used to:

♦ Expand the amount of data that can be reliably captured.

♦ Reduce the cost of gathering data.

♦ Eliminate or minimize human clerical processes.

♦ Reduce the time in data gathering.

♦ Increase the accuracy of the data collected.

CASE IN POINT

Many supermarkets use scanning technology, such as point-of-sale (POS) terminals, to record the exact contents of a customer's purchase. As a result, management knows the cashier, exact items and quantities purchased, sales price of each item, time of day, register number, store location, and amount of change given to the customer. In addition, if a credit card is used for payment, a great deal of information can be accessed regarding the customer. Gathering and entering this data by hand is both infeasible and subject to numerous input errors. A byproduct of using scanning technology is the elimination of inventory counts to determine what to order. Quantity on hand is automatically updated as each sale event occurs. The exact type and quantity of goods sold can be tallied by the computer and the information needed to order more merchandise can be sent automatically by the computer to the company warehouse or suppliers each day, week, month, or whenever management chooses.

This case illustrates the tremendous contribution input technology is making to business and information processes. Today, organizations can collect data in ways that were either cost prohibitive or entirely impossible a few years ago. Although many input components reliably capture a variety of natural input (e.g., speech, pointing, and pictures), the software required to control these devices lags hardware component capability. Continued advances in speech recognition, vision processing, scanning, and other input-related technologies will greatly reduce the complexity of both instructing the computer and recording input data.

Output

A major product of an information system is useful output. The typical output is information to help decision makers plan, evaluate, and control the organization. The objective is to present accurate, timely, complete, and accessible information in various formats.

Many output devices are available to present information in *hard-copy* (paper) or *soft-copy* (nonpaper). The most familiar types of output devices are monitors (using CRT or LCD[10] technology) and printers. Trends in output device development include improved accessibility and ease in providing high-resolution, user-defined output, while integrating multiple forms of media (particularly mixing sound and pictures with animation). Integrating various media is called *multimedia.* The objective of multimedia is to make the output more useful by providing stimulation to more than one human sense at a time. Examples of output devices for sight, touch, and sound include monitors, projection systems, plotters, and speakers, as shown in Exhibit F–5. Such sophisticated forms of output require equally sophisticated software. As in most areas of computing, hardware capacity is well ahead of the software in achieving natural forms of output, but software development is progressing.

One exciting benefit of newer input and output technology is its ability to communicate with people who require alternative forms of communication. Specifically, multimedia and printing technology provide output for sight- and hearing-impaired persons far more efficiently than ever before.

Memory

Data and instructions are needed to perform any computer task. Memory provides short-term storage for instructions and data during processing. While humans have fairly limited

EXHIBIT F–5

Computer Output Devices

Monitor

Projection

Printer

Fax/modem

Speaker

---

10 CRT stands for cathode ray tube. The newer generation of monitors are liquid crystal displays (LCD). Graphics controllers are being used to enhance the graphics displayed on monitors.

memory and processing capacity,[11] computers have the ability to maintain and process millions (or even billions) of instructions and pieces of data simultaneously.

For computers, memory is measured in units called *bytes.* A byte is roughly the equivalent of a single character. For example, the word *hello* requires five bytes of memory for storage—one byte for each of the five letters. Each memory location within a computer has a unique address. Computer memory is measured in units of thousands of bytes (*kilobyte*), millions of bytes (*megabyte*), billions of bytes (*gigabyte*), or even trillions of bytes (*terabyte*).

Memory is also measured by its speed. *Memory speed* refers to how quickly data and instructions can be stored, moved, and retrieved. The common measurement unit for memory speed is a *nanosecond* (one-millionth of a second). A lower number of nanoseconds means less time is required to perform tasks associated with managing memory. Generally, the greater the memory speed, the greater the price of the hardware.

Examples of physical memory devices in our office example include a note pad (for a manual system) or what is called *RAM* (random-access memory) and *ROM* (read-only memory) in a computer system. RAM is used to store data and instructions during processing and is only available when the computer is turned on. This would be akin to the memory of the accounts payable clerk in our office example. Once the power to the computer is shut off, or even interrupted for an instant, the instructions and data in RAM are lost. You can expand a computer's RAM by adding additional memory chips to the computer.

ROM is used to permanently store the low-level instructions that control the basic operations of computer systems components or software applications. ROM instructions are written by the computer manufacturer and are typically transparent to computer users.

The objective of advances in memory technology is to remove any processing limitations due to inadequate amounts and speed of memory. This is being pursued along two fronts, one dealing with physical memory (hardware related), the other dealing with virtual memory (software related).

On the hardware side (physical memory), great strides are being made in microelectronics to develop smaller and faster electronic storage devices. Some researchers are even working on utilizing molecules of hydrogen as computer memory. We will likely see tremendous breakthroughs in physics and electrical engineering that will continue to expand the size and speed of memory for computer processing.

On the software side (virtual memory), we are now able to quickly swap between main memory and secondary storage devices, which we will discuss in a moment. Memory swapping (the ability to quickly transfer data from secondary storage to main memory) makes it appear to the user as though there is an unlimited (virtual) supply of available memory. Hence the common term *virtual memory.* Over the years, great strides have been made in developing a computer's ability to swap between main memory and secondary

---

11 See G. A. Miller, "The Magical Number Seven, Plus or Minus Two: Some Limits on Our Capability for Processing Information," *The Psychological Review* 63, no. 2 (March 1956), pp. 81–97.

storage. As a result, in *some* computing environments, processing is relatively unconstrained by memory speed and size.

One restriction currently faced by developers of computer technology is the use of electromagnetic technology (i.e., electronic signals). The problem with electromagnetic technology is it is fairly volatile and is subject to interference from radio and other electromagnetic devices. Furthermore, electromagnetic technology generates tremendous heat, which can cause the failure of computing components. However, we may soon see the use of processing devices that utilize light rather than electronic signals for processing. Light has the advantage of being more stable for computing, storage, and communication and does not generate heat like electromagnetic signals.

Storage Devices and Storage/Access Methods

Efficiency in data processing requires the ability to store data and processing instructions for future use. Storage devices are occasionally called *secondary storage* because they are used in addition to the main memory that we just discussed. Storage devices differ from memory in that they are able to retain data even when the power to the computer is turned off. When needed, items in storage can be retrieved and placed in memory for use during processing.

Cost is another difference between memory and storage. Byte for byte, memory is much more expensive than secondary storage. For example, if one megabyte of memory were to cost $100, you could expect the same amount of storage to cost as little as $2 or even 20 cents depending on the type of storage device. As in the accounts payable example, data are often stored on low-cost storage devices (file drawers) until they are needed for processing. At that time, items are transferred to the more limited and expensive memory (the desktop) for processing. The same is true in a computerized environment.

Storage capacity, as with memory, is measured in size and speed. Storage size is measured in bytes, while speed is measured in *milliseconds* (thousandths of a second). Notice the significant difference between storage speed, measured in thousandths of seconds (milliseconds), and memory speed, measured in millionths of seconds (nanoseconds). Storage devices store and retrieve data and instructions slower than memory because most secondary storage uses mechanical devices while memory devices do not. Because mechanical devices involved in storage devices require physical movement they are much slower than memory devices that simply store and direct electronic signals. The most common type of computerized storage device is the *disk*. There are several types of disks ranging from removable floppy disks, that can store several hundred thousand bytes of data, to optical disks that can store several billion bytes of data on the same size or surface area.

Most disk technology is really quite simple. As shown in Exhibit F–6, most disks are partitioned in four ways: by surfaces, by tracks, by sectors, and by bytes.[12] Each magneti-

---

12 Fixed, removable floppy and optical disks use these types of tracks. CDs and DVDs, optical disk technologies that we will discuss later in this section, use a single spiral track.

EXHIBIT F–6

Disk Storage Technology

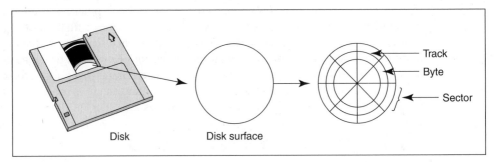

Disk   Disk surface   Track   Byte   Sector

cally coated disk typically has two *surfaces* (top and bottom). Each surface is divided into a series of concentric circles called *tracks,* with each track being divided into segments called *sectors.* Lastly, each sector is divided into a certain number of bytes. As with memory, each unique combination of surface, track, sector, and byte provides a unique address. The addresses are kept in an index on each disk and are used to identify the specific location of information stored on the disk.

Data and instructions are written to and read from a disk using a disk drive. A disk drive is an electromechanical device that reads and writes the data and instructions to and from the disk. By magnetizing microscopic areas of the disk, large amounts of data and instructions can be stored on the surface of a disk. Disk technology is available in several forms. The common types of disks today include floppy disks (such as 3½ inch disks), removable high-capacity floppy disks (such as Zip disks), removable hard disks, fixed hard disks, and disk packs (or arrays). They vary only in their capacity (speed and size) and cost. As you would expect, typically, the greater the capacity, the greater the cost.

Other forms of storage technology include magnetic tape and microfiche. *Magnetic tape* is one of the cheapest forms of electronic storage. Magnetic tapes are made of a flexible plastic ribbon similar to audiocassette tapes. One side is coated with an iron-oxide material that can be magnetized. As with disk technology, electromagnetic pulses record data on microscopic locations on the tape. Tape technology is available in reels, cartridges, or cassettes.

A file that is stored on tape usually has a *header record* as the first record of the file that identifies the contents of the file. A *trailer record* is usually the last record of the file and contains summary information, like a control total, of the file contents. Following the trailer record is an *end of file marker.* Like the disk technology, tape technology involves electromechanical components to read and write tape content. Because a tape read/write head takes time to slow down and speed up when stopping and starting, tapes have *interblock gaps* (called *IBGs*). An IBG separates blocks or groups of records to allow for stopping and starting the tape.

Storage devices affect the types of storage and processing methods used by an organization. Originally, all data were stored and accessed sequentially. *Sequential storage* implies that records are stored one after another in some order (e.g., by customer number, date, invoice number, or employee number). *Sequential access* starts at the first record in the sequence and reads every record until the desired record is located. Because magnetic tape technology stores its content sequentially, data can only be read and written sequentially. Corrections, modifications, additions, or deletions require rewriting the entire tape and creating a new tape. For this reason, magnetic tape is cost-effective for archiving data, backing up data, or storing data that are only involved in sequential processing. Tape storage devices cannot be used when more direct storage and access methods are required.

With the invention of disk technology, alternative storage and access methods were introduced. Today, *random-storage* and *direct-access methods* dominate technology use. Random storage is a bit of a misnomer. Data are *not* stored in a random fashion so that there is neither rhyme nor reason to how data are organized. The word *random* refers to the fact that the ordering of records on a disk appears random in contrast to sequentially ordered records. An index of record locations or some other technique is maintained that allow data to be accessed in a random (nonsequential) manner. Direct access allows computers to retrieve any data item requested by the user without having to read all the previous records, regardless of where the record is physically located in a file. Corrections, modifications, additions, or deletions for random-storage and direct-access methods do not require rewriting the entire disk. Only the file or data item affected needs rewriting.

In addition to more traditional types of secondary storage, portable modes of storage are increasingly used. *Smart cards* are examples of such media. Smart cards have a memory chip that is used to store information. (These types of smart cards are referred to as *memory cards*.) Some smart cards also have processors built onto the card.

As with memory, the driving force behind advances in storage technology is speed and size. As never before, humanity is adrift in oceans of data. Although significant amounts of data and information are being digitized (stored in digital form), most of the available information today is still stored on paper that cannot be directly processed by a computer. Advances in storage technology are making it possible to maintain and access tremendous amounts of instructions and data for immediate computer processing. Two key technologies are pushing back today's storage limitations: optical technology and storage compression.

Optical technology for storage is a trend that shows great promise for offering effective storage strategies. Optical storage provides a cost-effective alternative to other storage technologies such as magnetic tape and microfiche. It is more reliable and accessible, and requires less physical space. Unlike magnetized disks, optical technology allows high-volume, direct-access storage because optical disks are written and read using laser (light) technology. Examples of this type of technology include CDs (compact disks) and DVDs (digital video disk or digital versatile disks). This technology is used to store vast amounts of data, sounds, and both still and moving pictures. CD technology is also available in recordable and rewritable media, while some vendors offer DVD-RAM. Many organizations are excited about the ability to use *imaging,* or optical image storage. This medium digitizes paper pictures and documents for use by information technology.

CASE IN POINT

Differences in storage capacities can be illustrated by contrasting how Michigan and Texas stored tax records. Michigan's Department of Treasury stored the paper tax returns of the five most recent years in 45,000 square feet of rented warehouse space on 15-foot shelves. The warehouse employed over 20 people to store and retrieve tax documents. In addition, they had another warehouse with over 100,000 square feet of storage space in which tax records over five years old were stored.

Meanwhile, Texas used microfiche technology to store every tax document ever submitted in a single room approximately 10 by 20 feet. More recently, the documents stored on microfiche have been stored on optical disks that require less than 10 cubic feet and are readily accessible via computer terminal to hundreds of Treasury Department personnel.

In addition to advances in optical storage, we are finding new ways to compress stored data. A variety of methods are available to store data in a fraction of the space previously required. Significant breakthroughs in storage compression coupled with similar advances in physical storage devices (primarily optical technology) should do a great deal to reduce the limitations of how much we can store and how quickly we can access content.

Processing

Converting input data into meaningful output requires a device that executes a set of instructions. We refer to executing instructions as *processing* and the device that performs the processing as a *processor.* The instruction categories are *operating systems* and *application programs.*

More than one processor can be used in an information system. The accounts payable example illustrated in Exhibit F–2 identifies two processors: the clerk (the primary processor) and the calculator (a coprocessor). Coprocessors are often used to perform specific types of instructions or work with specific types of data or media (e.g., performing mathematical calculations, generating graphics, or recording or producing sound). When the primary processor encounters a task requiring specialized processing, if a coprocessor is available, the task is handed off to it.

Processing devices execute instructions to convert input to output. Processing activities include recording input data, performing mathematical computations, and maintaining data files (e.g., updating, replacing, and deleting records). Examples of computer processing devices include the common calculator and the central processing unit (CPU)—the heart of the computer. CPUs are often called *microchips,* or just *chips.* When your friend says, "My new computer has the newest Intel Pentium processor," or, "My machine uses AMD's K6 processor," they are referring to the type of CPU in the computer. Today there are many CPUs available for small desktop computers and mainframe computers. As well, there are a growing number of specialized coprocessors that perform complex mathematical instructions, generate graphics, or facilitate more sophisticated forms of multimedia output (voice, pictures, or animation).

Processing is often identified by type: batch, online, or real-time processing. *Batch processing* accumulates a group or batch of data before it is entered and processed by the computer to update master files. *Online processing* means the input device is connected to the CPU and activity data are stored by the CPU in machine-readable form as they occur. *Real-time processing* denotes immediate response—transaction data are processed, the relevant files are updated, and a response is provided to the person conducting the business event while the event occurs. For further details about types of processing refer to the discussion in Supplemental Chapter B.

Computer processing power is often expressed in megahertz, a measure of processor speed. The higher the megahertz, the faster the processing speed. For example, a 266-megahertz machine is faster than a 100-megahertz machine. The number of instructions performed per second is another measure of computing power. The common unit of measure today is MIPS—*m*illions of *i*nstructions *p*er *s*econd. It is not uncommon for microcomputers to have the ability to perform several MIPS. To give you an idea of what it means to perform even 1 million instructions in a single second, imagine writing 50 instructions on a single sheet of paper. To write 1,000,000 instructions would require 20,000 pieces of paper; 20,000 pages at 600 pages per inch is a stack of paper approximately 33 inches high (or about 2.75 feet or about 84 centimeters).

Another measure of processor capacity is its processing word size. The *word size* refers to the number of bits a processor can process at once. The larger the word size it can handle, the more efficient (and faster) the bus or processor. For example, a 16-bit processor (a processor that can process up to a 16-bit word size at a time) is less efficient than a 32-bit bus. The earliest microprocessors were 4- and 8-bit processors. Most new computers today are 32-bit processors, but look for 64-bit machines to follow soon.

Not only is the power of the individual processor increasing exponentially, the computer industry is developing sophisticated methods for processors to work together. Cooperative processing comes in two flavors: distributed processing and parallel processing.

Distributed processing has actually been around for some time. It involves linking geographically separate computers, dividing large tasks into smaller parts that can be performed separately, and bringing together the finished results. This is the same concept used in building cars, building a house, or completing a group project. One processor serves primarily to coordinate the work of several others.

On the other hand, *parallel processing* involves the coordination of several processors within a single computer to perform several related tasks simultaneously. Parallel processing environments require very sophisticated software to coordinate the task performance of the various processors. However, the results are startling in terms of the increased processing capacity of a computer.

You might be asking yourself, What is driving all this advancement in processing technology? Simply stated, users want more speed! As people become more familiar and creative with the use of information technology, they have an insatiable desire for greater processing capacity. What is amazing is that the computer industry is delivering the processing power users keep asking for: instantaneous processing.

Communication Channels

The hardware peripherals shown in Exhibits F–1 and F–3 (input, output, storage, and memory devices) are connected to the CPU using communication channels. Communication channels are the routes by which data and instructions are transported among components. The communication channel connecting memory and the CPU is the internal circuitry of the computer, called the *bus* or *channel*. Bus capacity, like processor capacity, is also measured in terms of its word size. As with processors, a 32-bit channel has greater communication capacity than a 16-bit channel.

Earlier we stated that computing environments have changed from the days when all processing was performed in a centralized EDP department where users used remote devices to communicate with a mainframe processor. During that period, terminals were the primary equipment used to send and receive communication signals. *Dumb terminals* perform input/output (I/O) functions only, while *intelligent terminals* have I/O and processing capabilities.

Today, users want accessibility to data and information regardless of their location or time of day. Organizations want to input, process, and receive output in real time, as business activities occur. This is accomplished by using communication technology. Advances in communication technology allow tremendous flexibility in the way computer systems are physically configured. Communication technology allows a CPU to be connected to other CPUs, or other input, output, and storage devices regardless of their location provided they share a common communication channel.

CASE IN POINT

The AT&T Wireless Services data network gives you a convenient and efficient route to both personal and business information when you're not at your desktop computer. As a mobile worker, you may have very unique needs, so AT&T has developed different ways to meet them. They have developed the revolutionary, new AT&T PocketNet® service that lets you access your Email, calendar, and address book with a new generation of wireless phones.

Originally, networks were developed to facilitate simple data exchange and sharing of peripherals (i.e., printers and disk drives). Today's networks are far more extensive, allowing connectivity, shared application processing, and transport of various types of communications such as voice, video, and multimedia.

Communications networks range from localized, such as local area networks (LANs), to more geographically dispersed networks, known as WANs. *Local area networks (LANs)* are networks that connect computers and peripherals within a fairly small geographic area (e.g., a building or floor of a building). *Wide area networks (WANs)* connect computers and peripherals over large geographic areas. Several WANs cover the entire globe providing communication between computing devices virtually anywhere in the world. Several companies today provide electronic message and information services to allow communication between individuals and companies and to provide information about current stock market returns, airline travel, weather, sporting events, and so on.

Communications networks include both hardware and software. Hardware includes personal computers, mainframes, workstations, printers, scanners, disk drives, and more. *Network operating system software* (located on a network storage device called a *server*) controls all the components and flow of communications on the network. Each network device is connected to the network with some type of *network interface* or *adapter card* that enables the device to send and receive communications on the network communications medium.

LANs are configured using a variety of topologies. The *LAN topology* denotes the path that communications physically travel to transfer data and access LAN hardware components. These include:

- *Star.* All terminals are connected to a central computer. The Ethernet model uses this configuration.
- *Hierarchical.* Terminals are connected in a treelike or organization chart pattern.
- *Ring.* Terminals are connected in a closed or sequential loop. The token ring model uses this configuration.

In addition to topologies, LANs are defined by the type of protocols used to govern how LAN media are accessed and controlled.[13] Two types of LAN access protocols are *contention* and *token passing.* Contention protocols instruct network nodes to listen and see whether the communication channel is in use. If it is not, the node is allowed to send messages. Sometimes, two or more nodes begin their messages at the same time and collisions occur. Token passing protocols are designed to limit collisions. When token passing is used, a node is allowed to control the communication channel only when it is in possession of a special packet called a *token.* When a node is finished with the token, it passes the token (and thus control) to another network node.

How do data travel from one location to another? Data can travel using *conducted media* or *radiated media.* Examples of conducted media include electrical impulse conductors such as twisted pair (e.g. telephone network) wires or coaxial cable (normally used for cable television). Conducted media also include light conductors such as fiber optics. One type of radiated media includes radio frequencies such as broadcast, microwave, satellite, spread spectrum, and cellular. There are also light frequencies of radiated media (of which infrared communications is an example).

The *bandwidth* of a medium reveals the amount of data transmission capacity. The larger the bandwidth, the more the data capacity of the communication channel or media. The *transmission mode* measures the quantity of data sent and received. *Asynchronous*

---

13 A *protocol* is a set of rules that govern sending and receiving communications.

transmission transmits one character at a time with a start bit preceding the bits of the character and a stop bit at the end of the character. *Synchronous transmission* is continuous (the characters are not "padded" with start and stop bits), and thus is faster.

The equipment that transmits data also differs in terms of method. For example, *simplex devices,* such as televisions, perform one-way data transmission. *Half duplex devices,* such as CB or ham radios, perform two-way transmission, but only one direction at a time. Finally, *full duplex devices* (such as telephones and interactive cable television) perform two-way transmission simultaneously.

There are a number of other specialized hardware devices that enable communication. *Line-sharing devices* allow more than one network device to share a single communication channel. Examples include multiplexors and concentrators.

Another type of hardware is *modems.* Modem is shorthand for modulator/demodulator. Computers think digitally. Many communications are sent over telephone lines that transport the data in wave form. The modem is the device that takes a digital signal, converts it to wave form to travel over the phone line, then converts it back to digital form. *Baud rate* is the term used to describe the speed of the data transmission. The higher the baud rate number, the faster the modem (because it can carry more bps, bits per second). At this writing, the current modem standard is the V.90, with a speed of 56 kbps (kilobits per second). Although the listed speed is 56K, phone regulations limit top-end communications at 53K and some phone lines maximize at 46 kbps. There are other types of modems. Users can purchase cable modems (available from cable operators for communications services), wireless modems, digital subscriber lines (DSL) modems, and integrated services digital network (ISDN) modems.

Other hardware that enables communications includes repeaters, bridges, switches, routers, and gateways. Although the line that differentiates these products is blurring, the devices have traditionally provided different features. *Repeaters* give network signals a boost so that they can travel further. *Switches* are devices that physically connect two networks, enabling them to act as one virtual network.[14] An even more sophisticated device for connecting networks of different types is a router. *Routers* can provide connectivity of network segments. In addition, they can determine the most efficient route for sending communications. Finally, *gateways* are devices used to connect one type of network to another type of network (e.g., connect a LAN to a mainframe).

Such examples of communication hardware and software have changed the way organizations communicate both within and with the outside world. As indicated previously, computing originally was centrally located (known as *centralized processing and computing*) in large rooms filled with mainframe equipment. Users accessed the mainframe computer for all processing activity. Advances in communications equipment and personal computers allowed the growth of distributed processing. *Distributed processing* refers to linking geographically dispersed computers using a communications network. With distributed processing, users can perform some processing from their own site (referred to as

---

14 If two networks are of the same type, the physical connection of the two networks can be facilitated by a less sophisticated device called a *bridge.*

a *remote site*), in addition to time-sharing processing support from the host or main computing site. Today, many organizations are enhancing the notion of distributed processing by using a model known as *client/server computing.*

Whereas distributed processing is primarily associated with mainframe computing and some limited use of personal computers, *client/server computing* makes more extensive use of today's advanced personal computers and communications.[15] Client/server computing is actually a plan for distributing work among various computing devices. The term *client* refers to the end user or machine that can request resources across a network. The term *server* refers to the supplier or repository of data and/or computing resources (i.e., the provider of requested resources). The term *server* can apply to one or more of a large variety of machines including powerful workstations, LANs, mainframes, or minicomputers. Clients attach to a network to access network resources. Client machines often handle the user-interface software and perform some or all of any data capture and data entry tasks. Server categories include print servers, file servers, computing servers, database servers, and web servers. For example, a client may send a data query (a request for data) to a server. The server provides a central database (and the security and control of the data) from which clients can query and retrieve data. The server downloads the requested data to the client for processing. If the processing is performed to update the data, the client uploads the revised data to the server. Servers can also provide other resources in addition to processing and databases. These include sharing of large disk drives or other peripherals, and access to messaging services or communication links.

To further facilitate communications, an *information superhighway* is the goal of many people. Several countries, including the United States, are trying to establish information superhighways. Private industry and the government hope to nurture the development of a communications network that will merge a variety of information offerings, and make them accessible to private homes, businesses, or via an array of communication devices. Information suppliers will include television, movies, interactive games, phone, interactive shopping, library, databases, news and information services, financial information services, video catalogs (available at video rental stores), and classified advertisements. The vision is to have these services reside on powerful file servers and individual users will select the type and timing of their information access. No longer will the user have to use different media to access the different types of information. Information superhighways will change the nature of several industries that are currently separate, such as the cable and phone industries.

Many people view the Internet as the best current solution to the need for an information superhighway. The *Internet* is the world's largest (and still growing) worldwide communications network. The Internet originated as a vehicle for the sharing of university and government research resources. As you know, that has changed dramatically. The Internet is now an international collection of interconnected networks.[16] The *World Wide Web*

---

15 This movement from mainframe use to more personal computer use is called *downsizing.*

16 You may have also heard of *Internet2.* Internet2 is a way for the government and academe to recapture the Internet of old. It is an infrastructure under development by the U.S. government and more than 100 universities. *Internet2* is the term used to describe the many projects underway to create a next-generation Internet designed for education and scientific research.

(WWW) is the graphical interface for accessing and distributing information on the Internet. The WWW provides special hypertext links to jump from one Internet location to another. An Internet site address is denoted by its *uniform resource locator* (URL).

Most people surf the Internet using a *web browser.* Most web pages are designed with some form of *hypertext transfer markup language* (HTML) code. *Hypertext transfer protocol* (HTTP) transfers HTML and other components from the servers on the WWW to your browser client.

When people speak of the Internet, they often use the term TCP/IP. *TCP/IP* is shorthand for *transmission control protocol/Internet protocol.* As previously mentioned, *protocol* refers to the rules dealing with how data are transmitted over the media that connect network devices. TCP/IP is the Internet protocol suite, and is also referred to as the *protocol of open systems.* TCP/IP divides data into packets and control information, communicates the intended destination, verifies receipt of data at the end of the transmission, and reconstructs the data to its original form.

The TCP part of TCP/IP provides transport functions, which ensures that the total amount of bytes sent are received correctly at the other end. The IP part of TCP/IP provides the routing mechanism, providing information about the destination of transmitted messages. Other examples of the TCP/IP protocol suite include:

- FTP (file transfer protocol) allows a user on one computer to transfer files to and from another computer over a TCP/IP network.
- SMTP (simple mail transfer protocol) is the protocol for Internet Email. This protocol governs the transfer of Email messages among computers. Internet Email was originally intended for unformatted text, which is known as *ASCII text.* Later, MIME (multipurpose internet mail extension) was created. MIME is a method for sending nontext files, thus allowing Email to include formatting, color, sound, and so on.
- Telnet protocol provides terminal emulation. This allows a personal computer or workstation to emulate a variety of terminals connected to mainframes and midrange computers.

The Internet has provided a medium for various communication trends and new forms of networks. For example, *intranet* is an organization's private version of the Internet. Organization employees access the intranet via the organization's LAN. Using a web browser, personnel can access information stored on the organization's computer. *Extranet* is the term used to describe a virtual network that enables an organization to connect its network to business partners, vendors, suppliers, and customers. The Internet has also facilitated the growth of some technologies. *Telephony* is an example. Telephony is the conversion of sound into electrical signals, transmitting it within cables or via radio and reconverting it back into sound. However, the greatest impact of the Internet to date may well be the growth of *electronic commerce.*

Electronic commerce (EC) in a general sense involves any commerce facilitated by electronic means. In today's world, that includes most commerce. However, electronic commerce is often used as a term to describe the following modes of commerce: electronic data interchange and commerce over the Internet or Web. EC includes business-to-business activities, as well as business-to-consumer activities.

Electronic data interchange (EDI) is the exchange of information between organization computers. For example, organization A's computer executes a purchase by contacting organization B's computer system. This type of electronic commerce was traditionally carried out on non-Internet communication media, but the current trend is to use the Internet as the infrastructure to execute EDI transactions. Web-based commerce ranges from simple marketing, to 24-hour seven-day-a-week customer support, to full execution of revenue, acquisition, and conversion business process events. In short, electronic commerce is having a profound impact on organization structures, products, business strategies, and business models.

As this section illustrates, the impact of increasingly extensive use of communication technology by organizations and customers cannot be overemphasized. Communications is so important that legislation has been passed that impacts the future of the industry. The most notable is the *Telecommunications Act of 1996.* This act deregulated wired and wireless communication in the United States with the objectives of increasing competition, reducing rates in the long run, and generating new services. The act has created changes in the telecommunications markets. For example, companies previously known as cable companies now offer telephone services, while some traditional telephone providers offer Internet access. Computer companies are entering the cable market. These types of activities, as well as a large number of significant mergers, are shaping the telecommunications industry.

Researchers for PricewaterhouseCoopers have proposed that "One of the most pervasive issues IT executives face is sustaining network performance in the explosion of network-based applications and traffic volume." Communications deals with more than hardware and software issues, it also involves management issues. Communication technology is allowing organizations and individuals to operate in very new and different ways. Such advances are changing the way people work, when they work, and where they work. For example:

♦ It is possible to sit with a portable microcomputer in your cabin in the mountains and write a textbook about accounting information systems. In addition, you can send messages and access processing and storage resources across the world.

♦ An organization can electronically pay for purchases without creating any physical documents.

♦ Employees can perform many responsibilities away from the organization's main office and still maintain close communication with other employees who may or may not be at the organization's main office.

CASE IN POINT

Electronic communications are affecting the way companies make their financial information available to users and to capital markets. In an effort to expedite information flows from companies to financial markets, many publicly held companies are subject to SEC electronic-filing requirements. EDGAR (Electronic Data Gathering, Analysis, and Retrieval System) is accelerating the processing and review of financial information by the SEC staff.

The power of even the simplest computer system can be increased exponentially by connecting it with more powerful computing resources using today's communication technology. As with hardware, the full capabilities of communication technology depend on equally advanced software. Advances in communication technology are having a significant impact on information technology. Today, computer and communication technology are so closely intertwined that each area greatly enhances the capacity and usefulness of the other. Although we have experienced significant strides in integrating computer and communications technology, we undoubtedly have seen only the tip of the iceberg in terms of what will occur during the coming years.

THE BUSINESS VALUE OF INFORMATION TECHNOLOGY

The components of a computer system are closely related. To this point, we have only talked about the performance of various components in engineering terms (e.g., MIPS, nanoseconds, and bytes). Having reviewed the purpose and the direction of advancement for each technological component, we are left with the question, What is the business value of all this information technology? The answer to this important question is found by analyzing the impact of technology on the business. To determine the business value of information technology, you should ask questions like the following:

- Does the technology provide more useful information to information customers?
- Does the technology improve business and information processes?
- Does the technology enhance the ability to control the risks of business and information processes?

A simple yes response is not adequate. We must identify and illustrate the value of the technology in business terms. If these questions are answered and illustrated affirmatively, you should then ask:

- Do the benefits provided by the technology exceed its costs?

Sometimes the answers to these questions are fairly straightforward but most of the time they are not. One reason for the complexity in measuring the value of technology is the difficulty in measuring the amount of work a computer can perform. The idea of measuring a computer's work in business terms was first proposed by IBM. They advanced the concept of throughput to counter claims of better performance by competitors using engineering measures (like MIPS) of performance.

Throughput measures the amount of work a computer performs in a given period of time—typically a minute. Examples include how many transactions are recorded, how many invoices are processed, or how many telephone calls are processed per minute. Throughput is a measure of the collective performance of technology in business terms, rather than computer terms. Therefore, rather than focusing on the performance of individual components, the focus is on determining the performance of the system and how well it satisfies the organization's needs. This requires a balance of technological components to solve business problems.

Not properly balancing the various technology components will result in a very poor measure of throughput. For example, having a very powerful processor with only a very small amount of memory can hamper the productivity of the system. Conversely, having a very efficient input device while using a relatively weak processor can also limit throughput.

One of the major problems in increasing a system's throughput for business applications is the performance of input and output devices. Input and output devices, often referred to jointly as *I/O,* are slower than a computer's CPU.[17] Even with tremendous strides in increasing I/O processing, I/O performance is still far behind some of the most primitive CPUs. Printing, the most common form of output today, is mechanically intensive and will likely never perform at the rate of internal CPU processing.

The difference between input and output device speeds causes an *I/O bottleneck.* The I/O bottleneck will continue to be a problem until two problems are solved:

- People reduce their dependence on paper-based information delivery.
- Storage and I/O components reduce their dependence on mechanical devices.

The I/O bottleneck can be reduced by dedicated I/O processors and by multitasking. *Dedicated I/O processors* increase throughput by unburdening the CPU of the details of managing I/O processors. When the CPU encounters any I/O task, it passes the task to the dedicated processor. When the task is completed, the dedicated processor signals the CPU that it is ready for another job. Multiple I/O devices may require the use of several dedicated processors that are controlled by a single CPU. As a result, system throughput is greatly enhanced.

Multitasking focuses on keeping the CPU busy while the slower I/O devices are working. We use multitasking while performing many everyday tasks. You probably use multitasking when you cook a steak dinner. You first wash and prepare the potatoes and place them in the oven. While the potatoes cook, you set the meat in your favorite marinade sauce and prepare the salad. As the potatoes near completion, you place the steaks on the preheated grill. As the steaks cook, you set the table and steam fresh corn on the cob. When the potatoes, corn, and steaks are all cooked to perfection you sit down with your favorite person and enjoy a wonderful meal.

Figuratively speaking, the same thing is accomplished with computers when they work on several different tasks (like formatting a disk, printing a file, recalculating a spreadsheet, and performing a database query) at the same time. In a multitasking environment, the processor quickly switches among a variety of tasks while waiting for the slower I/O devices to perform their functions. As a result, the throughput of the computer is greatly enhanced.

DIRECTIONS IN TECHNOLOGICAL ADVANCEMENT

Today's business professionals live in an exciting time. We have seen many advances in information technology and will continue to see more. Rather than sit and watch the world

---

17 Think of your brain (your processor) and your ability to write information on a piece of paper. Which is faster: your brain's ability to send information, or your hand's ability to write the thoughts on paper?

go by, it is important to note three significant directions of technology advances and the effect such advances will have on you and your organization:

1. *Adapting technology to human users.* The computer industry has learned a significant lesson: computers must adapt to the way humans work and communicate. For years, the emphasis has been on teaching people how to adapt in a technology world. The frenzy over computer literacy is a byproduct of this concern. However, computer, not human, adaptation will be the rule for the future. Improvements in voice and vision processing alone could make the computer a far less ominous resource to millions of people.

2. *Smaller is better.* The days of centralized processing with entire rooms dedicated to computer processing are less common. Computers with the processing power of yesterday's giant computers now conveniently fit in a briefcase. Computer developers now speak of entire systems residing on a single chip.

3. *Light-based computing.* The advantages of light as a computing medium (as compared to electromagnetic-based computing on disk or tape) are great. Using light in computers could be as significant as the invention of the computer itself. This could enhance the portability, reliability, and performance of computing technology. We appear poised for a technology that can do as much to revolutionize computers as did the microprocessor in the early 1980s.

CASE IN POINT

In 1990, AT&T's Bell Laboratories shocked the computing world with the announcement of a functioning computer processor that utilized optical, rather than electronic, signals.[18] Bell Lab's announcement could introduce a whole new era of computing. The advantages of using light rather than electricity are significant.

Unlike an ordinary computer, which processes information by moving electrons through its wires, an optical computer would "think" by shuttling fine beams of low-power laser light among a maze of mirrors and lenses. As in an electronic computer—or one made of Tinkertoy parts, for that matter—the operation of the machine would ultimately produce the logical operations that are necessary to solve problems.

The idea of using light beams in computers has long tantalized electrical engineers. The power of a computer depends on the speed of its components and how densely they are connected, and light seems ideal in both cases. Particles of light—photons—are the fastest things in the universe. They don't need wires in which to travel, and they don't interfere with one another: Beams of light can pass through each other unscathed.

The lack of interference among light beams allows researchers to cram thousands of information channels into a tiny space. Bell Labs' optical switches are so tiny that more than 2,000 can fit inside the letter *o*.

Many other predictions could be made regarding the future of computing technology. So where is all this technology headed? Progress will yield more optimal information

---

18 See "Computing's Bright Future," *U.S. News & World Report*, February 12, 1990, p. 55.

technologies that work toward achieving four goals (shown in Exhibit F–7): instantaneous processing, infinite storage, seamless connectivity, and intelligent software.

Instantaneous Processing

At the heart of more optimal information technology is the ability to perform instructions instantaneously. Instructions range from displaying a graph on a monitor, to summarizing an organization's financial position, to retrieving information for a manager faced with an acute problem. Therefore, the concept of instantaneous processing involves:

Performing any type of instruction instantaneously, regardless of the task.

Instantaneous processing is by far the greatest bottleneck to having a more optimal technology. Tremendous advances have been made in processing power over the past five years. However, as the abilities of technology become more and more sophisticated, so do the needs of users.

Infinite Storage and Instantaneous Access

The increasing volume of data that relate to every day decisions calls for infinite storage and instantaneous access. The concept of infinite storage and instantaneous access involves:

EXHIBIT F–7

Goals of Optimal Information Technologies

Seamless connectivity

Instant access

Intelligent software

Instantaneous processing

Infinite storage

> *Storing any quantity of information you need indefinitely, and allowing immediate access to create real-time information.*

Information customers demand an immense amount of information about an organization's operating environment and activities. With each passing day, we have access to volumes of additional information about what is happening and what is being discovered. At the same time, information customers demand more and more useful information. Without a means for storing and retrieving the available information, we waste a valuable resource that could significantly alter how an organization or an individual functions.

Seamless Connectivity

One of our most significant advancements has been the merger of computers with telecommunications technology. The concept of seamless connectivity is this:

> *Any computing device can freely communicate with any other computing device regardless of location and without the user having to direct when and how the various resources are being utilized.*

Seamless connectivity extends beyond linking processors, as with today's distributed processing systems. Additionally, it conceives of a world in which one can access a processing, storage, memory, input, or output device regardless of its location. When processing and storage technology are shared, the computational power of computer technology is significantly enhanced.

The idea of seamless connectivity may seem unrealistic by today's standards. However, the use of satellite and cellular communication technology is moving us toward a seamless-connectivity environment. As one cellular provider is already advertising, "Imagine: No Limits." Such seamless connectivity will enable the information superhighways of tomorrow.

Intelligent Software

Remember, without instructions the physical components of information technology are nothing more than expensive paperweights. The thought of creating intelligent software has been the focus of thousands of researchers and software developers for decades. Although successes have been limited, we are progressing toward relatively intelligent software.

Although we may never reach the four characteristics of a perfect technology in absolute terms, we have seen tremendous advancements in relative terms in just the past decade. We expect this trend to continue.

The Effect of More Optimal Technologies

What do the advances toward more optimal technologies mean to an organization or an accounting professional? Basically:

1. Technological advances redefine what might be considered a skill or a critical organization activity. Over the past 30 years, the computer has been used to automate, or even eliminate, many tasks once considered the domain of an expert. For example, until recently, humans at IBM classified fixed assets for depreciation purposes. Now, an expert system is used to determine the ideal classification, and the system performs the work of dozens of accountants at a fraction of the cost.

2. Technology allows knowledge workers to concentrate on being more creative and imaginative. Before the advent of computer technology, humans typically had only two ways to model something: with words or with mathematics. Both have advantages and disadvantages. Using words is a natural form for expressing understanding of something. However, words are often imprecise and subject to misinterpretation. Conversely, mathematics is quite precise, but for most types of communication, it is fairly cumbersome. The computer provides an alternative way to model the environment. The computer facilitates precision of thought while providing a much more natural means of expressing ideas for the common person.

3. Technological advancements will continue to break down physically imposed societal boundaries. Technology will continue to remove the need to be physically present to participate in many activities. To some extent we have already seen this occur. For example, in many areas, you need not appear personally to renew an automobile registration, order merchandise, or even attend a college class. You can go to your local photocopy shop and telecommunicate with friends and family from your hometown. As a result, accountants can expect to meet and work in groups with other persons from geographically dispersed locations.

4. Technological advances enable changes in organizational processes. More important than completing tasks and processes more efficiently, computer technology allows organizations to rethink both *what* they do and *how* they do it. Using the computer to perform the same old tasks in the same old ways is a tremendous waste of computing potential. Just think of being able to perform any instruction instantaneously, accessing any available information, and utilizing processing and storage power regardless of its location. This capability provides the opportunity to be much more creative in using technology. With more optimal technologies, organizations need not feel limited in efficiently and effectively providing customers with valuable goods and services. The reengineering efforts underway provide the opportunity to change everything organizations do, from manufacturing to employee development.

Today's use of computing resources is akin to our current use of the human mind—only a portion of its potential has been tapped. The thought of being able to control a resource (the computer) that can perform several million instructions each second is nearly inconceivable for most of us. However, as we continue to speed toward optimal technology, we will continue to underutilize this resource unless we rethink how we plan, control, and evaluate business activities. Hopefully, as you study the development of information systems in this book, you will become much more creative and imaginative in your use and application of technology.

DON'T START THE COMPUTER REVOLUTION WITHOUT ME

Although the need to understand information technology exists, we caution anyone from getting on the "computer technician" bandwagon. We have two reasons for this position:

1. It is extremely difficult for an accountant, or any other professional, to remain completely current with *all* the latest technology while also staying current in professional and organizational issues. Accounting professionals are not paid for detailed information about information technology; they are paid to measure business activity and control risk. Some have greatly profited over the past few years by becoming familiar with information technology at a very detailed level. It is arguably more important, however, to understand how and when to use and apply technology to solve business problems and provide improved information products. The objective of this and the next supplement are to help you acquire such a skill—a strategic-level understanding of information technology.

2. Staying current on the minute details of information technology has marginal value. Accounting professionals are not paid for an engineering level of IT knowledge. They are paid to provide useful information to information customers and enhance the value creation ability of an organization. Being able to identify opportunities to apply information technology is far more valuable to an accountant than being able to recite detailed engineering facts about information technology.

In their book *The Cognitive Computer,* Roger Schank and Peter Childers provide some useful observations about how much professionals should know about technological details. They use the example of automobile technology to suggest how much we should know.

In the early days of the automobile, people who owned a car needed to understand the details of how it worked. Why? Because the car was not reliable and would often break down. Many people were stranded along the roadside when they were unable to perform their own repairs or maintenance. To be an effective user of early automobile technology you needed to have a working knowledge of the technology itself.

Use of automobile technology today requires more attention to understanding the purpose and value of the automobile than understanding the engineering details. Few of us understand the details of fuel injection, antilock brakes, collision air bags, or basic combustion technology. However, there are millions of people worldwide, with and without a detailed engineering knowledge of automobile technology, that effectively use automobile technology every day.

Schank and Childers suggest the same is happening with information technology. In the early days of computing, users needed a detailed knowledge of how the computer worked because it was not very reliable or well understood. Initially, humans were trained to work with computers by focusing on technical computer issues. The key was to understand the details of computer technology and adapt the way you work to fit the technology. Now, technological advancement, coupled with an increased understanding of how humans work, reason, and interact with machines, has caused developers to adapt their products to humans. We have only seen a glimpse of what is possible when computers become more adaptive to human users.

Staying Informed of IT Advancements

There are several ways you can keep abreast of information technology and its business use:

- *Read technology reviews/executive summaries.* Several hard-copy and online magazines or information services are available that routinely provide both detailed and executive-level reviews of hardware and software technology. These require little time to review and often provide good examples of the value of technology. (If you get lost in the terminology, refer to a computer glossary such as http://www.techweb.com/encyclopedia or http://wombat.doc.ic.ac.uk/foldoc/index.html.)

- *Ask questions.* Realizing you cannot, and probably should not, spend too much time becoming an IT techie, we suggest you ask questions of those who do seem to understand the technology. However, don't get bogged down with the megahertz, megabytes, and MIPS. Ask questions about how the new technology improves its purpose (input, process, output, memory, storage, communication, or instruction) and its potential value to the organization (providing more useful information, reengineering business and information processes, or better controlling risk).

- *Experiment.* As frightening as it may appear, nothing takes the place of personal and organizational experimentation. We are not suggesting you try every little gadget that hits the street, nor that you experiment by applying them to actual business processes as they occur. Either approach could be both intrusive and dangerous. However, controlled experimentation is critical to see how information technology might be used.

- *Use your professional resources.* The AICPA routinely conducts technology conferences and publishes technology resources. You can check out the offerings at http://www.aicpa.org. For example, refer to the AICPA Task Force publication entitled "Information Technology Competencies in the Accounting Profession: AICPA

Implementation Strategies for the IFAC International Education Guideline No. 11."
Also, the AICPA publishes top technologies lists for accountants each year. These lists
provide guidance to accounting professionals on which technologies they should
investigate. For example, refer to the following lists published by the AICPA in
1998.[19]

Top Ten Technology Issues

1. Internet, intranets, private networks, extranets.
2. Year 2000 issues.
3. Security and controls.
4. Training and technology competency.
5. Electronic commerce.
6. Communications technologies (general).
7. Telecommuting/virtual office.
8. Mail technology.
9. Portable technology (notebooks/palmtops).
10. Remote connectivity.

Top Ten Technology Issues for Tax

1. Internet, intranets, extranets, private networks.
2. Training and technology competency.
3. Electronic document submission.
4. Communications technologies (general).
5. Mail technology.
6. Security and controls.
7. Remote connectivity.
8. Image processing and document management.
9. Telecommunications/virtual office.
10. Electronic document storage.

Top Ten Technology Issues for Consulting

1. Year 2000 issues.
2. Internet, intranets, extranets, private networks.
3. Training and technology competency.
4. Communications technologies (general).
5. Electronic commerce.

---

19 Make sure you check out the 1999 list.

6. Mail technology.

7. Portable technology (notebooks, palmtops).

8. Strategic technology planning.

9. Remote connectivity.

10. Business process reengineering.

Top Ten Technology Issues for Accounting, Auditing, and Assurance Services

1. Security and controls.

2. Year 2000 issues.

3. Electronic commerce.

4. Auditing electronic evidence.

5. Training and technology competency.

6. Electronic audit work papers.

7. Internet, intranets, extranets, private networks.

8. Portable technology.

9. Electronic document authentication.

10. Continuous auditing.

Top Technology Issues for Financial and Operational Management

1. Year 2000 issues.

2. Security and controls.

3. Internet, intranets, extranets, private networks.

4. Training and technology competency.

5. Electronic commerce.

6. Communications technologies (general).

7. Mail technology.

8. Strategic technology planning.

9. Technology management.

10. Disaster recovery.

Top Emerging Technologies

1. Agents (intelligent agents, focusing agents, filtering agents).

2. Push technology.

3. Smart cards.

4. Voice systems (voice/speech recognition, text to speech).

5. Auditing electronic evidence.

Every day we see evidence of powerful results when creativity and technology collide. The following are just a few examples.

CASE IN POINT

Aging cash registers, rising wages, and higher food prices have forced the fast-food industry to go leaner and meaner with information systems. The latest entrant in the fast-food grand prix is Wendy's International, Inc. In an attempt to get more and faster information a PC is placed in the back room of each store.

The PC takes information from the store's point-of-sale register at the end of the day, dials up a mainframe at company headquarters, and dumps the day's data. Among other things, Wendy's uses the data to plan faster and more efficient delivery of inventory and to supply 35 regional offices.[20]

CASE IN POINT

Some businesses can manage their price list on the back of an envelope. But price setting at Alamo Rent a Car, Inc., is a superhuman effort. That's why the company turned to expert-system technology to maintain more than 4 million different rental rates on a

fleet of 110,000 vehicles. At least 5,000 rates must be changed every day. The expert system can analyze the enormous number of rental rates faster and far more efficiently than a battalion of market analysts.[21]

We suggest two words for accounting and other business professionals to consider—carpe diem (seize the day). By acquiring and using a strategic, conceptual understanding of information technology, the opportunity exists to significantly increase the profession's value to organizations, but accounting professionals must be willing to make the investment.

CONCLUDING COMMENTS

This supplement has omitted a critical information technology component: instructions. An information system (computerized or manual) cannot process data and produce output without a set of instructions. Instructions and processors are needed to operate each component of a computerized system. The more useful the set of instructions, the more useful the information system. Instructions for a computerized information system are delivered as software. Supplemental Chapter G covers the various types of software and their effect on business and accounting. As discussed in this supplement, the bottleneck in developing useful computer systems is developing useful software. Hardware technology today is ahead of software technology. Some liken currently available software to attempting to use kerosene to fuel today's space vehicles—it can't even get the hardware off the ground even though it does burn!

---

20 "Wendy's Turns to PCs to Beef Up Operations," *PC Week,* February 12, 1990, p. 121.
21 "Expert Systems Drive Rental Rates," *PC Magazine,* June 3, 1991, pp. 59–61.

As you will see in Supplemental Chapter G, the real secret to successfully using and applying information technology is software, not hardware. Software has the potential to make the effect of even the most advanced computer hardware much more profound.

CHECKLIST OF KEY TERMS AND CONCEPTS

Asynchronous transmission	Hierarchical LAN configuration
Charles Babbage	Hypertext transfer markup language (HTML)
Bandwidth	Hypertext transfer protocol (HTTP)
Batch processing	Imaging
Baud rate	Infinite storage
Bit	Information superhighway
Bridge device	Input
Bus	Input/Output (I/O) bottleneck
Byte	Instantaneous access
Compact disks—Read only memory (CD-ROM)	Instantaneous processing
Central processing unit (CPU)	Intelligent software
Centralized processing and computing	Intelligent terminal
Channel	Interblock gaps (IBG)
Client	Interface or adapter card
Client server model	Internet
Communication channels	Internet2
Concentrator	Intranet
Conducted media	Key verification
Contention LAN access protocol	Kilobyte
Co-processor	LAN controlling software
Dedicated Input/Output (I/O) processors	Laser technology
Direct access	Light based computing
Disk sector	Line sharing devices
Disk track	Local Area Network (LAN)
Distributed processing	Magnetic disk
Dumb terminal	Magnetic ink character recognition (MICR)
Electronic commerce	Magnetic tape
Electronic data processing (EDP)	Megabyte
Electromagnetic technology	Megahertz
Extranet	Memory
File server	Microprocessor
File Transfer Protocol (FTP)	MIPS
Full duplex transmission device	Modem
Gateway device	Multimedia
Gigabyte	Multiplexor
Half duplex transmission device	Multitasking
Hardcopy	Nanosecond
Hardware	Network interface or adapter card
Header record	Network operating system software
	Offline

Online	Server
Online processing	Simple Mail Transfer Protocol (SMTP)
Optical character recognition (OCR)	Simplex transmission device
Optical technology	Smart card
Output	Softcopy
Parallel port	Software
Parallel processing	Source document
PEN based computing	Star LAN configuration
Point of sale (POS) device	Storage
Processor	Storage compression
Protocol	Switch device
Radiated media	Synchronous transmission
Random access memory (RAM)	Tape tracks
Random storage	TCP/IP
Read only memory (ROM)	Telephony
Real-time processing	Telnet protocol
Rekeying	Terabyte
Remote site	Throughput
Repeaters	Token passing LAN access protocol
Ring LAN configuration	Trailer record
Router device	Turnaround document
Scanning technology	Uniform resource locator (URL)
Seamless connectivity	Virtual memory
Secondary storage	Web browser
Sequential access	Wide area network (WAN)
Sequential storage	Word size
Serial port	World Wide Web (WWW)

REVIEW QUESTIONS

1. Define each of the terms in the *Supplement F Checklist of Key Terms and Concepts*.
2. What is the focus of a strategic, conceptual understanding of information technology?
3. List the objectives of input devices and procedures.
4. What are the trends in input device development?
5. Give four examples of input devices.
6. List the objectives of output devices and procedures.
7. What are the trends in output device development?
8. Give four examples of output devices.
9. Distinguish between memory and storage devices.
10. Describe the various types of (secondary) storage devices.
11. Which storage method(s) can you use with tape technology?

12. Which access method(s) can you use with tape technology?

13. Which storage method(s) can you use with disk technology?

14. Which access method(s) can you use with disk technology?

15. What two key technologies are currently pushing back storage limitations?

16. Describe and contrast batch, online, and real-time processing. Explain how each type of processing affects the timeliness of data stored in computer files.

17. What is the difference between distributed and parallel processing?

18. Give four examples of information highways.

19. What is an information superhighway?

20. What was the purpose of the Telecommunications Act of 1996?

21. How do you determine the business value of IT?

22. What causes the I/O bottleneck?

23. Describe and explain two methods for reducing the I/O bottleneck.

24. Explain what is meant by "instantaneous processing."

25. Explain what is meant by "infinite storage."

26. Explain what is meant by "seamless connectivity."

27. Explain what is meant by "intelligent software."

DISCUSSION QUESTIONS

1. How can information technology affect organizations?

2. How does a strategic, conceptual understanding differ from being computer literate?

3. Why do we advise you to focus on the use or impact of technology rather than on technology itself?

4. True or False: "By implementing technology into your organization, you achieve success." Justify your response.

5. Why do some organizations measure throughput? What is the significance of a system's throughput to the organization?

6. What does it mean for an accounting information professional to be technologically adept?

7. Select two teams to debate "whether there will ever be an optimal or perfect technology."

8. Is it more important to have a literacy of current information technologies, or the knowledge of how information technologies help business perform more effectively? Explain.

9. Is there a relationship between the ability to reengineer business and information processes, and advances in information technology? Explain.

10. Which is more important: hardware or software?

11. Will the exposure to information technology you receive in school sustain you throughout your career? Explain.

12. What is the difference between extranet, intranet, Internet and Internet2?

13. Why do you think the AICPA has focused on technology as one of its top five core services and on technological adeptness as one of its top five core competencies?

MINICASES AND OTHER APPLIED LEARNING

1. Visit a computer store and collect information about three of the following information technology components:
   output
   input
   processing
   memory
   storage
   communications channels
   instructions
   input

Required:

Prepare a three-page summary and prepare a ten-minute oral presentation of your findings.

2. Refer to current business and computer periodicals (e.g., *Business Week, Computer World, PC Week,* or *InfoWorld*) and find information about some current development in two of the following areas:
   output
   input
   processing
   memory
   storage
   communications channels
   instructions
   input

Required:

Write a one-page executive summary and prepare a five-minute oral presentation of your findings.

3. Contact a local organization and interview a knowledgeable manager to find an example of how information technology has helped the organization support decision-making or redesign processes.

Required:

Prepare a one-page executive summary and prepare a five-minute oral presentation of your findings.

4. Refer to current business and computer periodicals (e.g., *Business Week, Computer World, PC Week,* or *InfoWorld*) and locate descriptions or case study examples of how information technology has helped an organization perform one of the following:
   a. develop new products or services.
   b. enhance decision effectiveness.
   c. enable change.
   d. market goods and services.
   e. reengineer a business process.

Required:

Write a Case in Point (such as those found in the chapter) that describes your example.

5. Go to your library or search on the Internet to find articles describing the star, hierarchical, and ring LAN topologies. Identify the advantages and disadvantages of each of these topology types.

Required:

Prepare a short report (one to two pages) summarizing your findings.

Information Technology: Software Applications

SUPPLEMENT OBJECTIVE

The objective of this supplement is to introduce the fundamentals of computer software including the concepts behind communicating with the computer, various software types, and software's impact on organizations. This supplement also discusses future software trends, as well as the potential value of advances in software technology. After studying this supplement, you should be able to:

* Explain the concepts behind computer instructions.
* Describe the generations of programming languages.
* Identify different types of computer software.
* Describe application software commonly used by individuals and organizations.
* Develop a strategy for keeping current with software developments.

THE NEED TO BECOME FAMILIAR WITH SOFTWARE TOOLS

Computer hardware by itself has little value to an organization. Without software, it is nothing more than metal, plastic, wire, and silicon. Furthermore, computer hardware does exactly what it is told, asks no questions unless told to ask, and does not stop executing instructions until it is specifically told to stop. Every single task to be performed by hardware requires some form of programmed instruction. A series of computer instructions is referred to as *software* or a *computer program.*

Advances in the capability and performance of hardware technology are typically well ahead of software technology. Both hardware and software advancements take an extended period of time, but software is developed using existing hardware at the time the software project begins. As the software is being developed, additional advancements are made in hardware technology. Thus, there is a constant gap between what the hardware technology *could* do, and what it *can* do because software products take additional time to fully utilize hardware potential.

Business solution developers should focus on the software component of technology for several reasons:

* Software enables an organization to utilize the potential of information technology. Greater value can be added to products and services when an organization effectively utilizes information technology and software is the key to effectively utilizing available technology.
* Software enables an organization to enhance the personal productivity of employees, customers, and suppliers. Software packages such as spreadsheets, word processors, presentation graphics, databases, web tools, documentation packages (e.g., process

modeling software), grammar and writing aids, tax packages, accounting and auditing references, decision support tools, and statistical packages enhance personal productivity.

♦ An organization's information system is characterized more by software than the hardware components used to execute user instructions. Software defines the organization's information system used to plan, execute, and evaluate its processes.

Business solution developers should focus on *how* software is used to implement information system architectures, rather than the software itself. The value of software is *not* which particular language or software package is used, but rather *how* a package or language is used to implement a particular architecture.

The nature of the business should drive technology investments. The first step, therefore, is to correctly understand the organization including its industry, competitors, external environment, products, and services and how these products and services are delivered to customers. With this understanding, one can more effectively plan the information system architecture. Next, software needed to create the desired architecture is selected or developed and the hardware is chosen to run the selected software. There are a variety of software options that can be used to effectively implement a given architecture. Regardless of the software chosen, organizations should not allow software to distract from their mission of implementing computer applications to help plan, execute, and evaluate their strategic and operational processes.

THE VALUE OF SOFTWARE

The value of computer software lies in its ability to help the organization do something better, such as improve management's decisions, efficiently provide goods and services to customers, or improve the effectiveness and efficiency of decisions, operations, and information processes. Merely having more information does management little good if it does not improve their decisions.

Organizations today are not simply looking for software. They are looking for solutions to business problems. There are literally thousands of software packages, but very few real business solutions. Software can contribute toward a valid solution in the following ways:

♦ By improving organization workflows. Good software choices improve operating, information, and decision processes (i.e., an organization's workflow components). Too often, software choices hamper rather than improve workflow by institutionalizing antiquated processes that consume too many organization resources and stifle organizational and individual efforts to change.

♦ By providing real-time, useful information. Software solutions store, maintain, and make available the information decision makers need to plan, execute, and evaluate organization activities. Without useful information, there is little chance an organization will survive in today's competitive world, let alone optimize its operations and opportunities.

- By improving organizational and individual capacity to identify and control (in real time) business and information risks. Constructive software choices provide flexibility to change and aid in the effort to balance operational efficiency and effectiveness.
- By achieving organization strategy. Valid software enables organizations to accomplish goals and strategies. True solutions adapt to human and organization needs and objectives, rather than forcing humans and organizations to adapt to structures and processes mandated by a particular rigid technology.

These are rigorous standards by which to measure computer software's value and much of today's software falls short of these standards. During the coming years, however, efforts to develop and implement software will focus increasingly on developing technology that meets these and other criteria.

Useful software is not cheap. Organizations should expect to spend as much money on software as on hardware, if not more (especially when you consider software upgrades and support). Users often struggle deciding whether to make or purchase software for their business applications. Advances in software development tools have made it easier and less expensive to develop applications in-house. However, the decision to make or buy application software requires careful consideration.

INSTRUCTING THE COMPUTER

Humans communicate through the use of language. For example, in Spain, people use Spanish, Catalan, or Euskera depending on the region in which they live. Any human language utilizes written symbols (numbers, letters of an alphabet, and special characters), voice, facial expressions, or hand signals to communicate. Anyone familiar with a second language appreciates the complexity of using different languages to give instructions.

Instructing a computer also involves learning and using a language the computer understands. However, unlike human languages, there have traditionally been only two things the computer understands: the presence of an electrical impulse and the absence of an electrical impulse. This two-state environment is called *machine language* and is often represented by 1s and 0s. All computer instructions and data for input, storage, and processing must be represented by a series of 1s and 0s before the computer can process them.[1]

In the early days of computers, instructions had to be written in machine language, which is very difficult and time consuming. Imagine yourself trying to communicate with someone else using only strings of 1s and 0s. Errors were easy to make and difficult to identify. As a result, only people with extensive computer knowledge and good programming skills could communicate with the computer.

In an attempt to make the computer easier to use, alternative means of instructing computers have been developed. We will overview several categories of software, including:

---

1 These two states could change to four states in new computers. New technological advances could enable machines to store four electrical states rather than on–off.

- Programming languages.
- Operating system software.
- Communications software.
- Application software.

Programming Languages

To develop applications, you must choose a computer language. Just as there are a variety of human languages, there are a variety of computer languages. There are also computer language standards. Two associations identified with creating computer programming language standards are the International Organization for Standardization (IOS) and the American National Standards Institute (ANSI).

Since the inception of computers there have been successive generations of programming languages. Each new generation was developed to compensate for an existing weakness. This section examines the basics of various generations of computer languages.

First Generation Programming Languages Despite the variety in programming languages, the computer only understands machine language. *Machine language* is another name for *binary code,* and it is commonly called the *first generation programming language.*

As previously indicated, computers operate with electricity so data and processes are represented by the presence or absence of electrical impulses. Traditionally, everything is represented using this on–off binary set of signals. Inside the CPU, electronic switches are turned on or off by modifying the voltage of the electrical impulses. In memory or on storage devices, data are stored as microscopic magnetized elements with either a positive or negative electrical charge. Each of these states (on or off, high or low, positive or negative) is represented symbolically as a 1 or a 0. At the most fundamental level, the computer simply processes and stores strings of 0s and 1s that are referred to as *binary code.*

Using binary code, strings of 0s and 1s are combined into patterns that represent a variety of symbols (letters, numbers, and special symbols). Each 0 or 1 is called a *bit* (short for *BI*nary digi*T*). Typically, bits are combined into groups of eight to form a *byte.* Each byte represents one character—a single digit number, letter of the alphabet, or special character.

With an eight-bit byte, you can represent up to 256 different characters using different combinations of 0s and 1s. Having eight digits, each having two states, allows up to 256 (2^8) different combinations. For example, the following table gives you an idea of how various symbols are represented using different patterns of binary code:

Symbol	Binary Code
1	11110001
-	01100000
A	11000001

Instructing a computer using binary code involves telling the computer every little step to accomplish, even the most basic task. For example, instructing the computer to add two numbers (e.g., 2 + 4) requires each of the following instructions:

1. Place the binary code for 2 in a memory address A.
2. Place the binary code for 4 in a memory address B.
3. Add the contents of A and B using binary math.
4. Place the sum of A and B in memory address C.

Memory addresses A, B, and C are used by the computer's central processing unit (CPU) while executing the instructions. To access the sum, the computer retrieves the binary code stored in memory address C.

Imagine for a moment, being required to use only binary code (machine language) to communicate data or instructions to a computer. This simple example illustrates that using binary code is a tedious task that requires a working knowledge of the details of how the CPU performs processes and how memory is organized and utilized. No wonder only a few people were able to program computers initially. Obviously, most users today lack the time and interest to understand how to communicate with a computer using machine language. Fortunately, several advancements have been made in computer programming languages that make programming much less painful.

The initial breakthrough in making human/computer interaction more natural came when computer scientists realized that the computer could perform the task of translating nonmachine language instructions into machine language. As a result, subsequent generations of computer languages were developed.

Second Generation Programming Languages   Second generation programming languages, called *assembly languages,* represent the first effort to develop a more humanlike language to communicate with the computer. Assembly languages are specific to each type of computer. For example, computers using the Intel, Motorola, and DEC Alpha CPUs each have their own assembly languages. Each assembler instruction translates to one machine language instruction. Assembler code is very powerful and fast. However, because it requires the same detailed level of instruction, a great deal of time is required to program at the assembly level. An example of an assembly-level program is shown in Exhibit G–1. If the logic of this example is not very clear to you, then you will understand why third generation languages were developed.

Third Generation Programming Languages   Third generation programming languages moved toward the development of *procedure-oriented languages*. As the name implies procedure-oriented languages describe processing procedures to be performed by the computer using English-like vocabulary. Unlike assembly language, procedure-oriented languages are machine independent, meaning it is possible to translate them into machine code to run on many different types of computers.

The advantages of procedure-oriented languages include their more common language constructs and their ability to combine several machine-level instructions into a

EXHIBIT G–1

Assembly Language

```
105 Loop   DS      OH
106        GET     TRAN
107        LR      R11,R1
108        LA      R10,ISRECORD
109        MVC     ISKEY,TXKEY
110        PRINT   GEN
116        WRITE   ECB1, KN, NAMEFILE, ISAMAREA, "S", (R11)
117+       CNOP    0,4
118+       BAL     1,*+30
119+ECB1   DC      A(0)
120+       DC      BL1"10"
121+       DC      BL1"000001000"
122+       DC      AL2(0)
123+       DC      A(NAMEFILE)
124+       DC      A(ISAMAREA)
125+       DC      A(0)
126+       DC      A(0)
127+       DC      AL2(0)
128+       ST      R11,20(1,0)
129+       L       15,NAMEFILE+92
130+       BALR    14,15

132        WAIT    ECB=ECB1
133+       LA      1,ECB1
134+       LA      0,1(0,0)
135+       SVC     1

137        CLI     ECB1+24,X"00"
138        BE      LOOP
139        TM      ECB1+24,B"00001100"
140        BNZ     HRDWRERR
141        TM      ECB1+24,B"00100000"
142        BO      NOSPACE
143        TM      ECB1+24,B"00000001"
144        BO      INVALID
145        B       LOOP
```

single procedural-level instruction. Although a vast improvement over machine-level and assembler languages, procedure-oriented languages still do not use natural forms of human communication. Thus, the number of people who can easily learn to program with these languages is still limited. Examples of procedure-oriented languages include BASIC, FORTRAN, COBOL, Pascal, PL/1, and C. The following is an example of COBOL code commands:

> WRITE ISAM-RECORD INVALID KEY
> GOTO ERROR-RTN

As you can see, it is far less cryptic than assembly-level language, but is still not a completely natural language. Procedure-oriented languages describe the procedures—the detailed, fixed steps necessary to complete tasks and solve problems. Each minute computer function or action is delineated by a line or program code. *Program files* detail the explicit instructions of the input, process, and output necessary to record, maintain, or report information. Program files contain interdependent modules of processing, known as *subroutines*, as well as several types of logic, including If-Then-Else logic, Do loops, and For loops. (Refer to Exhibit G–2 for examples of programming logic.) In addition to program files, programmers create separate data files for use by the programs. *Data files* contain the data elements manipulated by program file instructions.

Currently, programmers can purchase a variety of tools to augment traditional third generation programming languages. These tools reduce the time necessary to develop application programs and help programmers customize screens, specify report formats, organize data, and even generate computer program code. Although such tools can enhance programmer efficiency, the tools are typically computer environment specific. This results in little uniformity across computing platforms.

A newer wave of third generation languages includes object-oriented languages. Traditional programs written in older third generation languages perform tasks specific to a particular function. This decreases the ability to reuse program code in other application programs. Today, programmers have a programming alternative. *Object-oriented programming* (OOP) is more flexible than traditional programming. In traditional programming, data are maintained separately from the processes and logic that define the data's behavior. In OOP, a problem is modeled as a group of interacting objects. An object includes both data that capture the behavior and properties of the things in the real world that they represent and the instructions for operating on or manipulating the data. These instructions are called *methods*. Program messages are written to initiate the methods embedded in an object (i.e., to request an object state change or to request that a value be returned).

Because object-oriented code is based on general, real-world behavior rather than task-specific actions, programmers can frequently reuse object-oriented code in different application programs. For example, a Print object in a program to record, maintain, and report sales data could be the same as a Print object in a program that records, maintains, and reports data about fixed assets. Being able to reuse code greatly reduces the time and effort required to develop valid, effective programs.

EXHIBIT G–2

Sample Program Logic

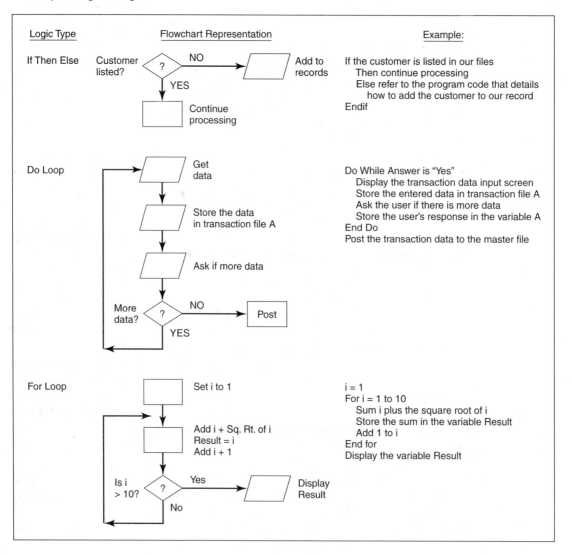

Logic Type	Flowchart Representation	Example:

If Then Else	Customer listed? ? NO → Add to records / YES ↓ Continue processing	If the customer is listed in our files
		    Then continue processing
		    Else refer to the program code that details
		        how to add the customer to our record
		Endif

Do Loop	Get data → Store the data in transaction file A → Ask if more data → More data? NO → Post / YES	Do While Answer is "Yes"
		    Display the transaction data input screen
		    Store the entered data in transaction file A
		    Ask the user if there is more data
		    Store the user's response in the variable A
		End Do
		Post the transaction data to the master file

For Loop	Set i to 1 → Add i + Sq. Rt. of i Result = i Add i + 1 → Is i > 10? Yes → Display Result / No	i = 1
		For i = 1 to 10
		    Sum i plus the square root of i
		    Store the sum in the variable Result
		    Add 1 to i
		End for
		Display the variable Result

Collections of objects are often assembled into what is called a *class library.* The idea behind class libraries is to provide programmers with a template for creating a repository of objects that can be used to assemble a variety of applications. Once an object class is defined, new objects can be created that inherit the attributes common to the object class.

For example, suppose you created an object class called *human.* If you created an object called *woman* and classified it as belonging to the human class, the woman object would inherit all human class attributes. Application developers today are providing libraries of objects from which you can choose various features. For example, instead of publishing a word processor that has every imaginable feature, you might simply select an object that allows you to view and edit text, another object that allows you to bold text, and others that allow you to bold, underline, save, convert, or spell check text. The objects you select can then be "snapped" together to provide the functionality you desire. So, in addition to being able to reuse objects, they can be used in a variety of ways depending on the needs of the individual or organization. Current examples of object-oriented tools include C++, Smalltalk, and JAVA.

Fourth Generation Programming Languages

Fourth generation programming languages concentrate on delivering a complete application development environment to the nontechnical user. Attempts at providing an integrated development tool have resulted in mixed success. Many fourth generation languages are still very complicated and are time-consuming and challenging to learn and use.

Examples of fourth generation languages include client server development tools. Client server computing concepts are discussed in Supplement F. CASE (Computer Assisted Software Engineering) tools are another example of fourth generation languages. These tools are intended to assist in the modeling and design of the software component of an information system. CASE tools can assist with a variety of tasks, including modeling data flows, processes, entities, and relationships, as well as creating data documentation. Original versions of these tools met with limited success but newer versions are more user friendly and can be used with other development support tools.

The intended advantage of fourth generation languages is rather obvious—end users are given a tremendous amount of power to develop computer programs. Characterized by more intuitive language construct commands, fourth generation languages do not require as much input, process, and output detail as third generation languages. To illustrate, consider the following simple example of a fourth generation structured query language (SQL):

> Select Customer-Name, Address, Telephone#
> From Customer
> Where Zip=95470

The command would result in a list of customer names, addresses, and telephone numbers for all customers with a 95470 zip code. Specifying the same instructions in first, second, or third generation languages would require far more code to communicate the same request.

Fifth Generation Programming Languages

Many people characterize programming languages that concentrate on embedding intelligence in computer applications as fifth generation languages. Truly intelligent machines have been imagined for many years.

There is a concerted effort under way to make software more intelligent. For example, computer programs exist today to help diagnose complicated medical problems, design production processes, configure computer systems, and control space vehicles. These types of software are far more ambitious than simply managing and editing text material. Many applications are available today to help evaluate loan applications, identify potential candidates for a job, schedule personnel, and detect employee fraud and theft.

The goal of intelligent software is to perform tasks normally considered to require human intelligence (e.g., the ability to make a credit decision, identify potential fraudulent transactions, or determine the best way to classify a recently purchased asset). Intelligent software is commonly affiliated with an area of research called *artificial intelligence.* Artificial intelligence applications exhibit human intelligence and behaviors (e.g., robotics, neural nets, voice recognition, expert systems, and natural and foreign language processing). Ultimately, some developers hope to give computers the ability to learn or adapt through experience, much like human experts who acquire expertise over time and experiences. Other developers feel that the potential of computing is not *artificial* thinking or intelligence, but rather *applied intelligence*—the art of knowing how to use programmed intelligence.

The move to make software more intelligent will greatly expand the usefulness of computers to the accounting professional. Although a few successful applications have been developed, we have probably seen little of what is possible in this area. Nonetheless, intelligent software will likely have a profound effect on organizations and accounting, freeing individuals from performing tasks that the computer could more easily perform. As a result, fewer humans will perform mechanical tasks and more humans will participate in creative efforts requiring the human touch. To date, accounting and auditing have been affected most by the development of expert systems. Only recently have we begun to make progress toward delivering truly intelligent computing devices.

Translating Computer Languages

Advances in programming languages were necessary to translate more natural languages to machine language that can be understood and processed by the computer. This was critical because application programs enable users to harness the power of the computer. As computer language generations evolve, they become more foreign to the computer. Languages that use human—or nonmachine—instructions must be translated back to machine language that the computer understands.

The process of translating instructions into machine language is illustrated in Exhibit G–3. The translation process begins with *source code,* the instructions written by the programmer using something other than machine language. Translation software converts source code into machine language, called object code. Finally, the computer executes the *object code.* This simple idea of having the computer translate instructions spawned the whole computer language development toward making human/computer communication more natural.

There are three basic types of computer language translators: *assemblers, compilers,* and *interpreters.* As you might suspect, an assembler translates assembly language into

EXHIBIT G–3

Language Translation

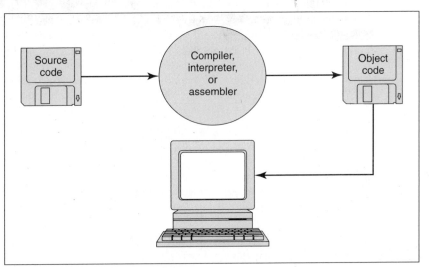

machine language. Compilers and interpreters translate procedural language into machine language. The difference between compilers and interpreters is that compilers translate an entire program prior to the computer processing any portion of it, while interpreters translate and execute program code line by line. With a compiler, a completely new file is created containing the object code. This file can be saved and executed the next time the program is run. This avoids having to recompile the program each time the computer program is executed. No file of object code is created with an interpreter; the program is interpreted and executed line by line each time the program is run. Typically, compiled (or object) code runs faster than code that is interpreted because all the translating occurs before attempting to execute the instructions.

Examples of Software Program Errors   Computers can perform such tasks as printing payroll checks, recording sales transaction data, retrieving a customer's account balance, or delivering messages to other individuals. After identifying a task for the computer to perform, someone must describe, in detail, how the task is to be performed. *Computer programmers* then translate the detailed instructions into a computer program to accomplish the task.

Writing computer instructions is called *programming* or *coding*. For many people, programming is tedious, unfulfilling, and even unpleasant. One reason programming is so aggravating for many people is that the computer is very exacting in executing instructions—even erroneous or unintended instructions. Because humans do not tend to be as exacting in specifying instructions, programs often contain errors. There are at least two types of programming errors: *syntax errors* and *semantic errors.*

The computer can only execute what is precisely communicated using the computer's syntax (grammar and vocabulary). *Syntax errors* are execution errors, in which the computer is unable to understand the grammar or vocabulary of the instructions, which prevent program execution. The following example illustrates differences between correct and incorrect COBOL code and the errors identified by the compiler as it attempts to create the object code:

Correct Code	Incorrect Code
STOP RUN.	STOP-RUN.
WRITE PRINT-LINE.	WRTE PRINT-LINE.
ADD B C TO D.	ADD (B + C) TO D.

Sample Error Messages from running the incorrect code are:

STOP-RUN.
Undefined symbol STOP-RUN

WRTE PRINT-LINE.
Undefined symbol WRTE

ADD (B + C) TO D.
Unrecognizable word or literal (
Unrecognizable word or literal +
Unrecognizable word or literal)

Semantic errors are logical errors—the syntax of the instructions is correct but it instructs the computer to perform undesirable tasks or to perform desirable tasks incorrectly. Semantic errors frequently occur in human communication. For example, suppose you have a visitor who is unfamiliar with the idioms of the English language. She goes on and on telling you how much she admires a Ming vase you received as a gift from your mother. Finally you become annoyed and tell her to "knock it off." If she is standing too close to the vase, you may quickly see that the syntax of your communication was correct, but the semantics were not, as she knocks the vase to the floor with a puzzled look on her face wondering why you wanted her to destroy such a beautiful piece of art.

Because semantic errors have valid program grammar but invalid logic, the code will execute, but will produce incorrect, often dangerous, results. An example of a semantic error is instructing the computer to add, rather than subtract, the amount of a check from your checking account balance. After a period of time, you may find yourself in real trouble. Although the syntax was correct, the semantics of the instruction were not.

Compilers and interpreters make programmers aware of syntax errors, but have limited intuition and judgment to identify the semantic errors. The task of finding and correcting errors in a computer program is called *debugging*.

CASE IN POINT

The word *debugging* has an interesting origin. In the early days of computing, computers would often require an entire room to house the vacuum tubes, wires, and electrical components. While developing a computer program, one of the teams pioneering the use of the computer could not understand why a certain program was not working. After several people reviewed the set of instructions, they decided to check the execution of the program through the hardware of the computer. Because the computer was open to view, they could trace the electronic signals through the physical components of the computer. Finally, they found the problem—a moth (as in a flying insect) had become wedged between the contact points of a circuit in the computer. Thereafter, whenever a program was not executing correctly they would say, "we've got another bug in our program." The term stuck and today we have the word *debugging*.

Fortunately there are many talented people who enjoy programming and are very good at writing and debugging computer programs. For some people, it is like solving a mystery loaded with intrigue and wonder. However, with today's programming languages, it takes someone with a certain disposition and aptitude for detailed logic to both enjoy programming work and to be productive.

Over time we expect the ability to program will become more and more accessible to even naive computer users. One thrust in software development and research is to provide programming tools for common computer users who understand what they want the computer to do (the semantics) but do not understand the syntax of communicating with computers.

Such progress has two implications for the business and information professionals. First, giving an end user the ability to write code could prove as risky as giving a loaded cannon to a child. Just because a program executes it does not mean it is correct. Programs should be critically evaluated, especially programs developed by end users with minimal experience or training in programming. Second, advances in programming languages and tools enable business and information professionals to more easily instruct the computer. This allows business and information professionals to concentrate their training efforts on the more critical component of program development—carefully delineating the computer requirements necessary to complete tasks. Furthermore, they have the opportunity to shift their focus from a program language emphasis to discovering ways to more effectively employ information technology.

Operating System Software

Programming languages are used to develop software programs of all types, including operating systems, application development software, and a variety of application programs. An *operating system,* often called *system software,* is the set of computer programs that manage basic computer operations by coordinating and commanding the hardware components. More specifically, the operating system performs tasks such as controlling execution of program instructions by the CPU, managing data storage in both memory and secondary storage devices, and managing communication between the CPU, its peripherals, and other computers.

In addition to managing the hardware operations as data are processed and moved, operating system software "talks to" a second category of software, application software. As we discuss later, application software performs specific tasks (e.g., a program that helps you maintain personal finances, or a program that records an organization's credit customer charges and payments).

The operating system accesses a set of instructions that reside inside a machine's *ROM* (read-only memory). ROM contains the machine's BIOS (Basic Input/Output System), which is used to start the computer. Typically, the remainder of the operating system is loaded into memory from a disk or tape device when the computer is turned on. The process of loading the operating system is known as *booting the computer.* This term comes from the early days of computing in which the instructions now residing in the BIOS had to be loaded manually into the computer when the computer was first turned on. This set of instructions was referred to as the *bootstrap,* from the metaphor of putting the computer's work boots on to get it ready to do some work.

Over the years, operating systems have evolved from a small set of primitive instructions to an elaborate collection of sophisticated programs. Developing an operating system requires a detailed understanding of the inner workings of the computer. Although operating systems are becoming more powerful, they are at the same time becoming much easier to use.

There are almost as many operating systems as there are computer hardware manufacturers. For larger computers such as department or enterprise servers, some of the more popular operating systems include OpenVMS, MVS, OS400, Microsoft NT, Novell NetWare, OS/2, and Unix. On smaller desktop and personal computers there are a variety of operating systems such as OS/2, DOS, Macintosh Operating Systems, and Windows.

A fundamental change in operating systems in past years was the migration toward a graphical user interface (GUI), which allows the user to command the computer using icons,[2] rather than typing text instructions on the keyboard. The GUI interface has proven much more intuitive to users because users do not have to remember commands to be typed to copy files, run programs, or access a network. This trend has made computing technology far more accessible to much larger groups of users including young children. Another trend has been to incorporate web server software and support for Internet protocols.

To aid in developing business systems, operating systems support a variety of programming languages and utilities. *Utility software* enhances file and systems management by performing tasks such as creating, copying, moving, and renaming files; monitoring

---

[2] An *icon* is a small pictorial representation of an object that is displayed on the computer screen. If you want to execute Excel you merely double-click the mouse with the pointer on the small picture representing the Excel software package. This is much easier than having to locate the appropriate subdirectory and execute the software by typing the program's name, as would be required in a DOS environment.

password access; or tracking system usage. Users can purchase utility packages to increase their ability to control the operating environment. Such packages include security packages, backup utilities, search routines, system diagnostic tools, recovery routines, or virus detection and protection. Over time, manufacturers continue to incorporate more utilities into newer releases of operating systems. We expect most of the best utility functions to be incorporated into the better operating systems of the future.

During the coming years developers will continue to improve the features and power of operating system products. Eventually, the look, feel, and functionality of operating systems will become more standardized, allowing users to move more freely from one computer to another and from one network to another (including intranets, the Internet, and other information highways). In addition, operating systems will continue to become much more flexible in their ability to interact with users through voice, visual, and tactile methods of communication.

The primary effect of advances in operating systems on organizations, management, and information professionals is in providing easy-to-learn and powerful computing environments. This helps everyone take greater advantage of applicable technology, resulting in the application and use of information technology in more areas and by more people (many with very little computer experience and training).

Communications Software

Supplemental Chapter F discussed the hardware developments in data communications. Now we will review advances in communication software. Connectivity is a fundamental need for successful use of technology today. In response to this need, we are watching an explosion of activity dealing with computer networking.

The merger of telecommunication and computer technologies is one of the most important developments in information technology. This *convergence* has resulted in a variety of connectivity software:

- *PC to PC* software allows two personal computers to share data, pass messages, or share resources such as a hard disk or printer.
- *Local area network (LAN)* software connects several personal computers located in a close proximity to one another and coordinates their interaction. Primary advantages of LAN software include sharing peripheral devices (e.g., printers, hard disks, and modems), thereby reducing the cost of buying peripherals for each individual computer, and facilitating communication among computer users by passing data and messages electronically.
- *PC to host* software allows a personal computer to interact with a large host computer. The host can reside in the room next door or on the other side of the world. The primary advantages of PC to host software are access to the power of large host computers for complex computing tasks, message passing among a variety of widely dispersed people, and the ability to centralize the recording of transaction data.

- *Wide area network (WAN)* software allows computers to interact across a wide geographic area. There are several networks that link computers throughout the world and make it possible to access a variety of computer resources regardless of what is available locally. WAN software facilitates worldwide communication among computer users. As a result, it is possible to collect data from throughout the world and communicate it to central sites where enterprise information is maintained.

- *Client/server* software enables the client/server communication model, discussed in prior supplements. The software allows clients (e.g., users on workstations or personal computers) to access data and processing capacity from servers (e.g., LAN file servers, mini or mainframe servers). The client and server(s) are connected via a network. The server maintains data and processing requests from clients. Often more than one server is created, with each server performing specialized processing tasks. Clients are able to access the processing power of the server or servers, and perform work online in real time. Client/server software is often applied to empower personal computers to perform tasks previously performed primarily on mainframes.

- *Web/Internet* software enables users to navigate the Internet, develop web sites, and participate in web based computing.

Until the mid-1990s connectivity technology tended to be rather proprietary and specific to the various types of connections (e.g., PC to PC, PC to host, WAN, LAN, client/server). Therefore, connecting all an organization's computers was more fantasy than reality. By the mid-1990s significant strides were made in making connectivity technology much less proprietary. In the future, we will see the development of standards that facilitate the sharing of objects across a variety of architectures and computing platforms.

Communication can increase the value of the computer to organizations by enabling them to construct communication configurations that best suit their desired information flows. As a result, communication technology (both the hardware and software) has made the collection and distribution of computing and information resources possible throughout the physical and virtual world (i.e., cyberspace).

Application Software ✔

For most users, operating systems and utilities are not terribly useful in and of themselves. Most users measure the value of the computer by assessing its utility in performing business tasks. Business problems can range from the mundane (typing memos, sending messages, or recording transaction data) to the complex (coordinating personnel schedules on a project, estimating the cash flow effects of a potential capital acquisition, or estimating the sales of a new product). With each year, users and software developers learn valuable lessons regarding how to create more useful software. Increasingly, users are learning to think of their computers as information storehouses and access tools, rather than as document-creating tools (word processors).

Application software includes the vast variety of programs written to process user requests to enter, update, store, query, or report information. Application software is available for many different tasks such as creating charts, managing enormous stores of data, speaking, creating simulations of buildings and products, and even managing building security and heating. Increasingly, application software, like operating system software, is moving from character-based user interfaces (CUI) to graphical user interfaces (GUI). A computer's user interface defines how the user interacts with the computer (e.g., menus, screens, keyboard, and helps).

Character-based user interfaces support text-based commands that are usually entered on a keyboard. Often these environments do not support WYSIWYG (What You See Is What You Get). The development of <u>GUI</u> environments provides the foundation for a much more flexible computing environment. GUI products use a variety of methods for communicating with the computer, including sound, pictures, animation, video, and simulations. Much work is needed to coordinate and control simultaneous use of different applications and data types. Watch for developers to continue to work toward more transparent and friendly user interfaces in the future.

For the most part, computers have concentrated on processing character-based symbols—numbers and words. However, a tremendous amount of work is focusing on the development of products that process multiple media forms (e.g., voice, text, pictures, and video). Today, we have the forerunners of software that allow users to record, edit, and manipulate sound, pictures (both still and moving), and animation. Using very simple tools, elaborate interactive applications are available to teach children about biology, math, and computers, or to assist mechanics in repairing cars. At a very reasonable price, children and adults can purchase products such as interactive encyclopedias on CD-ROM. These encyclopedias include hypertext and hypermedia features.

Hypertext allows users to link related textual information. For example, a child can read a passage from the encyclopedia and by clicking on a highlighted word, the encyclopedia displays additional information about the highlighted concept. *Hypermedia* features expand these capabilities by adding graphics, video, voice, animation, and pictures to the environment. Using the encyclopedia example again, a child could retrieve information about the Reverend Martin Luther King, Jr. By clicking on a picture icon, the child could view a portrait of the civil rights crusader. Clicking on a movie icon could display a short video clip such as a clip of the march on Washington, and clicking on a sound icon could cause a portion of King's "I Have a Dream" speech to flow from the computer speakers.

Although some exciting applications are already available (e.g., sitting at your computer to send a fax, watch television, answer your phone, or drive down the information highway), today's software products are really quite primitive in comparison to what is possible. Each year, developers are less constrained by the software available to implement desired business applications. Increasingly, a business professional's imagination and creativity is all that will limit the potential of application system design.

A complete discussion of application software would become overwhelming, and quickly outdated. Rather than attempting to provide a comprehensive review of application software, the following sections overview some relevant examples of personal productivity tools and business application software.

Sample Personal Productivity Tools   The workplace is becoming automated as organizations integrate information functions using such tools and techniques as teleconferencing, electronic mail, word processing, databases, graphics, and spreadsheets. More and more, employers expect new hires to be comfortable with (and have the ability to quickly learn) the features available in personal productivity tools such as spreadsheets, web browsers, database management systems (DBMSs), word processors, graphics packages, and presentation tools. Familiarity with other tools such as documentation tools (flowcharting and data flow diagram tools), tax packages, accounting and auditing references, decision support tools, and statistical packages enhance your value as a professional.

Software is intended to provide a platform for developing business solutions with little or no technical knowledge of lower-level communication software. Originally, software packages could be easily classified into application types. For example, spreadsheet packages and database packages offered separate and different application characteristics. Today, these lines are blurring. Increasingly, software packages incorporate and integrate a variety of characteristics that were previously embedded in separate application packages. Spreadsheet packages now include database, word processing, and programming capabilities. There are a large number of software tools available today, and the list is ever changing. We will provide a quick overview of a sample of the many platforms available. We encourage you to investigate the market on your own and become acquainted with the resources available to you, your competitors, and your clients.

Financial modeling tools   What-if questions are constantly asked while planning, controlling, and evaluating an organization's activities. For example, What if sales decrease, instead of increase, during the period? or What if inflation is 5% instead of 3.5%? or What if the interest rate changes before we secure our loan? Each of these questions can alter the analysis of a decision maker and are, therefore, important questions to answer. Completing several complex what-if tasks with only a pencil and paper is tedious and impractical. There is a variety of software that enables what-if analysis. Among the many types, *electronic spreadsheets* are probably the most popular.

A spreadsheet is like an electronic columnar pad with a built-in calculator and several useful functions for manipulating data. The workspace is divided into rows and columns, the intersection of which creates a cell. Each cell can contain text, data, formulas, or functions. Using some very simple commands, users can create helpful tools to aid decision making.

The primary effect of spreadsheets on accounting has been to expand the ability to do sensitivity analysis—model what-if scenarios. Accounting analysis involves tremendous amounts of financial information that must be summarized and analyzed in a variety of ways. Using spreadsheet technology, individuals are able to perform sophisticated analyses of complex business problems such as justifying the purchase of a large piece of capital equipment, determining the cost of a product, or negotiating the terms of a loan.

CASE IN POINT

Spreadsheet software is probably the single biggest contributor to the initial explosion of personal computers in the early 1980s. The first spreadsheet, called Visi-Calc, ran on the Apple II computer. A team of individuals led by Mitch Kapor at VisiCorp created it. Suddenly, people found they could build fairly sophisticated models and perform sensitivity analysis by changing one or more of the model's parameters and see the effect throughout the entire model. People rushed to take advantage of this new technological wonder.

After some disagreements with VisiCorp management, Mitch Kapor left and started his own company called Lotus Development Corporation. Soon they released Lotus 1-2-3™, one of the first programs released for the new IBM personal computer (PC). 1-2-3 was an instant success and soon made Lotus the largest software developer for the PC. Since then, many other companies have written spreadsheet software, improving upon what Lotus began.

Today there are several spreadsheet programs available for a variety of computers. Many are integrated and bundled with other software into software packages such as Microsoft Office, Microsoft Works, or Lotus Works. Most new spreadsheet programs go far beyond the initial copy of VisiCalc by including such features as graphics presentation, macro languages, spreadsheet linking, database functions, object linking and embedding, and import/exporting capabilities. Many also have powerful programming languages, such as VisualBasic, built into the program features.

Database management system software (DBMS)   A cross between application software and operating system software, a *DBMS* allows users to integrate and maintain a variety of data and programs previously stored in separate applications. This is a vast improvement over the original method of developing and maintaining applications.

DBMSs allow programmers to create a computing environment where one logical data pool is accessed by numerous application programs. DBMSs are written to develop data structures and manage user and programmer access to an organization's data pool. These packages coordinate the bits and bytes physically stored by the computer and the data views requested by users. (Refer to Supplemental Chapter C for a discussion of data-oriented modeling and DBMS software types.)

Unlike original databases that stored text data only, current DBMS products increasingly store a variety of data formats (including pictures, voice, graphics, and video). Intelligent databases are being developed to provide more data validation than the validation explicitly coded in application programs. Finally, object-oriented databases (OODB) allow processing instructions to be stored with data in the data pool and facilitate a variety of complex, real-world relationships between objects.

Web browsers   *Web browsers* are used to access the massive system of multimedia computer resources that are geographically dispersed around the world. The two most popular browsers are Microsoft's Internet Explorer and Netscape's Communicator (an expansion of their Navigator product). Like other products discussed in this section, browsers are increasingly becoming bundled as part of a software suite, and in some cases, are integrated with the operating system software.

Business Application Software   Organizations use a variety of software to help plan, control, and evaluate business activities. This software includes *transaction processing software,* decision support software, and executive information systems. The first application software, and still one of the most important, processed accounting transactions. This software captures, stores, and processes business transactions and prepares general purpose financial statements. *Decision support software* (DSS) helps decision makers analyze data and predict the impact of decisions prior to choosing a decision alternative. *Executive information systems* (EISs) provide management with information from internal and external sources, including real-time consolidations and summaries of transactions.[3]

Many new application programs have been developed over the years. There are so many it is not possible to discuss them all, but let's review a few types of business application software.

General ledger (GL) software   Of all the software applications used in business environments, traditional general ledger (GL) software is most closely identified with the accounting function. When organizations first began using information technology, the tasks associated with the general ledger were among the first automated. Initially, the cost of creating a general ledger program was very high. However, the reduced head count and increased performance more than justified the expense.

Traditional GL software automated various features of the manual bookkeeping approach and made the process more efficient and reliable. Particularly with larger organizations, GL software reduced the time spent collecting transaction data and preparing financial statements. However, GL software is becoming a smaller and smaller part of the software picture. Chapter 3 detailed the criticisms levied against the traditional general ledger approach in describing organization activities. As a result, organizations are developing new methods for recording and reporting transaction data.

Production management systems   Nowhere has information technology impacted organizations more than on the production floor. Production management systems help organizations plan, evaluate, and execute the production process. Whether the organization is preparing a newspaper for print or building cars, information technology is being used extensively. In many organizations production costs are declining while quality is increasing. In addition, decision makers are receiving better information to manage the production process.

Order/sales entry   Order or sales entry software handles customer orders and the sale of products and services to customers. Order/sales entry software is becoming increasingly popular, particularly among retailers. Sales are executed more efficiently and reliably and the resulting sales data provide organizations with a valuable information resource. Using

---

3 Supplemental Chapter C includes a discussion of a trend in executive information system support: data warehouses.

product scanners, organizations are building large stores of data describing customers' buying activities, product movements, and various other data about sales and orders.

Inventory management   This software handles the acquisition, storage, control, and movement of inventory. Currently, many companies are integrating the inventory system with the production system in an attempt to reduce the amount of idle inventory on hand. The movement today is toward *just-in-time inventory* management. The idea is to coordinate inventory shipments from a vendor or to a customer so inventory is delivered or produced exactly when it is needed—no sooner, no later. As a result, organizations are significantly reducing the amount of inventory being stored and thereby reducing operating costs. Achieving this level of coordination requires the use of sophisticated information technology.

Human resource management   Human resource management software manages information about employee hiring, training, scheduling, compensation, benefits, and termination. The management of human resources is an increasingly complex and critical area of the business. Software is being developed to help organizations better maintain and utilize their human resources.

Enterprise resource planning software   Application software components are being integrated and bundled to service the entire organization. Organizations want software solutions that span across functional boundaries. They want tools that are integrated, flexible, and process focused. *Enterprise resource planning* software helps fill these needs. (These systems were discussed in Chapter 3.) Originally introduced predominately in larger corporations, ERP systems (sometimes referred to as corporatewide applications) are also being implemented in an increasing number of medium-sized firms. These packages are comprised of a number of individual modules. The packages can support a variety of tasks including supply chain management, inventory management, logistics, human resource management, finance, accounting, manufacturing planning, sales, and distribution. The tools include support for facilitating information flows between the organization and its trading partners, suppliers, and customers. These packages often include the tools to support global operations, and can facilitate the use of Internet and intranet resources. Examples of ERP vendors include SAP, Oracle, Geac, Baan, PeopleSoft, J.D. Edwards, and Computer Associates.

Groupware   Organization participants include humans who work individually, in groups, or in teams. As a result, software developers are adapting their products to allow people to work together to complete organization tasks. *Group decision support software* (GDSS) coordinates group members involved in collaborative decision making. *Groupware* is the term often used to describe software that allows workers to coordinate efforts and collaborate on various tasks and projects. Examples of groupware activities include interactive group meeting and video teleconferencing software. Groupware software includes Lotus Notes, Microsoft Exchange, Oracle's InterOffice, and Novell Groupwise, to name a few.

Other software used to enhance organization productivity   Many other productivity tools are available. Examples include *workflow software,* used to graphically represent, document, and define business processes. This software is useful in analyzing and automating business processes. *Document management software* aids in organizing any data resource stored electronically. Today, the term *document* is not simply reserved for sales invoices or receipts. In computing circles, the term is used to describe many information resources stored electronically, such as spreadsheets, graphics, and video. Document management software assists users in searching for, retrieving, and maintaining organization documents.

Interestingly, more and more of these categories of personal, group, and organization productivity tools are converging, or becoming integrated. With the explosion of technology during this information age, individuals and organizations sometimes feel overwhelmed with the amount of data and information available. The challenge now is to make sure the truly useful information is accessible and used in an effective manner. Increasingly, the key is not to simply produce more information, but to glean the insights or knowledge that is available from that information. Thus, *knowledge management software* is increasingly critical within organizations. The Patricia Seybold Group, a noted IS consulting organization, has defined the knowledge continuum as:

Data + Context = INFORMATION + Experience = KNOWLEDGE

The objective of knowledge management technology strategies is to find the knowledge that is gained from the volumes of information that organizations are now more capable of producing.

FUTURE DIRECTIONS FOR SOFTWARE

In an age of virtual reality (e.g., cyberspace simulation and computer-generated worlds), increased software experience elevates user expectations and demands on software evolutions. Thus far, our discussion of software has highlighted a variety of future development issues, including:

- The need for tools and methods that enable more rapid, efficient application development.
- The shift from a department processing and data storage model to an enterprise perspective.
- The desire to allow computer users (clients) to control processes rather than having processes control the user.
- The need for improved user interfaces and communication of a variety of data forms.
- The need to facilitate communications globally and throughout cyberspace.

HOW TO TAKE ADVANTAGE OF INFORMATION TECHNOLOGY TODAY

Hopefully, you are asking yourself, How can I become familiar with, let alone take advantage of, such a dynamic technology? We suggest at least three things:

Read and/or Watch IT Programs and Videos

Today we have a variety of computer industry periodicals specifically designed to help you keep abreast of what is happening with computer technology. Paper and online periodicals such as *PC Week, InfoWorld,* and *ComputerWorld* provide current news about hardware and software. There are a number of online news services, and there are services that summarize and customize IT news per individual preferences. As with most everything else, it is hard to become familiar with a topic without investing some reading time. Alternatively, there are numerous television programs and videos that discuss and demonstrate advances in information technology.

Physically or Electronically Attend Technology Demonstrations, Workshops, and Conferences

It is one thing to read articles or watch videos about information technology, but quite another to actually see a live demonstration. Demonstrations are really quite accessible. There are a variety of national and international technology conferences (e.g., Comdex or Networld), often simultaneously transmitted and distributed electronically. Nearly every major city sponsors some kind of technology show much like auto and recreational equipment shows. At these shows vendors provide continual demonstrations of their technologies. In addition, most retailers of information technology provide workshops for those who purchase their products and those who wish to pay a fee for instruction. Finally, many universities offer free short courses in technology. Contact your university computer support personnel. Attending the available demonstrations, workshops, and conferences will help you catch the vision of what is possible.

Use the Technology

Imagine trying to learn how to drive a car by simply reading or watching videotape. Just like driver's education class, you have to get on the road and actually drive. The same is true with technology. Although reading about and seeing information technology is helpful, you need to actually use technology to learn to command its power. By combining reading with experimentation, you quickly become a fairly sophisticated user of a powerful resource that can greatly simplify your life. At a minimum, you should use computer technology to write reports, letters, and memos, prepare financial worksheets, and even maintain lists of telephone numbers and addresses. As you experiment with the available technology, you quickly discover its potential and understand the direction of technology advancement. This experience also helps you acquire skills that can differentiate you in a competitive job market.

There are no true shortcuts or warp zones to get and keep you informed about technology. In the end, it will require a commitment and a great deal of sweat equity on your part. However, we can promise that your investment in learning and staying current can pay large dividends.

CONCLUDING COMMENTS

As we have tried to emphasize throughout these supplemental chapters, technology is changing every aspect of our lives. Expect to see an even larger variety of new and improved software products performing more and more tasks. However, unless we experiment with new and innovative software, we will not discover its true potential.

Remember that a business's needs—rather than hardware or software capabilities—should dictate the information system architecture. Information technology (hardware and software) provides the foundation for today's information systems and information professionals. Like an architect's plans for a house, which could be built using stone or wood, a variety of software tools are available to develop a particular business application. The key to the power of software is *how* it is used to implement information system architecture.

We conclude our review of technology with a reminder: Do not make the mistake of basing your system architecture dreams only on today's technology. Technology (both hardware and software) is rapidly changing, and things that are not possible today may be possible tomorrow. Keep looking forward and dreaming of what can be. Then you can play a key role in developing new and exciting business solutions.

CHECKLIST OF KEY TERMS AND CONCEPTS

American National Standards Institute (ANSI)

Application software

Applied intelligence

Artificial intelligence

Assembler

Assembly language

Basic input/output system (BIOS) ✓

Binary code

Bit

Booting the computer

Business application software

Byte

Character-based user interface (CUI)

Class library (of objects)

Client/server software

Communications software

Compiler

Computer aided software engineering (CASE)

Computer instructions

Computer languages

Computer programmers

Database management system (DBMS) software

Data files

Debugging

Decision support software (DSS)

Do loop

Document management software

Enterprise Resource Planning software

Executive information system (EIS)

Fifth generation computer language

First generation computer language

For loop

Fourth generation computer language

General ledger software

Graphical user interface (GUI)

Group decision support software (GDSS)

Groupware

Hypermedia

Hypertext

Icon

If Then Else logic

Intelligent software

International Organization for Standardization (IOS)
Internet/web software
Interpreter
Knowledge management software
Local area network (LAN) software
Machine language
Multimedia
Object code
Object-oriented data bases (OODB)
Object-oriented programming (OOP)
Operating system software
PC to host software
PC to PC software
Procedure-oriented computer language
Program
Program files
Programming

Programming language
Read only memory (ROM)
Second generation computer language
Semantic error
Software
Source code
Spreadsheet
Structured query language (SQL)
Subroutine
Syntax error
System architecture
Third generation computer language
Utility software
Web browser
Wide area network (WAN) software
Workflow software
WYSIWYG

REVIEW QUESTIONS

1. Define each of the terms in the *Checklist of Key Terms and Concepts.*
2. List four contributions software should make to an organization.
3. What language does a computer understand?
4. List and contrast the different generations of programming languages.
5. What drives the need to develop a new generation of programming language?
6. Describe the methods computers use to translate instructions from source code to machine language or object code.
7. How do you instruct a computer?
8. List and describe the two types of computer programming errors. Give an example of each.
9. Contrast program files and data files.
10. What is the purpose of using CASE tools?
11. Explain what is meant by object-oriented technologies.
12. What is the purpose of a computer's operating system software?
13. List five examples of communications software.
14. Define application software.
15. Describe examples of personal productivity software tools.
16. Describe each category of business application software discussed in this chapter.

DISCUSSION QUESTIONS

1. List some business uses for the following software packages:
   a. Financial modeling tools (Spreadsheets)
   b. Word processing
   c. Communications
   d. Presentation software
   e. Web software

2. Why does this supplement argue that accounting professionals should focus on software, rather than hardware, components of technology?

3. True or False: The key to good computing is which software package you use. Explain your response.

4. Is it always beneficial to acquire new software? Does computerization always equate to positive business solutions?

5. The chapter suggests several ways to take advantage of information technology today. Most of these suggestions require some learning outside the classroom. Why don't universities simply teach you all the software relevant to your specialty area?

6. You just purchased the latest version of your favorite software. In a few months, you know the company will unveil a new or updated version of the package. Why are companies always changing their software?

7. Some people have commented on the paradox of software: Programmers need faster computers to make better software. What is the effect of this gap between hardware and programmer capability?

8. From your experiences, what distinguishes a user friendly package from a package that is not user friendly? Is the user friendliness of a software package a function of the computer's power?

9. When you remove the shrink wrap from a new software package, are you guaranteed that the package will work properly? Can a package appear to execute properly and still cause problems?

10. Select two teams to debate the following opinion expressed by an accounting major: "I don't have to spend my time learning various computer software packages or improve my information technology knowledge. The firm I get a job with will train me on their specific software and hardware."

11. Karen is a powerful Lotus 1-2-3 user, however, her company is changing to the Excel spreadsheet package. Is Karen's spreadsheet experience and Lotus 1-2-3 expertise wasted?

12. Is operating system software or application software more useful to a typical computer user?

13. What effect has (and will have) groupware had on accounting and organizations?

14. What effect has (and will have) intelligent software had on accounting and organizations?

15. What effect has (and will have) multimedia had on business organizations?

16. What effect has (and will have) increased used of communications had on accounting?

MINICASES AND OTHER APPLIED LEARNING

1. To acquire more familiarity with the breadth and depth of application software, visit stores that sell computer software and look through published software advertisements for descriptions of a product in two of the following categories:

   a. Financial modeling tools (spreadsheets).

   b. Word processing.

   c. Communications.

   d. Presentation software.

   e. General ledger packages and other financial packages.

   f. Database management systems.

   g. Web/Internet software.

   h. Enterprise Resource Planning software.

   i. Groupware software.

   j. Other types of business software in which you are interested.

Required:

Prepare a report that describes the features of the two software packages you chose.

2. Visit a local organization and research how they use software from each of the following categories:

   a. Financial modeling tools (Spreadsheets).

   b. Word processing.

   c. Communications.

   d. Presentation software.

   e. General ledger packages and other financial packages.

   f. Database management systems.

   g. Web/Internet software.

   h. Enterprise Resource Planning software.

   i. Groupware software.

   j. Other types of business software in which you are interested.

Required:

Write a summary detailing your findings.

3. Through your university computer resources center, at a store, or at a local business, view demonstrations of packages in three of the following software categories with which you are not very familiar:

   a. Financial modeling tools (spreadsheets).

   b. Word processing.

  c. Communications.

  d. Presentation software.

  e. General ledger packages and other financial packages.

  f. Database management systems.

  g. Web/Internet software.

  h. Enterprise Resource Planning software.

  i. Groupware software.

  j. Other types of business software in which you are interested.

Required:

Write a two-page summary to describe what you learned.

4. In groups, review the professional accounting literature and locate five articles about software and how it is impacting accounting. Make a short presentation that summarizes your findings.

5. Assess your personal productivity skills and develop a plan to enhance your skills to make you more marketable. Write a one-page summary of your plan.

INDEX

Andre Gray

(301) 996-6537